THE PAPERS OF
BENJAMIN FRANKLIN

SPONSORED BY

The American Philosophical Society
and Yale University

Silas Deane

THE PAPERS OF

Benjamin Franklin

VOLUME 23   *October 27, 1776, through April 30, 1777*

WILLIAM B. WILLCOX, *Editor*

Douglas M. Arnold, Dorothy W. Bridgwater, Jonathan R. Dull, Claude A. Lopez, and Catherine M. Prelinger, Associate Editors

New Haven and London YALE UNIVERSITY PRESS, 1983

Funds for editing this volume of The Papers of Benjamin Franklin *have been provided by the Andrew W. Mellon Foundation, the J. Howard Pew Freedom Trust, the American Philosophical Society, and the National Historical Publications and Records Commission under the chairmanship of the Archivist of the United States. For all these sources of support the editors are most grateful.*

Published with assistance from the National Endowment for the Humanities.

Library of Congress catalog card number: 59–12697
International standard book number: 0–300–02897–0

Printed in the U.S.A.

10 9 8 7 6 5 4 3 2 1

Administrative Board

Thomas C. Cochran, American Philosophical Society, *Chairman*
Whitfield J. Bell, Jr., American Philosophical Society
Carl Bridenbaugh, American Philosophical Society
Edmund S. Morgan, Yale University
John G. Ryden, Yale University Press
Lawrence W. Towner, Newberry Library
William B. Willcox, Yale University, *Secretary*

Advisory Committee

Thomas Boylston Adams
Thomas R. Adams
Charles Braibant
Prince Louis de Broglie
I. Bernard Cohen
John C. Dann
Gaylord Donnelley
Morris Duane

Sir Frank C. Francis
Andrew Heiskell
David C. Mearns
Sir Owen Morshead
Howard H. Peckham
John E. Pomfret
Robert E. Spiller

Editor's Note

Two staff members left, to our deep regret, while this volume was in preparation, Jennifer Lovejoy and Joy Sylvester. We wish them well.

Contents

French surnames and titles of nobility often run to great length. Our practice with an untitled person is to provide all the Christian names at first appearance and then drop them; a chevalier or noble is given the title used at the time, and details are provided in a footnote.

*Denotes a document referred to in annotation

ix

CONTENTS

xxiii

xxvii

CONTENTS

List of Illustrations

Contributors to Volume 23

The ownership of each manuscript, or the location of the particular copy used by the editors of each rare contemporary pamphlet or similar printed work, is indicated where the document appears in the text. The sponsors and editors are deeply grateful to the following institutions and individuals for permission to print or otherwise use in the present volume manuscripts or other materials which they own.

INSTITUTIONS

Algemeen Rijksarchief, The Hague
American Philosophical Society
Archives de l'Académie royale des sciences, Paris
Archives du Ministère des affaires étrangères, Paris
Archivo Historico Nacional, Madrid
Bibliothèque municipale, Mantes
British Library, London
Connecticut Historical Society
Thomas Gilcrease Foundation, Tulsa
Harvard University Library
Haverford College Library
Historical Society of Pennsylvania

Johns Hopkins University Library
Henry E. Huntington Library
Library of Congress
Morristown National Historical Park
Musée national de la coopération franco-américaine, Blérancourt
National Archives
New York Public Library
Public Record Office
Rutgers University Library
Staatsbibliothek Preussischer Kulturbesitz, West Berlin
University of Pennsylvania Library
University of Virginia Library
Yale University Library

INDIVIDUALS

Dr. Joseph E. Fields, Joliet, Ill.
David Holland, London

Method of Textual Reproduction

An extended statement of the principles of selection, arrangement, form of presentation, and method of textual reproduction observed in this edition appears in the Introduction to the first volume, pp. xxiv–xlvii. What follows is a condensation and revision of part of it.

Printed Material:

Those of Franklin's writings that were printed under his direction presumably appeared as he wanted them to, and should therefore be reproduced with no changes except what modern typography requires. In some cases, however, printers carelessly or willfully altered his text without his consent; or the journeymen who set it had different notions from his—and from each other's—of capitalization, spelling, and punctuation. Such of his letters as survive only in nineteenth-century printings, furthermore, have often been vigorously edited by William Temple Franklin, Duane, or Sparks. In all these cases the original has suffered some degree of distortion, which the modern editor may guess at but, in the absence of the manuscript, cannot remedy. We therefore follow the printed texts as we find them, and note only obvious misreadings.

We observe the following rules in reproducing printed materials:

1. The place and date of composition of letters are set at the top, regardless of their location in the original printing; the complimentary close is set continuously with the text.

2. Proper nouns, including personal names, which were often printed in italics, are set in roman except when the original was italicized for emphasis.

3. Prefaces and other long passages, though italicized in the original, are set in roman. Long italicized quotations are set in roman within quotation marks.

4. Words in full capitals are set in small capitals, with

initial letters in full capitals if required by Franklin's normal usage.

5. All signatures are set in capitals and small capitals.

6. We silently correct obvious typographical errors, such as the omission of a single parenthesis or quotation mark.

7. We close a sentence by supplying, when needed, a period or question mark.

Manuscript Material:

a. *Letters* are presented in the following form:

1. The place and date of composition are set at the top, regardless of their location in the original; the complimentary close is set continuously with the text.

2. Addresses, endorsements, and notations are so labelled and printed at the end of the letter. An endorsement on a letter is to the best of our belief by the recipient, a notation by someone else.

b. *Spelling* of the original we retain when in English, and correct it in brackets or a footnote if it is abnormal enough to obscure the meaning: "they where [were]." The most common such abnormalities in French are omitting apostrophes where they belong or inserting them where they do not belong, and running two words together or separating a single word. These vagaries cannot be handled in the same way without disfiguring the text or overburdening the annotation, and we silently correct them: "d'ans les qu'els jai resté 8 ans edemy" becomes "dans lesquels j'ai resté 8 ans e demy."

c. *Capitalization* we retain as written, except that every sentence is made to begin with a capital. When we cannot decide whether a letter is a capital, we follow modern usage.

d. Words underlined once in the manuscript are printed in italics; words underlined twice or written in large letters or full capitals are printed in small capitals.

e. *Punctuation* has been retained as in the original, except:

1. We close a sentence by supplying, when needed, a period or question mark. When it is unclear where the sentence ends, we retain the original punctuation or lack of it.

2. Dashes used in place of commas, semicolons, colons, or periods are replaced by the appropriate marks; when a sentence ends with both a dash and a period, the dash is omitted.

3. Commas scattered meaninglessly through a manuscript are eliminated.

4. When a mark of punctuation is not clear or can be read as one of two marks, we follow modern usage.[1]

5. Some documents, especially legal ones, have no punctuation; others have so little as to obscure the meaning. In such cases we silently supply the minimum needed for clarity.

f. *Contractions and abbreviations* in general are retained. The ampersand is rendered as "and," except in the names of business firms, in the form "&c.," and in a few other cases. Letters represented by the thorn or tilde are printed. The tailed "p" is spelled out as per, pre, or pro. Symbols of weights, measures, and monetary values follow modern usage, as: £34. Superscript letters are lowered.

g. *Omitted or illegible words or letters* are treated as follows:

1. If not more than four letters are missing, we supply them silently when we have no doubt what they should be, and otherwise with a bracketed question mark.

2. If more than four letters are missing, we supply them in brackets, with or without a question mark depending on our confidence in the insertion.

3. Other omissions are shown as follows: [*illegible*], [*torn*], [*remainder missing*], or the like.

---

1. The typescripts from which these papers are printed have been made from photocopies of the manuscripts; marks of punctuation are sometimes blurred or lost in photography, and it has often been impossible to consult the original.

4. Missing or illegible digits are indicated by suspension points in brackets, the number of points corresponding to the estimated number of missing figures.

5. When the writer has omitted a word required for clarity, we insert it in brackets and italics.

h. *Author's additions and corrections:*

1. Interlineations and brief marginal notes are normally incorporated in the text without comment, and longer notes with the notation [*in the margin*] unless they were clearly intended as footnotes, in which case they are printed with our notes and with a bracketed indication of the source.

2. Canceled words and phrases are in general omitted without notice; if significant, they are printed in footnotes.

3. When alternative words and phrases have been inserted in a manuscript but the original remains uncanceled, the alternatives are given in brackets, preceded by explanatory words in italics, as: "it is [*written above:* may be] true."

4. Variant readings of several versions are noted if important.

Abbreviations and Short Titles

AAE	Archives du Ministère des affaires étrangères.
AD	Autograph document.[1]
ADS	Autograph document signed.
AL	Autograph letter.
Almanach des marchands	*Almanach général des marchands, négocians, armateurs, et fabricants de France et de l'Europe et autres parties du monde* . . . (Paris, 1779).
Almanach royal	*Almanach royal* (91 vols., Paris, 1700–92). Cited by year.
ALS	Autograph letter signed.
Amer.	American.
APS	American Philosophical Society.
Archaeol.	Archaeological.
Assn.	Association.
Autobiog.	Leonard W. Labaree, Ralph L. Ketcham, Helen C. Boatfield, and Helene H. Fineman, eds., *The Autobiography of Benjamin Franklin* (New Haven, 1964).
Bachaumont, *Mémoires secrets*	[Louis Petit de Bachaumont], *Mémoires secrets pour servir à l'histoire de la république des lettres en France, depuis MDCCLXII jusqu'à nos jours; ou, Journal d'un observateur* . . . (36 vols. in 12, London, 1781–89).
Balch, *French in America*	Thomas Balch, *The French in America during the War of Independence of the United States, 1777–1783* (trans. by Thomas Willing Balch *et al.*; 2 vols., Philadelphia, 1891–95).

1. For definitions of types of manuscripts see above, I, xliv–xlvii.

BF	Benjamin Franklin.
BF's accounts as commissioner	Those described below, p. 20.
BFB	Benjamin Franklin Bache.
Bigelow, *Works*	John Bigelow, ed., *The Works of Benjamin Franklin* (12 vols., New York and London, 1904).
Biographie universelle	*Biographie universelle, ancienne et moderne, ou histoire, par ordre alphabétique, de la vie publique et privée de tous les hommes qui se sont fait remarquer* ... (85 vols., Paris, 1811–62).
Bodinier	From information kindly furnished us by Capt. Gilbert Bodinier, Section études, Service historique de l'Armée de Terre, Vincennes.
Boyd, *Jefferson Papers*	Julian P. Boyd *et al.*, eds., *The Papers of Thomas Jefferson* (19 vols. to date, Princeton, 1950–).
Burke's Peerage	Sir Bernard Burke, *Burke's Genealogical and Heraldic History of the Peerage Baronetage and Knightage with War Gazette and Corrigenda* (98th ed., London, 1940). References in exceptional cases to other editions are so indicated.
Burnett, *Continental Congress*	Edmund C. Burnett, *The Continental Congress* (New York, 1941).
Burnett, *Letters*	Edmund C. Burnett, ed., *Letters of Members of the Continental Congress* (8 vols., Washington, 1921–36).
Butterfield, *Adams Correspondence*	Lyman H. Butterfield *et al.*, eds., *Adams Family Correspondence* (4 vols. to date, Cambridge, Mass., 1963–).
Butterfield, *John Adams Diary*	Lyman H. Butterfield *et al.*, eds., *Diary and Autobiography of John Adams* (4 vols., Cambridge, Mass., 1961)

Chron.	*Chronicle.*
Clark, *Wickes*	William Bell Clark, *Lambert Wickes, Sea Raider and Diplomat: the Story of a Naval Captain of the Revolution* (New Haven and London, 1932).
Cobbett, *Parliamentary History*	William Cobbett and Thomas C. Hansard, eds., *The Parliamentary History of England from the Earliest Period to 1803* (36 vols., London, 1806–20).
Col.	Column.
Coll.	*Collections.*
Commons Jours.	*Journals of the House of Commons* (233 vols. to date, [London,] 1803–); vols. I-LI are reprints.
Crout, "Diplomacy of Trade"	Robert R. Crout, "The Diplomacy of Trade: the Influence of Commercial Considerations on French Involvement in the Angloamerican War of Independence, 1775–78" (Ph.D. dissertation, University of Georgia, 1977).
Cushing, *Writings of Samuel Adams*	Harry Alonzo Cushing, ed., *The Writings of Samuel Adams* ... (4 vols., New York, 1904–08).
'D	Document unsigned.
DAB	*Dictionary of American Biography.*
Deane Correspondence	*The Deane Papers; Correspondence between Silas Deane, His Brothers and Their Business and Political Associates, 1771–1795,* (Connecticut Historical Society *Collections,* XXIII; Hartford, Conn., 1930).
Deane Papers	*The Deane Papers,* 1774–90 (5 vols.; New York Historical Society *Collections,* XIX-XXIII; New York, 1887–91).
DF	Deborah Franklin.

Dictionnaire de bio-graphie	*Dictionnaire de biographie française* ... (15 vols. to date, Paris, 1933–).
Dictionnaire de la no-blesse	François-Alexandre Aubert de La Chesnaye-Dubois and M. Badier, *Dictionnaire de la noblesse contenant les généalogies, l'histoire & la chronologie des familles nobles de la France* ... (3rd ed.; 19 vols., Paris, 1863–76).
Dictionnaire historique	*Dictionnaire historique, critique et biblio-graphique, contenant les vies des hommes illustres, célèbres ou fameux de tous les pays et de tous les siècles* ... (30 vols., Paris, 1821–23).
DNB	*Dictionary of National Biography.*
Doniol, *Histoire*	Henri Doniol, *Histoire de la participation de la France à l'établissement des Etats-Unis d'Amérique. Correspondance di-plomatique et documents* (5 vols., Paris, 1886–99).
DS	Document signed.
Duane, *Works*	William Duane, ed., *The Works of Dr. Benjamin Franklin* ... (6 vols., Phil-adelphia, 1808–18). Title varies in the several volumes.
Dubourg, *Œuvres*	Jacques Barbeu-Dubourg, ed:, *Œuvres de M. Franklin* ... (2 vols., Paris, 1773).
Dull, *French Navy*	Jonathan R. Dull, *The French Navy and American Independence: a Study of Arms and Diplomacy, 1774–1787 (Princeton, 1975).*
Ed.	Edition or editor.
Etat militaire	*Etat militaire de France, pour l'année* ... (36 vols., Paris, 1758–93). Cited by year.
Exper. and Obser.	*Experiments and Observations on Electric-*

ity, made at Philadelphia in America, by Mr. Benjamin Franklin . . . (London, 1751). Revised and enlarged editions were published in 1754, 1760, 1769, and 1774 with slightly varying titles. In each case the edition cited will be indicated, e.g., *Exper. and Obser.* (1751).

Ferguson, *Power of the Purse*
Elmer James Ferguson, *The Power of the Purse: a History of American Public Finance* . . . (Chapel Hill, N.C., [1961]).

Fitzpatrick, *Writings of Washington*
John C. Fitzpatrick, ed., *The Writings of George Washington* . . . (39 vols., Washington, D.C., [1931–44]).

Force, *Amer. Arch.*
Peter Force, ed., *American Archives: Consisting of a Collection of Authentic Records, State Papers, Debates, and Letters and Other Notices of Publick Affairs* . . . , fourth series, March 7, 1774 to July 4, 1776 (6 vols., [Washington, 1837–46]); fifth series, July 4, 1776 to September 3, 1783 (3 vols., [Washington, 1848–53]).

France ecclésiastique
La France ecclésiastique pour l'année . . . (15 vols., Paris, 1774–90). Cited by year.

Freeman, *Washington*
Douglas S. Freeman (completed by John A. Carroll and Mary W. Ashworth), *George Washington: a Biography* (7 vols., New York, [1948–57]).

Gaz.
Gazette.

Gaz. de Leyde
Nouvelles extraordinaires de divers endroits, commonly known as *Gazette de Leyde*. Each issue is in two parts; we indicate the second as "sup."

Geneal.
Genealogical.

xl

Gent. Mag.	*The Gentleman's Magazine, and Historical Chronicle.*
Gipson, *British Empire*	Lawrence H. Gipson, *The British Empire before the American Revolution* (15 vols., New York, 1939–70; I-III, revised ed., N.Y., 1958–60).
Gruber, *Howe Brothers*	Ira D. Gruber, *The Howe Brothers and the American Revolution* (New York, 1972).
Hillairet, *Rues de Paris*	Jacques Hillairet, pseud. of Auguste A. Coussilan, *Dictionnaire historique des rues de Paris* (2nd ed.; 2 vols, [Paris, 1964]).
Heitman, *Register of Officers*	Francis B. Heitman, *Historical Register of Officers in the War of the Revolution* . . . (Washington, D.C., 1893).
Hinshaw, *Amer. Quaker Genealogy*	William W. Hinshaw, *Encyclopedia of American Quaker Genealogy* (6 vols. Ann Arbor, Mich., 1936–50).
Hist.	*Historical.*
Hutchinson, *Diary*	Peter O. Hutchinson, ed., *The Diary and Letters of His Excellency Thomas Hutchinson, Esq.* . . . (2 vols., London, 1883–86).
Idzerda, *Lafayette*	Stanley J. Idzerda *et al.*, eds., *Lafayette in the Age of the American Revolution: Selected Letters and Papers, 1776–1790* (4 vols. to date, Ithaca, N.Y., and London, [1977–]).
JCC	Worthington C. Ford *et al.*, eds., *Journals of the Continental Congress, 1774–1789* (34 vols., Washington, 1904–37).
Jour.	*Journal.*
JW	Jonathan Williams, Jr.
L	Letter unsigned.

xli

Larousse, *Dictionnaire universel*	Pierre Larousse, *Grand dictionnaire universel du XIXe siècle* . . . (17 vols., Paris, [n.d.]).
Lasseray, *Les Français*	André Lasseray, *Les Français sous les treize étoiles, 1775–1783* (2 vols., Paris, 1935).
Lee, *Life of Arthur Lee*	Richard Henry Lee, *Life of Arthur Lee, LL.D., Joint Commissioner of the United States to the Court of France, and Sole Commissioner to the Courts of Spain and Prussia, during the Revolutionary War* . . . (2 vols., Boston, 1829).
Lee Family Papers	Paul P. Hoffman, ed., *The Lee Family Papers, 1742–1795* (University of Virginia Library *Microfilm Publication* No. 1; 8 reels, Charlottesville, Va., 1966).
Lee Papers	*The Lee Papers*, 1754–1811 (4 vols.; New-York Historical Society *Collections*, IV-VII; New York, 1872–75).
Lewis, *Indiana Co.*	George E. Lewis, *The Indiana Company, 1763–1798: a Study in Eighteenth Century Frontier Land Speculation and Business Venture* (Glendale, Cal., 1941).
Lopez, *Mon Cher Papa*	Claude-Anne Lopez, *Mon Cher Papa: Franklin and the Ladies of Paris* (New Haven and London, [1966]).
Lopez and Herbert, *The Private Franklin*	Claude-Anne Lopez and Eugenia W. Herbert, *The Private Franklin: the Man and His Family* (New York, [1975]).
LS	Letter signed.
l.t.	livres tournois.
Lüthy, *Banque Protestante*	Herbert Lüthy, *La Banque protestante en France de la Révocation de l'Edit de Nantes à la Révolution* (2 vols., Paris, 1959–61).

xlii

Mackesy, *War for America*
Piers Mackesy, *The War for America, 1775–1783* (Cambridge, Mass., 1965).

Mag.
Magazine.

Mass. Arch.
Massachusetts Archives, State House, Boston.

Mazas, *Ordre de Saint-Louis*
Alexandre Mazas and Théodore Anne, *Histoire de l'ordre royal et militaire de Saint-Louis depuis son institution en 1693 jusqu'en 1830* (2nd ed.; 3 vols., Paris, 1860–61).

Morton, *Beaumarchais correspondance*
Brian N. Morton and Donald C. Spinelli, eds., *Beaumarchais correspondance* (4 vols. to date, Paris, 1969–).

MS, MSS
Manuscript, manuscripts.

Namier and Brooke, *House of Commons*
Sir Lewis Namier and John Brooke, *The History of Parliament. The House of Commons 1754–1790* (3 vols., London and New York, 1964).

Naval Docs.
William B. Clark, William J. Morgan, *et al.*, eds., *Naval Documents of the American Revolution* (8 vols. to date, Washington, D.C., 1964–).

Nouvelle biographie
Nouvelle biographie générale depuis les temps les plus reculés jusqu'à nos jours . . . (46 vols. Paris, 1855–66).

Pa. Arch.
Samuel Hazard *et al.*, eds., *Pennsylvania Archives* (9 series, Philadelphia and Harrisburg, 1852–1935).

Pa. Col. Recs.
Minutes of the Provincial Council of Pennsylvania . . . (16 vols., Harrisburg, 1851–53). Volumes I–III are reprints published in Philadelphia, 1852. Title changes with Volume XI to *Supreme Executive Council.*

Phil. Trans.
The Royal Society, *Philosophical Transactions.*

xliii

PMHB	*Pennsylvania Magazine of History and Biography.*
Price, *France and the Chesapeake*	Jacob M. Price, *France and the Chesapeake: a History of the French Tobacco Monopoly, 1674–1791, and of Its Relationship to the British and American Tobacco Trade* (2 vols., Ann Arbor, Mich., [1973]).
Proc.	*Proceedings.*
Pub.	*Publications.*
Rakove, *Beginnings of National Politics*	Jack N. Rakove, *The Beginnings of National Politics: an Interpretive History of the Continental Congress* (New York, 1979).
RB	Richard Bache.
Rev.	*Review.*
Sabine, *Loyalists*	Lorenzo Sabine, *Biographical Sketches of Loyalists of the American Revolution . . .* (2 vols., Boston, 1864).
Sibley's Harvard Graduates	John L. Sibley, *Biographical Sketches of Graduates of Harvard University* (Cambridge, Mass., 1873–). Continued from Volume IV by Clifford K. Shipton.
Smith, *Letters*	Paul H. Smith *et al.*, eds., *Letters of Delegates to Congress* (8 vols. to date, Washington, D.C., 1976–).
Smyth, *Writings*	Albert H. Smyth, ed., *The Writings of Benjamin Franklin . . .* (10 vols., N.Y., 1905–07).
Soc.	Society.
Sparks, *Works*	Jared Sparks, ed., *The Works of Benjamin Franklin . . .* (10 vols., Boston, 1836–40).
Stevens, *Facsimiles*	Benjamin F. Stevens, ed., *Facsimiles of Manuscripts in European Archives Re-*

xliv

	lating to America, 1773–1783 (25 vols., London, 1889–98).
Taylor, *Adams Papers*	Robert J. Taylor *et al.*, eds., *Papers of John Adams* (4 vols. to date, Cambridge, Mass., 1977–).
Trans.	Translator or translated.
Trans.	*Transactions.*
Van Doren, *Franklin*	Carl Van Doren, *Benjamin Franklin* (New York, 1938).
Van Doren, *Franklin— Mecom*	Carl Van Doren, ed., *The Letters of Benjamin Franklin & Jane Mecom* (American Philosophical Society *Memoirs*, XXVII, Princeton, 1950).
W&MQ	*William and Mary Quarterly*, first or third series as indicated.
Ward, *War of the Revolution*	Christopher Ward, *The War of the Revolution* (John R. Alden, ed.; 2 vols., New York, 1952).
Waste Book	BF's accounts described below, p. 000
WF	William Franklin.
Wharton, *Diplomatic Correspondence*	Francis Wharton, ed., *The Revolutionary Diplomatic Correspondence of the United States* (6 vols., Washington, D.C., 1889).
Willcox, *Portrait of a General*	William B. Willcox, *Portrait of a General: Sir Henry Clinton in the War of Independence* (New York, 1964).
WTF	William Temple Franklin.
WTF, *Memoirs*	William Temple Franklin, ed., *Memoirs of the Life and Writings of Benjamin Franklin, LL.D., F.R.S., &c. . . .* (3 vols., 4to, London, 1817–18).
WTF's accounts	Those described below, p. 19.

Note by the Editors and the Administrative Board

The period of the mission to France requires changes in the ground rules that have hitherto governed the edition. The surviving documents from the eight and a half years of that mission are roughly two and a half times as numerous as those for the remaining seventy-five years of Franklin's life. It was clear from the start of the editing, therefore, that the French material would have to be more rigorously selected and less exhaustively annotated than that of previous volumes,[1] or the series would never come to an end. We have considered many methods of selection, and chosen the one that we believe will best serve the purpose of the edition. We continue to print in full everything that came from Franklin's pen, except for trivial jottings, and everything that throws light on his official activities and his unofficial and multifarious dealings with individuals. We take notice of everything that does not fall within this category, yet is within our rubric of communications to and from him; here, however, we condense in various ways.

One way is by grouping. Sometimes letters of little significance to Franklin were interconnected to form a cluster, as when one elicited another and that perhaps another; here we select a single document to print or summarize, and discuss in our annotation the others that belong with it.[2] Sometimes letters that to the best of our knowledge were inconsequential, in the literal sense of producing no results, are related by their common subject matter, like requests in the early period for a military commission, or later for appointment as a consul; here we print a single specimen, and discuss in our annotation the other items in the group.[3] Some letters, equally inconsequential, cannot be assigned to any cluster or group; these we résumé as briefly as possible. When Franklin responded, directly or indirectly, the letter was by definition consequential; we print or summarize it if we believe it warrants such treat-

1. See above, I, xxxv–vi.
2. For examples see below, Lutterloh to BF, Jan. 3, and the commissioners to Rullecourt, Jan. 10.
3. The one example in this volume is Blondel to BF below, Jan. 13.

ment, and otherwise describe it in annotating the response. When a document appears only in annotation, its repository is given there. It is also listed in its chronological place, in the table of contents and in the text, with a reference to the page on which it is discussed; if it was written after the period covered by the volume, and future editors do not wish to deal with it further, it will appear under its date with a reference back to the earlier volume.

Our canons of selection, needless to say, are not precise formulas but only guidelines. Applying them requires judging every document that is not of obvious importance, and judgment is inherently subjective. Selectivity also changes with the changing character of Franklin's mission and of his attitude toward it: a letter may illustrate the clamorous demands upon him when he first arrived, and a similar letter may be redundant once he became inured to the clamor. Our focus is on the concerns that were central to him at any given period. As they shifted, some peripheral material becomes more relevant, some less; and we endeavor to select accordingly.

We have reduced the editorial apparatus in various ways. Cross-referencing within the volume has been kept to the minimum needed to supplement the index. Source identifications do not in most cases make the distinction, often impossible in photographed manuscripts, between copy and letterbook copy; the only letterbooks that we cite are those kept by the writers themselves. Little biographical detail is supplied about people who can be found in standard sources; when they cannot, we furnish such information as we have, on the ground that the interests of future scholars are unpredictable. News from abroad, particularly about the American war, often mixed true and false, and we do not try to sort out the mixture unless the news had some significance for the commissioners. Headnotes trace the outlines of major negotiations, such as those over tobacco, but most of the multitudinous details of military purchases, shipping, and similar business are left to speak for themselves; here the documents, in effect, annotate each other. These changes eliminate a number of texts that by earlier standards would have been published in full or in résumés, relegate to annotation material that has little bearing on Franklin's mission, and focus editorial information and explanation on what directly involved him. The result is to reduce the bulk of the documentary mountain in a way that maintains, we believe, the quality and usefulness of the edition.

Introduction

Franklin's arrival in France caused a sensation. By the time he reached Paris the city was buzzing with rumors: he had come with a small fortune in gold, to put his grandsons in school and then buy himself a Swiss château for his retirement; he had come to negotiate a treaty with France or, failing that, with Britain; he had come to sue for peace, just as he had earlier tried to reach a settlement with the Howes. These reports went the rounds of the diplomatic corps. The Parisians were so busy with conjecture, the Russian Minister informed St. Petersburg, that the police posted orders in all the taverns and coffee houses not to discuss American affairs.[1]

The report about negotiating a treaty with France was of course true. The rumored alternative of treating with Britain was partly true: the threat of doing so was a sword in the commissioners' armory, and one that turned out to be made of paper; when they waved it at Versailles, it made no impression. Neither did their effort to conclude a treaty. The expectations with which they began were dashed when Vergennes refused to see them, except once in secret, and showed no interest in their terms. He also brushed aside the requests that they had been instructed to make, for eight ships of the line and a loan of £2,000,000; but he did keep communications open through an intermediary, arranged before long for clandestine financial help on a much smaller scale, and gave them a vague intimation of more to come. This hint led them to the reckless conclusion, duly reported to Philadelphia, that France would pay the interest on emissions of American paper money. France had no such intention, but hope easily took root in the suave ambiguities of Versailles.

The commissioners' immediate concern, once the hope of French intervention faded, was with the problem of procurement. They had to find shipping, arms, uniforms, and the wherewithal to pay for them; and this necessity raised two

---

1. Nina N. Bashkina *et al.*, eds., *The United States and Russia: the Beginning of Relations 1765–1815* ([Washington, D.C., 1980]), pp. 39–40.

crucial questions. With whom were they to deal, and how were they to finance their dealings? The first question was answered in instalments. The French merchants initially in touch with the commission were those whom Franklin met in Nantes and who took him in charge there, and those whom he found in Paris already working with Silas Deane. Some of these men, as the present volume demonstrates, were much in evidence at the start and then faded from sight; others loomed larger as time passed. The documents themselves do not tell what was happening, but the story is there between the lines.

When Franklin landed on December 3 at the Breton village of Auray, exhausted by the hardships of his voyage, he was a stranger in a strange land. He had no friends in the provinces, and no one expected him; his ability to communicate was limited, for although he could read the language he could scarcely speak it or understand it when spoken, and had to rely on Temple's schoolboy French. The party set out for Nantes, and there they were almost monopolized by Pierre Penet. He was a merchant who had gone to America in search of business, met Franklin in Philadelphia a year before, and then returned in the spring with a list of the colonists' needs.[2] He must have been as welcome to the travelers as they were to him. He spoke some English himself, and had an interpreter at hand in Nathan Rumsey, a young American trading in the town. Penet's partner, Jacques Gruel, promptly moved the party to his country house near Nantes. There Franklin rested for a week before setting out for the capital, and by accident or design was isolated from other and more important Nantais merchants. He did meet two who were later closely associated with the commission, Montaudoüin and Schweighauser, but too briefly to satisfy them; Penet and Gruel, with Rumsey in attendance, took up most of his time. Penet went further. He accompanied the party when it took to the road again, and in Paris he put the commissioners in touch with his banker, a M. Sollier, who for a time handled their finances.

Arthur Lee arrived from London just after Franklin reached the capital, and the three began their work. Much of it was

2. Above, XXII, 311.

conditioned at the start by what Deane had been doing since his own arrival the previous July. He had made contact with a number of entrepreneurs who offered to supply American needs, and these the commissioners inherited. Three were particularly in evidence during the early months. One was Franklin's old friend Barbeu-Dubourg, whose dream of handling the whole American trade had now evaporated; but he still hoped against hope for some morsel of business. The second was the man who had shattered the dream and become the government's secret agent, Caron de Beaumarchais. The third was Le Ray de Chaumont, a wealthy merchant who was in touch with Vergennes and through whom Deane was obtaining gunpowder. None of these men lost any love on the others, and their antagonisms seem to have affected Franklin's relations with them. Dubourg resented Beaumarchais for superseding him; Beaumarchais regarded Dubourg and Chaumont as ineffective meddlers; Chaumont apparently kept his feelings to himself, but he soon managed to take Franklin under his wing and, before long, under his roof. The commissioners' contact with Beaumarchais was primarily through Deane, for reasons to be discussed shortly; their dealings as a group were with Chaumont and, for a time, with Penet and his friends in Nantes and with Thomas Morris, the agent there for the secret committee.

Almost immediately Penet and his circle became suspect. In mid-January Jonathan Williams, who had appeared from England in time to join his greatuncle's party on the road to Paris, was sent to Nantes to discover what was going on; he reported unfavorably on Penet's reputation, financial standing, and collaboration with Gruel. Soon afterward Arthur Lee, on his way to Spain, wrote even more unfavorably about Thomas Morris. The commissioners began to detach themselves from the whole group. Sollier, Penet's banker, ceased to be theirs. Rumsey was in their bad books by the time he sailed for home in April; so were Penet, Gruel, and Morris before the spring was out. Morris was an incompetent drunkard, and he and Rumsey had been only peripheral connections. Penet, Sollier, and Gruel had played much more of a part, but they did not have the resources to sustain it. They were small fry, and the commissioners' situation called for major figures—merchant princes like Chaumont, or an agent of the court like Beaumarchais, or great bankers like the Grand brothers, one of whom took over Sollier's former role. Only such men had the requisite governmental connections and, equally important, the wealth that enabled them to extend credit. The questions of whom the commissioners dealt with and how they financed their dealings became, once the need for credit was established, two sides of the same coin.

The necessity of credit was slow to show itself, because at the start an easier source of revenue seemed ready to hand. Cash was obviously in short supply: the commission had little beyond what it got from selling captured ships and cargoes; Congress had none to send; the French treasury was providing a mere pittance. But American tobacco promised to remedy this shortage. Congress could buy the tobacco at home with paper currency, and exchange it in France for war supplies; the only problem was how to effect the exchange. That problem, however, soon proved insoluble. The farmers general, who administered the tobacco monopoly in France, expected to buy the crop there; but not enough ships were available, the commissioners soon realized, to run it through the British blockade. The solution of sending French merchantmen to the Chesapeake the farmers rejected, presumably because they knew that it might embroil France in the war. Negotiations were foundering on this issue when rising tobacco prices in Virginia precluded any contract for a fixed sum. Although one was in fact signed, it was a mere screen for another advance from the government.[3] The commissioners were forced to realize that tobacco was not going to finance the war, and that their only hope of doing so was, aside from whatever Versailles might provide, through credit from French merchants.

That hope depended in the long run on how creditors assayed the chance of American success. When the commission first set to work, after Washington's recent disasters and the flight of Congress to Baltimore, the chance looked slim indeed. It looked somewhat better as soon as word arrived of

3. See the headnote below, March 24.

Trenton and Princeton, but even that vital news came indirectly. The commissioners could not function to good purpose, as they were well aware, unless they were kept up to date on what was happening at home; and for months they heard nothing whatever. They complained loudly, as Deane had complained before them. "We have had no Information of what passes in America but thro' England, and the Advices are for the most part such as the Ministry chuse to publish. Our total Ignorance of the truth or Falshood of Facts, when Questions are asked of us concerning them, makes us appear small in the Eyes of the People here, and is prejudicial to our Negotiations."[4]

Their commercial negotiations were central, but many others made demands on their time. They began to arrange for having warships built in the Netherlands. They listened to a horde of adventurers, offering everything from undisclosed secret weapons to a plan for raiding British commerce from some deserted Mediterranean islands. Above all they were besieged by Frenchmen who wished to serve in the American army. Here again Deane had set the stage. His reception of commission-seekers had been cordial, and had reached its climax in his commitment to Tronson Du Coudray, the talented and temperamental engineer, who had been made an American general and authorized to take with him a group of junior officers;[5] his conduct infuriated the commissioners before he finally left. They continued, nevertheless, to engage a few more engineers and artillerymen, as they had been instructed, and dispatched these recruits with the connivance of the French government. As the news spread, it kindled expectations in the officer corps at large. Franklin, better known than his colleagues, was inundated with requests from all over France; most of the writers asked him for commissions, but a few were ready to go as volunteers, sometimes even at their own expense, on the chance of finding a berth when they arrived.[6] He seems to have ignored almost all of them. He occasionally

4. To the committee of secret correspondence below, March 12.
5. Above, XXII, 462n.
6. See the headnote below, Jan 13.

took notice of a man with strikingly good connections, such as a protégé of Turgot or of the senior marshal of France, and might even interview him, but always to discourage; the most he provided was a letter of introduction that said, with great politeness, nothing at all.[7]

Although the French government could connive at the departure of a few recruits without compromising its neutrality, the first appearance of United States warships posed a tougher problem. The Treaty of Utrecht committed France to forbid such ships' remaining in port or selling their prizes. When Lambert Wickes and Franklin arrived in the *Reprisal* with two captured British vessels, Versailles managed to evade its obligations: the frigate refitted at leisure, despite threats from the authorities that it would have to put to sea, and the captures found clandestine buyers. This official tolerance encouraged the commissioners to experiment further, first by sending Wickes on a cruise that netted more prizes and then, at the end of the period covered in this volume, by providing him with a small squadron for a second cruise. The game was dangerous, but they had been told to play it: the committee of secret correspondence had instructed them to test French acquiescence until they found out how far it would stretch.[8] Vergennes knew the limit if they did not: he would tolerate what they were doing as long as they kept it decently concealed.[9] This essential condition seems to have eluded them, for they soon pushed beyond what the market would bear; the consequences will be apparent in the next volume.

How far Franklin's work as commissioner affected his social life in these early months is impossible to say. He might have been expected, if he had the leisure, to explore the intellectual world of Paris by cultivating the ties that he already had, with Dubourg, Elie de Beaumont, Jean-Baptiste Le Roy, and his fellow members of the Académie royale des sciences. Prob-

---

7. BF's view of these letters is suggested by his parody of one: below, April 2.

8. Above, XXII, 667–9.

9. He implied as much to the French Ambassador in London: Stevens, *Facsimiles*, XV, no. 1488.

ably he did, but little is on the record. Dubourg's letters are almost entirely on business, and Elie de Beaumont and Le Roy seldom appear. The Academy is scarcely mentioned, although we know that Franklin attended his first meeting soon after he arrived.[10] His old friendships endured; of that there is abundant later evidence. What this volume reveals is the making of new acquaintances.

One man who should have been among them was not. Beaumarchais had worked closely with Deane, and as the principal agent in providing war supplies was important to all the commissioners. He was a man of letters, furthermore, with a sense of humor that might have been expected to appeal to Franklin. Yet they saw almost nothing of each other, and by the Frenchman's account this was entirely the American's doing. Before Franklin arrived Beaumarchais offered him, through Deane, his services as a guide to the delicate situation in which they were all involved. Yet Deane's fellow commissioners, Beaumarchais protested a few weeks later, refused to show even common courtesy to their country's most useful friend; and by the end of the year he complained that Franklin had never once set foot in his house.[1] Perhaps Deane, the expected go-between, kept the two men apart for reasons of his own; perhaps Dubourg and Chaumont had some responsibility for their friend's coolness. In any case Franklin clearly declined a relationship that he might, given Beaumarchais' position, have been well advised to cultivate.

If this was imprudent, one imprudence is understandable in a newcomer to the intricacies of the Parisian world. Franklin's previous visits had brought him briefly into touch with a small circle of philosophes, but he knew little of French society. Now he was exposed to it at many levels, and had to feel his way on unfamiliar ground; he was beginning a new phase of his education, while always in the limelight. Within a few weeks

10. See the note on Milly's dinner invitation below, Jan. 8.

1. Morton, *Beaumarchais correspondence*, III, 19, 59; IV, 307, where the letter is misdated 1778. It says that BF explained his conduct in a way that makes no sense: he did not want to appear critical of what Deane had done before his arrival.

of his arrival, according to one observer, an engraving of him had become the fashion for the mantelpiece. The intelligentsia of Paris sought him out, and found him loath to give news of America but constantly praising it; its beauty had made heaven jealous, he said, and brought the scourge of war. "Nos esprits forts l'ont adroitement sondé sur sa religion, et ils ont cru entrevoir qu'il étoit de la leur, c'est-à-dire, qu'il n'en avoit point."[2] Mme. du Deffand invited him to her salon (there or elsewhere he made the acquaintance of a young visiting member of Parliament, Charles James Fox).[3] He dined with the duc de La Rochefoucauld, and was soon working with him on translating the new American constitutions. Jacques Paulze, one of the farmers general, arranged for him a tour of the King's library. Aimé Feutry, inventor and littérateur, bombarded him with ideas and verse. Last and far from least, Le Ray de Chaumont took him in hand, and before long engineered his move to the rural quiet of Passy, where he was surrounded by neighbors who soon became friends.

Passy solaced him in the trials of his new life. He was wrestling with financial and diplomatic problems in a fog of uncertainty, and while pestered day in, day out, by importunate favorseekers. Whom to trust? What weight to put on anonymous warnings? How best to publicize the American cause with no news of what was happening to it? How to plumb, most important of all, the intentions of Versailles? Past experience was of little direct help. His years in England had changed him from a provincial politician into a colonial spokesman, but not a policy-maker; and North and Dartmouth had been transparent by comparison with Sartine and Vergennes. His recent months in Philadelphia had taught him much about the politics and logistics of the war, but nothing about how to induce foreigners to finance it. Yet in one respect the past had served him well. It had forced him repeatedly to learn new ways, and learning had kept him limber. Otherwise he would never have

2. Bachaumont, *Mémoires secrets*, x, 29; see also p. 11.
3. For the salon see Wilmarth S. Lewis, *et al.*, eds., *The Yale Edition of Horace Walpole's Correspondence* (48 vols., New Haven, 1937–83), VI, 385–7; for BF's contact with Fox see Strahan to BF below, Jan. 23.

been resilient enough, in his seventies, to continue his education.

Even when the mountain of material in the French period is reduced to manageable proportions, editorial problems remain. The number of enclosures separated from covering notes, and of unidentifiable correspondents, is far greater than hitherto. So is the mass of undated letters and memoranda; some can be given a plausible date, and others assigned with reasonable confidence to a year or at worst to a bracket of years, but still others may belong anywhere. These problematic documents vary widely in importance, and a few of them may fall into place as the editing progresses. Yet no amount of research, even when combined with stalwart conjecture, is going to eliminate a residuum of significant mysteries.

That disorderly residuum, however, is insignificant by comparison with what has been put in order. The French mission is the least explored period of Franklin's life, not because of the lack of evidence but because of its chaotic abundance. Our files at the start were filled with unknown writers, incomprehensible references, and hints at obscure transactions. Two staff members have been working on this jumble, one for almost thirty years and the other for a decade, and have done wonders with it. Their research has put the vast majority of documents into context, and has identified most of the minor figures who crossed Franklin's path. The remaining task is to winnow the wheat of his life from the chaff. When that is done, we have every reason to hope that his years in France will be for the first time fully documented and open to exploration.

Chronology

October 27, 1776, through April 30, 1777

1776

October 27: BF sails for France on the *Reprisal*.

November 29: The *Reprisal* anchors in Quiberon Bay.

December 3: BF, WTF, and BFB land at Auray.

December 4: BF and his party at Vannes.

December 7: BF and his party reach Nantes.

December 14: The *Amphitrite* sails from Le Havre.

December 15: BF and his party leave Nantes with Penet.

December 20: BF at Versailles.

December 21: BF and his party reach Paris and lodge at the Hôtel d'Entragues.

December 21, 30: The committee of secret correspondence sends new instructions to the commissioners.

December 22: Arthur Lee arrives in Paris.

December 26: The Battle of Trenton.

December 28: The commissioners meet secretly in Paris with Vergennes.

Between December 30 and January 8: BF moves to the Hôtel d'Hambourg.

C. December 31: The *Amphitrite* returns to Lorient.

1777

January 1: Congress names BF commissioner to Spain.

January 4: BF and Arthur Lee have an interview with the Spanish Ambassador.

January 5: The commissioners formally request French aid.

January 9: Louis XVI approves the response to the commissioners.

January 13: Gérard reads the commissioners the King's response.

January 14: JW arrives in Nantes.

January 24: The *Amphitrite* sails again.

January 24–February 13: The cruise of the *Reprisal*.

January 28: BF has agreed to move to Passy.

February 5: The Pennsylvania Assembly re-elects BF to Congress.

February 12: The commissioners sign an agreement with Captain Boux on shipbuilding.

February 13: The commissioners sign an agreement with Duportail and other engineers.

C. February 27: BF moves to Passy.

March 14: Capt. Hammond arrives in Paris with dispatches.

March 24: The commissioners sign a tobacco contract with the farmers general.

March 27: The commissioners purchase arms from Montieu.

April 1: The commissioners sign an agreement with Chaumont to provide for their packets.

April 3: Arthur Lee returns from Spain.

April 8: Wickes and Nicholson leave Paris for their cruise.

April 17: William Hodge purchases a cutter at Dunkirk.

April 21: The *Lexington* is ordered to join Wickes's cruise.

THE PAPERS OF
BENJAMIN FRANKLIN

VOLUME 23

October 27, 1776, through April 30, 1777

From Charles Lee

ALS: National Archives

Dear Sir,   Camp at Philipsburg. Novr. the 6th 1776

The Gentleman who will deliver you this was as I understand sent by Congress to General Washington. He was to have given specimens of his abilities as Engineer and been recommended accordingly. Whether He is a great Engineer or no I cannot pretend to say, as He has had no fair opportunity of displaying his talents. The few small works He has thrown up have been in haste, at the same time labouring under the disadvantage of not being able to explain himself to the workmen. From the little I can judge of him He is a Man of capacity and knowledge, and I am told by his Countrymen that his Fort lies in surveying Georgraphically and military a Country. I know not any kind of Officer more wanted in America than a Military Surveyor of those parts which are likely to be the scene of action. General Washington and Myself have therefore concurr'd in opinion that He shoud begin with the Jerseys and if He gives satisfactory proofs of his talents in this line, to recommend him to Congress for this important Office. I must beg leave to recommend him to your Protection and Patronage and request that you will furnish him with the necessary instruments. And as I am so well acquainted with your liberal way of thinking and manners it will be unnecessary to desire you to show him all possible personal civilities. So far for Monsr. Imbert.[1] You will naturally expect something from me on our present situation. We have by proper positions brought Mr. Howe to his ne plus ultra. He has therefore apparently given all hopes of taking us Prisoners as, I believe, He lately sanguinely promised himself. Monsr. Imbert, as you know

1. Jean-Louis Imbert was a French engineer who had come from Martinique on the *Reprisal*; Gen. d'Argout had strongly recommended him and three other Frenchmen, none of whom spoke English, and Bingham had persuaded Wickes to take them to Philadelphia. Congress sent Imbert to New York to test his competence, and Washington suggested that he work on fortifying the highlands of the Hudson. Nothing came of the idea, apparently, and Lee returned him to Philadelphia. This letter to BF was laid before Congress, which referred it to the board of war. Above, XXII, 618; Lasseray, *Les Français*, I, 244–5; *JCC*, V, 783; VI, 968; Fitzpatrick, *Writings of Washington*, VI, 214.

French, will be able to explain the circumstances of both Armies. The spirit of our present Troops is upon the whole good,[2] and if America is lost, it is not in my opinion owing to want of courage in your Soldiers, but pardon me, to want of prudence, in your High Mightiness's. Adieu, God bless you, My Dear Sir, live long and make your Country and Frinds as happy, as you have render'd yourself admirable in the eyes of all good and sensible Men. Yours most sincerely   CHARLES LEE

Addressed: To Dr Benjamin Franklin / Member of the Continental / Congress. / from Camp wth / General Washington

Endorsed: 1776 Novr 6th. General Lee by a Monsr. Imbert

Notation: Letter[?] from Gen. Lee to Benjamin Franklin Nov 6. 1776.

From Michel-Alain Chartier de Lotbinière[3]

ALS: National Archives[4]

Chatam, au Cap Cod, 11[–20] Novembre, 1776.

Monsieur:

Me voici enfin au comble de mes souhait, puisque depuis deux jours je suis sur votre continent, et à même de pouvoir parvenir jusqu'à vous sous peu à Philadelphie, sans avoir à courir les risques que j'ai couru depuis mon départ de St. Pierre, ainsi que vous le pourrez voir en parcourant la lettre cy-jointe pour mon fils.[5] Je vous aurai, monsieur, la plus grande obli-

2. After the inconclusive Battle of White Plains Howe had marched off westward, leaving the Americans in the dark about his intentions. The spirit of Washington's troops was in fact at low ebb. Willcox, *Portrait of a General,* pp. 113–14; Freeman, *Washington,* IV, 235–7.

3. He was a voice out of BF's past, for he had written him more than a quarter-century before: above, V, 504–5. As far as we know they had had no contact since. The French Canadian seigneur claimed that Vergennes had sent him to the United States to observe; he returned to France in the summer of 1777. *Dictionnaire biographique du Canada.*

4. We have silently supplied a few illegibilities in the MS from the text printed in Force, 5 *Amer. Arch.,* III, 642–3.

5. His son Louis has joined the American army as a chaplain during the Canadian campaign, and was still in service: *JCC,* V, 645 and *passim.* The father, apparently misinformed, thought he was a prisoner, and in the enclosed letter reproached him for his recklessness, but offered to procure his release by taking his place. Force, *op. cit.,* cols. 644–5.

gation de vouloir bien la lui faire remettre le plûtost possible, dans la supposition toutefois qu'il soit encore dans vos provinces, autrement je vous prierois de vous la réserver jusqu'à ce que j'aie l'honneur de vous voir; et dans le cas où il fut encore avec vous, j'espere que vous aurez la bonté de le faire venir à Philadelphie pour le tems où je pourrai m'y rendre.

J'ai séjourné à Paris et Versailles plus de deux mois, avant de me porter à St. Malo, d'où j'ai pris mon embarquement pour St. Pierre de Miquelon. J'ai eu pendant ce séjour nombre de conférences avec M. de Vergennes, ministre des affaires etrangeres, ainsi qu'avec d'autres personnages importans en France, qui m'ont paru prendre constamment le plus vif intérêt à la réussite de vôtre cause. Je puis même vous assurer que la chose alloit au point, qu'il eut semblé qu'elle les affectoit plus que leurs propres affaires; mais c'est ce dont nous nous entretiendrons plus au long, pendant mon séjour à Philadelphie.

Je ne vous cache pas, Monsieur, que je désirerois beaucoup le reste de ma famille avec vous à présent, je serois dans le cas d'agir beaucoup plus ouvertement, que je ne le pourrai jusqu'à ce que j'aie tiré Madame de Lotbiniere et ma fille du pais où elles sont au moment; et pour y parvenir plus promtement, mon idée seroit de faire passer de suite mon fils en Canada, moi tenant sa place tant qu'il seroit absent, qui muni des instructions que nous pourrons lui donner, parviendra peut-être à nous les amener promtement: en attendant vous devez croire, par le zéle que vous m'avez connu pour la cause commune, que je ne m'épargnerai pas sur le conseil, d'après les connoissances que j'ai des lieux sur lesquels il me semble que vous devez diriger toutes vos vues, aussitost que vous aurez reduit l'ennemi que vous avez en face à ne pouvoir plus agir offensivement; et comme il vous reste bien peu de tems pour voir finir la campagne, je croirois que vous n'avez rien de mieux à faire avec cet ennemi, que de le resserer le plus que vous le pourrez, mais de n'engager avec lui aucune affaire generale qui, perdue, diviseroit toute votre armée sans espérance de la pouvoir rassembler à tems, afin de prévenir la désunion, que je n'apperçois desja que trop dans la colonie actuelement attaquée, par le peu que l'on m'en a dit depuis que je suis ici, sur laquelle je savois des Londres qu'on comptoit pour ne pas dire qu'on en étoit desja certain, et qui je le crois a décidé le projet d'attaque: il vous est necessaire plus que jamais, je le pense, de vous conduire à la Fabius, poussant toujours vos vivres derriere vous, et dévastant le pays que vous [avez] abandonné; par ce moyen vous êtes certains de consommer votre ennemi, qui ne pouvant se raffraichir ni se recruter dans votre pais, se réduira dans le cours de l'hiver à un nombre bien peu respectable; et vous savez mieux que moi, qu'il est impossible à l'Angleterre de fournir une seconde armée, à une dépense aussi exhorbitante que celle-ci.

J'aurois bien souhaitté, monsieur, être muni, avant mon départ de Boston, d'ordres assez précis pour voler le plustost possible jusqu'a vous, avec deux domestiques que j'ai, et mes équipages. J'ai l'honneur d'être, avec l'attachement le plus particulier, et la plus grande consideration, monsieur, votre très humble et très obeissant serviteur,   LOTBINIERE

P.S. De la Baye de Boston pret à arriver à cette ville ce Mardi, 7 heures du soir 19 Novembre 1776.

N'ayant pû trouver ni poste ni occasions certaines pour Boston à Harrwich, où j'ai sejourné malgré moi du lundi au samedi de la derniere semaine, non plus qu'à Plymouth, où un vent forcé de nord ouest nous a retenu jusqu'à ce matin, j'ai été réduit à porter moi-même la présente lettre jusqu'ici. Si nous arrivons ce soir à Boston comme je l'espere, je la ferai passer de suite à la poste; autrement ce sera demain des le matin, et on m'assure qu'il sera encore tems à 9 heures. Je ne sai combien j'aurai, monsieur, de jours à attendre votre reponse; je prévois n'être en état de laisser Boston que lorsque je la recevrai, car la goellette qui m'a apporté de St. Pierre à Chataim en est à peine partie, et ma chaise n'en poura sortir que dans 6 ou sept jours pour le plustost, qui sera le tems ou vraisemblablement cette goelette y arrivera, devant passer à Well-Fleet (au Cap Cod) où elle doit rester 3 ou quatre jours: ainsi je crois ne rien hazarder, vous annonçant que je ne laisserai cette ville qu'après avoir eu de vos nouvelles. Vous savez, monsieur, combien je vous suis attaché et à quel point je vous considere.   C.L.

Je profiterai du tems que je resterai à Boston pour voir la suite des ouvrages, tant à la ville et au-dehors, que dans la Baye, s'il m'est possible de parcourir le tout, et si'il m'est permis de le faire. Je vous en dirai mon sentiment, lorsque j'aurai l'honneur de vous voir.

Boston, 20 Novembre, 1776.

J'apprend à l'instant que Monsieur Franklin est parti pour se rendre en France.[6] J'aurai une obligation infini à Monsieur le Président du Congrès, à qui j'ai l'honneur de présenter mon respect, de faire usage de cette lettre comme si elle lui étoit addressée, et de vouloir bien suppléer au defaut de M. Franklin pourtant [pour tout] ce qu'elle contient. J'espere qu'il voudra bien m'honorer d'un mot de résponse. J'ai l'honneur d'être son très humble serviteur,   L.

Addressed: To / the Hon. Benjamin Franklin Esq. / &c., &c., &c. / at Philadelphia

Notations: From Monsieur Lotbiniere at Boston / From Monsr. Lotbinier Boston / [Mon. Lot]biniere Nov. 11. 1776

From Jan Ingenhousz

ALS: American Philosophical Society; duplicate: Staatsbibliothek Preussischer Kulturbesitz, West Berlin

Dear friend.   Vienna in Austria Nov. 15. 1776

Since I received your kind lettre dated Marsch 18, 1774,[7] great things have happened, of which your country is the theatre. That country is become the seat of horror and bloodshed, which I took to be the seat of tranquillity and happiness, and which I was formerly much inclined to chuse as a quiet retreat

---

6. He got the news just as the post was taking the letter and its enclosure, and wrote this note on the outside, he explained to Hancock on Dec. 4; he went on to give his credentials for proffering military advice, which he did at some length along the lines sketched in this letter. *Bulletin des recherches historiques*, LIV (1948), 115–118.

7. The letter (above, XXI, 147–9) was the most recent one that survives to BF's old friend, now physician to Maria Theresa; Ingenhousz had written several times thereafter, but as far as we know not since October, 1774: *ibid.*, pp. 216–17, 336.

in an approaching old age. This sceme has often had more wight upon my mind, than I trusted to communicate even to the best of my friends. My plan was to settle there in the mean time some children of my brother.[8] Not long ago I was asked advice by a very sensible man about his purchasing a little estate in the Neighbourhood of Philadelphia worth £2000, which he thought could be acquired for a thousand Pound St. during these troubles, which he expected would soon been setled. But it seems he is very much mistaken. What dismal scene of confusion anarchy and bloodshed exhibits this once happy climate! which did seem to be destined by the Author of Nature for the abode of tranquillity, the asilum for those who are persecuted for religious principles, and the only seat of undisturbed human felicity. A natural inclination, warmed by a sense of gratitude make me take a freindly share in every thing which befalls great Brittain and the colonies. I considered them as one country, the only, where men enjoyed in full all those liberties which they derive from nature, and which are consistent with a well regulated society. You made me consider them as one nation, tho divided thro different climates, which aught to have one common interest, as it is or aught to be gouverned by the same laws and to have one common seat of gouverment, which you thought should better remain, where it allways was, than to be transferred within the colonies. You told me more than once that no more distinction should be made between a man residing in England and one residing in North America, than between the inhabitans of London and cheffield. Knowing from your own mouth this to be your principles, I found myself often obliged to defend your conduct before the most Respectable Persons, who were verry willing to adscribe in a great great measur to you this unhappy contest and all the bloodshed of which it has been allready and may be still the cause. Will this dreadfull storm at last subside and end in a calm, as human affairs commonly do? or will it end in a total subversion of things? Will

8. His only brother, Louis, an apothecary in Breda, had a son who became a doctor there. Julius Wiesner, *Jan Ingen-Housz, sein Leben und seine Wirken* ... (Vienna, 1905), p. 14.

all the industrious labour of your ancestors employed in changing those wildernisses in the happyest abode for civilised men, at once been rendered useless, and their so newly erected cities converted again into uninhabited deserts? I shudder at the very thaught of such horrid catastrophes, of which no exemple has ever happened upon the surface of the earth.

Whatever may be your chief business at present I hope you have not entirely forgot your old friends. If he, how [who] is the most respectfully and sincerely attached to you, may claim some preference, I may expect the favour of a few lines and be informed of the state of your health, and of that degree of happiness or unhappiness which may at that period of time have befallen your country; that I may be qualify'd to give some satisfactory answer to those illustrious persons, who very often inquire about you, and ask whether and what news I got from you, which [with] whom they know I have been so many years intimately acquainted. I should be very glad to know at the same time, who [how] your Nephew does our fellow traveller with Mr. Canton,[9] and what is become of your son the governour of New Jersey. You promised me to send me a copy of your apology, but I have heard nothing about it since.[1]

Sir John Pringle and some of our other English friends let me sometimes hear from them. I expect the same kindness of you, tho separated from you by a great deal more land and sea. If I could expect that in the middel of the horrors of a civil warr you reserved some hours to philosophical poursuits, I should intertain you with some experiments upon air and other matters, which I made some time ago, some of which, I hear, are to be publish'd in the philosophical trans.

The Second volum of Priestley upon air is full of new matter and seems to open a large field to philosophers. Electricity is dayly advancing everywhere. Mr. Walsh has at last found out the method of making an Electric spark visible from a

9. A reference to Ingenhousz's tour of northern England in 1771 with BF, JW, and John Canton: above, XVIII, 101, 113–16.

1. BF's promise (above, XXI, 148) to send him the tract on the Hutchinson letters, presumably when it was in print, had not been redeemed because it was never finished or published.

Gymnotus of Surinam.[2] The new electrical machine, called by the discoverer, one mr. *Volta*, an Italien gentleman, *Electrophorus perpetuus* affords much matter of speculation. Some Electricians, thinking that the phenomena of this machine do not consist with your principles, have attempted to establish new ones; but I think them in the wrong. As the present troubles may possibly have prevented you getting some knowledge of this discovery, I think it may [my] duty to give you a Slight idea of its nature. It consists of two plates of metal, or wood, past-board or other matter covered with metal. One of them is covered with a thin coat of Rosin mixed with some wax and turpentin (for to make it less brittel) about one or 2 lines thick. The oter has a glas tube, stick of sealing wax, or silk strings fastened to its upper surface for to insulate it. The plate covered with rosin is put upon a table with the Rosin upwards and rubbed with a dry hand, a piece of leather or a hair skin. The other plate is put upon the rosin and touched with the finger, a spark issues out of it, and if the under plate is touched at the same time, a shock is felt. The upper plate being lifted up prouves to be strongly electrical positively, and the under plate negatively (if placed upon an electric stand) the upper plate, after a spark has been taken out, being let down again upon the rosin and touched as before becomes again electrical, and thus the electric force once excited may be kept a life years togeather. If a charged fial is slided over the surface of the rosin by taking it by the nob the electricity is very much increased. If insteat of one plate coated with rosin you take two, and slide the upper plate alternately over the surface of them, taking allways the spark from it when it is placed upon the rosin, both under plates become very strongly electrical the one communicating to the insulated plate a positive, the other

2. Ingenhousz's publication, "Easy Methods of Measuring the Diminution of Bulk, Taking Place in the Mixture of Common Air and Nitrous Air . . . ," appeared in the *Phil. Trans.*, LXVI (1776), 257–67. For the second volume of Priestley's work see above, XXII, 347 n. John Walsh, the experimenter with electrical fish (above, XIX, 160), had demonstrated to fellows of the Royal Society the sparks emitted by a gymnotus: Wilhelm Biedermann, *Electro-Physiology* (Frances A. Welby, trans.; 2 vols., London, 1896–98), II, 358.

a negative electricity, so strong, that at last the insulated plate
being lifted up discharges it self with a crakeling noice upon
the metal of the under plate (which last experiment is not yet
published).[3] Some years ago I contrived a very strong electrical machine. It consisted of a disk of pastboard 4 feet diameter
thoroughly dryed then impregnated and covered with linzeet
oil varnish, and whirled round verticaly, and rubbed by hair
skins in the way my flat machines are rubbed. The sparks
from the surface of such a pasteboard were about 2 feet long,
and when collected upon a metal prime conductor of 6 or 7
feet long, they were allmost unsufferable, tho they were but a
few inches long. By placing several such disks one after an
other and cushions between them, wirled round upon the same
axis, the electricity was much increased.[4]

You will be surprized to hear that I am maried with a Dutch
Lady, the sister of Mr. Jacquin professor of botany and chem-
istry in this University, and well known in the learned world
by his various botanical and chemical Works. But you will
perhaps not approuve that I took one, who is but 5 years
younger than I. However, after a great deal of reflexions I
thaught that such a wife did suit me bettre at my age than a
young girl.[5] This changement in my life will not prevent me
from visiting my friends in England.

I enjoye sometimes the company of one Mr. *Kauffman* from
Philadelphia, who studies physic here, and intends to settle in
his native country.[6]

3. This is the first appearance in our volumes of Alessandro Volta (1745–
1827), one of the greatest electrical scientists of the age. For a brief description of his electrophore and its significance see the article on him in the
Dictionary of Scientific Biography. Ingenhousz subsequently published experiments to reconcile BF's theories with the evidence produced by the electrophore: *Phil. Trans.*, LXVIII (1778), part 2, 1027–48.

4. Ingenhousz described this machine in *ibid.*, LXIX (1779), part 2, 659–
73, as an improvement on the earlier one that is discussed above, XIX,
190 n.

5. In 1775 Ingenhousz, at the age of 44, had married Agathe Maria Jacquin (d. 1800?), the sister of Nikolaus Josef Jacquin. Wiesner, *op. cit.*, p. 42;
see also the sketches of Ingenhousz and Jacquin in the *Dictionary of Scientific
Biography*.

6. Joseph Cauffman (1755–78) was a Philadelphian who had been educated in Europe for the past decade and had just taken his medical degree

As your unhappy contest with the mother country is not yet setled, I find a great difficulty to forward this lettre to you. I thaught it advisable to send two copies of it, as it is more than probable that one of them will be lost. I will venture to send one by England, if sometimes it may be taken with the Males of New York, where to all appearance the king's troops will keep their winter quarters. I will send the other over Amsterdam to S. Eustatius.[7] It will not be so difficult for you to direct lettres to me, either by the way of England, where they may best be delivred to the Imperial Ambassadour, or over S. Eustatius, or directely to Amsterdam to the care of Mr. *Hermanus Volkmar*, who will have the care of this lettre.

I hope your first news will be that of peace being restored, for I fear, that, if things are not soon be brought to an end, other powers will meddle in the affair and embroil whole the globe of the earth; which then will be the third warr one after an other, original from North America. How glorious would it be to you to be the chief means of stopping the streams of human blood, which are likely to flow still from these terrible misunderstandings. I am most sincerely Dear friend Your most obedient humble Servant and affectionat friend

J. INGEN HOUSZ

Addressed in another hand: To / Doctor Benjamin Franklin / at / Philadelphia
Notation: Ingenhouss Nov. 15. 1776.

From Anthony Wayne   ALS: Historical Society of Pennsylvania

Dear Sir   Ticonderoga 15th Novr. 1776
Yesterday An express Arrived here from Albany giving Intelligence that Gene. Howe with the British fleet and army had

---

from the University of Vienna. BF did not know him, but received a long-winded letter from him the following spring, asking for advice: below, April 23.

7. The copy sent to England was returned to him, and he forwarded it with his letter below of Jan. 29; it is, we assume, the ALS printed here. The duplicate, which differs in some details of wording, came to light in a German auction in 1882 and then disappeared until 1923, when it was presented to the Preussische Staatsbibliothek; it now belongs to the western division of that library.

passed Kings Bridge and from Appearances seemed as if he Intended to penetrate into Jersey or proceed up the Hudson's River the truth of this you will know much better than we at this Distance.[8] However Genl. St. Clair with the first Pennsa. and the 1 and Second Jersey Regts. whose times are about expiring are now on their March to Albany and will be at hand to Cooparate with our Other troops in that Neighbourhood in case of Necessity. We are Ordered to keep post at this place until we know the designs of Howe, and have Certain accounts of the Situation of the Enemy in this Quarter which we expect every hour from a boat and Scouts sent down the Lake for that purpose. Carlton and Burgoyne have tacitly acknowledged that they were afraid the Americans *would fight* and that they themselves were not so fond of it. Otherwise why Retreat so percepetately after Vanquishing our fleet without attempting anything by Land? It was not for want of Sufficient force. They realy out Numbered us far and had the Entire Command of the Lake.[1]

I may now with truth Assure you that for two weeks after their Arrival at Crown Point we had not more than 5,500 men fit for duty, of which not more than 3,000 were on this side the Lake, or could be had in case of Action, with the Risque of loosing mount Independence.[2]

The day must shortly come when these facts will be known to the World. What excuse, what Reason can be assigned by those Blustering sons of War, for thus shamefully flying from so small a force and from a People whom they effected so much to Dispise?

Had they Attempted to Storm, disgrace and ruen would have been their Portion; but had they Invested the place provissions and other Necessaris would have failed us. We had not one Barrel of flower on this Ground 4 days since. When I see you I can unfold a tale that will Astonish you.

8. The intelligence was in a letter from Schuyler, at Albany, to Gates at Ticonderoga: Force, 5 *Amer. Arch.*, III, 658.

1. For the British victory at Valcour Island and subsequent withdrawal see William M. Fowler, Jr., *Rebels under Sail: the American Navy during the Revolution* (New York, 1976), pp. 192–211.

2. Across from and commanding the fort. For the situation to which he refers see above, XXII, 540–2, 586.

For the present I must Inform you that our people through hard fatague without Necessaries[?] and totally Destitute of the Conveniences[?] of life, if kept a few weeks longer on this Ground, will not be able to reach home; nor can we expect them to reenlist with so Gloomy appearance of want and misery before them. But were they to be Recalld and this post garrisnd for the Winter by fresh troops, they would to a man Inlist during the War. Indeed they offer to engage Immediately on Condition that we pledge our Honour of their being suffered to go home for a few weeks during the Winter; and two of those fellows who have Survived thorough this hard Campayn are equal to three of the best fresh troops that can be Raised. On the Contrary if other Colones are Indulged in having all their men called home, whilst the Pennsylvanians are Continud here until their time's expire, we shall produce a Wretched Army from our State in place of the best, which is the case this present year.

Col. Hartly[3] an Officer of Real merit who carries this give you full and true Information on this head or any other whatever[?] Relating to this place and Army. I have not time to read what I have wrot you will excuse any error, and believe me yours most Sincerely   A WAYNE

Notation: 15th Novr. 1776 Docr. B Franklin

From Jean-Baptiste Le Roy[4]

Copy:[5] Massachusetts Historical Society; copy: National Archives

Aux galeries du Louvre a paris ce 28 9bre 1776
Les occasions de vous assurer de mes sentiments invariables pour vous Monsieur et cher confrere, me sont toujour infiniment pretieuses. Je profite en consequence et avec empressement du depart de M. le chevalier de Preudhomme de Borre

3. For Hartley see *ibid.*, pp. 189 n, 540.
4. We have hitherto spelled him "LeRoy" because that seemed to be the way he wrote his name; by now, however, he is clearly separating the words.
5. Made, according to a notation on the MS, by a clerk of Silas Deane.

pour avoir l'honneur de vous ecrire et pour vous dire combien j'aÿ eté enchanté d'apprendre qu'au milieu de tout le poid immense des affaires de l'amerique votre santé se soutienne toujour aussÿ bonne. M. le chevalier de Borre qui vous remettra cette lettre, est un homme de qualité du pais de Liege qui sert depuis 36 ans dans nos Troupes qui a fait quatorze campagnes de guerre etant depuis vingt ans lieutenant colonel d'infanterie et sur le point d'etre fait brigadier, en outre il ÿ a 32 ans qu'il a la commission de capitaine de cavalerie. Enfin pendant toute la guerre derniere, il a eu sous son commandement deux bataillons. M. le comte d'herouville qui etoit le bras droit du Marechal de Saxe et un de nos meilleurs lieutenants generaux et des plus distingués, m'a parlé de M. le chevalier de Borre comme d'un tres bon militaire et qui entend particulierement la composition et la formation des corps.[6] J'aÿ eté bien aise de vous prevenir de ses talens pour que vos generaux l'emploient comme il doit l'etre, il est essentiel que vous aiez des officiers qui entendent bien a discipliner des corps a les faire manoeuvrer et a les bien mener a la guerre et selon M. d'herouville vous trouverez tout cela dans M. le chevalier de Borre. J'aÿ l'honneur de vous le recommander d'ailleurs comme un galant homme qui sur le recit que je luÿ ai fait de vous sera enchanté d'avoir l'honneur de vous connoitre. Adieu Monsieur et cher confrere, conservez toujour je vous prie quelque amitié pour un homme de l'autre monde qui vous sera attaché par les sentiments les plus sincers jusqu'a son dernier soupir. Signé

Le Roÿ

Copie d'une lettre ecrite a M. francklin, addressée au Congrés a philadelphie

6. Philippe-Hubert, chevalier de Preudhomme or Preud'homme de Borre, left Paris two days after this was written, sailed on a ship that put back, and reached America in March. He was commissioned a brigadier general and served until 1779, when he became disgruntled and returned to France. Lasseray, *Les Français*, II, 367–70. For Antoine de Ricouart, comte d'Hérouville de Claye (1713–82), a writer as well as general, see Larousse, *Dictionnaire universel* under Hérouville.

Editorial Note on Franklin's Accounts

Franklin, when he arrived in France, began to keep accounts even before he began to write letters. His first entries are dated December 3, the day he set foot ashore; they show how much money he had on hand and what he paid for the boat from the *Reprisal* to Auray.[7] These humdrum details started a collection that grew and grew over the years. The financial records of the commission throw a great deal of light on how it functioned, but they are bewildering in their variety and dismaying in their bulk. They touch on everything from the funding of the war to the small details of housekeeping at Passy, and are so voluminous, and often so repetitive, that a detailed treatment of each is more likely to confuse than enlighten.[8] Many of them are Franklin documents, however, and clearly within our rubric. We limit ourselves here to discussing their general character, and to noticing those that bear on the period of this volume; future editorial notes will notice others that bear only on later periods. We use relevant information to annotate our documents and, where the information is important but not specifically relevant, summarize it briefly in these editorial notes. They deal only with accounts that directly involve Franklin: those that he kept himself, that others kept for him or jointly with him, and that European bankers and businessmen kept of their transactions with him and his colleagues. Those that do not directly involve him, such as Silas Deane's or Beaumarchais' in the present period, we use in annotation where needed but do not discuss further.

Only some of the accounts that deal with any given period were drawn up at the time, by Franklin and his entourage or by the commissioners' business associates. Others were compiled years later, for submission to Congress or by committees or agents of that body after it began to keep a close eye on the activities of its emissaries abroad. These official accounts derive from earlier ones, of which most survive but a few apparently do not, and are colored by the later setting. They rearrange some items and omit others, presumably those for expenses that either an auditor would not allow or that had already been paid; what Franklin submitted for his settlement with Congress, furthermore, must have been influenced by the

---

7. See the headnote on the next document. The entries are in the Waste Book, described below.

8. Many of these are available in two microfilm editions, that of BF's accounts in the APS and that of the Papers of the Continental Congress in the National Archives.

16

accusations and partisan bickering, particularly in 1779, over the commissioners' financial dealings. This later record, in other words, contains much the same material as the earlier but deals with it differently. We take notice here or in subsequent volumes of all accounts we have located, no matter when they were composed, that are relevant to the period of the volume.

The commission engendered controversy long before 1779. Arthur Lee was quick to convince himself that his two colleagues, for reasons of their own, were excluding him from their transactions, in which they were using public funds extravagantly and irresponsibly. "A thousand times have I desired that the public accounts might from time to time be made up, to which I have as constantly received evasive or affrontive answers."[9] When John Adams arrived in Paris in 1778 to succeed Silas Deane, he was appalled by the state of those accounts. Business had been conducted so unmethodically, he concluded, that "it was utterly impossible to acquire any clear Idea of our Affairs." He laid much of the blame on Franklin, in part for high living and in greater part for bad bookkeeping,[1] and the latter charge is important to any consideration of the commission's finances.

In 1781 Temple Franklin, who had been laboring for years over the accounts, pointed out areas in which they had been scrupulously kept.[2] In specific instances this was true, but in general the extant bookkeeping is chaotic. During Franklin's years in London it had been excellent, but thanks only to young Jonathan Williams.[3] His greatuncle was not well endowed with the necessary tidiness, and what little he had diminished with time. "In Truth I found myself incorrigible with respect to *Order*," he admitted near the end of his mission in France, "and now I am grown old, and my Memory bad, I feel very sensibly the want of it."[4] He may have felt the want, but seems to have made no great effort to remedy it. During the early years of the mission Temple took care of the household expenses, Deane of most of the commercial transactions. If Franklin concerned himself in detail with such matters, little evidence survives. He apparently made one attempt, mentioned below, to have his bookkeeping organized in the same comprehensive way as in London; but the project was abandoned. And for good reason. His French

9. Lee, *Life of Arther Lee*, II, 50.
1. Butterfield, *John Adams Diary*, IV, 77; see also pp. 53, 88, 107–9, 111.
2. WTF to John Adams, Jan. 11, and to JW, Aug. 24, 1781, Library of Congress.
3. See above, XI, 518–20.
4. *Autobiog.*, p. 156.

mission involved incomparably more men than his English, merchants as well as fellow commissioners, and incomparably larger sums of money. To bring these transactions together into the neat and narrow compass of the London "Journal" and "Ledger" would have been a herculean task.

The descriptive list that follows includes all the extant accounts, to the best of our knowledge, that relate to the five months covered by the volume. Most are mere notations of payments and receipts, but several attempt the kind of double-entry bookkeeping found in the "Journal" and "Ledger." The first seven on our list are Franklin's, some his alone and some his colleagues' as well, and the remaining three are those of merchants and businessmen with whom the commission dealt; each group is arranged in order of probable composition.

Only a few make any attempt to distinguish between public and private expenditures. The first were those for Congress, like what Franklin had laid out in London for Massachusetts; the second were salaries and expenses for the day-to-day support of the commissioners. Congress was responsible for both and eventually, after the furor over Deane's financial conduct, tried to define them in its resolutions of August 6, 1779, which set specific salaries and subjected expenses to strict accounting and audit by a Congressional agent;[5] later versions of Franklin's accounts reflect these resolutions and subsequent Congressional attempts to compensate him and his colleagues. A third category of his expenses also appears from time to time, what may be called personal because Congress had no responsibility for them. He still had funds with his English bankers; although soon after his arrival in France he transferred more than £1,000 to Paris, he retained a small balance in London.[6]

5. *JCC*, XIV, 928–9.

6. As late as January, 1777, Browns & Collinson had £878 in BF's account in London. He had ordered these funds transferred to John Sargent in 1775 (above, XXII, 71–2), but apparently the order was not carried out. Soon after he reached Paris BF moved £800 from London to Germany, Girardot & Cie., leaving £78 with his British bankers, and deposited with the Parisian firm the £222 he had received in his settlement with the Walpole Co.; by late March he had 23,800 *l.t.* in his French account. Waste Book, entries under March 22, 1777; Walpole to BF below, Feb. 10, 1777; Fragment of a Journal and Ledger, p. [2] of first section. Benjamin Vaughan, during a visit to Paris in the winter of 1776–77, borrowed 40 guineas and subsequently deposited that amount to BF's London account, bringing it to £120. Waste Book, entries under Feb. 8 and 26, 1777.

I. Waste Book, December 3, 1776, to March 10, 1779: American Philosophical Society. 10 pp.

This volume is a running record of Franklin's disbursements, public, private, and personal (labeled "self") jumbled together, with a brief description of each; the first page also has receipts arranged in a separate column. The entries are in both Franklin's hand and Temple's, and are not totaled; they are the basis for many of the later reworkings of Franklin's accounts, described below. The old man kept a careful eye on what he might charge his son for Temple's rearing, and an intriguing feature of the document is William's initials by such items. These were obviously added in 1785, the only time when father and son met after 1775.

II. Fragment of a Journal and Ledger, December, 1776, to April, 1777: American Philosophical Society. 19 pp.

The first three pages resemble the London "Journal" except that the entries, which are those in the Waste Book slightly reorganized, are undated. The final sixteen pages, prefaced by an alphabetical index of individuals and firms, rearranges the material in the first three as the London "Ledger" does that in the "Journal." Both sections are in Temple's hand. Between the two is the bulk of the volume, which is a quite different account: personal expenses from the fall of 1785 to the spring of 1787. Franklin must have tried at the start of his mission to continue his English practice of double-entry bookkeeping, dropped the idea after four months, and used the blank pages much later for another purpose.

III. William Temple Franklin's Accounts, January 16, 1777, to February 23, 1779: American Philosophical Society. 47 pp.

This is a running account in Temple's hand.[7] It opens with the receipt of 2,400 *l.t.* for household expenses; a few weeks later came 4,800, and the funds were periodically renewed; every so often Temple balanced expenditures against them. Between late February and mid-November, 1777, only a few minor entries appear. John Adams took charge of supervising the accounts after his arrival, and several times noted that he had verified them. William Franklin later initialed entries, as in the Waste Book, for Temple's expenses.

7. Two other versions, on which this is based, are in the APS, one of 32 pp. in WTF's hand and the other of 39 pp. in an unidentified hand and signed by him. The first ends on Aug. 12, 1778, and was apparently copied and slightly revised to make the second, which bears a final note by WTF of Sept. 14, 1778, that a copy was delivered for John Adams' examination.

IV. The Pillets' Accounts, March 2 to August 11, 1777: University of Pennsylvania Library. 41 pp.

The document is two separate manuscripts that form a single running account, by the pair who managed the Passy household. The outlays are for food, kitchen utensils, servants' traveling expenses, small gifts to the poor, postage, etc., and are invaluable in documenting the day-to-day operation of the household and the comings and goings of its members. The size of the staff cannot be determined from such material, but a number of servants are mentioned in other accounts.

V. Franklin's Accounts as Commissioner, December 3, 1776, to October 4, 1778: American Philosophical Society. 23 pp.

This is the most complete of four extant versions,[8] and was presumably compiled from the other three in response to the Congressional resolutions discussed above. Most of the material in the Waste Book reappears here in a different form, except that personal expenditures are deleted. Public and private ones are made comprehensible, but are not clearly distinguished: public payments, to prisoners of war or for American propaganda, are jumbled together with payments for the household. The first section of the document is a summary of the eleven separate accounts that follow, which are Franklin's own and those he kept jointly with Deane and Adams (Lee does not appear); all of them show the same mixture of public and private. Seven of the eleven are for money paid out, four for money received. Two of the seven are "taken from Joint-Expence Book" and two of the four "extracted from Expence Book"; these seem to be references to a book or books now lost.

8. We may for convenience call our document A and the others B, C, and D. Those others, to judge by internal evidence, were earlier and were for the most part incorporated in A; but B and C have entries after the terminal date of A. These are explained by BF's appointment as minister plenipotentiary on Oct. 4, 1778: he continued to keep accounts as commissioner until he learned the following spring of his new position. B (14 pp., University of Pa. Library) is draft versions of several sections of A; the latest entry is Feb. 23, 1779. C (4 pp., Hist. Soc. of Pa.) is divided into two sections, the first an earlier version of BF's private expenses listed in A and the second an interesting but incomplete table of the periods when the other commissioners, Deane, Lee, and Adams, were considered members of the Passy household. D (4 pp., *ibid.*) is one section of A in a draft version.

VI. Thomas Barclay's Review of Franklin's Accounts, December 3, 1776, to June 20, 1785: Library of Congress. 29 pp.

In 1782 Congress, pursuant to its decision three years before, appointed Barclay to try to settle its accounts with its agents abroad.[9] He examined Franklin's, and this document was the result. It served as a model, for Barclay gave the present copy to Thomas Jefferson, as a note by Jefferson attests, to guide him in his bookkeeping while minister to France. The review is based on document V and adds little to the information contained there, but includes entries after 1778 and is differently and in many ways more logically organized. Receipts and disbursements are in opposite columns; a series of sub-totals are included; and the final balance indicates 7,533 livres due to Franklin. That result did not satisfy him or the American government: Barclay, he believed, had omitted some allowable expenses, whereas the United States treasury insisted that Barclay should have provided documentation.[1] The upshot was that a final settlement was still hanging fire when Franklin died.

VII. Franklin's Private Accounts, December 3, 1776, to June 20, 1785: Library of Congress. 3 pp.

This three-page account in an unidentified hand is confined to personal and housekeeping expenses, and was compiled after Franklin's return to America, probably by some one in the treasury, as part of the prolonged attempt at a settlement. The bulk of its entries are for the years from 1776 to 1778, but it contains nothing new; it is an editing of Documents V and VI. The post-1778 entries are brief, but will be useful in the annotation of later volumes.

VIII. Jacques-Barthélémy Gruel's Account with Franklin and with the Commission, December 7, 1776, to February 8, 1777: Harvard University Library. 1 p.

A list of disbursements, in a clerical hand, that Gruel made to Franklin and his colleagues. The account distinguishes between payments on behalf of one of the commissioners and on behalf of the commission as a whole; a pencilled note indicates that 3320 *l.t.* were for Franklin out of a total of 4965. Gruel took a commission

9. *JCC*, XXIII, 728–30; E. James Ferguson, *et al.*, eds., *The Papers of Robert Morris* (5 vols. to date, Pittsburgh, Pa., 1973–), III, 263. See also Ferguson, *Power of the Purse*, pp. 179–202.

1. *Ibid.*, p. 195; Van Doren, *Franklin*, pp. 764–6.

of one half of one percent. The final entry is Jan. 19, and a note by Gruel of Feb. 8 attests that the debt was transferred to Congress.[2]

IX. Sollier's Accounts, with Franklin and the Commission, January 10 to February 20 and April 4 to August 1, 1777: Harvard University Library. Two documents, 1 p. and 3 pp.

Sollier ·was the Parisian banker for Penet, Gruel, and Thomas Morris,[3] and briefly for the commissioners as well. The first account begins with an undated order from Gruel to pay the commissioners 36,606 *l.t.* On February 26 Sollier still had 12,859 *l.t.* on hand, after numerous payments to Franklin and his colleagues and after taking the same commission as Gruel, one half of one percent.[4] He returned the balance to the commissioners, but did not thereby end their relationship: the three-page account, which he sent to Arthur Lee, lists additional disbursements to them during the spring and summer. Even after August, when Ferdinand Grand became their principal banker, they continued to deal on occasion with Sollier.[5]

X. Ferdinand Grand's Accounts with Franklin and Deane, January 31 to June 10, 1777: American Philosophical Society. 1p.[6]

In an unidentified clerical hand. The first entry began the commissioners' dealing with the man who became their bulwark as well as their banker, and served the American mission throughout the war and after. The accounts, which enter debits and credits, are in two parts; one ends on April 28, when expenditures and receipts balanced at 562,071 *l.t.*, and the other on June 10, when the balance was 1,503,250. Grand's extended accounts, beginning on June 10, 1777, and ending on February 11, 1779, will be discussed in our next volume.[7]

2. Another copy of this account, lacking the note, is in the University of Pa. Library.

3. For Sollier's relationship with Morris, the only one not fully documented in this volume, see Stevens, *Facsimiles*, III, no. 272.

4. The 36,606 *l.t.* came from the sale of the indigo brought by the *Reprisal*; the 12,859 were what remained. BF's note in the Waste Book, Feb. 26, 1777.

5. Indicated by numerous entries in the Waste Book.

6. A two-page partial copy in another hand and endorsed by BF, April 28 to June 10, 1777, is also in the APS.

7. On Feb. 3, when Arthur Lee was leaving for Spain, the commissioners instructed Grand to furnish him a letter of credit for 72,000 *l.t.*, and two days later authorized the banker to pay any one of them from funds that they had entrusted to him jointly. Both notes are in a copy in the Harvard University Library of the extended accounts from June 10. Another and

To Jacques Barbeu-Dubourg

Translation: Archives du Ministère des affaires étrangères

Franklin's crossing on the *Reprisal* with his two grandsons, William Temple Franklin and Benjamin Franklin Bache,[8] was imprinted on his memory as long as he lived. He "was badly accommodated," he wrote years later, "in a miserable vessel, improper for those northern seas, (and which actually foundered in her return,) was badly fed, so that on his arrival he had scarce strength to stand."[9] He had to subsist on salt beef, because the fowls offered him were too tough for his teeth; boils plagued him, and a skin ailment that was apparently psoriasis spread over much of his body.[1] Despite these troubles and a singularly rough voyage, his curiosity was unimpaired: he again tested the temperature of the sea to locate the Gulf Stream. The *Reprisal* made good time. On November 29 she was in Quiberon Bay, but contrary winds kept her from sailing up the Loire to Nantes. On December 3, therefore, the old man and the two young ones left the ship in a fishing boat, and landed that evening at Auray on the Breton coast. Franklin listened to the boatman speaking Breton and recognized only one word, that for "devil"; it was the same as the Welsh, and he had heard that the two languages were so similar that speakers of one could understand the other. The landing at Auray was unpropitious: the wretched village could provide no carriages; one had to be sent for and arrived the next day.[2] Before the travelers started on their way to Nantes, Franklin wrote Du-

---

derivative set of Grand accounts, which is occasionally useful in our annotation to supplement his running accounts, is well catalogued in the Papers of the Continental Congress in the National Archives. It consists of summaries made in the mid-1780's of the banker's accounts with BF, the other commissioners and ministers, and European businessmen, and has entries that antedate Grand's formal relationship with the commission.

8. WF's situation, and WTF's years with his grandfather in England, explain why BF took the sixteen-year-old with him; BFB, who was only seven, went to receive a European education. See Lopez and Herbert, *The Private Franklin*, pp. 213, 215–6.

9. Smyth, *Writings*, IX, 696. The trip, he told Sally and RB in 1785, "almost demolish'd me": *ibid.*, p. 327.

1. Bigelow, *Works*, VI, 211. BF had suffered the same afflictions during his mission to Canada: above, XXII, 442 n.

2. WTF, *Memoirs*, I 309–10. The details come from a journal, now lost, which BF kept.

bourg. With his letter he enclosed the two that follow, to Silas Deane and Thomas Morris.

Auray en Bretagne le 4. Xbre. 1776.

Mon cher bon ami sera bien surpris de recevoir une lettre de moi datée de france, quand ni lui ni moi ne nous y attendions. Je suis parti de Philadelphie le 26. 8bre. dernier sur un vaisseau de guerre appartenant au Congrès, et en trente jours nous sommes venus jetter l'ancre dans la Baye de Quiberon. Nous avons pris chemin faisant deux vaisseaux anglois que nous avons amenés avec nous.[3] Le vaisseau est destiné pour Nantes, mais les vents étant contraires pour entrer dans la Loire, nous avons attendu quelques jours dans la Baye, jusqu'à ce qu'impatient de mettre pied à terre, j'ai profité de l'occasion d'un bateau pour venir ici, d'où je me rendrai par terre à Nantes, où probablement je resterai peu de jours. Apprenant que la poste part d'ici ce soir, je saisis cette occasion pour vous saluer, ainsi que ma chere Madame Dubourg, Mesdemoiselles Priheron et Basseport, que j'espere avoir bientôt le plaisir de trouver en bonne santé.[4]

Je suppose que Messieurs Deane et Morris ont l'honneur d'être connus de vous, et comme je ne sais pas leur adresse, je prends la liberté de leur adresser à chacun un mot sous votre couvert, et je vous prie de le leur faire remettre. J'aurai soin de vous rembourser toutes vos dépenses.

Je vois que vous avés eu de mauvaises nouvelles de nos affaires en amerique; mais elles ne sont pas vraies. Les anglois à l'aide de leurs vaisseaux ont gagné un pied à terre dans deux îles,[5] mais ils ne se sont pas étendus dans le continent où nous les tenons en respect. Notre armée étoit à un mille ou deux de la leur, lorsque je suis parti, et retranchées l'une et l'autre. Dans différentes escarmouches qu'il y a eu dernierement entre des partis de 500 et de 1000 hommes de chaque côté, nous avons toujours eu l'avantage et les avons chassé du champ de bataille avec perte, notre feu faisant plus de ravage que le leur.

3. The *George* and *La Vigne*: Clark, *Wickes*, pp. 98–9.
4. Marie-Catherine Biheron and Madeleine Basseporte were old friends: above, xv, 115; Lopez, *Mon Cher Papa*, pp. 225–6.
5. Presumably Long Island and Manhattan.

Sur mer nous avons extrêmement molesté leur commerce en prenant un grand nombre de leurs vaisseaux des Indes Occidentales qui entrent journellement dans nos ports. Mais je ne veux pas m'arrêter sur cet objet jusqu'au moment où j'aurai le plaisir de vous voir.

Notation: B. Franklin à Barbeu Dubourg Traduit de l'Anglois

To Silas Deane

Translation: Archives du Ministère des affaires étrangères

When Franklin wrote this letter he was, as far as we know, ignorant of Deane's activities since leaving Bordeaux the previous June.[6] Those activities were multifarious, as might be expected of a man who was the agent for a consortium of American merchants under contract with the secret committee as well as the representative of the committee of secret correspondence in dealing with the French government, and who had also been permitted, if not encouraged, to engage in transactions of his own. He failed, for lack of cash, to obtain the goods that the secret committee had expected for presents to the Indians.[7] His private ventures were also failures; nothing came of a contract to sell tobacco, or of his hope of forming a large international syndicate to handle American trade. He did arrange some kind of partnership with Edward Bancroft, the American stockjobber who was becoming a British agent, but it yielded no immediate returns.[8] These schemes, hard as he tried to hatch them, proved to be china eggs.

As agent of the committee of secret correspondence, and hence of Congress, Deane was equally energetic and more successful, although success created problems for the future. His lack of funds was paralyzing only until the French and Spanish governments extended him credit through Roderigue Hortalez & Cie.; he then entered into contracts for arms and supplies, and ships to carry them. He also contracted, on his own authority, with four French officers to be major generals in the American army, and proposed to Ver-

6. The only communication that BF saw before he sailed was, we believe, Deane's letter to Morris of June 23: above, XXII, 487–90.

7. *Ibid.*, p. 354; *Deane Papers*, V, 386, 394–405.

8. *Ibid.*, I, 176, 233–5, 286, 421; Crout, "Diplomacy of Trade," p. 120; Price, *France and the Chesapeake*, II, 704–5; Ferguson, *Power of the Purse*, pp. 83–5; Bancroft's account with Deane, Jan. 1777–July 1779: Conn. Hist. Soc.

sailles his own terms for a commercial agreement.[9] He besieged American friends with advice, much of it worthless, on what course the United States should take.[1] His optimism was strong enough to carry across the Atlantic, and it induced Congress to issue instructions that were unrelated to European realities[2] and later caused a great deal of trouble for him and his fellow commissioners.

Auray en Bretagne le 4. Xbre 1776

Je viens d'arriver à Bord du Reprisal, Capitaine Wickes, petit vaisseau de guerre appartenant au Congrés, nous sommes dans la Baye de quiberon attendant un vent favorable pour aller à Nantes. Nous quittames le Cap le 29. d'8bre et nous n'avons mis que 30. jours de terre à terre. Je restai a Bord trois jours aprés avoir mis à L'ancre, esperant pouvoir aller jusqu'a Nantes avec le vaisseau, mais le vent continuant d'etre contraire, je suis venu icy pour aller par terre à Nantes.

Le Congrés vous a nommé en Septembre et Mr. Jefferson et moy, pour negocier un traité de Commerce et d'amitié avec la Cour de france. Mr. Jefferson alors en Virginie refusa, sur quoy Mr. arthur Lée, actuellement à Londres, fut nommé à sa place. Notre vaisseau a apporté de L'indigo pour le Compte du Congrés pour la valeur d'environ £3000 sterling, qui doit être à nos ordres pour payer nos dépenses; le congrès nous a de plus assigné £7000 sterling pour le même objet, et que le Comité nous fera passer le plutôt possible. Je me trouve ici aussi près de Paris que je le serai à Nantes, mais je suis obligé de m'y rendre pour m'y pourvoir d'argent pour mon voyage, et pour prendre mon bagage qui est resté à bord du vaisseau. Mais je tâcherai de vous rejoindre le plutôt que je pourrai. Je me propose de garder l'incognito sur mon caractere jusqu'à ce moment, et jusqu'à ce que je sache si la Cour voudra recevoir

---

9. *Deane Papers*, I, 229–32, 343–5, 359–64, 409–11.

1. For an example see *ibid.*, pp. 395–9.

2. In his letter of Oct. 1, 1776, to the committee of secret correspondence Deane urged that American privateers retaliate against the Portuguese for their government's expulsion of American ships; he also gave assurances that American warships might be outfitted in French ports, that commissioners from the United States would be welcomed in a number of European capitals, and that he could obtain a loan on most favorable terms: *Deane Papers*, I, 290–1, 293–4. Congress acted on all these suggestions: *JCC*, VI, 1035–7, 1054; VII, 8; below, the committee of secret correspondence to the American commissioners, Dec. 21.

des Ministres des Etats Unis. J'ai plusieurs lettres du Comité pour vous, que je ne vous envoye point, parceque je sais qu'elles contiennent des affaires de conséquence, et que je suis incertain de la sureté de cette voie. D'ailleurs comme je compte prendre la poste à Nantes j'imagine que cela ne fera pas trois ou quatre jours de différence. Nous avons rencontré à la mer deux Brigantins, l'un Irlandois et l'autre Anglois, que nous avons pris, et que nous amenons à Nantes. Je ne sais si le Capitaine obtiendra la permission de les y vendre, parceque cela pourroit être contraire aux traités qui subsistent actuellement entre les deux couronnes. Ils sont de la valeur d'environ £4000 sterling.[3] Nous avons eu un passage difficile, et je m'en sens affoibli; mais j'espère que le bon air que je respire à terre me rétablira bientôt, et que je pourrai voyager avec célérité, de vous joindre à Paris et de vous y trouver en bonne santé.

p.s. Si vous pouviés par quelque voie sure apprendre à M. Lee sa nomination, cela feroit [*sic*] très bien. Peutêtre la meilleure voye seroit-elle celle du Département des Affaires Etrangeres et de l'Ambassadeur de France; celle de la poste ordinaire ne seroit pas sure.

Je vous prie de me procurer un logement.

Notation: B. francklin à Silas Deane traduit de Langlois

To Thomas Morris[4]

Translation: Archives du Ministère des affaires étrangères

Aurai en Bretagne le 4. Xbre 1776.

Je suis arrivé ici à bord du Reprisal, Capitaine Wickes, qui est maintenant à l'ancre à la Baye de Quiberon, où il attend le

3. BF was more uncertain about the treaty violation than the fact warranted: permitting the ships to be sold would have flatly contravened Article 15 of the Anglo-French commercial treaty signed at Utrecht in 1713. The Americans solved the problem by acting without permission. A surreptitious sale was arranged, and the prizes brought roughly £1,700: Clark, *Wickes*, pp. 101–2, 105.

4. The younger half-brother of Robert Morris and agent for the secret committee in Nantes; see above, XXII, 544 n. The young man, despite Silas Deane's efforts to get him to take up his post, was still amusing himself in London: *Deane Papers*, I, 400, 419.

vent pour remonter à Nantes. J'ai apporté beaucoup de lettres et de gros paquets pour vous, et comme je compte partir de Nantes en poste, j'espere avoir le plaisir de vous les remettre. J'en joins seulement une ici, étant douteux que les autres ne fussent pas ouvertes à la Poste; et d'ailleurs elles couteraient fort cher. Si nos amis de Nantes le jugent nécessaire, je dépêcherai un exprès pour vous porter vos paquets et ceux de M. Deane, de maniere que vous les aurés peutêtre aussi promptement que si je vous les envoyois par la poste. Lorsque je suis parti, les armées, étaient très près l'une de l'autre à environ 18 milles de la Nouvelle York; mais il n'y avoit point eu d'action générale, quoiqu'on en attendît une tous les jours. Dans différentes escarmouches nos partis ont battu des partis ennemis de force égale et même supérieure, et notre armée est pleine de courage. Il arrive journellement dans nos ports un nombre de prises faites sur l'ennemi. Nous en avons fait deux dans notre traversée qui a été de trente jours.

Notation: B. Franklin à Thomas Morris Trad: de l'anglois

To Silas Deane

ALS: Connecticut Historical Society

On December 4, after writing the letters from Auray printed above, Franklin and his grandsons set out for Nantes, and reached Vannes late that evening. The journey, as Franklin described it, was not relaxing. "The carriage was a miserable one, with tired horses, the evening dark, scarce a traveller but ourselves on the road; and to make it more *comfortable*, the driver stopped near a wood we were to pass through, to tell us that a gang of eighteen robbers infested that wood, who but two weeks ago had robbed and murdered some travellers on that very spot." When the party left Vannes on the way to Nantes, they soon encountered other travelers; and Franklin was enough recovered to observe them with care. "On the road yesterday," he noted on the 6th, "we met six or seven country women, in company, on horseback and astride: they were all of fair white and red complexions, but one among them was the fairest woman I ever beheld. Most of the men have good complexions, not swarthy like those of the North of France, in which I remember that, except about Abbeville, I saw few fair people."

This letter to Deane, on the day the travelers reached Nantes, was written either before or after they were entertained with a sumptuous dinner. In the afternoon they moved to the nearby country seat of Jacques-Barthélémy Gruel, Penet's business associate, where they were immediately surrounded by crowds of visitors.[5] Although Franklin concealed his Congressional commission, as he says here, he was welcomed from the start as the representative of America.

My dear Friend   Nantes, Dec. 7. 1776

I wrote a Line to you on Wednesday last, from Auray (where I landed out of the Ship of War that brought me over) acquainting you with my Arrival and with our Appointment (jointly with Mr. Arthur Lee) to negotiate a Treaty of Commerce and Friendship with the Court of France, for which I have with me ample Instructions. I have acquainted no one here with this Commission, continuing incog. as to my publick Character; because not being sufficiently acquainted with the Disposition and present Circumstances of this Court, relative to our Contest with GB. I cannot Judge whether it would be agreable to her at this time to receive publickly Ministers from the Congress as such, and I think we should not embarras her unnecessarily on the one hand, nor subject ourselves to the Hazard of a disgraceful Refusal on the other. I therefore send you herewith a Copy of our Commission, that you may have time to consider and advise upon it before my Arrival at Paris, for which Place I shall set out as soon as I can, being oblig'd to wait here a little for my Baggage, which continues on board the Ship, and the Wind has not yet been favourable to bring her from Quiberon Bay into this River. We are impowered by a Vote of Congress, to live in such a Stile at Paris, as we shall find proper. A Cargo, suppos'd to the Value of £3000 Sterl. brought in the Ship with me is to be sold by our Merchants here, and the Produce is to be subject to the Drafts of the Commissioners towards their Expences. And the Committee have Orders to add to that Fund, till they make it up £10,000.[6] *I requested you to provide me a Lodging. If in the same*

5. WTF, *Memoirs*, I, 310. The direct quotations are from BF's now lost journal.

6. The Congressional resolutions were adopted on Sept. 28: see above, XXII, 629.

Hotel with you, it will be the more agreable.[7] I have with me two Grandsons; one about 16, who will serve me as a private Secretary; the other a Child of 7, whom I purpose to place in some Boarding School, that he may early learn the French Language. One Bed in the meantime may serve them both; but I must have them in the same Lodging with me till I can place the young one. M. Penet talks of accompanying me to Paris.[8] I suppose we may set out about the Middle of next Week, but cannot be certain, because it depends on my receiving my Baggage, and that depends on the Winds. In the mean time it would be a vast Satisfaction to me to hear from you, or meet you, but I do not see how it can be manag'd. I recommend to your Care the Informing Mr. Lee of his Appointment, by writing to him and conveying to him the Letters sent herewith, in the safest Way you can find. If thro' the Hands of the French Ambr: at London, it will be best perhaps to write only, keeping his Letters till he comes to Paris. For I know not what the seal'd one contains, and there is a Risque of its being inspected. Hoping soon for the great Pleasure of finding you well at Paris, I am, with sincere Esteem, Dear Sir, Your most obedient Humble Servant   B FRANKLIN

Honble Silas Deane Esqr

Endorsed: 1776 Benja: Franklins Letter Nantz. 7 Decr.

To the Committee of Secret Correspondence

ALS and copy: National Archives

Gentlemen,   Nantes, Dec. 8[–10]. 1776

After a short but rough Passage of 30 Days we anchor'd in Quiberon Bay, the Wind not suiting to enter the Loire. Capt. Wicks did every thing in his Power to make the Voyage comfortable to me; and I was much pleas'd with what I saw of his Conduct as an Officer, when on suppos'd Occasions we made Preparation for Engagement, the good Order and Readiness with which it was done, being far beyond my Expectation, and

---

7. These sentences are underlined in a different ink, perhaps by Deane; what seems to be a pointing hand is scrawled in the margin.
8. He did: see WTF to BF below, Dec. 24, 1776.

I believe equal to any thing of the kind in the best Ships of the King's Fleet. He seems to have also a very good Set of Officers under him: I hope they will all in good time be promoted. He met and took two Prizes, Brigantines, one belonging to Cork, laden with Staves, Pitch, Tar, Turpentine and Claret; the other to Hull, with a Cargo of Flaxseed and Brandy. The Captains have made some Propositions of Ransom, which perhaps may be accepted, as there is yet no Means of condemning them here, and they are scarce worth sending to America. The Ship is yet in Quiberon Bay with her Prizes. I came hither from thence 70 Miles by Land. I am made extreamly welcome here, where America has many Friends. As soon as I have recover'd Strength enough for the Journey, which I hope will be in a very few Days, I shall set out for Paris. My Letter to the President[9] will inform you of some other Particulars. With great Esteem, I have the honour to be, Gentlemen, Your most obedient and most humble Servant   B FRANKLIN

P.S. Dec. 10. I have just learnt that 80 Pieces of the Cannon, all Brass, with Carriages, Traces, and every thing fit for immediate Service, were imbark'd in a Fregate from Havre, which is sail'd: The rest were to go in another Fregate of 36 Guns.[1]

Honble. Committee of secret Correspondence

Endorsed: Nantes Decr. 8th. 1776

To John Hancock   ALS and copy: National Archives

Sir,   Nantes. Oct. [*i.e.*, Dec.] 8. 1776
    In 30 Days after we left the Capes of Delaware, we came to an Anchor in Quiberon Bay. I remain'd on board four Days, expecting a Change of Wind, proper to carry the Ship into the River Loire; but the Wind seeming fix'd in an opposite Quar-

9. The following document.
    1. The *Amphitrite,* the first of Beaumarchais' ships to sail, actually did so on the 14th. Several others were fitting out, and the *Romain* was expected to leave next. Both were merchantmen, not warships, and the *Romain* was the *Amélie* by the time she sailed. Roger Lafon, *Beaumarchais, le brillant armateur* (Paris, 1928), pp. 87–90; Morton, *Beaumarchais Correspondance,* II, 269–71; III, 30.

ter, I landed at Auray, and with some Difficulty got hither, the Road not being well supply'd with Means of Conveyance. Two Days before we saw Land, we met a Brigt. from Bourdeaux, belonging to Cork, and another from Rochefort belonging to Hull, both of which were taken. The first has on board Staves, Tar, Turpentine and Claret: The other Coniac Brandy and Flaxseed. There is some Difficulty in determining what to do with them, as they are scarce worth sending to America, and the Mind of the French Court with regard to Prizes brought into their Ports is not yet known. It is certainly contrary to their Treaties with Britain to permit the Sale of them, and we have no regular Means of trying and condemning them. There are however many here who would purchase Prizes, we having already had several Offers from Persons who are willing to take upon themselves all Consequences as to the Illegality. Capt. Wickes, as soon as he can get his Refreshments intends a Cruize in the Channel. Our Friends in France have been a good deal dejected with the Gazette Accounts of Advantages obtain'd against us by the British Troops. I have help'd them here to recover their Spirits a little, by assuring them that we shall face the Enemy, and were under no Apprehensions of their two Armies being able to compleat their Junction. I understand Mr. Lee has lately been at Paris, that Mr. Deane is still there, and that an underhand Supply is obtain'd from the Government of 200 brass Field Pieces, 30,000 Firelocks, and some other military Stores which are now shipping for America, and will be convoy'd by a Ship of War. The Court of England, Mr. Penet tells me (from whom I have the above Intelligence) had the Folly to demand Mr. Deane to be deliver'd up, but were refus'd.[2] Our Voyage tho' not long was rough, and I feel myself weakned by it: But I now recover Strength daily, and in a few days shall be able to undertake the Journey to Paris. I have not yet taken any publick Character, thinking it prudent first to know whether the Court is ready and willing

2. In August Beaumarchais had promised Congress the field pieces and 20,000 fusils; a month later Deane had raised the number of flintlocks to 30,000: Morton, *Beaumarchais correspondance*, II, 242; *Deane Papers*, I, 247. The British, as far as we know, did not request at this time that Deane be delivered to them.

to receive Ministers publicly from the Congress; that we may neither embarras her on the one hand, or subject ourselves to the Hazard of a disgraceful Refusal on the other. I have dispatch'd an Express to Mr. Deane, with the Letters I had for him from the Committee, and a Copy of our Commission, that he may immediately make the proper Enquiries, and give me Information. In the mean time, I find it is generally suppos'd here that I am sent to negociate, and that Opinion appears to give great Pleasure, if I can judge by the extream Civilities I meet with from Numbers of the principal People, who have done me the Honour to visit me. I have desired Mr. Deane, by some speedy and safe Means to give Mr. Lee Notice of his Appointment. I find several Vessels here laden with military Stores for America, just ready to sail: On the whole there is the greatest Prospect that we shall be well provided for another Campaign, and much stronger than we were the last. A Spanish Fleet has sail'd, with 7000 Land Forces, Foot, and some Horse. Their Destination unknown, but suppos'd against the Portuguese in Brasil. Both France and England are preparing strong Fleets,[3] and it is said that all the Powers of Europe are preparing for War, apprehending a general one cannot be very distant. When I arrive at Paris, I shall be able to write with more Certainty. I beg you to present my Duty to the Congress, and assure them of my most faithful Endeavours in their Service. With the sincerest Esteem and Respect, I have the Honour to be Sir, Your most obedient and most humble Servant   B FRANKLIN

Honble. John Hancock Esqr

Notation: Doctr. Franklyn. Nantes Decr. 8th. 1776.

To Jane Mecom   ALS: American Philosophical Society

Dear Sister   Nantes, in France, Dec. 8. 1776

I arrived here safe after a Passage of 30 Days, some what fatigued and weakned by the Voyage, which was a rough one;

3. The report of the Spanish fleet was substantially correct, but the French and the British naval preparations were much exaggerated; see Dull, *French Navy*, pp. 60–3, 75.

but I recover my Strength fast since my Landing, and shall be able I hope in a few days to undertake the Journey to Paris of about 250 Miles. If the Post Chaise here were as easy as the English, such a Journey would be no Difficulty. I hope you continue well and happy. Remember me affectionately to Cousin Jenney,[4] and to Mr. and Mrs. Greene. I am ever Your affectionate Brother   B FRANKLIN

You can have no Conception of the Respect with which I am receiv'd and treated here by the first People, in my private Character; for as yet I have assum'd no public One.

Addressed: To / Mrs. Mecom

From Nathan Rumsey[5]   ALS: American Philosophical Society

Monday, 12. O'Clock [December 9, 1776[6]]

Most respectable Sir

The Wind being favorable for Capt. Wicks has prevented my Setting out for Quiberon Bay this morning as proposed, least my Journey should be in vain; but should he not be in by tomorrow morning, think of setting out.

Mr. Penet and Self beg your Excuse for not attending to

4. Presumably Jane's granddaughter, Jane Flagg; she had married a relative of the Greenes three days before BF wrote. Above, XXII, 495–6.
5. The son of William Rumsey of Bohemia, Md., and the nephew of Benjamin Rumsey, a Congressional delegate. Hodge & Bayard of Philadelphia sent young Rumsey to France in 1776 to purchase war supplies for Congress. He reached Paris by way of Bordeaux (where he supposedly arrived with Deane), accompanied Penet to Nantes, and then went on a tour in search of commercial contacts; British intelligence followed his movements, though it characterized him as a man of small ability. Stevens, *Facsimiles*, XIII, nos. 1340, pp. 3–4; 1346, p. 2; 1350, p. 2. He soon returned to Nantes, was associated with Penet, and solicited business from the Maryland convention. On his father's death he inherited a considerable estate in Maryland, and sailed for home at the end of April, 1777. *Md. Hist. Mag.*, LXVII (1972), 155 n; *Naval Docs.*, III, 1103; VI, 499–500; William H. Browne *et al.*, eds., *Archives of Maryland* (72 vols.; Baltimore, 1883–1972), XII, 386–7; *Magruder's Maryland Colonial Abstracts, . . . 1772–1777* (reprint; Baltimore, 1968), no. 101; JW to the commissioners below, April 28.
6. The only Monday during BF's stay in Nantes.

dine with You, but our Letters intended for Cap. Rawlins[7] hope will plead our Excuse, as they have engaged us this morning. We propose doing ourselves the honor of waiting on You at 4 O'Clock this afternoon. With the Utmost respect I am Esteemed Sir Your Most obedient Servant

NATHAN RUMSEY

Addressed: Honorable / Doct. Benjamin Franklin

Notation: Nathan Rumsey

From Jean François Ubetius[8]

ALS: American Philosophical Society

⟨Turin, December 10, 1776, in French: I met you several times in London, some seven years ago, and now take the liberty of writing to recommend the bearer, Thomas Negroni, who has a burning desire to serve the colonies on his own. He comes from a good family in the Duchy of Milan, and his zeal and courage in emigrating to America entitle him to be considered as born there.[9] Your admirer and colleague, Father Beccaria, adds his recommendation to mine. I should like to come to Philadelphia myself, to see you again and spend the rest of my days there, but the voyage would be extremely harmful for me. Endorsed by Franklin: "Ubetius recommending the young Italian."⟩

7. Presumably Thomas Rawlins of Philadelphia, who had been plying for some time between America and Nantes; see for example *Naval Docs.*, VI, 1079.

8. Or Giovanni Francesco Ubezio, a physician of some distinction and the author of a work on smallpox, who has not appeared before in this series.

9. Negroni never made the voyage. Perhaps he went to France en route, learned of BF's arrival and delivered the letter, then stayed on. In any case he was giving Italian lessons to WTF by late 1778, and was in bad health; at some point "le Maleureux Negroni," close to destitution, wrote BF to ask for help. Negróni to WTF, Nov. 2, 1778, and to BF, undated, APS.

35

Franklin's Account of Payments for Benjamin Franklin Bache

December 12, 1776–September 6, 1780   See page 112n

From James Hutchinson[1]   ALS: American Philosophical Society

On board the Ship Sally Thursday morning

Dear Sir   [December 12, 1776?[2]]

We are Just proceeding to sea with a fair Wind, which we hope may continue, and carry us safely out of the Bay of Biscay; your dispatches I received from Mr. Pennet and shall not fail to take Care of them should we arrive in Philadelphia, and on the other hand should we be so unfortunate as to fall into the hands of any of the Piratical Cruisers of Britain they shall be sunk. Present my Compliments to Mr. Pennet tell him I shall ever remember his Civilities to me during my stay at Nantz. With wishes for your success and happiness I remain Dear Sir Yours &c.   JAMES HUTCHINSON

Addressed: Dr. Benjamin Franklin / at / Mr. Gruels / Nantz / favoured by / Mr. Le Bourg

Notation: J. Hutchinson

From Augustin Mottin de la Balme[3]

ALS: American Philosophical Society

Bordeaux le 14e. decembre 1776 chez la veuve

Monsieur   roger près la Bource

Au moment ou je me rejouissois d'avoir en mains deux lettres

1. For the young doctor, who had studied under Fothergill, see the *DAB*. His meeting with BF and return to Philadelphia are discussed by Whitfield J. Bell, Jr., "James Hutchinson (1752–1793): a Physician in Politics," in Lloyd G. Stevenson and Robert P. Multhauf, eds., *Medicine, Science and Culture: Historical Essays in Honor of Owsei Temkin* (Baltimore, Md., 1968), pp. 270–3. Gruel's accounts (above, pp. 21–2) show a payment in December of 120 *l.t.* to "Hockinson" for his passage.

2. The most probable date because it was the last Thursday before BF left Gruel's country house, to which the note was sent.

3. Silas Deane had introduced Lieut. Col. Mottin de la Balme (1736–80) to the secret committee and to Congress the previous October as an expe-

36

de recommandation pour vous remettre a philadelphie, la re-
nommée qui precède vos pas m'a appris votre arrivee a nante
ou dit-ons vous devez sejourner. Frustrés de mon Esperance
souffrés que j'aie L'honneur de vous Les Envoyer et vous prier
de vouloir bien reparer un peu la perte que je crois faire en
vous, d'un protecteur aussi respectable que generalement
honnorés. L'inffluence qu'à justes droits vous avez, sur les affaires de l'amerique, n'exige qu'un mot de votre part en ma
faveur, de grace, Monsieur, veuillez le prononcer; j'ose dire
que je merite quelques retours par le singuiller Désir que j'ai
de combattre pour la libertés des honnettes Colons et de cap-
tiver votre suffrage. Dans cette attente je suis avec le plus profond respect Monsieur Votre tres humble obeissant Serviteur
Mottin de la Balme Cape. de Cavalerie

Mr. de franklin a nante ou a paris chez Mr. deane.

Notation: de la Balme, Bordeaux 14 Xb. 1776.

From Louis Lestarjette[4]   ALS: American Philosophical Society

Honourable Sir,   [Before December 15, 1776[5]]
I take the liberty of offering you my best Services in this
kingdom being extremely well versed in both English, and
French languages, especially in the French as my mother tongue
and brought up in the College of the four Nations at Paris[6]
where I was eight Years. Capn. Cochran and myself married

---

rienced cavalry officer and theoretician, whom he had recruited and whose
expenses he was paying: *Deane Papers*, I, 328–9. The Frenchman was delayed at Bordeaux, for reasons unknown, until mid-February, and had time
to receive the recommendation that he is requesting here; see BF to Hancock below, Jan. 20. La Balme's subsequent career is sketched in Lasseray,
Les Français, II, 329–36.

4. A merchant of some consequence in South Carolina, to judge by scattered references to him in the *S.C. Hist. and Geneal. Mag.*, XXXVIII–IX, *passim*;
LXXII, 22.

5. *I.e.*, before BF left Nantes. He apparently accepted the offer in this
letter; his Waste Book records, under Feb. 8, a payment to Lestarjette on
Jan. 4 for expenses of the journey to Paris.

6. Founded by Mazarin and one of the most prestigious in France.

two Sisters in South Carolina.[7] I came over with him in the Vessel which he commands, merely to serve the Province in doing the affairs of that Vessel, and explaining to the French merchants the nature of our trade, and the manufacturing the different goods proper for that Country. I have fulfill'd my mission, and Capn. Cochran can inform you of my Character. Mr. Dean also has seen a Sketch of my abilities in Paris where I went with Capn: Cochran, and was constantly with Mr. Dean for whom I interpreted the different transactions that were going on at that time. It is not the case with you, Sir, Speaking and Writing the French language properly; but your time will be so much taken up at Paris in matters of Conversation that it wou'd be morally impossible for you to undergo the whole fatigue. I speak and write the French language, I may Say with elegance, and I have nothing else in View in offering to Stay with you, than to Serve the just Cause of America which is become my native Land. It is neither necessity or any motives of interest that lead me to open myself to you on that Subject. I am well Settled in Charlestown where I have a wife and two Children in whom I place all my happiness, and who I dare Say long for my return, but Sir, I wou'd sacrify many enjoyments of life to be attached to so illustrious a Gentleman ingag'd in so noble a Cause, and whom the whole world admires. The Vessel I came in is to Sail in about a forthnight. Only Say a word, and I'll Stay.[8] I may venture to advance that you cou'd not easily meet with a French American of my Capacity, and to whom you may intrust the most Secret affairs. I am with the most profound Veneration Honourable Sir, Your most humble Servant.   LIS. LESTARJETTE

Addressed: The Honourable / Doctr. Frankling

Notation: Lestargette

7. Robert Cochran, the owner of a Charleston shipyard, had been commissioned captain and given command of the S.C. brigantine *Notre Dame* the previous August. His wife was born Mary Elliot. *Naval Docs.*, VI, 212; *S.C. Hist. and Geneal. Mag.*, XXXIV, 67 n.

8. He stayed for a time. By Jan. 16 he was back in Nantes, lodging with Beaumarchais' agent Peltier and awaiting another ship; the one he had

From Charles-Frédéric Bedaulx

ALS: American Philosophical Society

Bedaulx (1752–79/80) appeared in passing in the previous volume, as the carrier of a letter to Franklin from Nicholas Barker of Rotterdam.[9] He was a Swiss soldier of fortune, the scion of an old family. "Je n'ay ni Seigneurie, ni titres a lui laisser," his mother wrote to Franklin, "mais seulement une suit d'ayeux de noble et bonne race qu'il ne dementira pas."[1] He began his military career at an early age, according to his own account, for he served in Europe for twelve years and rose to be a captain in the Dutch army before he decided to go to America.[2] His first attempt landed him in an English jail, from which he soon escaped to France. Silas Deane tried to obtain him another passage, and he says here that he expects to leave soon. He was in company with Baron de Kalb and others. Beaumarchais suspected him for some reason and made efforts to stop his departure, whereupon Bedaulx became impatient. Two days after writing this letter he was on his way to Paris to see Franklin,[3] to whom he sent an undated letter from a Parisian hotel: obstacles had been put in his way but left him undiscouraged; he still had enough money to pay his passage, and would be grateful for an interview. On March 6 he wrote again from Paris, to say that he had not gone to Passy for fear of being troublesome, and to ask that he be referred to some of Franklin's friends in America; on Deane's order he was departing two days later.[4] At some point Franklin apparently did see him, assured him that Congress would take him into its service, and reinforced the assurance with a letter to the secretary of the board of war. Bedaulx eventually sailed from Bordeaux in late March, along with Kalb and Lafayette.[5]

In Philadelphia he met a chilly reception. He kept refusing a rank less than what he thought he deserved until December, 1778, when

---

come in had already sailed: *Deane Correspondence*, pp. 64–6. He finally left for home at the end of February, but was back again in Nantes by the following August: jw to bf below, Feb. 27; Anne Izard Deas, ed., *Correspondence of Mr. Ralph Izard* . . . (New York, 1844), p. 322.

9. Above, XXII, 611.

1. Dec. 21, 1777, APS.

2. Bedaulx to Congress, Feb. 2, 1778, National Archives.

3. Kalb to Deane, Dec. 18, 1776, *Deane Papers*, I, 432.

4. The first letter is dated only Saturday; both are in the APS.

5. The letter to Congress cited above.

sustained efforts by Pulaski to recruit him for his legion won him a lieutenant colonelcy.[6] He went south with the Legion in 1779, but his health was failing; after the siege of Savannah he asked leave to resign and go home.[7] The request came too late; some time during the winter he died in Charleston.[8]

Sir.   Havre-de-Grace the 16th Xber 1776.

Being inform'd of your arrival in Europe I take the liberty to send you the inclosed letter. I was charg'd with it at Rotterdam, by Mr. Barker, one of your acquintances when I embark'd my self to America this three Months ago.

Having been taken by the English, I found an opportunity to come to France, where I had the honour to see Mr. Dean to whom I showed the said letter which I had been so happy to preserve from the perquisition of the English.

I'm to set out again to your Country, in hopes of finding an opportunity to use my Sword in the cause of the liberty against the Oppressors.

Excuse me sir for the liberty I take to write you. Mr. Dean will give you an exacter account of me.

I'm sir with the greatest respect, sir your most humble and most obediant servant   C. BEDAULX.

6. *Ibid.* and Bedaulx' subsequent letters to Congress of Feb. 4, Oct. 22, Nov. 17, 1778; Pulaski to Congress, [Nov.] 15, 25, Dec. 3, 4, 1778, all in the National Archives; *JCC*, XII, 1210. See also Idzerda, *Lafayette*, I, 10, 18–19, 76–81, 83–5.

7. To Congress, Oct. 25, 1779, National Archives. The letter was from Charleston; he had therefore survived the siege of Savannah, where a later report had him killed in action: R.R. Livingston to Dumas, Nov. 28, 1781, National Archives.

8. The chevalier de Segond to Congress, [1784,] National Archives. Rumors of Bedaulx' death were going around Europe in late 1780. A.-A.-J. Feutry inquired of WTF about them on Nov. 1, 1780, and an undated note to BF from the abbé Morellet made the same inquiry. Both are in the APS.

From Jane Mecom

ALS: American Philosophical Society

Goshon Chester County in Penselveny Decr. 16. 1776

My Ever Dear Brother

I was distres'd at your leveing us but as affairs have turned out I have bles'd God you were absent, and we have Reason to hope you are saif arived at your Port. On hearing the Enemy were advancing to wards us we thought it nesesary to Retire to this place where we hope we are saif and are very Comfortable.[9] I have another mercy to be thankfull for which has given grate ease to my mind, the Return of my son in Law Collas, who has by the Recomendation of Cousen Williams, and Capt. Faulkner, (who happened to be then in Boston) obtained the comand of a Contenental ship, Expects to go to France, and is the barer of this.[1] I hope He will aquit Himself properly in His station, I know nothing of His abilities but that He has allway borne a good charecter. Our Famely are all well, Will as Harty and as lovely as ever Says He wants to go to france to grand papa and He must send a Boat for Him. We shall be very Happy to hear from you, from Temple and Benny. Remember my love to them. I sopose your son and Daughter will write and Inform of all nesesary. I only add that I am as Ever your Affectionat sister   JANE MECOM

Addressed in different hands: Doctor Franklin / Favored by / Capt Collas

Endorsed: Family Letters 1777

9. "We" were she and Sally Bache and young William; see Sally's letter below, Feb. 23. The British were expected to advance on Philadelphia, but went into winter quarters in New Jersey.

1. While in Boston Peter Collas, Jenny's husband, must have obtained the recommendation of Jonathan Williams, Sr., and Nathaniel Falconer; the latter was by now a commissioner of naval stores: Van Doren, *Franklin—Mecom*, p. 169. Collas was almost certainly captured off the coast and imprisoned in New York; he was exchanged the following summer. *Massachusetts Soldiers and Sailors in the Revolutionary War* . . . (17 vols.; Boston, 1896–1908), III, 803; Jane to BF below, Aug. 18. If he carried this letter, he must have kept it with him and eventually sent it on its way, for BF acknowledged it on Oct. 5, 1777: APS.

From Philip Thicknesse[2]

ALS: American Philosophical Society

Sir   Calais Rue de Capuchin Decr the 16: 1776

My Being one of the indirect sufferers in the Cause of American liberty, I hope will plead my excuse in takeing this; My private misfortunes Sir fell upon me, for speaking, and sometimes writing, my honest sentiments, relative to your public ones. But I will not trouble you with the sorrows of an Individual, who I hope has the charge, and will protect millions. I shall therefore only say, that a few Scotch Lords *sent down* from St. James's, *out voted* that great, and good man, Lord Camden, and I was thereby defrauded of ten th[ousand]d pounds. The Enclosed printed papers will shew you *how*; and that I am now publishing by Subscription a Journey through France, and I entreat the honor of your name, and that of your Honorable Brothers, the Members of the Continental Congress of America as Subscribers to it![3] Nor do I ask it, from motives of parsimony, but to have it appear, to the present, and future generations; that I had the honor to mingle my afflictions along with brave men, who, like me, had seperated themselves from their mother Country rather than submit to the violation of their ancient Laws. I have the honor to be Sir your most Obedient and Devoted Humble Servant

PHIL. THICKNESSE

Addressed: To / The Honorable / Benjamin Franklin / President of the Continental / Congress of America / at Paris

Notations in different hands: Lett. from Phillip Thicknesse Calais Decr 16. 1776. / Thicknesse Papers to be answered

2. For this quarrelsome eccentric (1719–92), who for twenty years had been Gainsborough's patron, see the *DNB* and Philip Gosse, *Dr. Viper: the Querulous Life of Philip Thicknesse* (London, 1952).

3. He had hoped to acquire the money from his first wife's family, but had lost his case in Chancery and then, despite Camden's support, his appeal to the House of Lords. He considered himself a victim of the establishment, as the Americans were. The enclosures were doubtless three open letters, one signed by him and two pseudonymous, which an opposition newspaper, *The Crisis*, published on March 4, 25, and Aug. 12, 1775; they proclaimed that Chancery was lawless and the Lords corrupted by the King's friends. Thicknesse then left the country for a tour of France and Spain,

From Charles-Guillaume-Frédéric Dumas

ALS: American Philosophical Society; letterbook draft: Algemeen Rijksarchief, The Hague

Cher et respectable ami,   17e. Dec. 1776

Est-il bien vrai que vous soyiez arrivé? Puis-je le croire? Oui, car ni la mer, ni ses fatigues, ni ses dangers, ne sont rien aux yeux de l'homme vertueux et rare, qui ne vit que pour faire du bien au genre humain. Soyez donc mille fois le bien venu, et souffrez qu'en idée je vous embrasse de tout mon coeur. Vous venez, sans doute, mettre la derniere main à l'ouvrage que j'ai eu le bonheur de commencer, et que Mr. Deane a perfectionné. Vous venez annoncer l'indépendance et la souveraineté, offrir le Commerce et la bonne amitié des Etats Unis Américains, et demander en échange le réciproque. Tout cela sera écouté et accepté avec plaisir, j'en suis sûr. Quand tout cela sera ajusté et conclu, nous espérons, mon Epouse et moi, que vous nous ferez le même honneur que Mr. Deane nous a saintement promis,[4] et sur lequel nous comptons, de venir signer avec nous un bon Traité d'hospitalité de l'ancien temps. Alors, Monsieur, je vous rendrai compte, papiers sur table, de tout ce que j'ai fait en exécution des ordres dont vous m'avez honoré il y a justement un an, comme je l'ai déjà fait dans plusieurs Lettres successives que j'ai eu l'honneur de vous écrire par la voie prescrite de St. Eustache. Mais, de grace, avant tout, daignez me favoriser d'un mot seulement de réponse par premiere poste, afin que je ne doute plus du bonheur de vous avoir en Europe. Ma certitude à cet égard vient d'augmenter par la réponse d'un Ami de Rotterdam, à qui j'avois écrit avanthier, et qui me marque que la Lettre de Nantes existe reellement, est conforme à l'extrait de la Gazette,[5] et qu'il connoît ceux à qui

---

from which we assume he was returning home when he wrote this letter. With it he enclosed a printed prospectus, now in the APS, of the work that subsequently appeared as *A Year's Journey through France and Part of Spain* (2 vols., Bath and London, 1777.)

4. In his letter of Aug. 18, 1776: *Deane Papers*, I, 219.

5. Letters from Nantes published in the *Gazette de Rotterdam* of Dec. 14 brought "la bonne, l'importante nouvelle" of BF's arrival there and his departure for Paris, Dumas wrote Deane on the 17th: Algemeen Rijksarchief.

elle est écrite. La poste, qui va partir ne me laisse que le temps de vous assurer du parfait dévouement et respect Monsieur de votre très humble et très obéissant serviteur   CGf DUMAS

Pour Monsieur le Dr. Franklin

Notations: Lett. from Monsr CGf Dumas 17 Decr 1776 / Du Mas, Leyde 17 December 76

From Jacques-Barthélémy Gruel

ALS: American Philosophical Society

Monsieur   Nantes ce 17: Xbre: 1776.

Mr. Guerton directeur general des fermes, se presenta un instant aprés votre depart pour avoir l'honneur de prendre congé de vous, et de vous remettre une Lettre pour Mr. Roslin dont il avoit eté question dans la conversation que vous eûtes ensemble à la Barberie. Il m'a prié de vous l'envoyer, en consequence j'ay l'honneur de vous la remettre sous ce ply.

Mr. Roslin fermier general est chargé, par Mr. le Controleur general de tous les details qui concernent les affaires des ameriquains tant pour l'entrée des denrées du crû de vos colonies, que du chargement des navires que nous expedions.[6] En consequence nous nous sommes adressés à luy pour avoir une diminution sur les droits exhorbitants que payent les huiles de sperma ceti qui viennent de rhode island, et des environ. L'affaire est au conseil depuis trois mois, et n'est pas encore decidée, cela retarde l'expedition de Mr. Nicols, ce qui luy cause du prejudice; oserais-je, Monsieur, vous prier de luy en faire parler par Monsieur Moris, si vous ne croyés pas devoir le

6. Before BF left Gruel's country house, La Barberie, for Paris on Dec. 15, his host had apparently concluded that he and Penet were to be the principal agents for American commerce. Guerton was director in Nantes of the farm for import duties and the salt and tobacco monopolies; Hector-Edmé Roslin was a well connected banker and one of the farmers general. *Almanach royal,* 1777, p. 493; Lüthy, *Banque protestante,* II, 391; Yves Durand, *Les Fermiers généraux au 18ème siècle* (Paris, 1971), p. 529. The farm began to make contact with BF, in other words, almost immediately after his arrival. The reason was doubtless the expectation of a lucrative trade in tobacco; see the headnote on Dubourg's memorandum below under Jan. 9.

44

faire vous-même. Il seroit interessant que nous eûssions une reponse decisive afin de scavoir à quoi nous en tenir; nous demandons une diminution de moitié sur les droits, vû le bas prix de ces huilles en france, et les forts droits qu'elles payent en entrant.[7] Ces raisons puissantes empechêront par la suitte l'importation de cette denrée en france, ce qui ne peut que prejudicier au comerce. Il est donc d'un avantage reciproque que M.M. les fermiers generaux diminüent leurs droits sur cette denrée: vos observations à ce sujet ne pouront qu'etre d'un grand poids, et determineront vraisemblablement ces messieurs a satisfaire a notre demande.

Le navire le Succés Capitaine handerson est entierement dechargé, les alleges qui apportent icy les marchandises ne sont pas encore toutes arrivées.[8] Une seule chargée de 159 boucauts de tabac est actuellement en decharge, les autres vont suivre. J'aurai soin à ce que tout soit mis en bon etât en magazin, et aurai l'honneur de vous donner successivement avis de toutes les operations qui interessent le congrés: vous pouvés, Monsieur, vous reposer entierement sur mon exactitude.

M.M. les fermiers generaux desirent avoir non seulement cette cargaison de tabac, mais encore ils proposent de faire un traité pour leur approvisionement annuel. Cette affaire ne peut qu'etre avantageuse au congrés. Il seroit sûr du debouché de tous les tabacs du continent; beaucoup de negociants demandent egalement a achepter la cargaison du Succés. Ils la feront valoir sans contredit plus cher que M.M. les fermiers generaux; j'en ecris par ce courier a M.M. Moris et penet afin qu'ils prennent vos avis sur ce qui convient de faire. Je me conformeray à ce que vous aurés decidé, et attendray vos ordres pour la livraison de la cargaison du Succés. Le tabac du Succes

---

7. Capt. Nichols was a Nantucketer who had arrived at Nantes in September with a cargo of whale oil from Nicholas Brown & Co.: *Naval Docs.,* VI, 618. That grade of oil was not popular in France, and 20% of the price of a recent cargo had been absorbed by the duty: James B. Hedges, *The Browns of Providence Plantations, Colonial Years* (Cambridge, Mass., 1952), p. 235.

8. James Anderson was a merchant captain from Philadelphia, where he and Wickes had recently been fellow initiates in a Masonic lodge: Clark, *Wickes,* pp. 86, 105.

sera achepte icy pour l'Etranger de 13. a 14. sols et peut-etre 15 la livre. Je ne sçais ce que M.M. les fermiers generaux pouront en offrir, vous etes sur les lieux, et à même d'entendre leur propositions. Je me conformeray exactement à ce que vous voudrés bien me marquer à ce sujet.

Je me suis acquité, Monsieur, de votre commission auprés de nos Dames. Elles sont on ne peut pas plus sensibles à votre gracieux souvenir et me chargent de vous faire agreer ainsy que Mr. de Chavigny[9] leur civilités respectueuses.

J'attendray avec impatience de vos nouvelles, et apprendray avec bien de la joie votre heureuse arrivée, et en bonne santé dans la capitalle. Je suis avec Respect Monsieur Votre tres humble et tres obeïssant serviteur   J GRUEL

J'apprends dans le moment l'arrivée au bas de la rivierre de la fregate la Represaille Capitaine Mr. Witkes; Mr. harris vient de monter, et m'a remis les trois lettres cy inclus que je prends la liberté de vous adresser.[1] Mr. Rumcey a vendu de Quiberon les cargaisons, et les prises. La Represaille n'a a bord que vingt deux pieces eau de vie, tout le reste a eté vendû comptant. Mr. Rumcey en rendra compte; Mr. harris m'a dit qu'il ne seroit icy que dans quatre ou cinq jours. A son arrivée j'auray l'honneur de vous informer de toutes ses operations à quiberon relativement à ces deux prises. J'envoye à bord de la represaille prendre les indigo, et les effets qui vous appartiennent que je soigneray avec exactitude. La fregate n'a besoin que d'eau qu'elle va prendre, et aussitôt elle sortira.

Notation: Lett. from J Gruel Nantes Decr 17. 1776.

From Gruel   ALS: American Philosophical Society

Monsieur   Nantes ce 18: Xbre:1776

J'ay eû l'honneur de vous ecrire le 16: Courant, et de vous informer de l'arrivée en cette rivierre du navire la concorde Capitaine. Mr. harris.

<hr>

9. Chavigny, according to M. de Sallier-Dupin of the Bibliothèque municipale at Nantes, was Mme. Gruel's maiden name.

1. Lieut. Robert Harris was Wickes's first officer: Clark, *Wickes*, pp. 14, 105–6.

Monsieur de Basmarein, frere de mon neveu, qui etoit venu de Bordeaux pour vous presenter ses devoirs,[2] aura l'honneur de vous remettre la presente; pourois-je esperer, Monsieur, que vous voudrés bien luy permettre de vous assurer de ses respects, et pendant son sejour en la capitalle, de cultiver votre bienveillance que j'ose vous demander pour Luy.

On est venû m'annoncer l'arrivée du navire la Marie Elizabeth Capitaine Mr. yong mouillé aujourdhuy en rivierre, sans doute le Capitaine montera demain.[3] Si j'apprends quelque chose de nouveau avant le depart du Courier, j'auray l'honneur de vous en faire part. Je suis avec Respect Monsieur Votre tres humble et tres obeïssant serviteur   J GRUEL

Endorsed: Lett. from J Gruel Decr 18. 1776.

To Silas Deane   ALS: Connecticut Historical Society

Versailles, Friday, Dec. 20. 1776 4. P.M, a la belle Image
[*Torn*: My dear Friend?]

Finding myself too much fatigu'd to proceed to Paris this Evening, *and not knowing whether you have receiv'd my Letter wherein I requested you to provide me a Lodging,* I have concluded to remain here to-night. If you are in Paris, I hope to hear from you to-morrow Morning before I set out, which will hardly be till about Noon. With the sincerest Esteem, I have the Honor

2. The Basmarein who had come from Bordeaux, in other words, was the brother of a nephew known to BF. The latter, a nephew by marriage, will reappear in later volumes. He was Pierre-Jacques Reculès de Basmarein (1744–1806), of the Bordeaux firm of Reculès de Basmarein & Raimbaux, one of the leading merchant houses in France and one that was soon actively involved in the American war. Louis XV had recognized Basmarein's promise, and had helped arrange his marriage with a great heiress from St.-Domingue, Marie-Magdeleine-Victoire Gruel. The brother introduced here was probably the abbé Pierre-Martial Reculès de Poulouzat, a member and clerical counsellor of the parlement of Bordeaux and also active in the family firm. Robert Castex, "L'Armateur de La Fayette: Pierre de Basmarein . . . ," *Revue des questions historiques,* CII (1925), 83–9; William Doyle, *The Parlement of Bordeaux and the End of the Old Regime, 1771–1790* (New York, [1974]), pp. 12, 135, 322.

3. Capt. Peter Young, of Philadelphia, had arrived with a consignment from Congress: Rumsey to BF below, Dec. 31.

to be, Dear Sir, Your most obedient humble Servant

B FRANKLIN

Honble. Silas Deane Esqr

Notation: Doct. Franklin 20 Dec 1776

From Bérard Frères & Cie.[4]

ALS: American Philosophical Society

⟨Lorient, December 20, 1776, in English: When our friends in Nantes told us of your arrival with a consignment of tobacco, we ordered them to buy it if for sale. Your agent cannot treat, they tell us, "without your answer expected." We will give you the best bargain you can anticipate. You may find out about our firm from Germany, Girardot & Cie. or Tourton & Baur, the two leading bankers in Paris.[5] We will pay in cash or in drafts on Paris, Amsterdam, or London; and on whatever terms may be fixed between us we will thereafter, for the duration of the war, take any amount of leaf tobacco delivered at Lorient. We offer a higher price than the farmers general, and assured means of payment. Your ships will be safe here from the government, and we can supply all the articles that the colonies may require. Please tell us your price and conditions of sale, and do not dispose of the consignment until you have our answer.

We should be glad to talk with you, as we have proposals that cannot be committed to paper. If you are returning to Nantes, one of us will meet you there. If you winter in Paris, Germany, Girardot & Cie. will communicate our views. We stand ready to make advances at any time, and you may trust us.⟩

---

4. A firm of some consequence. It did not succeed in entering the tobacco negotiations, but later had considerable dealings with the commissioners. The brothers Bérard established themselves at Lorient in 1775 and engaged largely in the East India trade: Lüthy, *Banque protestante*, II, 440–1.

5. They were indeed; see *ibid.*, II, 402–4; I, 80–3, 412–13.

From [the Comte de Lauraguais?[6]]

L: American Philosophical Society

Sir   [Before December 21?, 1776[7]]

I congratulate your arrival with an intelligence of the first moment, which you will apply with your wonted caution. Mr. de morande is secretary to m. beaumarchais, and brother to a refugee of the same name in London, lately acquitted *in the Kings bench*, of a suit by the chev. d'Eon, and known by every body to be a man *a tout faire*. There is also m. Charles parker forth of somerset street portman sq. some time past and, now in paris intimate with all three, who conveys (by Lord stormonst messenger) to lord mansfield all the transactions and equipments of the court of france for america, the ships, description, name, force and cargo of mr. du Coudrays expedition at havre, &a. Mr. b—m—was to have come to england, but it was found that mr p—F—could more convenient go to france.[8] You are too wise to neglect this because anonymous.

Addressed: dr. Franklin / paris. / by the hands of Silas deane ecq.

Notation: Intelligence

---

6. For the comte see above, XIX, 86 n; XXII, 468 n. As a friend of Arthur Lee he saw a good deal of all the commissioners; although the letter is not in his hand, he seems to us the most likely author. He was jealous of Beaumarchais, he had some contact with Nathaniel Parker Forth (even though he mistook his first name), and he was fond of feeding information behind the backs of those concerned; see Stevens, *Facsimiles*, VIII, no. 782; XVIII, no. 1691. He was in Paris when BF arrived or soon after, for as early as Jan. 8 Stormont referred to the great intimacy between the two: *ibid.*, XIV, 1410, pp. 1–2. This evidence is not conclusive, but it is at least suggestive.

7. The fact that the note was left with Deane suggests to us that it was written before BF's arrival in Paris.

8. M. de Morande was in fact Jean-Baptiste-Lazare Théveneau de Francy. His brother in London was Charles Théveneau de Morande, indeed "a man *à tout faire*," and one whom Lauraguais detested. Charles Eon de Beaumont, Chevalier d'Eon, the brother-in-law of BF's winegrowing acquaintance the Chevalier O'Gorman (above, XIX, 86 n), was a notorious adventurer and transvestite. Brian N. Morton, "Beaumarchais, Francy, Steuben, and Lafayette: An Unpublished Correspondence . . . ," *The French Rev.*, XLIX (1975–

49

The Committee of Secret Correspondence to the American Commissioners

LS: American Philosophical Society, New York Public Library, University of Virginia Library, British Library;[9] AL (incomplete draft[1]): American Philosophical Society; three copies: American Philosophical Society, National Archives, Library of Congress

This letter was in response to Deane's of October 1, which was the first word from him in Paris that reached Philadelphia.[2] He complained hotly that he was not being kept in touch with developments at home;[3] hence the committee's long discussion of them. He also made a number of suggestions which, two days after his letter was read in Congress on December 21, elicited the resolutions that were enclosed with this reply.[4] Those Congressional actions put new burdens on the commissioners: a quarrel with Portugal, though it came to nothing; the commissioning of privateers; and the attempt to negotiate with Versailles a loan of impossible magnitude.

---

6), 943–59; Ernest A. Vizetelly, *The True Story of the Chevalier d'Eon ...* (London, 1895), pp. 88, 247–8; for Morande and Eon see also Larousse, *Dictionnaire universel.* Nathaniel Parker Forth was Lord North's unofficial emissary to Maurepas, and was known in Paris as Stormont's spy; the following April he approached Francy, apparently without success, to betray Beaumarchais: Stevens, *op. cit.*, VI, no. 640, p. 3; VII, no. 670, p. 26; XV, no. 1514. "b—m—" is clearly Beaumarchais himself. Du Coudray (above, XXII, 462 n), after collecting men, weapons, and supplies in ports from Dunkirk to Marseilles, had left Le Havre on Dec. 14 on the *Amphitrite* with a cargo of arms and ammunition. See Stevens, III, no. 240; XIV, no. 1405; WTF to BF below, Jan. 9; Roger Lafon, *Beaumarchais, le brillant armateur* (Paris, 1928), p. 87. The ship soon returned to port and left again without Du Coudray, as will be seen; but he and most of his officers eventually found their way to America, and constituted the largest group of French recruits before 1778.

9. A fifth LS, in the Haverford College Library, is now reported lost.

1. In the hand of Richard Henry Lee.

2. His earlier letter, of July 20–Aug. 18, had been lost at sea: above, XXII, 487 n.

3. "For Heaven's sake, if you mean to have any connection with this Kingdom, be more assiduous in getting your letters here." *Deane Papers*, I, 288.

4. See the headnote on BF to Deane above, Dec. 4. The decision to send commissioners to various European courts, mentioned there, was not taken until Dec. 30.

Baltimore in Maryland 21[–23] Decemr. 1776
Honourable Gentlemen

After expressing our Hopes, that this will find you all three safely fixed at Paris, we proceed with Pleasure to acknowledge the Receipt of Mr. Deane's Letter of the 1st. October. When we reflect on the Character and Views of the Court of London, it ceases to be a Wonder, that the British Embassador, and all other British Agents, should employ every means, that tended to prevent European Powers, but France more especially, from giving America Aid in this War. Prospects of Accommodation, it is well known, would effectually prevent foreign Interference, and therefore, without one serious Design of accommodating on any other Principles, but the absolute Submission of America, the delusive Idea of Conciliation hath been industriously suggested on both Sides the Water, that, under colour of this dividing and aid-withholding Prospect, the vast British Force, sent to America, might have the fairest Chance of succeeding; And this Policy hath in fact done considerable Injury to the United States, as we shall presently shew by a just Detail of this Campaign, for it is not yet ended.

You know Gentlemen, that at the Moment a Potent Land and Marine Force was preparing to be sent here, an Act was passed for appointing Commissioners, who, too many expected, were to give Peace to America. As therefore the War might be soon concluded, so were our military Arrangements accomodated, and the Troops taken into Service the last Spring, consisting of regular Corps, and Bodies of Militia, were all engaged for short Periods. With these the Campaign began in various Parts of North America. Dr. Franklin is so well acquainted with the Progress of the War in Canada previous to his Departure, that we need only observe, the Campaign has ended as favourably for us in that Quarter, as we could reasonably expect. The Enemy, having been able to pierce no further than Crown-Point, after a short Stay, and reconnoitring Genl. Gate's Army at Ticonderoga, thought proper to recross the Lake, and leave us in quiet Possession of those Passes. General Gates, having left a proper Force at Ticonderoga and on the Communication, retired with the rest of his Troops. New York and its Neighbourhood, not being defensible by an

Army singly against a strong Land and Sea Force, acting in Conjunction, was of Necessity yielded to the Enemy after some Contest, General Washington retiring, until the Situation of the Country above Kingsbridge no longer enabled the Enemy to receive Aid from their Ships. Genl. Howe having stopped here, and Genl. Carlton at Crown-Point, effectually disappointed the great Object of joining the two Armies, the latter, as we have said, returning to Canada, and the former retreating from the White Plains towards NYork gave us a favourable Prospect of seeing an happy End put to this dangerous Campaign. However many Causes have concurred in producing an unlucky reverse of Fortune, the Nature of the Country, the uncommon Fineness of the Weather, even to this day, and above all the short enlistments, which gave the Soldiery an Opportunity of going home, tired as they were with the Operations of an active Summer. When Genl. Howe retreated from the White Plains, he halted his whole Army on the North River, between Dobbes's Ferry and Kingsbridge, where he remained for some time. Having effected so little of the great Business, that brought him here, and the Season allowing him time for it, most Men were of Opinion, that the next Attempt would be to get Possession of Philadelphia by a March through the Jerseys, whilst a Fleet should be sent up the Delaware to facilitate the Enterprize. To guard against such a Maneuvre, Genl. Washington crossed the North River with all the Battalions that had been raised to the Westward of it, leaving Genl. Lee with the Eastern troops to guard the Pass of the Highlands on Hudson's River. In this Situation of Things Mr. Howe made a Sudden Attack on Fort Washington with the greatest Part of his Army, and carried it with considerable Loss; here he made near 3000 of our Men Prisoners. By this Event it became unnecessary longer to hold Fort Lee, or Fort Constitution, as it was formerly called which is on the West Side of North River, nearly opposite to Fort Washington. It had therefore been determined to abandon Fort Lee, but before the Stores could be all removed, the Enemy came suddenly upon it, and the Garrison retreated, leaving some of their Baggage and Stores behind. About this time Genl. Howe became possessed of a Letter (by the Agency of some wicked Person, who contrived to get it from the Express) written by Genl. Washington to the Board of War, in which he had given an exact Account, when the Time of Service of all our Batallions would expire, and his Apprehensions, that the Men would not reinlist, without first going home to see their Families and Friends. Possessed of this Intelligence, The opportunity was carefully watched,[5] and a vigorous Impression actually made at the very Crisis, when our Army in the Jersies was reduced to 3000 Men by the Retiring of Numbers, and the Sickness of others, and before Militia could, in this extensive Country, be brought up to supply their Places. The Enemy marched rapidly on, through the Jerseys, whilst our feeble Army was obliged to retreat from Post to Post, until it crossed the Delaware at Trenton, where about 2500 Militia from the City of Philadelphia joined the General. Since Genl. Howe's Arrival on the Borders of Delaware, various Maneuvres and Stratagems have been practised to effect a Passage over the River, but they have hitherto failed. General Washington's small Army is placed along the West Side of Delaware from above Coryell's Ferry to within 14 Miles of Philadelphia, which, with the Gondolas, one Frigate of 32 Guns, and other armed Vessells in the River above the Cheveaux de Frize, cover the Passage of it. Genl. Lee, (who had crossed the River with as many of the Eastern Troops, as could be spared from the Defence of the Highlands, either to join Genl. Washington or to act on the Enemies Rear, as Occasions might point out) was the other day unfortunately surprized and made Prisoner by a Party of 70 Light Horse, who found him in an House a few Miles in the Rear of his Army with his Domesticks only. This Loss, though great, will in some degree be repaired by Genl. Gates, who, we understand, has joined the Army commanded by Genl. Lee, and who, we have reason to think, has by this time effected a Junction of his Force with that of Genl. Washington. As the Militia are marching from various Quarters to reinforce the General, if the Enemy do not quickly accomplish their

5. This letter and other dispatches were stolen weeks before the retreat across New Jersey; see Fitzpatrick, *Writings of Washington*, VI, 237 n. We have no evidence that the theft had the least effect on Howe's planning.

Wishes of possessing Phila., we hope not only to save that City, but to see Genl. Howe retreat as fast as he advanced through the Jerseys. Genl. Clinton, with a Fleet, in which it is said, he carried 8000 Men, has gone from New York through the Sound; some suppose for Rhode Island, but neither his Destination or it's Consequences are yet certainly known to us.[6] Thus, Gentlemen, we have given you a true Detail of the Progress and present State of our Affairs, which, although not in so good a Posture as they were two Months ago, are by no means in so bad a way, as the Emissaries of the British Court will undoubtedly represent them. If the great Land and Sea Force, with which we have been attacked, be compared with the feeble State, in which the Commencement of this War found us, with respect to Military Stores of all Kinds, Soldiers Cloathing, Navy, and Regular Force; and if the infinite Art be considered, with which Great Britain hath endeavoured to prevent our getting these Necessaries from foreign Parts, which has in part prevailed the Wonder will rather be, that our Enemies have made so little Progress, than that they have made so much.

All Views of Accommodation with Great Britain, but on Principles of Peace as Independent States, and in a Manner perfectly consistent with the Treaties, our Commissioners may make with foreign States, being totally at an end since the Declaration of Independence and the Embassy to the Court of France, Congress have directed the Raising of 94 Batallions of Infantry, with some Cavalry. Thirteen Frigates from 24 to 36 Guns are already launched and fitting, and 2 Ships of the Line with 5 more Frigates are ordered to be put on the Stocks.[7] We hear the Levies are going on well in the different States. Until the New Army is collected, the Militia must curb the Enemies Progress. The very considerable Force, that Great Britain has

6. Rhode Island was captured, and for the next three years was a British naval base.

7. For recent Congressional resolutions authorizing the raising of troops and the construction of warships see *JCC*, V, 762; VI, 970, 981, 994, 1025. No ship of the line and only one of the new frigates ever saw service; see William M. Fowler, Jr., *Rebels under Sail: the American Navy during the Revolution* (New York, [1976]), pp. 246–8.

already in N America, the Possibility of recruiting it here within their own Quarters by Force and Fraud together, added to the Reinforcements, that may be sent from Europe, and the Difficulty of finding Funds in the present depressed State of American Commerce, all conspire to prove incontestibly, that if France desires to preclude the Possibility of North America's being ever reunited with Great Britain, now is the favourable Moment for establishing the Glory, Strength, and Commercial Greatness of the former Kingdom by the Ruin of her ancient Rival. A decided Part now taken by the Court of Versailles, and a vigorous Engagement in the War in Union with North America, would with Ease sacrifice the Fleet and Army of Great Britain, at this time chiefly collected about New York. The inevitable Consequence would be the quick Reduction of the British Islands in the West Indies, already bared of Defence by the Removal of their Troops to this Continent. For Reasons herein assigned, Gentlemen, you will readily discern, how all important it is to the Security of American Independence, that France should enter the War as soon as may be, and how necessary it is (if it be possible) to procure from her the Line of Battle Ships, you were desired in your Instructions to obtain for us,[8] the speedy Arrival of which here, in the present State of Things, might decide the Contest at one Stroke. We shall pay proper Attention to what Mr. Deane writes concerning Dr. Williamson and Mr. Hopkins, and we think the ill Treatment, this Country and Mr. Deane have recieved from these Men strongly suggests the Necessity of invincible Reserve with Persons coming to France as Americans and Friends to America, whom the most irrefragable Proofs have not removed all doubt about.[9] The British Recal of their Mediterra-

8. Above, XXII, 630.

9. For Dr. Hugh Williamson see above, X, 266 n. Deane had expressed suspicion of him in general terms. Either it was well grounded, or Williamson was playing a devious game: in August he surprised the British Ambassador, Lord Stormont, by calling on him and saying that the Americans were grossly misled to expect help from any European power; if he could only get home, he added, "he could be of real use." Stevens, *Facsimiles*, XIII, no. 1346. But his later conduct seems to have been above reproach: Smith, *Letters*, VI, 458 n. He sailed in fact from Nantes with Hutchinson, whose letter is above, Dec. 12. Joseph Hopkins, of whom Deane repeatedly com-

nean Passes is an Object of great Consequence, and may require much Intercession with the Court of France to prevent the Mischiefs, that may be derived to American Commerce therefrom; but this Subject has already been touched upon in your Instructions on the Sixth Article of the Treaty proposed to be made with France.[1] As all Affairs, relàtive to the Conduct of Commerce and Remittance, pass through another Department, we beg Leave to refer you to the Secret Committee, and Mr. Thomas Morris their Agent in France, for every Information on these Subjects. The Neighbourhood of Philadelphia having, by the Enemies Movements, become the Seat of War, it was judged proper, that Congress should adjourn to this Town, where the Publick Business may be attended to with the undisturbed Deliberation, that it's Importance demands. The Congress was accordingly opened here on the 20th. Inst.[2] As it is more than probable, that the Conference with Lord Howe on Staten Island may be misrepresented to the Injury of these States, we do Ourselves the Pleasure to inclose you an authenticated Account of the whole Business which the Possibility of Dr. Franklin's not arriving renders proper. This Step was taken to unmask his Lordship, and evince to the World, that he did not possess Powers, which, for the Purposes of Delusion and Division, had been suggested.

Mr. Deane's Proposition of Loan is accepted by Congress, and they have desired two Millions sterling to be obtained, if possible. The Necessity of keeping up the Credit of our Paper Currencey, and the variety of important Uses, that may be made of this Money, have induced Congress to go as far as 6 Per Cent, but the Interest is heavy, and it is hoped, you may be able to do the Business on much easier Terms. The Re-

---

plained, was a New Englander who had first served in the British army and then become a brigadier in the French; he had recently appealed to Vergennes to be sent to join the American army, where he would keep an eye on French interests. Stevens, *op. cit.*, no. 1348.

1. The instructions are above, XXII, 626. The passes, issued by the British Admiralty under treaties with the Barbary states, provided some protection against corsairs; see George L. Beer, *The Old Colonial System, 1660–1754* (2 vols.; New York, 1912), I, 124–7.

2. The motion to move to Baltimore passed on Dec. 12, and the motion to return to Philadelphia on Feb. 27: *JCC*, VI, 1027; VII, 164.

solves of Congress on this Subject are inclosed, and your earliest Attention to them is desired, that we may know as soon as possible the Event of this Application. Another Resolve Inclosed will shew you that Congress approve of Armed Vessels being fitted out by you on Continental Account, provided the Court of France dislike not the Measure, and blank Commissions for this Purpose will be sent you by next Opportunity. Private Ships of War, or Privateers, cannot be admitted, where you are, because the Securities, necessary in such Cases to prevent irregular Practices, cannot be given by the Owners and Commanders of such Privateers. Another Resolve of Congress, which we have the Honor to inclose you, directs the Conduct to be pursued with Regard to Portugal.[3]

We have Nothing further to add at present, but to request, that you will omit no good Opportunity of informing us, how you succeed in your Mission, what Events take place in Europe, by which these States may be affected, and that you contrive us in regular Succession some of the best London, French, and Dutch Newspapers, with any valuable political Publications, that may concern North America. We have the Honor to be with great Respect and Esteem Honorable Gentlemen your most Obedient and Very Humble Servants

BENJA HARRISON
RICHARD HENRY LEE
WILL HOOPER
JNO WITHERSPOON

In Committee of Secret Correspondence

P.S. The American Captures of British Vessels at Sea have not been less numerous or less valuable, than before Dr. Franklin left us. The Value of these Captures have been estimated at two millions.

Endorsed by Franklin: Letter from Committee of Correspondence Dec. 21. 1776 State of Affairs

3. Deane had recommended loosing privateers against Portuguese shipping; see the note on BF to Deane, Dec. 4. On Dec. 23 (hence our bracketed date for this letter) Congress directed the commissioners to ask whether Lisbon had excluded American trade or confiscated American ships, and if so to protest firmly to the Portuguese Ambassador: *JCC,* VI, 1035–6.

From [Henry Hugh Fergusson[4]]

AL: American Philosophical Society

Saturday Evening 9 [December 21?, 1776[5]]

Mr. Fergusson presents compliments and wishes all happiness to doctor Franklin. He takes the liberty to send this card to doctor Franklin, to congratulate him on his safe arrival in Paris. Mr. Fergusson would be much obliged to doctor Franklin could he condescend to name an day and an hour when Mr. Fergusson could have the honour to personaly pay his respects to him was it for ever so short a time to make a few domestick enquiries after Mrs. Fergusson and his friends in Pennsylvania.

Addressed: To Doctor Franklin

Notation: Ferguson

From Gruel

ALS: American Philosophical Society

Monsieur   Nantes ce 21: Xbre. 1776.

J'ai pris la liberté de vous ecrire par M. de Basmarein frere de mon neveu. Je luy ai recommandé de vous presenter ma lettre sitôt son arrivée a Paris. J'ose esperer, Monsieur, que vous trouverés bon qu'il profite de vos bontés, et qu'il vous assure quelque fois de ses respects pendant le sejour qu'il fera en la capitalle.

J'ay eû l'honneur de vous informer par ma susditte de l'arrivée en cette rivierre du 18: courant du navire la Marie-Elizabeth

---

4. Identified by the handwriting, which is sui generis. Fergusson has appeared before as the husband of Elizabeth Graeme, to whom WF had once been attached; the Scot had family interests in Britain that took him there from Philadelphia in September, 1775, carrying a letter from BF to JW, and he stayed in Europe until March, 1777. Above, VII, 177 n; XXI, 538 n; XXII, 198; *PMHB*, XXXIX (1915), 306. We suspect that he was the "Mr. Ferguson" who came to Paris the previous September and acted as a messenger between Edward Bancroft and Silas Deane: *Deane Papers*, I, 237.

5. The other note from Fergusson below, under Dec. 26, appears to have been his second to BF. If we are correct in our dating of it, and if this one was earlier, Fergusson must have been writing on the day BF reached Paris.

Capitaine Peter young: J'ay celui de vous remettre cy joint l'etât de son chargement.

Le navire la fanny Capitaine Sieur Willem Tokely passé de Boston en 28. Jours est arrivé ce matin. Mr. schweighauser a qui ce batiment est adressé a sans doute l'honneur de vous informer de son chargement qui consiste en 226 boucauts tabacs, et 2000ers merein;[6] le Capitaine ne rapporte rien de nouveau des affaires de Newe york, mais on dit que les armateurs ameriquains ont pris 11. batiments de transport anglois sur dix neuf destinés pour l'armée du general howe. Voila ce qui s'est debité.

Dans le moment les trente cinq bariques Indigo arrivent icy, je les ferai mettre en magazin jusqu'a ce que vous m'ayés donné vos ordres. J'attends la semaine prochaine vos malles que Mr. Wilckes me fera passer par un homme de confiance, je les soigneray avec exactitude.

Mr. Wilckes m'a fait l'honneur de diner hier chez moy, nous avons decidés ensemble qu'il ne resteroit pas long temps en rivierre. Il a besoin de quelques rafraîchissements, je les luy enverray lundy; je luy ai remis les deux pieces d'or dont vous m'avés chargé. J'ay egalement fait envoyer à bord les deux bariques vin d'equipage que vous m'aviés chargé de faire passer.[7]

Mr. Rumcey n'a pas encore parû, j'ignore toutes ses operations relatives aux prises, a son arrivée j'auray l'honneur de vous informer de tout.

Cy inclus une lettre qui m'est venû par la poste. Je suis avec Respect Monsieur Votre tres humble et tres obeissant serviteur

J Gruel

Notation: Lett. from J Gruel Nantes 21 Decemr 1776.

6. He meant, we assume, "deux milliers merein," or around 2,000 barrel staves; Schweighauser's letter of the 23rd put the number at 1,500. The *Fanny* had sailed from the Chesapeake in July, with a cargo of tobacco on Congress' account, but an American privateer had intercepted her on the supposition that she was bound for London; this contretemps delayed Tokely's departure until November. *Naval Docs.*, V, 138–9, 1090; VI, 1360; VII, 104.

7. White wine that was BF's gift to the crew of the *Reprisal*: entry of Dec. 23 in Gruel's account (above, pp. 21–2).

From Jean-Gabriel Montaudoüin de la Touche[8]

ALS: American Philosophical Society

Monsieur   Nantes 21 xbre 76

Voici une lettre qui m'a été addressée pour vous de Bordeaux. Je suis bien fâché que vôtre depart m'ait privë du plaisir de vous avoir a diner, comme vous m'en aviés flatté. C'eut êté une grande satisfaction, et un grand honneur pour moi. J'espere que quelque bonne circonstance nous procurera l'avantage de vous revoir dans nôtre bonne ville. Vous avés vû combien tous les honnetes gens s'interessent a la cause Ameriquaine. Je comptois Monsieur, vous faire presenter chéz moi par mon fils les vers que je joins ici, c'est une foible expression des sentiments que vous inspirés.

J'ai un ami a Paris nommé Mr. Bendet qui a êté longtems anploié dans les affairres Ministerieles. Il a encore beaucoup de relation avec le Ministere. Il demeure au Chateau des Thuileries au Pavillon de flore. Je pense qu'il pouroît vous être utile dans vos operations. Si vous voulés prendre la peine de vous aboucher avec lui j'ai tout lieu de croire que vous en serés très content. En attendant je lui ecris pour vous recommander. J'ai aussi, Monsieur, a Paris une Cousine Germaine qui est connue dans la Republique des lettres, c'est Madame Duboccage qui demeure rüe St. honoré vis avis les Jacobins. Quand vous voudrés vous delasser de vos occupations, je suis sur qu'elle vous recevra avec grand plaisir.[9]

Il vient d'arriver deux Navires de vôtre païs. L'un est parti quelques jours après vous. Les Armées etoient toujours en presence. L'autre aporte du Tabac. Je suis avec un respect infini Monsieur vôtre très humble très obeïssant Serviteur

MONTAUDOÜIN
Corresp. de L'Acad. Roy. des Sciences

Quand vous verrés, Monsieur, Messieurs Duhamel, Le Roy,

---

8. See above, XXII, 332 n. His brother Arthur, mentioned there, apparently did not correspond with BF or the commission.

9. Marie-Anne Le Page, dame Duboccage (1710–1802), was a poet famous in her day and crowned with laurel by Voltaire; see Larousse, *Dictionnaire universel*.

de L'Acad. des Sciences, et Mr. Delor[1] je vous prie de leur dire mille choses pour moi.

Portrait Docteur Benjamin franklin

Ce Sage nous a fait connoître
les effets merveilleux d'un feu subtil, et prompt
ressort de la nature, et son ame peût être
plus d'un laurier couvre son front:
il a fait a philadelphie
un temple a la philosophie,
un Thrône pour la liberté,
de L'Europe bientôt bannie;
dans les deux mondes respecté
il est par son heureux genie,
ses moeurs douces, sa bonhomie,
son ton, et sa simplicité,
sur tout pour sa philanthropie,
L'honneur de L'Amerique, et de L'humanité.

Addressed in another hand: A Monsieur / Monsieur Bn. franklin / des accademies des Sciences de / Philadelphie Paris &ca / L'un des presidents du congres / continental & president de celui / de Pensilvanie / A Paris

Notation: Lett. from Monsieur Montaudoins Nantes 21 Decr 1776.

From [Samuel Wharton][2]   AL: American Philosophical Society

Dear Sir   London December 21st 1776
I take the earliest Opportunity of expressing my sincere Congratulations on your safe Arrival in France. An Event of

---

1. Jean-Pierre-François Guillot-Duhamel (1730–1816) was a mineralogist: *Index biographique des membres et correspondants de l'Académie* ... (Paris, 1954), p. 165. Delor has appeared often in previous volumes.

2. Identified by the writing as well as the subject matter. This is the first extant letter since Dec. 23, 1775, from BF's old associate in the Walpole Co. Wharton had come to England in 1769 as an agent, with William Trent, of the American promoters, and stayed until 1779. At the time of this letter

the greatest Importance to all America, and particularly regarding your own personal Safety; As the Resentment of your and our Country's Enemies is not in the least abated, and They would have exceedingly rejoiced, If one of their Cruizers had conveyed you to this despotick Shoar: But Thanks to that all gracious Providence, Which has hitherto, so wonderfully animated and supported you in the great Cause of an oppress'd, virtuous, and gallant People. Your unexpected Arrival in France has afforded Administration much Uneasiness, and made a vast Noise through the City. The three per centum Consol. fell half per Centum on that Account,[3] and if a general Insensibility, and Ignorance, blended with a savage Vindictiveness against Us, did not prevail over the whole Kingdom, all the subtle Arts of the Minister and his Friends, could not keep Them, as high as They are; They however continue to deceive the People with the foolish Idea of a Reconciliation being effected by the two Brothers, during the Winter, or That General Howe will before the Spring, totaly rout the grand American Army; and the News just arrived of his success near Kingsbridge, affords Them favorable Ground to establish that Idea.

The Minority in both Houses, a little before their Adjournment, declined attending Parliament; But it was neither a formal Secession, nor done by Agreement between the Heads of the different Parties in Opposition, of Course, as might have been expected, it made little Impression on Administration; and especialy, as each Party remains as unconnected, and jealous of the other, as When you was here; But Yet most of Them write in discovering Disapointment and Displeasure, at the Declaration of Independence, as it deprived Them, of what They esteemed, Their best stepping Ladder into Office.[4] The

his activities in the Company were drawing to an end; see Walpole to BF below, Feb. 10, 1777. But Wharton had a number of other business interests, mentioned in a note below; he was also in touch with prominent members of the opposition, as he makes clear, and kept BF and friends in America informed of developments in London.

3. Consols, established in 1751, were the funded securities of the British government; their market value was considered a barometer of the national credit.

4. He was right about the opposition. The earlier reasons for its fragmentation (above, XXI, 306–7, 549) persisted and grew stronger as the

confidential Language nevertheless of a few of the Leaders in Opposition, such as No. 34. 35. 193, and 206 . . . ,[5] is, That if America Persists in her Resolution of Independence, The Situation of the Kingdom requires, That no Time ought to be lost, before a federal Union is made with Her; But the Pride and Ignorance of the Court and Nation are yet too high, to listen to such Wise Tho' humiliating Council, and nothing, in my Opinion, but the honest Adversity, or Dread of a Union with France and Spain (on the part of America) will awaken No. 125 of 72 from his brutal Lethargy. Lord Chatham declines fast, and it is generaly thought, will never be able again to assume a publick Character. He foretells the greatest Calamitys to be experienced by the Kingdom, in consequence of the rash and unjust Measures prosecuting against the American States. Mr. Deane is in Possession of his Prediction; It is founded in Experience and Wisdom.[6] The Losses occasioned by the successes of our Privateers, will be felt at the yearly Settlement in January, much to the Injury of commercial Credit. Several Failures are expected to follow from these Captures. At New Lloyds' They have a List of 160 Vessels taken by our Cruizers,[7] and doubless They do not know the Names of all,

---

movement toward American independence made the "Ladder into Office," that of reconciliation, more and more ephemeral. "I do not know how to wish success to those whose Victory is to separate from us a large and noble part of our Empire," wrote Edmund Burke. "Still less do I wish success to injustice, oppression and absurdity." Quoted by Frank O'Gorman, *The Rise of Party in England: the Rockingham Whigs, 1760–1782* (London, [1975]), p. 348. The frustration of this dilemma, which culminated in some members' withdrawing from Parliament, is described in *ibid.*, pp. 336–53.

5. Suspension points in the original. He explains the code numbers at the end of the letter, but we do not have the list of names and numbers and can rarely identify a reference.

6. The prediction, whatever it may have been, was not made in the House of Lords, where Chatham had not spoken since the failure of his conciliatory plan in February, 1775. Five months later he warned the peers in no uncertain terms: "if an end is not put to this war there is an end to this country." Quoted in Basil Williams, *The Life of William Pitt, Earl of Chatham* (2 vols., London, etc., 1913), II, 317.

7. New Lloyd's Coffee House was the center of marine insurance: Charles Wright and C. Ernest Fayle, *A History of Lloyd's from the Founding of Lloyd's Coffee House to the Present Day* (London, 1928), pp. 107, 156.

which are taken, and yet They compute the British Loss, at a Million Sterling. The Impress goes on heavily, and Lord Sandwich begins to find, and acknowledge, That it is impossible to man twenty Sail of Men of War, Whilst the Transports are detained in America. In Truth, The Nation *cannot* furnish Seamen for the Navy, The Transport Service, and for carrying on its *remaining* Commerce; And if a large Fleet is required, In Addition to what is employed in America, either the Transport, or Merchant Service, or perhaps both of Them, must be sacrificed to it. It is fortunate however for the Admiralty, That One hundred and Thirty Sail of Transports were, *from their leaky State*, obliged to be sent hither to be repaired, otherwise the impressing Parties would have been a long Time, before They could have procured, as many Men, as are on Board these Transports: But for farther Particulars relative to the Plans of Administration, and the State of the Kingdom, I must beg the Favor of referring you, to our Friend Dr. Bancroft.[8] Last Spring I wrote you many Letters, after the Ones I sent you by Mr. Cumming, But I fear several of Them were intercepted, and particularly One, conveying to you, a circumstantial Account of what Passed between Lord Howe and Me on the Subject of America, and what were the real Designs of Administration. I now send you under Cover, a State of the Conference between his Lordship, and Myself, and I would fain flatter myself, That my Propositions, (when considered, in Reference to the Time They were made) may meet your Approbation. I acted for the best, and thought, I was discharging a Duty I owed to my Country.

From the Moment I was favored with your kind Letter of Septr. 1775, (Which I considered, and therefore circulated

8. BF's old protégé (for whom see above, XVI, 224–5 n) has not appeared in our texts for almost a year. Although Bancroft was frequently in Paris he was based in England, where he was involved with Wharton in both stock speculation and the affairs of the Walpole Co.; see above, XXII, 149–53, and below, Wharton to BF, Jan. 17, 1777. His close ties with Silas Deane as well as BF were useful to him as a speculator and also, although Wharton did not know it, as a British agent. The formal agreement between Bancroft and Paul Wentworth, acting for Whitehall, is conjecturally dated December, 1776, in Stevens, *Facsimiles*, III, no. 235.

among the Great, as a fair Warning, as well to Administration, as to their Opponents, of What would happen, if They delayed to do immediate and substantial Justice to America) I was convinced of the indispensable Propriety, and Necessity of the Colonies asserting their Independence, and Therefore I have faithfully and zealously endeavoured as far as was in my Power, To countenance, and support it, And May I add, That I shall be happy, While I remain in Europe (Which will be for a few Months) to dedicate my poor Abilities, If you think They may be usefully employed, To the service of our Country? I lament exceedingly the mistaken Conduct of Mr. Galloway, my Brother, and too many of our former Friends (on Political Subjects) in Pennsylvania.⁹ My Correspondence for many Months, on that Head, has been very offensive to Them, and They blamed my liberal Communications, and Sentiments; But I have been long convinced of the arbitrary System and sad Depravity of this Court and People, and That if the Liberties of America were to be saved and Perpetuated, It must be done by the Americans Themselves, and Not by any Man, or Set of Men of this Country; And Therefore I have been inexpressibly rejoiced, in Perusing the new Forms of Goverment in the several American States, and especiely That of Pennsylvania, because it communicates *equal* civil, and religious Liberties to *all*, and particularly establishes an Equality of Representation in *all* the Counties, on a broad and fair Basis; Thereby destroying the narrow System of the Quakers, and emancipating the Inhabitants of a Majority of the Counties from the partial Views, of Sectarian Politicans. Lord Camden highly extolls the New Form of Goverment of Pennsylvania and says, That the bad Part of the British Laws is therein wisely corrected; and let me add, That the highest Honor and Thanks are due *to you*, for effectuating a Form of Goverment, so wonderfully replete with true Wisdom and Liberality.¹ With the sincerest Respect,

---

9. Galloway had resigned from Congress and opposed the new revolutionary regime; Thomas Wharton and other prominent Quakers were coming under suspicion, and within less than a year several of them were exiled.

1. "The narrow System of the Quakers" was that which had developed under Penn's charter of liberties; it was modified by the reforms in the spring of 1776 (above, XXII, 479) and destroyed by the constitution, which

Permit me to assure you, That I am dear Sir Your very affectionate and faithful humble Servant

PS. If you should have any Letters for me, either Now or hereafter, Pray never trust Them by the Post; as all my Letters are stoped by Administration. Dr. Bancroft has a Dictionary to explain the Numbers used in the foregoing Letter, and when He leaves France, He will give you a Copy it. The Doctor will enquire of you and write me, if you should not have Leisure to oblige me therein, How my Family were, When you left Home.

Dr. Franklin.

Notations: Intelligence from London / Lett. from London Decr 21. 1776

Barbeu-Dubourg: Memorandum for the American Commissioners

AD: American Philosophical Society

[After December 21, 1776[2]]

M. D. propose a Messieurs F. D. et L. de leur faire des avances soit de draps, soit de fusils (du modele de 1763, controllés et tirés des propres magazins du Roy) pour la valeur de trois cent mille livres tournois, a condition que ces Messieurs lui fourniront en retour des tabacs de Virginie et de Mariland pour pareille somme, bien entendu que les achats seront faits de part et d'autre avec fidelité et œconomie.

---

established representation of the counties according to taxable population and provided for periodic reapportionment. Wharton was not alone in his opinion of BF's role in framing the new government but was, we believe, exaggerating it; see *ibid.*, pp. 514–15.

2. This memorandum seems to us impossible to date except as we have, because its simplicity offers little clue to when it was written. War supplies are to be delivered to a French port, tobacco to an American. The question of how one commodity was to be exchanged for the other, as explained in our headnote below under Jan. 9, was the great stumbling block when negotiations over tobacco began; and Dubourg ignores it. He may have had a number of reasons for doing so, including naïveté or desperation, but in our opinion the most likely one is that he was writing soon after BF's arrival, before the full magnitude of the shipping problem had become apparent.

Si l'on accorde aux facteurs et commissionaires d'une part certains droits de commission a raison de tant pour cent, on en accordera de semblables aux facteurs et commissionaires de l'autre part.

M. D. livrera les fusils, ou les draps, dans un port de France des plus commodes pour en faire l'embarquement. M. F. D. et L. livreront les tabacs dans un port du continent de l'Amerique des plus convenables au même objet.

Chacun fera transporter a ses risques, perils et fortunes ce qui lui aura eté fourni et livré ainsi.

Et la fourniture d'une part fera la solde de la fourniture de l'autre part, et on demeurera quitte à quitte.

From the Comte d'Estaing[3]   L:[4] American Philosophical Society

[After December 21, 1776, and before February 27, 1777[5]]
Mr. le Comte destaing est venut pour avoire l'honneur de voire Mr. franklin et luy demandere sy y pouras avoire un Momant deudiance [d'audience] demain sur les 9 h. edemie 10 h. du matin.

Addressed: A Monsieur / Monsieur franklin Docteur, ancien membre / Du Congrés Général Des états unis de / L'amerique, en son hotel / A *Paris*.

3. Charles-Henri, comte d'Estaing (1729–94), had made his name as a soldier in India and was soon to become more famous as an admiral. When Arthur Lee and Lord Shelburne came from London together soon after Deane's arrival in Paris, William Carmichael testified in 1779, the French court feared that Shelburne would learn its secrets through Lee; d'Estaing thereupon warned Deane to remember that the Parliamentary opposition was intent on coming to power, not on serving the American cause: *Deane Papers*, III, 441–2. At some time before news of American independence reached France, d'Estaing translated a memorandum from Carmichael to Vergennes: Stevens, *Facsimiles*, VII, no. 647. These activities suggest that the Count was an emissary between Versailles and the Americans, and help to explain his desire to get in touch with BF.

4. It is not in d'Estaing's hand; the freakish spelling suggests that he had a servant write it.

5. While BF, that is, was staying at one of his hotels in Paris before the move to Passy. We have no other ground for dating the note.

From the Chevalier de Kermorvan

ALS: American Philosophical Society

[After December 21, 1776, and before February 27, 1777[6]]
Monsieur

Instruit par le public du passage de mon frere vers les in-surgens vos Compatriotes;[7] j'ai ecri a Messieurs De Montau-doüin freres Negotians a Nantes pour me faire part si il etoit vrai qu'il eût passé a L'amerique sur leurs vaisseaux, et m'in-former, s'il etoit possible, de son existence ou de sa mort; ils m'ont repondû que Reccomendé par vous lors de votre pas-sage a Nantes,[8] ils s'etoient chargés de le faire passer par la sollicitation d'un Medecin de paris,[9] mais que depuis ils igno-roient les evenemens qui avoient suivis son depart relative-ment a sa personne; j'oserois donc vous prier Monsieur, de m'instruire de son sort present, les inquietudes que j'ai a ce sujet, et les embarras de famille, que sa presence faciliteroit Beaucoup, par l'alternative ou nous sommes de son existence ou de sa mort, me forcent a vous supplier de me mander au vrai ce que vous en sçavez par vos correspondances. J'espere donc, Monsieur, que vous voudrez bien vous faire instruire de ce qui le regarde et que par suite de cette bonne volonté pour lui, vous voudrez bien me faire part de vos decouvertes; je sens qu'il vous faut un certain temps pour prendre ses infor-mations, mais d'apres cela j'ose me flatter Monsieur, que vous ne me refuserez pas la Grace que je vous demande, et que vous voudrez bien vous laisser convaincre des sentimens de la Plus respectueuse recconnoissance. J'ai l'honneur d'etre Mon-sieur, avec respect Votre tres humble serviteur

LE CHEVALIER DE KERMORVAN

6. The bracket of dates is the same as for the preceding document.

7. The other and better known chevalier de Kermorvan (about this one we know nothing) had sailed for America in the early spring of 1776: above, XXII, 390.

8. Kermorvan must have misread the letter, for this phrase makes no sense. The Montaudoüins perhaps wrote that BF, when they saw him in Nantes, had good things to say of the other Kermorvan. This would have been understandable, for the two had had considerable contact in America.

9. Dubourg.

Mon adresse est a Mr: le chevalier De Kermorvan a Guim-
gamp en Basse Bretagne

Addressed: a Monsieur / Monsieur francklin / Docteur a son hôtel / A Paris

Notation: Kermoran M. De

From ———

[after December 21, 1776] See page 104

Marginalia in a Pamphlet by Josiah Tucker

MS notations in the margins of a copy in the Library of Congress of
[Josiah Tucker,] *A Series of Answers to Certain Popular Objections, against
Separating from the Rebellious Colonies, and Discarding Them Entirely; Being
the Concluding Tract of the Dean of Gloucester, on the Subject of American
Affairs* (Gloucester, 1776).

These are the first marginalia by Franklin that deserve extensive
treatment since those that we assigned to 1769–70, a relatively placid
period of his life. After his return to America in 1775 he was plunged
into a maelstrom of activity from which he did not emerge for years.
He continued to read, but he seems to have lacked the time if not
the energy to annotate anything he read except this pamphlet. The
reason for the exception is probably that Tucker was his *bête noire.*
One of the Dean's earlier effusions had drawn the fullest and angri-
est rebuttal in any of his marginalia, and since then the two had had
an unproductive controversy by letter,[1] which doubtless prepared
Franklin to differ with anything Tucker might say.

In *A Series of Answers* the author developed his long-standing the-
sis, that the mother country would gain rather than lose by letting
America go, through the economic argument that the colonies after
independence would remain within Britain's commercial orbit. Although his tone was as abrasive as usual, his points were not so
much polemics as predictions. Franklin could have come on the
pamphlet as soon as he reached Paris, for it was published in England in mid-November.[2] He could just as well have read it at any

1. See above, XVII, 348–80; XXI, 83–5, 121–3, 125–8, 486.
2. *Public Advertiser,* Nov. 15, 1776.

69

time thereafter; his comments give no clue to a date. Neither do they touch on the Dean's central argument. Franklin presumably assumed, as the French did, that Anglo-American economic ties would not outlast the political ones; but the marginalia confine themselves almost entirely to more trivial issues.

The pamphlet begins with a preface and introduction and ends with a long conclusion. Franklin commented only on the early objections and answers, less than a quarter of the whole; his opening remarks were written in pencil and have faded to the verge of legibility, and the subsequent ones in ink are so compressed that we cannot always be sure of our readings. The method of presentation is the same as in previous volumes. In the right-hand column the printed text is paraphrased and drastically condensed, and only words or phrases that Franklin noted are in quotes; gaps to accommodate the marginalia do not indicate any break in the summary, and italics represent Franklin's underlining. The comments in the left-hand column are verbatim insofar as they can be deciphered.

[On or after December 22, 1776]

Objection I: How will British merchants and manfacturers recover their property and debts in the event of a separation?

Answer 1: In that event the debtors, who now blame the English government for their troubles, will have to blame their one.

[*Cropped*] Sir, and the Necessity[?] on the part of the British Creditors[?] to prevent[?] American Commerce [*cropped*] full[?] Prooff thereof.[3]

Answer 2: English creditors have always had more trouble in recovering in America than anywhere else in the world.

---

3. Even without the cropping this note is now almost completely illegible. Years ago, when the penciling may have been less faded, we received two readings from the Library of Congress, one by John C. Fitzpatrick; they differ with each other, and both are extremely tentative. We have amalgamated them according to our guess at what can still be seen, but key words must be missing.

A groundless
Supposition

Answer 3: After separation each colony will become "independent, and a jealous Rival, of its Neighbour. No common Cause or common Interest will unite them together," and because of their commercial competition each will have an incentive for honest dealing.

Ridiculous. He
confutes this
Nonsense Him-
self. [p.]28[4]

Answer 4: If any state should fail "to do Justice to the English Merchant or Creditor, a few small Ships or War sent to their Coasts, not to make Conquest, but Reprisals according to the Law of Nations, would soon teach them to be more observant of the Rules of Justice and good faith, than they are disposed to be. And the other Provinces, their Neighbours and Rivals, instead of arming in their Defence, would rejoice at their Chastisement."

Objection II: How can the West Indies be preserved from American conquest in case of separation?

Answer 1: The northern and southern colonies hate each other. "And nothing prevents this from breaking out into Action even at present, but the Apprehension of common Danger. Remove, therefore, this Apprehension, and then there will remain no central Attraction uniting them in one common League or general Association." Without such a league they cannot make the conquest.

How idotic[?]
these Remarks!
[The] Existence
of [the] conti-
nental
[Con]gress is
full[?] Evidence
[to] the Con-
trary.

Answer 2: If some of them should confederate, the others would oppose them and call for aid

4. See BF's note below, beginning "P. 17."

from Britain, which would hold the balance of power.

Answer 3: Even if they all confederated, other areas would attract them more.

Answer 4: The loss of the West Indies would only force British merchants to look elsewhere for sugar, and might put an end to slavery in the islands.

Objection III: How can the colonies, when independent, be kept from becoming a major naval power?

Answer 1: We can prevent any of the states from swallowing the rest.

Answer 2: The American coast south of the Chesapeake is not fit for large ships of war, and north of it has few good harbors.

Answer 3: The inhabitants of the coastal regions, which are less fruitful than the interior, will have their hands full in maintaining their authority over the increasing population of the back country.

Answer 4: Even if America should become powerful at sea, its interests would lie in not provoking Britain.

Objection IV: Will not the animosity of the war prevent future Anglo-American trade?

Answer 1: If so, the sooner the separation the better; our victory would only produce another revolt and another war, as has been pointed out by the authors of *Common Sense*, "supposed to be Dr. Franklin and Mr. Adams."

Answer 2: The merchant's universal rule is that "self Interest needs no Reconciliation: For Trade is not carried on for the Sake of Friendship, but of Interest." The mother country has never been able to prevent colonies from trading wherever they can to advantage. "We have now

P. 17 for apparent Contradiction to all which is here asserted.

the whole Force of the British Empire collected together: We have also as much Assistance as our Money can procure from foreign Powers: All our Men of War, Frigates, and Tenders; and most of our Transport-Ships are completely armed: All of them are stationed on the Coasts of America, in order to prevent the Colonists from carrying on any Trade of any Sort to our Detriment." Yet they trade almost wherever they please. *"How then shall we*

See p. 17.

be able to restrain their Commerce and Navigation, when this great and formidable Armament shall be removed?"

Answer 3: The Americans demonstrated "the Easiness of a Pacification with public Enemies, where private Interest is concerned on the opposite Side. For notwithstanding all their doleful Lamentations against Spanish Depredations, Spanish Cruelty, and French Incursions,

Childish.

they reconciled it to their Consciences to trade with those very French and Spaniards, when it was their private Intetest so to do, during the hottest of the War; and even to furnish them with Ammunition and warlike Stores for the Destruction of the English, their only Protectors and Benefactors in that very War."

Answer 4: Past experience shows that animosities fade fast after a war. "No sooner had the Dutch and Spaniards separated peaceably from

That is, When the Spaniards recognized their Independence.

each other, than they became mutual good Customers." A few years later they even allied against the French.

Answer 5: Anglo-American trade rests on the abundance of British capital and credit; the Americans have enjoyed this advantage more than any others, and in time they will "find by Experience, that in quarrelling with the English, they have quarrelled with their best Friends. Let them therefore go wherever they please, and try all the Nations on the Globe. When they have done, they will suppliantly return to Great Britain, *and entreat* to be admitted into the Number of our Customers, not for ours, but for their own Sakes."

Why entreat, When according to our Author, Self Interest needs no Reconciliation? See p. 28.[5]

Objection V: If we lose the northern colonies, where shall we procure naval stores? Answer 1: Where else will those colonies sell their stores? "Were we to withdraw our Bounties, it would be an exceeding difficult Matter for the Colonies to find any vent at all for these Articles."

Nothing can be more Ridiculus than this Assertion. The past Price of Naval Stores is a prooff thereof.

Answer 2: Other mercantile nations "are supplied with all these *Articles at a moderate Price, and without Bounties.* What therefore should prevent the English from being supplied from the same Source, and on as good Terms?"

But Where are they so supplied? Surely by the Americans. Answer. They must be supplied by the Allies of North America.

Answer 3: "The English Navy receives much greater, and *more necessary supplies* from the Northern States of Europe than from the Northern Colonies of America." Oak planking "is *chiefly* imported . . . from Germany, Dantzick, and the other Ports of the Baltic: *The Iron* (if any wanted besides our own) is brought from Sweden and Russia; and the Hemp almost altogether from Russia, and its con-

Not true.

This is most fallaciously stated.

5. Answer 2 to Objection IV.

The Quantity supplied by America, greatly lessened the Price and Quantity of Articles, Which Great Britain bought of Russia, Sweden, &c. And Which She must hereafter be *dependant* on these Kingdoms for. Most absurdly erroneous.

quered Provinces. Yet we have most absurdly and impoliticly loaded both the Iron, and Hemp of those Countries with heavy, discouraging Taxes, in order to favour the Iron and Hemp or ungrateful America. As to Masts, Yards, and

Deals, they may in general *be purchased cheaper* in Norway, Sweden, and in some Parts of Russia, Quality for Quality, than in North-America," although their price on the English market has been raised by ill-judged bounties.

Britain, by losing the Affections and Commerce of the Colonies, will be reduced to her former dependant Situation on *Sweden* and other Northern Powers for *Tar and Pitch*, and not only at their own Prices, But Silver and Gold, instead of British Manu-

Answer 4: Pitch and tar originally came from Sweden. *"But the Swedes were so impolitic* as to *lay an exhorbitant Duty on* the Exportation of their Pitch and Tar, presuming that the English could find no other Supplies." Britain then, instead of looking elsewhere in Europe, favored the colonies by offering bounties.

75

facturies, (as was the happy Case of the Trade with the Colonies) must be exported out of the Kingdom to pay for the necessary Articles *of Pitch and Tar.*

When Great Britain or the West India Islands shall acknowledge the Independence of the Colonies, There can be no Doubt but They will plentifully supply them with Provisions, and Lumber. But until such Recognition is made, The Islands will be in a very perilous distressful Situation; And must be properly supplied with them from any European Markets.

Objection VI: In case of separation, where shall we get lumber and supplies for the West Indies?

Answer 1: The Americans illegally supplied the West Indian possessions of other powers even in wartime. "Tell me therefore, why the North-Americans, *after a peaceable* Separation, will refuse to supply our Sugar Islands (whilst they supply others) if they shall be as well, or better paid for what they bring? And tell me also, when did they supply them with any one Article whatever, without being well paid for it?"

Then They
must of Course
attend less to
the making
Sugar &c.

Salt Fish "out of
their Own
Plantations,"
(i.e. the West
India Planta-
tions) is rather
curious.

They may sup-
ply Them in
Degree, with
these Articles;
But the Prices
would be so ex-
horbitant as to
ruin the West
India Platns.

They will cer-
tainly Never
permit British
Merchants to
deprive Them,
as heretofore,
of the greater
part of the
Price, Tobacco
usually sold for.
They will send
their Tobacco to

Answer 2: The inhabitants of the West Indies "may still raise great Quantities of most Sorts of Provisions within their own Plantations."

Answer 3: If these inhabitants have trouble "in supplying themselves *out of their own Planta-tions* with Flour, Bread, Biscuit, Beef, Pork, *Salt-Fish*, Oats, Pease, and Beans, then Great-Brit-ain and Ireland can supply them with all these

Articles in great Abundance, either from their own Stores, or from Stores imported."

Objection VII: In case of separation, where shall we get rice and tobacco?
Answer 1: The question rests on two suppo-sitions, that "the Virginians and Carolinians will not sell *Tobacco* and Rice to English Merchants for a good Price, and ready Money," and that Tobacco can be grown nowhere else. Will any man in his senses affirm either of these?

the several
Ports in Eu-
rope, Where
the British Mer-
chants used to
send it, and
They will ex-
change it for or
lay out the Pro-
ceeds of it, in
the purchase of
Linens, Woollens
&c, at much
cheaper Prices
Than British
Merchants for-
merly were ac-
customed to
make Them
pay.

The respective
European States
will certainly
never permit
the Land neces-
sary to raise
Corn for the
Subsistence of
their Subjects,
to be applied to
the Culture of
Tobacco. The
General Scarc-
ity of Corn in
Europe for
many years, un-
doubtedly con-
firms this Sup-
position, and

Answer 2: Almost any country in Europe could grow sufficient tobacco 'if permitted by its respective Legislatures so to do." In England itself there were once extensive and increasing plantations of tobacco, but the government forebade them by acts of Parliament in order to favor the colonies.

more especialy, as America, when in an independant Situation, can abundantly supply all the European Govents (except England) with Tobacco.

This is too whimsical to require a Serious Answer.

Answer 3: As for rice, much of *"the swampy Coast of Guinea"* would produce it in abundance if the inhabitants were encouraged to do so instead of being sold into slavery; they would also consume at least four times as much British manufacturers as they do as slaves.

From William Alexander

ALS: American Philosophical Society

My Dear Sir   Dijon 22d Decr 1776

I can hardly express my surprise on first hearing of your arrival, And Altho' motives are here assigned for your Journey which I will not beleive unless you Confirm them yourself, That safety is your object,[6] and I will only believe you, because I think you one of the few Politicians, to whom Lying will be unnecessary. Be that as it will, my hypothesis is already formed, but without Entering into such Abstruse Matters, I conceive it very possible that you may find it convenient to be retired for Some litle time, were it but for a few weeks perhaps untill the British Parlt meets after the Holidays. If this or any other Motive can Induce you to Come the length of Dijon I write you My Dear Friend to offer you a sanctuary, which I am Sure when you are in it, will be Agreeable. I am here in a very Comfortable House with a very Good

6. "Many of the French are already persuaded that he comes here not only as a fugitive, but as one who is watching an opportunity to obtain his Pardon, and who will correspond openly with the Congress, and secretly with the English Ministry." Stormont to Weymouth, Stevens, *Facsimiles*, XIV, no. 1402.

spare Room for one I Love, I have only with me two very Excellent young Girls who will Consider you as another Father.[7] You can be much, or litle in society as you please. And you can have the Company of a few very Ingenious and worthy Men, Or a More Briliant Company, if you incline part of both, or none of Either If you please. I can offer you the use of Some of the Best private libraries in France. Living is here good and Cheap. It will not Cost me more than 2 *l.t.* per day to Entertain you like a Prince.

I have no English servants so that It might be possible for you to remain incognito If you desire it, by assuming another name. I have even Contrived a vehicle for your Correspondence in case you should have any of a secret Nature. There are two post Coaches a week from Paris. The Charge of travelling from thence will be about 3 Louis. The distance is about the same as from Paris to Dover. I think I have now left you but two Excuses, Pleasure or Business, for I put health out of the Question with your Constitution. I will Come and fetch you If you desire it, Tho' I woud leave my two Girls with reluctance but we will all Come some stages to meet you. So let me know your resolution. Your friends in England were all well about a fortnight ago, I mean all those I know. Williams you probably know is very agreeably Setled with the Blunts and will work his way.[8] He is my faithful Correspondent for American news, and behaves so as to deserve and Obtain the love of all who know Him.

With regard to myself I Shall say the less, that I am in print [*interlined*: for the use of my friends] tho' not publishd,[9] but my history Since you left us is a litle romance, which you shall

7. Bethia (1757–1839) and Mariamne (1758–1809).

8. See above, xxii, 268–9. Alexander had not heard that jw was no longer settled, but had joined BF on the road to Paris; see the note on WTF to BF below, Dec. 24. Silas Deane said soon afterward that jw came to France to visit BF because England, where Americans were unpopular, was disagreeable to him: *Deane Papers,* II, 148. In fact, however, he must have come before he knew that BF had landed; if that news had reached him in London, he could not have arrived in time to intercept his greatuncle en route to Paris.

9. Something to do, we assume, with his complex litigation at home; whatever was in print seems to have remained unpublished.

see at meeting, at present I Shall only Say that your two Last Thousand pounds were paid in a Jail, so that money Matters are even between us,[1] tho' there is a large account in my heart, that never will. It will be in the Mean while a Satisfaction to know that I have been always Very happy and still preserve my old system That time and Patience will with propriety of Conduct, bring about every desireable end. My Antagonists say I am very obstinate which I hope is the worst They can say of me.

In case we are not to meet let me know my Dear Sir If I can be usefull to you. You know perhaps better than myself what I am fit for, and in any thing you will desire, but high Treason You may Command me [*interlined*: and that I will only Commit when I go to America] were It even necessary to go to England for you. The more you Employ me the more you will oblige me and that you may not think the Compliment too great know that I am studying Law and Anatomy thro' sheer Idleness. In case you can make me of use I can contrive a resource for the Girls for a Month or two. I conclude this long letter by assuring you, That you have no friend who is more Entirely Yours Than Your most obedient humble Servant

WILLIAM ALEXANDER

My address is a Monr Alexandre Hotel de st Louis a Dijon as I know not your address I Send this under Cover of my friend Mr. Lumisden a very worthy and Ingenious Man who knows Paris well and I am Sure will have a pleasure in being usefull to you.[2] He is the single Person in Paris That knows any thing of me or my affairs and can give an account of both and of Dijon where he did me the favour to spend a few days with me.

Notation: Lett. from W Alexander Dijon 22 Decr 1776

1. He was paying back the loan discussed above, XIX, 315–16; XX, 342.
2. Undoubtedly Andrew Lumisden (1720–1801), who had been secretary to the Pretender but had broken with him in 1768; Paris was the Scot's headquarters. *DNB*.

The American Commissioners to the Comte de Vergennes

Vergennes   ALS:[3] Archives du Ministère des affaires étrangères

Sir   Paris, Dec. 23. 1776[4]

We beg Leave to acquaint your Excellency, that we are appointed and fully impowered by the Congress of the United States of America, to propose and negotiate a Treaty of Amity and Commerce between France and the said States. The just and generous Treatment their Trading Ships have received, by a free Admission into the Ports of this Kingdom,[5] with other Considerations of Respect, has induced the Congress to make this Offer first to France. We request an Audience of your Excelly. wherein we may have an Opportunity of presenting our Credentials; and we flatter ourselves, that the Propositions we are instructed to make, are such as will not be found unacceptable. With the greatest Regard, we have the Honour to be, Your Excellency's most obedient and most humble Servants   B Franklin
                                        Silas Deane
                                        Arthur Lee

His Excelly. the Count de Vergennes.

To [Dumas]   Reprinted from *The Port Folio*, III (1803), 294.

Dear Sir,   Paris, December 23, 1776.

I have only time to say that I am arrived here well, and happy to learn, by your favour of the 17th, that you are so. I enclose a letter to you from the committee, and I shall write

---

3. In BF's hand.
4. BF had joined Deane in Paris on the 21st, and Lee had arrived the next day. The commissioners lost no time in requesting an audience to begin their mission, and Vergennes saw them on the 28th. Force, 5 *Amer. Arch.*, III, 1415; BF to the committee of secret correspondence below, Jan. 4.
5. A diplomatic exaggeration: the French government had tacitly encouraged American traders, but they had had considerable difficulty in purchasing and loading war supplies. Crout, "Diplomacy of Trade," pp. 70–88, 109–12, 122–3, 129, 144–6.

to you more fully in a few days.[6] With great esteem, I am ever yours, affectionately,   B. FRANKLIN.

From Jean-Daniel Schweighauser[7]

ALS: American Philosophical Society

Monsieur   [December 23, 1776[8]]

J'espere que vous aurez eu un heureux voyage jusques à Paris, et je l'apprendrai avec la plus grande satisfaction. Je regrette infiniment de n'avoir pu avoir celle de vous rendre plus souvent mes devoirs icy.

Maintenant j'ai l'honneur de vous écrire la presente pour vous faire part de l'arrivée icy du Navire La fanny Cap. Tokely chargé pour compte des Etats Unis de L'amerique de 226. Bariq. de Tabac et 1500 pièces de Merrain (soit Staves).

Il est parti de Plimouth près de Boston le 21. 9bre et est entré en notre riviere avanthier sans aucune mauvaise rencontre en mer n'ayant vu que 4. navires de loin qu'il n'a pas cherché a reconnoître. Il n'apporte non plus aucune nouvelle qu'il se soit passé quelque chose d'essentiel entre les armées à L'amerique.

L'honorable Committé me donne ordre de vendre au mieux possible les Susdits Tabacqs qui sont tres demandés de L' Etranger, et il paroit que notre Ferme generale en a egalement besoin ainsi on en tirera un bon prix.

Depuis votre départ il en est aussi arrivé une Cargaison adressée à Mr. Pennet par le Navire La Marie Elisabeth Cap. Young.

Des passagers venus avec le Cap. Tokely rapportent que le Navire Le hancok et Adam Cap. Smit que j'ai expedié d'icy

6. BF mislaid this note and enclosed it with his below, Jan. 28. The letter from the committee of secret correspondence, of Oct. 24, 1776 (Yale University Library), merely asked Dumas to continue his correspondence and to send regular shipments of English and European newspapers.

7. See above, XXII, 314–15 n.

8. The *Fanny* arrived at Nantes on Dec. 21; see Gruel's letter of that date. Schweighauser says here that she arrived the day before yesterday.

étoit arrivé à Dartmouth;[9] j'en suis bien charmé pour les Interests des Etats unis, et l'honorable Committé aura au moins eu de mes nouvelles.

Si vous aviez quelques ordres à me donner je serai tres flatté que cela me procure les moyens de vous prouver en touttes occasions mon sincere devouement et le profond respect avec lequel j'ai l'honneur de me dire Monsieur Votre tres humble et tres obeïssant serviteur   J. D. SCHWEIGHAUSER

Addressed: To / The honourable Doctr / Franklin / at / Paris

Notation: Lett. from J D Schweighauser Nants no date

From the Marquis de Courtanvaux[1]

AL: American Philosophical Society

Ce mardy [December 24 or 31, 1776, or January 7, 1777[2]]. Le marquis de Courtanvaux envoye sçavoir des nouvelles de Monsieur francklein et l'assurer de son respect il espert avoir l'honneur de l'aller voir l'un de ces jours.

Addressed: A Monsieur / Monsieur francklein / a l'hotel d'antragues / rue de l'Université

From William Temple Franklin

ALS: American Philosophical Society

Honored Sir,   Versailles Decr. 24th. 1776
Mr. Gerrad not being in town, I waited upon Count Vergennes, and delivered him the Letters, which he put in his

9. The *Hancock and Adams*, Capt. Samuel Smith, was the ship that carried Boisbertrand (above, XXII, 469 n) as well as a cargo of precious stores; she was captured by an American privateer, and the delay in her voyage raised a storm: Smith, *Letters*, V, 491–3.

1. The soldier turned scientist who had entertained BF during an earlier visit to Paris: above, XV, 34. A few later notes from the Marquis indicate that their social relationship continued at least through 1778.

2. The three Tuesdays between BF's arrival and his move to the Hôtel d' Hambourg.

Pocket,[3] and desired I would call upon him for his answer, at 9 OClock tomorrow morning; so that I purpose staying here to night and have taken the Liberty of keeping the Carriage and Servants. Present my respects to Messrs. Deane and Lee and believe me Honored Sir Your dutiful Grandson

W. T. FRANKLIN.

PS. I have wrote to Mr. Chaumon,[4] that I purpose to keep the Carriage.

Addressed: To / Dr. Franklin / à L'Hotel Dentragues[5] / Rue Université / à / Paris.

Notations: dix huit Sols au porteur la presente rendüe a neuf heures du Soir ce jourd'huy 24. Decembre 1776.

W T. Franklin Versailles Decr 24. 1776

3. Conrad-Alexandre Gérard (1729–90), later the first French minister to the United States, and his younger brother, Joseph-Mathias, directed the two political bureaus of the ministry of foreign affairs: John J. Meng, ed., *Despatches and Instructions of Conrad Alexandre Gérard, 1778–1780* . . . (Baltimore, Md., 1939), pp. 33–42. The Minister normally used Gérard, it will be seen, as his channel of communication with the commissioners. Their letter above of Dec. 23 was one of those that WTF delivered; the other was probably a covering note from Deane to Gérard of Dec. 24, now in the APS.

4. The first appearance of a man with whom BF worked as closely as with any Frenchman. Jacques-Donatien Le Ray (1725–1803) was a wealthy merchant from Nantes, who had added "de Chaumont" to his name after buying the château of Chaumont-sur-Loire in 1750. He had held a number of administrative posts, and was in close contact with Vergennes. In August, 1776, he had acquired the Hôtel de Valentinois at Passy, which soon became BF's home; see the headnote below, under Jan. 28, on the agreement between the two. Deane no doubt introduced them as soon as BF's party reached Paris, for while sole agent he had obtained saltpetre and gunpowder from Chaumont. These had been paid for, but the Frenchman continued to furnish the commissioners with military supplies "before we had provided any apparent Means of Payment." BF to Richard Henry Lee, April 12, 1785, National Archives. See also *Deane Papers*, III, 166; Lüthy, *Banque protestante*, II, 452–6; Lopez, *Mon Cher Papa* pp. 123–8.

5. BF and his grandsons arrived in Paris at 2 P.M. on Dec. 21, Mme. du Deffand reported to Horace Walpole the next day, along with Pierre Penet, JW, and a "tutor": Wilmarth S. Lewis *et al.*, eds., *The Yale Edition of Horace Walpole's Correspondence* (48 vols., New Haven, 1937–83), VI, 383; the "tutor" was undoubtedly the interpreter, Lestarjette, whose letter is above

85

From Gruel

ALS: American Philosophical Society

Monsieur   Nantes ce 24: Xbre: 1776.

J'ay l'honneur de vous confirmer les trois lettres que j'ay eû celui de vous ecrire depuis votre depart de cette ville. Je me flatois d'avoir aujourd'huy la satisfaction d'apprendre votre heureuse arrivée en la capitalle, mais j'ay eté frustré dans mon attente. Je souhaite que votre santé ne soit pour rien dans ce retardement, et desire apprendre par le prochain courier, que vous etes arrivé a Paris sans accident.

Mr. Rumsey est icy de dimanche au soir, il a l'honneur de vous ecrire par ce courier pour vous instruire de toutes ses operations relatives à la vente des deux prises. Il m'a remis divers effets sur Paris, et sur cette ville montants ensemble a 27000 *l.t.* et un reçu de 3000 *l.t.* de Mr. Wilcken. Ces susdits effets sont payables partie fin Janvier, et partie fin fevrier prochains. Je garderai cette somme à votre disposition, il vous plaira m'indiquer l'employ que j'en dois faire. Je me conformeray à vos ordres.

Mr. Rumcey a gardé pour luy le plus grand des deux batiments pour prix de 9600 *l.t.* convenû avec Mr. Wilcken. Par ce moyen le montant des deux prises, navire, et cargaison compris, est de la somme de 39600 *l.t.*

J'ay fait remettre à Mr. Wilcken 48 *l.t.* pour etre distribués selon vos intentions aux garçons de chambre de la fregate la represaille.

J'ay en ma possession vos trois malles, et une caisse qui m'ont eté envoyé de la fregate. Je vais les faire plomber afin qu'elles ne soient pas visitées en route, je les ferai partir vendredi prochain par la messagerie à l'adresse de Mr. Sollier[6] qui vous les fera parvenir à leur arrivée.

Les 35. quarts d'Indigo de la fregate sont icy en magazin, je vous prie de me marquer si vous voulés que je les vende de

---

under Dec. 15. BF and the boys lodged for a time at the Hôtel d'Entragues. By Jan. 8 they had moved to the nearby Hôtel d' Hambourg, where Silas Deane was staying.

6. Gruel's and Penet's Paris banker, who subsequently handled the receipts from the indigo mentioned in the next paragraph; see the note on Arthur Lee's letter below, Feb. 22.

suitte, il est d'une assés bonne qualité, Il ne manquera pas d'achepteurs il s'en est même deja presenté. Je suis avec Respect Monsieur Votre tres humble et tres obeïssant serviteur

J GRUEL

On m'a remis en Bourse une copie de la declaration faite à l'amirauté de cette ville par le Capitaine du Brigantin la vigne, vous l'avés cy inclus; elle ne m'inquiete pas beaucoup, vous en ferés l'usage que vous jugerés propre.[7]

Notation: Lett. from J Gruel Nants 24 Decemr 1776.

From Nathan Rumsey   ALS: American Philosophical Society

Honorable Sir   Nantes 24th. Decemr. 1776.

Upon my arrival here from Auray I had the Honor of receiving your's of the 15th. Inst. the Contents of which shall be fully and punctually observed.

M. Delamain who loaded the Prize from rochfort and was part owner, is in Nantes: has spoke to me relative to the Vessel and Cargo, which last he says was his property and says he cannot conceive that Cap. Wicks can by any means detain french property. He has this day made a Declaration in the Admiralty office against his Cap. Cap. Wicks, and Penet and Rumsey a Copy of which Mr. Gruel sends you by this post.[8] I have refered Delamain wholly to Cap. Wickes for his Satisfaction, and Wicks is apprised to give that Satisfaction to no person but such as are authorised from Court, but least any unexpected Difficulties should arise Cap. Wickes is ready to sail at a half hour's warning.

I doubt not, sir but your presence at Court will quickly decide these Affairs in our favor. I had the honor of writing You from Auray which you will receive by this post.

I this day examined the Trunk according to your request and carefully packed the Clothes in brown paper. The Key Mr. Gruel takes in Charge to send; the Trunks also.

7. The declaration is printed in *Naval Docs.*, VII, 804–5.
8. Rumsey was inaccurate: Delamain laid before the court a declaration by his captain against Wickes and the others; see Clark, *Wickes*, p. 107.

Mr. Gruel will have informed You before this of the Arrival of two Vessels here laden with Tobacco. With the Compliments of the Season I am Honorable Sir, Your Most obedient Humble Servant   N. RUMSEY.

Addressed: The Honorable / Doctor Benjamin Franklin / at / Paris

Notation: Lett. from N Rumsey 24 Decemr 1776.

From "une Personne Honneste"[9]

AL: American Philosophical Society

Ce 25 Xbre 1776

Une personne honneste, et dont le nom ne serait pas connu de Monsieur le docteur franclin, aurait un service a Luy demander, et pour cela le suplie de Luy Mander quel heure dans la matiné, elle pourait parler à monsieur franclin de vendredy ou de samedy, c'est une personne qui demeure a la campagne et qui vousdrait bien ne pas faire un voyage inutile.

Addressed: A / Monsieur / Monsieur Le docteur franclin / a lhotel d'antragues, rüe de / Luniversité, faubourg st germain

From Henry Hugh Fergusson

ALS: American Philosophical Society

[December 26?, 1776[10]]

An Express arrived last night to Lord Stormont with an account of a defeat of the americans, the English said to have lost 200 men, to have taken 74 pieces of Cannon and at the time the news came off a party of the Americans consisting of

9. The writer, although he or she lives in the country, somehow knows within four days BF's Paris address, and is thus one of the earliest of the favor-seekers who pestered him for years to come.

10. On Dec. 20 Lord Weymouth sent Stormont the news that the Americans had abandoned their lines at Kings Bridge; on Dec. 25 the Ambassador acknowledged the letter: Stevens, *Facsimiles,* XIV, nos. 1398, 1401. Although Weymouth did not mention Fort Washington, the arrival of his dispatch must have precipitated this note.

1400 said to be surrounded in fort Washington.

H. Fergusson

The affair said to have happened the 24 octor.

Addressed: Doctor Franklin

Notation: Ferguson

From [Ralph Izard[1]]   AL: American Philosophical Society

Dear Sir   London 27th: December 1776.

I heartily congratulate you on your arrival in Europe. The Gentleman who will present this to you is the son of Mr. Henry Laurens of South Carolina the Vice President of the Province. He is warmly attached to the cause of his Country, and desirous of being presented to you.[2] I am happy in having it in my power to do him so acceptable a piece of service. With the greatest regard I am Dear Sir Your most Obedient Servant

Notations: R. Izard / R. Izard to BF. London 27. Decr 76

The American Commissioners to the Conde de Aranda[3]

ALS:[4] Archivo Historico Nacional; draft: Harvard University Library

Sir   Paris, Hotel d'Entragues, Dec. 28. 1776

We wish to inform your Excellency, that we are directed by the United States of America, to cultivate the Friendship of

1. This was presumably BF's first word after reaching France from the man who was later a thorn in his side. In our brief note on Izard above, XXI, 158 n, we misinterpreted the *DAB* and said that he went to Paris in 1776; in fact he and his family crossed the Channel at the end of July, 1777: Anne Izard Deas, ed., *Correspondence of Mr. Ralph Izard* . . . (New York, 1844), pp. 319–20.

2. John Laurens (1754–82), who later played a brief role in BF's mission, had been studying law in London and was returning home by way of France. If he passed through Paris it was a hasty visit, for he sailed from Bordeaux for St. Domingue at the end of January: *ibid.*, p. 238; see also the *DAB*.

3. For the Spanish Ambassador see above, XXII, 468 n.

4. In BF's hand.

the Court of Spain, with that of France. For that purpose, as well as to pay our personal Respects to your Excellency, we purpose to wait upon you to-morrow, or on any other Day that will be more convenient, and at any Hour that your Excellency may be pleased to appoint.[5] We have the Honour to be, Your Excellency's most obedient and most humble Servants

B FRANKLIN
SILAS DEANE
ARTHUR LEE

Plenipotentiaries from the Congress of the United States of North America

His Excellency the Count d'Aranda Ambassador of Spain

Francis Mackay to Franklin and Silas Deane

ALS: American Philosophical Society

Paris a Lhotel de Luynes ruë du Colombié this 28th:
Gentlemen   Xbre 1776
I would be glad to have the pleasure of meeting you or one of you incognito, therefore be so good as to appoint an hour, and where, that I may have the opportunty of acquainting you of things which would not be proper for me to commit to Papers. I am Gentlemen Your most obedient and most humble Servant   FRANCIS MACKAY
Late Surveyor General
of the Woods in Canada

You will find my name in the Court Callender Quebec Government[6]

Addressed: To / Doctor Frankling and / Dean Esqrs / L hotel dentrague

Notation: Francis Macay 28 Decr 76

5. A brief interview, chiefly concerned with privateers and prizes in Spanish ports, took place at the end of the month; see Aranda's dispatch to Grimaldi of Jan. 13, 1777, in Juan F. Yela Utrilla, *España ante la independencia de los Estados Unidos* (2nd ed.; two vols., Lerida, 1925), II, 34–5. Another dispatch from the Ambassador of the same date describes a more significant interview on Jan. 4: below, Jan. 13.

6. He was indeed listed in the *Royal Kalendar*, and remained in it from 1770 to 1780.

From Gruel

ALS: American Philosophical Society

Monsieur   Nantes ce 28: Xbre: 1776.

Je ne suivrai point l'usage, ni ne vous ferai de compliment du jour; le sentiment ne connoit pas ce language; je me bornerai à vous exprimer la sincerité des voeux que je forme pour vous en ce nouvel an: je vous souhaite, monsieur, une continuation de parfaite santé une issue satisfaisante dans vos glorieux projets, et l'accomplissement en entier de tout ce que vous pouvés desirer; j'ose egalement vous demander la Continuation de votre bienveillance, je tacherai de la meriter par mon sincere, et inviolable attachement.

Toute ma famille se joint à moy, et me charge de vous faire agreer les souhaits qu'elle fait pour tout ce qui peut contribuer à votre entiere satisfaction pendant le Cours de l'année Nouvelle, elle vous prie d'etre bien persuadé de la sincerité de ses voeux, et de permettre ainsy que moy que Messieurs vos fils trouvent icy les mêmes voeux que nous faisons unaniment pour tout ce qui peut leur etre agreable.

Mes amis Messieurs Tourton & Baur Banquiers à Paris, dont la reputation Egale l'honeteté, et la solidité en tout genre, desirent d'avoir l'honneur de vous voir, ils m'ont ecrit, et me prient de vous engager de leur permettre de vous presenter leurs devoirs, et de vous offrir leurs services; j'ose esperer, Monsieur, que vous voudrés bien leur donner la permission de cultiver votre connoissance pendant votre sejour en la capitalle; je leur remêts en consequence par ce courier une lettre pour vous,[7] persuadé que vous voudrés bien leur faire acceüil. Je suis avec Respect, Monsieur, Votre tres humble et tres obeïssant serviteur   J GRUEL

J'ay envoyé un exprès porter une lettre a Monsieur Wilcken. Je la crois de vous, elle m'est venû par ce courier, j'ay crû reconnoitre votre cachet, ce qui m'a determiné à expedier un exprès, crainte qu'elle ne fut pressée, elle sera rendüe aujourdhuy à 4. heures.

Cy joint la relation d'un Capitaine parti de Dartsmouth le

---

7. Gruel's note, of the same date and also in the APS, says merely that the bankers will present it along with the offer of their services.

17: 9bre. dernier. Je m'empresse de vous la faire passer, ce Capitaine est arrivé a Bordeaux le 24. Courant.

J'ay eû aujourd'huy arrêt entre mes mains de la part des chargeurs du navire la vigne qui a ete pris par la fregate la represaille. Ces messieurs se disant chargeurs, et proprietaires des vins et eaux de vies chargés dans le susdit batiment, pretendent à une somme de soixante quatre mille livres montant du susdit chargement. Ils demandent en outre celle de seize mille livres pour le navire, et une indemnité de dix mille livres. Ils paroissent porter leur pretention bien haut. Je vais constituer Procureur, et renvoyer ces Messieurs à Mr. Wilckes; je pense que vû le Bon vent la fregate aura mis dehors; j'auray l'honneur de vous instruire des suittes de cette affaire.

Notation: Lett. from J Gruel Nants 28 Decr 1776.

From Gruel

December 28, 1776 See page 91n

From the Chevalier Hamilton[8]

AL: American Philosophical Society

Dec 28. 1776.

The Chevalier Hamilton has the Honour to present his best Compliments to Dr. franklin on his Safe Arrival at Paris.

8. We have been tempted to guess that this was Sir William Hamilton, the British envoy to Naples (above, xx, 78 n), dictating to a French amanuensis who mishandled English. Sir William was on home leave at the time: Brian Fothergill, *Sir William Hamilton, Envoy Extraordinary* (London, [1969]), p. 147. But we have found no hint that he visited Paris that winter, was ill for three months, or knew the people to whom the writer refers. Another tempting guess has been Charles Hamilton of Painshill, with whom BF had had some contact years before (above, x, 251, 333); if he were the writer, his long friendship with Lord Holland might account for BF's meeting Charles James Fox, Holland's son. But that Hamilton was apparently not knighted, and the objections to Sir William apply equally to him. We are forced to assign the note to an unknown acquaintance of BF, perhaps a Frenchman of Jacobite descent, who has not appeared before and to the best of our knowledge does not reappear.

The Chevr. has for this three months bin very ill, and his present Convalessence does not permit to stir out of doors, otherwaise he should with pleasure have personnely waited on Dr. Franklin and informe him of some news from Messrs. Brown & Whitford, and in return should have Desir'd the favour of Dr. F., to informe the Chevr. how the late Mis Grahme and her hosbend at Philadelphia do,[9] and anything that Dr. franklin can think of in this part of the world the Chevalier hamilton begs he would Comand him, at Monsieur Brousse Conseilier a la Cour des Aide dans son hotel rue la Vererie. Begs the favour of an Answer.

Addressed: To / Dr. Benj Franklin / rue Jacob. faubourg St G / Paris

Louis Lebègue de Presle Duportail to the American Commissioners

ALS: American Philosophical Society

This is the first appearance of one of the important French volunteers. The American army suffered from a dearth of engineers, and the commissioners had been instructed to obtain four competent ones.[1] Duportail (1743–1802) had graduated from the military school at Mézières and joined the corps of engineers at the age of eighteen. In 1776 he completed a new set of regulations for the corps, as part of the reforms initiated by Saint-Germain, so that his name was to the fore. He had the government's permission to go to America, as he indicated in his letter below of January 2. His offer began three weeks of bargaining with the commissioners, and it was March before he and three companions sailed for Philadelphia by way of St. Domingue. The bargain turned out to be a good one for the United States. Duportail, unlike most of the French officers who had pre-

---

9. For Thomas Brown and his partner in the wine business in Craven St., BF's old friend Caleb Whitefoord, see above, X, 171–3; XX, 412. Elizabeth Graeme Fergusson was in America. Her husband had gone to England on business and was at the moment in Paris; see his notes above under Dec. 21 and 26.

1. Above, XXII, 628; below, BF to the Sieur de Lauron, June 6, 1777.

ceded him, was of such value to the American army that he rose to be a general.[2]

[December 29, 1776[3]]

Mr. Duportail Capitaine au Corps du genie avec un grade de major des troupes de la marine a l'honneur d'offrir ses services à messieurs les deputés des colonies unies. Il ne demande que la certitude d'etre employé dans un grade superieur et ne fait aucune condition pour les appointements. Si on le desire, il menera avec luy deux officiers du même corps d'un grade inferieur au sien et qui seront choisis pour leurs talens et leurs connoissance. Messieurs les deputés voudroient bien luy indiquer les moyens d'y passer et luy donner sur cela tous les renseignemens necessaires. Il se trouvera pret dès qu'on le desirera.

Mr. duportail Capitaine au Corps du genie à l'hotel du Cheval Rouge A *versailles*.

From Joseph-Etienne Bertier[4]

ALS: American Philosophical Society

Monsieur   à l'oratoire ce 29 décembre 1776

Il me tarde bien qu'un rheume et un crachement de sang n'arrêtent pas l'empressement que j'ay d'aller marquer en persone le respect, l'attachement, et la reconoissance dont je suis et seray toute ma vie pénetré pour l'illustre Mr. franklin. J'espère que le Seigneur exaucera bientôt mes voeux, et que je vous exprimeray de vive voix, ce que je souhaiterois que vous pussiés lire dans mon coeur où il est bien gravé que je suis avec un attachement inviolable Monsieur Votre très humble et

---

2. Lasseray, *Les Français*, I, 272–7; Elizabeth S. Kite, *Brigadier-General Louis Lebègue Duportail, Commandant of Engineers in the Continental Army* ... (Baltimore and Philadelphia, 1933).

3. See Duportail's letter below of Jan. 2, in which he refers to his propositions of "last Sunday," Dec. 29.

4. During an earlier visit to Paris BF had received kindnesses from Father Bertier, and thereafter had helped to procure his election to the Royal Society: above, xv, 33.

très obeissant serviteur   BERTIER père de l'ora[toire]

Addressed: A Monsieur / Monsieur Franklin hôtel / d'Entra-
gue / *rue de l'Université*

Notation: Bertier, Paris, 29 Xb. 76.

From Benjamin Vaughan[5]   AL: Library of Congress

Decr: 29h:, 1776

B. Vaughan presents his best respects to Dr: Franklin and in-
closes him some papers for perusal *at his leisure.* He sends them
for several reasons. To shew, first, that neither his head nor
his heart have been unoccupied upon the subject of America;
to prove in the next place, under what disadvantages every
man enters upon the subject, without *information* from thence;
and to enable him also to judge of the confidence which Dr:
Franklin is to repose in him.[6] The letters are the *result* of thought,
but were for the most part committed to paper in haste; particularly No. 1 which he begs (if read at all) may be read last.

Addressed: Dr: Franklin.

[*A possible continuation is printed below under Sept. 19, 1777.*]

From [Duportail][7]   AL: University of Pennsylvania Library

[After December 29, 1776.]

J'ai l'honneur de vous envoyer, Monsieur, un etat imprimé des
officiers du Corps du genie afin que vous puissiéz vous assurer
que vous n'avéz pas un seul de nous. D'un autre coté si vous
consultéz quelque militaire instruit et sans prévention, il vous
dira qu'aucun officier d'artillerie comme d'infanterie ne peut
remplacer l'ingenieur pour ce qui concerne l'attaque et la de-

5. As early as January, 1775, BF had referred to Vaughan as "my particular Friend" (above, XXI, 442), but this note is the first that is extant in a
correspondence that went on for years.

6. "Him" in this clause must be BF. Vaughan's particular reason, we assume, for wanting to win confidence with the enclosures, now lost, was
that BF had then accepted him as his editor; see Vaughan's letter below, Jan.
27.

7. Identified by the handwriting as well as the contents. This note clearly
followed his first overture on Dec. 29.

fense des places, leur tracé et leur construction ainsi que pour le tracé et la construction des retranchements et de tous les ouvrages dont on fait usage à la guerre. J'ajouteray que dans une guerre defensive comme la vôtre l'art de l'ingenieur est de la plus grande importance, puisqu'une ville mal fortifiée, un poste mal retranché peuvent estre decisifs contre vous. Je n'ay toujours d'autres propositions à faire que celles que j'ai mises par ecrit chéz vous. Ce n'est pas la fortune que je cherche, monsieur, c'est la gloire ainsi que des connoissances et de l'experience. A ce motif se joint l'interêt que je ne puis m'empecher de prendre à votre cause et la liberté du nouveau monde est un oeuvre auquel je serois flattée de contribuer.

J'attendray, monsieur, votre reponse quelques jours. Si vous êtes disposé a recevoir l'offre que j'ai l'honneur de vous faire, et que vous ayéz quelque personne de ce pays chargée de traiter ces sortes d'affaires, je vous seray obligé de me l'indiquer, parceque le secret rigoureux qu'on exige de moy me defend de paroistre souvent chéz vous. J'ai l'honneur d'etre &c.

Notation: M. [*blank in* MS] Versailles

The Committee of Secret Correspondence to the American Commissioners

LS: American Philosophical Society; Haverford College Library; LS without postscript: Joseph E. Fields, Joliet, Ill. (1958); AL (draft[8]): American Philosophical Society; copies: Historical Society of Pennsylvania; National Archives (two)

The military defeats that had followed consistently on the Battle of Long Island, and had brought the British so near Philadelphia that Congress had fled to Baltimore, changed the mood of the delegates. The change showed itself immediately after the committee's letter above of December 21. On the 24th Congress appointed a committee to form a plan for obtaining foreign assistance, on the 28th and 29th debated its report, and on the 30th adopted a series of resolutions that embodied a new approach to foreign policy. Gone was the old optimism, which assumed that French assistance could be had by the offer of a treaty and the promise of neutrality if that

8. In the hand of Richard Henry Lee.

treaty brought France and Britain to war. Now the commissioners were authorized to offer much more: military help in obtaining joint control of the fisheries and dividing Newfoundland, while the United States annexed Cape Breton and Nova Scotia; a joint monopoly of American trade with the West Indies; and, if more were needed, a Franco-American assault on British possessions in the Caribbean for the benefit of France alone. Spain was to be offered a commercial alliance and, in return for American use of the Mississippi and the port of Pensacola, military aid in conquering that port and a declaration of war against Portugal. Congress resolved at the same time to widen its circle of friends: commissioners were to be sent, as Deane had suggested, to the courts of Spain, the Empire, Prussia, and Tuscany.[9] These offers to the Bourbon powers gave the original commissioners bargaining points which in fact aroused little interest. The appointment of new commissioners was equally fruitless. They arrived in Paris, discovered that the courts to which they were accredited had no intention of receiving them, grumbled at cooling their heels, importuned Franklin for money, and made a nuisance of themselves.

Honorable Gentlemen   Baltimore 30 Decemr. 1776
You will be pleased to receive herewith copies of our letter of the 21st. Inst. and of it's inclosures, which we recommend to your attention. Since that letter was written, General Washington, having been reinforced by the Troops lately commanded by General Lee and by some Corps of Militia, crossed the Delaware with 2500 men, and attacked a body of the enemy, posted at Trenton, with the success that you will see related in the inclosed hand bill. We hope, this blow will be followed by others, that may leave the enemy not so much to boast of, as they some days ago expected, and we had reason to apprehend.

Upon mature deliberation of all circumstances, Congress deem the speedy declaration of France and European Assistance so indispensibly necessary to secure the Independence of these States, that they have authorized you to make such tenders to France and Spain, as, they hope, will prevent any longer delay of an event, that is judged so essential to the well being of North America. Your wisdom, we know, will direct you to

9. *JCC*, VI, 1054–8.

make such use of these powers, as will procure the thing desired on terms as much short of the concessions now offered as possible; but no advantages of this kind are proposed at the risk of a delay that may prove dangerous to the end in view. It must be very obvious to the Court of France, that if Great Britain should succeed in her design of subjugating these States, their Inhabitants, now well trained to arms, might be compelled to become Instruments for making conquest of the French Possessions in the West Indies; which would be a sad Contrast to that security and commercial benefit, that would result to France from the Independence of N. America.[1]

By some accident, in removing the papers from Philadelphia to this place, the Secretary of Congress has mislaid the additional instructions formerly given you, by which you were impowered to negotiate with other Courts besides France.[2] We think it necessary to mention this to you, lest the paper should have got into wrong hands, and because we wish to have a copy sent us by the first good opportunity.

We observe, that Mr. Deane sent his dispatches for this Committee open to Mr. Bingham, but, though we have a good opinion of that Gentleman, yet we think him rather too young to be made acquainted with the business passing between you and us, and therefore wish this may not be done in cases of much importance.

The next opportunity will bring you the determination of Congress concerning the persons, that are to be sent to the Courts of Vienna, Prussia, Spain, and the Grand Duke of Tuscany. In the mean time it is hoped, that through the medium of the Ambassadors from those Courts to that of France, you may be so fortunate, as to procure their friendly mediation for the purposes proposed by Congress.[3]

1. This sentence went beyond the intentions of Congress; it condensed two paragraphs in the report of the ad hoc committee that were deleted in the ensuing debate: *ibid.*, p. 1055.

2. Those of Oct. 16: above, XXII, 629–30.

3. Congress had directed the commissioners to request, through the ambassadors of the Emperor and the Grand Duke, that those courts use their influence to secure an end to Britain's hiring of foreign troops and the recall of those already in America. *JCC*, VI, 1057–8. That directive must have been enclosed, or the sentence would have been unintelligible. The other reso-

Our Andrew Doria of 14 Guns has taken a King's Sloop of war of 12 guns after a smart engagement. In our last we say, the Enemy made near 3000 Prisoners at Fort Washington, but the number is fixed at 2634. The *West Indiamen* taken by our Cruisers amount to 250 Sail.

The Scarcity of Ships here is so great, that we shall find much difficulty in making the extensive remittances to France, that we ought, in due season, and therefore it will, in our opinion, be an object of great importance to obtain the consent of the Farmers General to send to Virginia and Maryland for any quantity of Tobacco they may chuse, or to the State of North Carolina for any quantity of Naval Stores, which may be wanted for publick use, or to supply the demands of private Merchants. The terms, both as to quantity and price, you will endeavour to learn, and let it be made known to us with all possible expedition, that you may receive an answer thereon.

The Captain of the armed vessel, that carries these dispatches,[4] has orders to deliver them himself to you in Paris, and his vessel will expect his return in a different port from the one he arrives at. He will take your directions about his return, and receive your letters. But the anxiety prevailing here to know your success renders it proper, that he should return with all possible dispatch. Wishing you health, success, and many happy years we remain Honorable Gentlemen your most obedient and very humble Servants   Benja Harrison
Richard Henry Lee
Jno Witherspoon
Will Hooper

p.s The number of prisoners lately taken in the Jersies is about 1100 and Gen. Washington is now advancing upon the enemy who are retreating thro the Jersies towards New York.[5]

---

lutions were undoubtedly sent as well; those relating to France are mentioned in the endorsement.

4. Larkin Hammond in the schooner *Jenifer*.

5. The postscript was later than Dec. 30. It reflects, with a 10% exaggeration in the number of prisoners, Washington's letter to Congress of Dec. 29, just before he recrossed the Delaware to Trenton, and that dispatch was

Endorsed by Franklin: Letter from the Committee of Correspondence dated Dec. 30. 76. Relation of Gen. Washington's Proceedings in N Jersey Propositions to France Business to be done / Write to propose that the Congress would insure French Vessels.

Two Notes to Franklin at the Hotel d'Hambourg [between December 30 and February 27, 1777]

ALS: American Philosophical Society

These brief communications, from men of some distinction, are undated, but have an address that provides a bracket of plausible dates. We know that Franklin was at the Hotel d'Entragues until December 29 and at the Hambourg by January 8; hence he moved at earliest on December 30. He arrived at Passy on or about Feb. 27.[6] These notes might have been written at any time between.[7]

received on Dec. 31. Fitzpatrick, *Writings of Washington,* VI, 451–3; Smith, *Letters,* V, 697 n.

6. The latest surviving letter written in Paris and addressed to him at the Entragues is Bertier's above, Dec. 29, and the first to the Hambourg is Dalibard's of Jan. 8; the change of hotels could have been at any time between those dates. BF's move to Passy is discussed in our note on his agreement with Chaumont below, under Jan. 28. On March 2 he wrote Arthur Lee that he was returning almost daily to see Deane at the Hambourg, where he might still have been addressed; but the wording of these notes suggests to us that the writers knew he was living there.

7. We have omitted two other short notes to BF at the Hambourg, because they have no significance that we can discern; both are in the APS. The first is from 'an English Gentleman" (who we hoped against hope was Charles James Fox, but was not), asking for an interview. The second is from a Mr. Hooper: he is leaving for Orléans, and asks "Mr. Frankland" to forward an enclosure to America and send word of his whereabouts for his brother's sake. An undated letter, signed "J. Hooper" and addressed to Passy, is also in the APS and belongs, we conjecture, to the period of this volume. He thanks BF for his assistance, announces that he is returning to America because he has property to attend to and is of no use to his country in Europe, and asks for a note to secure him passage. The only clue to his identity is the reference to his brother, who seems to have been known to BF. But two Hoopers qualify, Robert Lettis and William. The former had been associated with WF as a surveyor, and the latter had served with BF on the committee of secret correspondence. Both had brothers, Jacob in one case and John in the other, about whom nothing seems to be known. *PMHB,* XXXVI, 64; above, XIX, 352 n; XXII, 638 n; Smith, *Letters,* I, 523.

A M A U R Y,

Tient l'Hôtel de Hambourg, meublé dans le plus nouveau goût, grands & petits Appartemens & Jardin, avec une belle vue dans un des plus beaux Jardins de la Ville, & avec de bonnes Écuries & Remises, rue Jacob, Fauxbourg Saint-Germain, A Paris. On y parle Anglois.

A M A U R Y,

Keeps the Hôtel de Hambourg, ready furnished, in the neatest Taste, with an exceeding pleasant view into a neighbouring garden and his own and with very good Stables and Coach houses, in Jacob Street Suburbs of S. Germain, at Paris. The English Tongue is spoke at his house.

A Business Card Advertising the Hotel d'Hambourg

I. From Michel Adanson[8]

ce jeudi à 9 h. du matin

Mr. Adanson a l'honneur de présenter ses respects très-humbles à Monsieur Franklin, en lui envoiant son adresse qu'il a oublié de lui laisser; et il le prie de vouloir bien la communiquer à Monsieur Daine avec l'assurance de son respect.

Addressed: A Monsieur / Monsieur Franklin / à l'hôtel *d'hambourg,* / *ruë Jacob*

II. From John Greenwood[1]

Fryday morng. Hotel de la Providence Rue d'Orleans
St Honoré.

Mr. Greenwood presents his respects to Dr. Franklin will do himself the pleasure of waiting on him on Sunday morning to know if he has any comands. Mr. G. leaves Paris on Sunday.

Addressed: Monsieur / Mons: Franklin / Hotel d'Hambourg / Rue Jacob. / F. St. Germaine.

Notation: Greenwood

From "an English Gentleman"

[between December 30, 1776, and February 27, 1777]

See page 100n

From [J.] Hooper

[between December 30, 1776, and February 27, 1777]

See page 100n

8. This is the only extant communication between BF and the distinguished botanist (1727–1806). The two were fellow members of the Académie royale des sciences, but the only interest that we know they shared was in reformed spelling. Larousse, *Dictionnaire universel.*

1. BF had apparently known the American-born artist, who by this time was living in London, since 1761 (above, IX, 357); but this is the only extant communication between them. Greenwood was an art dealer as well as painter, and we assume that he was in Paris on business. The following April he was back again; see BF to Cushing below, May 1.

From J. Mosneron l'Aîné[2]   ALS: American Philosophical Society

⟨Nantes, December 31, 1776, in French: I pay homage to the Archimedes and Solon of his country, known throughout the world. The press of business and callers while you were here kept me from trying to push through the crowd; I was afraid of becoming one more favor-seeker. The philosophe whom I know through your works will, I trust, approve of my asking advice about the following project. Six months ago I had the idea of loading a ship for America, as long years of family experience equip me to do, but I fear she will be captured en route from the Leeward Islands. Although your small ships make the passage safely, no vessel in this port remotely matches them for speed and handling. Your clear-sightedness and knowledge of the area will perhaps suggest ways to succeed that elude me, and I have as much confidence in you as in my best friend.

Tell me whether you think my plan reasonable, and if so what the best means are of forwarding it. I must also know to what American port or ports the ship should be directed, and what cargo she should carry; it would likewise be helpful if the captain had letters from you to the principal merchants of the area. Please let me have your answer as soon as possible; none but you and me will see it. An admirer of yours can scarcely fail to be an honest man. If I had been a mason I should have prided myself on helping to build the Parthenon; you are raising a structure of liberty that will be equally famous down the centuries, because it ensures the greatness and felicity of one-eighth of the world.⟩

2. His family, one of the most prominent in the mercantile community of Nantes, was engaged in the transatlantic trade; see Jean Tarrade, *Le Commerce colonial de la France à la fin de l'Ancien Régime* ... (2 vols., Paris, 1972), I, 129, 189; Patrick Villiers, *Le Commerce colonial atlantique et la guerre d'indépendance des Etats-Unis* ... (New York, 1977), pp. 404–5. He subsequently had some business dealing with the commissioners; see JW's letter to them below, June 3, 1777.

From Nathan Rumsey

ALS: American Philosophical Society

Honorable Sir   Nantes 31st. Decemr. 76

I have the pleasure of informing you of the Arrival of a Brigt: Yesterday in the Loire loaded with Tobacco from George Town on Sassafras River in Maryland. In her comes passenger Mr. Robert Maise of Philada. who has been with me to day. She left the Capes of Virginia the 15th Novemr., spoke a Plymouth Privateer the 28th of Novemr. at Sea out 7 Days from Boston who told him that Major Rogers had been defeated in Connecticut with his party raised against us on Long Island,[3] that the Royalists had retired into New York to winter Quarters. Nothing from the lakes since our Defeat at Crowpoint which you were acquainted with before leaving the Continent. He reports no other matters of any consequence. Mr. Maise sups with me this Evening, and should he communicate any thing that may merit your Attention, I shall not fail to give you the particulars, as I shall of every piece of Intelligence. Inclosed is a Letter which Mr. Maise put into my hands. Since your Departure from hence is also arrived Cap. Young of Philada. and another Vessel from Plymouth, on Acct. of Congress, the Cap. and Sailors of which last have forsaken her and are going to England. She is consigned to Mr. Schweighauser and he is in Doubt how to act. It would give me pleasure Mr. Morris was here. Mr. Gruel speaks no english and I am prodigiously hurried, without any Directions or powers to act. A Dutch Transport is lately arrived, an English officer passenger put in her I conjecture to prolong the freight. The officer has protested against the Cap. here for not proceeding on his Voyage and insists he shall not stir untill Gov-

3. "Maise" was Robert Mease, a Philadelphia merchant and the brother of Washington's clothier general, James Mease: *History of the Friendly Sons of St. Patrick* ... (Philadelphia, 1892), p. 122. At the end of October the Pa. Council of Safety had issued Robert and Matthew, another brother, blank letters of marque for privateers to be bought and outfitted in Europe: *Naval Docs.*, VI, 1478. Matthew went to England for a time, and reached Paris in early June; see his note to BF below, June 9, 1777. Maj. Robert Rogers, BF's old acquaintance, had raised a corps of rangers that was with Howe's army; on Oct. 22 he was attacked near White Plains but scarcely defeated. Ward, *War of the Revolution*, I, 258–9.

103

ernment have dischargd him here. He fears Cap. Wickes will take the Vessel going out. With the utmost respect I am Honorable sir Your Most obedient Humble Servant.

NATHAN RUMSEY

Addressed: The Honorable / Doctor Benjamin Franklin / chez Mons. Sollier Banquier / a / Paris

Notation: Lett. from N Rumsey Nantes 31. Decr 1776.

From ———— : a Memorandum

AD: Historical Society of Pennsylvania

After Franklin reached Paris he received a number of unsigned, undated proffers of services or advice. Many may have gone into the wastebasket, but five that appear to have come soon after his arrival are among his papers. Three of these we have identified, if only tentatively, and discuss elsewhere. One of the remaining two is a brief note in English, perhaps incomplete, warning Franklin to sign nothing that is not in that language; otherwise ambiguities are sure to arise in dealing with foreigners, and "one may take the Gingerbread for the Baker."[4] The second is the memorandum below. It impressed Franklin enough to elicit his approving endorsement. The author, who was clearly no admirer of Beaumarchais and his works, was writing after the first sailing of the *Amphitrite* in December, and apparently not long after; hence the tentative date. This may well have been the memorandum to which Le Roy refers approvingly in his note below under Jan. 9.

Note pour M. Francklin.

[December, 1776?]

La Cause des Americains a interressé, echauffé mon coeur. Quelle difference en effet de nos guerres entreprises pour quelques limites inconnues où au moins Indifferentes aux peuples qui y contribuent, d'avec la guerre que s'est vüe forcée de soutenir une nation entiere qui combat pour sa liberté, après avoir épuisé auprès de la mère patrie toutes les voyes praticables de moderation et de soumission même pour obtenir

4. APS.

d'être traitée sur le pied d'égalité que l'interest propre de la metropole devoit lui assurer à jamais.

Connu depuis longtems En Europe par ses decouvertes interessantes en Phisique et par la superiorité avec laquelle il a deffendu les interests des colonies, M. francklin arrive en france chargé des pouvoirs du Congrès général.

La confiance de cette assemblee fait assez l'éloge de ses lumieres et de ses talents. Mais peutêtre ignore-t'il quelques details dont je puis croire que la connoissance lui sera utile pour le succès de sa mission.

En Amerique L'interest de tous decide la volonté generale. Dans les gouvernements d'Europe au contraire presque toujours l'interêt General cede a L'interest particulier.

Tous les Peuples ont l'amour de la liberté dans le coeur. La Nation françoise l'a peutêtre autant qu'aucune autre de la terre.

Les françois ont vu avec entousiasme les efforts qu'a faits l'Amerique Septentrionale pour se soustraire à L'oppression dont elle etoit menacée et, à part toute espèce de rivalité, la nation en general verroit avec la plus grande satisfaction le Gouvernement donner aux états unis les secours que cette partie du monde est en droit d'attendre de tous les peuples auprès desquels la cause de l'humanité est encor en quelque recommandation.

Mais comme nous venons de le faire pressentir le Voeu general ne sera pas consulté. Le gouvernement peut seul prendre une determination et il ne peut pas convenir a tous ses membres d'adopter les mesures vigoureuses dont les circonstances paroissent devoir assurer le succès.

L'Esprit d'ordre du Roy lui fait craindre la guerre comme un obstacle à ses vües d'économie et au bonheur de ses peuples, ce qui l'empeche peutêtre d'apprecier surement les ressources immenses de son Royaume. Il est donc fort douteux que la proposition que fera Mr. francklin a notre ministère de faire la guerre a L'angleterre en soit favorablement accueillie. On peut même croire qu'il ne s'ouvriroit pas entierement avec lui a ce sujet.

Mr. francklin peut cependant le demander, insister même par tous les motifs connus de L'interest de la france a prendre ce parti qui lui convient d'autant plus que son alliance avec la cour de Vienne lui assure a peu près la paix sur le continent.

Dans le cas où on lui fera une reponse dilatoire il doit presser pour qu'on lui donne au moins des secours cachés d'argent et pour qu'on lui permette de faire partir sans délai ce que Mr. Deane peut avoir rassemblé d'effet de toute espèce, ainsi que de se pourvoir de toutes les choses qu'il scait être le plus urgent de fournir à son Pays.

La publicité qu'ont donnée a toutes leurs operations les personnes chargées de L'expedition des deux vaisseaux du hâvre, a infiniment nui a la cause. Le Gouvernement s'est crû compromis et obligé de tout suspendre. C'est un avertissement de ne confier a L'avenir qu'a des gens du metier c'est a dire a des negocians surs et discrets toutes les expeditions de ce genre. On doit au surplus a Mr. Deane la justice de convenir qu'il n'a pas été en son pouvoir de ne pas se servir de personnes qui lui etoient données par le gouvernement et dont il ne pouvoit d'ailleurs prevoir ni même supposer l'indiscretion.

Aux menagements recemment adoptés par le Gouvernement pour dissiper les plaintes du ministère anglois succederont bientot il faut l'esperer des mesures plus satisfaisantes.

En attendant on pense que Mr. francklin ne peut mieux faire que de s'occuper des moiens de remplir avec succès et celerité dès qu'on le lui permettera, toutes les cases du Tableau qu'on suppose qu'il apporte avec lui de ce qui peut manquer en tout genre a l'armée Americaine.

Ce tableau a du être fait sur les lieux d'après le plan d'operations pour la campagne prochaine, Le nombre des troupes a i emploier et les moiens de les i entretenir.

On ne doute point que la pluspart des officiers françois qui sont passés jusqu'ici a L'armée americaine n'y aient porté un esprit d'insubordination et des pretentions énormes qui n'auront pas permis d'en tirer le parti qu'on a du s'en promettre. Mais on ne doit pas s'en inquietter. Rien ne sera plus aisé que de les employer de la maniere la plus utile dès qu'ils auront des chefs de leur nation d'un grade superieur, d'un nom et d'un merite connus.

Tout depend donc du choix de ces Chefs.

Il est probable qu'il se presentera des officiers des plus hauts grades, même de ceux qui ont de la reputation a la guerre qui s'offriront pour aller servir la cause americaine. Mais il faut aux Colonies Angloises des deffenseurs qui aient quelque chose de plus que la valeur et les Talents militaires: C'est a dire des chefs honnêtes gens, dont la probité et la rigide austérité de Moeurs contiennent tous les sous-ordres et puissent s'attirer La confiance et l'estime des troupes et des habitans des Colonies.

Si pour detourner L'attention du veritable objet de sa mission importante, M. francklin croit devoir paroitre s'occuper moins des interests de sa patrie que de repondre à L'empressement avec lequel il est recherché dans cette ville immense, on lui offrira un million de diners, mais où il ne trouveroit pas une Guinée pour le Service du Congrès. Il sçaura sans doute se tenir en garde contre les steriles Cajoleries des Grands, des scavants et des femmes qui auront chacun un personnage à lui reccommander. Il scait que le Salut de son pays ne doit pas être remis dans des mains quelconques sans les plus serieuses reflexions.

Endorsed: Good Advice

From the Committee of Secret Correspondence

LS: Library of Congress; University of Pennsylvania Library; copies: Library of Congress, National Archives (four)

Honorable Sir   Baltimore 1 January, 1777

Congress relying on your wisdom and integrity, and well knowing the great Importance of the Case, have appointed you their Commissioner to negotiate a treaty of friendship and commerce with the Court of Spain. The Idea of Congress on this Subject you will find in the instructions of Congress sent by this opportunity to yourself and the other Commissioners at the Court of France. Your Commission for this special service we have now the honor to inclose you.[5] We are

5. The committee was anticipating formal Congressional approval of the new instructions and BF's letter of credence as commissioner to Spain; see the next headnote.

with great Respect and Esteem Honorable Sir Your most obedient and very humble Servants   BENJA HARRISON
    RICHARD HENRY LEE
    JNO WITHERSPOON
    WILL HOOPER

Doctor Franklin

Endorsed: Letter from Committee of Correspondence to B.
Franklin, acquainting him with his Appointment to the Court
of Spain Jan. 1. 1777

The Continental Congress to the American Commissioners: Letter of Credence

January 2, 1777   See the following note

The Continental Congress: Letter of Credence for Franklin as Commissioner to Spain

DS: American Philosophical Society, Archivo Historico Nacional; draft:
National Archives

On December 30 Congress decided to offer a military alliance to
France and to Spain, and to send commissioners to Madrid and other
European courts. On January 1 Franklin was named the commissioner to Spain; the reason for choosing him, he believed, was nothing more than that many months earlier a son of the King had sent
him a present. On January 2 Congress issued Franklin, Deane, and
Lee a new commission authorizing them to negotiate with France
for a military alliance, and at the same time approved the letter of
credence that follows.[6]

[January 2, 1777]
The Delegates of the United States of Newhampshire, Massa-
chusets-bay, Rhodeisland, Connecticut, New-york, New-jersey,

6. *JCC*, VII, 8–10; BF to Lee below, March 21. For the present see above,
XXII, 62, 298. We do not print the joint commission (Harvard University
Library) because it is, except for its references to France and the omission
of the sentence about BF's powers there, identical with this one.

Pensylvania, Delaware, Maryland, Virginia, Northcarolina, Southcarolina and Georgia to all who shall see these presents send Greeting.

Whereas a friendly and commercial connection[7] between the subjects of his most catholic majesty the king of Spain and the people of these states will be beneficial to both nations, know ye therefore, that we confiding in the prudence and integrity of Benjamin Franklin one of the delegates in Congress from the state of Pensylvania and a commissioner from these united states to the court of France, have appointed and deputed and by these presents do appoint and depute him the said Benjamin Franklin our commissioner, giving and granting to him the said Benjamin Franklin full power to communicate, treat, agree and conclude with his most Catholic Majesty the King of Spain or with such person or persons as shall by him be for that purpose authorised, of and upon a true and sincere friendship and a firm, inviolable and universal peace for the defence, protection and safety of the navigation and mutual commerce of the subjects of his most Catholic Majesty and the people of the united states and also to enter into and agree upon a treaty with his most Catholic Majesty or such person or persons as shall be by him authorised for such purpose for assistance in carrying on the present war between Great Britain and these united states and to do all other things which may conduce to those desireable ends, and promising in good faith to ratify whatsoever our said commissioner shall transact in the premisses. Provided always that the said Benjamin Franklin shall continue to be possessed of all the powers heretofore given him as a commissioner to the Court of France from these states, so long as he shall remain and be present at the said Court.

Done in Congress at Baltimore the second day of January in the year of our Lord one thousand, seven hundred and seventy seven. In testimony whereof the president by order of the said Congress hath hereunto subscribed his name and affixed his seal. JOHN HANCOCK

7. The commissioners' original letter of credence (above, XXII, 634–5) here read "a trade upon equal terms." The rest of the paragraph until the final sentence followed the earlier wording, as did the commissioners' new letter of credence, except for the added clause about a treaty of assistance.

Attest Chas Thomson secy.

Endorsed: Commission appointing B. Franklin to the Court of Spain. 2d Jany 1777.

From Duportail[8]

ALS: American Philosophical Society

Monsieur   Versailles le 2 janvier 1777

Je desirerois avoir reponse sur la proposition que j'ai eu l'honneur de vous faire dimanche dernier, parcequ'il me faut prendre certaines mesures en consequence tant pour moy que pour les officiers du corps dont je vous ay parlé. Il me paroit d'ailleurs absolument essentiel de nous entendre sur tout cecy afin que vous, monsieur, ou les personnes qui vous secondent ne recevièz pas les propositions d'un plus grand nombre d'officiers que celuy auquel il sera *permis* d'executer ce projet. Cela auroit des inconvenients de toutes sortes.

Si votre reponse est telle que je la desire, j'iray à paris pour prendre des arrangemens plus positifs. J'ai l'honneur d'etre avec la plus respectueuse consideration Monsieur votre tres humble et tres obeissant serviteur   D.P.TL

P.S. Je vous prie instamment, Mr., de ne point laisser sortir de vos mains cette lettre non plus que l'ecrit de dimanche dernier.

Notations: Versailes 2d Jan. 1777 / D. pt / De Portail

From Henry Emanuel Lutterloh[9]

ALS: American Philosophical Society

Sir!   Paris Jany the 3d 1777.

Yesterday I forgot to acquaint You, that my journey is undertaken unknown to any body, and to do it properly to avoid

8. See his first letter above, Dec. 29.

9. A retired German major, despite the notation on this letter, who rose to be an American colonel. On Jan. 8 he wrote again to BF, along with the other commissioners, to repeat his request and enclose another account of his past career; it added that he had married and resigned his commission while in England, and in 1776 had done some recruiting, apparently for

all manner of inquiry and Suspition, I traveled to here under my Mothers family Name as Monsieur de Luders, and I told my friends in Holland I did go back to Wittgenstein to my Recruits. Therefore would beg to call Me so in your direction if a Note is Send to me as below.

Nobody knowes Me here, nor do they know I am an officer.

I thought, and am still of opinion, that if anny thing should be undertaken in Germany or in the North, it ought to be kept a profound Secrat.

On my part every Service which I undertake and promisse to do, shall be faithfully, and exactly executed, according to the Commands with which you honour Me. I have served all the late War from a Leutn. to a Major, and was two Campaygns an Aide Camp, and Brigade Major to His Serene Highness Prince Ferdinand, So that I know that business. After the War was over I was Send an Agent for the Reigning Deuke of Brunswick to the Court of London, So that I acquainted with the Ministeriale affairs liekewise. And that I was where I had the honour to be acquainted with you in London! And if I had not left that Servize i should bee a Colonell in the Brunswick Servize and Marched with his Troops.

I must liekewise tell you, it would be a great difficulty to get Men and officers out of Germany without leave of the Severall Princes and Reiging Counts, but those I have allready

Brunswick, but had abandoned it. He offered, if commissioned colonel, to raise a regiment or more in Germany, and to take charge of American propaganda there. On Jan. 21 he suggested to the commissioners that, if they bought a ship and provided him funds, he would man her with the best of his Germans and load her with good rifles. All these letters are in the APS.

On Jan. 23 BF gave him a letter of introduction to his old friend, Michael Hillegas, and soon afterward money for his trip. Hillegas to BF, March 17, 1778, Hist. Soc. of Pa.; entry under Feb. 8, 1777, Waste Book. The Major arrived in Nantes without enough funds, and did not finally sail until late March. JW to BF below, March 6, 25. In May he joined the American army, where he was soon promoted to colonel and made a deputy quartermaster general. He served throughout the war, and afterward settled in the United States and was instrumental in founding the German Society in New York. Fitzpatrick, *Writings of Washington*, VIII, 145, 179–81, 328; XI, 102; Lutterloh to Mifflin, Oct. 16, 1777, National Archives; *Annual Report of the German Society of the City of New York for the Year 1883* (New York, 1884), pp. 6–7.

got with great Espences and are Established with so Maney officers. And as Your Country allways will Want Men, even to Supply the present Losses, I think such an Establishment worth any Attention. I could liekewise form hereafter maney other plans. Having the honour to be with great Respect, Sir Your Most obedient and most humble Servant   H E LUTTERLOH.

My direction is Pour Monsieur de Lüders. a l'hotell de Espagne Rue Dauphine

Notation: Coll Lutteloch Paris Jan. 3. 1777.

From Jacques-Donatien Le Ray de Chaumont

ALS: American Philosophical Society

[Before January 4, 1777[1]]

Nous avons vu ce matin, Monsieur, avec vostre petit fils unne pension qui peut convenir au Benjamin, si le compte que vostre petit fils vous en rend peut vous determiner, comptez sur toutte ma surveillance.

Un gentilhomme francais qui a commandé unne troupe de volontaires en pologne demande a passer avec sa troupe en amerique et servir vos braves americains, il luy faudra cent ecus par volontaire, il en conduira soixante qu'il commandera en qualité de Colonel, et ses volontaires recevront la solde que vous donnez aux meilleures troupes. Ce Colonel a de Bons et Excellents Repondants.[2] Un homme d'importance doit venir

1. Dated by the beginning of BFB's stay in Passy for his schooling at the pension of a M. d'Hourville. Another *maître de pension*, a Parisian by the name of Gadolle, tried to obtain the boy and WTF for pupils; two undated notes from him survive, one enclosing a prospectus. Passy, thanks no doubt to Chaumont, was selected; BFB had a new suit made for the occasion, and arrived at the pension on Jan. 4. BF's account of payments for him, Dec. 12, 1776–Sept. 6, 1780; Hourville's receipted bill, Jan. 8, 1777. All these documents are in the APS.

2. This was undoubtedly Philippe-Charles-Félix Macquart, baron de Rullecourt, a soldier of fortune from the Austrian Netherlands. He had been in the Spanish and French services before entering the Polish, and was now full of ideas for aiding the Americans. The previous September he had proposed to join them with six hundred men. Chaumont and Dubourg seem to have been involved, and Beaumarchais asked Vergennes'

Lundy me demander vostre Reponse vous pouvez compter que cette troupe servira bien parcequ'elle sera composée de gens determinés a vaincre ou mourir. Je suis avec le Respect dues [dû] a vos vertus Monsieur vostre tres humble serviteur

LERAY DE CHAUMONT

Notation: de Chaumont sans datte

From ——— Gadolle: Two Notes and Prospectus

[before January 4, 1777]   See page 112n

To the Committee of Secret Correspondence

ALS and copy: National Archives

Gentlemen,   Paris Jan. 4. 1777.

I arrived here about two Weeks since, where I found Mr. Deane. Mr. Lee has since join'd us from London. We have had an Audience of the Minister, Count de Vergennes, and were respectfully receiv'd.[3] We left for his Consideration a Sketch

---

advice about introducing Rullecourt to Deane. In December the British Ambassador reported that this plan had been stopped. The Baron then concocted a much wilder scheme, but none of his various projects came to anything. He eventually rejoined the French army, and was killed in an attack on Jersey in 1781. Lasseray, *Les Français,* II, 494–6; Morton, *Beaumarchais correspondance,* II, 254; Stevens, *Facsimiles,* XIV, no. 1393, pp. 2–3; the headnote on the commissioners to Rullecourt below, Jan. 10.

3. This audience, which the commissioners had requested in their letter above of Dec. 23, took place secretly in Paris on the 28th. According to Vergennes, it was neither long nor very interesting. BF apparently did the talking for his colleagues; he presented the plan of a commercial treaty and promised a memorandum on the state of American affairs. "Le personnage paroit intelligent, mais très circonspect, cela ne m'etone pas." Vergennes to Aranda, Dec. 28, 1776; Archivo Historico Nacional. What did surprise him was how little the Americans were requesting; he correctly interpreted this modesty as confidence that close commercial ties with France and Spain would by themselves bring those countries into war with Britain. Doniol, *Histoire,* II, 114–5. The Minister for his part assured them that their commerce would receive all the facilities compatible with Anglo-French treaties; to make clear what he meant he read them the article restricting the access of privateers to French ports and barring the sale of their prizes. Vergennes to the commissioners below, July 16, 1777.

of the propos'd Treaty. We are to wait upon him tomorrow with a strong Memorial requesting the Aids mentioned in our Instructions.[4] By his Advice we had an Interview with the Spanish Ambassador, Count d'Aranda, who seems well dispos'd towards us, and will forward Copies of our Memorials to his Court, which will act, he says, in perfect Concert with this. Their Fleets are said to be in fine Order, mann'd and fit for Sea. The Cry of this Nation is for us; but the Court it is thought views an approaching War with Reluctance. The Press continues in England.[5] As soon as we can receive a positive Answer from these Courts we shall dispatch an Express with it. I am, Gentlemen, Your most obedient humble Servant

B Franklin

The Committee of Secret Correspondence

Lambert Wickes to the American Commissioners

ALS: American Philosophical Society

Gentlemen,   Nantz January 4th, 1777.

I this day received yours 26th. Decemr. and shall pay due Attention to the Contents thereof.[6] I shall emeadiately proceed for port L'Oriont and Execute that Bussiness and make my report Accordingly, as soon as possible. I shall take particular Care to Send my letters as you Direct and all my Letters will be directed to the Honourable Doctor Franklin, untill I get your firm Approbation, for directing as you shall think proper. If you think it absolutely Necessary for me to Come to Parris, Shall come up emeadiately after I Come from L'Oriont. From

4. Their first letter to Vergennes below of Jan. 5; as explained in the headnote there, they were not allowed to present it in person.

5. The French navy was far from ready. The British, nevertheless, were sufficiently alarmed to have inaugurated a general press the previous October. Dull, *French Navy*, pp. 66–8; Gruber, *Howe Brothers*, p. 165.

6. The letter has been lost, but Wickes sketched the contents in a letter of Jan. 24 to the committee of secret correspondence (*Naval Docs*, VIII, 544–5): the commissioners directed him, when ice in the Loire prevented the *Reprisal* from leaving on its cruise, to go to Lorient and inspect three ships there that were offered for sale. See also Clark, *Wickes*, pp. 114–15.

Gentlemen Your most Obliged humble Servant

LAMBT. WICKES

From Jan Ingenhousz   ALS: American Philosophical Society

Dear Sir   Vienna January 4th 1777.

A little time ago I sent you a lettre by the way of London
in hopes it should soon Come to your hands in America. But
a few days ago I was informed by the newspapers and private
lettres that you are arrived at Paris. This piece of news as
astonishing as unexspected was very agreable to me, being
happy to understand, that you are safe and in good health and
that I have some hopes to meet you once more upon this
world. As I make no doubt but my friend mr. Collard secretary
to the Dutch Ambassadour will have allready forwarded my
lettre to Paris,[7] I will not take up your time to mention any
thing more of it. Tho I do not know, whether your coming
upon our continent has for its object the happy reunion between the Mother country and the colonies (which I have so
much the more hope is the case, as I know it was your constant opinion that the colonies should keep the seet of Gouverment out of their country, and which I wish so much the
more, as I should be happy to see, that after you have so well
deserved of mankind in general allready, you should accumu-
late your reputation with the immortal glory of having quelled
a civil warr, prevented the effusion of more human blood and
the fall of a mighty and generous nation) or a quiet enjoye-
ment of the remaindre of your days, I am highly reioyced to
be informed of your arrival, and I have the greatest reason to
regreat my not accompagning my Imperial Master to France.
You will most probably see this Monarch in disguise of a Private man, and I make no doubt but he will converse with you
upon many subjects and mention my name.[8]

7. The letter is above, Nov. 15. Ingenhousz had intended to send one
copy of it via the Imperial Ambassador, but it went instead to the Dutch
Embassy and was returned to him; see his letter below of Jan. 29.

8. Joseph II had been elected Holy Roman Emperor after his father died
in 1765, and was co-regent with his mother, Maria Theresa, of the Haps-
burg dominions. His trip to France incognito to visit his sister, Marie An-
toinette, was postponed until April.

If I had been informed of your undertaking this voyage my desire to see you again would have overcome my natural shiness and even aversion to ask favours for my self, and would have emboldened me to ask him the favour of taking me with him. This is now too late. But I could go by my self, and indeed I am strongly inclin'd to it. His Ser. Heighess the Prince Louis de Rohan, who being Ambassadour here honour'd me with his acquaintance and good countenance, offers me just now by a lettre an appointment in his Palais in purpose to give me a fair oportunity to meet you.[9] I should like to accept of his offer and take the same oportunity to see our common friends of London, where my private affaires call me; for, as I have still my whole inheritance of my father in the stocks, and bankrupties become frequent, I dare scarce to trust my money in their hands.[1] If some family of distinction desired me to inoculate their children, I should have a good excuse to ask leave to set out for that purpose. Towards the month of may I am requested to inoculate at Ratisbonne two children of the Reigning Prince of Tour and Taxis.[2] I could make a Trip to Paris and London before that time. I will shut this lettre into that of the Prince Rouhan, and propose him my sceme. He may possibly find some body who would desire me there.

However this sceme may succeed, permit me to claim the Priviledge of an old friend, sincerely and respectfully attached to you, who desires for return of his affection a lettre of answer as soon as possible. I am dear sir Your Most obedient humble servant   J. INGEN HOUSZ

Addressed: a Monsieur / Monsieur Benj. Franklin / Membre de l'Academie Royale / des Sciences de Paris, de la Societé / Royale de Londres &c.&c. / presentement / a Paris.

9. Louis-René-Edouard, Prince de Rohan (1734–1803), had been recalled from Vienna in 1774. For the future Cardinal Bishop of Strasbourg, a principal in the affair of the diamond necklace and one of the outstanding clerical rakes of his day, see Larousse, *Dictionnaire universel.*

1. Ingenhousz's father had divided his estate between his two sons; see the *Dictionary of Scientific Biography.* Jan, we presume, had invested the proceeds in stocks during his four-year stay in England in the 1760's.

2. Carl Anselm, Fürst von Thurn und Taxis; the family controlled the German postal system. See Max Piendl, *Thurn und Taxis, 1517–1867* (Regensburg, 1967).

Notations: Dr Ingenhousz / Ingenhouss. January 4. 1777. / Letters from Dr. Ingenhousz to BF.

From Lambert Wickes

ALS: American Philosophical Society

Sir,   [January 4, 1777]
    I sent your Things up imeadiately, to the Care of Mr. Grewel [Gruel], Who told me he would send them forward for you directly, As I was on Shore when the order Come for your things they made a Mistake and Sent your Old Wooden Box also, this I hope you'll excuse as I did not find it out time enough to prevent it Coming to Parris. I remain with Much respect Your Most obligd Humble Servant   LAMBT WICKES

PS. Please make my Compliments to Mr. Franklin and Master Benjamin.   L: W:

Addressed: To / The Honble. Dr. Benja: Franklin Esqr / at / Parris

Notation: Captn. Weeks Nantz January 4th 1777

Memoir on the State of the Former Colonies

AD:[3] Archives du Ministère des affaires étrangères

[Before January 5, 1777[4]]
Memoir concerning the present State of the late British Colonies in North America.

1. *With regard to their Union.*
    All their humble Petitions for Redress of Grievances being rejected, and answered only by an Act of Parliament confiscating their Estates, and declaring their Lives forfeited; and

3. The binding of the AD now hides the ends of many lines; we have silently supplied missing words from Stevens, *Facsimiles*, VI, no. 614.
    4. We believe that the commissioners brought with them to Versailles their first letter to Vergennes of the 5th, which immediately follows; they delivered it that evening along with the memorandum, as explained in the headnote. Even if they wrote the letter, which is in BF's hand, before leaving Paris that morning, he would not have had time to compose this document as well.

117

the War being carried on against them with uncommon Cruelty, by burning their defenceless Towns in Winter, exciting Slaves to rise against their Masters, and Savages to assassinate and massacre their inoffensive Husbandmen; the several Colonies, exasperated to the last degree, call'd loudly upon the Congress to declare an Independence. The Congress, after mature Deliberation, have done it; the several Colonies have since approv'd and confirm'd that Declaration, and have accordingly form'd their separate Constitutions as independant States: A general Confederation is also plann'd by the Congress, whereby, for general Purposes and the common Defence, the Power of the whole is united in that Body. A Copy of that Instrument of Confederation is hereunto annexed.[5]

There are nevertheless in each Colony some who have not heartily concurr'd in this Revolution. They consist chiefly of Traders who are put out of Business; of People from England and Scotland who have not been long settled in that Country; or of such Natives as have held Offices under the former Government, or are afraid of the Consequences that may follow a Conquest. The Number of these latter is not at present great, but may increase if any considerable Success should attend the British Army. The Harmony among the Members of the Congress and between the Congress and the several States, was perfect when Mr. Franklin left America, [*in the margin*: Octr. 26] and was likely to continue so.

2. *With regard to their Strength.*

The Congress have resolv'd 88 Battallions for the ensuing Campaign, each Battalion to consist of about 780 Men. A Copy of this Resolution is annex'd.[6] They have a Squadron of small Ships at Sea, which have greatly annoy'd the English Commerce. They have 13 Frigates of 32 to 36 Guns, just built, most of them rigg'd and nearly ready for Sea, but some want Guns and Anchors. Cannon of Iron are casting in different

5. BF had with him the draft Articles of Confederation that had emerged from the Congressional debate the previous summer (above, XXII, 121), for he gave the Spanish Ambassador a French translation of the text that is now in the Archivo Historico Nacional.

6. *JCC*, V, 762.

Places, as large as 18 pounders; but the Workmen not being yet perfect in the Business, many of the Pieces fail in the Proof, which occasions a Want of Cannon from Europe. A number of Privateers are also out against the Enemy. Abundance of Fishermen being put out of their Employment by the War, enter in the Frigates or engage in the Privateers.[7]

The Number of Souls in the 13 United States, is commonly estimated at 3,000,000. Perhaps that Estimate is too high at present; but such is the rapid Increase of People there, thro' early Marriages, that it cannot be long before that Number is exceeded, the Inhabitants having been generally found to double themselves by natural Generation every 25 Years; and in a quicker Proportion in those Colonies that receive an Accession of strangers. So that probably Men will not be wanting to continue this War.

3. *As to their Agriculture, and Commerce.*

The Agriculture has not hitherto been much lessen'd by the War: those who are not in Arms working more diligently; so that the Country is full of Provisions, and cheap. Some Diminution there has been in the Planting of Tobacco, from a Prospect of less Demand, but more Cotton and Flax has been raised, as being immediately wanted for Clothing. The Commerce is for the most part stopp'd from two Causes; the Fear of Captures by the English, and the Want of Ships to export the Produce; the Merchants of the middle and more northern Colonies, who used to export Wheat, Flour, Fish, and other Provisions, having sold most of their Ships to Europe when they foresaw the Stoppage; and the British Ships which used to carry the Tobacco from Virginia and Maryland, and the Rice Indigo, Pitch and Tar from the Carolina's and Georgia, to the Number of 500 Sail, being withdrawn, and our Carpenters now employ'd in building Frigates and Privateers, very little Trade can be carry'd on. A few Ships only have been sent to Europe and the French Islands, for Arms and Ammunition, on

---

7. Inexperience in cannon-founding hindered arming the frigates, and competition from the privateers hindered manning them: William M. Fowler, Jr., *Rebels under Sail: the American Navy during the Revolution* (New York, 1976), pp. 237–8, 281.

Account of the Congress, some of which have been taken either going or returning. Those who would trade with us should therefore bring Ships.

The Commerce of the 13 States has increas'd in a much greater Proportion than that of the Number of People, because at the same time that they have grown more numerous, they have also become richer, and abler to pay for richer Manufactures. This Commerce before the War amounted to about Five Millions of Pounds Sterling, and employ'd between 8 and 900 Sail of Ships. England has lost this Commerce. It may now, *with all its future Increase*, be gain'd by France and Spain if they will protect it; and they will thereby be as much strengthen'd, in the Vent of Manufactures and Produce, Increase of Wealth and Seamen, &c. as England will be weaken'd, whereby the Difference will be doubled. The Tobacco, &c. which France and Spain cannot consume, they may vend with Profit, to the rest of Europe.

It is to be apprehended, that if the Commerce of America is much longer obstructed, the Party who dislike the War will be so strengthen'd as to compel the rest to Accommodation with Britain. For the other Party, tho now by far the most numerous, and who are for continuing the War till the Independence is establish'd, until they have oblig'd Britain to make Reparation for the Injuries she has done us, will be weaken'd by the want of Commerce, as, without it, Taxes cannot so well be rais'd for Supporting the War, nor the Troops so easily cloath'd and armed.

Notation: avec la lettre du Docteur Franklin au Ministre Vergenes du 5. Janvier 1777.

The American Commissioners to Vergennes

ALS: Archives du Ministère des affaires étrangères; copy: Harvard University Library.[8]

On Sunday, January 5, the commissioners went to Versailles. That evening they sent a brief note to Vergennes asking for an audience

8. The ALS, in BF's hand, lacks some words as in the preceding document, and we have silently supplied them from the copy.

on Monday morning.[9] Such an interview in the spotlight of the court would have been quite different from the previous clandestine meeting in Paris,[1] but the idea never seems to have occurred to them that publicizing American demands might be unwelcome to the Minister. It was. He had no intention of complying with their request, and asked Gérard either to see them on Tuesday, again in Paris, to find out what they wanted, or to put them off by promising a response "quand j'aurai pris des ordres."[2] Instead his assistant, in a note to Deane written only an hour after the commissioners' note, offered to see them himself immediately.[3] They must have assumed, although he did not say so, that he was acting in the Minister's stead.

The other developments of that evening are not clear. Deane wrote Gérard, perhaps while the latter was writing him, perhaps on receipt of his note, to say that he was too ill to leave his hotel and to ask for an interview there, either immediately or in the morning.[4] The next day Gérard offered to see him wherever and whenever convenient.[5] At the same time he acknowledged receipt of the present letter from the commissioners and of the memoir that is the preceding document.[6] His two notes in conjunction suggest that the letter and memoir were not delivered in person because no interview took place.

9. The following document.

1. For which see BF to the committee of secret correspondence above, Jan. 4.

2. Stevens, *Facsimiles*, VI, no. 616; see also Doniol, *Histoire*, II, 116–17.

3. Harvard University Library.

4. Stevens, *op. cit.*, VI, no. 615. This letter was not directly connected with the commissioners' business at Versailles. In December the court, under strong British pressure, had ordered Beaumarchais' three ships held at Le Havre. The order had arrived in time to stop two of them, but the *Amphitrite* had already sailed. Deane complained to Vergennes on Jan. 1 that the artillery purchased for the United States was being detained; he was assured in the name of the King that all difficulties would soon be removed. *Ibid.*, nos. 611–12; see also Doniol, *Histoire*, II, 62. He had not received this promise when he reached Versailles on the 5th, but learned instead, from whom we do not know, that the *Amphitrite* had put back and was now forbidden to leave. *Deane Papers*, I, 449. He then wrote his note to Gérard, saying nothing about the other commissioners and asking for an interview to explain why his complaint had gone unanswered. On the 8th he heard that the ships might sail, but only on condition that they carry no artillery: *ibid.*, p. 452.

5. *Ibid.*, p. 450.

6. The demands in their letter were politely tabled: Gérard to the commissioners below, Jan. 6.

When did the commissioners write their letter? After they learned that Vergennes would not receive them, it might be argued, in order to convey in writing what they had expected to discuss. But the argument does not stand up. Franklin referred the day before to a "strong Memorial" that they were about to present to the Minister, requesting assistance according to their instructions.[7] They scarcely had time, furthermore, to compose such a document after Gérard's seven-o'clock note informed them by implication that they were not going to see his superior. We are convinced, therefore, that they wrote their letter earlier, probably before going to Versailles, and later added the place and date.

Versailles Jan. 5. 1777.

To his Excellency the Count de Vergennes, one of his most Christian Majesty's principal Secretaries of State, and Minister for foreign Affairs.

The Congress, the better to defend their Coasts, protect the Trade, and drive off the Enemy, have instructed us to apply to France for 8 Ships of the Line, compleately mann'd, the Expence of which they will undertake to pay. As other Princes of Europe are lending or hiring their Troops to Britain against America, it is apprehended that France may, if she thinks fit, afford our Independent States the same kind of Aid, without giving England just Cause of Complaint: But if England should on that Account declare War we conceive that by the united Force of France, Spain and America,[8] she will lose all her Possessions in the West Indies, much the greatest Part of that Commerce that has render'd her so opulent, and be reduc'd to that State of Weakness and Humiliation, she has by her Perfidy, her Insolence, and her Cruelty both in the East and West, so justly merited.

We are also instructed to solicit the Court of France for an immediate Supply of twenty or thirty Thousand Muskets and Bayonets, and a large Quantity of Ammunition and brass Field Pieces, to be sent under Convoy. The United States engage

7. BF's letter to the committee of secret correspondence, cited above.
8. This seemingly casual phrase anticipated instructions not yet received. All that the commissioners were empowered to offer in case of war, as far as they knew, was American neutrality: above, XXII, 627 n.

for the Payment of the Arms, Artillery and Ammunition, and to defray the Expence of the Convoy.[9] This Application is now become the more necessary, as the private Purchase made by Mr. Deane of those Articles, is render'd ineffectual by an Order forbidding their Exportation.

We also beg it may be particularly considered, while the English are Masters of the American Seas and can, without Fear of Interruption, transport with such Ease their Army from one Part of our extensive Coast to another, and we can only meet them by Land-Marches, we may possibly, unless some powerful Aid is given us, or some strong Diversion made in our favour be so harass'd, and put to such immense Expence, as that finally our People will find themselves reduc'd to the necessity of Ending the War by an Accommodation.

The Courts of France and Spain may rely with the fullest Confidence, that whatever Stipulations are made by us in case of Granting such Aid, will be ratified and punctually fulfill'd by the Congress, who are determin'd to found their future Character, with regard to Justice and Fidelity, on a full and perfect Performance of all their present Engagements.

North America now offers to France and Spain her Amity and Commerce. She is also ready to guarantee in the firmest Manner to those Nations all their present Possessions in the West Indies, as well as those they shall acquire from the Enemy in a War that may be consequential of such Assistance as she requests.[1] The Interest of the three Nations is the same. The Opportunity of cementing them, and of securing all the Advantages of that Commerce, which in time will be immense, now presents itself. If neglected, it may never again return.

9. For this and the instruction about ships of the line see *ibid.*, pp. 627–8, 630.

1. This sentence is ambiguous. It might mean that the United States would guarantee French and Spanish possessions against British attack, but in that case the commissioners were contravening both their instructions and, in the absence of any American navy worth mention, the dictates of common sense. A more probable meaning is that the United States would not "molest" those possessions; an instruction to that effect applied only to Spain (*ibid.*, p. 628), but the commissioners may have stretched it to cover France as well.

We cannot help suggesting that a considerable Delay may be attended with fatal Consequences.   B FRANKLIN
SILAS DEANE
ARTHUR LEE

Plenipotentiaries from the Congress of the United States of North America.

Notation: [Du] Docteur Franklin [au] Ministre Vergennes [177]7. Janvier 5. Traduction ci-jointe.

The American Commissioners to Vergennes

AL:[2] Archives du Ministère des affaires étrangères

Versailles Jany. 5th 1777. 6, OClock in the Evening Dr. Franklin, Mr. Dean, and Mr. Lee, present their most respectful Complimts. to the Count de Vergennes; and request an audience of his Excellency, to-morrow morning, at such hour as he shall be pleas'd to appoint.

Notation: 1777. Janvier 5.

Conrad-Alexandre Gérard to the American Commissioners

Copies: American Philosophical Society; Library of Congress

A Versailles le 6 Janvier 1777
On desireroit qu'on voulut bien suspendre la Communication du Memoire signé contenant des Demandes particulieres. On aura l'honneur de prevenir du Moment ou elle pourra se faire. En attendant on pourroit se borner a faire Part du Memoire d'Eclaircissemens relatif a l'etat des Choses en Amerique, ainsi que des Pieces qui y sont annexées.[3]

Notation: M. Gerard a MM. les Deputés.

2. In BF's hand according to Stevens (*Facsimiles*, VI, no. 613), but actually in Arthur Lee's. We have silently supplied from Stevens a word obscured in the MS as now bound. For the background of the commissioners' request see the headnote on their earlier letter to Vergennes of the same date.
3. The "Memoire signé" is above, the commissioners' first letter to Ver-

From Louis-Joseph Plumard de Dangeul[4]

AL: American Philosophical Society

Moonday. [Jan. 6?, 1777[5]]

M. de Dangeul is below desiring to pay his visit to Mr. doctor francklin, and woud have him so good as to remember that in 68. (London) m. de Dangeul was one of his assidue servants and hearers, at his Lodgind, and at M. le Chevalier Pringle at their assemblies in the evening.[6] He has some particular words to deliver to him.

From Jeremiah Terry[7]   ALS: American Philosophical Society

Sir.   Hotel de Luxembourg 7th. Jany. 1777

I set out from London the 2d. Inst. and arrived here about 4. o'Clock this Evening. My Principal Business is to learn a

---

gennes of Jan. 5, and the "Memoire d'Eclaircissemens" is BF's under the same date.

4. A political economist and author of *Remarques sur les avantages et les désavantages de la France et de la Gr. Bretagne, par rapport au commerce* . . . (2nd ed.; Leiden, 1754). On Jan. 9 he wrote again (APS), this time partly in French and partly in English, to say that BF had not come to see him, to inquire about the Doctor's health, and to ask whether he was coming that morning. With this second note, presumably, he forwarded one that he had received from a M. Guillard, dated merely Tuesday [Jan. 7?], enclosing a pamphlet by an old and unnamed friend of his, which he hoped Dangeul would approve. "Vous voudrés bien alors le remettre to this great Republicain." APS. Our guess is that Guillard was Nicholas-François, the well known playwright. He does not appear again in BF's papers; neither does Dangeul except for his dinner invitation below, under Jan. 13.

5. The present note, introducing himself, is clearly earlier than that just cited of the 9th, and the January date seems more probable than a Monday in late December.

6. Dangeul seems to have brought to London a paper nominating him for the Royal Society and signed by French members, which BF and Pringle also signed; but the nomination did not go through. Above, VIII, 358.

7. A Virginian who had been a trader on the Mosquito Coast, and who had come to London at the end of 1774. He attempted while there to secure for himself the superintendency of the Coast, and his failure to do so seems to have embittered him; in any case he devoted himself thenceforward to

125

more Satisfactory account of my Countrymen in America, than I have been able to do in England, for which Purpose if you will Signify when you will be at leasure I will do myself the Honor to wait on you.[8] In the meantime I remain with great respect Sir Your unknown Humble Servant   JER. TERRY

Addressed: His Excellency Benjn. Franklin

Notation: J. Terry 7 Jan 77.

[The American Commissioners]: Memoir [for Vergennes]   D:[9] Archives du Ministère des affaires étrangères

Memoire.   [*c.* January 8, 1777[1]]

The situation of the United-states, require an immediate supply of Stores of various sorts, of which a proportion of Military for the opening and supporting the coming Campaign.

Vessels or Ships belonging to the United-States cannot be procured, and if they could, the Danger and Risque would be very great.

Difuculties have arose at the different Ports, where Military

---

the effort to bring the area under Spanish rather than British sovereignty. He is said to have come to Paris to enlist BF's support, and to have obtained it in an interview. He returned almost at once to London, consulted with the Spanish Ambassador, and then left in April for Madrid, where he received enough backing so that he eventually crossed again to Central America; but nothing came of his design: William S. Sorsby, "The British Superintendency of the Mosquito Shore, 1749–1787" (doctoral dissertation, University of London, 1969), especially pp. 201, 230 *et seq.*

8. In a second note, written the next day from a different hotel and also in the APS, Terry says that he is returning very shortly to England, and asks BF for a half-hour's private conversation and an introduction to Deane if the latter's health permits. Neither that note nor this establishes that Terry saw BF, let alone received encouragement from him.

9. In WTF's hand, according to Stevens (*Facsimiles* VI, no. 609). We are inclined to agree, but the misspellings and the botched opening sentence are surprising.

1. The second sentence paraphrases one in a letter of that date from Deane to Gérard: *Deane Papers,* I, 452. The other commissioners had already supported Deane in their first letter to Vergennes of Jan. 5, by pointing out the effect of restraining his shipments of supplies; and we assume that he persuaded them to elaborate the point in the present memorandum.

Stores have been collected and Objections made to their being shipp'd for the United-states in French ships though Charter'd on Account of the States, in the name of private Persons, by which great Delay has been already occasioned, and the Damages in consequence will be irreparable, unless speedily relieved. Prudence dictates that ships charged with Stores for the United States should appear as if bound for other Ports at Peace with Great Britain, but at the same time Captns. of such Ships are unwilling, (after giving security in France, that they will Land such stores, in some French Port) to go for North America without assurances of indemnity.

To Remedy these Difficulties it is with submission requested, that Warlike stores already purchased or that may hereafter be purchased for the United States, may be shipp'd in French Ships for the said United States, directly, and if Political purposes render it necessary that surety should be given for Landing them in some Port belonging to France, that the Captains giving such surety may by some means be satisfied of an Indemnity should they land them in the Ports of the united States.

To enforce this Request, it need only be Observed that without this, or some Measure effecting the same Design, the United States will be disappointed of the Stores they expected. The actually sending them to the West India Islands, will be no relief, as the risque from thence to the Continent is as great, or greater than from Europe direct.

NB. The Stores in the Amphitrite, those ready to be Shipp'd from the other Ports, are now detain'd by the above Obstacles.[2]

Lutterloh to the American Commissioners: Letter and Memorandum

January 8, 1777 See pages 110–11n

2. The other ports were Le Havre and Nantes. *Deane Papers*, I, 451.

From Thomas-François Dalibard[3]

AL: American Philosophical Society

ce Mercredi matin 8. Janv. 1777.
M. Dalibard a l'honneur de souhaiter le bonjour à Monsr. Le Docteur franklin et de lui adresser M. de Roussille qui desire avoir l'honneur de le voir et de s'entretenir avec lui pour quelques expéditions qu'il voudrait faire dans l'amérique septentrionale.[4] M. Dalibard suplie Monsieur franklin de vouloir bien accorder à M. de Roussille quelques momens d'entretien, il lui en aura la plus sincere obligation.

Addressed: A Monsieur / Monsieur Le Docteur franklin / à L'hôtel de hambourg Rue Jacob / fbg. St. Germain

From the Comte de Milly[5]

AL: American Philosophical Society

a paris le 8: janvier 1777
M. le comte de Milly de l'academie des Sçiences de paris est venu pour avoir l'honneur de voir Monsieur le docteur franklin et le prier de lui faire l'honneur de diner ches lui lundy 13: de ce mois, avec plusieurs de ses confreres qui seront tous fort aise de voir de près le grand homme qu'ils ont admiré de loin.
M. le comte de Milly demeure rüe dauphine la 2me. porte

---

3. For BF's old acquaintance see above, IV, 302 n.
4. Presumably the Pierre Roussille whose first voyage, the following spring, got him into trouble. He was captured at sea, and imprisoned for two years in England; on his release he appealed to BF for help: March 30, Dec. 27, 1780, APS.
5. Nicholas-Christiern de Thy, comte de Milly (1728–84), was a former soldier who had become a chemist, writer, and dabbler in the occult: Larousse, *Dictionnaire universel.* He was the father-in-law of Jean-Baptiste Le Roy (above, XIX, 111 n), a fact that may account for the promptness of his offer to introduce BF to some of the Parisian scientific world. In an undated note (APS) Milly invited WTF, whom he styled "Monsieur franklin le neveux," to the same dinner party. Two days after the party BF attended his first meeting of the Academy; Milly was also there, perhaps to introduce him. Archives de l'Académie royale des sciences, feuilles de présence de 1776 à 1780, Jan. 15, 1777.

cocherre a droite en venant du pont neuf dans la même maison de M. jombert le pere[6] Libraire du Roi.

Addressed: A Monsieur / Monsieur le docteur / franklin, de la-cademie / Royale des Sciences de paris &c & / A paris

From ——— d'Hourville: Receipt

January 8, 1777   See page 112n

From Jeremiah Terry

January 8, 1777   See page 126n

Barbeu-Dubourg: Memorandum for the American Commissioners

AD: American Philosophical Society

This memorandum is the first account of the negotiations over tobacco that had been going on before Franklin's arrival, and that were expected to play a crucial part in financing the war. No other American export was in such demand in France; if military supplies were to be traded for commodities, the only commodity available was tobacco. The committee of secret correspondence, writing to Deane the previous October, had expected to deal with the farmers general;[7] and a contract with them remained one of the commissioners' major aims. The farm was a syndicate of financiers, one of the most elaborate and efficient bureaucracies of the *ancien régime*, that was responsible for collecting taxes on goods and for administering the state monopolies of salt and tobacco.[8] For the latter the farmers paid the government twenty-four million livres a year, and the maximum sale price was fixed; the syndicate therefore had to have a sufficient supply or face bankruptcy. When it discovered that it could not obtain what it needed from Britain, it started looking for American sources, among them the commissioners.

6. Charles-Antoine Jombert was not only a bookseller and printer but also, like Milly, a writer of some note; see Larousse.
7. Above, XXII, 645.
8. See Price, *France and the Chesapeake,* I, 427–32.

British firms had hitherto controlled the bulk of the trade: their agents had bought the crop in the Chesapeake area, and their ships had carried it to France. Now that the war had eliminated these middlemen, a direct commerce in tobacco promised to be enormously lucrative; and French and American entrepreneurs jostled for a share of it. Some of the Frenchmen, such as Barbeu-Dubourg, hoped to substitute connections for resources; others, such as Chaumont in particular, had better connections and far greater resources. American merchant houses and consortia, like Willing & Morris and Alsop & Company, hoped to do business both for themselves and for Congress. The farmers initially negotiated with the commissioners, with the secret committee through Thomas Morris, and with Dubourg; and the negotiations came to nothing. The main problem was transport. The crop could not be shipped in American vessels; they were too few, and British cruisers too prevalent. The commissioners had a ready answer: send French ships for it. The farmers refused; they were as well aware as the Americans that such a move would stir the hornets' nest in London, and that Versailles was not yet ready to risk war. The protracted negotiations were consequently unrealistic,[9] and the commissioners' idea that tobacco might finance the war was a pipe dream.

[Before January 9?, 1777[1]]

M. Penet m'ayant chargé de negocier avec la ferme génerale des tabacs, je pris des arrangemens avec M. Paulze.[2] Sa lettre du 22 may 1776 en fait foi. J'en rendis compte à M. Deane à son arrivée, et m'en tins là pendant longtems.

M. Deane à qui on avoit proposé à Bourdeaux un autre plan fit peu d'attention à mes representations.

Au mois d'août M. Paulze me recrivit à ce sujet, je communiquai immediatement sa lettre à M. Deane qui parut alors s'en occuper tout de bon. Nous fumes ensemble chez M. Paulze qui lui offrit même des avances pecuniaires. Nous lui fimes esperer des cargaisons abondantes de tabacs pour les mois de xbre. Jr. et fr. M. Deane se chargea d'y pourvoir efficacement,

---

9. For an able analysis of the situation see *ibid.*, II, 700–17.

1. The date when the commissioners opened their negotiations with the farmers general. We assume that Dubourg submitted his memorandum before that, to bring the Americans up to date on what had already happened.

2. Jacques Paulze (1721–1994), Lavoisier's father-in-law, had been a farmer since 1768 and was currently the director of the tobacco department.

et sur les instances de M. Paulze, je lui en garantis l'execution par une lettre du 20 août.

M. Paulze m'a rappellé cette lettre, et en a reclamé les effets par la sienne du 9e. x bre. dernier à l'occasion des tabacs arrivants à Nantes. Je l'ai fait attendre jusqu'à l'arrivée de M. franklin.

Les prix de ces tabacs devoient être evalués à l'amiable suivant nos conventions, au moyen de quoi la ferme generale ne devoit point s'adresser à d'autres.

M. de Chaumont est venu à la traverse, et pour s'attirer tout ce commerce, il a offert un prix avantageux des tabacs arrivés, et fait entendre à M. Deane et consorts qu'il falloit tirer parti de la detresse où se trouvoient les fermiers generaux.

Persuadé qu'il ne falloit pas les vexer si fort, ni les obliger à chercher d'autres ressources, j'ai speculé à mon tour sur toutes les parties qui ont rapport à cet objet; et promis de faire venir en Societé avec des personnes honnetes et solides, tant françois qu'Americains, 20,000 bouccauts de tabac à raison de 7. sols la livre, moyennant de grandes avances pecuniaires de la part de la ferme generale, ou à 8 sols la livre sans avances de sa part. Et cette proposition avoit été bien reçue et le marché devoit en être arreté en definitive Samedi 4e. Jr. 1777.

Mais sur ces entrefaites M. de Chaumont ayant demandé une entrevue avec le Comité de fermiers generaux chez M. de Trudaine pour le jeudi 2e. jr. ou leur donna des inquietudes sur l'execution des promesses de la Societé, ou au moins sur leur accomplissement aux epoques marquées; M. de Ch. fît echouer notre affaire, et ne reussit pas mieux dans la sienne propre.[3]

Il paroit que les fermiers generaux ont traité avec des hollandois et autres, pour tirer de diverses contrées de l'Europe des tabacs d'une qualité au dessous de la mediocre, mais qu'au

---

3. Jean-Charles-Philibert Trudaine de Montigny (1733–77), *intendant des finances*, was in charge of four departments of the farm. Larousse, *Dictionnaire universel*; Suzanne Delorme, "Une famille de grands Commis de l'Etat . . . ," *Revue d'histoire des sciences*, III (1950), 104–9. Beaumarchais agreed that Chaumont's intervention with the committee had been effective, and so reported to Vergennes on Jan. 13: Morton, *Beaumarchais correspondance*, III, 33.

moyen de leur privilege exclusif, ils debiteront également, et se moqueront des cris du peuple.

Il m'a paru necessaire que M. fr. soit bien imbu de ces faits pour en faire usage suivant sa Sagesse dans la conversation qu'il doit avoir avec M. de Trudaine.

Au reste la Societé proposée peut toujours avoir lieu. Non seulement M. de Chaumont veut la renouer, mais je vis hier un autre de nos principaux adjoints qui m'encouragea beaucoup à la refondre sur un plan un peu different, en offrant d'y mettre de plus gros fonds, en tant que besoin seroit.

Endorsed: M. Dubourg

Negotiations over Tobacco between the American Commissioners and the Farmers General: Two Documents

(I) D: Archives du Ministère des affaires étrangères; copy: American Philosophical Society; incomplete copy, Harvard University Library.[4]
(II) AD (draft): American Philosophical Society

On January 9 the commissioners met with a committee of the farmers general to begin negotiations for a tobacco contract. The agenda of that meeting, or the product of it, was written questions from the farmers and replies from the commissioners, on two of which the farmers made observations that raised further points. Paulze forwarded these observations, presumably with the questions and answers, to Vergennes on January 10. The commissioners then delivered a written answer to the observations, in which they suggested that the farmers send their own ships to carry American war supplies to the Chesapeake and receive the tobacco. Paulze forwarded this answer to the Minister on the 13th, with a note informing him

4. We print the D, but for the sake of clarity reverse the questions and answers; in the original they are in the righthand and lefthand columns respectively. The copies are not, strictly speaking, copies at all. The one in the APS omits a small amount of material, and rearranges much of the rest without affecting the substance. In the one at Harvard, made by Arthur Lee, the questions are in French, and the farmers' lengthy observations on the answer to the fifth are omitted; the commissioners' replies are in English, and vary in minor details from our French translation.

that the negotiations had broken down.[5] The first document we publish is confusing in its title and its two opening questions, which deal with tobacco over which the commissioners, as they point out, have no control; all the rest, however, the questions and answers and the farmers' observations, relate to consignments that the commissioners expect to receive. The second document, undated but obviously between January 9 and 13, is Franklin's draft of the commissioners' answer to the observations.

I.

[A Paris Le 9. Janvier 1777[6]]

Au Sujet de tabacs arrivés a Nantes pour le compte du Congrès.

Demandes faites par Les fermiers Generaux	Reponses faites par MM. Francklin Dean et Lée.
1mo. Les Tabacs arrivés à Nantes sur les navires le Succès, l'Elizabeth et la Fanny sont ils à la disposition et pour le compte du Congrès ou pour le compte des particuliers?	1mo. Les Tabacs arrivés sont pour compte du Congrès, mais ils sont destinés à remplir des engagements contractés avec des Negocians d'icy.
2°. MM. Francklin et Dean peuvent ils en traiter, ou M. Morris est il le seul qui ait droit d'en disposer?	2°. MM. Francklin et Dean n'ont pas la disposition de ces Tabacs.
3°. Le congrès a t il des tabacs à sa disposition dans les Colonies unies, ainsy que M. Dean l'a assure dans le mois de Septembre dernier et que M. Morris l'a confirmé le 29. Decembre dernier?	3°. M. Dean se rapporte au mémoire qu'il a délivré a M. Paulze, et par lequel il paroit qu'il a été mal entendu.

5. Paulze's letter to Vergennes of the 10th, which we have not located, is mentioned in his of the 13th in the AAE.
6. Supplied from the APS copy.

4°. MM. Francklin et Dean sont ils disposés à traiter avec les fermiers généraux et sans l'intervention de personne a des prix et conditions raisonables et de bonne foy pour les Tabacs arrivés et pour ceux qui arriveront sans aucune exception?

4°. MM. Francklin, Dean et Lée souhaitent de traiter avec MM. les fermiers généraux, avec toute la bonne foy possible, à des conditions raisonables et sans l'intervention de personne; Mais il n'est point en leur pouvoir de disposer d'aucuns Tabacs, excepté de ceux qui seront envoyés d'après les arrangemens qui seront pris et qu'ils auront annoncés au congrès.

Observations des fermiers généraux sur la réponse faite au 4e. article par MM. Francklin, Dean et Lée.

MM. Francklin, Dean et Lée sont ils suffisament autorisés pour traiter des à présent au nom du Congrès avec les fermiers Généraux pour tous les Tabacs qui arriveront en france, ou seront-ils obligés d'écrire au Congrés pour faire autorisé ce Traité?

Dans quel tems pourront ils recevoir la ratification du Congrès, si elle est nécessaire?

A quelle époque commencera le traité pour la livraison des Tabacs qui arriveront en France?

A quel prix et conditions veulent ils traiter?

5°. Veulent-ils ou peuvent-ils traiter d'une quantité quelconque de Tabacs rendus dans les ports des Colonies unies de L'Amérique et prêts à être embarqués et à quel prix?

5°. MM. Francklin, Dean et Lée ne cherchant aucun profit de commerce pour le congrès, proposent à MM. Les Fermiers généraux, en premier lieu, d'envoyer des Agens resider dans les provinces qui fournissent des Tabacs, pour y vendre les articles qui leur seront indiqués par ces Messrs. comme les plus nécessaires dans les cir-

constances présentes des
Etats unis, et au prix que les
besoins et la concurrence des
Acheteurs produiront.

Et ensuite se prévaloir des
avantages que la même concurrence des Vendeurs leur
donneront pour acheter des
Tabacs.

Ils déclarent de bonne foy
qu'ils ne voyent rien de
mieux pour remplir les vues
reciproques des parties inté-
ressées. Ces agents seront
certains de la protection du
Congrès et de toutes les
facilités que le Gouvernement pourra leur donner sur
les lieux pour transiger leurs
affaires; mais dans le cas ou
ce parti ne conviendroit pas à
Messrs. les fermiers généraux, MM. Francklin, Dean
et Lée s'engageront pour le
Congrès de procurer avec
toute la célérité possible
20 000 Boucauts de Tabacs
dans les differents magazins
de la Virginie et du Maryland
ou les Anglais étoient en
usage de les recevoir, au prix
de 4 sols tournois par livre,
en échange de munitions de
guerre, lainages, uniformes,
draps, toiles pour chemises,
tentes et toiles à voile qui
seront achetés par les agents
choisis par MM. Franklin,
Dean et Lée, et payés par

MM. les fermiers généraux, qui les transporteront dans leurs vaisseaux.

Cet echange sera fait sur ce pied, que pour chaque 4 sols montant des factures des marchandises passées au prix d'achât, on fournira une Livre pezant de Tabac, étant entendu que les fraix et risques du transport des marchandises dans les ports Américains et des Tabacs des endroits ou ils seront délivrés seront à la charge de MM. les fermiers généraux.

Si cette proposition est agrée, on s'attend que les vaisseaux qui porteront les marchandises feront voile aussitôt possible, leurs cargaisons devenant necessaires pour l'ouverture de la Campagne prochaine, et les Cotes d'Amerique etant moins exposées pendant l'hyver aux vaisseaux anglais en croisière.

MM. Francklin, Dean et Lée ont établi le prix des Tabacs à 4 sols comme le plus bas auquel ils pensent qu'il sera possible de les acheter.

Mais si le prix courant étoit plus bas dans les provinces à Tabacs, ils offrent très volontiers de stipuler que MM. les Fermiers généraux jouiront des plus bas prix auxquels il sera possible de les obtenir.

Observations des fermiers généraux sur la reponse faite au 5eme. Article par MM. Francklin, Dean et Lée.

Le parti proposé d'envoyer des agens pour vendre des marchandises de France dans les Colonies unies et y acheter des Tabacs ne peut convenir aux fermiers généraux, parcequ'ils ne pourroient envoyer que des Agens Ecossois en état de parler la langue et instruits des détails du commerce et que ces Agens ne seroient pas reçus dans les Colonies et que des Agens Francois ne pourroient remplir l'objet proposé.

La 2de. proposition faite par MM. Francklin, Dean et Lée de procurer aux fermiers généraux 20.000 Boucauds de tabacs dans les différens Magazins de la Virginie et du Maryland ne répond pas exactement à la 5e. question. Il y étoit question de Tabacs rendus dans les ports des Colonies unies et prêts a être embarqués et non pas des tabacs rassemblés dans les Magazins. Cet expédient rentre alors dans la 1ère. proposition d'envoyer des agens et laisse subsister le même embarras. Ou les agens prendroient ils des voitures pour faire conduire les Tabacs des Magazins dans le lieu d'embarquement, ces agens ne connoissant ni le pays ni la langue seroient une année entière à se procurer les secours nécessaires. Il n'y a que le Congrès ou des personnes sur les lieux choisies de sa part qui puissent etre chargés de tous ces détails.

3°. Le prix des Tabacs dans les Magazins de la Virginie et du Mariland est beaucoup trop haut a 4 sols argent de France, a moins qu'on ait en vue des Tabacs des crus d'York et James rivers de Virginie, ou de Patapsico et Patukant pour le Maryland. Mais comme la principale consommation des fermiers généraux est en Rappanhanook, en South Potomack, North Potomack et en Cherser et Choplank, le prix proposé doit être réduit au moins d'un quart, et les fermiers généraux pourroient offrir 4 sols par livre des Tabacs rendus à bord des navires dans les ports des Colonies unies, moitié des premiers crus et moitié des crus inférieurs, ou 3 sols pour un quart de ces premieres qualites et les trois quarts des inférieures.

4. La forme d'echange proposée n'est ni juste, ni raisonable. 4 sols de marchandises de France au prix des factures rendues dans les Colonies représentent au moins 12 sols. Les Tabacs des Colonies ne valent au plus haut prix que 4 sols. Ce seroit donc échanger 12 sols. contre 4 sols et la lezion seroit énorme. Tous les risques de l'aller et du retour seroient à la charge des fermiers généraux, et les Colonies unies jouiroient sans risques d'un bénéfice de 200 per cent.

Ce n'est donc pas ce que MM. Francklin, Dean et Lée ont entendu et leur proposition est mal énoncée.

Ils ont sans doute voulu dire que 4 sols de marchandises rendues dans les colonies seroient echangées contre une livre de Tabacs, mais alors ce n'est ni sur le prix d'achat, ni sur le prix des factures que l'évaluation peut être faite, mais sur le prix courant dans les colonies au moment de l'arrivée des navires.

Alors l'augmentation dans le prix des marchandises compenseroit le fret et les risques et il seroit juste que les fermiers généraux en fussent chargés.

On peut encore présenter cette proposition sur une autre face. Lorsque MM. Francklin, Dean et Lée avertiront les fermiers généraux qu'il y a dans un port désigné des Colonies, un chargement de Tabacs à leur disposition les fermiers généraux en remettront le prix à raison de 3 sols ou 4 sols par livre suivant la qualité des Tabacs à ces Messieurs, qui acheteront ainsi qu'ils jugeront à propos des marchandises, autres que des armes et munitions, qui seront chargées sur les navires frétes ou achetés par les fermiers généraux. Il sera convenu d'un prix de fret et ces MM. feront assurer les risques ou ils seront à leur charge; comme le fret et les risques des Tabacs au retour seront à la charge des fermiers généraux.

En un mot il doit y avoir une égalité entière. Le congrès livrant le Tabac pris dans les ports des Colonies au prix d'achat ou à une somme fixe, qui le représente, les fermiers généraux ne peuvent etre tenus que de livrer dans les ports de France les marchandises données en echange, ou la valeur en argent au choix du congrès, mais les risques du retour étant à la charge des fermiers généraux pour le tabac qui leur appartient, les risques de l'aller doivent être à la charge du congrès pour les marchandises qui lui appartiendront au moment de la livraison ou du payement en argent.

Il y a encore une voye plus simple. La ferme générale echange de l'argent ou des marchandises remises en France contre des Tabacs livrés en Amérique. Voila ou peut se terminer toute la négociation. Les fermiers généraux s'arrangeront comme ils jugeront à propos pour faire venir leurs Tabacs en France et le Congrès aura la même liberté pour faire rendre en Amérique, les marchandises qui luy auront été fournies ou qu'il aura achetées avec l'argent des fermiers généraux.

Tout se réduit donc à ces deux articles.

Le 1er. convenir d'un prix pour les Tabacs rendus en France.

Le 2d. fixer un prix pour les tabacs pris dans les Colonies.

MM. Francklin, Dean et Lée sont priés de donner une prompte réponse sur ces différentes propositions.

6°. Peuvent ils ou veulent ils traiter d'une quantité quelconque de Tabacs rendus à St. Domingue, la Martinique, Cayenne, St. Pierre de Micquelon ou St. Eustache et à quel prix pour chacune de ces Isles?

6°. MM. Francklin, Dean et Lée ne pourroient point traiter pour des Tabacs rendus dans les Isles a des conditions aussy favorables.

7°. Préfèrent ils de traiter pour une quantité quelconque de boucaults de Tabacs qu'ils se chargeront de faire transporter en France à un prix convenu? Dans ce cas les fermiers généraux offrent de leur faire des avances jusques à concurrence de la somme convenue, en donnant par ces Messieurs les suretés suffisantes. Les fermiers généraux se rembourseront de leurs avances sur le

7°. Ils sont trop incertains que le Congrès puisse se procurer des vaisseaux pour transporter des Tabacs dans les ports de France, pour s'y engager, et ils ne peuvent penser a donner d'autres suretes, que celles de leurs pouvoirs et Lettres de Créance qu'ils tiennent du Congrès.

prix des Tabacs à mesure de
leur arrivée et continueront
d'avancer la même somme
avec les mêmes précautions.

II.

[Between January 9 and 13, 1777]
Messrs. F. D and Lee, cannot treat for all the Tobacco which
may arrive in France; a great part of it will come on Account
of private Merchants, to discharge Debts. But they can assure
the F.G. that whatever Contract they make concerning Tobacco, in order to obtain immediate Supplies for the Armies
of the Congress, will be confirm'd and punctually executed by
the same.

The Proposal they made which is objected to as unjust and
unreasonable, viz. that the Farmers G. should be at the Risque
and Expence of transporting the Goods both to and from
America, did not, when they made it appear so to Messrs.
F. D. and Lee, who considered the Lowness of the Price, and
the Risque they propos'd to run of its being higher, as a sufficient Compensation. Besides the same Causes that could make
4 Sous worth of Goods in France worth 12. Sous in America,
would make 4 Sous worth of Tobacco in America worth 12
Sous when brought to France; which would annihilate the
supposed Loss. The English too who formerly carry'd on that
Trade, were always at the Risque and Expence both Ways in
War as well as Peace. But this Proposal, being only an Alternative to one they thought better for the F.G. viz. that of sending Factors, they readily waive it.

Chaumont to the American Commissioners

ALS: American Philosophical Society

Ce 9. Janvier 1777
M. de Chaumont a l'honneur d'informer Messieurs les deputés
du Congrès qu'il peut leur procurer deux cents milliers de sal-

pestres de l'inde pres a L'orient a soixante le quintal pareil a celuy qu'il a deja procuré a M. Dean payable en lettres de change acceptées sur Paris Londres Amsterdam Bordeaux ou Nantes. Il faut unne prompte décision parceque les Espagnols marchandent ce salpestre. Il vaut en hollande soixante dix huit livres quinze sols le quintal.   LERAY DE CHAUMONT

Notation: de Chaumont 9 Janv. 77

The Committee of Secret Correspondence to the American Commissioners

LS: American Philosophical Society; copies: Library of Congress; Yale University Library[7]

Gentlemen   Baltimore 9th January 1777

Captain Hammond having been detained longer than we expected,[8] furnishes us with an opportunity of giving you the information we have since our last received from the Army, thro a Committee of Congress left at Philadelphia; for we have yet had no regular accounts from General Washington. On the 2d. instant, General Washington having received information that the enemy were on their march to attack him at Trenton, ordered two brigades of militia to advance and annoy them on the road leading from Princeton to Trenton, who falling in with the enemy about 3 miles from the latter place, engaged them, but being overpower'd by numbers, made a retreating fight until they joined the main body who were drawn up on the heights west of a bridge that divides the village of Trenton nearly in two parts. The enemy attempting to force

7. The Yale copy has the following autograph notation: "Passy, Mar. 21. 1777. The above is a Copy of the Committee's last Letter. The preceding give an Acct. of the taking Prisoners 3 Battalions of Hessians at Trenton Dec. 26., of which I suppose you have already seen the particulars. BF."

8. Capt. Larkin Hammond, commanding the 10-gun schooner *Jenifer*, reappears a number of times after his arrival in Europe. He came of a prominent landed family in Maryland and was a captain in the state's navy. See Harry W. Newman, *Anne Arundel County Gentry* (Baltimore, 1933), pp. 214–15; Joshua D. Warfield, *The Founders of Anne Arundel and Howard Counties, Maryland* (Baltimore, 1905), p. 183; Smith, *Letters*, VI, 17 n.

the bridge were repulsed with loss by a body of men with artillery placed there to receive them. In the mean time some batteries being opened on the heights soon drove the enemy from that part of the Town possessed by them. Thus the affair ended for that evening. But General Washington having received intelligence that Gen. Howe was in person coming up to join his army with a strong reenforcement, directing fires to be made on the heights to deceive the enemy, decampt at midnight and made a forced march in order to meet Mr. Howe and give him battle before he joined his main body. About 3 miles short of Prince Town, the Van of our army fell in with 600 British Infantry Strongly posted behind a fence, and upon a hill, with artillery. They were attacked, and after a smart Engagement, routed, having lost 200 killed and taken prisonners; among whom, one Colonel, one Major, several Captains and subalterns were slain, and about 20 officers made prisoners. The fugitives were pursued thro Princeton where our army halted a while. In this affair 6 pieces of artillery with abundance of baggage fell into our hands. At Princeton it was learnt that Gen. Howe was not with this party, but that he remained at Brunswick with 3 or 4 thousand men. There being a considerable force in the rear, and our Men greatly fatigued with their march, and their baggage chiefly behind (it having been sent to Burlington) the General proceeded to Sommerset Court house that evening, a little to the Westward of the road leading to Brunswick, and about 7 or 9 miles from that place. Here we understand he expected to be joined by a body of 1500 or 2000 fresh troops and that his intention was to attack Mr. Howe in Brunswick. On friday morning, when the enemy at Trenton missed our army, they returned towards Princeton, but it seems, they left 3000 Hessians behind them, who following afterwards, were so fatigued with travel and want of food, that numbers were left on the road, and were straggling about the country in threes and fours. Many were taken by the Country people and brought in prisoners, many came to Trenton and surrendered themselves. The militia of Jersey were rising generally, and it was thought few of these Hessians would get back again. This is the present state of our information, and we hourly expect a well authenticated account of the whole, and of much greater successes. We shall endeavor to give you the speediest account of what shall further come to our knowledge from good authority. The above relation is taken from a Gentleman who was in the action, and who the Committee write us, is a person of sense and honor. The General has been too much engaged to write, and we suppose waits the final issue: We most earnestly wish you success in your negotiation, and are with perfect esteem, honorable Gentlemen, your most obedient and very humble Servants.

BENJ HARRISON
RICHARD HENRY LEE
in secret Committee

P.S. In the engagement near Princeton we lost 15 privates, one Colonel, and Brigadier Gen. Mercer a very good Officer and a worthy Gentleman.[9]

From Dangeul

January 9, 1777 See page 125n

From William Temple Franklin

ALS: American Philosophical Society

Honored Sir, Passy Jany. 9. 1777.

Mr. Chaumont desires me to inform you, that he has received a Letter from Mr. Montaudoin (whom you saw at Nantes) in which he mentions, and desires you may be informed of it; that there is a Scotchman arrived at Nantes, in a Dutch Vessel from New-York, who says, that General Howe had embarked ten thousand Men for the purpose of attacking Philadelphia.

Mr. Montaudoin likewise mentions that the 3d of this Month about 11 at Night he was much surprized at receiving a Visit from Mr. Decoudray who went from Harvre the fourteenth of December in the Amphetrite; that he had come into port in

---

9. For Hugh Mercer's earlier career see above, XXII, 526 n.

order to place ten or twelve passengers (out of 34) on board some American Vessels that were at Nantes, and that he was to set off the Day after for Port Louis.[10] I am Honored Sir your Dutiful Grandson   W T FRANKLIN.

Addressed: A Monsieur / Monsieur Franklin / Hotel D'anbourg, / ruë Jacob / Paris

Notation: W T. Franklin

From Le Roy

Jeudy matin [January 9, 1777?]

J'envoy savoir Mon cher Docteur des nouvelles de votre rhume. Hier au soir je voulus vous aller voir je ne pus trouver de voiture à cause du froid.

J'espere que M. Deane va mieux.[1] Vous savez combien je vous suis sincèrement attaché pour la vie.   LE ROY

J'ai lu hier un mémoire qu'on vous destine mais l'auteur a dans ce moment la goutte cruellement. Les vuës de ce mémoire me paroissent bien bonnes. J'aurai l'honneur et le plaisir de vous voir aujourdhui.

Addressed: a Monsieur / Monsieur Franklin / a l'hotel de Hambourg / ruë Jacob

The Baron de Rullecourt to the American Commissioners

[before January 10, 1777]   See the next headnote

10. The *Amphitrite* had put back into Lorient after seventeen days at sea because, according to Du Coudray, she proved to be inadequately equipped for the voyage. He and two of his officers and the captain of the ship then came to Nantes, supposedly to obtain charts and money. Du Coudray to Congress, Jan. 26, 1777, National Archives; Lasseray, *Les Français*, I, 106.

1. When the commissioners went to Versailles on Jan. 5 Deane was suffering from a fever that kept him to his room: Stevens, *Facsimiles*, VI, nos. 611, 615. Unless he was ill again later, Le Roy's remark strongly suggests the date we have assigned.

From L. B.

[before January 10, 1777]   See the next headnote

The Baron de Rullecourt: Proposed Agreement with Franklin

[before January 10, 1777]   See the next headnote

The American Commissioners to the Baron de Rullecourt[2]
Copy: University of Virginia Library[3]

This letter of appointment is the only dated record of one of the most bizarre schemes to which the commissioners ever lent themselves. A considerable amount of material about the plan is extant among Franklin's papers in the American Philosophical Society: two letters from the Baron to the commissioners, a proposed agreement between him and Franklin, and a memorandum to the Doctor from some one who identifies himself merely as "L.B." These documents are undated, but with one exception were undoubtedly written before the present letter. They are all related to that letter, even though we do not know precisely how, and for that reason we summarize them here.

What appears to be the earliest is a note from Rullecourt to the commissioners, to enclose a letter to them from the abbé Baudeau which they should answer promptly; a messenger will await their response at eight the next morning. The enclosed letter cannot be identified with certainty but was, we are inclined to believe, the memorandum mentioned above, entitled "Developpement de deux idées capitales communiquées au venerable docteur franklin par son serviteur et ami L.B."[4] The first idea is that an American embassy be established in Switzerland, with the writer as its secretary. The second, already explained to Dubourg, is for a Mediterranean cam-

2. See the note on Chaumont to BF above, under Jan. 4.
3. Two unsigned copies, with slightly different wording, are respectively in the APS and the British Library.
4. The abbé had been in contact with BF years before; hence he might have been expected to call himself his friend but scarcely "L.B." (unless for concealment) when his first name was Nicolas. See above, xix, 235–6 n.

paign: an ostensible commercial company based on Monaco, and using its flag, will collect ships and, with the secret consent of the King of the Two Sicilies, occupy and fortify the island of Lampedusa; the ships will scatter through the Mediterranean, and on a given date raise American colors and attack British commerce. The function of Lampedusa, and its garrison under Rullecourt's command, will be to protect the privateers once they have disposed of their prizes.

The proposed agreement between Franklin and Rullecourt appears to be somewhat later, for the base has shifted: Lampedusa, between Malta and Tunisia, has given place to the deserted Zaffarin Islands off the coast of Morocco. The Baron will hold them as governor for the United Colonies, and as soon as they are fortified will sail under the American flag against enemy commerce; he will have colonel's rank and will commission his own officers. His command will be at least five hundred men, with the same pay and maintenance as in the British army. Proceeds from prizes will be divided, part to defray the cost of the military establishment, part for the company providing the ships, and part for the soldiers and crews. Franklin will supply as far as possible sailors, supplies, etc., and Rullecourt will furnish the initial funds. Congress will ratify the agreement at the earliest feasible moment.

Rullecourt's second undated letter to the commissioners, probably written some weeks after the present letter of appointment, indicates that the secret was no longer between him and them. He had broached the scheme (if indeed it was the same one) to the man who could best ensure its success, M. "de Beaum . . . " Beaumarchais, to whom he presumably referred, had given a Delphic response: he would not meddle in the business but, if the commissioners asked him about it, would know what to reply. As for the rumor about Lord Stormont, Rullecourt added, it was doubtless false; in any case the suspicions of the British Ambassador would not outlast the Baron's departure.[5] There the story ends.[6] The newly enlisted

5. Not until late February, it seems, did Stormont get wind of the plan. It lay behind Arthur Lee's trip to Madrid, Paul Wentworth in London reported to Suffolk on March 3; Chaumont and Aranda were providing the money. The planners, Wentworth added two days later, were assuming the tacit support of Spain, which claimed sovereignty over the islands; the Moroccans might occupy them and defeat the whole scheme. Stevens, *Facsimiles*, II, no. 144; I, no. 54.

6. Two brief letters from Rullecourt to the commissioners, of Jan. 18 and 20 (University of Pa. Library), deal with obtaining a ship that seems to have been destined for America, and to have had no connection with the

American "Cheif of a Corps" remained in France, and the Zaffarin Islands remained deserted.

Sir,   Paris Jany. 10th. 1777
In the name and by the authority of the Congress of the United States of America, we take you into their service, as Cheif of a Corps, which you are to command, agreable to your plan, upon the deserted Zafarimes Islands.

We authorize you, as Commander in Cheif, to fortify and defend, the said Islands. And as we agree to your request to naturalize you and the officers of your Corps, you are allowed to carry the colours of the thirteen United States of America, and under them to combat their Enemies. Wishing you health and success, We are, Sir, Your sincere Friends

Signd. B. FRANKLIN
SILAS DEAN
ARTHUR LEE

To the Baron de Rullecourt Colonel of Infantry &c. &c.

From ———— Gloro   ALS: American Philosophical Society

⟨Hennebon, near Lorient, January 10, 1777, in French: I have served the Compagnie des Indes since 1752, and was returning from China in 1776 when my ship put in at Ascension Island to revictual and take on turtles. There I encountered a Mr. Benjamin Salter, out of St. Eustatius from Bermuda, waiting to make purchases from passing vessels. I made friends with him and sold him all I had brought with me, receiving two bills of exchange. The larger one, on a London merchant named William Cawthorne, was protested; Cawthorne was in debtors' prison and denied knowledge of the business. Salter knew that I faced ruin if not paid, and I trusted him so much that I never learned his address. I have since heard of a rich Philadelphia merchant of that name; can you give me infor-

---

Zaffarin scheme. The final extant letter from the Baron was on Sept. 7, 1777 (APS). In it he reverted to his proposal a year before to recruit a corps from those who had served with him in Poland, and from foreigners already in the United States.

mation, any means by which I may collect? Please do not let the ship's owners hear of my misadventure; they do not like such private business, although it is the only way that the underpaid can survive.)

From Nathan Rumsey

ALS: American Philosophical Society

Honorable Sir   Nantes Jany. 10th. 1777.

I have this day a letter from Mr. Guerin of Auray in which he requests me to let you know that he had forwarded for your perusal under Cover to the Count de Vergenes the Copy of a letter from the Admiralty officers of Vannes to those of Auray.

There appears to be a jealousy between these officers and Mr. Guerin, from the latter having ventured on such a purchase without their Consent; and they seem to be determined to give as much Trouble as possible.[7]

I doubt not, Sir, you have it in Your power to prevail with the Marine Officer to order those officers of Vannes to give over their researches, and to desist troubling Mr. Guerin, as, if these Matters are carried too far they may injure possibly the Sales of our Prizes hereafter. We have no Arrivall[?] since my last to You, and the Ice in this river drives so much that we cannot dispatch a single Vessel. With the utmost respect I am Honorable Sir your most obidient Humble Servant

NATHAN RUMSEY

Addressed: The Honorable / Doctor Benjamin Franklin / at / Paris.

Notation: N. Rumsey Jan 10. 77

7. Guérin had entered the office of the Intendant of Brittany as a clerk in 1758; he stayed there for thirty years, and eventually rose to be a *sous-chef.* Henri Freville, *L'Intendance de Bretagne, 1689–1790* (3 vols., Rennes, 1953), II, 16; III, 133. He had bought one of the prizes, a purchase of doubtful legality, and enlisted his brother in Paris to help in his troubles with the naval authorities. The brother wrote BF on Jan. 15 to urge him and Deane to solicit promptly, as BF had promised him the day before, the good offices of Sartine in settling the affair, and enclosed some news from Auray; on Jan. 30, in response to further news, he wrote again to repeat his urging. Both letters are in the APS.

From [Louis Dupas?] de Vallenais[8]

ALS: American Philosophical Society

Sir   Paris the 10th of January 1777

As you was very busy this morning, when I have been to present my respects to you: I would not be so bold as to disturb you; though I intended confering with you before my departure.

Mr. de Chaumont's Ship in which I was to embark has lately set sail; but I know there are several others ready to sail in two or three weeks time. They are directed to Mr. Grouet Merchant at Nante, which is your correspondent.

This present is to beg you the favour of guiving me also a letter for the said Mr. Grouet in order I may treat with him for the price of our passage to america. I bring a relation of mine along with me, which has been recommended to Mr. Dean by his commander in france.

Our intentions are not only to get in the american Service if it is possible; but we propose forming a solid establishment in the country very soon. We are determined to fix our dwelling place for Life in that free country.

Though we are born under the yoke of a despotic empire; Liberty, from our infancy, has ever been very dear to our hearts. It is with those Sentiments which are certainly valuable to every men who possess a little notion of themselves, I have the honour to be with profound respect Sir your most obedient and humble Servant   DE VALLENAIS

I beg your favour to present my [*torn*] to Mr. Dean, and my compliments to Mr. Williams.

I propose going too morrow morning in order to take my leave of you.

Addressed: A Monsieur / Monsieur franquelin / hotel de hambourg / rue Jacob fauxbourg / St Germain / A Paris

Notation: De Vallenas

8. He joined the American cavalry in 1777, at about the same time as La Balme, and became his aide with the rank of captain; he apparently quit the service in August, 1778. Fitzpatrick, *Writings of Washington*, XII, 373 n; Lasseray, *Les Français*, II, 462–3, where his Christian names are tentatively suggested.

[Samuel Wharton to Edward Bancroft] with a Postscript to Franklin[1]

AL: American Philosophical Society

Dear Sir   London January 10 1777

I am still without any of your Favors, although two Mails arrived Yesterday. I am wholly at a Loss to account for your not answering my several Letters, and can only ascribe it to Illness, or an Interception of Yours. I will however persevere in my Correspondence, While, I think, There is a possibility, of my being any Ways useful. The Report of ten thousand more Foreigners being to be sent early in the Spring to America (as I mentioned in my last) gains Ground, and it is now confidently said, They are to consist of Brunswickers Hessians, Hanoverians &c., and are to be commanded by Burgoyne, Who is to be employed to the *Southward.* It was this Morning affirmed in the City by Governmental People, That One hundred Sail of Transports are to be engaged for this Service. 82 has told all the 16, That Lord Cornwallis had obtained possession of Brunswick, without the least Opposition; That He found three Months provission for his Army there, was supplied by the Inhabitants, and neighbouring Farmers with Plenty of fresh Meat; and That the Retreat of the Provincials was so precipitate, They had not *Even broken the Bridges on the* Road thither; and That, as the Inlistment of the American Army was expired, The greater part of it, had returned to their respective Homes, and were determined, *not* to inlist again. It was currently asserted a few Days ago, That Doctor Price had received a Letter from Dr. Franklin, informing Him, That a Treaty had been signed between America, France and Spain. I was prevailed On to apply to Dr. Price, To know Whether there was any Degree of Truth in the report, and my Application was kindly answered, by the inclosed Letter from Him Which by Desire of 81, I send to 74, as a Confirmation of the Opinion, He last Year published. I understand from 81, That

---

1. Wharton is identified by the handwriting and the intended recipient by a change in the postscript: "your" was deleted and became "Dr. Bancroft's."

Dr. Price's Character is well known, and esteemed for Financial Knowledge by 227, and That a Use may Possibly be made of his Letter:[2] At all Events however, The sending it to You, can do no Harm. The Correspondence by the Post, grows daily more and more dangerous, and Uncertain, I wish therefore you would suggest to Dr. Franklin, That if a Courier was dispatched from Hence *to Calais*, on *Tuesdays*, as well as Fridays, It would afford a constant, certain and safe Mode of Communication twice a Week. The Expence could easily be settled between France and America. Pray desire the Favor of Dr. Franklin to send me some ostensible Name, Wherby I may safely write to Him any Thing of Importance.[3] My best Respects wait on the Doctor, and Mr. Deane. Adieu Yours affectionately   #

Friday Night 10. oClock.[4] Just as I was sealing my Letter, Dr. Bancroft's Favor of the 30th of December was brought to Me. The Mail, however, arrived *Wednesday* Night. The Letter had been opened; But as Nothing could be collected from it, It was after Two Days suffered to be sent to its Direction. I trouble my Friend Doctor Franklin with the foregoing, as Dr. Bancroft will most probably have left Paris.

Rullecourt to the American Commissioners

[after January 10, 1777]   See page 146

2. We cannot identify any of the people for whom the code numbers stand. What was "currently" reported (the adverb may also be read as "correctly") was beyond question erroneous. Richard Price's answering letter seems to have disappeared; whether it confirmed an opinion that he had published, probably in *Observations on the Nature of Civil Liberty*, or that 74 had published is, given Wharton's debonair attitude toward antecedents, wide open to conjecture.

3. BF promptly obliged by adopting the alias of M. François; see his letter to Mary Hewson below, Jan. 26.

4. Jan. 10.

[Duportail and the American Commissioners]: Memorandum on Terms of Service[5]

D: American Philosophical Society

[January 11, 1777]

1. M. de Portal demands to be at the Head of the Corps d'Ingenieurs in America: and under the Orders only of the General, or the Commander in chief in the Place where he may be.

2. He demands a Rank superior to that he enjoys at present, which is Major in the marine Infantry.

3. He proposes to take two Captains of the same Professions with him: to whom should be given in America the Rank superior.

4. That himself and his Friends shall be at Liberty to quit the Service and return to France when they please except in the middle of a Campaign.

The Gentlemen are willing to give the Chevalier de Portal the rank of Lieutenant Colonel and the Gentlemen he mentions that of Major, when their names are made known to them so that they may inform themselves of their qualifications which they shall do with every necessary precaution. They cannot do so much in justice to Gentlemen who have been from the beginning in the service of the States as to advance Strangers suddenly above them.

Notation in BF's hand: M. de P——l's Proposals

Lambert Wickes to the American Commissioners

ALS: American Philosophical Society

Gentlemen   Nantz January 11th. 1777

Immediately After the Receipt of your favr of 26th Decr. I Set out for L Orient and have Executed the Businss you Desird there in the best maner The time and Surcumstances Would

5. The first half of this memorandum is in WTF's hand, the second in Arthur Lee's. The document was undoubtedly the product of Duportail's interview with the commissioners on Jan. 11 (referred to in his letter below of the 12th), which seems to have settled only two of the Major's four conditions. He reiterated them all when he wrote the next day, with slight changes, and added four new ones.

Admitt. I have no Great Appinon of the 60 Gunn Ship As Shee is an Oald Ship and A very Slow Sailer. Another Very Great Objecktion is her Draft Water being to much for our American ports very few of our ports Would have Water Enoughf for her to Enter in at As Shee Will Draw 21 or 22 feet Water. I think the Friggates Are better vessails and much Better for our purpose as thier Draft Water Will be only 16 or 17 feet and Am perswaided they Will Sail much faster Esspetially the St. John. Shee is Entirely new built from the Keel and has All her Spars Riging Sails Anchors Cable and All other Materals Quite New. Shee has the Carrecktor of A prime Sailer they have prommised to Furnish A Compleat Inventory of All her Riging Sails Stores And materals Which I Exspect to Receive to morrow or Next Day and if Not Stopt by your order I Shall Immediately Set of for Parris on the Receipt of The Inventory. I have had A full veiw of the Ship and her Materals and Like her Well Her Materals are All new and of the first Qualety.[6] There is Another 36 Guns Friggate and a Ship that mounts 50 Guns on two Decks boath of these vessails have the Carrecktors of prime Sailors but I Am Affeard they Are too Antient and Tender for our purpose therefore they Would Want over Halling and a Good out fitt before they Could Go to See. The St. john is All new and May be fitt for Sea in a month or 6 Weeks She is mounted With 26 twelv pounders on one Deck and 10 Six pounders on the Quarter Deck and fore Castle her Dementions is 114 feet Keel 36 feet Beam 13 feet Hoald and 6 feet Between decks. I think they Can Well Afford to Sell this Ship for £12000 Sterling haveing formd my jugment on the best Information I Could Get of the prices of Ships and Materals at L Orient. I Dare Say provided it Suites you to purchase the Cargo you May Get her At that price the Cargo Consists Cheifly of Led Copper Cordage Canvis and Large Anchors Which is Much Wanted in America. I Was on bord of the Ship that Put into L Orient from Haver de grass[7] and found her So Much Lumbered and Short of provistion that I think they Did Well to put in and Get a

---

6. For Wickes's mission to Lorient see his letters to the commissioners above, Jan. 4, and for further negotiations about the *St. John* those below, Jan. 14 and 18.

7. The *Amphitrite*.

Supply. On findeing them So Crowded I Advised General Decorated [Du Coudray] to Leav Some of his most Useles officers behind Which he Did to Get Passages Elsewhere he has Dischargd 12 or 13 and Sent the Rest forward in the Ship. He Got Her Water'd and Supplyed With provistions As Soon As possible and Sent her of for fear of haveing her Stopt. he is to Come to Nantz and may Possibly be At Parris before he Leavs France. This Business I Performd at the Request of the General and thought it [*torn*] To Make my Report to you Accordingly. I Am With much Respect Gentlemen your most Obligd Humble S[ervant]   LAMBT. WICKES

Addressed: The Honorable / Doctor Benjamin Franklyn / at / Paris.

Notation: Capt Wecks Nantes 11 Jany 77

From Barbeu-Dubourg

[*c.* January 11, 1777]   See page 155n

From Thomas-Antoine de Mauduit, Chevalier du Plessis[8]

AL: American Philosophical Society

[*c.* January 11?, 1777[9]]

De Mauduit Chevalier du plessis, Lieutenant au corps royal d'artillerie, agé de 22 ans, né au plessis près Lorient en bre-

8. The chevalier (*c.* 1754–91) ran away from the artillery school at Grenoble, at the age of twelve, with two friends; they shipped as cabin boys to the Near East and came down with fever at Alexandria, where his companions died. He made his way to Constantinople, the French Ambassador sent him home, and he resumed his military training. Balch, *French in America*, II, 176–8. He went to America as a volunteer at his own expense, served with distinction in the Philadelphia campaign, and was breveted lieutenant colonel by Congress in January, 1778: *JCC*, x, 64. He sent a copy of the Congressional resolution, with thanks for BF's good offices and a request to pass on thanks to those who had recommended him: to BF, May 4, 1778, APS.

9. Du Plessis was in Nantes by Jan. 21, and clearly had by then BF's endorsement (see JW to BF below, Jan. 21, 27); we assume that he took ten

tagne brûle d'envie de passer chez les insurgens, il demande le même traitement qu'on a dejà fait aux officièrs de son grade qui y sont passé.

Depuis près de 8 ans il sert, au corps royal, s'est beaucoup appliqué a son métier, et se flate que ses generaux sont satisfaits de son zele.

Il jouit d'une excellente santé, et est habitué a toutes sortes de fatigues ayant dejà voyagé pendant 20 mois en europe, asie et afrique. Le jeune homme a si bonne volonté de bien faire, qu'il desireroit voir doubler son existence, pour les perdre au service d'une nation à qui il jure le plus entier devouement; le chevalier de Mauduit voudroit pouvoir exprimer dignement tout ce qu'il pense, mais il a le coeur si plein que lui seul a fait les frais de ce qu'il écrit dans ce moment-ci. Il éprouve combien l'esprit est muet quand le coeur parle.

Addressed in another hand: A Mr le docteur franclin / de boston / a l'hôtel d'hambourg rue jacob / fauxbourg st germain

Notation: Memoire sur le Sieur Mauduit

From Mauduit du Plessis

[*c.* January 11, 1777]   See the preceding note

To Mary Hewson   ALS: Yale University Library

My dear dear Polley   Paris, Jan. 12. 1777.

Figure to yourself an old Man with grey Hair appearing under a Martin Fur Cap, among the Powder'd Heads of Paris.[1]

---

days or so to obtain it, wind up his affairs, and reach Nantes. Support from the marquis de Courtanvaux may have facilitated his acceptance. At about this time Courtanvaux informed BF, through Dubourg, that he had equally good things to say about another artillery officer; Dubourg's note, undated and unsigned but identifiable by the handwriting, is in the APS. So is a note in Du Plessis' hand, giving his Paris address and saying that Dubourg and Courtanvaux have already spoken well of him.

1. This is the first appearance of BF's famous cap. He had brought it back from his journey to Canada months before, and wore it often during his first winter in Paris instead of the conventional wig; the public identified it with him, and it acquired symbolic status. See Charles C. Sellers, *Benjamin*

It is this odd Figure that salutes you; with Handfuls of Blessings on you and your dear little ones.

On my Arrival here, Mlle. Biheron gave me great Pleasure in the Perusal of a Letter from you to her.[2] It acquainted me that you and yours were well in August last. I have with me here my young Grandson Benja Franklin Bache, a special good Boy. I give him a little French Language and Address, and then send him over to pay his Respects to Miss Hewson.[3]

My Love to all that love you, particularly to dear Dolly.[4] I am ever, my dear Friend, Your affectionate   B F.

Temple who attends me here presents his Respects. I must contrive to get you to America. I want all my Friends out of that wicked Country. I have just read in s[ome?] Newspapers 7 Paragraphs about me, of which 6 were Lies.

To Thomas Walpole   ALS: David Holland, London (1955)

This letter, the first in a brief correspondence with Walpole during the next two months about the affairs of the Walpole or Grand Ohio Company, touches an important question: to what extent, if any, did Franklin's connection with the Company affect his conduct as a diplomat? He seems here to be severing the connection, but in fact he retained it; and it later brought him under suspicion, as he must have known it would. When Congress decided to create an expanded commission to negotiate peace, it refused at first to put Franklin on it because, as a member of the Company, he was interested "in territorial claims which had less chance of being made good in any other way, than by a repossession of the vacant country by the British Crown."[5] If the west were returned to Britain, in other

---

Franklin in Portraiture (New Haven and London, 1962), pp. 96–9. In late January, nevertheless, BF spent just over 100 *l.t.* for wigs: Waste Book, entry of Feb. 8.

2. Marie-Catherine Biheron was an old acquaintance of the Hewsons as well as of BF: above, XXI, 331–2.

3. The old dream that Benny would marry Elizabeth.

4. See BF's inquiries about Dorothea Blunt in his letter below, Jan. 26.

5. William T. Hutchinson *et al.*, eds., *The Papers of James Madison* (13 vols. to date, Chicago and Charlottesville, 1962–), V, 467; see also p. 470 n. Arthur Lee made the same point without mentioning BF: Burnett, *Letters*,

words, and if the Walpole grant were then revived in London, Franklin would stand to gain. No one can say for sure that he ignored these "if's." But the record of his relationship with the Company, meager as it is, suggests that he did. When he was asked for and submitted his resignation in 1774, the period of his major involvement was over. He had concluded the year before that part of the grant the Company was seeking, the cession to the "suffering traders" on which the Indiana Company based its claim, needed no confirmation by the crown.[6] In 1775–76 he supported moves to market land in America without recourse to London. It is unclear whether the moves were confined from the start to the cession from the Indians, or embraced the whole Walpole grant, which included that tract and what the crown had purchased; but by early 1776 the focus of attention was the tract.[7] In the years that followed, to judge by such meager evidence as there is, the promoters seem to have kept open both options: they maintained that their title to the Indiana grant was valid in itself, and they attempted to purchase from some American authority the rest of the Walpole grant or, failing that, to obtain compensation for their claim. Franklin is optimistic here about such a purchase from Virginia. Three years later, when that hope had evaporated, he and Samuel Wharton petitioned Congress for compensation.[8]

In the present letter he is asking to have back his money. He had paid Walpole £200 apiece for his and William Franklin's two shares. (Galloway's, which he had also handled, was now dissociated from them.) They were not shares in the modern sense of stock certificates, but shares in the land for which the Company was hoping; and shareholders paid pro rata assessments for the expected purchase from the British Treasury and for attendant expenses. These assessments Franklin had paid.[9] Now that the purchase was no longer expected, Walpole was settling the last expenses and returning each

---

VI, 331. Thomas P. Abernethy echoes this suspicion: *Western Lands and the American Revolution* (New York and London, 1937), p. 285; Cecil B. Currey carries it much further, without benefit of evidence: *Code Number 72: Ben Franklin Patriot or Spy?* (Englewood Cliffs, N.J., [1972]), pp. 267–9.

6. Above, XX, 302–4.

7. Above, XXII, 19, 102–3, 325–6.

8. Bigelow, *Works*, X, 346–71.

9. Above, XIX, 140; XX, 326 n. Galloway had reimbursed BF for this payment: Jour., pp. 50, 57; Ledger, p. 55. WF, as far as we can determine from his father's accounts, had not; what was left of the £400 was therefore BF's alone.

member the balance due him.[1] When Franklin received his reimbursement, his financial tie to the Company ended.

But his interest did not. He retained the right to two shares, from which he hoped his descendants would benefit—the right, that is, to participate in any future land grant that might come out of the Company's initial efforts. We have no evidence whatever that he expected such a grant to emanate from Whitehall, in the event that Britain won the war or at least retained the west. All his expectations after 1773, on the contrary, seem to have ignored the British government. In 1778, when he recovered his letter of resignation from the Company and the grant had long been a lost cause in Whitehall, he noted that the shares were still valid.[2] Two years later he petitioned Congress for compensation. There the record ends. Brief as it is, it indicates that he considered his land claims as an important part of his estate, perhaps important enough to risk their being misunderstood. It also suggests, in the absence of opposing evidence, that during the war he looked solely to American authority for furthering those claims.

Dear Sir,   Paris, Jan. 12. 1777

I hope this will find you and your amiable Family well and happy.

I left Major Trent well. He had Thoughts of applying to Congress relating to the Lands of our Purchase, but was dissuaded by Mr. Galloway.[3] I had some Information that Virginia, which claims all the Crown Lands within its Boundary, will not dispute that Purchase with us, but expects the Purchase-Money to be paid into their Treasury. It may be long before

1. See his letters below, Feb. 1, 10, March 5.

2. Above, XXI, 32–3. In the first days of 1778 BF dined with Deane, Bancroft, and Paul Wentworth at Le Ray de Chaumont's. The group offered bets, Wentworth reported, that America would be independent and "that Vandalia was to be the Paradise on Earth." Stevens, *Facsimiles*, V, no. 489. The possible rights of the crown seem, at least on that occasion, to have been on no one's mind.

3. Galloway had good reason to dissuade, because the application implied a degree of Congressional authority that was anathema to him. The political hopelessness of the proposal may have deterred Trent: if it had been made before the Declaration of Independence it would have evoked the same opposition that induced BF to withdraw his Articles of Confederation (above, XXII, 120–1), and if made later it would have exacerbated the controversy over the states' land claims.

these Matters can be adjusted;[4] and longer still before we shall see Peace. Had Lord Chatham's first wise Motion for withdrawing the Troops, been attended to by your mad Ministry; or his Plan of Accommodation been accepted and carried into Execution, all this Mischief might have been prevented. If that great Man be yet living, I pray you to present my affectionate Respects to him, and also to Lord Camden.[5]

As the Money I left with your good Brother[6] cannot now be of any Use to me in England, I request a Letter of Credit for the Amount on some Banker here: I mean the Money for my two Shares. That of Mr. Galloway's will remain for his Order.

I should certainly be glad to have a Line from you, but I cannot ask it, because it may not be convenient in your Situation. But I shall always be happy in hearing of your Welfare by any means, being with sincere Esteem and Affection, Your most obedient humble Servant   B FRANKLIN

Addressed:[7] Honble Thos Walpole Esqe / London / per favour of / Dr Bancroft

From [Duportail]   AL: American Philosophical Society

Monsieur   [January 12, 1777[8]]
J'ai l'honneur de vous envoyer quelques nouvelles conditions que je desirerois entrer dans notre arrangement avec celles que nous avons ecrites hyer. J'en useray de même s'il me vient encore à l'esprit quelque chose d'important qui doive estre arreté d'avance entre nous.

4. The information was wrong and the prediction right. Virginia had made clear, before BF's departure, that it would uphold its land claims: when the reorganized Indiana Co. attempted to market land in early 1776, the state convention put a stop to its operations. From 1779 on the promoters turned to Congress, again without success. Lewis, *Indiana Co.*, pp. [199]–222.

5. Walpole had been a channel of BF's communication with both Chatham and Camden in 1775: above, XXI, 519, 598–9.

6. Richard, for whom see above, XVI, 167 n.

7. The address could not be photographed and was supplied us by the owner.

8. So dated in his next letter below, Jan. 16.

Comme il est juste que vous prenièz de votre coté les informations necessaires sur ce qui me concerne, je vous prie de le faire avec les plus grandes précautions. Je suis d'ailleurs assèz connu des gens au courant des affaires, etant depuis six mois auprès du ministre de la guerre pour travailler à une nouvelle ordonnance du corps du genie qui va paroistre, et ce fait, s'il m'est permis de le dire, vous temoigne que je jouis de quelque consideration dans mon etat.

Je vous prie instamment, monsieur, de ne rien montrer à qui que ce soit d'écrit de ma main, parce qu'il est sur que, si le bruit se repandoit de mon depart pour l'amerique, le ministre ne me laisseroit plus sortir de france ny moy ny aucun officier du corps. J'ai l'honneur d'etre etc.

lere. Condition. Que le gouvernement des colonies unies me donnera un grade superieur [*interlined*: le brevet de colonel] à celuy dont j'auray le brevet en france au moment de mon depart.⁹

2°. Que je seray chef dans ma partie et qu'a l'armée et dans les places je ne repondray qu'au general où à celuy qui commendera en chef les troupes.

Dans le cas cependant ou l'officier qui est presentement à la tête du genie et moy nous trouverions dans le même lieu, je pourrois estre à ses ordres s'il avoit un grade superieur au mien où plus d'ancienneté dans le même grade.

Mr. de laumoy aura le brevet de lieutenant colonel.¹

3°. Que l'officier où les officiers du genie qui viendront avec moy recevront de même du gouvernement un grade superieur à celuy qu'ils auront en france au moment de leur depart.

Mr. de gouvion celuy de major.²

9. The interlineation has no caret; we have placed it where we presume he meant it to be. At the time he was a major, but expected soon to be breveted lieutenant colonel, as he was; see his letter below, Jan. 25.

1. Jean-Baptiste-Joseph, Chevalier de Laumoy (1750–1832), had been commissioned captain of engineers on Jan. 1. He received a brevet majority before sailing, when Duportail and Gouvion were promoted; see Duportail's letter below, Jan. 25. In the formal agreement below, Feb. 13, Laumoy was assured of a lieutenant colonelcy in the American army. By the end of the war he was a brigadier general. Lasseray, *Les Français*, I, 269–71.

2. Jean-Baptiste de Gouvion (1747–92) had been commissioned first lieutenant of engineers in 1771, and was breveted captain before his depar-

4°. Que les uns et les autres nous serons libres de quitter le service des colonies quand nous le desirerons, bien entendu pourtant que ce ne sera pas au milieu d'une campagne ou d'une besogne commencee. On voudra bien s'en rapporter sur cela aux sentiments d'honneur dont les officiers francois ont toujours fait profession.

Le gouvernement americain pourra de son coté nous remercier quand il le jugera à propos.

5°. Que dans le cas où nous serions pris par les anglois dans la traversée ou dans le pays, le Congrès emploira franchement et loyalement tous les moyens qu'il pourra pour nous procurer notre liberté.

6°. Qu'en general le gouvernement americain nous traitera à tous egards comme doivent l'etre des officiers qui sans que rien les y oblige viennent risquer leur vie ou leur liberté pour son service.

7°. Que les appointemens et traitements selon leur [*interlined, notre*] grade courront depuis le jour de l'embarquement en france.[3]

8°. Que Messieurs les deputés des colonies prendront les mesures necessaires pour que dans le vaisseau nous soyons logés et traités aussi bien que cela sera possible.

Ces messieurs voudroient bien me dire aussi quelles sont les choses dont il faut se munir pour l'habillement etc.

Comme dans l'etablissement d'une place considerable il faut des instrumens tels que graphometre, boussole etc. et qu'il n'y en à pas peut-estre dans le pays, il seroit à propos d'en faire l'achat. Si nous convenons avec ces messieurs, je chercheray tout ce qui peut m'etre necessaire dans l'exercice de ma profession.

ture; he went as a major and by the end of the war was a colonel. *Ibid.*, pp. 234–5.

3. The 2nd, 6th, and 7th articles are marked as if they have been deleted.

From Juliana Ritchie[4]

ALS: American Philosophical Society

Sir   Cambray 12th Janry. 1777.

The agreeable manner in which I lived for several years in the (once happy) Citty of Philadelphia made too deep an impression upon my mind for either time, distance or the vicissitudes of fortune to erase; you will not be surprised, Sir, after this declaration, when I inform you that the unhappy situation of the affairs of America, has caus'd me to pass many Days in painful anxiety, and sleepless nights since the commencement of the present warr with England, hopeing and fearing alternately, for the safety of the country in General but more perticulerly for the fate of those whom repeated acts of friendship and kindness rendered truely dear to my heart. It is from these sentiments that I take the liberty of addressing you Sir, being fully perswaded (from the knowledge I have of your amiable character) that you will not only pardon the freedom I am now takeing, but will allso keep the purport of this letter from the knowledge of any other Person, or otherwise I shall be involved in *great trouble*. But I am quite easy upon that head, knowing that it is to a Gentleman of integrity I am writeing, and therfore without further preface, I proceed to the purpose of this letter, which is to inform you Sir, that you are Surrounded *with Spies*, who watch your every movement who you Visit, and by whom you are visited. Of the latter there are who pretend to be friends to the cause of your country but *that* is a mere pretence. Your own good sence will easily infer the *motive* of *their conduct*. One *Party* assures that you are seeking aid and support from *this Kingdom* the other *Party* insinuate

4. This is the first letter in a correspondence that continued intermittently until 1782. We know little of Mrs. Ritchie beyond what she tells of herself. She may have known the Franklins years before in Philadelphia but, as she remarked in writing BF on March 5, 1780 (APS), had never met him. Smyth identifies her husband without explanation as William Ritchie, a Philadelphia merchant: *Writings*, VII, 11 n. The pair had separated in 1765, and she had gone home to London, where she befriended Elizabeth Graeme: *PMHB*, XXXIX (1915), 279–81. Mrs. Ritchie lived on a meager trust fund, and emigrated to Cambrai because a relative was abbess of the English Benedictine convent there and living was cheaper than in Britain: to BF, April 18, 1780, APS. BF's reply to the present letter is below, Jan. 19.

that you have given up *that Cause* and are makeing the *best terms* you can for the private advantage of your own family connections &c. I dare not be more explicit for weighty reasons to my self, but of the truth of what I inform you, you may strictly rely. As I am ignorant of your address I send this to Messrs. Le Normond & Co. Rue St. Honory to deliver to your own hand, and shall rejoice to know that you have received it safe. If at your leisure you favor me with a few lines, please to address me at Cambrai. That address will be sufficient as I have resided here for two years with five young Ladies of fortune (Doughters to my perticuler friends in England) who are all under my Care. We return to England in the spring season,[5] where if I can render you any acceptable service, to know your Commands will give me real pleasure. I make no doubt but you have many abler friends, but I am sure none more willing then my self. I hope you left Mrs. Franklin and your Do[ughter] well, an account whereof will give me pleasure.

I had a letter from my husband a few Days since, but He does not mention the affairs of America.[6] I have the honor to be with great esteem Sir your humble Servant

JULIANA RITCHIE

Benjn. Franklin Esqr.

Addressed: To be delivered into the / hand of Benjomin Franklin Esqr. / lately arrived at Paris from / America.

Notations: Mrs Ritchey Jany 1777 / Letter from Mrs Ritchey with the Answer in

5. But only for a time; the party returned to Cambrai and remained another year or so, after which Mrs. Ritchie stayed on by herself; see the letter of April 18, 1780.

6. Her husband's letters stopped late in 1777, and her mounting anxiety for word of him accounted for her later correspondence with BF. In the letter of March 5, 1780, she mentioned that Ritchie had been with the American troops, which makes us suspect that he was the William Ritchie who was a matross, or gunner's helper, and was blinded by exploding powder in November, 1777: *PMHB*, XLII (1918), 164–5.

The King's Answer to the American Commissioners

D and two drafts: Archives du Ministère des affaires étrangères

Vergennes had required time to consider the commissioners' propositions in their letter of January 5, but discussion of them began almost immediately in the highest circle of government. On the 7th some one, presumably at Versailles, wrote a longwinded memorandum on the crisis that confronted France. The hand cannot be identified, and the author spoke of himself as a private citizen; but the position he took was at bottom remarkably similar to Vergennes', and he appears to have been writing for the eyes of the King and his advisers. The United States had two alternatives, the author argued, either to obtain effective French assistance or to offer Britain, in return for recognition of American independence, a military alliance for conquering the French West Indies; if Versailles did assist, the British would be ousted from the Caribbean and lose half their power, which France would gain.[7] On the 8th the King and Maurepas saw a condensed version of the commissioners' letter.[8] At about the same time Vergennes made two drafts in his own hand of what became this reply; the second draft was presented to Louis on the 9th, in Maurepas' presence, and received royal approval.[9] Gérard then made a copy with insignificant changes, the text printed here. It in turn was approved, and four days later was read to the commissioners.

The anonymous memorandum of the 7th and the *réponse verbale* of the 9th reflect the dilemma in which the court found itself. Policy dictated avoiding a war for which the navy was not yet ready, but also avoiding an American rapprochement with Britain that would be disastrous for France. The memorandum emphasized the second point, and the gains to be won by direct involvement. The *réponse verbale* was more cautious: it renounced such involvement for the moment but only for the moment ("ce qui semble encore eloigné peut se raprocher"), and it ended with a promise of further "secours secrets." Although these were too secret to be put on paper, even a paper to be read aloud, Gérard explained the meaning; and what he told the commissioners accounts for the enthusiasm of their reply the next day.

7. Stevens, *Facsimiles*, VI, no. 619.
8. Doniol, *Histoire*, II, 118–19.
9. Stevens, *op, cit.*, nos. 621–2.

Reponse verbale aux Deputés du Congrés des États unis de l'Amerique septentrionale

Il a eté rendu compte au Roi du contenu du memoire de Messieurs les Deputés du Congrés de l'amerique.

Sa Majesté souhaiteroit que les circonstances lui permissent de se desaisir d'une partie de ses vaisseaux. Elle en feroit volontiers le sacrifice gratuit; mais elles exigent plutot que Sa Majesté s'attache à augmenter la masse de ses forces navales et c'est ce dont elle est occupee. On doit considerer d'ailleurs que l'envoi de 8. vaisseaux sur les parages de l'amerique n'y changeroient pas la face des affaires. Aussi puissament armés que les anglois le sont en Europe, ils envoyeroient bientot une escadre bien superieure qui reduiroit l'autre à l'inaction. La france en se pretant à cette requisition se compromettroit donc ouvertement sans qu'il en resultat aucun avantage pour la partie qu'Elle auroit voulu assister. Il ne faut pas se tromper; un secours ostensible est un motif legitime de guerre pour la nation contre laquelle il est administré.

Les memes raisons qui militent contre le pret des vaisseaux, s'opposent egalement à la concession des convois. Ceux-ci doivent etre la consequence et non pas le preliminaire de la guerre. Il seroit contraire a la dignité et à la justice d'une grande puissance d'y tendre par des moyens detournés. C'est par le sentiment et la necessité de ses grands interrets qu'elle peut et doit y etre conduite. Ce qui semble encore eloigné peut se raprocher; mais on ne peut anticiper sur le cours des evenemens. Il faut les attendre et se tenir en mesure d'en profiter. Ce sera le moment de s'entendre et de mettre des fondemens solides à une union, dont le desir est deja subsistant et qu'il sera d'autant plus facile de rendre indisoluble qu'il n'existe aucune vue de la part de la france et de l'espagne qui puissent froisser les interets des provinces unies et exciter leur jalousie ou leur causer des inquietudes.

La france et l'espagne faisant jouir les americains de toutes les facilités qu'elles accordent dans leurs ports aux nations amies font suffisament connoitre leur facon de penser pour les provinces unies. Que pourroit on exiger de plus d'elles? Ce n'est pas une guerre embarquée legerement qui pourroit former un point de reunion solide. Ce seroit plutot s'ecarter de l'objet qu'on doit se proposer respectivement et qui peut resulter du cours naturel des evenemens.

La france ne gene point les americains dans l'extraction des resources qu'ils peuvent se procurer par le commerce mais elle leur recommande de se conformer de leur part à toutes les regles prescrites sur le sens precis et rigoureux des Traités, auxquels le Roi ne veut point etre le premier à contrevenir. Il n'est pas possible d'entrer dans le detail des diverses fournitures dont on peut avoir besoin, mais Sa Majesté voulant marquer sa bienveillance et sa bonne volonté aux provinces unies, elle leur destine des secours secrets propres à etendre leur credit et à faciliter leurs achats.

Au bas est ecrit de la main du Roi *approuvé*.

Notation: Presenté au Roi en presence de M. le C. de Maurepas le 9. Janvier 1777. et aux dits Deputés par le Sieur Gerard le 13.

From the Baron de Bissy[1] and Dangeul

AL: American Philosophical Society

Paris ce 13. Janvier 1777.

Comme Mr. le Baron de Bissy en faisant ressouvenir Monsieur le Docteur francklin, aura peut être oublié de lui parler

---

1. Most of what we know about Stephano, Baron de Bissy, is in a memorandum that he addressed to the U.S. "Senate" on Dec. 15, 1776 (University of Pa. Library); a duplicate, dated Feb. 6, 1777, is in the APS and bears a notation by BF: "Memoire from a Person who has some Ingenuity, but seems at present a little *extra*. I was oblig'd to promise a Friend that I would send it to Congress. [*In another hand:*] B. Franklin." Bissy, according to his memorandum, came of a Lombard family and was in his late forties, with an English wife and four children. He was an inventor and artilleryman who had served on land and sea; he claimed to have a secret weapon, as yet untested in action but of enormous power, and gave no hint of what it was. He asked to be a lieutenant general (he was then a captain) with a staff of fifty, all captains or higher, whom he would recruit; Congress would pay their expenses from the day of enlistment, and each would receive a land grant proportioned to his rank. This was the bizarre document that BF reluctantly forwarded. Bissy later invited him to witness a demonstration of his weapon: below, Sept. 14, 1777. It was probably a new kind of oar for

de l'heure de diner chez M. de Dangeul, laquelle sera *Two o'clock precisely Tomorrow*.[2] On lui en renouvelle l'avis: Mr. le Docteur n'y trouvera que quatre ou cinq amis de M. de Dangeul et des Insurgens, y compris le Baron de Bissy. M. de Dangeul fancied that it would be more convenient and agreeable to him, to whom he present his best compliments. Moonday, 14 Jany. 1777.

M. francklin.

Addressed: A Monsieur / Monsieur franckelin / à l'hotel d'ambourg / Rue Jacob.

From —— Blondel de Lantone[3]

ALS: American Philosophical Society

This letter is the first in a series from writers who sought, to the best of our knowledge unsuccessfully, employment in the American armed services either for themselves or for others, usually their sons. We publish the earliest letter as a sample, and summarize here the others that fall within the scope of this volume.[4] They seem to have produced nothing, not even an answer from Franklin; but they do throw some light on his situation, and more on that of the French military in the wake of the reforms by which Saint-Germain, the Minister of War, had reduced or eliminated a number of army units. The letters came from men about whom we have little or no information and who were presumably unknown to Franklin. Unless otherwise noted they are all among his papers in the American Philosophical Society.

warships. Bissy had been pestering the Academy with this idea since 1774; three successive committees investigated it, and it was gently but firmly rejected. Archives de l'Academie royale des sciences, procès-verbaux, XCVI (1777), July 19, Nov. 23, Dec. 23.

2. The note to this point is in an unidentified hand; the rest is in Dangeul's.

3. Or Blondel des Moulins, a young Norman who had been in the gendarmerie and later became a captain in the regiment of Maine. Bodinier.

4. The letters that had no results continued for years, and we plan summaries like this one in future volumes. The fullest discussion of the entire group of unsuccessful commission-seekers is Catherine M. Prelinger, "Less Lucky than Lafayette: a Note on the French Applicants to Benjamin Franklin for Commissions in the American Army, 1776–1785," *Western Soc. for French History Proc.*, IV (1977), 263–70.

These writers, it must be remembered, were only a small sample of the suitors whom Franklin had to endure. Many others insisted on seeing him, and they made his life miserable. "You can have no Conception how I am harrass'd. All my Friends are sought out and teiz'd to teaze me. Great Officers of all Ranks, in all Departments; Ladies, great and small, besides professed Sollicitors, worry me from Morning to Night. The Noise of every coach now that enters my Court terrifies me. I am afraid to accept an invitation to dine abroad, being almost sure of meeting with some Officer or Officer's Friend, who, as soon as I am put in good Humour by a Glass or two of Champaign, begins his Attack on me."[5]

Five days after Blondel's letter a comte de Macdonald, captain in the regiment de Foix at Pau, writes in what he thinks is English to explain that his family, of Scots origin, has long been settled in France, and that he is so well known in his own right that the court wishes to keep him at home. He encloses a memorandum of his services, and asks to bring two officers to America with him. The Americans, he adds, were mistaken in assuming the offensive without sufficient artillery; he has a plan that will enable a small army to take advantage of a large one.[6]

On January 27 Briant de Peinquelein, a captain of infantry,[7] writes from Quimperlé in Brittany. The welcome given his relative, the chevalier Mauduit du Plessis, shows that all applications are not, as rumored in the provinces, being automatically refused. He offers his services, provided the terms are satisfactory; although he is no needy mercenary, he cannot be expected to make war at his own expense. He is young, vigorous, independent, and full of good will.

The next day another man writes from Quimperlé, a former officer in the Compagnie des Indes named Pierre Buisson de Basseville; the letter is in English, enclosing a memorandum in French. His service on privateers during the previous war cost him four years' imprisonment in England, where he learned the "tong"; since then he has been in India on Company business and is about to sail for China unless he can obtain a position with the Americans. On March

5. Smyth, *Writings*, VII, 81–2.

6. Charles-Edouard-Frédéric-Henry Macdonald (born 1745) was a Jacobite, as his first two Christian names imply. He was commissioned a lieutenant in the French army in 1757 and a captain in 1776; later he served under the d'Estaing at the siege of Savannah (where his brother was in the British garrison), and left the army in 1785. Bodinier.

7. Probably François-Hyacinthe, born in 1750; he served in the royal Breton grenadiers. *Ibid.*

3, having had no answer, he writes again to suggest that he be given command of a privateer.

On February 6 one de Bruni,[8] captain of light horse, writes a more personal letter from Paris. He recently saw Franklin to ask his help in locating a M. de Chermont, chevalier de Saint-Louis, who went to Portugal and disappeared, perhaps into the American service; Chermont's wife (whom he does not deserve) is anxious about him. De Bruni and a friend of his had hoped to join the American army but learned, no doubt from Franklin, that no more officers were wanted. They now desire to become American citizens; they are wealthy and well born, a far cry from those adventurers "qui n'ont d'autre resource que dans les tentatives hazardeuses du désespoir."

On February 24 a man who signs himself du Breüil fils, a *réformé* by the abolition of the provincial regiments,[9] writes from Fort Nieulay in Picardy to ask how he can obtain a commission. On March 5 Barbier de St. Georges, a former army officer now with the mounted police, requests from Carhaix in Brittany a cavalry commission. On the 28th a Captain de Jousserant, formerly of the royal grenadiers and now living in the Bordelais, offers his services. On or about April 8 the chevalier de Mazancourt, a former captain of dragoons *réformé*, applies for employment suitable to his rank and birth; a note dated April 8 from his cousin's wife, the comtesse de Mazancourt, asks that the two of them interview Franklin "sans l'importuner."[10] Another *réformé*, named Butor, writes the next day from Poitou to say that he loves to make war, of which he has had twenty years' experience, and what will Congress offer him? "C'est un garson d'un ésprit solide, age de quarente ans."

On April 16 an Italian soldier of fortune, Louis Gioanetti Pellion, formerly in the court of the King of Sardinia, writes a long letter from Turin to detail his military experience all over eastern Europe (he is twenty-three) and to explain that he would like to join the Americans for the next campaign because it would be more "intheressante, et avantageuse" than joining the British.[11] On the 17th the

8. Thomas-Edmé, born in 1738. *Ibid.*

9. They had been reconstituted from the militia in 1771 as a military reserve, and suppressed in 1775; *État militaire* for 1772, pp. 315–17; for 1776, p. 306; for 1777, p. 289.

10. The chevalier was Baptiste-François-Joseph and the comtesse Victoire-Thérèse Hardouin de Beaumois: *Dictionnaire de la noblesse.*

11. He remained in the Sardinian army until 1808, served for six years under Napoleon, and then returned to his former allegiance. Bodinier.

chevalier Jean-Baptiste-Guillaume Leprévôt de Basserode, a retired captain in the regiment de Languedoc who served with distinction under Montcalm in 1758, writes from Tonnay-Charente, near Rochefort, to request that he be commissioned at least a lieutenant colonel; the Americans will never have cause to reproach him "tant sur ma conduite de bonnes moeurs que sur mes dévoirs militaires."[12] On the 26th a Jean-Annet Chabreu Duparquet writes from Languedoc; he tosses off the names of numerous generals who know him, and suggests that the court be asked to brevet him a brigadier. He was one of the most persistent of the commission-seekers; this letter was followed by three others in May, one of them enclosing a memorandum on how the war should be conducted.[1] The last letter in this group is from a M. Eÿraut, who writes from Nantes on April 27 in hope of employment on an American warship; he tells little of himself because the bearer will explain to Franklin "l'homme que je puis etre."

The other group of letters we omit is from those who recommend relatives or friends; if the latter wrote as well, their applications have not survived. The first recommendation is from the marquis du Buat, a captain of cuirassiers stationed in Brittany, who suggests on January 21 that the chevaliers de Louvigny and Lefer, captain and sublieutenant respectively in his regiment, would be useful as colonel and captain in the American army; another former captain, unnamed, is also interested. An undated note probably written in January (Library of Congress) from the famous mathematician and member of the Académie royale des sciences, Étienne Bézout, supports the application of an artillery officer by the name of Villemont. On March 1 a nobleman in Champagne, Bergere, inquires what truth there is in the report reaching that part of the world of the terms that Congress is offering. His three sons, all *réformés*, want to go to America in the belief that they will be commissioned at a rank above what they have had, and given good positions and three-year leaves. The nobility of Champagne is not rich; he can pay only for the equipment and journey to the port of embarkation. On the 4th Jean-Paul Grandam, in Bordeaux, recommends an unnamed German, who has been forced into exile and who speaks good French.

On March 17 a Major Gastebois, in the Bordelais, explains that

12. He was born in 1724, was made a chevalier for his service in Canada, and retired in 1766: *ibid.*; Mazas, *Ordre de Saint-Louis*, I, 488. On June 17, assuming his unanswered letter had miscarried, he sent BF a copy.

1. He was born in 1710: Bodinier. His other letters are of May 10, 15 (with enclosure), and 22.

the duc de Duras[2] has requested from Franklin two companies for the Major's sons, lieutenants *réformés* in a provincial regiment, and that the American has inquired whether they speak English. They do not at the moment, but with any encouragement the father will send them to Bordeaux, where they will learn the language in three months. For a long time they have been seeking employment from Deane, through M. Gradis of Bordeaux.[3]

One La Barberie writes from Paris on April 2 to remind Franklin that, when they dined together at Dubourg's the previous day, their host said that Barberie *fils* wanted to go to America, and Franklin promised him letters of introduction. Chaumont and M. Poissonier[4] would recommend the young man, but his father thinks that unnecessary now that Franklin has offered his good offices.[5] "Mon fils," he adds in a postscript, "a l'honneur d'etre gentilhomme." On April 5 another father, the sieur Montée, chevalier de Saint-Louis, asks from Lille Franklin's help for his son, aged twenty-two, the eldest of seven and in a sad situation after the abolition of the provincial regiments. On the 13th still a third father, de Gailhard, writes from Pamiers, the capital of Foix, to intercede for his son, also *réformé*. "C'est un jeune homme qui joint à un goût décidé pour les armes, une figure noble et une taille de cinq pieds cinq pouces." "Mon fils," a postscript adds, "partira nanti de son certifficat de noblesse."[6]

These letters as a whole suggest a few tentative conclusions. One is that the news of an American market for officers spread far and wide with considerable speed. Another is that the *réformés* applied more because they wanted to improve their rank and their fortunes than because they professed, as Blondel did, any love for the American cause; what he called "la vie oiseuse" was weary, stale, flat, and above all unprofitable. A third is that the criteria for acceptance in the American forces appeared to the applicants to be the same as in France. "Mon fils a l'honneur d'etre gentilhomme." "Une taille de cinq pieds cinq pouces ... nanti de son certifficat de noblesse." Even

2. For this marshal of France see Larousse, *Dictionnaire universel*.

3. His sons were Martial and Jean: Bodinier. Gradis was a prominent Jewish merchant; see Paul Butel, *Les Négotiants bordelais* ... (Paris, 1974), p. 190 and *passim*.

4. Above, XIX, 328 n.

5. The son was Julien-François La Barberie de Saint-Front, born in 1755 in Falaise, Normandy. Bodinier.

6. Two recommendations similar to these we treat separately because they touch on other matters: below, Boux to the commissioners, Feb. 14, and Georgel to BF, April 9.

the few candidates who spoke English did not understand the language of the new world; why should they?

Monsieur   a Moulinnes ce 13 janvier 1777

Les motifs qui ont determiné les Bostoniens a se soustraire a la tyrannie angloise me paroissent si conformes au droit naturel, que j'ay souvent ambitionné d'etre aportée de leurs offrir les services d'un citoyen qui d'abord s'étoit voüé au service de sa patrie, mais que des raisons que je vais vous detailler, Monsieur, ont reduit a mener depuis un an unne vie oiseuse si indigne de tout etre pensant. Lors qu'il a plú a sa majesté de supprimer sa maison militaire ou je servois depuis huit ans, je n'ay rien eú de plus pressé que de voler aupres du ministere pour le suplier de me mettre a portée de continuer ma carriere dans un des regimens soit d'infanterie soit de cavalerie ou il pourroit se trouver place; mais malheureusement pour moy elles se sont toutes trouvées remplies.

Ce qui m'engage a saisir l'occasion ou vous etes deputé dans nos etats, pour vous demander dans vos armées l'employ que je jugerez convenable a un offitier de huit ans de service. Vous serez peut-etre surpris, Monsieur, du peu d'alentour que je prens pour vous faire ma demande, mais j'ay toujours regardé la methode la plus simple, comme la plus directe, et la plus sure pour parvenir aupres d'un homme qui a sçú se faire admirer jusques dans le continent le plus eloigné du sien, par la force et la beauté des discours qu'il a prononcé au milieu d'une assemblée a laquelle il vouloit enfin faire connoitre le droit des gens. J'ose donc vous suplier, Monsieur, si vous octroyez ma demande, de m'honorer d'unne reponce. Dans l'instant je me rendray à Paris pour vous y faire ma cour et vous prouver par des certificats authentiques la verité de ce que je vous annonce. Je l'attens avec bien de l'impatience et suis avec respect Monsieur Votre tres humble et tres obeissant serviteur   BLONDEL

Mon adresse est a M. Blondel ancien gendarme de la garde du roy au chateau de Moulinnes pres et par St. hilaire du harcouët basse Normandie.

Notation: Blondel, Moulinnes 31 Janv. 77

From Michaël Kôváts de Fabricÿ[7]

ALS: American Philosophical Society

⟨Bordeaux, January 13, 1777, in Latin: I am Hungarian, trained in the Prussian army, where I rose from the ranks by merit and valor to be chief officer of the Guards. I have come here on my own to offer my services to Congress. Through the help of M. Fadeville, a merchant of this city and a supporter of the American cause, I have secured a passage with Captain Whippy; I beg you to send me a passport and recommendation to Congress. Companions are joining me here, and you will serve our common cause by expediting, through M. Fadeville, their passage as well.[8] Because I am not yet fluent in English or French, I must write in German or Latin.⟩

MICHAËL KÔVÁTS DE FABRICÿ.

The Conde de Aranda to the Marqués de Grimaldi:[9]

Extract   Copy and incomplete draft:[1] Archivo Historico Nacional

Excmo. Sr.

Muy Sr. mio: a consequencia del Oficio antecedente dirè a V Ea, que viendo no se me explicaba el Dr. Franklin no ob-

---

7. A member of the Hungarian nobility who served Maria Theresa in the War of the Austrian Succession, entered the Prussian service, and fought in the Seven Years' War until his resignation in 1761. After a visit to Poland he returned to Austria, was tried for treason and acquitted, and settled again in Hungary until 1776, when he left for Bordeaux by way of Leipzig. He sailed on the *Catharina of Darmouth* on Feb. 25, 1777: Fadeville to Hancock, May 8, 1777, National Archives. In May Congress accepted his services; in April, 1778, he was appointed a colonel in Pulaski's Legion, helped organize and train the cavalry, and was killed in action before Charleston on May 11, 1779. László Eszenyi, *Faithful unto Death: the Life and Heroic Death of Michael Kovats de Fabricy* . . . (Washington, D.C., 1975), which contains the full text and translation of this letter.

8. Fadeville sent Kôváts' letter to some one, probably Silas Deane, for delivery to BF. In a covering letter of Jan. 14 he praised the Hungarian as a soldier and a man, explained that the companions were two or three officers who had served with Kôváts in the Prussian army, and asked what to do if they arrived after his departure. APS.

9. Grimaldi (1720–86) had resigned as the Spanish foreign minister several months before, but remained in office until the Ambassador to the Holy

stante su promesa, le hice entender que desearia hablarle, y efectivamente vino acompañado de Arthur Lee la noche del sabado 4 del corriente.

Por la dificultad de entendernos me parecio, que seria mui del caso valerme del Conde de Lascy Ministro plenipotenciario del rey en la Corte de Petersbourg, y alojado en mi casa, quien posehe la lengua Inglesa; para que aclarase a Franklin, y Lee la inteligencia de los puntos que se tocasen, si no los concebian bien, y a mi igualmente por la explicacion de ellos.

"Preguntè al Dr. Franklin, quando entregaria el papel de proposicion para la España, respecto a que avia proporcion de dirigirlo."

Respondio que lo tenia ya formado, faltando solo el confrontar su copia; y averse retardado, por haver estado algo indispuesto Mr. Dean.

"Si dicho papel contenia alguna cosa diferente del entregado a la Francia."

Respondio, que no, y ser identico, como tambien conforme a las ordenes que tenia del Congreso.

"Si no avia alguna diferencia precisamente, atendiendo a que la posicion de los dominios de España, y sus nombres siempre exigian uncontexto, que avia de variar del de la Francia."

Respondio, que estaba autorizado del Congreso, para tratar con cada una de las dos Cortes segun sus intereses, y con plenos poderes para quanto ocurriese.

"Como es que sin hallarse aun asegurados de su independencia, y sin estar tampoco reconocidos aun por estas potencias, venian proponiendo tratados, quando todo el mundo crehia que la venida del Dr. Franklin se dirigia mas presto à solicitar auxilios, que los ayudasen hasta conseguir su reparacion."

Respondio, que por medio de semejante tratado verian la potencia que quisiesse ser su Amiga de veras; y que hasta averse asegurado de esta calidad, no avian crehido conve-

---

See, the conde de Floridablanca, returned from Rome to succeed him.

1. The first page and a half of the copy is in Aranda's hand; his draft omits the first two paragraphs and ends where our extract does. Both have notations from which we have supplied the date. For the full text of the dispatch see Juan F. Yela Utrilla, *España ante la independencia de los Estados Unidos* (2 vols.; Lérida, 1925), II, 39–48.

niente entrar en el punto de necesidad, tanto mas que su situacion aun no era tal, que necesitasse imediatamente auxilios directos.

"Si era cierto que avian recivido ya socorros de este reino; si avia partido el Amphitrite; y si otros dos bastimentos que debian seguirle, lo hacian, o se suspendian."

Respondio: que de esta Potencia no havian recibido socorros algunos; que por medio de una Compania se les havian provisto diferentes generos, armas y municiones; que tambien se avian recivido oficiales a su Servicio; y que en todo esto no avia hecho la Francia otra cosa, sino el no oponerse, y dejar libertad de practicarlo: que el Amphitrite avia salido, y crehia averse suspendido la salida de los otros dos buques.

"Quales serian los auxilios, que mas les urgian en la actualidad."

Respondio, que cañones de Bronze, y buques de guerra, respecto à que los bastimentos que tenian hasta ahora, eran inferiores en feurza à los Ingleses; y bien que eran muchos sus armadores, y havian hecho cantidad de presas hasta el importe de millon y medio de libras Sterlinas segun computo hecho en el mismo Londres; como no podian presentarse à las naves de guerra Inglesas, siempre era una inferioridad que necesitaban reparar: tanto mas que los Ingleses con sus muchas naves de guerra, y las de transporte cubiertas de ellas, estaban en estado de llevar sus Tropas, y viveres à qualquiera parte de aquel continente.

"Por que no hacia de una vez para la Corte de Madrid todas las explicaciones que tuviesse que hacerle; respecto a que por la distancia no havia la proporcion de manifestarlas de un dia a otro, como se podia practicar en Versailles, sabiendo desde luego tambien sus respuestas."

Respondio que en esta consideracion entragaria otro papel, que contendria quanto se le avia indicado; que si convenia que uno de sus Compañeros diputados pasase a Madrid, lo haria desde luego.

A esto le dije, que el hacerlo, o no era libre en ellos; pero que no se adelantaria tanto, porque entre si tendrian que entenderse por los Correos ordinarios; y la Corte de Madrid en qualquiera proposicion que reciviesse, querria consultarla con la de Paris; siendo mejor hacer aqui las explicaciones, porque ya se comunicarian a Madrid con el dictamen de esta Corte, y le repeti, que si lo querian, que so propondria à Madrid. Hicieron ambos con este motivo muchas demonstraciones de respeto acia el Rey Catolico, y que su principal fin era el de convencer que de su parte anhelaban su proteccion.

"Si hacian algun Comercio con los dominios Españoles de America."

Respondieron que antes estando bajo la dominacion Britanica hacian alguno por la parte de la Jamaica, pero que en estos tiempos no lo practicaban.

"Si tenian muchos Oficiales Extrangeros."

Respondio que el maior numero era de franceses, algunos Alemanes, y un Polaco: que al principio havian pasado algunos desde St. Domingo, y otros trasferidose desde los Puertos de Francia: aviendo tenido el pensamiento de levantar tres regimentos en el Canada; pero inutilizadose por averlo ocupado los Ingleses. Que mantenian dichos Oficiales asalariados, bien que sin emplearlos.

"Si no entraria la mala inteligencia en los miembros del Congreso."

Respondio mui sucintamente que no.

Para abrirles un poco el animo, y que no extrañassen las questiones que se les havian hecho, les dije, que se dirigian à tomar una luz del estado en que se hallaban; y que reciprocamente podian preguntar lo que les pareciese, pues en lo que yo pudiesse corresponderles, se les diria con franqueza, como tambien, si no me hallasse en estado de contextarles.

Entonces me preguntaron, si tenia probabilidad, que la rusia acordasse un Cuerpo de tropas à la Inglaterra contra los Americanos, en tono de hacerles mucha impresion este recelo: y les dije, que las noticias publicas de gazeta havian hablado de ello, pero que nada mas se sabia.

Expusieron, que el Congreso avia embiado à Cadiz seis cargamentos de su cuenta dirigidos a la casa Inglesa de Buick, y Compañia, la qual se resistia a sus pagos; siendo este caudal urgente, porque el congreso lo havia destinado, para hacer en Francia las compras que necesitaba: y preguntaron, que medio auvia de conseguir de dicha casa tan justa satisfaccion, respecto à que se negaba a toda contextacion sobre este asunto.

Les dije si seria acaso una especie de represalla como casa

Inglesa, por descubiertos que otros negociantes de las Islas Britanicas tendrian con los Americanos; y a esto respondieron, que no podia ser, pues la correspondencia de los particulares nunca se avia cortado, antes bien vigilado el congresso, en que se mantuviese con toda exactitud; de tal modo que en su propio bastimento avian venido varias letras de Cambio para el Comercio de Londres. Se les explicó pues, que el modo de solicitar el cobro de la Casa de Buick, seria el presentarse un particular con los conocimientos de su deuda, y poderes necesarios, pidiendo ante el tribunal que correspondiesse el pago de lo que se les debiesse; y que en este caso se podria buscar un apoyo de la autoridad, para que se les administrasse justicia sin demora.

Translation[2]

Excellency, Dear Sir: [January 13, 1777]
    With regard to my last communication,[3] I wish to inform you that, when Mr. Franklin did not get in touch with me as promised, I let him know that I should like to see him; and finally he came, accompanied by Arthur Lee, on Saturday night the 4th instant.

    Because of the language difficulty I thought it would be helpful to ask Count Lascy, the King's minister to the court of St. Petersburg[4] and a guest in my house, who knows English, to clarify for Franklin and Lee the meaning of what I said, in case they misunderdstood me, and similarly for me the meaning of what they said.

    "I asked Dr. Franklin when he could deliver the paper of proposals to Spain, so that it could be forwarded."

2. The Spanish, like Giambatista Beccaria's Italian (above, xx, 356), leaves the translator the alternatives of reproducing circumlocutions and vague constructions or of taking liberties with the text to bring out the meaning; we have chosen the latter course, and have had invaluable assistance from Prof. Gustavo Correa of Yale. For any misinterpretations we are solely responsible.

3. Utrilla, *op. cit.*, 33–5. The Ambassador had first seen the commissioners on Dec. 29 at Vergennes' instigation, Bancroft reported to London: Stevens, *Facsimiles*, I, no. 7, pp. 3–4.

4. The conde de Lacy, who was wintering at Paris en route to St. Petersburg, had three interviews with the commissioners: *loc. cit.* For this diplomat of Irish extraction see Larousse, *Dictionnaire universel.*

He answered that he already had the paper in shape, and all that was needed was to check the copy; this had been delayed by Mr. Dean's indisposition.[5]

"Did the paper contain any points different from that delivered to France?"

He said no, it was identical, and also accorded with his instructions from Congress.

"Was there not some kind of difference, inasmuch as the position and names of the Spanish dominions required variations from the text addressed to France?"

He was authorized by Congress to deal with each court according to its interests, he answered, and to make decisions as necessary.

"How is it that they are proposing treaties, without being yet assured of their independence or of recognition by these powers, when every one thought that Dr. Franklin's trip was rather to seek assistance in reaching that objective?"

They would discover by such treaties which power wanted to be a true friend, he answered. Until they knew this they had thought a discussion of their needs inappropriate, particularly as the situation did not yet require direct and immediate help.

"Had they in fact already received help from this kingdom, had the *Amphitrite* sailed, and were the other two shipments that were supposed to follow going to be sent or delayed?"

He replied that they had not received assistance from this power. Through a company they had received supplies of different kinds, arms and ammunition, and officers for their service; France had merely refrained from interfering. The *Amphitrite* had sailed; the departure of the other two ships, he thought, had been suspended.

"What assistance is most urgently needed at this point?"

Bronze cannon and warships, he answered, because those they had were much less effective than the English. Although they had numerous shipyards and had captured English vessels to the value of a million and a half sterling, according to London's own estimate, they were still unable to confront the

5. Deane was ill with malaria, according to the Ambassador: Utrilla, p. 46.

English warships. This inferiority must be remedied, particularly because English transports protected by men-of-war could carry troops and supplies to any part of the continent.

"Why did he not pull together all the points that he was supposed to put to the court of Madrid, since distance precluded what would be possible in Versailles, questions and answers on a day-to-day basis?"

He replied, in the light of this suggestion, that he would submit another paper containing all the points at issue.[6] If one of his fellow commissioners might appropriately go to Madrid, he would of course do so.

I answered that this was up to them but that it would not save much time, because they would have to correspond with each other by ordinary mail, and the court of Madrid would want to consult with Paris on any proposal received, so that the points might better be made here and communicated to Madrid. But if they wished, I repeated, this idea could be transmitted to Madrid. Both of them took the occasion to express their respect for his Catholic Majesty; their chief aim was to demonstrate a desire for his protection.

"Could they trade to any extent with the Spanish dominions in America?"

They answered that previously, under British control, they had had some trade through Jamaica, but at present had none.

"Had they many foreign officers?"

The majority were French, he replied, and some Germans and one Pole. They had come at the beginning either through St. Domingo or from French ports, with the intention of raising three regiments in Canada; but this plan had come to nothing because of the English occupation. They kept such officers on the payroll even when they were not used.

"Did members of Congress misunderstand what was going on?"

6. BF saw Aranda on the 8th, and gave him French translations of his memoir to Vergennes of the 5th and of the proposed American Articles of Confederation; they are now in the Archivo nacional historico. He had no paper for Spain, and according to the Ambassador asked to be excused because he had, in Deane's absence, no one about him whom he could trust. Utrilla, *loc. cit.*

He answered succinctly no.

I told them, to be encouraging and to prevent surprise at the questions asked them, that those questions were meant to clarify their situation, and that they in turn might ask any they wished; I would either answer candidly or tell them that I could not answer.

They then asked me, in a tone that strongly implied anxiety, whether Russia was likely to furnish England with troops to use against the Americans. I told them that the *Gazette* had made some mention of this, but that nothing more was known.

They said that Congress had sent six shipments on its account to the English house of Buick & Company in Cadiz, which was refusing to pay.[7] The matter was urgent, because Congress had earmarked the money for necessary purchases in France; they asked how payment might be extracted, when the company answered no inquiries.

This might be reprisal by an English firm, I suggested, for outstanding American obligations to British merchants. That could not be, they answered: private dealings had never been interrupted; on the contrary, they had been carefully maintained by Congress, and its shipments had arrived with letters of credit on London. I explained that the way to collect from the Buick firm was to file a brief giving the details of the debt, with the necessary documentation and powers of attorney, and to ask the court for payment. They might thus invoke the help of the authorities in obtaining prompt justice.

The American Commissioners to Gérard

AL: Archives du Ministère des affaires étrangères; copy:[8] Harvard University Library

The commissioners are here acknowledging, on the surface, the King's message that Gérard had transmitted to them the day before. Their gratitude, however, had little to do with the message, which offered

7. We can find no mention of the name, or of another company that fits the description. The usual consignee at Cadiz was Duff & Welsh, but all the obvious sources are silent on such a contretemps with that firm.

8. Both are in the hand of Arthur Lee; the differences in wording and punctuation are inconsequential.

them nothing beyond a vague promise, at the end, of help in purchasing supplies. What they are in fact acknowledging is Gérard's verbal definition of that promise, not to be mentioned on paper by either side, as a loan of two million livres under the guise of contributions from well-wishers in France.[9]

Paris. Jany. 14th. 1777.

We thank Monsr. Gerard, for the polite and explicit manner in which he has communicated his Majesty's Message.

We beg to return our most grateful sense of the gracious intentions, which his Majesty has had the goodness to signify towards our States; and to assure his Majesty, that we shall ever retain the warmest gratitude for the substantial proofs he has given us, of his regard; and that we will, in due time, endeavour to impress our Constituents, with the same sentiments.

We feel the strength of the reasons, his Majesty has been pleasd to assign for the conduct he means to hold; and the magnanimity of his motives. We beg leave to assure his Majesty, that we shall at all times, and in all things endeavor to conform ourselves to the views he has opend to us; as nothing is farther from our intention, than to precipitate his Majesty into any measures which his royal wisdom and justice may disapprove. And if in any thing we shoud contravene these

9. "Jan. 14, 1777. Commissioners returned Thanks to Mr. Gerard for the 2 Million granted by his Majesty." Notes compiled by WTF for BF "Relative to the 2 Millions granted in Jany. 1777," Jan. 14–Dec. 18, 1777, Library of Congress. The loan was in quarterly installments, without interest or date of termination; see the commissioners to the committee of secret correspondence below, Jan. 17. Price suggests that the government made this decision only after Vergennes learned on the 13th that the commissioners and the farmers general had failed to reach agreement on a tobacco contract; the loan was thus a substitute: *France and the Chesapeake*, II, 710–12. The commissioners implied the same thing in their letter below of March 12 to the committee of secret correspondence. Although the loan might not have been made if a tobacco contract had been signed in early January, the decision was reached while negotiations were still under way. The King's answer to the commissioners was approved on the 9th, and on the 12th Vergennes, in writing to his ambassador in Madrid, defined precisely the secret aid mentioned in it. AAE, Correspondance politique, Espagne, DLXXXIII, 40–2.

purposes, we shall always be happy and ready to amend it, according to the advice and direction of Government.

The Secret Committee to the American Commissioners

ALS: American Philosophical Society; LS: American Philosophical Society, Harvard University Library; copies: Library of Congress, British Library.

Honorable Gentlemen   Philad. Jany 14th. 1777

I have the honor to enclose herein a Copy of two Resolves of Congress passed the 19th and 29th Novr. by which the Secret Committee are directed to import two hundred and twenty Six Brass Canon and Arms and equipage compleat for three thousand Horse. You'l observe they are also directed to Confer with the Canon Committee as to how many they can provide here of the Field pieces,[1] but we pay little regard to that part, well knowing they will not be able to procure proper Metal for many of them.

Therefore I must request in the Name and on behalf of the Secret Committee that you will Contract immediately for these necessary supplys and send them out to these States by Various conveyances as quick as possible indeed I hope you may procure some line of Battle Ships to come out with them and then there will be little danger of their coming safe. I most sincerely hope the Court of France may be disposed to favour all our Views, that they will accomodate you with sufficient loans to pay for these and all other Stores we want from Europe for altho we have plenty of Valueable produce that wou'd soon provide you with ample Funds if we cou'd get it exported safely, yet the difficultys and impediments we meet with render it impossible to get it away half fast enough. Nothing in our power shall be left undone and Mr. Thos. Morris will be ordered to supply you with Money fast as he receives it from the Net proceeds of our Consignments.[2] I have the honor

1. For these Congressional actions see the *JCC*, IV, 55; VI, 963, 992, 1064.
2. The secret committee to Thomas Morris of this date, APS.

to be, with great esteem and regard, Honorable Gentlemen
Your most obedient Servant

ROBT MORRIS,
Chair Man of the Secret Committee

PS These resolves wou'd have been sent long since but our
Port has been long blocked up by British Men of War and the
Confusion we were put in on the Rapid March through the
Jersey and near approach to this City by the Enemy, put it
totally out of our power to forward any dispatches for some
time past.   R M

original

To The Honorable Benjn. Franklin, Silas Deane and Arthr Lee
Esqrs. Commissioners &c Paris

Endorsed by Franklin: Letter from Commee Jan. 14. 1777

Thomas Morris to the American Commissioners

ALS: Connecticut Historical Society

Gentlemen   Nantes. January 14th. 1777

I embrace this opportunity of Captain Nicholsons return to
Paris to acquaint you with my arrival here yesterday about
four O'Clock in the afternoon. Mr. Penet having some bussiness at Orleans, detained us at that place a few hours, which
together with the badness of the roads rendered it impossible
for us to make greater dispatch than we did.³ I have now the
pleasure to acquaint you that best part of the Tobacco is disposed of at a price that will neat [net] about 13 Sous per lb.
Two of the Ships are near ready to take onboard their return
Cargoes which are now in store waiting. I expect one of them
the Success Captain Anderson will be dispatched in 10 days
from this date, for your government in preparing any Papers
you may have to send to America. Captain Wickes has been

3. For Samuel Nicholson, an old friend of Wickes who had received his
naval commission a month before, see the following letter and the *DAB*.
Penet was returning from Paris, where he had gone with BF; Morris was
taking up his post at Nantes as agent for the secret committee.

at Port L'Orient and will write you fully with respect to the Ships you desired him to examine there, and an Inventory of the 36 Gun Frigate will be sent to Paris, and as Captain Nicholson will be on the Spot, he can form a judgement of the situation that Ships in, and what may be still necessary provided you determine to purchase her.[4] I shoud be glad to know your sentiments with respect to any prizes that may be sent into any of the French Ports by American Privateers, and wether you are of oppinion they will meet the protection of the Court of France. I shall keep you regularly advised of every occurrence here, and in the mean time remain with much respect Gentlemen Your most Obedient Servant   THOS. MORRIS

PS. As Captain Nicholson does not go to L'Orient the letters for Mr. Bromfield[5] will be sent to him by Express this forenoon.

Benjn. Franklyn, Silas Deane & Arthur Lee Esqrs. Paris

Addressed: To / The Honble. Benjn: Franklin Esqr. / at / Paris

Notation: Nantes Jany 14th 1777 Letter from Thos. Morris Esqr

Lambert Wickes to the American Commissioners

ALS: American Philosophical Society

Gentlemen   Nantz january 14th. 1777
   I have bin Waiting Ever Since I wrote you Last for the Inventory of St. john and have not Recd. It yet therefore Conclude Mr. Gourlade has Sent it forward for Parris.[6] Captn.

4. A description of the frigate, in French, is among BF's papers in the APS, and is printed in translation in *Naval Docs.*, VIII, 526 n.

5. Thomas Bromfield, the Boston merchant who had recently come to France from England, and was about to sail home with a cargo: above, XXI, 157 n; XXII, 161 n.

6. Jacques-Alexandre Gourlade, of Lorient, had had a brilliant military career in India and then become a director of the Compagnie des Indes; after its suppression he remained one of the leaders in the Indian trade: Meyer, *Noblesse bretonne*, I, p. 418. He was changing the name of his ship to the *Comte de Maurepas*, and had actually sent the inventory to Wickes the day before; the latter forwarded it with his letter below, Jan. 18.

Nicholson Arrivd here yesterday and produc'd your Instrucktions to him concerning the vissiting and Inspecting the Ships at L Orient. But I think I have Done Everything that Captn. Nicholson Could Do Was he to Go there therefore have Conclded That it is Best for Captn. Nicholson to Return Immediately To Parris and there to Assist you in pointing out the Defisencyes of Stores and Materals agreable to Inventory. I Think you had best get Captn. Nicholson to Make What Addition he may think Neadfull or Nessesary to the Inventory And Agree With those Gentlemen to furnis All Stores And materals and fitt the Ship out fitt for Sea as it Will Be in their Power to Do it much Cheaper and Quicker than We Could possibly Do it our Selves. My Reason for Mentioning this Matter is that It May be Conducted With More Secrecy Than it Could be Done provided Captn. Nicholson or my Self was to Attend the fiting This Ship as they have Spies In Every port Who would Giv Immediate Information to the Court of Brittain Whome We may Reasonably Suppose Would giv orders for Blocking her Up and thereby Render her Useless. I Beg Leav to Recommend Captn. Nicholson To your Notice as a Gentleman of Good fammely Who has Bin Regularly Bred to the Sea and think him Well Qualified to Command A Ship of Warr. He Was very Acttiv in the Begining of our Unhappy Disputes in his Cuntrys Cause and Continnued So Untill the Nesessity of his business oblig'd him to Go to London Where he has bin ever Since Idle for Want of Employment. This Inconvenency I hope you'l Soon Remedy by Employing him in the Service of the United States Of America and there by put it in his Power to Make Good His Lost Time. As Captn. Nicholson Will be there to Assist you I hope it Will not be Nessesary for me to Come To Parris. I Am Now All Ready fited for Sea and only Wait To be informed by you Whether our prizes Will Be Recd. and protected In french ports or not as I May Take my Measures Accordingly. Youl pleas Inform of this As Soon as possible As I only Wait your orders and Answer to this and then procead on A Cruize Immediately. I Should be much Obligd for All other Nessesary Informations in your Power. I Remain With much Respect Gentlemen your Most oblig'd Humble Servant   LAMBT. WICKES

P.S. If you think it Nessesary I Should Come to Parris I Will Set of Immediately on Recving your Orders.   L.W.

To Doctr Franklin Sileas Dean Arthur Lee Esqrs.

Addressed in another hand: To the Honble Benjn. Franklin Esqr. / Paris

Notation: Capt Weekes Nantes Jany 14. 77

From Meschinet de Richemond, fils

ALS: American Philosophical Society

⟨La Rochelle, January 14, 1777, in English: Respect for the brave defenders of American liberty makes me want to establish contact with them. But they have hitherto seemed ignorant of our harbor, and used Nantes or Bordeaux instead. This haven is safe, frequented by ships of all nations and particularly those from French America, and a good market for indigo, rice, fish oil, and furs. Our brandy is almost as good as that of Cognac. We export all manufactured articles, and gunpowder is made nearby. Mr. Schweighauser and others will assure you that I deserve your trust. I should be glad to assist American ships if you will send them here.[7]⟩

From Nathan Rumsey

ALS: American Philosophical Society

Honorable Sir   Nantes Jany. 14th. 1777.

Yrs. of the 6th Instant by Mr. Penet, and of the 11th. by Mr. Williams I safely rec'd. I am happy that Messieurs Morris and Penet are safely arrived. The papers respecting the Prizes I have put in Mr. Morris's hands. Nothing material has been

7. One J. J. Garnauld, banker in Paris, delivered this note to BF and received from him the names of Philadelphia houses to which Richemond might write. The letters had already gone off, Garnauld informed BF on Feb. 21 (APS), and added that Richemond's experience and talent for business would enable him to carry out the most important transactions with credit. He himself was leaving for La Rochelle, he added, within the week.

agitated with respect to a reclamation since I had the Honor of writing to You last. Cap. Cod has offered to purchase his Vessel of Cap. Wickes, but he is too late: He applied both to Mr. Gruel and Self first, but as we looked upon his application as intended to entrap by gaining an acknowledgement from us that we had something to do in the Matter we always refered him to Cap. Wickes. Pratchell has been seen with a Lawyer, but Nothing has yet Transpired.[8] But should any thing result from it, I shall not fail to give You every particular according to your request. I shall duly inform Mess. Penet and Gruel of the 300 Louis rec'd by you on their Accts. of Mr. Sollier. I shall always Sir be proud of your Correspondence and sensible of the Honor, In the Course of which any Intelligence You may please to give me You may depend shall be honorably kept to myself. With the Utmost respect I am Honorable Sir Your Most obedient Humble Servant

NATHAN RUMSEY

Addressed: The Honorable / Doctor Benjamin Franklin / at / Paris. / per Cap. Nicholson.

Notation: Nathan Rumsey Jan 14. 77.

From Jonathan Williams, Jr.

ALS: American Philosophical Society

This is the first letter in Williams' extensive correspondence from Nantes. He went at Deane's suggestion, and expected to return as soon as he had inspected the stores that Peltier, the agent of Hortalez & Cie., was loading on the *Mercure*.[1] But he also had other tasks assigned him. One, to judge by this and the following letter, was to investigate Penet, his relations with Gruel, and his failure to work with Schweighauser. Another, to judge by later letters, was to keep an eye on Thomas Morris, about whom, even though he had just arrived, the commissioners were clearly uneasy. They kept Wil

8. Cod was master of the *George*, James Pratchell of *La Vigne*: Clark, *Wickes*, 98–9.

1. The commissioners had heard a rumor that the stores were of bad quality and badly packed. *Deane Papers*, I, 451–2; II, 148–9. JW was advanced 480 *l.t.* for expenses: Waste Book, entry of Jan. 12.

liams in Nantes on these assignments, and he was soon acting as their agent. His difficulties, combined with his lack of self-assurance, generated a prodigious volume of letters, to Franklin and to the commissioners; and their delays in answering augmented his anxieties.

> Nantes 14th Janry 1777. Tuesday 1 oClock

Dear and honored Sir

I arrived here last evening about 10 oClock and am now writing at Mr. Pennetts who with Mr. Morris I find arrived a few Hours before me.[1] I have been with Mr. Montardoine and Mr. Shweighaussen from whom I have received every offer of civility, and do not doubt but I shall be able to collect the best Information upon every subject that affects the American Interests; at present I have nothing conclusive enough for a proper Report, but I shall see Mr. Rogers this Evening, who returned with the Amphitrite and without being so pressing as to discover my Reasons for Enquiry, I hope to obtain full Information with regard to that Ship.[2]

I have been at Mr. Peltier (Mr. Beaumar[chais'] Agent)[3] but have not yet seen him. I shall however meet him on 'Change and shall not lose a moment's Time in the Execution of my Business.

I dispatch this by Capt. Nichelson but I propose to write you more fully by post this Evening.[4] I am with best Respects to Mr. Deane and Mr. Lee Your dutifull and Affectionate Kinsman   J WILLIAMS JUNR

I address this to you only, because as Capt. Nich[olson] is

2. In other words an explanation of why the *Amphitrite* had put back to Lorient after sailing from Le Havre. Nicholas Rogers was a Marylander who, on Deane's initiative, was going as an aide to Du Coudray; he eventually became a lieutenant colonel in the U.S. army. *Ibid.*, I, 367; Morton, *Beaumarchais correspondance*, III, 25–6 n; Alexandra L. Levin, "Colonel Nicholas Rogers and His Country Seat . . . ," *Md. Hist. Mag.*, LXXII (1977), 78–82.

3. M. de Sallier-Dupin, of the Bibliothèque municipale at Nantes, informs us that Jean Peltier became Peltier-Dudoyer by adding his wife's name after their marriage in 1758; the firm's name also appears as Pelletier Dudoyer: Morton, *op. cit.*, III, 86.

4. The letter that follows; for Nicholson see Morris to the commissioners above, Jan. 14.

waiting, I am obliged to write with too much Haste for a regular Report.

I see Capt. Weeks here who says he waits to know whether prizes are admissible into french ports.

Addressed: Doctor Franklin / a l'Hotel de Hambourg / Rue Jacob / a Paris.

Notation: J. Williams 14 Janry 77

Jonathan Williams, Jr., to the American Commissioners[5]

ALS: University of Virginia Library

Gentlemen   Nantes 14 Jan. 1777

Since writing this morning by Capt. Nicholson I have been with Monsr. Peltrier, who informs me that the Vessell is at the mouth of the River, where it seems all Vessells of Burden are obliged to load. She is not yet loaded but there are several Cases of Fusils gone from hence to the Ship, and Monsr. Peltrier expects a Barge loaded with Bales to come down the River this Week which has hitherto been detained by the Ice. Mr. Peltrier and myself are to set off tomorrow morning for the Ship, and we expect to be able to return the next day. I shall pay particular regard to your Instructions on this head, and as the Ship is not yet loaded I shall have better opportunity to inspect into the Quality of the Goods, that done I shall do my best Endeavours to hasten her Departure. Mr. Peltrier appears very willing to submit to my Inspection, which gives me hopes that it will turn out satisfactory, but this the Event must determine. I understand from him that the Amphitrite is not yet gone from l'orient, but that she waits only for a Wind, and from what I have yet been able to learn it seems that the want of provision, occasioned by false Calculation and a multiplicity of Passengers, is the principal Cause of her return: whatever other Cause I can find out shall in due time be reported. I understand that Monsr. Coudrais is gone to paris and

5. We print this out of the usual order because it was written after the preceding letter.

proposes to go to America in the Mercury,[6] in which Case I shall be glad to be notified, as I shall observe the verbal Instructions of Mr. Deane at parting, which were to suffer no passenger to go in the Ship without a written Direction from you. I am the more particular in this as I apprehend I shall have many applications, and I should be sorry either to refuse those you choose should go, or to permit those you do not, in which I can only be governed by your Instructions.

I have seen Mr. Pennett and Mr. Morris. The former is very civil and attentive to me but I shall keep myself as independant in that Respect as I can.

I understand by Mr. Montardoine and Mr. Schweighaussen that the two last Cargoes of Tobacco were sold from 71 to 76 Livres per hundred wt. and that good Rice would sell for 30 Livres per hundred. I find that I shall be able by means of Mr. Schweighaussen to obtain very particular Information about Mr. Pennett, but in that Information some allowance may be made for a Difference between them, it seems by him that the Cause of this Difference is on account of a Discount which is allowed here for paying ready money, which Mr. S thinks should belong to the Congress but which Mr. P. thinks he has the right to take; it is to this and to the dislike of being too closely examined, that Mr. Schweighaussen attributes Mr. Pennetts Application to Mr. Gruel, instead of himself as he has managed business for the Congress before. But I must gain more information in this particular, before I can venture a decisive Opinion about it.

I find that Mr. Peltrier wishes to keep all his Business as secret as possible for Fear, I suppose of some stoppage if too much noise is made. I shall comply with his desire except to Mr. Montardoine and Mr. Schweighaussen both of whom ap-

6. Du Coudray, by his own account, still hoped while in Paris to sail on the *Amphitrite*. He made the trip to confer with BF, who he believed had superseded Deane, about dispatching military supplies waiting in other ports—and no doubt also, as he did not say, about confirming his previous arrangements with Deane. He consulted with the two commissioners and was delighted to find them working together. Du Coudray to Congress, Jan. 26, 1777, National Archives. Deane gave the committee of secret correspondence a highly critical account of this trip: *Deane Papers*, I, 464–5.

pear to me good men, and to them I shall conduct without reserve. I have the Honour to be with the greatest Respect Gentlemen Your most obedient and most humble Servant

JONA WILLIAMS JUNR

The Honourable The Deputies of the United States

Notations: Mr Williams Nantes Jany. 14th. 1777 / Jona. Williams to Deputies U.S. (14 Jany. 1777.)

From ——— Guérin

January 15, 1777   See page 148n

From Jean de Ternant[7]   ALS: American Philosophical Society

Sir   Bordeaux 15 Jr. 1777

I am but just arrived at Bourdeaux after a dangerous Illness and shall have scarce time to buy the goods I Intended to carry with me before our vessel sails. Such a hasty departure makes me doubtful of receiving the letters you promised to send me for North america. However if they could not reach me before I leave this port, Messrs. Pecholier, freres Negotiants;[8] at whose house you will be kind enough to direct them, will forward them to me very carefully by another vessel that will sail some days after ours for the same place (The Cap francois) where I shall spend a month or six weeks and wait for your letters. . . .[9]

---

7. The chevalier de Ternant (born 1751) had clearly been in touch with BF in Paris and, if only because he was an engineer, had no doubt been promised letters of recommendation. The young man was at the beginning of what proved to be a distinguished career. He did not appear in America until he joined Washington's army at Valley Forge in the spring of 1778; perhaps he was delayed by a return of the illness he mentions here, for bad health plagued him. He acted as chief subordinate of Baron Steuben, who confirmed the impression this letter gives that Ternant spoke perfect English. At the end of the war the chevalier returned to France a full colonel, and in 1791 began a brief term as minister to the United States. Lasseray, *Les Français,* II, 433–6.

8. They forwarded this letter with theirs below of the 18th.

9. Suspension points here and later are in the original.

If I can be of any use to you in any thing whatever, you may depend upon my ardent desire of defending the rights of humanity and supporting with all my might, those who have so generously stood in defence of them. . . . I have a thousand things to say; and some useful plan to propose; but prudence forbids me intering here into any particulars. . . . I must wait for a better opportunity. I wish you success in your Negotiation. . . . The new spanish minister Count florida-Blanca whom I know, and who was formerly a counsellor will undoubtedly serve your cause with an unremitted ardour.[1] I am very respectfully sir, Your most obedient humble servant   TERNANT

chez Messrs. Pecholiers freres Negotiants à Bordeaux.

Notation: Ternant Bordx. 15 Jan 77.

From Chaumont

ALS: American Philosophical Society

Monsieur   Passi ce jeudy 16. Jer. 1777.
   M. Bernier et gourlade qui vendent avec moy la fregatte que vous avez fait visiter par le Capitaine Lambert Vickes me prient de leur envoyer promptement vostre decision;[2] Ils veulent vendre cette fregatte quatre cents mile livres. Il fait beau tems, venez diner avec nous amenez vos deux confreres et nous concluerons. J'ay l'honneur d'estre avec Respect Monsieur vostre tres humble et tres obeissant serviteur   LERAY DE CHAUMONT

M frankelin

Notation: de Chaumont, Passy 16 Janv. 77

   1. José Moñino y Redondo, conde de Floridablanca (1728–1808), was returning from his embassy to the Vatican to become the King's chief minister, a position that he retained for the next fifteen years.
   2. See Wickes to the commissioners below, Jan. 18. For Gourlade's fellow director of the Compagnie des Indes, Pierre Bernier (1715–93), see J. Conan, *La dernière Compagnie française des Indes, 1785–1875* (Paris, 1942), p. 193.

From Nicholas Davis[3]

AL: American Philosophical Society

[*c.* January 16, 1777[4]]

Mr. Davis's most respectful Compliments wait on Mr. Franklin begs leave to acquaint him that he is waiting below in the Coffee Room till Mr. Franklin is at leisure when Davis would be glad of the favour of speaking to him.

—— Franklin Esqr.

From [Duportail]

AL: American Philosophical Society

Monsieur   versailles le 16 janvier 1777

Comme je ne trouve point à vous proposer d'autres conditions principales de notre arrangement que celles exposées dans ma derniere lettre du 12, je vous seray obligé de les examiner et m'instruire le plustôt possible du party que vous prenèz. J'ai absolument besoin de scavoir à quoy m'en tenir sur tout cela et d'ailleurs, selon ce que vous m'avèz fait l'honneur de me dire, je n'aurois pas plus de temps qu'il ne m'en faudroit pour me preparer au depart. J'ai l'honneur d'etre etc.

a l'hotel du Cheval Rouge Ruë du vieux versailles A versailles.

Vous pouvèz, monsieur, si vous le preferez m'ecrire en latin

Notation: M. Portail Engineer

3. One of the Americans who got money from the commissioners on false pretenses; see their letter to the committee of secret correspondence below, Feb. 6. Davis almost invariably reappears in this and subsequent volumes in a bad light. He said—and what he said cannot be trusted—that he was the son of a Boston distiller who emigrated to Jamaica in 1755, later went to England to take holy orders, and returned to the island for a decade of "excellent good living." To BF, May 3, 1779, APS.

4. The date when the commissioners gave Davis 720 *l.t.*, for which he signed a receipt (Library of Congress). BF did see him in January, according to the letter just cited, and presumably at this time.

The American Commissioners to the Committee of Secret Correspondence

LS and two copies: National Archives; copy: South Carolina Historical Society

Gentlemen   Paris. Jany. 17[-22]. 1777.

We joined each other at this place on the 22d. of December and on the 28th. had an Audience of his Excellency the Count De Vergennes, one of his most Christian Majesty's principal Secretarys of State and Minister for Foreign Affairs. We laid before him our Commission with the Articles of the proposed Treaty of Commerce. He assured us of the protection of his Court, and that due Consideration should be given to what we offered.[5] Soon after we presented a Memoire on the present situation of our States, drawn up at the Ministers request, together with the Articles of general Confederation and the Demand for Ships of War agreable to our Instructions. Copies of all these Papers were given by us to the Count D'Aranda his Catholic Majestys Ambassador here, to be communicated to his Court.[6]

We are promised an Answer from this Court, as soon as they can know the Determination of Spain, with which they mean to act in perfect Unanimity.

In the mean time we are endeavouring to expedite several Vessels laden with Artillery, Arms, Ammunition and Cloathing, which we hope will reach you in time for the Campaign, tho' unfortunately one Vessel which Mr. Dean had sent so laden has put back after having been three Weeks at Sea. She is however now sail'd again.[7]

The Ports of France, Spain, and Florence (that is Leghorn

---

5. From "had an Audience" to this point is underlined in the LS and both copies, and in the LS the paragraph below beginning "In the mean time" is lined in the margin. We suspect that these emphases were supplied in Philadelphia.

6. See above, BF to the committee, Jan. 4, and BF's memorandum to Vergennes, Jan. 5, and Aranda to Grimaldi, Jan. 13.

7. No doubt the *Amphitrite*, even though she did not sail until the 24th.

in the Mediterranian) are open to the American Cruisers, upon the usual Terms of Neutrality.

We find it essential to the establishment and maintenance of your commercial Credit in Europe, that your Concerns of that kind should be in the Hands of the most respectable men in the different Countries. From the Observations we have made, Mr. Myrtle is not of that Description and we are sorry to say that the irregularities of Mr. Thomas Morris renders it absolutely necessary that some other person shoud be immediately appointed in his place.[8] We also think it adviseable that you should be so far upon your guard with respect to Monsr. Pennet, as not to deviate from the original Contract made with him; as we cannot learn that he is known to be a Person of Substance. At the same time it is justice to say that he appears to be active, industrious and attentive to your Interests. He is indeed connected with a very good House in Nantes, M. Gruel, but we know not the Terms of that Connection, or how far Mr. Gruel is answerable.[9]

It seems to us that those houses which are connected in great Britain are to be avoided.

It would be useful if we had some blank Commissions for Privateers: and we therefore wish that some may be sent us by the first opportunity.[10] As Vessels are almost daily arriving from America at the Ports here, we conceive advices of the

8. For Merckle and Morris see above, XXII, 534–5 n, 544 n. We have now adopted Merckle's spelling of his name. Deane's private warnings to Robert Morris about his brother's conduct did not arrive until after this dispatch was laid before Congress. Robert rose to complain of such public exposure, and to insist that he had authorized Deane to confirm the young man in his position or dismiss him. In private Morris gave full vent to his anger at Deane and BF; he had expected more friendship from them both, but would now correct his error. He had reports from Nantes, he added, that the commissioners were trying to oust his brother in the interests of BF's nephew, JW. *Deane Papers*, II, 77–80.

9. Arthur Lee pointed out to the committee a few weeks later that Montaudoüin and Schweighauser were the two Nantais merchants of highest standing and most influence with the government; Gruel was at a lower level, and Penet lower still: Wharton, *Diplomatic Correspondence*, II, 269.

10. Deane had made this recommendation to the committee before BF's and Lee's arrival: *Deane Papers*, I, 377.

Proceedings in the Campaign might be frequently contrived[1] to us, so as to enable us to contradict the exaggerated representations made by the English of their Successes; which standing uncontroverted have a considerable influence upon our Credit, and upon our Cause.

Great efforts are now making by the British Ministry to procure more Troops from Germany. The Princes in Alliance with France have refused to lend any, or to enter into any Guarantee of Hanover which England has been mean enough to ask, being apprehensive for that Electorate if she should draw from it more of its Troops. Four more Regiments, two of them to be Light Horse, are raising in Hesse, where there has been an Insurrection on account of Drafting the People; and now great sums of Money are distributed for procuring Men. They talk of 10,000 Men in all to be sent over this Spring.[2] These things do not look as if England was very confident of Success in the next Campaign without more Aid.

The Hearts of the French are universally for us, and the Cry is strong for immediate War with Britain. Indeed every thing tends that way, but the Court has its reasons for postponing it a little Longer. In the mean time preparations for it are making. They have already a Fleet of 26 Sail of the Line, mann'd and fit for Sea; Spain has 17 Sail in the same state, and more are fitting with such Diligence, that they reckon to have 30 sail in each Kingdom by the month of April.[3]

This must have an immediate good Effect in our favour, as it keeps the English Fleet at Bay, coops up their Seamen, of whom they will scarce find enough to man their next set of Transports, will probably keep Lord Howe's Fleet more together for fear of a Visit, and leave us more Sea Room to prey upon their Commerce, and a freer Coast to bring in our Prizes, and also the supplies we shall be able to send you in consequence of our agreement with the Farmers general, which is, that the Congress shall provide, purchasing bona fide at the lowest price possible, 20 thousand Hogsheads of Tobacco in

---

1. Presumably in the old sense of discovered.

2. The cabinet had decided to hire 4,000 more mercenaries, but less than 1,300 were forthcoming: Mackesy, *War for America*, p. 111.

3. The preparations that were actually being made were less impressive; see Dull, *French Navy*, pp. 63–4.

Virginia and Maryland at the Publick Warehouses in those States, for the Ships which they the Farmers general shall send, and that those Tobaccoes shall be brought to France at their Risque and in their Ships. They understand the Price is not likely to exceed 3 or 4 french Sous in America; but we do not warrant that it shall cost no more, tho' we hope it will not. Upon these Conditions we are to have half the supposed price advanc'd immediately and the Opportunity of Shipping Warlike stores on board their Ships at your Risque and paying reasonable Freights: the rest is to be paid as soon as advice is received that the Tobacco is Shipt.

The Desire of getting Money immediately to command the preparatives for the ensuing Campaign, and of interesting so powerful a body as the Farmers general, who in fact make the most Efficient part of Government here, and the absolute part in all Commercial and money'd Concerns, induced us to concede these Terms which may possibly in the Estimate of the price of the Tobacco be low; but which upon the whole we judg'd necessary, and we hope will be advantageous.[4]

So strong is the inclination of the wealthy here to assist us that since this Agreement we are offered a Loan of two Millions of Livres, without Interest, and to be repaid when the United States are settled in Peace and Prosperity; No Conditions or Securities are required, not even an Engagement from us. We have accepted this generous and noble Benefaction. 500,000 Livres or one Quarter is to be paid into the Hands of our Banker this Day, and 500,000 more every three Months.[5]

As the Ships we were ordered to hire or buy from this Court cannot be obtain'd, it being judg'd absolutely necessary to keep their whole Naval force ready at home in case of a Rupture, we think of purchasing some else where, or of building, in order as far as possible to answer the Views of the Congress. Of this we shall write more fully in our next.

In the mean time, we cannot but hint, that this seems to us

4. This news was wishful thinking. No agreement had been reached, as the commissioners admitted in their postscript; and, as they did not admit, none was in prospect. See the headnote above, Jan. 9, and Price, *France and the Chesapeake*, II, 711–12.

5. The source of the loan was a fiction; see the commissioners to Gérard above, Jan. 14.

a fair Opportunity of supporting the Credit of the Paper Money you borrow; as you may Promise payment in Specie of the Interests, and may draw upon us for the same with all Confidence.

We cannot for several weighty Reasons be more explicit at present; but shall hereafter.

Present our Dutiful Respects to the Congress and assure them of our most faithful Services. We are Gentlemen Your most Obedient Servants
B FRANKLIN
SILAS DEANE
ARTHUR LEE

Duplicate

P.S. Jan. 22. Our Agreement with the Farmers general is not yet signed, and perhaps some small Changes may be made in it; but as those will probably not be very material, we wish measures may be taken immediately for the purchase of the Tobacco. We shall send by the next Opportunity a Copy of the Contract.

We have receiv'd the Five hundred thousand Livres mentioned above, it is now at our Disposal in the Hands of our Banker; who has orders to advance us the second Payment if we desire it, and he is ready to do it. We are on the Strength of this, in Treaty for some strong Ships.

10,000 French Troops are on their March to Brest. But America should exert herself as if she had no Aid to Expect but from God and her own Valour. Another Campaign will ruin her Enemies.

Notations: Copy No 3 / Franklin Deane Lee to the Comttee Jany. 17–22 1777

The American Commissioners: Receipt for Money from the French Treasury[6]

ADS: Archives du Ministère des affaires étrangères

At Paris, this 17th Day of January, 1777.
We the underwritten, Ministers plenipotentiary from the Congress of the United States of America, do hereby acknowl-

6. The loan discussed in the preceding letter.

edge, that we have received of Mons. Micaut d'Harvelay, Garde du Tresor Royal,[7] the Sum of Five Hundred Thousand Livres, Money of France. Witness our Hands,   B Franklin
                                                            Silas Deane
                                                            Arthur Lee

Jonathan Williams, Jr., to the American Commissioners

ALS: American Philosophical Society; letterbook draft:[8] Yale University Library

Gentlemen   Nantes Jan. 17. 1777
    The two last days have been employed in going to Painbeuf (about 30 miles hence) examining the Mercury, and returning to Nantes. I have the pleasure to inform you that what I have hitherto seen is very satisfactory, the Mercury appears to be a very good Ship, 7 Years old, burden 300 Tons (Mr. Peltrier thinks 350,) 78 feet Keel, 26 feet Beam, 10 feet in the lower hold under the Beams, and 5 feet 4 Inches betweendecks; she was new sheathed about 6 months ago, and upon that sheathing has another sheathing of Deal to prevent the Worms from penetrating. Her Riggin is in general very good, part of it new, she has 4 Cables each 120 Fathom, 1 of them has never yet been wet, another almost new; the other two about half worn; she has 10 anchors from 12 to 1500 wt. besides a good Hauser and Kedge, two suit of Sails, some of which entirely new; in short I see no cause of Complaint, either of the Ship or the manner in which she is provided. She has accomodation for 4 and can have for 6 passengers in the great Cabin, and places may be made for 10 or 12 more between Decks, but in the latter Case she must have so much less Cargo as these places

7. Joseph Micault d'Harvelay held his position in odd-numbered years from 1755 to 1785; see John F. Bosher, *French Finances, 1770–1795 . . .* (Cambridge, 1970), pp. 89–90. A receipt in slightly simplified form for the second quarterly installment of the promised two million livres, signed on April 3, is in the Yale University Library.

8. The draft, dated the 16th, differs somewhat in wording, is badly mutilated in places, and is incomplete.

can be well filled. The number of Passengers should be known as early as possible, that a sufficiency of provision may be provided. Mr. Peltrier promises [me] that he will have rather more than less than 4 more but if I stay here, I shall see this myself. She has at present on board a quantity of Bricks well stowed for Ballast, and 1000 barrells of powder, she is now taking in Cases of Arms and Bales of Blankets &c. All her Cargo is ready. I have examined the Fusils which turn out very much to my satisfaction, but have taken 3 from different Cases and ordered them to [be] pack'd and sent to Paris for your own Inspection. The Bales I have yet opened are only Caps, which appearing well pack'd as to their preservation, but very ill as to [their] Bulk, having two coverings, and a large quantity of straw between, which appears to me useless. The Blankets particularly are pack'd too loosely, according to the english method they would have been squeezed into half the Compass, and the covering of straw would have been saved. I shall examine the Bales of Cloth &c. tomorrow. Mr. Peltrier says that she shall be ready to sail in 8 Days and if nothing unforseen happens I think this very practicable. I should here observe that Mr. Peltrier is the Shipper of the Goods only so knows nothing of the quantity and Quality of the Contents, (except of the Arms). They are sent from Orleans on Account of Mr. Morrice Mercht at Paris, so that Mr. Monthieu must see that the Invoices and necessary papers are sent here in time, if there is no delay in these particulars the ship may be dispatch'd as above.[9] Her Guns are only 3 pounders, she has 14 of them, but I think it would have been better if they were larger. It is reported here that there will be a stoppage at l'orient, I hope it is without Foundation or that the Amphitrite will get away before it comes, she was not sail'd the 15th, but I understand it is only the Wind that detains her, and I hope soon to hear of her Departure.

It may not be amiss to desire Mr. Monthieu to procure some

9. Morrice was possibly a M. Morice in the Rue Saint-Denis, listed as a wholesale cloth merchant in *Almanach des marchands*, p. 375. Carié de Montieu, who had formerly been engaged with Dubourg in supplying arms (above XXII, 464 n), was now associated with Hortalez & Cie. in supplying ships: *Naval Docs.*, VII, 691–2.

good Charts if they are to be had at Paris least they should be wanted, I have not yet examined the Captains, but I shall enquire about it tomorrow, when I intend to have the pleasure of writing to you again. I have the honor to be Gentlemen Your most obedient Servant   J WILLIAMS JUNR

The Honorable The Deputies of the United States.

Notation: Jona Williams Nantes Jany 17. 1777

From the Chevalier d'Anmours[1]

ALS: American Philosophical Society

Sir   Bordeaux Jnry 17. 1777.
    Madam La Marquise de Saineville, has Sent me, inclos'd in one of her letters, another, which at her Recommandation, and that of Mr. l'abbé Raynal, you were So good to write in my favour to Mr. Moris, your friend in Philadelphia.[2] Your Réputation, Sir, makes me acquainted with its Value, and that Value Engages my most Sinceres Sentiments of Gratitude. Accept my thanks for it, and my offers of Service in a Contry where I intend to pass some time; and where I should think my Self exceedingly happy, were it in my power to give you

1. Charles-François-Adrien Le Paulmier d'Anmours (1742–1807) had spent some years in England and America and returned home in 1773. Through the Chevalier de La Luzerne, a relative, he made contact with Vergennes in September, 1776, gave him several memoranda on American affairs, and was eventually authorized to go to Philadelphia as an unofficial observer. He subsequently became a French consul, and lived out his life in the United States. See the sketch of him (in which his name is misspelled) in the *Md. Hist. Mag.,* V (1910), 38–45; Kathryn Sullivan, *Maryland and France, 1774–1789* (Philadelphia, 1936), pp. 39–45.

2. The marquise de Gérente de Senneville (or, as she spelled herself, Jarente de Sainneville) was a relative of d'Anmours, the daughter of the marquis de Senas et d'Orgeval, and the wife of the baron de Senneville, *lieutenant de vaisseau;* see her letter below, April 30, and *Dictionnaire de la noblesse,* IX, 163. BF had been in indirect touch with Raynal, the well known philosophe, in 1773 (above, XX, 448); the phrasing suggests that he had recently been in more direct contact. The letter to Robert Morris has disappeared.

a Proof of the high Sentiments of veneration and Respect with which I am, sir your most humble and most obedient servant

LE CH[EVALIE]R D'ANMOURS

Mr. B. franklin in Paris.

Addressed: À Monsieur, / Monsieur Franklin / *à Paris.*

Notation: D'Anmoeurs

From [Samuel Wharton³]   AL: American Philosophical Society

Dear Sir   January 17th 1777

My last was the 14th,⁴ since Which I have not been favored with a Line from your Side. Every Day more and more confirms your just Observation, That "implacable Malice and Hatred" would soon (in Case of Separation) take place of mutual affection, and Friendship. In the politest and best Families of this City, and among Even the most gentle, and humane of the fair Sex, So unhappily and effectuely have politicks reversed their Natures, You hear Them rejoice at the Butchery of Americans, and wish the most cruel Punishments exercised On Them, for Alass! They have been taught to consider Us, as a Race of ignorant, ungrateful, brutal Cowards. All Ranks

3. Identified as usual by the handwriting and contents.

4. Unless this letter was to BF and has since been lost, it was one of that date that is now among his papers in the APS, addressed to a Mon. Benson; in that case Wharton, to judge by his phrasing here, assumed that BF would read it. It was Benson who later revealed to Whitehall the existence of the Franco-American treaty, and his identity has caused confusion from that day to this. He is said to have been Silas Deane. A British agent leaped to that conclusion when he found a number of letters to Benson in Deane's lodgings in May, 1777, and Julian Boyd accepted the conclusion: "Silas Deane: Death by a Kindly Teacher of Treason?," 3 *W&MQ,* XVI (1959), 322–3. This identification, however, is unwarranted. In 1778 Wharton addressed five letters to Benson about their joint speculations in stocks; four are in the British Library (Feb. 24, March 13, April 21 and 28) and one in the APS (May 19), and some of these refer to Deane as a third party. We are confident that he was writing to Edward Bancroft as Benson. In early 1777 Bancroft was still living in England, and on his visits to Paris presumably lodged with Deane, as he had the previous summer: *Deane Papers,* I, 209–10.

of People joyfully anticipate the Operations of next Campaign. Howe and Carlton, They say, will separate the Colonies inclusive, and southwardly of New York, from those to the Northward of it. These are devoted to Destruction: The united Calamaties of Carnage, and Devastation are to be inflicted on Them; for They alledge, They excited Rebellion in all the Colonies, entertain and promote Anti-Kingly Notions of Government, are of very little Use to the Kingdom, Purchasing scarcely any of its Manufactures, and essentialy interfering with it's Fisheries and Commerce; And with Respect to the Middle and southern Provinces, It is graciously intended, after a moderate Chastisement, To pardon their Revolt, In Consideration of their being *profitable* Planters, and large Consumers of British Manufactures. These are the flattering Wishes, and benevolent Intentions of these Islanders. Can Americans forget or forgive Them? No. They will, I trust, disapoint Them, and shew by their Unanimity, Perseverance and Fortitude, That They know the Value of, and will maintain, Their Freedom; and the Independence of their Country.

Yesterday a Committee of West India Merchants, consisting of twenty five, waited upon Lord Sandwich, and desired the Convoy for the West Indies might be postponed for a little While. It was agreed to. The Committee took Occasion to complain to his Lordship of the great Losses, The Merchants had suffered by American Captures, and delivered Him a List of West India Vessels (Only) taken, To the Value, of *One Million and Eight hundred thousand pounds*, and stated to his Lordship, How very much commercial Credit suffered in Consequence of it.

Do you not imagine, The Capture of Transports, and other Vessels, amount, at least, to half a Million More? People in Office say, That Colonel Faucit has engaged 5000 Wirtemburghers, In Part of the Quota of Troops, To go to America.[5]

A Ship yesterday arrived from Augustine, and brings the dismal News of the Cherokees, and Creeks, at the Instigation of the Governor of East Florida, and Mr. Stewart, The Super-

5. Col. William Fawcett, or Faucitt, had negotiated with German rulers the earliest treaties for mercenaries. *DNB* under Fawcett.

intendent of Indian Affairs, having in One Day taken Seven hundred Scalps from the inoffensive, frontier Families of the Carolina's and Georgia. The inhuman Governor, it is said, was alarmed, and relented, at the Sight of these savage bleeding Trophys, and dispatched Expresses to stop the farther Massacre. But by his Bribes and wicked Misrepresentations, the prowling Murtherers had been stimulated into Action, and their brutal Career would not easily be arrested.[6] Can America Ever be reconciled to the *Primary* Author of this Tragedy? It is impossible. My Soul detests Him, as a most sanguinry, deceitful and obstinate T—a—t. I was desired by 81 to hint to you, That Government is furnished by the Jew, who lived, (When I was in America) in Peter Evans's large House in Second Street, opposite to Holt's the Sadler (DF.) with every Transaction at Philadelphia. He is Permitted to appear as a Friend to the Views of the Congress, in Order to acquire the best Intelligence.[7] If Dr. B. should not have left Paris, When this Letter gets to Hand, He should be very careful of his Papers. He had better return by the Way of Brighthelmstone. It is publickly talkd of, That He is *with you.* I enclose you an Extract, from Davilla's History of the Civil Wars in France,[8] to shew, that Ambassadors *were Publickly* received at the French Court, from the revolted States of the Low Country. My best Respects wait on 57. I am dear Sir Your most Affectionate Friend.

#

Prices of Stocks this Day
Bank 130 to 137⅞

6. For John Stuart and the beginning of these Indian incursions see above, XXII, 642–3.

7. This warning had some color of justification. David Franks, who has appeared occasionally in earlier volumes, was Peter Evans' son-in-law. He was supplying prisoners of war, as agent for a British contractor and with the authorization of Congress and of Gen. Howe, and had visited New York on this business. American authorities subsequently banished him for the duration of the war. Edwin Wolf, 2nd, and Maxwell Whiteman, *The History of the Jews of Philadelphia from Colonial Times to the Age of Jackson* (Philadelphia, 1956), pp. 33, 38, 47, 86–92, 181–2. We have no evidence that he was a spy, but his activities and British contacts made him suspect.

8. Enrico Caterino Davila, *Historia delle guerre civili . . .* , first published in 1630, had numerous later editions and translations.

3 percents consol. at 12⅛
India   172¾
Navy   2¼ to ⅜ Discount

PS. The officer, 236, Whom Dr. B. and I recommended to you about twelve Months ago,[9] is returned from Philadelphia, by the Way of Nants, and I am told, When in Paris, about ten Days ago, waited upon Lord Stormont, and gave a very sad account of the Situation of the People, as to their Union in Philadelphia and other Parts of America, as well as the American Army; In short, He represents, That He was courted by the Congress to accept of being Engineer General to their army and some other high Post. But He told me yesterday, He positively refused all their offers, as He was persuaded, They coud not long maintain their Independence, as their army was badly constituted, both as to officers and Soldiers &c. I perceive He is a disapointed Man, speaks from Resentment, and will endeavour to recommend Himself to administration. I wish Dr. B. may bring an account of his Propositions to the Congress and Conduct at Philadelphia, That so He may be confronted with Them. I send you by the Courier, the Daily papers, from Monday to this Day inclusive. I am dear Sir, yours sincerely   #

If Dr. B should have left Paris, before This Letter reaches you, be pleased to let the within Letter be sent to Him in London, by the *Courier*, and not by the Post.[1]   #

Rullecourt to the American Commissioners

January 18, 1777   See pages 146–7n

9. Elias Wrixon; see above, XXII, 306n.
1. We cannot identify the enclosure. It could scarcely have been the letter to Benson of Jan. 14, discussed above, because it remained among BF's papers; it contained largely London news, furthermore, which Bancroft would not have needed on his return.

Lambert Wickes to the American Commissioners

ALS: American Philosophical Society

Gentlemen   Nantz January 18th. 1777.
Inclos'd you have a letter and Inventory of the Frigate the
Count of Maurepat. It is the same Vessell that I saw at L Or-
iont and Calld the St. John. I think her Inventory is very short
and will want a Large Addition if fitted for a Ship of War. The
Defishencys I Hope will be pointed out by Capt. Nicholson
When translated into Inglish. I hope Capt. Nicholson will be
able to make the Necessary Addition but least he should not
be Able to recollect all the Necessary Articles, I shall readily
and willingly Give all the Assistance in my Power. I think the
Price very high, but submitt that to your Superior Judgment.
I shall be very glad to hear from you as soon as Possible. Mr.
Gourlade is Desireous of having the Fitting of this Ship and I
have promised to Recommend him to your Honours for this
Service, as I am perswaded he will do it on as Good if not
better terms then any Other person at that port and with more
Secrecy. He also mention'd two Officers whom he can Rec-
commend as proper persons for Officers for said Ship. As to
the Officers I Shall Referr him to you for Answer as well as
for fitting the Ship out. From Gentlemen Your Most Oblidg'd
Humble Servant   LAMBT. WICKES

The St. john is 114 feet Keel 36 feet Beam 13 feet Hold 6 Ditto
Between Decks. She has only Made one voige and is Now All
New Built her Riging Spars Sails Anchors Cables and All other
Stores and Materals are All New and of the first Quality. Her
guns Appear very Good but ought To be prov'd previous to
their being put on bord. This precaution Will be Hily [Highly]
Nessesary as the Guns has bin Laying by Some time. If the
Inventory is Not At Parris I Will Desire Mr. Gourlade to Send
it Immediately or Will Send it my Self if it Comes to my hands.
                                                L. WICKES

The [*illegible*] Capt Wickes is not Certain about but it is the
Ship that is Owend by Messr. Thomaire[?] M[*illegible*] Gourlade She is now on the Stocks where she was rebuilt and[?]
can not be got down the River before next Spring which will
be in Febry.

Memo of Ship

Addressed in another hand: To / The Honble. Benjn. Franklin Esqr. / at / Paris

Notations: Capt Weekes Nantes Jany 18 77 / Letter from Capt. Wickes.

Jonathan Williams, Jr., to the American Commissioners
ALS: University of Virginia Library

Gentlemen   Nantes Jan. 18. 1777

In your instructions to me you mention another Vessell which Mr. Beaumarchais proposes to send to America with Stores, but I can gain no Information of any such Vessell, Mr. Peltrier tells me he knows nothing about it. There is indeed a Ship (the St. Dominique) which Mr. Peltrier bought at the same time that he bought the mercury, and which he is to load on account of Mr. Monthieu for St. Domingo. If this is the Ship in question I will examine her particularly; she is at present strip'd, and they are taking off her deal Sheathing caulking her &c., so that being full of workmen and just come from a guinea Voyage she appears in her dishabile, but I understand she is only 18 months old and has been but one Voyage. She is not so burdensome as the mercury, but is better calculated for a fast Sailor: from her construction I imagine she will excell in this. The mercury being of a flatter construction, and fuller under her Quarters, will not sail so well upon a wind, but before it or with the Wind upon the Quarter she will sail well. I hear that Mr. Beaumarchais Secretary[2] will be here in a few days from l'orient so perhaps I shall be farther informed from him.

By all the information I have yet obtain'd it appears that the want of provisions and room for so many passengers is the principal Cause of the amphitrites return, if there is any other cause I hope I shall find it out. I am told that they were obliged to lay on the bare decks for want of bedding &c. I thought

2. Francy.

that passengers always took care of themselves in this particular, but if it is otherwise expected by those who go in the mercury (if you allow any to go) I beg to be informed by return of post, least these preparations should occasion delay.

I have been this morning with Mr. Peltrier and examined two Bales of Cloth, 1 of Baise, and 1 of Hose. I pitch'd upon 4 indifferent numbers, and caused those identical ones to be opened to avoid the possibility of being deceived. I find all in very good order, and as I have before observed very well pack'd except as to bulk, but if you pay Freight by measure I think by having them in future closly pressed, and twice covered without any straw between, a third part of this expence might be saved. Tomorrow I shall examine the Linnens &c.

I inclose a manifest of the Cargo which is full sufficient to load the Ship. Mr. Peltrier fears she will not be able to take all for want of room, it may therefore be well to have no passengers between decks that all the Goods may be crowded in if possible, and accordingly if I receive no orders from you to the Contrary, I shall have all filled.

There is one part of your Instructions the execution of which will be very painfull to me, as I fear it will turn out very little to your or my satisfaction, I mean that which relates to Mr. Pennett. Without making any Enquiry about him, I am continually hearing things to his disadvantage, whether all I hear is well founded or not I can't determine, but I shall attend particularly to the proof of those stories that affect his probity, before I venture a Report; I therefore beg to be excused on this Head, 'till they are better ascertain'd. The sum of the other part of his Character here, is extravagance, idleness, and ignorance. The splendour of his appearance and pursuit of pleasure seems in some measure to justify the first; but the others may proceed from prejudice. Mr. Morris has been here so short a time that as yet he is little known. I have the honor to be with the greatest Respect Gentlemen Your most obedient Servant   J WILLIAMS

The Honble The Deputies of the United States

Notations: Mr. Williams Nantes Jany. 18th 1777 / Jonan. Williams to Hon: Deputies U.S. (18 Jany 1777.)

From Henry Echlin[3]

ALS: American Philosophical Society

Sir   Prison of the Abbaie St. Germain. 18th. Jany: 1777

Tho' I have not The honour of being personally known to you, I thus venture to address you, not as a Country man, but as a fellow creature, who is reduced by a Captivity of upwards of three years; by Sickness, and Every sort of Evil to the last degree of unhappyness. I am thus compel'd to have Recourse to this most humiliating method of Subsisting. Your Reputation of humanity is as well establised, and does you as much honour, as that of your Extensive Learning, Knowledge and unequalled understanding, and Experience. To whom then can I better address myself In this moment of accumulated ill? In happier days I had occasion to prove myself a Lover of Liberty and an Ennemy to oppression. In my sad situation my way of Thinking is of little Consequence. The unhappy have no freinds. The Bearer will Receive your Commands. I shall always Remain with equal Gratitude and Respect Sir your most obliged obedient servant   HENRY ECHLIN

Addressed: A Monsieur / Monsieur Francklin / A: *Paris.*

Notation: Echelin 18 Jan 77. from Prison

From the Duchesse d'Enville

January 18, 1777 See page 213n

From the Comte de McDonald: Letter and Memorandum

January 18, 1777 See page 168

---

3. An Irish baronet (1740–99) who spent years in jail for debt; the relief provided by friends, including Horace Walpole, proved only temporary. He later returned to England and changed his name, but went on squandering his estate. Wilmarth S. Lewis *et al.*, eds., *The Yale Edition of Horace Walpole's Correspondence* (48 vols., New Haven, 1931–83), VII, 110 and *passim*; Pierre Manuel, *La Police de Paris dévoilée* ... (2 vols., Paris, [1791]), II, 260–2; John R. Echlin, *Genealogical Memoirs of the Echlin Family* (2nd ed., Edinburgh, [1882]), p. 52. BF made some reply, we do not know what, and Echlin sent him a list—perhaps of those who might help to buy him out of jail; Echlin wrote again on the 28th (APS) to ask to have the list back.

From Jacques Paulze[4]

AL: American Philosophical Society

Paris le 18 janv 1777.

M. Paulze souhaite le bonjour à M. francklin et lui rapelle la promesse qu'il a faite a M. Grand de lui faire l'honneur de diner chés lui mardi prochain 21 de ce mois avec M. son petit fils et MM. Dean, Lée et autres des MM. du Congres qui voudront lui faire cet honneur.

Addressed: A Monsieur / Monsieur le Docteur f[ranklin] / hotel D'hambourg / rue Jacob.

From Pecholier Frères

ALS: American Philosophical Society

⟨Bordeaux, January 18, in French: Our good friend M. Ternant, who sailed for Cap Français on the 15th, sent us the enclosed letter for you,[5] which we hasten to send on. If you wish to write him by us, we will forward your letters with the same promptness.⟩

From Jonathan Williams, Jr.

ALS: American Philosophical Society

Dear and honoured Sir   Nantes Jan. 18. 1777

I have written the inclosed because I feel myself very uneasy least I should be liable to the charge of double dealing but if you do not think a longer silence will be construed to my disadvantage, I confess it appears best that the Letter should not go. You know my only motives, and can best judge of the probability of my return or stay, I therefore beg the favour of

4. See Dubourg to BF above, before Jan. 8. The host for whom he was writing was either the prominent Parisian banker Rodolphe-Ferdinand, usually known as Ferdinand, Grand (1726–94), or possibly his older brother and fellow banker, the Chevalier Isaac-Jean-Georges-Jonas, known as Georges (1716–93), whose base was Amsterdam but who was frequently in Paris. Both men became of crucial importance to the commissioners and will appear with corresponding frequency. For the background of the house see Lüthy, *Banque protestante*, II, 339–42.

5. The letter above, Jan. 15.

you to send it to the post or not as you shall think best.[6] I am your dutifull and affectionate Kinsman   J WILLIAMS JUNR

Addressed: A Monsieur / Monsieur Franklin LLD / a l'Hotel d'Hambourg / Rue Jacob / a / Paris

Notation: J. Williams 18 Jan 77.

To [Juliana Ritchie[7]]   ALS (draft): American Philosophical Society

Madam,   Paris, Jan. 19. 1777.

I am much oblig'd to you for your kind Attention to my Welfare, in the Information you give me. I have no doubt of its being well founded. But as it is impossible to discover in every case the Falsity of pretended Friends who would know our Affairs; and more so to prevent being watch'd by Spies, when interested People may think proper to place them for that purpose; I have long observ'd one Rule which prevents any Inconvenience from such Practices. It is simply this, to be concern'd in no Affairs that I should blush to have made publick; and to do nothing but what Spies may see and welcome. When a Man's Actions are just and honourable, the more they are known, the more his Reputation is increas'd and establish'd. If I was sure therefore that my Valet de Place was a Spy, as probably he is,[8] I think I should not discharge him for that, if in other Respects I lik'd him.

The various Conjectures you mention concerning my Business here, must have their Course. They amuse those that make them, and some of those that hear them; they do me no harm, and therefore it is not necessary that I should take the least Pains to rectify them. I am glad to learn that you are in

6. The lost enclosure must have been a letter to his London partner, Walter Blunt. For the partnership see above, XXII, 268–9. The young man was still not sure on which side of the Channel his future lay, to judge by his phrasing here, and wished to keep open, if he could with propriety, the option of returning to the sugar business in London. BF forwarded the letter to Blunt, and soon after JW wrote his partner a second time: below, BF to JW, Feb. 5, and JW to BF, Feb. 16.

7. The letter is in reply to hers above of Jan. 12.

8. BF originally wrote "was a Spy, and I like"; he then interpolated "as probably he is."

a Situation that is agreeable to you, and that Mr. Richie was lately well. My Daughter and her Children were so when I left them, but I have lost my dear Mrs. Franklin now two Years since. I have the Honour to be very respectfully Madam, Your most obedient humble Servant   BF

From [Duportail]   AL: American Philosphical Society

Monsieur   paris le 19 janvier 1777

Faute d'entendre suffisamment l'anglois et plus encore de le lire non imprimé je n'ay pu comprendre la Reponse que vous m'avèz fait l'honneur de m'adresser à versailles. J'esperois trouver icy un de mes amis qui y auroit suppleé mais comme il est absent je suis obligé d'avoir Recours à vous même. Cependant autant que j'ai pu deviner il me semble que vous n'acceptez point mes conditions et que vous dites ne pouvoir me donner le brevet de lieutenant colonel ny de major. Or vous jugèz bien, monsieur, que quand la Cour me donne à moy un grade superieur pour m'engager à passer chèz vous, ce n'est pas apparemment pour que je consente a y servir comme subalterne, et assurement vous ne trouveréz aucun officier du corps du genie et qui y soit sur un bon pied sans les avantages que je demande. Peut estre trouverèz vous des gens qui se diront ingenieurs sans l'etre ou qui n'ayant paru qu'un instant chèz nous n'auront pas eu le temps d'etudier nos places et en avoir tiré les principes de la fortification.

Au reste, monsieur, si j'ai bien compris votre Reponse vous pouvèz vous epargner de me l'écrire. Votre silence la confirmera. Si je vous avois mal entendu, alors ayèz la complaisance de m'en instruire en latin, s'il vous plait, ou en francois. J'ai l'honneur d'etre etc.

D'icy à un mois mon adresse est à l'hotel de hollande Ruë du bouloy

Si notre commerce finit icy, je vous prie monsieur de bruler toutes les lettres et ecrits que vous avèz de moy.

From Mathurin-Jacques Brisson

[before January 20, 1777]   See page 432n

To John Hancock

ALS and copy: National Archives; copy: British Library

Dear Sir,   Paris, Jan. 20. 1777

The Bearer Capt. Balm[9] is strongly recommended to me, as a very able Officer of Horse, and capable of being extreamly useful to us, in forming a Body of Men for that Service. As he has otherwise an excellent Character, I take the Liberty of recommending him to my Friends as a Stranger, of Merit, worthy of their Civilities, and to the Congress as an Officer who if employ'd may greatly serve a Cause which he has sincerely at heart. With great Respect I have the Honour to be Sir, Your most obedient humble Servant   B Franklin

Honble John Hancock Esqr

Notation: Jany 20. 1777 Letter from Doctr Franklin to the Presidt. of Congress recommendg. Lt. Col de la Balme

The Duc de La Rochefoucauld[1] to Franklin and Silas Deane

ALS: American Philosophical Society

This is the first communication from a man who, with his mother, soon became part of Franklin's circle, and who corresponded with him intermittently for the rest of the Doctor's life.[2] Franklin had met

9. The Captain was at the time a lieutenant colonel, presumably by brevet; see La Balme to BF above, Dec. 14. He was given the same rank in the American army, after serving briefly as a volunteer, and was then promoted to colonel and made inspector general of cavalry. He resigned his post in October, 1777, fought thereafter on the frontier, and was killed by Indians near Detroit. Freeman, *Washington*, IV, 539; Lasseray, *Les Français*, II, 329–35.

1. Louis-Alexandre, duc de La Roche-Guyon et de La Rochefoucauld (1743–92), whose great-great-grandfather was the author of the *Maximes*, was prominent among the enlightened nobility. "He is the pearl of all the Dukes," Crèvecoeur said of him years later, "a Good Man and an most able Chemyst." Boyd, *Jefferson Papers*, VII, 376. He later played a part in the reforms of the National Assembly, and was one of the liberal aristocrats whom the Revolution destroyed; a mob stoned him to death in 1792.

2. For BF's relations with the mother and son see Lopez, *Mon Cher Papa*, pp. 185–9. The Duchess, in a note of Jan. 18 (APS), invited BF to dinner on the 23rd; her son was a widower and living with her.

the mother, the duchesse d'Enville, on one of his earlier visits to Paris, and the son at a dinner in London in 1769; but the connection seems to have been casual.[3] It was renewed as soon as the American arrived in France. He brought with him, and forwarded to Vergennes in early January, the draft Articles of Confederation.[4] They were promptly translated for publication, probably by La Rochefoucauld himself; and he forwarded the copies mentioned here. Later, as will be seen, he and Franklin collaborated in translating a number of state constitutions.

20th January. [1777].
Le Due de la Rochefoucauld presents his compliments to Mr. franklyn and Mr. dean and has the honour to send them 50. Exemplars of the American Confederation translated: this traduction will be publicated in the Journal *Des Affaires de l'Amérique*,[5] but these 50. have been separately tied for being offered to the two honourable Gentlemen.

Rullecourt to the American Commissioners

January 20, 1777   See pages 146–7n

Dumas to the American Commissioners

ALS: American Philosophical Society; letterbook draft:[6] Algemeen Rijksarchief, The Hague

Dear Sirs,   21e. Janvr 1777
    Depuis mes deux Lettres du 22 et 26e. Nov. qui sont, je pense, celles dont Mr. Deane m'accuse la réception dans la

3. Above, XIX, 127, where the mother appears as the Duchess of Rochefoucauld; XVI, 33 n.

4. BF's memorandum above under Jan. 5.

5. *Affaires de l'Angleterre et de l'Amérique*, III, cahier XIV, clxxix–cxcii. For a description of this periodical, which was closely connected with the government and is a bibliographer's nightmare, see Butterfield, *John Adams Diary*, II, 354–5 n. BF paid for his subscription on Feb. 8: entry of that date in the Waste Book.

6. The draft omits the lengthy quotations, but otherwise has no significant variations from the ALS.

sienne du 13e. Dec. J'eus l'honneur de lui en écrire une autre le 17e. du dit Dec. et enfin une dans les derniers jours du même mois de l'année passée, dont j'ai oublié de marquer sur mon memorandum la date précise.[7]

Sans aucune nouvelle de votre part, Messieurs, depuis la susdite du 13e. Dec., je crois ne devoir plus différer de vous faire part de ce qui s'est passé depuis ce temps entre moi et le Commis d'une grande maison commerçante,[8] avec qui j'ai jusqu'ici correspondu pour les affaires dont vous m'aviez chargé en Décembre 1775. Ce Commis, chargé des affaires de la Maison jusqu'à l'arrivée d'un autre Facteur,[9] m'écrivit le 24e. December passé la Lettre suivante, que je reçus à Utrecht, où j'étois pour quelques affaires

"Je vous suis très obligé, Monsieur, de la Lettre que vous avez eu la bonté de me communiquer (c'étoit celle de Mr. D. du 13e. Dec.) Je vous prie de ne point vous lasser de m'honorer de ces marques de confiance. J'ai prévenu, Monsieur, quelqu'un qui vient de m'arriver, que je respecte, et à qui j'ai l'honneur d'être attaché depuis longtemps, que je vous présenterois à lui, et qu'il seroit aussi aise que moi, de profiter de votre connoissance. Je vous prie en conséquence d'arranger un voyage dans quelques jours, et de m'en prévenir."

Sur une telle Lettre, je laissai tout, je courus à La Haie et lui écrivis, que j'y attendois ses ordres. J'en reçus le billet suivant, daté du Dimanche (29e. Dec.) au soir

"Si vous pouvez me faire l'honneur, Monsieur, de venir me voir demain Lundi à midi et demi, j'aurai celui de vous entretenir de ce qu'il seroit inutile d'anticiper dans cette réponse."

Je fus donc présenté le lendemain, comme un homme zélé pour nos amis, discret, et plein de bonne volonté, dont on avoit déjà tiré de bonnes lumieres. Mr. le Nouveau Facteur me

7. Deane's letter of Dec. 13 is in the *Deane Papers*, I, 419, and Dumas' of the 17th is in the APS; the letter in late December seems to have disappeared.

8. A veiled reference to the abbé Desnoyers, the chargé d'affaires at the French embassy: above, XXII, 406 n.

9. A new ambassador had been appointed and arrived in late December, Paul-François de Quélen, duc de La Vauguyon (1746–1828), for whom see Larousse, *Dictionnaire universel*.

reçut fort gracieusement, et me dit que je lui ferois plaisir de correspondre avec lui, et de venir le voir de temps en temps, comme j'avois fait à l'égard de Mr. le Commis. Il me demanda, s'il étoit vrai que Mr. Frankl. étoit venu s'établir avec sa famille en France? Je lui répondis, que je ne savois rien de ce que Mr. F. étoit venu faire en F. mais que mon opinion étoit, qu'il y étoit plus pour les affaires de ses amis, que pour les siennes propres. Il me fit quelques questions encore touchant les opérations des Royalistes, auxquelles je répondis comme je pus; on annonça une visite, et je me retirai.

Peu après j'écrivis la Lettre suivante à Mr. le Commis, du 8e. Janvier 1777

"Je reste encore ici jusqu'à Lundi matin. Je suis toujours sans recevoir aucune Lettre de mes amis; et par conséquent hors d'état de rien présenter d'intéressant à Mr. le Facteur. Celle-ci n'est donc que pour vous prier, Monsieur, de vouloir bien me dire comment je dois m'y prendre lorsque j'aurai de quoi; c'est-à-dire, s'il est nécessaire que j'observe le cérémonial en signant mon nom, ou si l'on préferera, comme Vous avez fait, Monsieur, que j'omette cette formalité. Comme elle m'exposoit en cas que quelqu'une de mes Lettres se fût perdue avant de parvenir, j'ai profité avec reconnoissance de cette dispense; mais je n'oserois m'en prévaloir auprès de Mr. le Facteur, sans sa permission.

"A dire vrai, je ne dois pas m'attendre que mes amis m'écrivent rien de leurs affaires actuelles: car ou ils ne devront point le faire; ce qui seroit fort bon: où ils n'auront rien à m'en dire; ce qui seroit mauvais. Je ne vois aucun milieu entre ces deux extrêmités, quant à l'emploi qu'ils pourroient faire de moi ici. P.... est à présent le centre de tout ce qui devra éclorre; et je conçois, que le moins qu'il en transpire avant la maturité, ne sera que le mieux.

"Si les affaires de mes amis étoient désespérées, ce qu'à Dieu ne plaise, M. F. feroit fort bien de s'établir avec sa famille en France, et moi aussi, si j'en avois les moyens. Mais, malgré les triomphes apparents des vainqueurs du jour, je suis fort éloigné de croire le respectable Docteur dans la nécessité de revêtir le triste personnage d'exilé en France: au contraire, tout me persuade qu'il y rend les plus grands services à sa patrie.

"Je compte, Monsieur, sur la promesse que vous avez bien voulu me faire, de me prévenir du temps de votre futur départ, afin que je puisse venir vous remercier de toutes vos bontés pour moi comme pour mon Epouse, et recevoir vos bonnes directions sur la meilleure maniere de poursuivre et terminer son affaire en Dauphiné.

"Je présente mes profonds respects à Mr. le Facteur. Soyez bien persuadé, Monsieur, que celui, plein de reconnoissance, que nous avons pour vous mon Epouse et moi, durera autant que nous-mêmes."

Il me répondit sur le champ ce qui suit,

8e. Janv.

"Je vous suis très obligé, Monsieur, des nouvelles marques de votre souvenir et de vos bontés.

"Je préviendrai la personne considérable, que vous nommez, de la maniere dont vous finirez vos Lettres, et qui pourra être une simple dénomination, telle que *Celui qui vous fut présenté dès le commencement de votre arrivée*, ou *L'habitant de l'Académie de Leyde*, ou *L'Ami des Col* . . .

"Je conçois jusqu'ici le silence de vos liaisons. Peut-être que cela ne durera pas.

"Voulez-vous bien, Monsieur, assurer Madame de mes respects, et de mon zele pour le succés de ses justes prétentions vis-à-vis de Mr. son frere?"

Ces prétentions de mon Epouse, sont une vieille affaire qu'elle a réellement en france, et que j'ai mise en train il y a quelques mois, non seulement pour en tirer quelque parti par la circonstance; mais aussi, et sur-tout, pour me servir de voile aux yeux des curieux indiscrets.

Voila, Messieurs, ce que j'ai cru devoir vous communiquer, non pour que vous entriez là-dessus avec moi dans aucune explication, mais pour que vous en jugiez et profitiez pour vous-mêmes. Je ne reçois plus rien de Londres, quoique j'aie fait sentir suffisamment au correspondant que vous m'aviez donné là, combien ses Lettres m'aident à rendre essentiellement service à nos amis.[1] Mais peut-être vous écrit-il à vous-

---

1. Arthur Lee ended his correspondence, of course, when he left London for Paris.

mêmes autant et plus qu'il ne m'en écrivoit ci-devant à moi. En ce cas je suis tout consolé. Mr. Carmichaël ne m'écrit pas non plus. Je ne sai s'il est encore en Allemagne, ou de retour auprès de vous; s'il vit, s'il se porte bien, s'il fait de bonnes affaires, s'il m'aime toujours, je continuerai d'attendre patiemment qu'il se ressouvienne de m'écrire.[2]

Je vous ai prié dans ma derniere, Messieurs, de m'adresser vos Lettres à l'avenir sous couvert de *Mr. De Visme Marchand de vin à Leyde.* Je vous réitere cette priere, par la raison que j'ai déjà dite. Je ne saurois vous dissimuler, que je languis extrêmement d'avoir de vos Lettres, quand elles ne me diroient rien autre, sinon, que vous aimez toujours, Messieurs, celui qui est avec le respect le plus sincere, et avec l'attachement le plus indépendant de la fortune, Votre très humble et très obéissant serviteur   DUMAS

Leide 21e. Janv. 1777.

Notation: Dumas 21. Janry 1777.

[Duportail] to the American Commissioners

AL: American Philosophical Society

Messieurs   paris le 21 janvier 1777

Je suis bien faché d'avoir entendu précisément le contraire de ce que vous me faisièz l'honneur de m'ecrire et que cela nous ait fait perdre un temps pretieux: mais je vais tacher de le reparer. Je pars ce soir pour versailles afin de scavoir les intentions du ministere, car (ainsi que je crois vous l'avoir dit) il me parut la derniere fois s'etre un peu refroidi et desirer que je suspendisse l'execution de mon projet.[3]

Je vais ecrire aussi à nos messieurs pour avoir leur derniere Resolution après quoy je vous donneray leur nom, mais j'ose reponde d'avance de leurs talens et (ce qui n'est pas indiffe-

2. For William Carmichael, whom Deane had sent to Berlin, see above, XXII, 487 n.
3. The "ministere" was undoubtedly the Minister of War, the comte de Saint-Germain.

rent) de leur caractere. Assurement vous vous feliciterèz quelque jour de les avoir. J'ai l'honneur d'etre etc.

Lutterloh to the American Commissioners

January 21, 1777   See page 111n

Jonathan Williams, Jr., to the American Commissioners

ALS: American Philosophical Society

Gentlemen   Nantes Jan. 21. 1777

I have finished my examination of the Mercurys Cargo and have patterns of the several kinds of Goods, which I shall shew you at my return: I have opened in all ten Cases and Bales and find them in good order.

The last Lighter Load of Goods will be ready to go to the ship tomorrow morning, and I hope to include in it all the provisions &c.; by the common Course of things these will be alongside the 23d in the Morning and then I hope we shall not require more than 3 or 4 Days to finish. I mean however in this Calculation to except bad weather and other unforseen events.

The Capt. has luckily procured a Chart of the Coast from Newfdland to N York but we are still in want from thence southward. I shall set down with the Captain this evening to examine this Chart, and conclude measures about apparent orders and other necessary papers for St. Domingo; I fear I shall not be able to get a pilot but I will do my best endeavour.

I hope by return of my Courier to know your Intentions about the passengers Monsr. DuCoudray proposes to send, and I shall take care to observe them strictly. Monsr. Le Chavalier de mauduit de Plessis is just arrived and I shall do all I can to assist him.[4]

4. See du Plessis' letter above, under Jan. 11. Du Coudray was much taken with the young man, whom he believed BF had sent to him, and soon afterward persuaded him to carry to Congress his letter of Jan. 26, now in the National Archives.

219

I have recvd. twenty Louis d'ors from Mr. Pennet on your account. I have the honor to be Gentlemen Your most obedient and most humble Servant   J WILLIAMS

The Honourable The Deputies of the United States.

Notation: Jona Williams Nantes Jany 21. 77

From Barbeu-Dubourg   AL: American Philosophical Society

Dubourg's inventiveness seems to have been his chief, if not his only, qualification as an entrepreneur. When he learned that the commissioners' negotiations with the farmers general had broken down on the issue of shipping, he returned to the "grande affaire" that he had mentioned in an earlier letter,[5] that of forming a company to bring the tobacco to France in its own ships; and he soon thought that success was in sight. All that remained, as he saw it, was to enlist Franklin as a member, to add luster to the scheme. He amplified his offer with a memorandum, the document following this one, which outlined the plan in more detail; and he obtained from the farmer general most concerned a letter to testify that Franklin's dual role would be no hindrance to negotiations with the farm.[6]

Mon cher Maitre,   A Paris ce 21 jr. 1777.

J'allois hier au soir pour vous dire, si je vous avois trouvé seul, que nous etions enfin au moment de la conclusion de la grande affaire de la fourniture des tabacs aux fermiers generaux à ma satisfaction; pour vous en rendre un compte detaillé, vous inviter à acceder à une societé peu nombreuse mais honnéte et solide, et en ce cas vous demander votre heure pour la signer aujourd'huy.

1°. Nous sommes convenus avec les fermiers generaux que je ne leur demanderai aucunes avances d'argent que je ferai venir à mes frais et risques des tabacs d'Amerique en quantité mediocre d'abord, que je ne continuerai qu'autant que j'y trouverai un benefice honnete, que si je puis le leur fournir a

---

5. Above, under Jan. 9.

6. Paulze [to Dubourg], Jan. 23, 1777, APS. BF did not accept the offer, but hoped that JW might join the company instead; this idea, too, eventually died aborning: Price, *France and the Chesapeake,* II, 709–9.

raison de 8 sols la livre, ils le payeront comptant à ce prix, et s'engagent à en prendre jusqu'a 20 mille boucauts sur ce pied, d'icy au 1er. avril 1778. Que s'il me revient à plus cher, je ne serai point obligé de le leur vendre, mais serai libre de le faire passer a l'etranger.

2°. Nous sommes convenus avec un Banquier de cette ville, et un Commerçant de Dunkerque, de former une societé pour faire ce commerce,[7] et de vous inviter à y acceder.

Cette societé fera un fond de plusieurs millions, pour equiper des navires, et envoyer des marchandises de France au Continent de l'Amerique septentrionale, et rapporter des ports de ce continent en France du tabac pour la provision de la ferme generale, et même pour en reverser dans les autres Etats de l'Europe; independamment des autres denrées et productions des Colonies que l'on pourra en tirer avec profit. Vous contribuerez plus ou moins à la formation de ce fond sans qu'on exige de vous que ce qui pourra vous convenir a cet egard. Et ce que vous en fournirez sera employé soit a acheter, et rassembler dans les ports des Etats unis, les denrées qui devront etre chargées le plus promptement possible sur les vaisseaux appartenants a la Société soit à faire construire en Amerique quelques vaisseaux pour le compte de la societé.

Chaque Associé se chargera de la gestion des affaires communes de la societé, autant que sa position le comportera, et que cela pourra convenir a son gout et a ses autres affaires. Et chacun prelevera un droit de tant pour cent d'interet pour son administration dans la partie dont il aura eté chargé; et la quotité de ce droit de gestion sera fixée aujourd'huy à l'amiable.

On se rendra mutuellement un compte fidele du tout, et sur le benefice total qui resultera de ce commerce, toutes charges frais et pertes deduites, on prelevera l'interet de l'argent avancé par chacun des Associés, lequel interét est fixé a cinq pour cent par an et le benefice excedent sera partagé en quatre portions egales, une pour chacun des Coassociés. Qu'en dites vous, Monsieur et tres cher Maitre? N'esperez vous pas, comme moi, qu'une societé ainsi formée procurera un debouché des denrées et marchandises des deux nations respectivement avanta-

7. See Dubourg to the commissioners below, Feb. 1.

geux? N'esperez vous pas que chaque associé y trouvera per-
sonellement un profit tres honnete, et vraisemblablement même
tres considerable? Nous ferez vous l'honneur d'y concourir?
Où jugez vous à propos que nous nous assemblions pour cet
effet aujourd'huy, et à quelle heure?

Notation: M. Dubourg Tobacco Scheme

[Barbeu-Dubourg]: Memorandum on Tobacco

AD: American Philosophical Society

[January 21?, 1777[8]]

Le commerce des tabacs pour la fourniture de la ferme generale offre a la societé qui l'entreprend dans les circonstances
presentes la perspective d'un benefice aussi assuré et plus considerable que jamais.

Avant les troubles qui ont divisé les Colonies de leur Metropole, les entrepreneurs de ce commerce achetoient le tabac
dans la Virginie et le Mariland à un prix moyen. Ils etoient
obligés de relacher, non sans frais, dans les ports de la grande
Bretagne. Ils vendoient leurs tabacs rendus en France cinq sols
la livre (tout au plus) avec trois mois de credit et ils ne pou-
voient remporter que tres peu de marchandises de France au
Continent de l'Amerique pour l'usage des Colons.

Depuis la guerre ouverte entre les Etats unis et la grande
Bretagne, le tabac est moins cher en Amerique. Les navires
qui en sont chargés n'ont plus à se detourner pour toucher a
l'Angleterre. Le prix en est arreté entre notre societé et la ferme
generale a 8 sols la livre argent comptant (ce qui fait 3 sols
par livre de plus qu'avant la guerre) et les memes vaisseaux
peuvent porter quantité de marchandises de France en Amerique avec un benefice considerable. Mais voicy le revers de la
medaille, la navigation d'un Continent a l'autre est tres peril-
leuse aujourd'huy. Ainsi il faut considerer si l'on ne peut pas
parer à ce danger, et à quoi doivent etre evaluées les precautions necessaires pour s'en garantir? Si elles ne peuvent pas
rencherir le tabac de 3 sols par livre, nous avons un gain assuré.

8. See the headnote on the preceding document.

On mandoit de Nantes et de Bourdeaux au mois d'octobre dernier que l'assurance des vaisseaux de France dans les etats unis de l'Amerique, ou des Etats unis en France, pourroit rouler entre 15 et 18 pour cent pendant les mois d'hiver ou les jours sont courts; d'où l'on inferoit qu'elle iroit de 20 à 25 pour cent pendant les mois d'ete ou les jours sont plus longs. Or 25 pour cent d'assurance, ou un quart de la valeur d'une denrée qui ne coûte vraisemblablement pas plus de deux sols, et qui certainement ne coute pas 4 sols la livre dans le pays ne rencherit pas le tabac d'un sol par livre.

Il s'ensuit evidemment de la que le tabac sur lequel on gagnoit honnetement à le vendre 5 sols la livre avant la guerre, pourroit etre vendu avec profit a raison de 6 sols la livre dans la conjoncture presente, et qu'en le vendant 8 sols cela fait deux sols par livre de benefice ulterieur, ou deux millions sur 20,000 boucauts, sans compter le benefice que l'on peut raisonablement se promettre sur les marchandises portées en retour par les mêmes navires, qui s'en retournoient presque a vide auparavant, benefice qui couvre tout au moins l'assurance des navires allants et venants.

Il est vrai que le tabac aujourd'huy à vil prix dans le Continent peut remonter un peu, et approcher d'avantage du prix commun, mais il n'est pas a craindre qu'il monte plus haut qu'avant la guerre.[9] C'est cependant cette unique apprehension qui a intimidé divers speculateurs, et ecarté nos principaux concurrens.

Il est vrai que la guerre peut eclater entre la France et l'Angleterre; ou que les Colonies peuvent rentrer sous la dependance de leur ancienne Metropole, quoique cela ne soit pas vraisemblable. Mais dans l'un comme dans l'autre cas, il dependra entierement de nous de continuer ce meme commerce, ou d'y renoncer, si nous craignons qu'il ne nous devint onereux.

Voila dans quelle position nous implorons les bons offices de Monsieur Franklin, et l'invitons à entrer dans notre Societé, si cela peut lui etre agreable.

---

9. On this crucial point Dubourg was wrong. Tobacco prices soared to the point where they made meaningless all contracts on fixed terms: Price, *France and the Chesapeake*, II, 715–16.

From the Marquis du Buat

January 21, 1777   See page 170

From Montaudoüin

ALS: American Philosophical Society

Monsieur   Nantes 21 Jer 77

Cette lettre vous sera remise par Mr. de L'Etombe Conseiller au Conseil Superieur du Port au Prince isle St. Domingue.[10] Ce Magistrat recomandable par son honnetete, ses moeurs, et ses lumieres a un grand desir de vous connoître. C'est un desir asses naturel, on aime a rendre hommage a la vertu, et a la science. Il m'a prié, Monsieur, de vous le recommander, et je le fais avec d'autant plus de plaisir qu'il est très bon a connoître. Je suis avec Respect Monsieur vôtre très humble obeissant serviteur   MONTAUDOÜIN

Addressed: A Monsieur / Monsieur le Docteur / Benjamin Franklin / deputé des états unis / hotel d'hambourg / ruë Jacob / à *Paris*

Notation: Montaudoin, Nantes, 21 jan. 77

From Jonathan Williams, Jr.

ALS: American Philosophical Society

Dear and honored Sir   Nantes Jan [21?,[11]] 1777

The inclosed is for the Deputies.[12]

I propose to expedite Monsieur Le Chevalier de mauduit du

10. This was, we assume, Philippe-André-Joseph de Létombe, who subsequently played a part of some importance in Franco-American relations. In 1779 he was appointed consul in Boston, and two years later took up his post. He returned home in 1793, survived the Terror, and in 1795 became consul general for the United States. Butterfield, *Adams Correspondence*, III, 287; IV, 90, 230; Boyd, *Jefferson Papers*, XIV, 64; Howard C. Rice, "French Consular Agents in the United States, 1778–1791," *Franco-American Rev.*, I (1936–7), 369.

11. JW's heading is in another ink, which suggests that it was added later. The suggestion is strengthened by the way he wrote the date: it was originally "Jan 27. 1778," and he then substituted for the digits "1777." Nantes on the 27th is impossible; he left for Paimboeuf the day before. The earliest possible date is the 21st, when Mauduit du Plessis arrived.

12. His letter to the commissioners above of Jan. 21 or, if he was writing a few days later, that of the 23rd.

plessis in the mercury, for I know of no better way and the warmth of his Reccommendation requires the best.

Altho' I can say nothing in alteration of what I have written to the Deputies about Mr. P,[1] yet I confess it creates an uneasy Reflection, for I hope it is no part of my Disposition to speak ill of another with pleasure; but I beg it may be understood as the Opinion others and not mine, for in that I shall be justified by all I have heard speak of him at Nantes, of myself I have no right to Judge. I am dear Sir most dutifully yours

J WILLIAMS

Addressed: A Monsieur / Monsieur Franklin LLD. / a l'Hotel d'Hambourg / Rue Jacob / a / Paris.

Notation: J. Williams Jan. 77.

Barbeu-Dubourg to the American Commissioners

AL: American Philosophical Society

23e. jr. 1777.

Dubourg a l'honneur de souhaiter le bonjour a Monsieur Franklin, Monsieur Deane et Monsieur Lee; et les supplie d'accorder une audience favorable a M. Bayard qui a des objets importans a leur communiquer, et sur l'honneteté et la solidité duquel ils peuvent compter avec la plus parfaite assurance.[2]

Notation: Notes of no Consequence

Jonathan Williams, Jr., to the American Commissioners

ALS: American Philosophical Society

Gentlemen   Nantes. Jan. 23. 1777.

I have the pleasure to inform you that the last Lighter went to the Ship[3] yesterday afternoon on board of which are all the

1. About Penet in his letter above of Jan. 18.
2. Bayard & Cie. was a Parisian firm of bankers and cloth merchants located at the Cloître Sainte-Opportune: *Almanach des marchands*, p. 373. This note suggests that Dubourg was already beginning his venture into supplying textiles and weapons, first mentioned in his letter to the commissioners above, under Dec. 21.
3. The *Mercure.*

provisions &c. except live Stock, which will be bought at Painbeuf. She is cleared at the Custom house and I hope will have all ready to heave up her anchor by monday. I shall go to her on sunday morning to give a last look and hope to see her undersail before I leave her. After this (my Business being finished) I shall set off for Paris unless I receive further Commands, in which Case, be it here or in any other Port, I shall obey with chearfulness and do my utmost to give you satisfaction. I am impatient to hear that the amphitrite is gone. We had a tolerable wind yesterday but it might not have reach'd L'orient. I gave mons. DuCoudray a Copy of the general Instructions when he went away, to be sure that the want of them should be no Cause of Detention.[4]

Having nothing more than what I have already written, I conclude with assuring you that I am very respectfully Gentlemen your most obedient Servant   J WILLIAMS JUNR

The Honourable The Deputies of The United States.

Notation: Mr Williams Nantes 23rd. Jany. 1777

From William Strahan   ALS: American Philosophical Society

Dear Sir   London January 23. 1777.

I take the Opportunity of our worthy Friend Mr. Strange[5] just to ask you how you do, and to acquaint you that all my Family are in perfect Health, and remember you with great

4. This statement clears up a misunderstanding of Deane's. He complained that Du Coudray had brought the ship's papers with him to Paris, thereby delaying her departure; Du Coudray said that he had left them with the ship. *Deane Papers*, I, 465, 467; Du Coudray to Congress, Jan. 26, 1777, National Archives. Both were apparently right: he took a copy of the papers and left the originals.

5. Undoubtedly the famous engraver, Robert Strange (1721–92). He had been angered by his exclusion from the Royal Academy, founded in 1768, and had been involved in controversies that got under his skin to the point where he moved his family to Paris, apparently late in 1775, and stayed there for five years. James Dennistoun, *Memoirs of Sir Robert Strange . . . and of His Brother-in-Law Andrew Lumisden . . .* (2 vols., London, 1855), I, 244–5; II, 175–80; see also the *DNB*. In 1779–83 BF had some correspondence with him and Mrs. Strange.

Esteem and Affection, particularly your Wife, who expects, as you are now so near, that you will soon pay her a Visit.[6] Sir John Pringle I see often. He is quite well (want of Sleep only excepted, which is a pretty constant Complaint with him) and is as sincerely attached to you as ever.

This is a Letter of Friendship, not of Politicks, therefore I shall not say a Word on the Subject; but only to express my Wish and Hope that Peace, Unity and Happiness may be quickly restored. I have not heard a Word *of* or *from* Mr. W. Hall for almost two Years.[7] I want sadly to know how his Mother and all the Family are in these turbulent Times; but I know not how to learn, unless you can assist me.

I hear that you saw my Colleague Mr. Ch. Fox frequently. You would find one of the cleverest Fellows of his Years you ever knew in your Life.[8] I am, with a lively Remembrance of our old Friendship, Dear Sir Your affectionate humble Servant

WILL: STRAHAN

Addressed: Dr. Franklin / at / Paris / By Favour of / Mr. Strange

Notation: W. Strahan

From Louis Garanger

January 24, 1777 See page 432n

Jonathan Williams, Jr., to the American Commissioners

ALS: American Philosophical Society

Gentlemen   Nantes Jan. 25. 1777.

I am just informed that the amphitrite is at last gone, she sail'd yesterday morning at 7 oClock.

6. Strahan's youngest daughter Margaret: above, XVIII, 236.

7. David Hall's elder son was carrying on the *Pa. Gaz.*: above, XX, 88. BF answered this inquiry as best he could; an extract of his reply is below, Feb. 4.

8. Charles James Fox was already, at twenty-seven, a prominent member of the opposition. During his visit to Paris at the end of 1776, he later told the House of Commons, BF "honoured me with his intimacy" and discussed the war: Cobbett, *Parliamentary History*, XXII (1781–82), 514–5.

I have recd. Letters from Monsieur Du Coudray of the 22d and 23d Instant, by which I find he has sent me 7 officers and their Baggage; He names *4* for the *3* I agreed to take, and afterward 3 more, two of which he says are more necessary than even the Fusils and powder; all 7 have recd. advances. I have yet accepted but the first four, and I continue firm to my first plan. I shall do so 'till the last minute, when I believe I shall take the whole 7 as they come within Mr. Deane's exception, and as they are all picked as being the most important;[9] but in this I hold myself reserved, for were I at once to accept these 7 I should have 7 more in half an hour. The above Officers are yet to arrive in a Boat from L'orient, and in all probability they will be at painbeuf to day. I shall go thither tomorrow morning, and if the Vessell is ready and the wind good she shall sail on monday whether these officers are in her or not. In the latter Case I shall have them all upon me, but at all events I shall obey your orders and hope for your approbation and support. I have just parted with an officer whom I have point blank refused, this is the 2d, and before the Day ends I expect to be obliged to treat others in the same manner; I conduct however as civily as the rigour of the Determination will permit, for poor Fellows! I understand they are without the means of procuring even a Dinner. They ask me to certify their presence here, and my refusal, I tell them I shall never deny what is true, but I shall take care how I give certificates.

By some mistake the Letter to Mr. DuCoudray and the Capt. of the amphitrite were left out of Mr. Deane's Packet, but now the Ship is gone it makes no difference. The Letters to Mr. Conway and Mr. Rogers I have not been able to convey.[1] Mr.

9. Deane's original agreement with Du Coudray in 1776 had stipulated the assistants that the Frenchman was authorized to take with him: *Deane Papers*, I, 230–1. Deane's "Exception," no doubt included in the packet from him mentioned in the next paragraph, could well have been some amplification of that agreement. Only two French officers actually left on the *Mercure*: JW to the commissioners below, Jan. 29.

1. The only letter that we can identify is the one to Du Coudray, which was undoubtedly the blast from Deane printed in the *Deane Papers*, I, 467–8. Where Rogers was we do not know, but he stuck with Du Coudray and eventually sailed with him. For Thomas Conway, the Irish-born French officer who later played a controversial part in the War of Independence,

Du Coudray mentions to me that I am to go to l'orient to examine 3 Vessells which he mentioned in his memoire to you, if so I beg your particular Instructions, for otherwise I shall set off for Paris after the mercury is gone. I can't say positively that these officers threaten to complain, but their conversation seems to imply it.

Nothing is more difficult than to procure Charts of our Coast. I am however well supplied except from N York to Georgia, but here I want particular ones; the Captain will I hope arrive at Boston, if not he must do as well as he can with the general Charts (Mercators &c.). I can have here no other Invoices than the numbers of the Bales and what they contain, for as to price &c. we know nothing about it, as I have before observed to you.

I inclose you a protest that Mr. DuCoudray has made against the Captain of the amphitrite. Mr. Beaumarchas' Secretary announces me an Officer whom he calls a nobleman, and particularly charged [for] the mercury by Mr. Beaumarchais.[2] I shall flatly refuse him. I have the honor to be Gentlemen with great Respect Your most obedient Servant   J WILLIAMS

The Honourable The Deputies of the United States.

Notation: J. Williams Jan 25. 1777.

From [Duportail]   AL: American Philosophical Society

Monsieur   paris ce 25 janvier 1777

La Cour me permet d'executer mon projet et même en faveur de ce voyage et pour me recompenser d'un grand travail

---

see the *DAB*. He had been left in charge of the *Amphitrite* but left her, it is said there, and eventually departed from Bordeaux. This is erroneous. She sailed with him, according to his wife, and news reached Nantes in early July that she had brought him to America: Lady Conway to BF below, April 14; Anne Izard Deas, ed., *Correspondence of Mr. Ralph Izard . . .* (New York, 1844), p. 306.

2. The secretary was Francy. The quasi-noble officer was in all likelihood Beaumarchais' nephew, Augustin-François de l'Epine, who had changed his name to des Épiniers, sometimes spelled Epinières, and who aroused Du Coudray's contempt. The young man got to America, became an aide to Steuben, and returned home in the autumn of 1779. *Deane Papers,* I, 406–7; Fitzpatrick, *Writings of Washington,* XI, 356; Lasseray, *Les Français,* I, 100, 283–5.

pour le Corps qui vient d'être terminé, elle me donne le tître de lieutenant-colonel du Corps Royal du genie, comme j'auray l'honneur de vous le faire voir par le congé que je dois recevoir sous deux ou trois jours. C'est parce que j'avois lieu d'esperer cette grace que j'avois mis pour premiere condition que le gouvernement americain me donneroit un grade superieur à celuy que *j'aurois en france au moment du depart*. Ainsi puisque c'est celuy de lieutenant-colonel je demande donc chèz vous le rang de colonel. Comme j'ai obtenu pour mr. de laumoy mon premier compagnon de voyage le tître de major, je demande pour luy chèz vous le grade de lieutenant-colonel et pour mr. de gouvion mon second compagnon le grade de major ayant obtenu icy pour luy la commission de capitaine. Vous trouverèz sur l'etat du Corps ces officers dans les promotions de 1770 et 71. Il ne faut pas croire que ces officiers ne servent que depuis ces dates. Il y a toujours 5 ou six ans d'ecole et d'etudes avant l'epoque de la reception. Souvent même on a servi dans d'autres Corps. Aussi le plus jeune d'eux a plus de trente ans.

Si vous avèz d'ailleurs, messieurs, quelques moyens de vous informer *d'eux* que ce soit, je vous prie, avec le plus grand secret; car la moindre chose qui perceroit dans le public nous attireroit une defense de poursuivre notre entreprise.

Je vous seray obligé de me mander sur le champs si vous acceptèz mes propositions. Si je reçois votre reponse d'icy a six heures du soir, j'iray ce soir même chèz vous pour prendre des arrangements plus particuliers sur le voyage. Vous voudrèz bien me dire de quoy il faut principalement se munir &c. j'écriray ensuite a nos messieurs de se rendre icy et sous quinze jours au plus nous serons prets.

Si vous me mettèz dans le cas d'avoir l'honneur de vous voir ce soir, je vous prie, Monsieur, de m'en indiquer l'heure précise et de prendre des mesures pour que je n'y trouve aucune personne etrangere et qu'aucune autre ne survienne. Car je ne dois pas estre vu. J'ai l'honneur d'etre

A l'hotel d'hollande Rüe du bouloy

From the Comte de Sarsfield[3]

ALS: American Philosophical Society

Sir   January the 25th 1777

As I never will lose the memory of the honour I had of your acquaintance in london Some years ago, I am not less Confident that you have not quite forgotten it. I hope to be in paris within Some few weeks, and it will make me very happy to be able of assuring you my Self of my attachment and respect. In the mean while I beg leave, Sir, to present you my Brother.[4] He is also my best friend, he wishes very much the honour of being known to you, and will inform me of many particularities relating to you which I desire extremely to find at your Satisfaction. I am with the Greatest regard and attachment Sir your most humble and obedient Servant   SARSFIELΓ

Give me leave, Sir, to present my best Compliments to Mr. Deane.

Addressed: A Monsieur / Monsieur franklin / A Paris

Notation: Sarsfiel Jan 25. 77

From Jonathan Williams, Jr.

ALS: American Philosophical Society

Dear and honored Sir.   Nantes Jan. 25. 1777

I write the inclosed in haste as I have many things to see ready in order that I may get to the Ship tomorrow. I have got

---

3. A French officer of Irish extraction, who had known BF in London in 1767: above, XIV, 205. Sarsfield renewed the acquaintance in person and by correspondence when he arrived in Paris. His next note that survives is an AL of April 15, 1777 (identified by the handwriting; APS), to accompany two gazettes, which he asked BF to return.

4. Jacques-Hyacinthe, vicomte de Sarsfield, a French cavalry officer: *Dictionnaire de la noblesse*, XVIII, 292. He apparently called with this letter when BF was out, for he wrote on the back of it an invitation to dinner the following Saturday at his house. He, like his brother, had considerable subsequent correspondence with BF. The only item in it that may belong in this volume is a two-sentence note from the vicomte (APS) asking whether he may call at Passy the next day; it is dated "Vendredi 25 avril," and was therefore written in either 1777 or 1783.

a difficult Task to go through but I will acquit myself as well as I can and hope (obeying orders) you will not think my Conduct too rigourous. I am Your dutifull and Affectionate Kinsman   J WILLIAMS

I have not time to answer Mr. Alexanders Letter now.[5]

I am treated here with as much Respect as if I were the Nephew of a prince. So much is your name respected that I hear the Ladies of Nantes are about making an addition to their heads in imitation of your Hair Cap, which they intend to call *a la Franklin.*[6]

Addressed: A Monsieur / Monsieur Franklin LLD / Hotel de Hambourg / Rue Jacob / a Paris.

Notation: J. Williams 25 Jany. 77.

The American Commissioners to [Montaudoüin]

Copy:[7] Library of Congress

Sir: Paris, Jany. 26th. 1777

We are very much obligd to you for the information containd in yours of the 21st.

Mr. Williams's good sense will prevent him from being materially embarrassd by any manouvre employd to make him counteract our Instructions.

We cannot so entirely comprehend the obligation we have to the Mayor and Aldermen of your City, as to know in what terms to return it.[8] As it is probable one of our number will soon be in Nantes, he will be able to thank them in person. In the mean time we beg the favor of you, Sir, to make them our acknowledgements in such manner as you may think becom-

5. He had trouble in answering; see his letter to BF below, Feb. 16.

6. See the note on BF to Hewson above, Jan. 12.

7. In the hand of Arthur Lee. Montaudoüin's letter, now lost, may have referred to Beaumarchais' "Manouvre"; see JW to the commissioners above, Jan. 25.

8. The obligation concerned a reduction in the duty on tobacco; see Montaudoüin to the commissioners below, Feb. 13.

ing. We have the honor to be, with very great esteem, Sir, Your most obedient Servants.

Notation: Supposed to be to M. Montondoin Jan. 26.77.

The American Commissioners to Thomas Morris

AL:[9] Library of Congress

Sir: Paris, Jany. 26th. 1777

We have expected some Remittances from you to our credit, in consequence of the sales which have been made at Nantes.[1] You must be sensible how very unbecoming it is of the situation we are in, to be dependent on the credit of others. We therefore desire that you will remit with all possible expedition the Sum allotted by the Congress for our expences.

To Mr. T. Morris

Notation: Mr. T. Morris. Jan 26. 1777.

The American Commissioners to Samuel Nicholson

AL:[2] Library of Congress

Sir   Paris Jany. 26th: 1777.

You are directed to proceed to Boulogne, and there purchase, on as good Terms as possible a Cutter suitable for the purpose of being sent to America; on the purchase being made dispatch the Vessel to Havre du Grace to the Care of Monsr: Limozin, and agree in the Bargain to have her delivered at said Port at the risque and expence of the Original Owner, at which stipulate to make the payment; should you miss of one at Boulogne, proceed to Calais, and pursue the same Directions, if you fail there pass to Dover, or Deal, and employ a person

9. In Arthur Lee's hand.
1. Morris was under order from the secret committee to make these remittances: Smith, *Letters*, v, 388–9. The commissioners repeated their request in more peremptory terms in their letter below, Jan. 30. But Morris was having difficulties, which he explained in his letter below, Feb. 4.
2. In Deane's hand.

there to make the purchase as for Mr. Limozin of Nantes, at whose house the payment shall be made.[3] Your skill in Maritime Affairs will enable you to judge of the Vessel proper for Our purpose, in which We wish you to embark yourself for Havre, and on your Arrival, put the Vessel into the Care of Mr. Limozin to be filled with every thing Necessary for her to proceed the designed Voyage, at the same time directing Mr. Limozin to call her and speak of her as his Own, after which you will instantly set off for this Place to inform Us of your proceedings. Meantime you are on purchasing to write by the first post, not to Us, but to *Mr. LeGrand Banquier Rue Mont Mart Vis a Vis St. Joseph a Paris*, only saying in a few Words that you have made a purchase, and shall draw on him soon for the Money favor of Mr. Limozin or Words to that Purpose. This Letter will be shewn Us, and We shall regulate Our proceedings Accordingly. Should you be obliged on purchasing to pay at Dover, or Deal, Monsr: LeGrands Letter will give a sufficient Credit for the purpose. And at Calais, or Boulogne, you will address yourself, on the score of advice and assistance in Money Matters, To the persons to whom you will have Letters directed but on No other Account, and avoid hinting your proceedings or views to any one. But should Capt. Hynsen arrive from London and join you let him go in the Vessel you purchase, to Havre and there wait Our further Orders.[4] Should he arrive and no Vessel be purchased, in such Case procure him a passage to Havre, and Direct him to apply to Mr. Limozin for Our Directions. In the whole, we have to wish you to Make the Utmost Dispatch, and to conduct with the utmost secrecy and the Œcconomy consistent with hastening as fast as possible the Object in View.

Capt. Nicholson

Notation: Instructions to Capt Nicholson

3. André Limozin was the merchant in Le Havre whom the committee of secret correspondence had instructed the commissioners to use as agent of prizes: above, XXII, 667.

4. Joseph Hynson, a sea captain from Maryland who was Wickes' stepbrother, was then in London without a ship; the commissioners had selected him to carry their dispatches to America on the cutter that they expected Nicholson to acquire. Hynson was soon afterward approached by the British and enlisted as a secret agent. Clark, *Wickes*, pp. [161]-4.

To Mary Hewson
AL: Yale University Library

Dear Polley   Paris, Jan. 26[–27]. 1777

I wrote a few Lines to you by Dr. B. and have since seen your Letter to Jona. by which I have the great Pleasure of learning that you and yours were well on the 17th.

What is become of my and your dear Dolly? Have you parted? for you mention nothing of her. I know your Friendship continues; but perhaps she is with one of her Brothers. How do they all do?

I have not yet receiv'd a Line from my dear old Friend your Mother. Pray tell me where she is, and how it is with her. Jonathan, who is now at Nantes, told me that she had a Lodging in Northumberland Court. I doubt her being comfortably accommodated there.

Is Miss Barwell a little more at rest; or as busy as ever? Is she well? And how fares it with our good Friends of the Henckel Family?[5]

But principally I want to know how it is with you. I hear you have not yet quite settled with those People.[6] I hope, however, that you have a sufficient Income, and live at your Ease; and that your Money is safe out of the Funds. Does my Godson[7] remember anything of his Doctor Papa? I suppose not. Kiss the dear little Fellow for me, not forgetting the others. I long to see them and you.

What became of the Lottery Tickit I left with your good Mother, which was to produce the Diamond Earings for you? Did you get them? If not, Fortune has wrong'd you! For you *ought* to have had them. I am, my dear Friend, ever yours, with sincere Esteem and Affection.

If you write to me, direct for me thus *A Monsr. Monsieur François*, chez M. de Chaumont à Passy, près de Paris.

P.S. 27th Jany. They tell me that in writing to a Lady from

---

5. Dr. B. was presumably Edward Bancroft and the "few Lines" the letter above, Jan. 12. Dolly's two brothers were Sir Charles and Walter Blunt. For Mrs. Stevenson's move from Craven St. see above, XXII, 263 n, and for Mary Barwell and the Henckells respectively XVII, 194 n, and XIX, 152 n.

6. Hutchinson Mure and Richard Atkinson, from whose firm Polly was trying to obtain her legacy; see her letter above, XXII, 300–1.

7. William Hewson, who was then five.

Paris, one should always say something about the Fashions. Temple observes them more than I do. He took Notice that at the Ball in Nantes, there were no Heads less than 5, and a few were 7 Lengths of the Face, above the Top of the Forehead. You know that those who have practis'd Drawing, as he has, attend more to Proportions, than People in common do. Yesterday we din'd at the Duke de Rochefocault's, where there were three Dutchesses and a Countess, and no Head higher than a Face and a half. So it seems the farther from Court the more extravagant the Mode.[8]

Notation: Paris Jan 26. 77

La Rochefoucauld to Franklin and Silas Deane

AL: American Philosophical Society

[January 26?, 1777[9]]

Le Duc de la Rochefoucauld has the honour to send to Dr. franklyn and to Mr. Deane this letter which he has received few minutes after the two Gentlemen have been out of his house, and to make to them his sincere compliments on the departure of the Amphitrite: he begs them be so good to send back to him the letter after reading it.

8. Polly had commented, in the letter just cited, on the extravagance of London headdresses.

9. Our dating rests on one fact and one strong probability. The fact is that BF, presumably with Deane, attended a dinner party at the Duke's on the 26th; see the postscript of the preceding letter. The Duke, just after his guests had left, received the letter that he is enclosing for them and learned from it that the *Amphitrite* had sailed. She put to sea early in the morning of the 24th, JW wrote the commissioners the next day; in that case a courier, leaving at once and riding post haste, could have reached Paris late on the 26th; and that is probably what happened. But it is only a probability, because Du Coudray wrote to Congress on the 26th (National Archives) that he had tried to board the ship on the 25th and had been stopped by the *commissaire du port*, who had delivered him the King's order to rejoin his regiment. We believe that "25" was a slip of the pen, and that the episode occurred near dawn on the 24th. Du Coudray, we suspect, immediately sent La Rochefoucauld word of what had happened, in a letter that the Duke enclosed with this note. For the next piece of the story, as we conjecturally reconstruct it, see the headnote below, Feb. 3.

Ladies' Headdresses

From Pierre Duffy
ALS: American Philosophical Society

⟨St. Malo, January 26, 1777, in English: The writer, an Irish-man and Recollect friar, addresses his letter to Franklin as "Irish Gentle-Man" and informs him that he has a needy relative named Geene, Ginny, or Jeanne Franklin, the widow of "your Brother Robin Francklin" of Limerick. The letter is endorsed, apparently by Temple, "Jane Franklin pretended."⟩

From [Duportail]
AL: American Philosophical Society

Monsieur   paris le 26 janvier 1777

Je m'en vais quelques jours chèz moy à vingt lieües de paris disposer tout pour mon depart: ainsi passé midy demain, si vous avèz quelque chose à me faire scavoir ecrivèz moy, s'il vous plait, à l'adresse que vous trouverèz au bas de cette lettre.

J'ai reçu ce matin nos permissions du Roy et je vous les montreray pour que vous voyèz par vos yeux et puissièz certifier la verité des tîtres que nous prenons. Je vous prie même, si vous vous occupèz a dresser nos conventions, de faire mention de notre qualité icy parce que cela justifiera d'autant la concession que vous nous ferèz au nom de votre gouvernement, des grades convenus.

Je vais tout disposer pour estre pret à partir sous quinze jours au plus. J'ai l'honneur d'etre etc.

a pithiviers en gatinois[1]

Dès que mr. de gouvion sera à paris il vous ira voir.

To Joseph Priestley
AL (incomplete) and copy:[2] Library of Congress

Dear Sir,   Paris, Jan. 27. 1777

I received your very kind Letter of Feby. last, sometime in September. Major Carleton, who was so kind as to forward it

1. His family seat: Lasseray, *Les Français*, I, 272.
2. The copy, entitled "To Dr. Priestley," originally read "Extract of a Letter to Dr. Priestley (on American affairs)"; it omits the incomplete sentence at the end and adds BF's initials.

to me had not an Opportunity of doing it sooner.[3] I rejoice to hear of your continual Progress in those useful Discoveries. I find that you have set all the Philosophers of Europe at Work upon Fix'd Air; and it is with great Pleasure I observe how high you stand in their Opinion; for I enjoy my Friend's Fame as my own.

The Hint you gave me, jocularly, that you did not quite despair of the Philosopher's Stone, draws from me a Request, that when you have found it you will take care to lose it again; for I believe in my conscience that Mankind are wicked enough to continue slaughtring one another as long as they can find Money to pay the Butchers. But of all the Wars in my time, this on the part of England appears to me the wickedest; having no Cause but Malice against Liberty, and the Jealousy of Commerce. And I think the Crime seems likely to meet with its proper Punishment, a total Loss of her own Liberty and the Destruction of her own Commerce.

I suppose you would like to know something of the State of Affairs in America. In all Probability we shall be much stronger the next Campaign than we were in the last; better arm'd; better disciplin'd, and with more Ammunition. When I was at the Camp before Boston, the Army had not 5 Rounds of Powder a Man. This was kept a Secret even from our People. The World wonder'd that we so seldom fir'd a Cannon. We could not afford it. But we now make Powder in Plenty.

To me it seems, as it has always done, that this War must end in our favour, and in the Ruin of Britain, if she does not speedily put an end to it. An English Gentleman here the other day in Company with some French, remark'd, that it was Folly in France not to make War immediately: *And in England,* reply'd one of them, *not to make Peace.*

Don't believe the Reports you hear of our internal Divisions. We are I believe as much united as any People ever were, and as firmly. There [*remainder missing.*]

Notation by the copyist: Dr. Priestly Extr.

3. See above, XXII, 347–8 n.

Jonathan Williams, Jr., to the American Commissioners

ALS: American Philosophical Society

Gentlemen   Painbeuf Jan. 27. 1777

I was astonished on saturday Evening[4] to find that Mr. DuCoudray had returned to Nantes. As we were late for the Tide (the loss of which would have been the loss of a day) I came away without seeing him: Mr. Peltier tells me he has positive orders from Mr. Demontieu (which are given with your approbation) that if Mr. Du Coudray should come to Nantes to refuse him a passage.[5] I have no contrary orders, so in this I must acquiese, especially, as whether I will or no he (Mr. P) will refuse him.

Last Evening Mr. DuCoudray arrived here and shew me the Kings sign manual ordering him to his Regiment. This he says is the Reason of his not going in the amphitrite which sailed as I have before mentioned and he now demands a passage in the Mercury. I told him that there were orders forbidding it, without saying from whom they came. He desired I would sign a Refusal in form. I told him I would sign nothing, especially as it was Mr. Peltier not me that refused him. He said he would have nothing to do with Mr. Peltier and would protest against me.[6] I told him he may do as he pleased, and so it rests. Here is also the Chevalier de Borre, who shews me his Engagement with Mr. Deane and seems to be in dispair at his Situation: He was on board the amphitrite but Mr. DuCoudray obliged him to disembark, as he says. In this Situation are 11 officers, each claiming a Right and pretending that his Engagements are more valid and of more Consequence than all the others. I therefore think that I should do well to refuse all, and there appears such an Idea of Authority among them, that I believe this refusal would be for the good of the service; but

4. Two days before.
5. Montieu's association with Hortalez & Cie. enabled him to give orders to Peltier, Beaumarchais' agent.
6. He did protest, vehemently, in his letter to Congress of Jan. 26, 1777, National Archives.

the utmost that can be done, is to take 4 according to my first plan, and to avoid preferences to take them by Lot.[7]

The Ship is as full as she can be cramm'd and yet there are 40 Bales which will be left, notwithstanding this these people expect passages with their Domestiques and Baggage: Mr. DuCoudray alone has 15 Trunks.

I write on board where I am obliged to keep myself 'till the Ship gets under sail, which I hope will be this Evening.

Mr. DuCoudray sent on Board a Letter to Mr. Peltier charging him according to his Duty as *Garde d'artillerie* to come before his *superiour* officer (Mr. DC) before noon. The Stile and intent of this is to me unintelligible. As Mr. Rogers was going back I told him he might tell the Officers that I would take 4 and no more, who these 4 are to be they may determine among themselves, and as to Mr. D Coudray I could only refer him to Mr. Peltier who says with regard to that particular he is not at present under my orders. I therefore do not refuse him, but if he were to come on board the Captain would refuse him admittance.

I am in a very disagreeable Situation having only my own discretion for my Guide. I hope however you will not condemn my Conduct if it should not turn out to your wish when you consider that my aim is to give satisfaction as far as my abilities will allow. I have the honor to be Gentlemen Your most obedient Servant   J WILLIAMS JUNR

The Honourable The Deputies of the United States.

Notation: J. Williams 27 Jan. 77.

From ——— Briant de Peinquelein

January 27, 1777   See page 168

7. De Borre, whether or not he was chosen by lot, did get onto the *Mercure.* He was commissioned a U.S. brigadier general, served throughout the next campaign, and then resigned in disgust. Lasseray, *Les Français,* II, 367–70.

From Paulze

ALS: American Philosophical Society

Paris le 27. Janvier 1777.

M. Paulze fait mille complimens à M. Le Docteur franklin, il a l'honneur de le prevenir que la Biblioteque du Roy[8] lui sera ouverte Jeudi prochain 30. depuis onze heures jusques à deux, que MM. les Bibliotequaires s'empresseront de l'y recevoir et lui montrer tout ce qu'il est de rare. Il est à propos que M. franklin et sa compagnie se trouvent a onze heures precises à la Biblioteque.

From Benjamin Vaughan

ALS: American Philosophical Society

My dearest sir, Essex, January 27h: 1777.

Having a convenient opportunity[9] I have sent you the publications you desired. The maps I hope you will do me the favor to accept of.

Upon a reconsideration of the matter I shall cancel the whole impression of your political works, and wait for the additional pieces. I shall then have it my power to give a new arrangement, with a total omission of all notes, excepting such as mark the periods of publication and the like. To this I conceive you will have as little objection as myself. But you will please to recollect, that I have not yet got your remarks upon *paper currency*. And might not the American edition of Mr. *Galloway's* speech accompany the dialogue on slavery &c.? But I am still at a loss where to procure the paper about the twelve points of a senator.[1]

The letter to Mr. C: was safely delivered, and the forty gui-

8. In the former Hôtel Mazarin, rue de Richelieu, now incorporated in the Bibliothèque Nationale.

9. By Edward Bancroft; see his letter below, March 4.

1. BF's remarks on paper currency and preface to Galloway's speech are above, XIV, 77–87 and XI, 271–311; they appear in *Political Pieces* on pp. 206–21 and 418–64 respectively. The "Conversation on Slavery" (above, XVII, 37–44) Vaughan did not print. The paper about a senator leaves us bemused: it sounds like a commentary on *The Senator's Remembrancer*, which BF greatly admired (above, XVIII, 36 n); but we have no indication that he wrote about it, and Vaughan's edition contains no such paper.

neas paid into his hands in the name of Mr. Jonathan Williams Junr.: for which I have one of the tellers' receipt.[2]

All letters *to* this country are opened, and I suppose they are also opened *from* this country. While I write nothing treasonable against the minister, I have no fear of proclaiming to the world how much I am your respectful, grateful and affectionate   BENJN: VAUGHAN

P.S. We expect Dr: Price's pamphlet out soon, and I believe it may contain some extracts from a paper supposed to have been drawn up by you in Congress, June, 177[5][3]

List of books sent. Remembrancer from the beginning
                     Parliamentary Register from Ditto
                     Smith's Wealth of Nations
                     Philosophical Transactions
                     Pamphlet about Gen: Washington
                     Mr. Radcliffe's sermon on the fast.
                   ⎧ Holland and Pownall's Map of New York
Maps.   ⎨ Montresor's Ditto
                   ⎩ Map of the lakes[4]

Addressed: Dr: Franklin, / Hotel d'Hambourg, / Paris.

Notations: Mr. Vaughan / Vaugan Bn. January 27. 1777.

2. We assume that Mr. C. was the Collinson of Browns & Collinson, and that the letter Vaughan delivered him was from JW rather than BF. The latter presumably did not know what the transaction was about. JW was supporting an illegitimate son in England, but did not admit the fact until his letter below of June 7. Vaughan had been in Paris at Christmas (see his note to BF below, Sept. 18) and had doubtless been intrusted with the money then.

3. Price's work, *Additional Observations on the Nature and Value of Civil Liberty* . . . , was published on Feb. 20, and did contain an extract of BF's "Intended Vindication and Offer": above, XXII, 114.

4. Some items on this list, such as Adam Smith or the *Phil Trans.*, need no identification. The first series of books was John Almon's venture, *The Remembrancer, or Impartial Repository of Public Events* . . . , which began publication in 1775. The pamphlet "about" Washington was probably one or more of the spurious letters from him published in 1777, although we have found no printing so early in the year. The sermon was Ebenezer Radcliffe, *A Sermon Preached at Walthamstow, December 13, 1776, Being the Day Appointed for a General Fast* . . . (London, 1776). The three maps, all published in London in 1776, were Samuel Holland, *The Provinces of New York, and New*

From Jonathan Williams, Jr.

ALS: American Philosophical Society

Dear and honored Sir,   Painbeuf Jan. 27. 1777.

The inclosed will inform you how matters are here.[5] I feel myself uneasy least my Conduct should not be approved yet I think it is precisely according to orders. You will perhaps have representations from these officers to my prejudice as the part I act cannot but be offensive to them all, but however I may succeed I depend that you will believe my motive and not allow any Report from them to injure me in your Esteem. I am 30 miles from Nantes so have no body to advise me, but I shall continue firm to my first plan. I am in haste your dutifull Nephew   J WILLIAMS

Addressed: A Monsieur / Monsieur Franklin LLD / Hotel de Hambourg / Rue Jacob / a Paris.

Notation: J. Williams 27 Jany 77.

To [Dumas]

ALS: Library of Congress

Paris, Jan. 28. 1777

My dear Friend may be assured that the Omission of writing to him for so long a time either by Mr. D. or myself, was not in the least owing to any Want of Respect or Change of Sentiment towards him; but merely from the extreme Hurry we have been engag'd in ever since my Arrival, which has prevented our Writing to many other of our Correspondents. I now enclose several Letters, One of which was wrote by me when in Philada. and sent viâ Martinique. Mr. Deane has but this Day receiv'd it. Another that I wrote soon after my Arrival, which had been mislaid.[6]

Jersey . . . *Improved from the Original Materials, by Governor Pownall* . . . ; John Montresor, *A Map of the Province of New York* . . . ; and William Bassier, *A Survey of Lake Champlain Including Lake George.* . . .

5. His letter to the commissioners of the same date.

6. BF's notes were so brief that they scarcely qualify as letters: above, XXII, 646, and Dec. 23 in this volume. Both contain, as this one does, a promise to write more fully soon.

I hope you and yours are in good Health and good Spirits, as we are, not doubting of the Success of our Affairs with God's Blessing. We have nothing to complain of here.

I have taken a Lodging at Passy, where I shall be in a few Days;[7] and hope there to find a little Leisure, free from the perpetual Interruption I suffer here by the Crowds continually coming in, some offering Goods, others solliciting for Offices in our Army, &c. &c.. I shall then be able to write you fully.

Be of good chear, and don't believe half of what you read in the English Gazette. With great Esteem, I am ever Your most obedient Servant   BF

Notation: Frank lin

Franklin and Chaumont: Agreement about Board at Passy

D:[8] University of Pennsylvania Library

On January 28 Franklin intended, as he mentions in the preceding letter, to move to Passy within a few days. He was following his younger grandson, who at Chaumont's instigation had been put in boarding school there.[1] In fact the old man waited, for reasons we do not know, until the end of February, and this agreement on board might have been reached at any time in the intervening month; we assign it to the earliest plausible date.

Chaumont had had for some time the idea of bringing the commissioners under his roof. He had originally bought the Hôtel de Valentinois, he later wrote Vergennes, "pour y Loger gratuitement les ministres plenipotentiares du Congrès, et les preserver des Embuscades qu'on leur auroit tendues a Paris."[2] This was certainly stretching a point, for the previous August, when he made the purchase, there were no ministers; Deane was the nearest approach to one, and he stayed in Paris. But, once the commission began to operate, the country estate may well have assumed new importance to its owner and to Vergennes. Chaumont was in touch with Frank-

7. See the headnote on the next document. At about this time BF must have informed the Shipleys that he was moving, for Georgiana's letter below of Feb. 11 was addressed to him at Passy.

8. In WTF's hand.

1. See Chaumont to BF above, under Jan. 4.

2. Stevens, *Facsimiles*, XXII, no. 1985, p. 1.

Jacques-Donatien Le Ray de Chaumont

lin from the start and soon became, the British believed, the Minister's principal means of communicating with the Americans.[3] Moving them to Passy had obvious advantages from the viewpoint of the court: they would be less conspicuous and better insulated from the gossip-mill of the city than they were in the Hôtel d'Hambourg; their host could discreetly keep them in touch with the government's real position, as distinct from its ostensible one, and as discreetly watch over their comings and goings, their mail and their visitors. These considerations may or may not have been back of Chaumont's invitation. All we know is that Franklin acted on it in February, and that Deane followed in the summer; only Lee remained aloof.

The agreement says nothing about rent, because Chaumont was charging none, on the understanding that Congress would compensate him with a land grant at the end of the war.[4] The arrangements about board, if they ever went into effect, were of short duration. At some time between February 26 and 28 Franklin and his party arrived at the Hôtel de Valentinois.[5] On March 2 his major-domo began to lay in large supplies of food: meat, vegetables, fruit, wine, bread "pour les maitres" and "pour les gens." A great deal of equipment was also required, not only such obvious items as candles and shoebrushes and wax, but also a coffee mill, a "Diable" for roasting the coffee, a sugargrater, a feather duster for Franklin's desk, and even "quatre ballets [balais] pour les pots de chambre."[6] The new menage had many needs. It also had a setting of great charm. The Americans were housed in one of the garden pavilions of the Hôtel, which stood on a high bluff. Outside were terraces and gardens

3. *Ibid.*, III, no. 248, pp. 7–8; VII, no. 670, p. 10; XIX, no. 1718, pp. 1–2.

4. Smyth, *Writings*, VIII, 589. Chaumont and his family, Paul Wentworth reported a year later, intended to emigrate to America: Stevens, V, no. 439, p. 11. In 1782, when his financial position became precarious, he was allowed current and retroactive rent at 6,000 *l.t.* a year: Claude A. Lopez, "Benjamin Franklin, Lafayette, and the *Lafayette*," APS *Proc.*, CVIII (1964), 186–7 n.

5. The move may have consumed several days, and was probably completed on the 27th. Two charges appear for "the Horses at Passy," one on the 26th in BF's accounts as commissioner, and the other on the 28th in WTF's accounts; an entry of the 27th in the Waste Book records a settlement for final domestic expenses in Paris. For these accounts see above, pp. 19–20. Deane, also on the 27th, wrote that BF was "in the country in good health": *Deane Papers*, II, 13.

6. The Pillets' accounts (above, p. 20), entries under March 9.

leading down to the Seine, woods to walk in, and a view of Paris in the distance.[7]

[c. January 28, 1777]
Conventions.

1°. M. Franklin, et M. son petit fils payeront chacun la somme de six francs pour chaque Diner qu'ils feront ensemble ou separément chez M. De Chaumont. Ce qui fera, en supposant qu'ils y dinent tous les Jours, 4380 *l.t.* par An.

2 Ils ne payeront ces 6 francs par Diné, qu'autant qu'ils y dinent, comme de raison.

3 M. F. payera egalement Six livres, pour chaque Ami qu'il pouroit ameneroit [*sic*] diner chez M. De Chaumont.

4 Quand M. Franklin aura du Monde, et qu'il voudra faire Table a part, Il payera en entier le montant du Diner, qu'il lui aura été pourvu par Mlle. de Chaumont.

5 M. Franklin fournira le vin et autres Liqueurs, aux Diners qui se feront a part chez lui, et M. De Chaumont fournira les memes pour ceux qui se feront chez lui.

Montaudoüin to the American Commissioners

ALS: American Philosophical Society

Messieurs   Nantes 28 Jer 77

J'ai reçû la lettre dont vous m'avéz honoré le 21 de ce mois. Je ne crois pas qu'aucun particulier veüille entreprendre d'acheter, d'armer pour son compte le batiment en question, et de le livrer a ses risques dans quelque port de vôtre pais. On ne trouveroit pas d'assurances solides pour une telle en-

---

7. Smyth, *Writings*, VII, 223; BF to Mary Hewson, Jan. 10, 1780, APS; Howard C. Rice, Jr., *Thomas Jefferson's Paris* (Princeton, N.J., 1976), pp. 91–2; Meredith Martindale, "Benjamin Franklin's Residence in France . . . ," *The Mag. Antiques*, CXII (1977), 262–3, 269–71, and "L'Hôtel de Valentinois et ses environs au temps de Benjamin Franklin," Soc. hist. d'Auteuil et de Passy *Bulletin*, XV (1975–78), 7–14.

treprise, et les particuliers sont imprudens quand il faut courir
des risques aussi considerables. Mais ces risques peuvent être
tentés aisement pour le compte du Congrés sans qu'il paroisse
en rien dans l'expedition. De cette maniere je ne pense pas
que Le Gouvernement y voit obstacle, puisque voilà plusieurs
expeditions dans le même gout.

Je fus fort surpris, Messieurs, de voir arriver dans mon cabinet Dimanche dernier a 9 heures du matin Mr. Ducoudray.[8]
Je savois le depart de L'Amphitrite du 24. Je le croiois de mer.
Il m'aprit qu'il avoit eû ordre de ne pas partir sur ce batiment,
et qu'il alloit joindre le Mercure. Il me demanda une lettre
pour Mr. Williams qui etoit parti le même matin pour Painbeuf
pour expedier le Mercure. Je mandai a Mr. Williams qu'il me
paroissoit d'une grande consequence pour vôtre pais que Mr.
Ducoudray s'y rendit avec ses principaux officiers. Ce matin
Mr. Ducoudray m'est revenu, et m'a apris que Messieurs Williams et Peletier Dudoyer n'avoient pas trouvés convenable
qu'il s'embarqua sur ce batiment. Il est revenu avec tout son
monde vous ne tarderés pas a le revoir. Je suis bien touché de
ce contretems. Je crains qu'on n'ait pris l'effroi trop aisement.
Il paroît que l'agent qui a êtè envoié au Port Loüis pour le
depart de L'Amphitrite a êtè aussi peu circonspect que celui
qui a êtè au havre.[1] Je vous exhorte, Messieurs, a bien choisir
ceux a qui vous confiés vos interests. On ne peut mettre trop
de prudence dans des affairres de cette nature. Il paroît que
l'ordre expedié pour empecher le depart de Mr. Ducoudray a
êtè accordé aux importunités du Lord Stormont. Je suis avec
un respect infini Messieurs vôtre très humble et très obeissant
serviteur   MONTAUDOÜIN

Je prie très humblément Monsieur franklin d'agréer mes re-
mercimens de ce qu'il a eû la bonté de m'envoier. Voici une

---

8. Sunday was the 26th, a busy day for Du Coudray. He left Nantes for
Paimboeuf, was refused passage on the *Mercury*, and wrote the long letter
to Congress that is now in the National Archives.

1. The first agent mentioned was Beaumarchais' secretary, Francy, and
the second was Beaumarchais himself; see Louis de Loménie, *Beaumarchais
et son temps* . . . (2 vols., Paris, 1856), II, 135–40.

lettre de Mr. Williams.[2] Le Mercure a dû descendre hier au soir a St. Nazaire au bas de la Riviere. Le vent n'est pas bon aujourd'huy. Mr. Williams n'est pas remonté de Painbeuf.

Notation: Montaudoin, Nantes 28 Janv. 77

From Pierre Buisson de Basseville: Letter and Memorandum

January 28, 1777   See page 168

From Henry Echlin

January 28, 1777   See page 209n

From the Prince de Gallitzin[3]

ALS: American Philosophical Society

La Haye, ce 28. Janvier, 1777.

J'ose me flatter, Monsieur, que vous ne desaprouverez pas la liberté que je prens de vous ecrire, sans avoir en aucune facon

2. Perhaps the undated letter that we have assigned to Jan. 21. JW was using Montaudouin's house for his mail; see the address on BF's note to him below, Feb. 5.

3. "Gallitzin" is our best guess at a signature that is, as witness the notation, virtually indecipherable; in modern usage the name is Prince Dmitrii Golitsyn. However he spelled himself, the Prince (1738–1803) was one of the leading Russian intellectuals of his day. He had been Russian minister to France in the 1760's and was currently accredited to The Hague, and was not only a diplomat but also an author, experimental scientist, and friend of many philosophes. *Biographie universelle*; Larousse, *Dictionnaire universel*; Eufrosina Dvoichenko-Markoff, "Franklin, the American Philosophical Society, and the Russian Academy of Science," APS *Proc.*, XCI (1947), 152–3; Nikolai N. Bolkhovitinov, *The Beginnings of Russian-American Relations, 1775–1815* (Elena Levin, trans.: Cambridge, Mass., and London, 1975), pp. 16–17, 119–20. This letter is the only one extant between him and BF. It presumably elicited a reply, now lost, for two years later the Prince addressed further inquires to him through an intermediary: Keralio to BF, Jan. 19 and March 21, and to WTF, March 7, 1779, APS.

248

l'avantage d'être connu de vous. A titre d'un de vos plus sinceres admirateurs, j'ai cru pouvoir me permettre cette demarche: celui d'aimer les Sciences et de m'interresser veritablement à leurs progres, me donne même le droit de m'adresser à vous. Qui mieux que vous, Monsieur, pourroit décider si les idees que je me suis faites des Electricités *positive* et *negative* et du pouvoir attractive des *Pointes* sont justes ou non.

Vous voyez, Monsieur, que sans autre préambule, j'entre tout de suite en matière avec vous; mais auprés de Mr. de Franklin, les complimens trouvent, je crois, toujours peu de fortune. Je reviens donc à ce qui seul peut vous interresser de ma part.

Vous nous avez parfaitement bien prouvé l'existence et la difference des Effets des Electricités *positive* et *negative*; des occupations plus importantes vous auront vraisemblablement empeché d'y mettre la derniere main; qui seroit, de nous expliquer la cause de la difference de leurs effets.

M'etant fait une occupation toute particuliere de l'Electricité, et y ayant toujours suivi vos principes, je me suis fait des idées sur ces objets que je soumets d'autant plus volontiers à votre examen que je vous reconnois incontestablement pour le Juge le plus competent que nous ayons dans cette partie. Quelque soin que j'aie pris pour m'y confirmer par des experiences; quelques raisonnemens que j'aie faits pour y arriver, je serai le premier à avouer mon erreur, des que vous les desaprouverez. Voici le fait.

Axiomes tirés des ouvrages de Mr. de Franklin et confirmés par toutes les experiences.

1°. L'Electricité *positive* repousse, l'Electricité *négative* attire les Corps; ou, si l'on aime mieux, la première donne, la seconde reçoit l'Electricité.

2°. Toute Electricité a une Atmosphere.

Voici maintenant à quoi mes propres experiences m'ont conduit.

1°. L'Atmosphere de l'Electricité *positive* est plus forte, ou plus violente (si j'ose m'exprimer ainsi) c'est-à-dire, qu'independament de ce tourbillon qui doit caracteriser toutes les Atmospheres, celle-ci a encore des rayons; et cela, parce que le Corps electrisé dont elle emane, a une surabondance de fluide electrique. Aussi, rencontre-t-elle un autre Corps? elle le repousse, ou lui donne de son Electricité.

2°. Celle de la *Negative*, est plus tranquille: elle forme, tout simplement, un tourbillon autour du Corps. Aussi, des qu'elle rencontre un autre Corps, qu'elle l'entraine à lui. (NB: il s'agit ici, dans ces deux cas, de la rencontre des Corps non electrises).

Avec tout autre que vous, Monsieur, j'aurais cité quantité d'experiences qui confirment mon idée; avec vous, je me contenterai d'exposer la chose: sans tous mes raisonnemens, vous saurez à quoi vous en tenir. La seule experience que je me permettrai de vous recommander, c'est celle que nous faisons par le moyen de la Machine (ou de l'Electrophore) de Volta.[4] Nous adaptons une couple de bales de surau à la plaque d'en haut, et une autre couple à celle d'en bas. Une de ces couples s'electrise *positivement*, l'autre negativement. Les premieres se repoussent reciproquement, les autres se collent ensemble: ce qui, à mon avis, doit être le vrai resultât des Atmospheres que j'assigne à leurs Electricités respectifs.

Quant aux Pointes, je crois que tout Corps n'attire l'Electricité que lorsqu'il se trouve deja dans son Atmosphere. La raison pourquoi les Corps elevés sont plus souvent frapes de la foudre que ceux qui sont situés bas c'est que naturellement ils se trouvent plutot dans son Atmosphere. Spa en est un exemple frapant. De memoire d'homme on n'y a vu tomber le Tonnere. Cependant les orages y sont frequens, terribles mêmes. Les habitans attribuent ce pouvoir preservatif au son des cloches, mais à l'aspect du lieu, vous concevrez aisement ce qui les garantit. Spa est situe entre deux chaines de Montagne paralleles. L'une le couvre pour ainsi dire, l'autre en est à un quart de lieue. De maniere que de quel côté que le nuage arrive, son Atmosphere rencontre les Montagnes avant tout. Aussi le Tonnere fait-il des ravages continuels sur ces Montagnes, et epargne toujours Spa.

Arrive-t-il par l'ouverture des Montagnes? Le nuage ne manque jamais de se partager en deux, et de suivre une cime.

Or, la Pointe se trouvant dans l'Atmosphere, celle-ci trouve

4. See Ingenhousz to BF above, Nov. 15.

dans le sommet de cette Pointe un endroit plus à sa proximité que tout autre. Aussi tous les rayons de l'Atmosphere s'y portent-ils et la *Pointe* devient a l'egard de l'Electricité, ce que le Miroir ardent est a l'egard du Soleil. Le foyer du miroir rassemble les rayons du Soleil; la *Pointe* rassemble les rayons de l'Atmosphere, ou plutôt de l'Electricité même. La reunion ou plutot l'affluence prodigieuse de ces rayons se manifeste a notre vue, et c'est ce que vous appellez, Monsieur, *Vers luisant*.

Mais presentez à l'Electricité un Corps d'une certaine superficie: vous conviendrez que sur cette superficie il se trouve necessairement plusieurs endroits tout autant a la portee de l'Electricité que bien d'autres. L'Electricité se partage donc entre chacun d'eux, et travaillant par parties desunies, sa force est affoiblie, et elle penetre le Corps clandestinement (si je puis me servir de ce terme).

Quelques Phisiciens nient l'existence de l'Atmosphere electrique. À mon avis, Monsieur, quant même l'Electricité n'en produiroit pas, celle de la terre (qui naturellement environne tous les Corps) le deviendroit dès qu'elle se trouveroit autour d'un objet où l'Electricité est accumulée.

Quelques autres croyent qu'on se procure rarement l'Electricité naturelle par le moyen des cerfs-volans de votre invention. Je puis vous assurer, Monsier, que Mr. Dentan (ami de Mr. De Luc que vous devez avoir connu à Londres[5]) a elevé le mien ici en tout tems, en toute saison, à toute heure; et que jamais, mais au grand jamais, il n'a manqué de nous en donner. Mais les Phisiciens qui y ont travaillé sans succés, avoient eu aparament une corde troup courte: j'ai remarqué que la difference quelque fois est prodigieuse: il y a des tems où elle va de 100 à 150 toises.

Je finirai cependant, Monsieur, par vous faire des excuses sur mon indiscretion, et j'en commettrai, peut-être, une plus forte encore: c'est en vous priant en grace de m'honorer d'un mot de reponse, et de me dire franchement si vous aprouvez

5. Pierre-Gédéon Dentand or Dentan (1750–80), Swiss by birth, was a naturalist of some distinction. Jean-André Deluc (above, xx, 78 n), who had established residence in England in 1773, published a number of Dentand's treatises. *Nouvelle biographie générale* under Dentand; *DNB* under Deluc.

ou desaprouvez mes idées. Ma demeure est toujours à la Haye, où je suis Ministre de l'Imperatrice de Russie.

J'ai l'honneur d'être avec une estime des plus sinceres et la consideration la plus distinguée, Monsieur, Votre tres humble et tres obeissant serviteur   DIMITRI PRINCE DE GALLITZIN

à Mr. de Franklin

Notation: de Gattin, Lahaye 28. Janv. 77

Jonathan Williams, Jr., to the American Commissioners

ALS: University of Virginia Library

Gentlemen   Nantes Jan. 29. 1777.

My last was written on board Ship at Painbeuf, after sealing it Mr. Niver came on board and I repeated to him my offer to take 4 passengers. I told him to avoid giving any preference, they might settle among themselves either by Lot or otherwise who those 4 should be. He returned without deciding whether he would go or not.[6] The Wind having fail'd us the Ship could not sail that night, I therefore came on shore and found that Mr. DuCoudray and the great part of his officers had returned to Nantes, Mr. Rogers and 5 others remain'd. I again repeated my offer to Mr. Rogers, and particularly with regard to himself, he said he could not think of Going without Mr. DuCoudray unless he had orders so to do from Mr. Deane, and so the others had determined. As there then remained places, and as the Chevalier deBorre came within Mr. Deane's allowance I consented to his going in the Ship. The Chevalier duPlessis also took passage paying to Mr. Peltier 400 Livres: these 2 are all the passengers on board.

I thought it proper that the best Invoice that I could collect should be sent, I therefore took the liberty to write the inclosed Letter and sent with it.[7] This Letter with all yours, have

6. Nicolas Niverd, an engineer, did go but not in the *Mercure*, to judge by the last sentence of the paragraph; he was later commissioned a captain of artillery in the U.S. army: *JCC*, x, 119.

7. Doubtless JW to the secret committee, Jan. 27, 1777; a copy is in the *Lee Family Papers*, roll 3, frames 38–9.

a particular mark to distinguish their importance, which the
Captain only knows, and all Letters and papers that have any
relation to America are put into one packet. The passengers
also consented to deliver up their Letters of Recommendation
and every paper that related as above, which are also at the
sole disposal of the Captain. We directed him to tie a cannon
Ball to these packets so that in case of being unable to avoid
an Examination they may be sunk. The Captain has the sole
and supreme authority on board. As nothing more remain'd
to do, We returned to Nantes leaving strict orders with the
Captain to sail the next morning if possible, if it should be
calm we told him to tow down with the Tide, and I flatter
myself he is now out of the River. The Chevalier de Borre
voluntarily gave me the inclosed paper.

Mr. Du Coudray I hear is gone to Bourdeaux but I rather
think he is gone to Paris, if so you will no doubt hear his
account of my proceedings. With regard to him, I hope I shall
stand justified, for I did not refuse him; but as Mr. Deane appeared very much dissatisfied with his Conduct, as he had
such a quantity of Baggage which there was not room in the
ship for, as there was a positive order from the King for him
to return to his Regiment, and as the Letter to Mr. Peltier
announced him to have deceived all concerned and that you
had found him out tho' unhappily too late, I thought I had no
Right to take an active part in his Favour, more especialy as if
I had taken an active part it would have avail'd nothing, as in
this particular Mr. Peltier would not have obey'd my orders.
With regard to the other officers I confined Myself to Mr.
Deane's Discription of those that were to go and the Number
the Ship could conveniently take. If they did not choose to
accept my offer it is their Fault and not mine.

I mentioned in my last that we should be obliged to leave
out 40 Bales, but when we came to store the Water and Wood
we found ourselves obliged to leave out 43. Mr. de Francy is
arrived from L'orient and with Mr. Peltier is about buying a
Ship for these Goods and those that are expected, which will
amount to upwards of 200 Bales and some of them amasing
large ones. If they were closely press'd and pack'd without
straw they would not occupy above ⅔ the place they now

require. As by my Instructions I am not expected to make any Engagements either as to Ship or Cargo, I shall be a Spectator only of these operations, but justice obliges me to say that the Conduct of Mr. Peltier has been so satisfactory that I not only think him capable but disposed to do the best for all concerned. I have the Honor to be Gentlemen Your most obedient Servant   J WILLIAMS JUNR

PS The Mercurys provisions upon a Calculation of 5 months will afford upwards of 2 pound of meat and Vegitables per man per day, and 40 Gallons Water per head, which I think sufficient.

The Honourable The Deputies of the United States

Notations: Mr Williams Nantes Jany. 29th 1777. DeCoudray and french officers [*in another hand:*] to Hon: Deputies U.S.

From William Dodd[8]   ALS: American Philosophical Society

Sir   Jan. 29. 1777.

I make no Apology for troubling you with a request I have heretofore made, of conveying the inclosed Letter, if possible, to a worthy young Woman, who in an unfortunate Hour, went to America; and to whose fortunes and situation there I am a stranger.[9] Anxious for the success of the grand struggle in which you are engag'd, I cou'd have been happy in conversing with

8. An Anglican clergyman well known in London for his writings, philanthropies, sermons, and high living. Although his tone here suggests a previous acquaintance with BF, we have no evidence of it. Three days after writing this letter Dodd embarked on the forgery that led him to the scaffold in June, 1777. James H. Warner, "The Macaroni Parson," *Queen's Quarterly,* LII (1946), [41]–53; Gerald Howson, *The Macaroni Parson: a Life of the Unfortunate Dr. Dodd* (London, [1973]), p. 108 *et seq.;* DNB.

9. We are convinced in our bones (in other words without proof) that this was Ann or Anna Brodeau, who emigrated to Philadelphia with a small baby in 1775 and started a school that was recommended by BF and Robert Morris: above, XXII, 282. Dodd, according to a long-lasting rumor, was the father of the baby. She grew up to marry William Thornton, and at her death a newspaper described her, on her husband's authority, as the clergyman's daughter; her friends denied the statement but gave no evidence. *National Intelligencer,* Aug. 18, 22, 1865.

you, when I was at Paris; but you was not then arriv'd. If you shou'd see or converse with Mr. Mante who resides at Diepe, but is frequently at Paris, He knows my sentiments, and wou'd be happy to communicate with you.[1] I am Sir with very great Esteem Your obedient humble Servant   W. DODD

It is not possible to effect a *reconciliation?* How happy cou'd I be to be any way instrumental in it!

Addressed: Docr. Franklin / Paris.

Notation: Dr Dodd Jan 29. 77.

From Jan Ingenhousz   ALS: American Philosophical Society

Dear Sir,   Vienna Jan. 29. 1777.

As I recieved my lettre Directed to you at Philadelphia back from London because my friend thought it would not please me, when I should know you was at Paris, I send it you without opening it, tho you will now be acquainted with the philosophical part of it. As I referred to it in my last, which will have come to your hands by Abbe *Georgel*, I am affrayed you delay answering me till you recieve it, which I hope you will do after having perused it.[2] I am about to get conductors erected

1. Dodd had strange friends. Thomas Mante, or de Mante as he sometimes signed himself, was a writer on military affairs (*DNB*), an Englishman who had become a French citizen and been—and perhaps still was—a secret agent for both countries. He was certainly a French spy, Stormont reported in January, 1777, and the French believed that he was also working for the British. Frank Monaghan, "A New Document on the Identity of 'Junius,'" *Jour. of Modern History*, IV (1932), 69–70; Stevens, *Facsimiles*, XIV, no. 1413, p. 1. Mante did not see BF at this time. In September, 1778, when he was in prison in Paris, he wrote as a stranger to ask for money; BF obliged, and Mante continued intermittent pleas for help. See his letters in the APS of Sept. 3, 1778; Feb. 22, March 12, June 14, 1779; Jan. 10, 1780; and Jan. 1, 1781.

2. The two letters he is talking about are above, Nov. 15, 1776, and Jan. 4, 1777. The first was returned to him by the secretary of the Dutch embassy, as mentioned in the second; the latter was carried by the abbé Jean-François Georgel (1731–1813), who had been Rohan's secretary in Vienna and the ambassador, in effect, after the Prince's recall to France in 1774: Larousse, *Dictionnaire universel*; below, Georgel to BF, April 9.

upon the gunpowders magazines and some other buildings of the Emperour, who entrusted me alone with that affair. I follow entirely your opinion at the manner in which they are erected upon your Magazines at Purfleet.[3] Father Beccaria, whose writings are as obscure as yours are clear upon the subject of electricity, writes in a lettre dated Nov. the 1th the following article upon this subject. *Ego tamen in ea persto opinione: ante omnia metallo omni, quod hic est cautum, exui oportere, uti scribebam in litteris ad Beccarium.* I aknowledge I do not understand his meaning; but I thinck he is against the use of conductors.[4] I should like to write a little deduction containing the principal arguments, and facts, by which the utility of this practice is prouved. A such undertaking would be a part of my duty, as being entrusted with the direction of this undertaking. The Republic of Venise has just now asked the Emperour to get a thorough instruction made of the manner of building Gunpowder magazins, preserving the powder, and preventing mischief from lightning. As no body of the artillery Corps is able to give some tolerable explication upon this matter, they have allready applyed to me for to assist them. An thus I will be obliged to work at it. I expect the six last volumes of the Philos. Transactions, in which I will probably find some articles, which will be usefull to me in this undertaking. I will not abuse to much your patience in prolonging my lettre. I will only add, that I expect from you some good news, but above all to be informed of your health and happiness.

The next day of my writing to you may last, the journey of our Emperour was countremanded, and will perhaps be layd aside entirely. My journey to Ratisbon is fixed upon the 10 or 12 of April, if nothing hinders me, where I will inoculate the two sons of the Reigning Prince of *Tour and Taxis*, after which I should be very glad to take a trip to Paris and to have the

3. See above, XIX, 153 *et seq.*; XX, 122 *et seq.*

4. He was. The Latin is typically Beccarian; it may be rendered as "I therefore persist in my opinion that it is above all prudent to get rid of all metal, as I wrote in my letters to Beccari," referring to his work cited above, XXII, 675–6 n.

great satisfaction of enjoying your company.[5] I am with the greatest esteem Your Most obedient humble Servant

J. INGEN HOUSZ

Notation: Ingenhouss Jany. 29. 1777.

The American Commissioners to Thomas Morris

Copy: National Archives; copy: University of Virginia Library; AL (draft): Library of Congress[6]

Sir. Paris. Jan. 30th. 1777.

We are inform'd that the Cargoes at Nantes, have been disposed of some time past, yet we are still without any remittance from you. The Congress directed you to pay Mr. Dean for the purposes of our Embassy the sum of ten Thousand pounds; this you must consider as the first and most Important obligation of that kind on you; we therefore must urge your immediate Complying with this order of Congress, and that you remit to Mr. Dean this sum for our use. We have many occasions for money in the public service besides our subsistence, and[7] can by no means consider any partial or temporary supplies in that way as adequate to our purpose: Mr. Gruel, Mr. Montandoin or Mr. Schweighauser will undertake to remit the money hither, immediately on its being lodg'd in either of their hands, as we shall direct. We expect your answer by the first post, and are Sir, Your most obedient humble Servants (Signed) B FRANKLIN

SILAS DEANE
ARTHUR LEE

Paris Janvier 30e. 1777. *Endorsed:*[8] B. Franklin &ca.

5. See his letter above of Jan. 4.
6. The two copies are in the same hand and identical; the copyist noted that the original, now lost, was in BF's hand. The draft is Silas Deane's; it is dated Jan. 28 and lacks, as noted below, one clause in the letter as sent.
7. The preceding clause is omitted in the draft, which reads "We can by no means," etc.
8. The copyist noted that this was in Morris' hand.

From Gruel

ALS: American Philosophical Society

Monsieur   Nantes le 30: Janvier 1777

J'ay reçu en son temps la lettre que vous avés pris la peine de m'ecrire le 27 Xbre. dernier. Je suis ainsy que tous les miens tres sensibles aux choses obligeantes que vous nous dîtes, nous desirerions beaucoup que vos affaires vous permîssent de recevoir a la Barberie nos sinceres remerciments de votre gracieux souvenir, nous nous flatons que pour faire trêve à vos grandes occupations, vous nous donnerés la satisfaction de vous y posseder au retour de la belle saison. Vous y trouverés des amis qui vous sont toujours sincerement attachés, et qui ne cesseront de vous etre entierement devoues.

Je reçois l'honneur de la votre du 25: Courant par la quelle vous me demandés a quoy peuvent monter les indigo que j'ay reçu par la fregate la Represaille Capitaine Mr. Wilcken. Vous aurés eté instruit par Mr. Sollier que j'avois vendû cette teinture 7 *l.t.*, ce qui fait un bon prix vû qu'elle etoit chargée de poussiere et grabat, ce qui en diminue la valeur; le net produit se monte a la somme de 41571 *l.t.*: 17 s: 6: d: sur la quelle somme je vous ay compté icy celle de 2400 *l.t.* J'ay depuis fait divers petits debours pour votre compte dont je vous enverray la notte par le premier courier, mais il vous revient aux environs de la somme de trente neuf mille livres que vous devés toucher a Paris des mains de Mr. Sollier. Je luy ai remis cette somme, ainsy vous en pouvés disposer à votre gré, et de plus forte somme si vous le jugés a propos. Mon dit Sieur Sollier aura toujours des fonds à vos ordres.

Je suis occupé à expedier dans ce moment le navire le Chester Capitaine Sieur folger pour Nantuket, et le navire du Congrés [le] Succés Capitaine Sieur anderson pour philadelphie. Je vous prie de ne pas differer à m'envoyer vos depeches, je les recommanderay aux Capitaines.

Monsieur Williams votre neveu m'a fait le plaisir de me remettre un petit livre contenant les articles de confederation des treize Etats unis de l'amerique. Je les ay lû avec une vraye satisfaction. Je ne peux que vous faire mes justes et sinceres remerciments de votre souvenir. Je vous prie de me le continuer, et de me donner toujours une petite part dans votre bienveillance. Je la meriteray par l'inviolable attachement que je ne cesserai de vous voüer, ainsy qu'a tous ceux qui vous appartiennent.

Je garde votre lettre pour Mr. Wilckes. Je la luy remettray lorsqu'il reviendra, il a mis en mer samedi dernier 26.Courant.

Tous les miens reconnoissants comme ils doivent l'etre de tout ce que vous me chargés de leur dire d'obligeant, me chargent de vous faire agreer leur civilités respectueuses, ainsy Mesdemoiselles de la Selle qui ne sont pas moins sensibles que nous à votre gracieux souvenir. Voulés-vous bien faire mention de nous tous auprès de Monsieur votre fils franklin. Ces Demoiselles esperent qu'elles pouront cet eté converser avec luy en français, nous l'invitons tous à vous accompagner dans le voyage que vous nous flatés devoir faire cet eté à la Barberie, ce sera pour nous un surcroit d'une veritable satisfaction, c'est ce dont je vous prie d'etre bien persuadé. Je suis avec respect Monsieur Votre tres humble et tres obeïssant Serviteur   J GRUEL

Notation: Gruel, Nantes 30 Janv. 77

From ——— Guérin

January 30, 1777   See page 148n

From C. Bedaulx

[January, 1777?]   See page 39

From Étienne Bézout

[January, 1777?]   See page 170

The American Commissioners: Memorandum to Vergennes

ADS:[9] Archives du Ministère des affaires étrangères; copy:[1] Harvard University Library

This memorandum, most of it in Franklin's hand, marks a distinct departure from the position that he generally maintained. He "was from the first averse to warm and urgent solicitations with the Court of France," Silas Deane remarked years later. "His age and experience, as well as his philosophical temper, led him to prefer a patient perseverance, and to wait events, and to leave the Court of France to act from motives of interest only."[2] Perhaps the intelligence of British plans for the Chesapeake, fallacious as it was, jolted him for the moment out of his patient perseverance. Perhaps he deferred to the views of his fellow commissioners, as he had previously deferred to the views of Congress, and acted against his better judgment "that a Virgin State should preserve the Virgin Character, and not go about suitering for Alliances, but wait with decent Dignity for the applications of others."[3]

Paris Feby. 1st. 1777.

Messrs. Franklin, Dean, and Lee, Ministers from the Congress of the United States, beg leave to represent to his Excellency the Count de Vergennes.

That, besides the general alarming Accounts of the successes of the English against their Country, they have received authentic Intelligence, from England, that eight thousand Men, chiefly Germans, under the command of General Burgoyne, are to be sent, early in the Spring, to America; and to be employed with some Ships of War, in the Invasion of Virginia and Maryland.

That if not by some means diverted, from their Design; it will be in their Power to destroy a great part of that country, as the Houses and Estates of the principal Inhabitants are situ-

9. In WTF's hand through the opening of the next to last paragraph; the rest, from "his Majesty and his Ministers," is in Arthur Lee's hand.
1. With a notation, not in the copyist's hand, "presented by Mr. Lee alone at Versailles."
2. *Deane Papers*, V, 438.
3. To Arthur Lee below, March 21.

ated on the navigable Waters, and so separated from each other, as to be incapable of being defended from arm'd Vessels conveying Troops, the place of whose landing cannot be foreseen, and consequently Force cannot be assembled in all places sufficient to oppose them.

That great Danger is also to be apprehended from the Blacks of those Colonies, who being excited and armed by the English, may greatly strengthen the Invaders; at the same time that the fear of their Insurrection, will prevent the white Inhabitants from leaving their places of Residence, and assembling in such numbers for their own defence against the English, as otherwise they might do.

That the greater part of the Tobacco of those Colonies is probably collected, as usual in the Warehouses of the Inspectors, which are also situated on the navigable Waters, and will be liable to be taken, and destroyed by the Invaders.

That the Destruction of these two Colonies, may probably make a great Impression on the Minds of the People in the rest, who seeing no prospect of Assistance from any European Power, may become more inclined to listen to terms of Accomodation.

That the supplys of Arms and Munitions of War, which they have been made to expect from France, having been by various means delayed and retarded, are not likely to arrive before the Commencement of next Campaign, and may perhaps be dispair'd of, especially if those supplies are to be carried first to the French Islands.

That notwithstanding the Measures taken to convince the Court of Britain, that France does not countenance the Americans, that Court according to our information, believes firmly the Contrary; and it is submitted to the Consideration of your Excellency, whether if the English make a Conquest of the American States, they will not take the first Opportunity of shewing their resentment, by begining themselves the War that would otherways be avoided, and perhaps begining it as they did the last, without any previous declaration.

Upon the whole we cannot on this Occasion omit expressing our Apprehensions, that if Britain is now suffered to recover the Colonies, and annex again their great growing

Strength and Commerce to her own she will become the most formidable Power by Sea and Land that Europe has yet seen, and assuredly, from the natural Pride and insolence of that People, a Power to all the other States the most intolerable and pernicious.

We therefore would with deference submit it to the wisdom of his Majesty and his Ministers, whether if the independency of the united States of America and the freedom of a Commerce with them with the consequent diminution of british power, be an object of importance to all Europe, and to France in particular, this is not the proper time for effectual exertions in their favor; and for commencing that war, which can scarcely be much longer avoided, and which will be sanctifyd, by the best of justifications, that a much injurd and innocent people will thereby be protected, and deliverd from the most cruel oppression, and securd in the enjoyment of their just rights; than which nothing can contribute more to the glory of his Majesty and this Nation.

The critical situation of our country, will apologize for earnestly requesting your Excellency to grant us an interview as early as possible; when we may personally explain what we have stated above, and mention other subjects of great importance to both Countries.　　　　　　　　　　　B FRANKLIN
　　　　　　　　　　　　　　　　　　　　　　　SILAS DEANE
　　　　　　　　　　　　　　　　　　　　　　　ARTHUR LEE

Barbeu-Dubourg to the American Commissioners

ALS: American Philosophical Society

A Paris ce 1er. fr. 1777

MM. Dubourg, Debout et Compagnie,[4] ayant pris des engagemens pour fournir a la ferme generale vingt mille boucauts de tabac des crus de la Virginie et du Mariland, se proposent de

4. Debout was the Parisian banker referred to without name in Dubourg's letter above of Jan. 21, which explains the background of this one. The Dunkirk merchant mentioned there as a third partner apparently fell by the wayside.

porter de france dans les ports des Etats unis de l'Amerique des marchandises de fabrique françoise, pour rapporter en retour non seulement des tabacs, mais diverses autres denrées de l'Amerique, à l'avantage reciproque des deux nations.

Ils implorent avec confiance à ce titre la faveur de Messieurs Franklin, Deane et Lee, et la protection du Congrés continental, pour leur faciliter la vente et debit des marchandises Europeennes, et l'achat et aquisition des denrées Americaines à des prix justes et raisonables; et pour leur procurer et assurer la libre entrée et sortie des ports du Continent de l'Amerique, et la sureté de la navigation dans ses parages, autant que la conjoncture presente le comporte.

Ils s'efforceront de meriter cette faveur et cette protection par leur zele et leur fidelité, et par le plus grand empressement a pourvoir a tous les besoins que ces memes conjonctures occasionnent aux genereux habitans des Etats unis, et a leurs dignes et respectables Chefs. DUBOURG

Notation: M. Dubourg's Request

From Duportail

ALS: American Philosophical Society

Monsieur   pithiviers le 1er. fevrier 1777

Mr. de laumoy un de mes compagnons de voyage desirant avoir l'honneur de vous voir se presentera chèz vous lundi 3, a sept heures du soir, Je vous prie de vouloir bien donner des ordres pour qu'il soit reçu et que personne d'ailleurs ne le trouve chèz vous, ainsi que nous en sommes convenus pour moy même. Cet officier vous dira que nous esperons pouvoir estre vers le 15 de ce mois à nantes ou à bordeaux selon qu'il faudra s'embarquer à l'un ou l'autre port. Mais j'ose surtout de vous recommander de prendre le moyen qui nous expose le moins à estre pris ou, si nous avions ce malheur, qui nous expose le moins à de mauvais traitemens. J'ai l'honneur d'etre DUPORTAIL

Je compte estre mercredy au soir à paris toujours à l'hotel d'hollande Ruë du bouloy

From Thomas Walpole

ALS: American Philosophical Society

Dear Sir   Lincolns Inn Fields, 1st. feby 1777.

I was very glad to receive a testimony under your own hand of your kind remembrance of me, and I am obliged to you for the information you give me, relative to the Lands of our purchase in America.[5] When the charges incurred here upon that Object are finally settled, I shall send you an account thereof with a credit upon some House in Paris for the ballance. I hope this will be speedily, as I am and have been for some time past very impatient to get rid of a transaction where so many different persons are concerned, that I might be left at liberty to act for myself in it hereafter according to my own inclination and to the circumstances of the times.

If Lord Chatham was in a state of health capable of comfort I know nothing would give him so much as your testimony of his conduct on the opening of the important crisis to which the two Countrys have been driven, and I will communicate to him your observation as soon as a fit opportunity offers. Lord Camden sends you his best compliments and laments heartily with me that the restoration of peace is at so great a distance as you seem to apprehend.

All those who are friends to both Countrys think they have much reason to complain of the neglect with which they have been treated by America, in not having been made acquainted in some authentick manner with her real views and circumstances at the opening of this unhappy rupture, nor with a true representation of the events which have followed. The want of which advices it is thought has not been less prejudicial to the reputation of America in the eyes of the rest of Europe than in the public opinion here, as the friends of both Countrys have thus been deprived of all means of refuting the tales which have been imposed on the world by the artifice of Administration and which have principally contributed to the delusion of the people of England.

But these considerations are of small importance compared to that of the declaration of Independence extending itself not

5. See BF's letter above, Jan. 12.

only to the renunciation of all Allegiance but even to all connection with this Country in preference to any other. This measure so taken reduced the friends to the liberties of America to the single argument of resisting the War against her upon local considerations of a ruinous expence to the Nation in prosecuting a plan of Conquest which in its issue must be considered as very uncertain, and altho' we should be successfull, would be probably in its consequences prove[d?] more burdensome than profitable. May I add also that Shutting the door so fast against a reconciliation with this Country may make American Alliances with other Powers more difficult or give these at least a considerable advantage in negotiation.

These are the complaints of friends and my reflections upon them, but all I fear too late for any usefull correction or possible remedy, and all a person of my very small importance in these great matters dares to add is that he would think no office too mean, nor any endeavours above his ambition which could tend to put a stop to our dreadfull civil contentions. To expatiate further upon them with you Sir would be as if I doubted of the benevolence of your disposition being equal to your other great talents. But the contrary is so truly my opinion that I subscribe myself with the sincerest sentiments of esteem and affection Dear Sir your very faithful humble Servant   THOMAS WALPOLE

The American Commissioners: Two Resolutions

(I) DS and draft DS (incomplete); (II) ADS: all University of Pennsylvania Library[6]

The context of these resolutions is the commissioners' memorandum to Vergennes of February 1, in which they urged France to enter the war. Their instructions gave them almost no practical lev-

6. The two forms of (I) are apparently in WTF's hand; (II) is in Lee's. The draft DS of (I) omits the first paragraph and contains an interlineation, "or in the Absence of others, for any one of us," which is incorporated in the DS. Another signed copy of this draft and of the second resolution was reproduced in Parke Bernet Catalogue 1756, May 7–8, 1957, no. 130; it was purchased by Perc S. Brown and cannot now be located.

erage for achieving that end, and they were considering how far they could stretch the instructions. Congress had authorized them to promise, in the event of a French alliance, that neither party would make a separate peace without six months' notice to the other.[7] In the first of the commissioners' resolutions they authorize themselves, if need be, to promise no separate peace, or aid to the common enemy, or relaxation of effort while the war continues. This assumption of authority must have seemed to them, or at least to one of them, extremely dangerous; hence their dramatic pledge, three days later, to do whatever might be needful at the risk of liberty or life. Lee wrote this second resolution, and he was prone to drama if not melodrama. Perhaps his fellow commissioners expected some answer from Vergennes that would put their resolution to the test; more probably Franklin and Deane, for the very reason that they had no such expectation, were willing to humor Lee.

I.

Paris, Feby. 2d. 1777.

It is considered that in the present situation of things at the Courts of France and Spain, we find no probability of obtaining any effectual aid, alliance, or declaration of War against Great Britain, without the following stipulation; therefore

We the Commissioners plenipotentiary from the Congress of the United States of America, are unanimously of Opinion, that if France or Spain should conclude a Treaty of Amity and Commerce with our States, and enter into a War with Great Britain in consequence of that, or of open aid given to our States, it will be right and proper for us, or in absence of the others, for any one of us, to stipulate and agree that the United States, shall not separately conclude a Peace, nor aid Great Britain against France or Spain, nor intermit their best exertions against Great Britain during the continuance of such War. Provided always that France and Spain, do on their part enter into a similar stipulation, with our States.   B FRANKLIN
SILAS DEANE
ARTHUR LEE

7. Above, XXII, 627.

II.

Paris, Feby. 5th 1777.
It is farther considered, that in the present peril of the liberties of our Country, it is our duty to hazard every thing in their support and defence.

Therefore Resolvd unanimously,

That if it shoud be necessary, for the attainment of any thing, in our best judgment, material to the defence and support of the public cause; that we shoud plege our persons, or hazard the censure of the Congress by exceeding our Instructions, we will, for such purpose most chearfully risque our personal liberty or life.

B FRANKLIN
SILAS DEANE
ARTHUR LEE

Notation: Resolution of the Commrs. Feb. 2. 1777 likewise a Resolution of Feb. 5. 1777.

The Committee of Secret Correspondence to the American Commissioners

LS: American Philosophical Society; LS: Rutgers University Library[8]; draft: Harvard University Library; copies: National Archives (two), Library of Congress

Honorable Gentlemen   Baltimore 2 Feby. 1777

You will recieve inclosed copies of our letters of the 21st. and 30th. Decemr., and of the Resolves of Congress accompanying them. It concerns us not less than we are sure it will you, that you should have heard so seldom from us, but the vigilance of the British Cruisers has prevented our most earnest solicitude for this purpose. The manner, in which they now conduct their business, proves the necessity of the request made by Congress for the loan or sale of a few Capital Ships. The entrance into Delaware and Chesapeak being narrow, by placing one 40 or 50 Gun Ship for the Protection of their Frigates, they stop both our Commerce and our Corre-

8. Signed by Harrison, Lee, and Witherspoon.

spondence. Formerly their Frigates protected their Tenders, but now that we have Frigates, their larger Ships protect their Frigates; and this winter has been so uncommonly favourable that they have been able to keep the sea undisturbd by those severe gales of wind so usual off this Coast in the winter season. If we had a few line of Battle Ships to aid our Frigates, the Commerce of North America so beneficial to ourselves and so advantageous to France, would be carried on maugre the opposition of Great Britain. As we have not recieved any of those military Stores and Cloathing promised by Mr. Deane, we have much reason to fear, they have fallen into the Enemie's Hands, and will render a fresh supply quite necessary. Except Mr. Deane's favor of Septemr. 17th. which is but just now recieved, and that of October the lst.[9] we have not heard from him since the summer, so that we have been as destitute of European, as we fear you have been of true American Intelligence. The inclosed papers will furnish you with authentick accounts of our successes against the enemy since the 24th. of Decemr. They have paid severely for their visit of parade through the Jerseys, and these events are an abundant proof of British Folly in attempting to subdue North America by force of arms. Although the short inlistments had dispersed our Army directly in the face of an hostile force, and thereby induced a proud enemy to suppose their work was done, yet they suddenly found themselves attacked on all sides by a hardy active Militia, who have been constantly beating up their quarters, captivating and destroying their Troops, so that in the six or seven last weeks they have not lost much fewer than 3000 Men, about 2800 of whom, with many Officers, are now our Prisoners. Instead of remaining cantonned in the pleasant Villages of Jersey, as the inclosed authentick copy of Mr. Howe's order to Colonel de Donop (the original of which fell into our hands by the Colonel's flight from Burdenton[10]) will shew you, that General vainly expected would be the case, they are now

9. Deane's earlier letter was to Robert Morris and his later one to the committee: *Deane Papers*, I, 247, 287–94.

10. No doubt Howe's letter of Dec. 13 to Donop, commanding at Bordentown; the letter is printed in William S. Stryker, *The Battles of Trenton and Princeton* (Boston and New York, 1898), pp. 316–17.

collected upon the Brunswick Heights, where they suffer every kind of distress from want of Forage, Fuel, and other necessaries, whilst Genl. Washington's Army of Militia so environs them, that they never shew their faces without their lines, but they get beaten back with loss and disgrace. Being thus situated, we have reason to hope, that this part of their Army (and which is the most considerable part) will, by the end of winter, be reduced very low by deaths, desertion, and captivity. Genl. Heath, with a body of Eastern Troops, is making an impression on New York by King's Bridge, which we understand has obliged the Enemy to recal their Troops from Rhode Island, for the defence of that City.

The regular Corps, that are to compose the new Army, are making up in the several states as fast as possible; but Arms, Artillery, Tent Cloth, and Cloathing will be greatly wanted. For these, our reliance is on the favor and friendship of his most Christian Majesty. If you are so fortunate as to obtain them, the propriety of sending them in a strong Ship of War must be very evident to you Gentlemen, when you know, our Coasts are so covered with British Cruisers from 20 to 50 Guns, though but few of the latter. We believe, they have not more than two Ships of 40, and two or three of 50 Guns in their whole Fleet on the North American Station; and these are employed, one of them to cover a Frigate or two at the Capes of each Bay, whilst the rest remain at New York.

We beg leave to turn your attention to the inclosed propositions of Congress, and we doubt not, you will urge their success with that real and careful assiduity, that objects so necessary to the liberty and safety of your Country demand.

We are exceedingly anxious to hear from you, and remain with particular sentiments of esteem and friendship Honorable Gentlemen Your most obedient and humble Servants

BENJ HARRISON
RICHARD HENRY LEE
WM HOOPER
ROBT MORRIS,
at Philada.

Notation: From the secret Committee 2d Feby '77

From M. and Mme. de Saint Wast[1]

L:[2] American Philosophical Society

2. fevrier 1777. Ruë st. honoré vis avis les jacobins Monsieur franklin et monsieur son petit fils sont priés de la part de Mr. et Made. de st. Wast de leur faire l'honneur de venir diner chés eux mercredy prochain 5. fevrier.

The American Commissioners to Ferdinand Grand

February 3, 1777 See page 22n

Dumas to the American Commissioners

Letterbook draft: Algemeen Rijksarchief, The Hague

3e.[–14] fevr. 1777

Depuis mes deux Lettres de la fin de Dec. et du 21e. Janvr., dans la dernière desquelles je vous ai rendu compte des lettres reçues du commis de la Maison que vous savez, et de ma présentation au Facteur,[3] j'en ai reçu une autre du premier, dont voici copie.

La haie 21e. Janvr. 1777

"J'ai l'honneur de vous informer que je partirai demain, &c."

Le 30e. Janvr. je reçus la lettre de Mr. Carm[ichael] du Havre le 21e. Janvr.[4] Indépendamment du grand plaisir que m'a causé sa lettre en me donnant de ses nouvelles, j'ai été bien aise de profiter de cette occasion pour entamer la correspondance avec

1. M. de St. Wast had been a secretary of Louis XV and later, under Turgot, a tax official for the royal domain: Yves Durand, *Les Fermiers généraux au XVIIIe siècle* (Paris, 1971), p. 141; Edgar Faure, *La Disgrâce de Turgot* (Paris, 1961), p. 97. He and his wife were friends of Dubourg as well as Grand, and she sent BF dinner invitations on at least two later occasions, Feb. 16, 1778, and Nov. 26, 1781: APS.

2. In the hand of Ferdinand Grand.

3. The abbé Desnoyers and the new French ambassador, the duc de La Vauguyon.

4. Carmichael's to Dumas is in the *Deane Papers*, I, 465–7.

—— et j'écrivis à ce sujet la Lettre suivante 1er fevr. "Enfin il y a eu &c."

A cette Lettre j'en joignis une pour Mr. le Commis comme suit "1r fevr. Quoique je m'attendisse &c."

14e. fevr. 1777.

Ce qui précede étoit écrit, Messieurs, lorsque le paquet dont vous m'avez favorisé en date du 28e. Janv. me parvint le 4e. de ce mois. Il est superflu de dire combien il m'a fait plaisir. Je me mis tout de suite à copier et traduire celle de Mr. Lee, et je l'envoyai au Grand Facteur avec la lettre suivante: 6e. fev. "Dans l'esperance &c."

Le surlendemain, Samedi matin 8e. j'allai à Lahaie. En passant, je donnai moi-même au portier du grand facteur un paquet contenant copie et traduction des 3 Lettres de Mr. Franklin, des 1er. Octob. 23 Dec. 28e. Janv. dernier, comme aussi de celle du Comm. de la Corresp. Secrète du 24e. Octob. dernier avec une autre de moi, dont je n'ai pas gardé copie, où je marquai que j'étois prêt à montrer les originaux de toutes, et notamment de celle du Committé. Rendu de là chez moi, j'y trouvai la réponse du G.F. à mes deux précédentes, dont voici copie:

"J'ai reçu, M. les deux Lettres &c."

Une heure après, l'un des Secretaires du Gr. Fr. vint me dire de sa part qu'il m'attendoit à 5˙h. du soir. J'y fus reçu fort gracieusement. Il commença par me dire, qu'il m'étoit bien obligé, comme particulier, qui prenoit un intérêt de Spectateur à ce qui se passoit en Am. de lui communiquer ainsi les Lettres de mes amis, et qu'il me prioit très fort de continuer en ce sens: que si Mr. le Dr. Fr. étoit envoyé avec caractere pour traiter avec la France (ce qu'il ignoroit, et devoit ignorer), cela se passeroit sans doute entre Lui et le Ministere; par conséquent il ne pouvoit s'en mêler ici &c. Il n'en examina pas moins avidement les Lettres, surtout celle du Committé. Quoiqu'il me fît entendre qu'il n'envoyoit rien de ce que je lui communiquois, je sai à quoi m'en tenir. Je dois même être plus circonspect à présent que ci-devant: car j'écrivois plus familierement au prédécesseur, sachant qu'il corrigeroit dans ses extraits comme je l'en avois prié ce que le zele me faisoit quelquefois dire de trop, au lieu qu'à présent je sai que tout

271

seroit envoyé tel quel. Nous causames ensemble pendant une heure.

C'est à vous, Messieurs, à juger de l'utilité dont la continuation de cette liaison pourra être aux Etats Unis. Pour qu'elle puisse subsister, il faut que j'aie souvent des Lettres à communiquer. Les vôtres ne peuvent servir à ce but, ce me semble, qu'au cas que vous voulussiez faire parvenir indirectement quelque notion que vous ne vous soucieriez pas de dire directement; mais en ce cas je devrai toujours vous nommer, comme m'écrivant, ces choses par maniere de confidence. Il faudroit qu'il y eût à Londres quelqu'un de vos amis, qui pût m'écrire de temps en temps ce qui s'y passe derrière le rideau mieux qu'on ne peut le savoir par la Gazette: en ce cas il seroit bon que vous me missiez en liaison avec lui, en lui marquant de mettre sur ses Lettres *pour Mr. Delpueche* et de les fermer dans un couvert à l'adresse de Mr. *Alexandre Herman Marchand de Vin au Schotjen Dyk Rotterdam*; et de me donner aussi son adresse à Londres, si bien que nos Lettres parviennent surement.

Paris à Mrs. S.D. & B.F.

From La Rochefoucauld ALS: American Philosophical Society

This note, unlike the Duke's others to Franklin at the time, carries a sense of urgency; but the reason is not immediately clear. He encloses what he considers an important letter, which he wants kept secret; some of the news in it Franklin has doubtless heard already at Versailles. Du Coudray, under an alias, is somewhere in the offing.[5] These subjects seem unconnected. But we believe that a plausible assumption ties them together, and at the same time indicates a probable date. The assumption is that the missing enclosure and the note itself are about Du Coudray, and are the outgrowth of what had recently been happening to that harassed officer.

He was unsure, as he had reason to be, of his reception in the United States. As soon as he learned of Franklin's arrival in France,

5. Clearly still in France. If the Duke had been hoping for news of him in America, mentioning the alias would have been pointless.

he became eager to obtain from him a letter of recommendation to Congress; this was one of his motives, rumor had it, for ordering the *Amphitrite* back to Lorient.[6] He set out from there for Paris, where he saw the commissioners but, as later developments prove, did not obtain the letter he wanted. When he returned to Lorient ready to board his ship, he was stopped by an order to rejoin his regiment; the *Amphitrite* sailed without him. He decided to defy the order, and on the 26th went to Paimboeuf in hope of boarding the *Mercure*; again he was stopped, this time by Jonathan Williams.

Du Coudray's situation was critical, for unless he could leave France he was in danger of arrest for disobeying orders. He took off again for Paris, now under an alias, and arrived there on January 31. His main purpose was to secure passage and a change in orders that would permit him to sail.[7] In his need for help he apparently turned to the ministry of war,[8] but he also needed support from the American commissioners. Deane refused to have anything to do with him.[1] He had two possible channels for an appeal to Franklin, through La Rochefoucauld and the chevalier de Chastellux.[2]

Our assumption, which comes out of this background, is that some one, perhaps the chevalier or perhaps even Du Coudray himself, wrote to explain the predicament to the Duke, who responded by forwarding the letter with this covering note. In that case he did so on Monday, February 3, and the reason for his urgency is clear; he was ignorant of Du Coudray's whereabouts but aware that time was running out; the defiance of orders, he conjectured, was already known at Versailles.[3] His concern is understandable, and also con-

6. Morton, *Beaumarchais correspondance*, III, 19; *Deane Papers*, I, 462–3.

7. His side of the story is in his letter to Congress, Jan. 26, 1777, National Archives.

8. Beaumarchais to Vergennes, Feb. 3, Morton, III, 48.

1. *Deane Papers*, III, 162.

2. We do not know why La Rochefoucauld acted for him but only, as mentioned below, that he did. The chevalier de Chastellux (above, XXI, 505 n), a major figure in Rochambeau's subsequent campaigns, would have been a natural ally because in 1776 he had been Du Coudray's interpreter in negotiating with Deane: Lasseray, *Les Français*, I, 99.

3. Perhaps it was, but Beaumarchais forwarded it to Vergennes on the 3rd in the letter cited above. BF may then have been at Versailles, as La Rochefoucauld supposed; an entry of Feb. 8 in BF's Waste Book indicates that he had made a number of trips to court in January. The absence of similar entries thereafter may suggest that he discontinued the practice and kept in the background. He was not present when Arthur Lee delivered the commissioners' letter to Vergennes of Feb. 1; see the note on the copy of that letter. On the 8th Deane proposed to call on the Minister and leave BF in Paris to avoid attention: *Deane Papers*, I, 488.

sonant with what he did a few days later, when he and Chastellux interceded with Franklin and Deane and persuaded them, against the latter's better judgment, to give Du Coudray the letter of recommendation that he wanted.[4] Hence our assumption, although unprovable, fits the known facts.

Ce Lundi matin [February 3?, 1777.]
J'ai reçu ce matin la lettre ci jointe dont j'ai crû, Monsieur, qu'il seroit bon que vous fussiez instruit, quoique vous aiez pû apprendre à Versailles une partie de son contenu. Si j'avois sû votre adresse à Versailles, je vous l'aurois envoiée tout de suite; je la remets avec la mienne à un de vos Messieurs qui veut bien me promettre de vous la donner, si vous revenez ce soir, ou de vous la faire tenir, si vous ne revenez pas. Je vous prierai de ne la communiquer à personne, et de me la rendre à votre retour. Si j'apprens quelques nouvelles de M. du Coudrai, *M. le Blond*, j'aurai l'honneur de vous les transmettre tout de suite. Recevez, je vous supplie, mes voeux pour l'Amerique, et l'hommage de l'estime et de l'attachement avec lesquels j'ai l'honneur d'être, Monsieur, Votre très humble et très obeissant serviteur   LE DUC DE LA ROCHEFOUCAULD

Notation: Lett. from Le Duc de la Rochefoucauld monday morning.

From Richard Peters[5]   ALS: American Philosophical Society

Sir,   Baltimore Feby 3d 1777
I leave the enclosed open for your Perusal and beg if you can assist me on the Subject of it you will be so kind as to do

---

4. *Ibid.*, III, 162–3; the letter itself is below, Feb. 6.
5. The nephew of the clergyman of the same name who appears frequently in earlier volumes. Young Peters (1744–1828) was a graduate of the College of Philadelphia, a lawyer, and formerly an adherent of the proprietary faction. Since June, 1776, he had been secretary of the continental board of war. *DAB.*

it. I know not what Part of England Mr. Penn[6] is in but perhaps on Enquiry you can supply that Defect. I am with great
Esteem Your obedient Servant   RICHARD PETERS

Hon. B Franklin Esq

Addressed: The Honble Benjamin Franklin Esq / Paris

Notation: From Richd Peters Esqr

To William Strahan   Extract:[7] Henry E. Huntington Library

[Paris, February 4, 1777[8]]

Mrs. Hall and her Sons, whom you enquire after, were well
when I left Philadelphia. I was too much employed while there
to be often with them; but I heard that their Trade goes on as
successfully as ever.

Thomas Morris to the American Commissioners

ALS: Yale University Library

Gentlemen   Nantes February 4th. 1777.

I have received your several letters dated the 26th. and 30th.
Ultimo, and observe what you say with regard to such prizes
as may occasionally be sent into the different Ports of France
by our American Privateers which will serve for my government in future. As to money matters the sum you require to

6. Without the lost enclosure its subject remains conjectural. William Peters, Richard's father, was in England, no one in Pennsylvania knew where;
if still alive he had no financial resources. At some time during this winter
the son heard that he was dead, and later wrote BF about the report: May
31, 1778, APS. Our guess is that this is a covering note for a letter to Penn,
left open for BF to read, asking help to find the father. Richard Penn, the
former lieutenant governor of Pennsylvania, had gone to England in 1775,
carrying the Olive Branch Petition, and stayed there: above, XII, 94 n.

7. Quoted in Strahan to Mrs. Hall, April 7, 1778. She is identified above,
XVII, 101 n.

8. Strahan gave the place and date in quoting these sentences, which
were in BF's lost answer to his letter above of Jan. 23.

be paid Mr. Deane farr exceeds the net Proceeds of the three cargoes that are arrived here on account of the Congress, and notwithstanding they are all sold, I have not as yet touched one farthing of Cash on that account. The Cargo by the Fanny Captain Tokely came addressed to Mr. Schweighauser who is to be paid therefrom a Considerable sum he has for some time past been in advance for goods sent to America. The others by the Success Captain Anderson, and the Mary and Elizabeth Captain Young will produce together about 180,000 *l.t.*, and the cost of return Cargoes ordered back by these Ships which are already purchased and paid for will amount to 315,000 *l.t.*, consequently will leave Mr. Gruel in advance 135,000 *l.t.*. The orders I have from the Committee of Secrecy, relative to the application of the net Proceeds of the sundry cargoes to be addressed me, do not recommend any particular payment to be made in preferrance to another, but they desire I shoud endeavour to supply the different demands made on me in such a manner, as might prove satisfactory to their different Connections here, as well as those at Paris, Bourdeaux &c. and you May depend upon it I shall not deviate in the least from their instructions in this particular by making partial or temporary payments, but supply the money where most wanted, and in such sums as their remittances may enable me. And as it cannot now be long, before other funds arrive, I have concluded to remit you the net Proceeds of the Mary and Elizabeth's cargo, which you will receive during the Course of the ensuing week, in bills at sight on the Farmers General at Paris to the amount of 90,000 *l.t.* This will increase Mr. Gruel's advance to 225,000 *l.t.*, which is a Capital Sum and a Credit not easily obtained in the present Critical situation of Publick affairs. The amount of the Indico by the Reprisal has been remitted to Mr. Solier in the sum of 41,571 *l.t.* 17. 6 and he will account with you for the same. There is a Ship arrived at Port L'Orient with Rice and Indico, that left Charles Town So. Carolina the 20th. Decemr. last but brings nothing new. The Vessell carried into Gibraltar and onboard a rice cargo on a private account. I hope soon to acquaint you with the arrival of others on account of the United States of America. Captain Anderson is nearly ready to sail. He will wait for your dispatches which shall be carefully forwarded by Gentlemen Your most Obedient Servant   Thos. Morris

To The Honble. Benjamin Franklin, Silas Deane, and Arthur Lee Esqrs. at Paris

Jonathan Williams, Jr., to the American
Commissioners   ALS: American Philosophical Society

Gentlemen   Nantes Feb. 4. 1777.

Since I last had the pleasure of writing to you I have been employed in collecting information relative to shipping, and am sorry that I cant give you any expectation of procuring a Vessell ready built and fitted that will answer for a packet Boat. I have already mentioned two that are here but I apprehend you will think them too large. I have since seen a french Brig but she is so small and so out of repair that I can't think of recommending her. There is here a little Ship on the Stocks that I am sure is exactly what you want, she is not to be sold but I am informed that another like her may be built in 2 or 3 months. The cost of the Hull compleat I am told will be about 24,000 Livres, and I suppose her rigging &c. compleat for the Sea, will cost near as much more. Ready seasoned stuff may be had and while she is building her rigging &c. may be provided so that in about 3 months she may be ready for the Sea. I have desired a plan of her and two or three other different Constructions which if I return soon I will bring with me, if not I will transmit them. There is also here a new Ship that has never been at sea called L'Euole, 500 Tons, will carry 25 Guns; she is for sale if you want such a one.

The mercury left painbeuf the 30th and I hope to hear no more of her 'till I hear of her arrival, but as the Winds have been westerly for several Days past I fear she has not made great progress.[9]

I wait your orders for my return, and in the mean Time

9. The *Mercure* left St. Nazaire on Feb. 5 and arrived at Portsmouth, N. H., on March 17. Lasseray, *Les Français*, I, 368.

shall endeavour to gain all the Information I can on every commercial subject.

Nothing is doing relative to the remainder of the Goods, as Mr. Peltier waits orders for the purchase of another Ship.

Since writing on the other side I have received the inclosed Memorandum from a Builder; his prices seem to me extravagant, much more so than the Builder I saw this morning; when I have his memorandum I shall be able to make the Comparison. I have the Honor to be with the greatest Respect Gentlemen Your most obedient Servant.   J WILLIAMS JUNR

The Honorable The Deputies of The United States.

Notation: Mr Williams Nantes Febry 4th. 1777

The American Commissioners to Ferdinand Grand

February 5, 1777   See page 22n

To Jonathan Williams, Jr.   ALS: Yale University Library

Dear Cousin,   Paris, Feb. 5. 1777.

I receiv'd several Letters from you last Night, which I put into Mr. Dean's Hands, who answers them.[1] I forwarded yours to London; for M. Blount, some time since.[2] Since you are likely to stay at Nantes some time longer, I enclose some Letters receiv'd here for you. [*In the margin*: I shall enclose the mention'd Letters in one by Mr. Lee.] I think a Connection with Mr. S.[3] might be advantageous to you both, in the way of Business. Besides he is rich, and has handsome Daughters: I know not whether you can get one of them, I only know you may deserve her.

Mr. Lee, in his Way to the South of France, will call at Nantes.

1. The answer is in the *Deane Correspondence*, pp. 71–2.
2. BF may have already answered, in some missing letter, JW's troubled inquiry in his above, Jan. 18, about how to handle his relations with Walter Blunt. If not, this was a curt way to brush the problem aside.
3. Schweighauser.

He sets out to morrow or next Day, and will take our Dispatches for America. I am, ever, Your affectionate Uncle

B Franklin

Respects to Mr. Gruel, Penet, Rumsey, Morris, Mounandoin [Montaudoüin], and Schweighauser, as you happen to see them.

Addressed: A Monsr / Monsieur Williams / chez M. Montandoin / Negociant / à Nantes

Endorsed: Franklin Feb 5 1777

From Richard Bache   ALS: American Philosophical Society

Dear Sir   Philadelphia 5th. February 1777

We are now in daily expectation of hearing from you;[4] If I am right in my calculations, you have been gone from us fourteen weeks and upwards, and since your departure, our common Cause has under gone a variety of interesting changes and events, which no doubt, you will become acquainted with thro' the proper channel; our situation at one time was very alarming but thro' the assistance of divine Providence, and the exertion of our Militia, we have hitherto defeated the enemy's intention of possessing themselves of this City, and if we [can] get our Army raised in due time (and recruiting I am told, goes on very vigorously) we shall be an overmatch for them in the Spring. The Enemy at present possess Brunswick and Amboy, where they have their Transports ready to receive them in case they are drove off. We are daily attacking and harrassing their foraging parties and out-centries, and scarcely a day passes, that we do not [take] some Prisoners; the Scotch, from their frequent desertions, appear to be sick of the winter's campaign, and the Hessians complain heavily of being pushed into the Posts of danger, which as they are but hirelings, are no posts of honor to them, they fight not for honorable Victory. Plunder is their aim.

On the approach of the Enemy towards this City I had your Library packed up and sent to Bethlehem, where I intend it

4. See RB's next letter below, Feb. 28.

shall remain, 'till our public affairs wear a better aspect. I removed my Family, with such things only as were necessary to their comfort, about twenty-four miles from hence, to a place called Goshen in Chester County, having procured in a good farm house, two comfortable rooms for them. They yet remain there, and I shall not think of bringing them to Town 'till it can be done with the greatest safety, for Womens fears are soon alarm'd.[5] The Enemy may determine to pay us a visit in the spring by water, as well as by Land, if they should, I hope we shall be ready for them.

The hurry and confusion occasioned by the unsetled situation of our public affairs have prevented me from looking into, or medling with your papers or accounts, any further than removing them into a place of safety and 'till things become a little settled, this business must lye dormant. I suppose you have been informed from the Congress of their appointing me Post Master General (wh[ich they] did, soon after your departure) and of their reasons for su[ch action?] If they have not furnished you with their reasons, it is out of my power to do it; there is one that naturally occurs to me, but whether it is a good one or not, I will not pretend to determine, it is this, your Services may be required in France, for a much longer time, than you or I perhaps had any Idea of, when you left home, and the Congress soon after your departure sa[w as much?][6]

As soon as the Loan Office was opened, your money agreeable to your directions, was put out. It is said, that people in general think the Interest of 4 per Cent too low, and that from this cause they are rather tardy in carrying in their moneys. I have had some intimation that the Interest will be raised to 5 per Cent,[7] but I am of opinion that this will not work to any

5. See Sarah Bache to BF below, Feb. 23.

6. Congress appointed RB postmaster general on Nov. 7, 1776: *JCC*, VI, 931. We have found no discussion of the reasons, but RB was the obvious candidate because of his experience as well as his relationship to BF; as comptroller he had played a key role in the organization of the Post Office.

7. The 4% rate was established when the loan office was authorized, on the eve of BF's departure for France: *JCC*, V, 845–6. The rate was raised to 6% soon after RB wrote; see his letter below, March 10. We have found no record of BF's initial investment, mentioned here, but he said years later

good purpose in this State, for the tardiness of the monied People here, I am afraid pr[oceeds?] more from disaffection than any thing else, and it is certain that these People are monopolizing imperishable commodities at any prices, which is an Evil of so dangerous a nature that it ought to be remedied by our Legislature as soon as possible.[8] With most anxious expectation of hearing from you, and with unfeigned Love to yourself, Temple and Benny I subscribe myself Dear and honored Sir Your affectionate Son RICHD BACHE

Dr. Franklin.

Addressed: The Honble Dr. Franklin / One of the Commissioners at the / Court of France, from the United / States of America / Paris

Sir Philip Gibbes:[9] Minutes of a Conversation with Franklin

Copy:[10] Yale University Library

[On or before February 5, 1777.]

1st. Conversation. A Conversation with Doctor Franklin at Paris on the 5th of February 1777 or some days before.

---

that he subscribed £3,000 at the 6% rate and was credited with £3,037 in 1786: Smyth, *Writings,* IX, 635; Forrest McDonald, *We the People: the Economic Origins of the Constitution* (Chicago, [1958]), p. 63 and n.

8. The first Pa. statute against monopolizing was passed in January, 1778: James T. Mitchell and Henry Flanders, eds., *The Statutes at Large of Pennsylvania from 1682 to 1801* (17 vols., [Harrisburg,] 1896–1915), IX, 177–80.

9. We know little about Sir Philip (1730–1815) except that his family had been settled in Barbados since the early seventeenth century, and that he was created a baronet in 1774: *Burke's Peerage,* pp. 1081–2. He was prominent, at least by 1778, among the West Indian planters and traders in London: Sir John W. Fortescue, *The Correspondence of King George the Third . . .* (6 vols., London, 1927–28), IV, 233–4. He may have met BF there during the efforts to organize merchants' petitions in 1774–75; Gibbes makes clear that their acquaintance had been slight. Eleven months later he saw BF again, and again recorded their conversation: Jan. 5, 1778, Yale University Library. On that occasion BF read and accepted Sir Philip's written account, presumably this one, of the first interview.

10. We have silently corrected a few minor and obvious errors, such as the omission of closing quotation marks. The copy is headed by a note:

I opened my conversation with Doctor Franklin by saying, "My first visit, Sir, was to the Philosopher and the acquaintance. I shall now address you in another stile. I feel myself so much affected by this unhappy dispute between Great Britain and her Colonies, that I determined to avail myself of the little acquaintance I once had with you, to pray you would indulge me with some conversation on the subject. I know I am not entitled to your confidence; perhaps you may think I am not entitled to your communication. I beg, Sir, at once to set you at ease, by assuring you, that if you should judge it imprudent to answer me, or improper even to hear me, I shall rest satisfied with your caution." The Doctor kept silence, but gave attention: I went on; "Give me leave here to promise, that this visit is not made at the request of, or even in consequence of any communication I have had with any man whatever. I am unconnected, uninfluenced; I feel my[*self*] independent, and my conduct is directed by my own Ideas of propriety. It has always been my Opinion, that no man is of so little consequence, but that he may be useful, if he will be active. Upon this Occasion I determined not to be restrained by a timid caution from offering myself as an humble instrument, if I can be used, for the general good. I have all the predeliction for America, that is consistent with my attachment to Great Britain. I wish to see peace established upon such constitutional principles, as shall secure the permanent prosperity of both Countries. United, they continue for ever formidable; separated, they soon become weakened." Here I paused. The Doctor continued silent, but I thought attentive. The interval tho' short was awkward. I then proceeded; "The work of reconciliation is become perhaps difficult; but it is far from impracticable. I cannot presume to surmise what terms the King and the Parliament of Great Britain may be inclined to grant to America. But I think I hazard nothing in assuring you, that administration is sincerely disposed to conciliate with Amer-

---

"Minute of two Conversations between Dr. Franklin and Sir Philip Gibbes at Paris upon the subject of America during the War with Great Britain. From the Original MSS. in Sir P. G.'s handwriting communicated to Me in Octr. 1796. C.A." The writer of this note was Sir Philip's son-in-law, Charles Abbot, Lord Colchester, from whose library Yale acquired the copy.

ica. I know your Abilities Sir; I know your influence in America. You owe it to your country, who confides in you. You owe it to Heaven, to whom you are accountable, to employ all your powers to facilitate a reconciliation. This unfortunate business must be terminated. It must end either in absolute conquest by the Sword, or in an equitable Union by negotiation. The first is too horrible to think of. Let me then beseech you, Sir, to devise the means of making known to Administration the terms, which will satisfy America, or of applying to administration to sollicit the conditions which would be granted to America. I want to see a communication opened. I would by no means undertake to convey any thing directly from you to any person in Administration But if I could engage so much of your confidence as to be entrusted with the great outlines of Reconciliation, I think I could find the means of conveying them to Lord G.G.[1]" Here Doctor Franklin answered to this effect "I am much afraid Sir, that things are gone too far to admit of reconciliation. I am inclined to think that America would insist upon such terms, as Great Britain would not be disposed to grant." (I pass over the Doctors observations upon the harsh treatment of Great Britain to America, and the respectful conduct of America to Great Britain to a certain period. He concluded with saying) "We know that the King, the Ministry, and the people despise and hate us; that they wish the destruction, the very extirpation of the Americans. Great Britain has injured us too much ever to forgive us. We on our parts can place no confidence in Parliament; for we have no security for their engagements. We delayed the declaration of Independency as long as we hoped for justice from Great Britain. It was the people that called for it long before it was made the Act of Congress. It is made and we must maintain it if we can." Here I begged the Doctor to reflect, "that in cases not immediately within view, the ablest and best of men could only form opinions and take their measures upon the information they received. I wish Sir, said I, that you should be well informed of the sense of the people and the firmness of the Ministry. I speak to you as a man of honour, and tell it you

1. Germain.

283

upon the fullest persuasion, that however well inclined Administration may be, it is fixed and determined to prosecute the War with vigour, unless America will submit to reasonable terms. The resolution is taken in conformity with the temper of the people, whose liberal Grants seem to anticipate the demands of the Minister. The ministry and people look to the end, and will not withhold the means. Knowing then the power you have to contend with, Policy, Humanity, and every motive that ought to influence the human mind seem to conspire to direct America to sue for Peace." The Doctor replied, "I am not authorized to treat or to make proposals; besides this is a very improper time. Great Britain is now flushed with the Idea of victories gained in America. With respect to the power we have to contend with, we know it is formidable, but we know how far it can affect us. We have made up our Accounts in which we have stated the loss of all our towns upon the Coasts. We have already reconciled ourselves to that misfortune; but we know it is impossible to penetrate our country. Thither we are resolved to retire, and to wait events, which we trust will be favorable. We expect to be more powerfully attacked the next Campaign; but we know we shall be better prepared for our defence. What we wanted in the last campaign, we shall be fully supplied with in the next. You observed Sir, (he said) that Great Britain and America united were formidable. We feel the advantages, and wish to preserve the continuance of the union, for we know that separated both Countries must become weak; *but there is this difference, Great Britain will always remain weak; America after a time, will grow strong.*" At this pause I rose to take my leave. "I am sorry (I said) I cannot induce you to impart any thing to me, which I may hope to turn to the mutual advantage of the contending parties." He then said, "Tho, Sir, I am not impowered to say or do any thing, I can venture to declare it, as the resolution of America to treat upon no other footing than that of Independency. If Great Britain is disposed to grant Conditions, the proposal of them must come from herself. You may be sure none will ever come from America, after the repeated contempt shewn to her petitions. *A reconciliation founded upon a fœderal union of the two Countries may take place.* In that Union, they may engage to make peace

284

and war as one state, and such advantages may be granted to Great Britain in the regulation of commerce as may satisfy her."[2] In my last reply, I took the liberty to say, "I lamented much that Parliament, tenacious of dignity, had refused to receive the demands of America, and lost the happy moment of satisfying them. I hope Sir America pleased with the sound of independency will not prolong the War by a vain struggle for the word. If she can enjoy the advantages without the name, I hope she will learn to be wise and to be satisfied."

The American Commissioners to the Committee of Secret Correspondence

LS and copy: National Archives; copy: Harvard University Library

Gentlemen,   Paris, Feb. 6. 1777.

Since our last, a Copy of which is enclosed Mr. Hodge is arrived here from Martinique, and has brought safely the Papers he was charged with. He had a long Passage and was near being starved. We are about to employ him in a Service, pointed out by you, at Dunkirk or Flushing. He has delivered us three sets of the Papers we wanted; but we shall want more, and *beg you will not fail* to send them by several Opportunity's.[3]

A Private Company has been just formed here, for the Importation of Tobacco, who have made such Proposals to the Farmers general, as induced them to suspend the signing of their Agreement with us, tho' the Terms had been settled and the writings drawn. It seems now uncertain whether it will be revived or not. The Company have offered to export such goods as we should advise, and we have given them a List of those most wanted. But so changeable are Minds here on occasion

2. This suggestion, of which we have found no echo elsewhere, gives particular significance to Sir Philip's assertion that BF later approved it along with the rest of the account; but in doing so he pointed out that the time had passed by then for any such proposal.

3. It is impossible to tell whether this and later underlinings were in the original text. William Hodge carried copies of the proposed commercial treaty and of BF's credentials; and was charged with buying a privateer: above, XXII, 619 n. The sets of papers were blank commissions.

of news good or bad, that one cannot be sure that even this Company will proceed.[4] With an Universal Good Will to our Cause and Country, apparent in all Companies, there is mixt an Universal Apprehension that we shall be reduced to Submission, which often chills the purposes of serving us.

The want of intelligence from America, and the Impossibility of contradicting by that means the false news spread here and all over Europe by the Enemy, has a bad Effect on the minds of many who would adventure in Trade to our Ports, as well as on the Conduct of the several Governments of Europe. It is now more than three Months since our B.F. left Philadelphia, and we have not received a single letter of later Date, Mr. Hodge having left that place before him. We are about purchasing some Cutters to be employed as Packets. In the first we dispatch, we shall write more particularly concerning our proceedings here than by these Merchant Ships we can venture to do: For the orders given to sink letters are not well executed: One of our Vessels was lately carried into Gibraltar, being taken by an English Man of War, and we hear there were Letters for us, which the Captain just as he was boarded threw out of the Cabin Window, which floating on the Water were taken up: and a Sloop dispatch'd with them to London. We also just now hear from London (thro' the Ministry here) that another of our Ships is carried into Bristol by the Crew: who consisting of 8 American Seamen with 8 English, and 4 of the Americans being sick, the other 4 were overpowred by the 8 English, and carried in as aforesaid:[5] The Letters were dispatch'd to Court.

From London they write to us, that a Body of 10,000 Men, chiefly Germans, are to go out this Spring, under the command of Genl. Burgoyne, for the invasion of Virginia and

4. If the reference is, as we think, to Dubourg's scheme discussed in the headnote above, Jan. 9, the company did not proceed.

5. Although the episode at Gibraltar sounds like that which Carmichael reported to Deane on Jan. 24 (*Deane Papers*, I, 471), the ship mentioned there was from South Carolina, and would have been most unlikely to carry dispatches for the commissioners. We have found no trace of a ship taken to Bristol at this time, but two put in at other ports; see the commissioners to Germain below, Feb. 7.

Maryland. The opinion of this Court founded on their advices from Germany is, that such a number can by no means be obtained: but you will be on your guard. The Amphitrite and the Seine from Havre, and the Mercury from Nantes, are all now at Sea laden with Arms, Ammunition, brass Field Pieces and Stores, Cloathing, Canvas &c. which if they safely arrive will put you in a much better Condition for the next Campaign than you were for the last. Some excellent Engineers and Officers of Artillery will also be with you pretty early: Also some few for the Cavalry. Officers of Infantry of all Ranks have offered themselves without Number. It is quite a Business to receive the Applications and refuse them. Many are gone over at their own Expence, contrary to our advice: to some few of these who were well recommended we have given Letters of Introduction.[6]

The Conduct of our General in avoiding a decisive action is much applauded by the Military People here, particularly, Marshals Maillebois, Broglio, and D'Arcy; M. Maillebois has taken the pains to write his Sentiments of some particulars useful in carrying on our War, which we send enclosed.[7]

But that which makes the greatest Impression in our Favour here, is the prodigious success of our armed Ships and Privateers. The Damage we have done their west India Trade has been estimated in a Representation to Lord Sandwich by the Merchants of London, at £1,800,000 Sterling, which has raised Insurance to 28 Per Cent, being higher than at any time in the last War with France and Spain. This mode of exerting our Force against them should be pushed with Vigour. It is that in which we can most sensibly hurt them: and to secure a continuance of it we think one or two of the Engineers we send over may be usefully employ'd in making some of our Ports im-

6. See the headnote above on Blondel de Lantone's application, Jan. 13.

7. Only Broglie was a marshal; the other two were BF's colleagues in the Académie des sciences, and will frequently reappear. Among BF's papers in the APS is a long document endorsed, "Memoire, concerning Useless Expenses that many States put themselves to"; it is in French, addressed to Congress, Washington, and Franklin, and has to do with the organization of an army. If this was Maillebois' contribution to the cause, the commissioners doubtless enclosed a copy.

pregnable. As we are well informed that a number of Cutters are building to Cruise in the W. Indies against our small Privateers, it may not be amiss we think, to send your larger Vessels thither, and ply in other Quarters with the small ones.

A fresh misunderstanding between the Turks and Russia, is likely to give so much employment to the Troops of the latter, as that England can hardly expect to obtain any of them.[8] Her malice against us is however so high at present, that she would stick at no Expence to gratify it. The New England Colonies are, *according to our best information*, destined to Destruction, and the rest to Slavery under a Military government. But the Governor of the World sets Bounds to the Rage of Men, as well as to that of the Ocean.

Finding that our Residence here together is nearly as expensive as if we were separate; and *having Reason* to believe that *one of us might be useful at Madrid, and another in Holland, and some Courts farther northward*, we have agreed that Mr. Lee go to Spain, and either Mr. Dean or myself to the Hague. Mr. Lee sets out tomorrow having obtained Passports, and a Letter from the Spanish Ambassador here to the Minister there. The Journey to Holland will not take place so soon: The particular Purposes of these Journeys we cannot prudently now explain.

It is proper we should acquaint you with the behavior of one Nicholas Davis, who came to us here pretending to have served as an Officer in India, to be originally from Boston, and desirous of returning to act in defence of his Country, but thro' the loss of some Effects coming to him from Jamaica and taken by our Privateers, unable to defray the Expence of his Passage. We furnish'd him with 30 Louis, which was fully sufficient; but at Havre just before he sailed he took the Liberty of Drawing on us for near 40 more which we have been obliged to pay.[9] As in order to obtain that Credit, he was guilty of several Falsities, we now doubt his ever having been an Officer at all. We send his note and Draft, and hope you will

8. Hostilities between the Turks and Russians were reported in the *Public Advertiser* of Jan. 29 and Feb. 3.

9. See his note to BF above, under Jan. 16.

take proper care of him. He says his Father was a Clergyman in Jamaica. He went in the Seine, and took Charge of two Blankets for Mr. Morris.

We hope your Union continues firm, and the Courage of our Countrymen unabated. England begins to be very jealous of this Court; and we think *with some reason*. We have the Honour to be with sincere Esteem Gentlemen, Your most obedient and most humble Servants   B Franklin
                                                      Silas Deane
                                                      Arthur Lee

Notation: Franklin Deane Lee To the Comtee Feb 6. 1777

The American Commissioners to the President of Congress[1]

ALS[2] and copy: National Archives

Sir   Paris, Feb. 6. 1777

This will be delivered to you by M. de Coudray, an Officer of great Reputation here, for his Talents in general, and particularly for his Skill and Abilities in his Profession. Some accidental Circumstance, I understand, prevented his going in the Amphitrite; but his Zeal for our Cause, and earnest Desire of promoting it, have engag'd him to overcome all Obstacles, and render himself in America by the first possible Opportunity.[3] If he arrives there, you will I am persuaded find him of

1. For the background of this letter see the headnote on La Rochefoucauld to BF above, under Feb. 3. The letter was the result, as mentioned there, of the intercession of the Duke and the chevalier de Chastellux. We have no evidence that Du Coudray was present at their interview with the commissioners, when the letter was presumably signed, but if not they must have transmitted it to him immediately. It is unlikely that he had already left the city, as Deane later remembered (*Deane Papers*, III, 162), for he used the letter within a day or two; see the note below on Deane's signature.

2. In BF's hand.

3. Du Coudray wasted no time in finding an opportunity; he left in haste before he could be stopped, as Beaumarchais and Deane hoped he would be. By the 8th or thereabouts he was near Angers: Morton, *Beaumarchais correspondance*, III, 55. By the 13th he was in Nantes, and on the next day he was reported there to have sailed: Lee to BF and Deane below, Feb. 13, 14. A shipmate later provided a timetable of the voyage, according to which the sailing was no later than the 14th: *Deane Correspondence*, p. 89.

great Service not only in the Operations of the next Campaign, but in forming Officers for those that may follow. I therefore recommend him warmly to the Congress, and to your Countenance and Protection. Wishing you every kind of Felicity, I have the Honour to be, with the highest Esteem, Sir, Your most obedient humble Servant   B FRANKLIN
SILAS DEANE[4]

Honourable John Hancock Esqr Presedt of the Congress

Notation: Letter from Ben Franklin & Silas Deane 6 Feby 1777 per Mons Du Coudray read 3 June 1777 referred to the comee. on foreign applications[5]

From ——— de Bruni

February 6, 1777   See page 169

From Jean Girardot de Marigny[6]

AL: American Philosophical Society

6e. fevrier 1777

Mr. Girardot de Marigny a l'honneur de faire ses complimens a Monsieur Le Docteur franklin. Un de ses amis qui est hol-

---

4. Lee, as Deane remembered, was out of town: *Deane Papers*, III, 162. BF's use of the first person singular suggests that he did not expect his fellow commissioner to sign the letter. Deane did so with the greatest reluctance, and only after La Rochefoucauld and Chastellux had given their word of honor that no use would be made of it in France. Instead Du Coudray promptly divulged it to others, including Beaumarchais. Deane found this out and was furious. He protested to Chastellux at the breach of faith, and assured Beaumarchais that he hoped Du Coudray would never reach America. Beaumarchais forwarded Deane's letter in translation to Vergennes, with the complaint that Du Coudray was jeopardizing the secrecy of the whole operation. Deane to Chastellux, undated but after Feb. 6, *Deane Papers*, I, 468–9; Morton, *op. cit.*, III, 51, 54–5.

5. *JCC*, VIII, 412.

6. Girardot (d. 1796) was a prominent Parisian banker, a Protestant of Swiss extraction; he was a partner in what had been Germany, Girardot & Cie. and was becoming, through a process of reorganization, Girardot, Haller & Cie. Robert D. Harris, *Necker, Reform Statesman of the Ancien Régime* (Berkeley, Los Angeles, and London, 1979), pp. 5–6; Lüthy, *Banque protestante*, II, 233–4.

landois l'a prié de lui demander si Mr. Adams qui doit être a Philadelphie n'est pas originaire de la haie. Il paroit qu'on y est inquiet d'une personne de ce nom qu'on croit etre Mr. Adams actuellement en Amerique. M. Girardot sera fort obligé a Monsieur Le Docteur des Eclaircissemens qu'il pourra lui donner a ce sujet. Il fait mille complimens a Monsieur Deane et a Monsieur Lee.

Addressed: A Monsieur / Monsieur Le Docteur / franklin / hotel d'hambourg / *Rue Jacob.*/ hotel *Colbert*

Notation: Girardot Gill Paris 6 fevr. 78

From Emma Thompson[7] AL: American Philosophical Society

St Omar Febry the 6th. [1777]

Tho' your residence in Paris be proclamed in the public papers, (you arch Rebel) yet having left England some months ago, I should have known nothing of you but for a Mrs. Playdell who happened to lodge in the House with you at Paris. Oh tell me I pray you how were Mr. and Mrs. Barrow when you left America?[8] Did you see them were they safe, had they thoughts of returning to England? Do answer me let me bribe you to it and pay you now before hand in intelligence of your friends and Sweethearts left in England. Yes they are still so, naughty man, the good Man Wilkes and Wife in particular: I am sorry to tell you that nothing has yet been done for them and that wearied of their condition they have at length, he to the notory public business, She to take in Boarders. Her last letter directs my next address to her in Kingstreet Southampton Row. But your friends Mr. and Mrs. Cheap are not only *well* but well off too, have got a Prebendary at York and a something better in daily expectation but Docr. Huck disdaining all small matters except a Wife is now (upon my word tis true) just going to marry a little Miss Kensy quite a young

7. Clearly an old friend, but to our surprise we know nothing more about her than is revealed in this letter and BF's reply below, Feb. 8.

8. They had been acquainted with BF as early as 1766: above, XIII, 537 n.

Lady with a fortune of a Hundred Thousand Pds.[9] No I do not forget your good friend Stevenson who I think would have risqued all taring and feathering to have paid you a Visit in Philadelp., but now so near you what can prevent her seeing you? Nothing to be sure but the Weather, which stops me in my Rambles likewise. I left England early in November last hoping from air Exercise and dissipation to recover or mend at least my Health and Spirits most sadly depressed. Knowing little of the French Tongue I purposed getting on to Brussels as there are so many English families settled in there. But the Winter Season was too far advanced when I first sett out upon this scheme, so here I was stoped and shall continue for a month at least. Do you know any thing of Brussels? The people here tell me all things are dear there, and that Lisle will better answer all my purposes, tell me can one live comfortably there upon two Hundred pounds a year? I am very weary of this place tho the people are indeed more than civil to me. But I am out of temper I believe and associate but little with any of them. Mrs. Paine and Heathcott, (tho friends to your Cause) are yet my most welcome visiters. Three times a Week we do generally meet at Whist or Cribbage. I wish you would come and cutt in. I will give you your dinner tho you stay a month, and a Party Every Evening. Adieu I must invoke St. Patrick now before I get courage to sign my name, for tho native of a Country which he so bountifully blessd with proper assurance upon all occasions, yet I feel we do degenerate when long absent from it. For tho I know you a Rebel and myself a right Loyal, tho you deserve hanging, and I deserve pensioning Still I feel you my Superior, feel a return of the great Respect I ever held You in, and feel alas, unhappy, thinking I have been too bold, and that Emma Thompson may suffer in the mind of Dr. Franklin. She lodges at Madam Batiste Rue Commandant, St. Omar.

Addressed: To Docr Franklin / Paris

9. Israel and Elizabeth Wilkes have frequently appeared before, but Andrew Cheap and his wife have not since 1766: *ibid.* Dr. Richard Huck did not marry this heiress but another, in 1777, and as a consequence changed his name to Huck-Saunders: above, xv, 172 n.

From Jonathan Williams, Jr.

ALS: American Philosophical Society

Dear and honoured Sir,   Nantes February 6. 1777.

Inclosed is the proportion of the little Ship I mentioned in my last. The price you will find more reasonable than either of those proposed by the other Builder.

A Ship arrived the other day from Carolina; an Officer who came passenger in her is I suppose by this time with you, I am very sorry I did not see him.

I am much disappointed by not receiving Letters by the post to day, for I don't know what to do. By my Instructions I am to regulate my stay by Letters, therefore can't leave this place till I recieve orders, tho' I am now quite idle.

I apprehend that what passes at Nantes openly will be known in London, for here are several Englishmen and one very suspicious as to his Business. It will be a question whether my return to that Country will not be hazardous as to my person, I assure you however I have no desire to return if I can manage matters here either in a public or private capacity. If I possess any Talents that can in any way be serviceable to my Country they are at her service *Gratis*, I only ask a Subsistence; but if I can make any commercial Connection with an Individual I must make the best Bargain I can: what I mean to say is, that in the first Instance the Love of my Country will be my motive, in the last the desire of gaining a Fortune.

By advice from St. Domingo and Martinique powder is quite a Drug 35 sous per pound and so much of it that they are obliged to keep it on ship board for want of sufficient magazines. I am in haste Yours most dutifully and affectionately

J WILLIAMS J

Addressed: A Monsieur / Monsieur Franklin LLD / Hotel de Hambourg / Rue Jacob. / a Paris.

Jacques Boux to the American Commissioners

[before February 7, 1777]   See page 307n

The American Commissioners: Proposed Memorial to Lord George Germain

DS: Library of Congress; ADS (draft): Library of Congress[1]

To the Right Honorable Lord George Sackville Germaine, one of the Principal Secretaries of State to the King of Great Britain.

Paris Feby. 7th. 1777.

Whereas the Snow Dickenson with her Cargoe, which was the property of the Congress of the United States of America, was by an Act of Piracy, in some of her Crew, carried into the port of Bristol in England, and there as we are informed, was converted to the use of the Government of Great Britain; and the perpetrators of so base and dishonest an action, the Mate and Sailors, (who had hired themselves in Consideration of good Wages, and engaged faithfully to work the said Snow in her Voyage to France, but in their way treacherously[2] rose upon the Captain, and took the Vessel from him,) were rewarded instead of being punished for their wickedness.

And Whereas another Vessel with her Cargoe of Tobacco, being also the property of the United States, or of some Inhabitants of the same, was lately carried into the Port of Liverpoole, in England, by a similar act of Treachery in her Crew; and a third has in the same manner been carried into Halifax.[3]

We, therefore being Commissioners plenipotentiary from the Congress of the United States of America, do, in their

1. The DS is in WTF's hand. The ADS is largely in Lee's, and is signed by him as well as the other commissioners; it also has interlineations and a separate sheet of interpolations by BF.
2. The draft originally added "conspired."
3. For the *Dickinson* see above, XXII, 332–3. The second ship was the *Aurora*, bound for Nantes with dispatches and a cargo from the secret committee; she was seized by English members of her crew and sailed into Liverpool in late January: *Naval Docs.*, VII, 120–1; VIII, 555; *Public Advertiser*, Feb. 1, 3, 1777. The third was the *Molly*, an American prize captured off Newfoundland, which again was seized by members of her crew and taken to Londonderry in mid-January: *ibid.*, Feb. 1. The commissioners perhaps mistook the port because they caught only the reference to Newfoundland.

name and by their Authority, demand from the Court of Great Britain, a restitution of these Vessels and their Cargoes, or the full value of them; together with the delivery of the Pirates into our Hands to be sent where they may be tried and punished as their Crimes deserve.

We feel it our Duty to humanity, to warn the Court of Great Britain of the consequences of protecting such Offenders, and of encouraging such Actions as are in violation of all moral obligation, and therefore subversive of the firmest foundation of the Laws of nations.

It is hoped, that the Government of Great Britain, will not add to the unjust principles of this War, such practices as would disgrace the meanest State in Europe; and which must forever stain the Character of the British Nation. We are sensible, that nothing can be more abhorrent from the Sentiments and Feelings of the Congress of the United States, than the authorising so base a kind of War, as a retaliation of these practices will produce. We are, therefore, more earnest in pressing the Court of Great Britain, to prevent, by the Act of Justice which is demanded, the *retaliation*, to which necessity, in repugnance to principles, will otherwise compel.

And we hereby notify the said Court, that if the Justice demanded is not speedily obtained, a publick and general Invitation will be given to all Seamen intrusted with british Ships, to bring the same into the Ports of the United States, where the full value of them and their Cargoes will be fairly divided among the Captors, as Legal Prize.

We desire an Answer within four Weeks from the Date of this Demand.
B FRANKLIN
SILAS DEANE

Commissioners Plenipotentiary for the United States of North America

In Franklin's hand: Memorial to Lord G. Sackville not sent Feby. 7th. 77.

From Duportail

ALS: American Philosophical Society

Monsieur paris le 7 fevrier 1777
Je desirerois avoir l'honneur de vous voir pour arreter quelque chose au aujet de notre depart; je vous seray obligé de me recevoir aujourd'huy à sept heures du soir. J'ai l'honneur d'etre votre tres humble et tres obeissant serviteur DUPORTAIL

Addressed: A Monsieur / Monsieur francklin à l'hotel / d'hambourg Rüe jacob / *A paris*

The American Commissioners to the Committee of Secret Correspondence

ALS and copy: National Archives

Gentlemen Paris Feby. 8th: 1777
Since Our last We have received the inclosed Intelligence from London, which we take the earliest Opportunity of forwarding, in hopes it may be received with Our other Letters by Nantes.[4] A Vessel from So: Carolina, loaded by that state, which sailed the 20th December, is arrived at L'Orient with Rice and Indigo. As We were particular in Our last which was sent but yesterday, we have nothing material to add by this but are Gentlemen Your most Obedient and Very Humble Servants B FRANKLIN
SILAS DEANE

The hon. Messr: Morriss, Jay, &c, &c, Comr: Philadelphia

Addressed: To / the hon: / Messrs Morriss, Jay, Lee &c / Secret Com: of Congress / Philadelphia

Notation: Franklin & Deane to the Comtee Feb. 8. 1777

To Emma Thompson[5]

ALS (draft) and copy:[6] Library of Congress

Paris, Feb. 8. 1777
You are too early, Hussy, (as well as too saucy) in calling me Rebel; you should wait for the Event, which will determine

4. The letter is in Deane's hand; the intelligence was probably Bancroft's letter to him of Jan. 31, describing the imminent British threat to New England and preparations for war against France: *Deane Papers,* I, 479–81.
5. In answer to her letter above, Feb. 6.
6. We have supplied in brackets from the copy a passage now illegible in the draft.

whether it is a Rebellion or only a Revolution. Here the Ladies are more civil; they call us *les Insurgens*, a Character that usually pleases them: And methinks you, with all other Women who smart or have smarted under the Tyranny of a bad Husband, ought to be fix'd in *Revolution* Principles, and act accordingly.

In my way to Canada last Spring, I saw dear Mrs. Barrow at New York. Mr. Barrow had been from her two or three Months, to keep Gov. Tryon and other Tories Company, on board the Asia one of the King's Ships which lay in the Harbour; and in all that time, naughty Man, had not ventur'd once on shore to see her. Our Troops were then pouring into the Town, and she was packing up to leave it; fearing as she had a large House they would incommode her by quartering Officers in it. As she appear'd in great Perplexity, scarce knowing where to go I persuaded her to stay, and I went to the General Officers then commanding there, and recommended her to their Protection, which they promis'd, and perform'd. On my Return from Canada, (where I was a Piece of a Governor, and I think a very good one, for a Fortnight; and might have been so till this time if your wicked Army, Enemies to all good Government, had not come and driven me out) I found her still in quiet Possession of her House. I enquired how our People had behav'd to her; she spoke in high Terms of the respectful Attention they had paid her, and the Quiet and Security they had procur'd her. I said I was glad of it; and that if they had us'd her ill, I would have turn'd Tory. *Then*, says she, (with that pleasing Gaiety so natural to her) *I wish they had.* For you must know she is a Toryess as well as you and can as flippantly call Rebel. I drank Tea with her; we talk'd affectionately of you and our other Friends the Wilkes's, of whom she had receiv'd no late Intelligence. What became of her since, I have not heard. The Street she then liv'd in was some Months after chiefly burnt down; but as the Town was then, and ever since has been in Possession of the King's Troops, I have had no Opportunity of knowing whether she suffer'd any Loss in the Conflagration. I hope she did not, as if she did, I should wish I had not persuaded her to stay there. I am glad to learn from you that that unhappy tho' deserving Family the W's are getting into some Business that may afford them Subsistence. I pray that God will bless them, and that they may see happier Days. Mr. Cheap's and Dr. Huck's good Fortunes please me. Pray learn, (if you have not already learnt) like me, to be pleas'd with other People's Pleasures, and happy with their Happinesses; when none occur of your own; then perhaps you will not so soon be weary of the Place you chance to be in, and so fond of Rambling to get rid of your *Ennui*. I fancy You have hit upon the right Reason of your being weary of St. Omer, viz. that you are out of Temper [which is the effect of full living and idleness. A month in Bridewell, beating] Hemp upon Bread and Water, would give you Health and Spirits, and subsequent Chearfulness, and Contentment with every other Situation. I prescribe that Regimen for you my Dear, in pure good Will, without a Fee. And, if you do not get into Temper, neither Brussels nor Lisle will suit you. I know nothing of the Price of Living in either of those Places; but I am sure that a single Woman, as you are, might with Oeconomy, upon two hundred Pounds a year, maintain herself comfortably any where, and me into the Bargain. Don't invite me in earnest, however, to come and live with you; for being posted here I ought not to comply, and I am not sure I should be able to refuse. Present my Respects to Mrs. Payne and Mrs. Heathcoat, for tho' I have not the Honour of knowing them, yet as you say they are Friends to the American Cause, I am sure they must be Women of good Understanding. I know you wish you could see me, but as you can't, I will describe my self to you. Figure me in your mind as jolly as formerly, and as strong and hearty, only a few Years older, very plainly dress'd, wearing my thin grey strait Hair, that peeps out under my only Coiffure, a fine Fur Cap, which comes down my Forehead almost to my Spectacles. Think how this must appear among the Powder'd Heads of Paris. I wish every Gentleman and Lady in France would only be so obliging as to follow my Fashion, comb their own Heads as I do mine, dismiss their Friseurs, and pay me half the Money they paid to them. You see the Gentry might well afford this; and I could then inlist those Friseurs, who are at least 100,000; and with the Money I would maintain them, make a Visit with them to England,

and dress the Heads of your Ministers and Privy Counsellors, which I conceive to be at present *un peu dérangées.* Adieu, Madcap, and believe me ever Your affectionate Friend and humble Servant   BF

PS. Don't be proud of this long Letter. A Fit of the Gout which has confin'd me 5 Days, and made me refuse to see any Company, has given me a little time to trifle. Otherwise it would have been very short. Visitors and Business would have interrupted. And perhaps, with Mrs. Barrow, *you wish they had.*

To Mrs Thompson at Lisle

From Duportail   ALS: American Philosophical Society

Monsieur   paris le 8 fevrier 1777
    Toutes reflexions faites, je crois que les vaisseaux de nantes nous offrent plus de sureté et de commodités pour notre passage que le *paquebot.* Ainsi je choisis le premier moyen à moins que vous n'ayèz vous même fait des observations contraires; auquel cas je vous prierois de vouloir bien m'en faire part.
    J'ai eu l'honneur de vous parler de quelques instrumens necessaires à notre profession. Cela consisteroit en trois graphometres, trois boussoles, et trois alidades de planchettes. C'est l'affaire d'une quinzaine de louis. Il seroit à propos que vous les fissièz acheter ou si vous le desirèz je les acheteray et vous m'en rembourserèz le montant. Les instrumens appartiendront à l'état.
    Si vous voulèz, monsieur, lundy soir je me rendray chèz vous et nous signerons les conditions de notre arrangement.[7] Si vous prenèz la peine de les dresser d'avance, je vous prie d'y inserer notre titre en france et de laisser à la suite de nos noms veritables la place d'un autre nom que nous prendrons.
    J'ai appris aujourd'huy qu'un officier du corps à qui la Cour

7. The agreement was actually signed the following Thursday; it is below, Feb. 13.

vient *de donner sa retraite* doit vous offrir ses services.[8] Quelque party que vous prenièz à son egard je vous prie instamment de ne luy rien apprendre de notre depart. J'ai l'honneur d'etre votre tres humble et tres obeissant serviteur   DP

Notation: Papers concerning / M. du Portail.

From Jonathan Williams, Jr.

ALS: American Philosophical Society

Dear and honored Sir   Nantes February 8. 1777.
  I recvd your and Mr. Deanes Favour of the 5 Inst. and wrote a short Letter to Mr. D. by Mr. de Francy this morning. I shall do the best in my power for the Interest of the Concerned in everything that comes under my Direction.
  I am glad you approve of a Connection with Mr. S. I imagine I can form one in a commercial way, but as I have no capital I must only rely upon my Conduct, which I will always endeavour shall be such as to deserve your approbation; and if you think me deserving of your recommendation I imagine by your Interest in america I could obtain consignments, and thereby make my connection with Mr. S more serviceable than even with a Capital without such assistance. I don't mean by this to make myself burdensome to you, I only wish for such countenance as my conduct may deserve, and when that ceases to be agreeable to you, I can expect no farther encouragement.
  Nantes is very agreeable to me and I think I could be happy to stay here; I am very sensible of the advantage of an intimate acquaintance in so agreeable a Family as I find Mr. Shweig-

---

8. We are confident that he is referring to Du Coudray, whose orders to rejoin his regiment, if Duportail's information is correct, must have been rescinded by the 7th. We have no other evidence of this official change of heart except the fact that Du Coudray sailed a few days later. Had his previous orders still been in effect, he would presumably have been barred from the ship as he had been from the *Amphitrite.*

hausser's to be, and I will not as yet determine whether that circumstance may not add to my motive.[9]

I am endeavouring to provide Lodgings for Mr. Lee who I suppose will be here before you receive this. I am with the greatest Respect Your dutifull and affectionate Kinsman

J WILLIAMS

Addressed: A Monsieur / Monsieur Franklin LLD / Hotel de Hambourg / Rue Jacob / a / Paris

From J. de Sparre[1]   ALS: Historical Society of Pennsylvania

⟨Strasbourg, February 10, 1777, in French: I have had no answer to two letters to Mr. Deane[2] in which I told him, without going into details, about my project for aiding the colonies, and offered to come to Paris to explain it to him. I repeat the same offer to you. I was in America in the French service during the last war, and after that in the Russian; I am now in none. Neither am I a French subject; I was born in Germany and raised in England. Do what you please with me so that I may distinguish myself in America, which I long to do.⟩

9. The moment was opportune: Schweighauser had just lost a son-in-law who had been active in the firm, and was hoping for a replacement. J.-C.-F. Meinert to Thomas Dobrée, Feb. 9, and P.-F. Dobrée to his parents, Feb. 13, 1777: Library of Congress microfilm of the Pierre Dobrée Papers (Bibliothèque municipale, Nantes), roll 1.

1. He presumably belonged to a distinguished Swedish family that had intermarried with the French aristocracy; several members were officers in the Strasbourg garrison. *Dictionnaire de la noblesse; Etat militaire de France . . .* for 1777, pp. 279–80. This Sparre was pertinaceous as a letter-writer, although he never seems to have had an answer. He went on throughout the war pestering BF with a variety of offers, none of which as far as we know bore fruit. These letters, except as indicated, are all in the APS. They are of Feb. 21, 1777 (Hist. Soc. of Pa.), Feb. 28, 1777 (University of Pa. Library), May 3, 1777; Jan. 6, May 11, 30, 1778; Jan. 6, 1780; April 17, 1781; and March 1, 1783.

2. Of Oct. 24 and 28, 1776; the first is in the Hist. Soc. of Pa. and the second in the University of Pa. Library.

From Margaret Stewart[3]   ALS: American Philosophical Society

Sir   Callais 10 Febr 1777

After Your goodness to Me allready; I am Sorry I am under the necessity of troubling You again; which to beg You will lend me fivty Pounds; which I will most faithfully pay You on my arrival at Paris. I have been detained here Some time by being disapointed of Monney due to me in England. I have also a great deal due to me from my Brother; which I have the Senators Remembrancer as a Security for; which as yet has been of little Service to me; but I hope by Your protecttion it may be of Some in france; as Works of Merit meet with great prtection here; if You will honour me with an enswer to this you will Much oblige Your Obliged humble Servant

M STEWART

Pleas to adress Your Letter A Madame Madame Cavendish chez Monsieur Augustin Meurice Calais

Addressed: A Monsieur / Monsieur Dr Franklin / A Paris

Endorsed: Mary Stewart Calais 10 Feb. 77.

From Thomas Walpole   ALS: American Philosophical Society

Sir,   London the 10 feby 1777.

Mr. Wharton having signified to me by Letter that in the present unhappy Situation of Affairs in America he apprehends he cannot be of any use in the further Application to

---

3. All we know about her is what she tells of herself in this and subsequent letters. She was the sister of John Stewart, the creator of *The Senator's Remembrancer,* a publication that BF greatly admired (above, xvIII, 36–7). In 1774 BF had written to her to express this admiration and to offer his services, presumably in recommending the volume; she referred to this lost letter in hers of Jan. 8 and April 26, 1782 (APS). She apparently stayed in Calais for more than a year, for she wrote him from there on April 8, 1778 (Hist. Soc. of Pa.), to say that she could not get copies from England, and was still in financial straits and needed help; in that letter she gave her first name. In 1781–82 she renewed her pleas, and had the *Remembrancer* reprinted; BF ordered a dozen copies, which he apparently did not receive until 1788. See her letters, in addition to those cited, of Oct. 17, 22, 27, 1781; Aug. 23, 1782; Aug. 3, 1788: APS.

Government for Lands on the River Ohio, he therefore finally closed his Account on the 17th August last against my self and Associates, and sent me his Note of Charges, which are included in the inclosed State of your Account with me. I have been prevented from making out this Account 'till now, for want of being able to get sooner the Charges at the Public Offices, and those of Mr. Dagge, whereof you will find Copies here inclosed at length; and your part amounting to £5 17s. 4d. is carried to the Debtor side of your Account, reducing the Balance in my Hand to £111 8s. 9d. Inclosed is also the Account of William Franklin Esq. to whom there is likewise due a Balance of £111 8s. 9d. which Sums I am ready to discharge, on your returning my Receipts, or giving me any other proper Acquital.[4] I am Sir Your most Obedient Servant

THOMAS WALPOLE

To Benjamin Franklin Esq:

Notation: Walpole 10. Feby. 1777.

From Georgiana Shipley[5]   AL: American Philosophical Society

London February the 11th 1777

After near two years had past, without my hearing any thing from you and while I look'd upon the renewal of our correspondence as a very unlikely event, it is easier to conceive than express the joy I felt at receiving your last kind Letter. The certainty that you are in good health and spirits, and that you still remember your English Friends, is the greatest pleasure we can know during your absence. How good you were

4. BF asked Walpole to settle the account in his letter above, Jan. 12. Mr. Dagge, we assume, was Henry, for whom see above, XX, 310 n. In 1773 BF had paid £200 on each share, just over £177 for purchase money and the rest for expenses; when he left England he believed that this sum was still in Walpole's hands: *ibid.*, p. 326 n; memorandum book (above, VII, 167–8), entry of March 20, 1775. After the chance of a purchase evaporated, Walpole doubtless deducted final expenses and reduced the balance due to the figure mentioned here.

5. For BF's favorite among Bishop Shipley's children see above, XVIII, 200 n.

to send me your direction, but I fear I must not make use of it as often as I could wish, since my Father says that it will be prudent not to write, in the present situation of affairs.[6] I am not of an age to be so very prudent, and the only thought that occured to me was your suspecting that my silence proceeded from other motives. I could not support the idea of your believing that I love and esteem you less than I did some few years ago. I therefore write this once without my Fathers knowledge. You are the first Man that ever received a private Letter from me, and in this instance I feel that my intentions justify my conduct, but I must intreat that you will take no notice of my writing, when next I have the happiness of hearing from you. You say you are interested in what ever relates to this Family. My Father I think was never better than he is at present, both as to his health and spirits. My Mother has not been so well this last Summer, but I flatter myself, that she has now perfectly recovered, her late indispostition. Emily has only one daughter, a charming little girl, near fifteen months old, whom her Aunts reckon a prodigy of sense and beauty.[7] The rest of my Sisters continue in statuquo; whether this proceeds from the Men being difficult, or from *their* being difficult I leave you to determine. I often see many of your good Friends, need I add that you are the favorite subject of our conversation? They all love you almost as much as I do, as much I will not admit to be possible. Doctor P. made me extremely happy last Winter, by giving me a print of my excellent Friend. It is certainly very like you, altho it wants the addition of your own hair to make it complete.[8] But as it is I prize it infinitely, now the dear Original is absent. Pray have you met with Smiths Wealth of nations, if not, I venture strongly to recommend it to you. I have read only parts but propose shortly to read it

6. In the autumn of 1774 BF had been "a Letter in debt to Georgiana; which I will pay when I can" (above, XXI, 322). If he paid, as her phrasing implies, the letter has disappeared. So has the one to which she is replying; in it BF must have provided her with his new alias (for which see Wharton's letter above, Jan. 10) and with Chaumont's address.

7. For Emily's marriage see above, XVIII, 200 n.

8. Pringle had perhaps given her the Martinet engraving, of BF bewigged, that is the frontispiece of vol. XX.

regularly thro. His sentiments are liberal, and the Language clear and interesting, and this is the only book that has been lately publish'd worth mentioning, except Gibbons History of the rise and fall of the Roman Empire. It is written in a pleasing elegant manner, his scheme is to unite antient and modern history, an immense work which I wish he may have application to accomplish. I have been at lenght fortunate enough to procure the Economics, which I have read with great attention, as indeed every thing else I can meet with relative to Socrates,[9] for I fancy I can discover in each trait of that admirable Mans character, a strong resemblance between him, and my much-loved Friend, the same clearness of Judgement, the same uprightness of intention and the same superior understanding. I dined lately with Sir Wm. Hamilton,[1] he gave me an account of a new Electrical machine, invented in Italy. It is composed, of bees-wax a plate of metal and a plate of Glass. They are able to take a spark from it at ten inches distance, but he could not inform me why these bodies united produce this effect. Were you in England how happy should I be to have this as well as many other things explain'd by you, but I dont allow myself to entertain any hopes on this subject, as I much fear there is no reason to flatter myself with so pleasing an idea. *Envy* is reckon'd one of the foibles of our Sex. Till lately I thought I was exempt from it, but now I find a strong inclination to *envy* your grand-son the having it in his power to shew you any kindness and attention. Did my family know of my writing, my Letter would scarce contain the very many things, they would desire me to say for them. They continue to admire and love you as much as they did formerly nor can any time or event in the least change their sentiments. My paper now reminds me, that it is high time for me to conclude. Assure youself that every good wish for your happiness and prosperity attends you from this House. Adieu mon cher *So-*

9. The *Economics* was Xenophon's *Oeconomicus*, a treatise on household-management in the form of a dialogue between Socrates and Ischomachus; it had appeared in translation in [Robert Vansittart,] *Certain Ancient Tracts Concerning the Management of Landed Property* (London, 1767).

1. The British envoy to Naples; see the annotation of the chevalier Hamilton to BF above, Dec. 28.

crate, conservez vous pour l'amour de moi, et pour mille autres raisons plus importans. Je ne vous en dirai pas d'avantage pour aujoud'hui, mais je veux esperer de vous entretien plus a mon aise, avant qui soit longue. Pray write when ever a safe conveyance offers, since the receiving Letters is reckon'd very different from answering them. I must once more repeat, nobody knows of this scrall, a word to the wise, as poor Richard says. Febry the 11th.

Addressed: A Monsr. Monsieur Francois / chez M. de Chaumont / à Passy pres de / Paris[2]

Endorsed: From Miss Georgiana Shipley London 11 Feb 77

Agreement between the American Commissioners and Jacques Boux

DS: Yale University Library

Jacques Boux had achieved an eminence in the French navy remarkable for one who was not of noble birth. The government had called on him in 1771 for advice in reorganizing naval administration, and the following year had promoted him to *capitaine de vaisseau*. In 1776, however, a new minister shelved his suggested reforms and substituted others.[3] Boux, annoyed at this treatment, turned to Silas Deane and offered him plans for constructing American frigates.[4]

The commissioners were interested in the proposal as soon as they discovered that they had no chance whatever of obtaining, as instructed, eight ships of the line from the French government.[5] Boux was introduced to them, according to Lee, through Chaumont and the Grand brothers, who lauded him to the skies as "the most ingenious, the most disinterested, and the most honest man in France; zealous for our cause, and desirous of nothing so much as to get into our service, so entirely free from any selfish motive that he would go out of it naked, (such was the expression) as he came in." The commissioners could not understand some details of the plans

2. See the note on BF to Dumas above, Jan. 28.

3. Georges Lacour-Gayet, *La Marine militaire de la France sous le règne de Louis XV* (2nd ed., Paris, 1910), p. 428; Jacques Aman, *Les Officiers bleus dans la marine française au XVIIIe siècle* (Geneva, 1976), pp. 117–8; Dull, *French Navy*, 12–13, 58–60, 66–7.

4. *Deane Papers*, I, 342–3; III, 166.

5. See Vergennes' reply to the commissioners above, Jan. 13.

that he produced but found them plausible, and were persuaded that the frigates could be built most quickly and cheaply in the Netherlands.[6] Although the decision may have been economically sound, it led to future trouble.

Duplicata [February 12, 1777]

Observation 1.

Monsieur Boux ne se détermine a quiter les dousseurs de la retraite dont il jouit apres 30 ans de service, que parce que les circonstances semble l'appeller a un genre de Gloire, ausy Grand que nouveau. L'etablissement d'une puissente marine millitaire est l'objet qu'il se propose, et pour lequel il se deside a entreprendre tout ce qui peut etre honnorable pour y parvenir au mepris de toutes les peines et de toutes les fatigues qui en sont inseparable. La gloire adoussit tout et est la recompense de tout.

2.

Mr. Boux etant millitaire, il ne veut jamais sesser de l'être. Il demande a cette epoque à etre l'egal de l'officier le plus haut en grade dans la marine des Etats uny de l'amerique septentrionalle car il ne veut jamais renoncer au commandement des flotes et des escadres de cette marine, quoi qu'il en deviennent le legislateur et le ministre.

3.

Mr. Boux consent de bon coeur de se transporter partout ou besouin sera pour la construction des vaisseaux de guerre des Etats uny de l'amerique comme pour toutes autre mitions honorable.

6. Lee's journal, Oct. 3, 1777, printed in Lee, *Life of Arthur Lee*, I, 337. The present agreement was only a stage in the negotiations, which were not completed when Lee left Paris. One reason may have been that Boux was in uncertain health. At some point he sent the commissioners a line, undated, to say that he was too ill to go out but would be glad to have them come to him. APS.

4.

Mr. Boux demende qu'on ôbtiene du roy son agrement pour qu'il puissent quiter son pais et aller servir en amerique sans que les pensions dont il jouit luy soient rétiree.

5.

Mr. Boux demende de n'etre point chargé de faire vivre les ôfficier a bord du vaisseau qu'il commanda, voullant manger seul.

6.

Mr. Boux demande qu'il luy soit abendonné la nomination du capitaine ou des capitaines, des vaisseaux qu'il va faire construire, de meme que des 2 premier ôfficier de chaquns.

We reserve to ourselves the Nomination of the Captain and Officers of one of the Ships, leaving the other to M. Boux.[7]

7.

Mr. Boux demande pour son neveu une commission de Lieutenant de Vaisseau de la marine des Etats uni de l'amerique septentrionalle daté du jour qu'il quitera la marine du roy de france; avec les appointement reglé par le Congré.

8.

Que les frais de voyages de ce jeune officier, de meme que ceux de son sejour en holande pour [exécuter?] sou mes ordres les traveaux de constructions, ou tout autres luy seront payee convenablement.

At Paris, Feb. 12. 1777. The above Articles are agreed to by us, and we shall give M. Boux a Commission when he sails from Europe, appointing him a Commodore in the Service of the United States of America, with the Pay belonging to that Rank; and we agree that the Pay commence from the Day of his setting out from Paris in the Service of the said States.   B FRANKLIN
                                                                    SILAS DEANE

Notation: Agreement wh Boux

7. This and the final paragraph are in BF's hand.

Franklin and Silas Deane to Arthur Lee

Copy:[8] University of Virginia Library

Dear Sir   Paris Feby. 12th: 1777

We inclose this to Care of Messrs. Delaps hoping it will find you safe arrived in that City.[9] Nothing material has occurr'd since your leaving Us; Long Island is repossess'd by the Provincials, but we have not learned the Particulars. One thought we take this Opportunity of suggesting, should you be able to procure a sum of Money either on Loan, or otherways. To remove any Objection that may be made about the mode of supply, there need only to have an Order pass'd to Our Freind in Amsterdam, to hold such a sum at Our disposal, who will instantly advance it.[1] Or as Our Freind may not be known to those with whom you are to treat, or possibly the same Cautious mode may be pursued by them as by some others, There need only a Letter to the Spanish Ambassador at the Hague directing him to order Our Freind to advance the Sum agreed for. The Money if obtained must be raised in that Quarter, and No one can effect it with greater Secrecy or dispatch. We most heartily wish you may not be under the Necessity of having any Cover for what is so much for the Interest and honor of those you are to deal with to have transacted openly, but We have not the Choice of the mode, and the Object is so important that We must if possible obtain it by any means not dishonorable to Us. Wishing you a prosperous Journey We are Dear Sir your most Obedient and Very Humble servants   B FRANKLIN
                                              SILAS DEANE

Hon Arthur Lee Esqr.

8. In Deane's hand.

9. *I.e.*, Bordeaux. Lee had planned to start on his mission to Spain on Feb. 7; he reached Nantes on the 11th, and expected to leave on the 14th and be in Bordeaux by the 17th: the commissioners to the committee of secret correspondence above, Feb. 6, and Lee to BF and Deane below, Feb. 13.

1. The friend was Georges Grand: Price, *France and the Chesapeake*, II, 722. He was still in Paris, and may have suggested this way of handling a clandestine Spanish loan.

To Jan Ingenhousz

ALS: Yale University Library; incomplete draft and copy:[2] Library of Congress

My dear Friend,   Paris, Feb. 12[–March 6]. 1777

I received your kind Letter on the 4th of Jany. It gave me great Pleasure, as it inform'd me of your Welfare, and of the Continuance of your Friendship, which I highly value. If his Imperial Majesty's Journey to France is only postponed, and not entirely laid aside,[3] I hope I may still have the Happiness of seeing you, as I suppose it will not be so inconvenient to you to travel hither in his Suite, as it would be to go to England (as you wish to do) alone.

Mr. Collard has not sent me the Letter you mention, so that I know not the Contents of it, otherwise I should now answer it.[4] I have waited already too long in Expectation of it.

I long laboured in England with great Zeal and Sincerity to prevent the Breach that has happened, and which is now so wide that no Endeavours of mine can possibly heal it. You know the Treatment I met with from that imprudent Court: But I keep a separate Account of private Injuries, which I may forgive; and I do not think it right to mix them with publick Affairs. Indeed there is no Occasion for their Aid to sharpen my Resentment against a Nation, that has burnt our defenceless Towns in the midst of Winter, has excited the Savages to assassinate our innocent Farmers with their Wives and Children, and our Slaves to murder their Masters. It would therefore be deceiving you, if I suffer'd you to remain in the Supposition you have taken up, that I am come hither to make Peace. I am in fact ordered hither by the Congress for a very different Purpose, viz. to procure such Aids from European Powers for enabling us to defend our Freedom and Indepen-

2. The copy is of the draft, which contains the postscript with the first two paragraphs missing and the others rearranged.

3. BF must have heard this news in Paris; the letter he is answering did not mention postponement.

4. The letter above of Nov. 15.

dence, as it is certainly their Interest to grant, as by that means the great and rapidly growing Trade of America will be open to them all, and not a Monopoly to Britain as heretofore; a Monopoly, that if she is suffer'd again to possess, will be such an Increase of her Strength by Sea, and if she can reduce us again to Submission, she will have thereby so great an Addition to her Strength by Sea and Land, as will together make her the most formidable Power the World has yet seen, and, from her natural Pride and Insolence in Prosperity, of all others the most intolerable.

You will excuse my writing Politicks to you, as your Letter has given me the Occasion. Much more pleasing would it be to me to discuss with you some Point of Philosophy: And I am ready to promise you, that whenever you give me an Opportunity of enjoying that Pleasure in your Company, you shall not hear a Word from me on any other Subject, or against your Favourite Nation.

I have lately heard from our excellent Friend Sir John Pringle. He is well, except his *Insomnia*, which I fear grows upon him.

They tell me here that you are married. I congratulate you on that happy Change in your Situation. It is the most natural State of Man. I have lately lost my old and faithful Companion; and I every day become more sensible of the greatness of that Loss; which cannot now be repair'd. Present my respectful Compliments to your Spouse, and believe me ever, with sincere and great Esteem, My dear Friend, Yours most affectionately   B Franklin

March 6. Passy near Paris

Just as I had finish'd writing the above, I receiv'd your Favour of Jany. 29. with the other you had written to me in November last. Being exceedingly occupied here with Business, and moreover continually interrupted by the Civility of Visits, I have insensibly postpon'd to this time the Answer to those Letters, and have kept, unnecessarily, what I had written to go with that Answer. Excuse, my dear Friend, this Delay. Old Men, I find, are not so active as young ones.

With regard to securing Magazines of Gunpowder, I have seen no reason to vary from my Opinion since the Directions given for that at Purfleet. Possibly some Improvements may occur to you, when you are giving the Directions required of you, in which I wish you Success. There is a Paper of mine, in the French Edition, which contains some of the principal Arguments, Experiments and Facts, upon which the Practice is founded.[5]

You desire to know my Opinion of what will probably be the End of this War? and whether our new Establishments will not be thereby reduced again to Deserts? I do not, for my part, apprehend much Danger of so great an Evil to us: I think, we shall be able, with a little Help, to defend ourselves, our Possessions and our Liberties, so long, that England will be ruined by persisting in the wicked Attempt to destroy them. I must nevertheless regret that Ruin, and wish that her Injustice and Tyranny had not deserv'd it. And I sometimes flatter myself, that, old as I am, I may possibly live to see my Country settled in Peace and Prosperity, when Britain shall make no more a formidable Figure among the Powers of Europe.

As to the present State of our Affairs, which you desire to be inform'd of, the English have long boasted much in their Gazettes of their Successes against us; but our latest Advices are, that they have been repuls'd in their intended Invasion of Pensylvania, and driven back thro' New Jersey to New York, with considerable Loss in three Engagements; so that the Campaign probably will end pretty much as it began; leaving them only in Possession of the Islands, which their naval Strength secures to them; and we shall in the next Campaign be much better provided with Arms and Ammunition for their Entertainment on the Continent, where our Force is to consist of 84 Battalions.[6]

You put me in mind of an Apology for my Conduct, which had been expected from me, in answer to the Abuses thrown upon me before the Privy Council. It was partly written; but the Affairs of public Importance I have been ever since en-

---

5. Dubourg, *Œuvres*, I, 289–300; the original paper is above, xix, 244–55.

6. The three engagements were presumably the two at Trenton and the one at Princeton, after which the British fell back on Manhattan and its environs. Congress, the previous September, had authorized the raising of eighty-eight battalions: *JCC*, v, 762.

gag'd in, prevented my finishing it.[7] The Injuries, too, that my Country has suffer'd, have absorb'd private Resentments, and made it appear trifling for an Individual to trouble the World with his particular Justification, when all his Compatriots were stigmatiz'd by the King and Parliament, as being in every respect the worst of Mankind. I am oblig'd to you, however, for the friendly Part you have always taken in the Defence of my Character; and it is indeed no small Argument in my favour, that those who have known me most and longest, still love me and trust me with their most important Interests, of which my Election into the Congress by the unanimous Voice of the Assembly or Parliament of Pennsylvania the Day after my Arrival from England, and my present Mission hither by the Congress itself, are Instances incontestible.

I thank you for the Account you give me of M. Volta's Experiment. You judge rightly in supposing that I have not much time at present to consider philosophical Matters: But as far as I understand it from your Description, it is only another Form of the Leiden Phial, and explicable by the same Principles. I must however own myself puzzled by one Part of your Account, viz. "and thus the electric Force once excited may be kept alive Years together"; which perhaps is only a Mistake. I have known it indeed to be continued many Months in a Phial hermetically sealed, and suppose it may be so preserved for Ages; But though one may by repeatedly touching the Knob of a charg'd Bottle with a small insulated Plate like the upper one of the Electrophore, draw successively an incredible Number of Sparks, that is, one after every Touch, and those for a while not apparently different in Magnitude, yet at length they will become small, and the Charge be finally exhausted. But I am in the wrong to give any Opinion till I have seen the Experiment.

I like much your Pasteboard Machine, and think it may in some respects be preferable to the very large Glass ones constructed here. The Duke de Chaulnes has one, said, if I remember right, to be 5 feet in Diameter. I saw it try'd, but it happen'd not to be in Order.[8]

7. The incomplete text is above, XXI, 415–35.

8. BF presumably saw it during his visit to Paris in 1769, when he met the Duke (Boyd, *Jefferson Papers*, IX, 487–8); and it is the machine that John

You inquire what is become of my Son, the Governor of New Jersey. As he adhered to the Party of the King, his People took him Prisoner, and sent him under a Guard to Connecticut, where he continues but is allow'd a District of some Miles to ride about, upon his Parole of Honour not to quit that Country.[9] I have with me here his Son, a promising Youth of about 17, whom I brought with me, partly to finish his Education, having a great Affection for him, and partly to have his Assistance as a Clerk,[10] in which Capacity he is very serviceable to me. I have also here with me my worthy Nephew, Mr. Williams, whom you kindly ask after. The ingenious Mr. Canton, our other Fellow Traveller, I suppose you know is now no more.[11] God bless you, my dear Friend, and believe me ever, Yours most affectionately   B FRANKLIN

Dr Ingen Hausz

———— Boilau and Gilles de Lavallée to the American Commissioners[1]   ALS: American Philosophical Society

Mercredy ce 12 [–14] fevrier 1777

Mr. Boylau prie Messiers Dean franklin de faire remettre au porteur l'echantillon d'habit fusils sabre bonet &c, &c. qu'il a laissé chez eux. Il obligeront leurs tres humble Serviteur

BOILAU

Walsh described to him three years later: above, XIX, 190. Our note there, however, confuses the Duke with his son. The father, Michel-Ferdinand, was the electrician and a member of the Académie royale des sciences; he died in 1769. The son was primarily a naturalist; see his note below under Feb. 28.

9. See above, XXII, 551.

10. The draft reads "Secretary."

11. Nor had been for years; John Canton had died in March, 1772. Above, XIX, 89 n.

1. This was BF's introduction, as far as we know, to a business that subsequently tried his patience, the procurement of uniforms. Lavallée was a textile manufacturer, who after the war emigrated to the United States with the encouragement of BF, Jefferson, and others to try to establish cloth manufacture there; the attempt failed, and he returned to Europe in disgust. Boyd, *Jefferson Papers*, VIII, 377–9. Boilau was doubtless his business associate; he submitted, presumably on this occasion, two detailed price lists of a uniform and accoutrements, including musket and saber. The lists are not

14 fr. 1777

Donner au porteur si il vous plait toutte les choses apertenant a monseur Boileau.   DE LAVALLEE

Addressed: A Messieurs / Messirs Dean & franklin / Equrs / a lhotel dHambourg / rue Jacob

Notation: Boilau, Paris 14 fevri. 77

From [Duportail]   AL: American Philosophical Society

Monsieur   [February? 12, 1777[2]]

D'après ce que vous m'avèz fait l'honneur de me mander je me rendray aujourdhuy 12 du courant chèz vous entre six et sept heures du soir. J'ai l'honneur d'etre etc.

Addressed: A Monsieur / Monsieur francklin à l'hotel / de hambourg / rüe jacob / A *paris.*

Agreement between the American Commissioners and Duportail, Laumoy, and Gouvion

Copy: National Archives; draft: American Philosophical Society; transcript: National Archives[3]

---

in the same hand as this note, but his name appears at the foot of each, once as "Boilleau" and once as "Boilleaud." With them in the APS are an account in an unknown hand of where cloth can be obtained and at what cost, and a report in Chaumont's hand on his research into uniforms. The prices he gives are higher than Boilau's, but what is more interesting is his recommendation of a cloak that will double as a blanket, a cover for a trench, or, in some way not explained, a screen to conceal manoeuvers from the enemy. Chaumont's prices must have been satisfactory, for between July and October, 1777, he had 15,000 uniforms delivered to Bordeaux for the American army: Sabatier fils & Despres to BF, *c.* Aug. 29, 1783, APS.

2. The note reveals the day of the month. Duportail's negotiations with the American commissioners began on Dec. 19, and by March he was in Nantes; hence he must have been writing in January or February. His letters above of Jan. 12 and 16 give no indication of an interview with BF or any reason for one. On Feb. 12 there was ample reason: to discuss the formal agreement signed the next day.

3. The transcript, like the copy we print, is also misdated 1776; the draft is not dated. We have noted two substantive passages deleted in the draft, but not minor differences between it and the copies.

Franklin presumably approved this commitment to the three Frenchmen, and to La Radière four days later; but he soon came to regret the whole business. "I was concerned in sending the 4 Engineers," he wrote eight months afterward, "and in making the Contract with them: but before they went, I had reason to dislike one of them, and to wish the Agreement had not been made, for I foresaw the Discontent that Man was capable of producing among his Companions, and I fancy that if instead of America they had gone to Heaven it would have been the same thing."[4]

[February 13, 1777]

Agreement	Convention
1st. It is agreed that the Congress of the United States of America shall grant to the Chevalier du Portail now Lieutenant Colonel in the royal Corps of Engineers of France, the Rank of Colonel in their Service.[5]	1me. Le Congres des Etats unies de l'amerique donnera a monsr. Le Chevalier duportail Lieutenant Colonel dans le Corps royal du Genie de la France, le grade de Colonel dans leur [Service].
2d. The Congress of the United States of America will grant to Monsr. de Laumoy now major in the Royal Corps of Engineers of France, the Rank of Lieutenant Colonel in their Service.	2. Le Congres des Etats unies de l'amerique donnera a monsieur de Laumoy major dans le Corps royal du Genie de la France, le grade de Lieutenant Colonel.
3d. The Congress of the United States of America will grant to Monsr. de Gouvion now Capt. in the Royal Corps of Engineers of France, the Rank of Major in their Service.	3 Le Congres des Etats unies donnera a Monsieur de Gouvion capitaine dans le Corps royal du Genie de la France, le grade de Major dans leur Service.

4. To Lovell, Oct. 7, 1777, Mass. Hist. Soc.
5. A clause at this point in the draft was deleted: "being the rank superior to that of Lieutenant Colonel to which he is to be advanced in the service of France, the moment of his departure."

4th. Messrs. Le Chevalier duportail, de Laumoy, and de Gouvion, shall be at liberty to quit the Service of the united States provided it is not during a Campaign or during any particular service, unless ordered so to do by the King of France: and the Congress may dismiss them or any of them whenever they may judge it proper.

4me. Ces Messrs. serront libre de quitter le·Service des Etats unies quand ils le desireront; bien entendu pourtant que ce ne serra pas dans le milieu d'une Campagne, ou d'une besogne commencé, a moins qu'ils ne fussent appellés par le Roy de France, le Congres pourra de son coté les remercier quand il le jugera apropos.

5. If all or either of these Gentlemen should be made prisoners by the King of Great Britain the Congress shall use all due means to obtain their Liberty.[6]

5me. Dans le Cas que ces officiers serront pris par le Roy de la grande Bretagne Le Congres emploira toutes les moyens convenables pour les procurer leur Liberté.

6 These Gentlemen shall use all possible dilligence in preparing for their embarkation in order to reach Philadelphia or wherever else the Congres of the united States may be to obey their orders.

6me. Ces Messieurs se prepareront en toute dilligence a s'embarquer et se trouver a Philadelphia ou a quelque autre endroit où le Congres s'assemblera pour y attendre les ordres du Congres.

7 The pay of these Gentlemen shall be such as is given to officers of their Rank in the Service of the States of America, and shall commence from the date of this agreement.

7me. La paye de ces Messrs. serra la même que celle des officiers de leur rang dans le Service des Etats unies de l'amerique, elle commencera du Jour de la datte des presents conventions.

6. An article at this point in the draft was deleted, that Congress would cover their expenses if their pay did not begin until they arrived in America.

8th These Gentlemen shall procure and provide for their own passages in such Ships, and in such manner as they shall think proper.

8 Ces Messrs. se procureront leurs passages à leur propre depense, dans telles vaiseaux et en telle façon qu'ils le jugeront a propos.

The above agreement was entered into and concluded by us at Paris this 13 February 1776.

signed   B Franklin
S Deane
le che du Portails
Gouvion l'aîné
signé pour Mr. de Laumoy

Copy

Note Mr la Radiere was afterwards agreed with on the same terms with the within officers and is to be a Lieut. Colonel.[7]

Arthur Lee to Franklin and Silas Deane

als: Connecticut Historical Society

Gentlemen,   Nantes Feby. 13th 1777

I arrivd here the night before last, and shall proceed to-morrow. Your Dispatches I receivd from Mr. Montandouine, and they will go on board this day with the others, as the Ship is to sail to-morrow. Mr. Williams has purchasd another Ship, I think the Ct. Vergennes, of three hundred tons, which he expects to dispatch in three weeks. The demand we made upon Monsr. Sollier, had reachd Nantes before me, and was the talk of the Exchange.

Monsr. De Coudray is here incog: determind, as is said, to go by the west Indies. Monsr. Montandouine told me, De Coudray had shewd him a Letter of the strongest recommendation, signd by you, to the Congress, of a late date.[8] I cannot

7. See the agreement below, Feb. 17.

8. Another example of du Coudray's violating the promise of secrecy that had been the condition on which the letter had been provided; see the note on it above, Feb. 6.

help thinking his Orders to return to his Regiment are fictitious; for there is not an Army in Europe, in which an Officer
woud not be immediately broke for disobedience to such Orders. If they are real, he must be out of his senses to act as he
does. Mr. Rogers, I cannot find.

I am a little anxious about Baron Rullecour having our commission. Because as he has done toutes sortes des choses in
Poland, it is not impossible but he may sell it to the English
Ambassador, who will irritate the piratical States against us by
shewing them our design of seizing an Island which seems by
its situation to belong to some of them.[9] Mr. Morris promises
to attend to the remittances as fast as he obtains funds. I think
it was your opinion that Mr. Gruel shoud not be left too much
in advance, tho it shoud retard his remittances to you; but I
wish you woud write explicitly to him on the subject.

I have thankd the Mayor, who is a tres galant Homme.[1] Mr.
Morris, I am told, has sold the Tobacco to the Fermiers at 14
Sous; but it is a secret sale, and has greatly chagrind the Mer-
chants here, who think the best Bidder ought to have it at an
open sale. They say 15 Sous woud have been given for it. Mr.
Morris has not yet explaind this business to me.[2]

I hope to be at Bordeaux four days hence. I have the honor
to be, with the greatest esteem, Gentlemen, Your most Obedient Servant   ARTHUR LEE

Montaudoüin to the American Commissioners

Copy: Archives du Ministère des affaires étrangères

Nantes le 13. février 1777.

J'ai remis à Mr. Arthur Lee, qui arriva avanthier, les 2 lettres
que vous m'aviez adressées pour lui; Il m'a remis aussi celle
dont vous m'avez honnoré au sujet de l'avis que je vous ai

9. See the headnote above, Jan. 10.
1. He thanked him for the town's action on tobacco; see the following
document and *Naval Docs.*, VII, 582. The Mayor's name, furnished us by the
curator of the departmental museum of Loire-Atlantique, was Jean-Baptiste
Gellée de Prémion.
2. Lee knew more when he wrote his colleagues again the next day.

donné de la diminution sur les droits que MM. le Maire et les Echevins de notre ville ont accordée sur le tabac de votre pays. Nous venons de nous rendre MM. Arthur Lee, Williams et moi à l'hôtel de ville pour faire les remerciments convenables à Mr. le Maire, qui a témoigné toute sa sensibilité à cette démarche, et qui a assuré de toute la bienveillance de la Maison de Ville pour ce qui intéresse vos Américians.[3]

J'ai été enchanté, MM., de faire connoissance avec Mr. Arthur Lee, qui justifie très bien l'opinion que sa réputation m'avoit donnée de son mérite. Il vient diner demain chez moi avec Mr. Williams, et partira le soir pour Bordeaux.

Il y a ici un officier de la marine angloise, qui est venu il y a quelque tems de New-Yorck sur un bâtiment hollandois. Il se nomme Allen. Il y a toute apparence qu'il est en relation avec le Lord Stormont;[4] On va examiner s'il a des affaires qui exigent sa résidence ici, et voir s'il n'y auroit pas moyen de l'engager à s'en aller ailleurs.

MM. Lord et Jennings de la Caroline, qui sont ici, sont aussi venus avec nous chez Mr. le Maire.[5]

Nos négociants qui avoient sollicité des ordres à l'etranger pour achepter les Cargaisons de Tabac, ont été étonnés d'ap-

---

3. The two letters to Lee are missing. He carried with him, we assume, the commissioners' letter to Montaudoüin above of Jan. 26, which discussed the reduction in the Nantais duty on American tobacco.

4. David Allen was indeed providing information for Stormont; see Stevens, *Facsimiles*, XIV, nos. 1433, p. 2; 1444; 1450, p. 6.

5. Lee was in close touch with John Lloyd (1735–1807), who will reappear in later volumes. He was an English-born merchant and landholder in South Carolina, a former member of the local committee of correspondence, and a friend of Henry Laurens and Ralph Izard. Lloyd and his wife had arrived in Nantes from England on Feb. 3; the local merchants had received him cordially and put him in touch with Montaudoüin. Anne Izard Deas, ed., *Correspondence of Mr. Ralph Izard* . . . (New York, 1844), pp. 241–2, 246; *S.C. Hist. and Geneal. Mag.*, XXII (1921), 47 n; XX (1919), 83; Philip M. Hamer, George C. Rogers, *et al.*, eds., *The Papers of Henry Laurens* (8 vols. to date; Columbia, S.C., 1968–), III, 33 n; VII, 455–6. Edmund Jenings (above, XXI, 216 n) was in fact a Marylander, who had gone to England for his education and never returned; he is suspected of having been a double agent. His contact with Lee is interesting because the two, a few months later, began an active correspondence; see James H. Hutson, *Letters from a Distinguished American* . . . (Washington, D.C., 1978), expecially p. x.

prendre qu'on les avoit vendues à Paris. Ils doutent qu'on en ait donné là un aussi bon prix qu'on auroit obtenu ici.

Voici une lettre pour Mr. Franklin. (On la fournit; elle est d'Arthur Lee.)

Notation: Montaudouin, à Franklin, et Dean.

Jonathan Williams, Jr., to the American Commissioners
ALS: American Philosophical Society

Gentlemen   Nantes Feb. 13. 1777.

Upon examination of the Concord, her Inventory was found very deficient, those things which we thought would be a diminution of her price of at least 5000 Livres were not in her. It seems the owner has lately fitted out a large Ship for the Coast of Guinea and has taken from one to supply the other. This determined Mr. Peltier to purchase the Count de Vergennes which is of the same size and age; the difference between them is, that this Ship is not so sharp as the other, and will require some addition to her Riggin &c; but she is more burdensome, and cost 10,000 Livres less money.

No Time shall be lost in dispatching her which I expect to compleat in 3 Weeks from this Date, I mention this that the Charts and Dispatches may arrive in time.

Mr. Lee writes by this opportunity. I have the honor to be with the greatest Respect Gentlemen Your most obedient Servant   J WILLIAMS

The Honorable The Deputies of the United States.

Notation: Nantes 13th Feby 1777 J Williams Lettr.

From Elizabeth Wright[6]
ALS: American Philosophical Society

Honourd Sir   Pall mall London Febuy. th 13 1777

Your known Goodness of Heart and Generosity in Releiving and Suckouring the injured or oppres'd has Emboldned

6. The daughter of Patience Wright (above, XIX, 93) joined her mother in London at some time before November, 1775, and became like her a modeler in wax. *London Mag. . . .* , XLIV (1775), 555–6; Charles C. Sellers, *Patience Wright, American Artist and Spy . . .* (Middletown, Conn., [1976]), pp. 90, 225–6.

me to trouble you with the Case of Mr. Plat now a Prisoner
in Newgate, On a charge of High Treason Comitted in America, that thro your Means or influence his Frinds may be made
acquaintd with his Situation in order that they may take some
Precautions for his being acquited, or at least, that he may
Receive some Remittances for his Support in His Disagreable
Unhappy Confinement, which I am apprehensive will be of
some Continuence, as I fear this new Act that is now passing,[7]
is made allmost on Purpose to Detain Him with Several Others Nearly in the same Situation, Without Bail or Tryall as
Prisoners of Warr, to be Confined in the Severeest Maner, in
Goals, or Dungeons, as Criminals and God only knows where
it may End, Perhaps Hang'd. Wee was intimately Acquainted
with Mr. Plat in New York of Which Place He is A Native.
His Father was A Merchant There a Man of Fortune and un-
spotted Reputation and He Himself is a very Amiable young
Man, and A Credit to His Country. His Uncle of the same
Name, no Doubt Sir, you are Acquainted with, As He is One
of the Members of the Congress.[8] About 3 years Ago Mr. Plats
Father setled Him in Georgia at His own Request, where he
Purchased 5000 Acres of Land, intending to turn Planter, but
meeting with some Obstructions with Regard to Negros to
Stock His Farm He Entred into Trade And became much known
and Esteemed in Georgia as A Worthy Young Man. His Father
Came from New York to see him and unfortunately Died
whilest on the Vissit. His Mother A Brother and two Sisters
are now on Long Island and have not heard from Him since
He wrote them an Account of his Fathers Death. The 13th of

7. An act regarding arrest for treason or piracy, 17 Geo. III, c. 9, passed
on Feb. 17: *Public Advertiser*, Feb. 19, 1777.
8. Young Platt was born on Long Island in 1753; Elizabeth presumably
had a more than charitable interest in him, for after his release from prison
in 1778 she married him: Sellers, *op. cit.*, pp. 105–6, 118. A slim pamphlet,
*The Case of Mr. Ebenezer Smith Platt, Merchant of Georgia, Now Confined in Irons
in Newgate, on a Charge of High Treason* ([London, 1777?]), is now among
BF's papers in the APS; it must have been enclosed with this letter or with
Patience Wright's below of March 7, for in Platt's letter of March 10 he
assumes that it is in BF's hands. The uncle, Zephaniah Platt, was at this time
a member of the N.Y. provincial congress: *Biographical Directory of the American Congress, 1744–1961* ([Washington, D.C., 1961]), p. 1464.

Jully 1775 there Arived A Vessel in Savanah Harbour Commanded by A Captain Maitlord,[9] Laden with Goods and some Powder and Arms from Merchants in England Consignd to their Correspondents, Merchants in Georgia. The People of Georgia at that Time had just formd a Congress amongst themselves and began as well as the Other Provinces to be Divided into Liberty and tory Partys. The Merchants to whom the Goods were Consigned were of these different Oppinions. A Stoppage of Trade then takeing Place and Goods being rather Scarce the Congress Previous to the Arival of the Vessel Purchased the Goods of the Merchants at An Advanced Price, but rather against the Will of those of them who were in the opposition to the Congress, in Consequence of which the others fearing there might be any obstruction to the Landing the Goods or that Possibly a Mob might be Rais'd to Destroy or Prevent the Congress from obtaining them, applied to Mr. Plat with two other Gentleman to go on board the Vessel which Lay some Miles off and see that She was safe brought up to the Town and that none of the Goods should be Landed till Her Arival There. They gave them an order to the Captn. and Mate to Receive and Entertain them in the best Maner on Board. But they seeing the Captn. aterwards in Town shew'd Him the order, and as He was not going on Board again just then He gave them an order to the Mate, much to the same Purpose as the other, viz., to Receive and treat them well, and was very Polite and Friendly. But by what hapned afterwards it appears that He was rather Averse to the Congress haveing the Cargo. They staid on Board 6 Days, saw the Vessel brought up to the Town and Nothing Landed Except some Horses for Governor Campbell at Charlestown south Carolina. They then went on shore thought no more of it and Another Commite was sent in their stead, who Landed the Cargo. After Captn. Maitland had Cleard his Vessel in Georgia he set sail with a Cargo from thence for Jamaica and soon after Mr. Plat went as Merchant in a Vessel of His own which He had fitted out for the same Port leaving his Partner to superintend his Business and Prop-

9. Capt. Richard Maitland, in the *Philippa*, had left Deal on May 1: *London Chron.*, April 29–May 2, 1775.

erty in the Mean time. After his Arival in Jamaica He saw Captain Maitland There who was Exceeding Friendly to Him and invited Him to Make His home on Board His ship whilest He staid in Kingston. This offer He Declined but they frequently fell in Company with Each other and allways upon the footing of Friendship for about 8 weeks when they hapned one Evening to Meet in A Coffee House in a good deal of other Company amongst which was Captain Miller of New York, with several other Captains. Some of them had got a little heated with the Liquor and one Amongst the rest, gave as a Toast "Damnation to all Americans" to which Mr. Plat Reply'd, that No Gentlemen of Honour or Goodness could drink such a Toast as it was Repugnant to the Rules of Society, on which the other grew warm as well as some of the Company, and Mr. Plat fearing A Quarrel imediately Withdrew. Captain Maitland who by this time had grown warm with the Liquor and Conversation soon after His Departure, Cryd out "That Damnd fellow was one of them on Board my Ship at Georgia with an order from the Congress and Landed the Powder and Arms for them." Most of the Company was Exceedingly Pleasd at the Discovery and the next Day Reported it all over the town, not omiting the Governor Sir Bassil Keith[1] who imediately sent word to Captain Maitland that He ought to come and Exhibit an information against Mr. Plat. The Captn. having grown sober again was Exceedingly Sorry for what he had said and sent word to Mr. Plat that He wish'd he would absent Himself or Leave the Place. Elce He must be obliged to Comply with the Governors Comands. Mr. Plat Amazed, tho' indiffirent, at his information returnd Answer that His Business did not suit him to leave the Place at that Time, that He had nothing to dread from any information He Could make against Him, and that He was at liberty to act as he thought Proper in the Case. Mr. Plat was at that Time haveing Disposed of his Vessel and Cargo fitting out another for Turtling and fishing before His Return to Georgia. As He Lay off in

1. Sir Basil, the brother of Sir Robert Murray Keith, British Ambassador to Vienna, was governor from 1774 until his death in 1777; see George Metcalf, *Royal Government and Political Conflict in Jamaica, 1729–1783* ([London], 1965), pp. 182–98.

324

the River Prepared to Sail the Admiral's Boat Came allong Side and Askd for Mr. Plat the Captain Reply'd that He was on Board on which they imediately seiz'd the Vessel and Crew alledging it was on account of An information of Captain Maitlands against Mr. Plat, before the Governor. Mr. Plats Captain and Crew were set at Liberty about 3 weeks afterward, but Mr. Plat was Confind in Irons and for a fortnight Debard from Seeing or writeing to Any of His Friends, and treated with the greatest insolence and indignities by the Sailors. He was afterwards Permited to write to His Friends on shore who Procured for him a Habeas Corpus on which He was brought to Trial on the affadavit of Captn. Maitland His Mate and 3 of His Men who deposed that he had been on Board their Vessel in Georgia with an order from the Congress and Landed for them the Powder and Arms which the Governor Deem'd Rebelion and Treason but finding it rather Difficult to Prove He Deliverd Him intirely into the Admiral Gaytons Hands[2] who was both His Prosecuter and Goalor. Mr. Plat had a Negro Boy which with his own Cloaths they had when His Vessel was seiz'd Permitted Him to keep. Him He was oblidged to sell in order to defray the Expences of His tryal. Mr. Plats Council Pleaded that at the Time these goods Arived in Georgia that Province was not Declared in Rebelion, as this hapned in July and that Declaration was not made till in the fall and that as to Seizing His Vessel, the Act[3] intitled them to Seize American Privateers and did not Extend to A Private Vessel which had been cleard out for Turtling and Fishing. The admirals Council made their Cheif Plea wich was addressing themselves to the Judge, Pleas your Honour if your Honour should set the Prisoner at Liberty it will cost the Admiral 6000 Pound Damages for falce imprisment to which the Judge Reply'd "Well I acquit the Prisoner of the Charges laid to Him but Return Him on Board as an Able Bodied Seaman to do Duty in Consequence of a late Act that all Masters and Mariners so taken, should serve on Board His Majestys frigates in His Majesty's Service. To this it was answerd that

2. For Clark Gayton, commanding the Jamaica squadron, see the *DNB*.
3. The Prohibitory Act.

Mr. Plat was neither Master nor Mariner but Merchant on Board His own Vessel, that this the Captain and crew could Prove. But this Assertion was Evaded and he was again Caried on Board the Admirals Ship and from thence Remov'd to several others and after some time sent home by the Admiral under Pretence of tryal in England in order Chiefly to Secure Himself from Prosecution, which He fear'd had Mr. Plat been set at Liberty. He arived at Portsmouth after having been A Prisoner 10 Months and sent to London for A Habeas, obtain'd it but there was the greatest Precautions taken in order to Render it inefectual. He was Remov'd with the greatest Expedition into Another Vessel, but He still Persisting in desire to be Brought to Tryall, 2 of Sir Johnfeildin[g's[4] Men?] Was sent for Him to Portsmouth. He wa[s brought] to Town and Carry'd before Him but He not ch[oosing] to Medle with so intricate a Cause He was Carryd before another Majistrate and Comanded to Prison, with a charge of Treason tending to Piracy on the written affadavit of two of Captn. Maitlands Sailors Previously Prepared by Council and not appearing to Confront Him in a new, and diffirent Maner from that at Jamaica. A Copy of it Refused Him, and the Comitment wrote in such a Maner that his tryall Cannot be brought on till the Kings Pleasure wich no doubt according to this New Act will not be during the Warr unless He could be Exchanged for some English Prisoner. I could not help wishing you sir and his Uncle knew his situation, as it Distresses us Exceedingly tho he himself is Exceeding chearful under it and says that if it can in any respect conduce to the good of his country he shall bear it with Pleasure Even tho his Life was Required of him. If you Sir approve of it, I should Esteem it as a Favour if you would send this to his Uncle or whatever you think best. I Reman with the greatest Respect ELIZABETH WRIGHT

My Mother Brother Sister and Self desire our best Love and duty to You.

Addressed in another hand: Doctor Franklin

4. Fielding (1721–80) was the half-brother of Henry Fielding, and succeeded him as magistrate after his death: *DNB*; Ronald Leslie-Melville, *The Life and Works of Sir John Fielding* (London, [1934]).

The American Commissioners to Baron Schulenburg[5]

ALS:[6] The Thomas Gilcrease Foundation, Tulsa, Okla.

May it please your Excellency   Paris Feby. 14th: 1777

We have the honor of inclosing the Declaration of the Independancy of the United States of North America, with the Articles of their Confederation; which we desire you to take the earliest Opportunity of laying before his Majesty, the King of Prussia; At the same time We wish he may be assured of the earnest desire of the United States to obtain his Freindship; and by a free Commerce, to establish an intercourse between their distant Countries, which they are Confident must be mutually beneficial. The state of the Commerce of the United States, and the Advantages which must result to both Countries from the Establishment of a Commercial intercourse; We shall if agreeable to his Majesty lay before him. Meantime We take the Liberty of assuring your Excellency that the Reports of the Advantages gained by his Brittannic Majestys Troops over those of the United States are greatly exaggerated, and many of them without Foundation, especially those which assert that an Accommodation is about to take place, there being no probability of such an Event, by the latest intelligence We have received from America. We have the honor to be with the most profound respect Your Excellency's Most Obedient and Very Humble Servants   B FRANKLIN

SILAS DEANE

5. Friedrich Wilhelm von der Schulenburg (1742–1815) was a Prussian minister who served with one brief intermission from 1771 to 1806, and under Frederick II held simultaneously a great number of offices; the commissioners addressed him, we assume, as minister of trade. For his career see Bernhard Rosenmöller, *Schulenburg-Kehnert unter Friedrich dem Grossen* (Berlin and Leipzig, 1914). In 1776 he was involved in Deane's effort to obtain Prussian goods in return for American tobacco; the negotiations broke down, in part because the King was opposed to establishing commercial relations. Friedrich Kapp, *Friedrich der Grosse und die Vereinigten Staaten von Amerika* (Leipzig, 1871), pp. 15–21. The commissioners, as this letter indicates, refused to give up hope of overcoming all the obstacles in the way. Schulenburg politely discouraged them in his reply below, March 15, but they tried again on April 19.

6. In Silas Deane's hand.

Commissioners Plenipotentiary for the United States of North America

Addressed: To / his Excellency / Baron de Scolenborg

The Farmers General: Memorandum for the American Commissioners[7]

Copy:[8] Archives du Ministère des affaires étrangères

Du 14 fevrier 1777. Les Fermiers généraux avanceront deux millions aux termes proposés. Le premier million sera payé le 15 May préfix. Le second le 15 Aoust et ils en seront remboursés en Tabacs qui leur seront livrés dans les ports de france avant la fin de décembre prochain.

Le prix proposé de 4 s. la livre dans les Magasins de la Virginie et du Maryland est beaucoup trop considérable. Les fermiers généraux croyent être bien assurés que le prix courant des Tabacs des premiers crus de Virginie n'excede pas 12 *l.t.* le cent pezant, et celuy du Maryland est encore au dessous.

Il n'est pas possible en effet que les habitans de ces Colonies ayant des besoins sans autre ressource pour s'en procurer que leurs Tabacs et ayant plus de deux récoltes accumulées tiennent leurs Tabacs à un prix excessif.

Il en est de même du prix proposé pour le transport des Tabacs en france. Le Compte Simulé joint aux propositions ne l'établit qu'à 138 *l.t.* 8 s. quoiqu'on y ait porté une double commission et qu'on n'ait eu aucun égard au bénéfice que feront les marchandises de france qui seront achetées avec l'argent fourni par les fermiers généraux.

Enfin ce qui doit fixer toute Incertitude sur les prix c'est Le Marché qu'ont déja conclu les fermiers généraux et celuy que

7. In answer to one from them of Feb. 12, now missing, in which they seem to have offered a choice between tobacco at four sols a pound in the United States or at eight delivered in France. Price, *France and the Chesapeake*, II, 713. The commissioners' reply is below, Feb. 24.

8. Paulze had the memorandum copied, along with the commissioners' reply of the 24th and the farmers' response the next day; these copies he forwarded to Vergennes: *ibid.*, p. 714.

leur propose de conclure une Compagnie de Négocians très solvables à raison de 32 *l.t.* Le cent pezant poids de Marc de Tabac rendu en france payable en Lettres à Trois usances du jour de la livraison.[1]

D'après ces faits, dont les fermiers généraux donneront preuve, ils offrent de prendre tout le Tabac qui sera transporté en france à raison de 6 s. La Livre ou 30 *l.t.* pezant poids de Marc avec les réfractions, allouances et deductions ordinaires, en remboursement des deux millions de leurs avances, et après leur remboursement ils payeront au même prix Tout le Tabac qui arrivera en france en a[rgent] ou en Lettres sur leur Receveur général à un mois d'usance[?].

Lorsque les deux millions auront été acquittés et que l'excédent des Tabacs qui pourront arriver leur aura [été] remis de bonne foy dans le courant de cette année, ils [ne] feront aucune difficulté de renouveller le marché proposé pour les trois années suivantes, et de faire l'avance des trois millions qui sont demandés payables aux époques qui seront convenues.

Mais cette seconde avance qui présente un nouveau traité doit dépendre de l'exécution entiére du premier traité et ce n'est qu'à la fin de l'année ou au commencement de la prochaine qu'on peut s'en occuper.

Arthur Lee to Franklin and Silas Deane

ALS: American Philosophical Society

Gentlemen Nantes, Feby. 14th. 1777

Since my last, I have been informd of an agreement made between Mr. Morris and the Farmers general, by which he stipulates to let them have all the Tobacco which shall arrive in France during the war, on the account of the Congress, at seventy Livres a hundred. The ratification of this bargain they knew on the 30th of last month, which I think was about the time of their declaring off; and they were conducting the two negotiations at the same time. The price is good, but the un-

1. Lord Stormont believed that Arthur or William Lee was behind this mysterious company, but we know nothing more about it; see *ibid.*, p. 713.

certainty of arrivals will continue the same difficulties with regard to Funds.[2]

De Coudray is said to have saild for St. Domingo. There is nothing new here. I am, with great esteem Gentlemen Your most Obedient ARTHUR LEE

PS. I set out to-morrow.

Addressed: A Monsr / Monsr. le Docteur Franklin / l'Hotel d'Hambourg / Rue Jacob / Paris

Notation: A Lee to BF. & SD Nantes Feb. 14. 1777.

Lambert Wickes to the American Commissioners

ALS: American Philosophical Society

Gentlemen   Port Lewis[3] Feby. 14th 1777

This will inform you of my Safe arrival after a tolerable Successfull Cruize, having Captured 3 Sail of Brig's one Snow and One Ship, the Snow is a Falmouth Packet bound from thence to Lisbon she is Mounted with 16 Guns and had Near 50 Men on board, She Engaged Near an hour before she struck. I had one Man killed. My first Lieut. had his left Arm shot of above the Elbow and the Lieut. of Marines had a Musquet Ball lodged in his Wrist. They had Serveral Men wounded but none killed.[4] I am in great hopes that both my Wounded Officers will do well, as there is No Unfavourable Simptoms at Present; Three of our Prizes is Arrived and I expect the other two in to Morrow. As I am informed that there has been two American Private Ships Warr, lately taken and Carried into England, I think it would be a good oppertunity to Negotiate

2. On Feb. 15 Lee gave his views at greater length to the committee of secret correspondence. The U.S. objectives, he wrote, were to insure the export to France of produce that could not be carried in American bottoms, a supply of ready money in France for purchasing military supplies, and protection for shipping them. Morris' contract will not achieve those ends; it does not stipulate a cash advance for the tobacco, and ignores the problem of getting it to Europe. Wharton, *Diplomatic Correspondence*, II, 270.

3. Port Louis, adjacent to Lorient.

4. See *Naval Docs.*, VIII, 623–5; Clark, *Wickes*, pp. 128–32.

and Exchange Prisoners if it Could be done, but Submit to your better Judgments to Act as you think proper. I Should be very Glad to hear from you as Soon as Possible and Should be Much obliged if you Would Point out Some line or Mode for me to Proceed by, in Disposing of Prisoners and Prizes. As Nothing will be done before I receive your Answer to this, I hope you'll excuse my being more particular at Present, from Gentlemen, Your most oblig'd Humble Servant

LAMBT WICKES

To the Honble. Commissioners Dr. Benja. Franklin Silas Dean & Arthur Lee at Parris

A List of the Vessels and Cargoes take Vizt

No. 1, A Brig from Pool, bound to Cadiz with a Cargo of Cod Fish

　2, A Brig with Wheat and Flour from Dublin bound to Lisbon

　3, A Brig from Sheetland with Barley bound Cadiz

　4, Swallow Packet, bound from falm[outh] to Lisbon in Ballast

　5 A Ship from Bordeaux bound to London-Derry with Brandy, Claret and Hoops. Three of those are Arrived and the Other two are not farr Off.　　　L.W.

Addressed: To / The Honble. Dr. Benja: Franklin / at / Parris

Notation: Capt Weeks Port Louis Feby 14 77

From Boux　　　　　ALS: American Philosophical Society

⟨Paris, February 14, in French: I did not have time yesterday evening to tell you about a friend of mine who, at my earnest solicitation and out of attachment to me, has decided to enter the American service and take his whole family with him. He has served the King for forty-two years, been a chevalier de Saint-Louis for twenty-four and a major for sixteen, and is now a brevet colonel in the regiment du Cap; he will be a brigadier before his return to Saint Domingue. He is fifty-four, and his distinction and experience could be most useful to you. I have long been close to his family, whose fondness

331

for me has decided them to move to your country; and I hope you will not separate me from my old friends. His only condition is a rank higher than what he will hold when he leaves. If my friend M. Cornie were as close to me as M. le marquis de Bouillé, I should have no doubt of persuading him to follow me.[5] Once I rejoin my friends, America will become my country and theirs.

Please tell me approximately when you will be writing home, so that I may know whether I shall have time before my departure to make the plan of the ships for you to enclose with your letter.⟩

From C. W. K. and J. H. ALS (?): American Philosophical Society

This letter is a mystery to which we have no solution. The hand we cannot identify, but Franklin's endorsement makes us suspect that the bearer himself may have been the writer. The initials "C. W. K." suggest nothing to us. "J. H." may well be John Horne, better known later as Horne Tooke. In 1775 he had played a prominent part in raising a subscription in London for the dependents of Americans killed at Lexington and Concord, and two years later was tried and imprisoned for his part in that affair.[6] All that can be said with assurance is that Horne, if this letter is not a complete concoction, would have been a logical backer for Potter's mission to France.[7]

Israel Ralph Potter (c. 1744–1826) was a Rhode Islander who had

5. Bouillé was not the better known marquis, François-Claude-Amour, but an older one in the same family, Charles-Pierre-Antoine (1717?–80), who had been a chevalier de Saint-Louis since 1752: Mazas, *Ordre de Saint-Louis*, I, 425. He did not go to America but returned to his regiment in St. Domingue, where he died. Bodinier. "Cornie" was Louis-Dominique Ethis de Corny (1738–90), administrator and littérateur; he later went to the U.S. to make arrangements for the French contingent based on Rhode Island: Larousse, *Dictionnaire universel*; Howard C. Rice, Jr., and Anne S. K. Brown, *The American Campaigns of Rochambeau's Army* . . . (2 vols., Princeton, N.J., and Providence, R.I., 1972), I, 27 n.

6. *DNB* under Tooke, John Horne; for the subscription see above, XXII, 52 n.

7. But, unless he was trying to disguise himself, he was too literate to have written the letter. Potter apparently might have; he is said to have dictated the memoirs cited below: James G. Wilson and John Fiske, eds., *Appleton's Cyclopaedia of American Biography* (7 vols., Detroit, 1968).

fought at Bunker Hill. He then sailed in the Continental brig *Washington*, Captain Sion Martindale, and was captured at sea and imprisoned in England. After his escape he went to London, as mentioned here, and then made two visits to Paris. On both of them, according to his later account, he saw Franklin, who promised that if he returned he would be given passage to America; but the outbreak of war between France and Britain prevented this third trip.[8] His story is consonant with the suggestion in the present letter that he was in Paris to further, in some way not explained, the American cause in Britain. The crucial difficulty, however, is two entries in Franklin's accounts that February, both apparently covering the same disbursement of 120 *l.t.*: in one it was to "Potter, an American Prisoner escap'd from England, to help him home"; in the other it was to "Israel Potter and Edward Griffis, to bear their Expenses to Nantes."[9] Franklin believed, these entries indicate, that Potter was homeward bound; but how could he have believed so when he had this letter in his hands? That is part of the mystery.

Sr   Feaby 14th 1777

We Have Taken This oppertunity of writing To you by The bearer Hereof Hoping you are in good Health As we are at This Time by The will of god.

Sr we Have the Pleasure to Inform you That The bearer Hereof Isreal relft Potter was Taken Prisnor on board The Washington Commanded by Captain Marlinggal and Caried into Pounchmouth From which Pleace he gained his Libberty after sumtim of Confindment There and he is we Can Ashure you a man That is greatly to be Estemed For his Vallor and Zeal Which he Hath often Shewed For the Cause of his Country. For Atho he was A Prisnor Himself yet he gladly Accepted The oppertunity of being our searvant To go To Relive his brother Souldiers That where [were] in Prison in London Twice and Hath often Expressed The Greatest Desire to Re-

8. Henry Trumbull, *Life and Remarkable Adventures of Israel R. Potter ...* (Providence, R.I., 1824), pp. 50–2. These reminiscences provided Herman Melville with the material for his novel, *Israel Potter ...* (New York, 1855).

9. Waste Book, one of the entries under Feb. 8 (many of which bear other dates); WTF's accounts, entry of Feb. 25. JW's letter below of April 8 mentioned that Potter and his companion had not appeared at Nantes.

turn Again to Amarica but Could Not by Any means Efect it. But we Have sent him unto you and Have Asised [assisted?] him as well as we Could at Present. But as we and many other Friends are very Desirous to Know The True State of Afairs We Desire That he may Return as Soon as Possible As he will be The only Person That Can be Depended upon For That Purpose. For he knows And Hath been in great Part of England and as he Hath A Searvant with him he may Pass Very Safely and we Dought Not But he will. And we Can Asure you That you Have A great many Friends In England who will with us Asist To The utmost of Their Power in all Things. We are well known By The bearer who will give you A Perticular Acount of us. But The sooner he Returns The Better it will be For There is Like To be Troublesum Times in England Very Soon So No more at Present. We are your

C:W:K and J: H

To the Rev Mr F

Addressed: For Mr / Fran Paris / France

Endorsed: Israel Potters, pretended Letter from some Gentm. in England.

From the Marquis d'Osmond[1]

AL: American Philosophical Society

Vendredi 14 fevrier 1777.

Le Marquis d'Osmond, colonel commendant du regiment de Cavalerie d'Orleans, s'est presenté plusieures fois à l'hotel d'hambourg pour avoir l'honneur de voir Monsieur franclin où Monsieur dign; Les circonstances l'ont mal servi. L'un de ces Messieurs etoit incommodé l'autre etoit occupé. Le Mar-

---

1. René-Eustache, marquis d'Osmond (1751–1838), later achieved some distinction in the French diplomatic corps. He was minister to The Hague on the eve of the French Revolution, and after the Restoration was ambassador to Turin and then to St. James's: Larousse, *Dictionnaire universel*. We suspect, without proof, that he wanted to see BF on behalf of his younger brother, Marie-Joseph-Eustache, who never joined the American army but did serve with the French, as aide-de-camp to the marquis de St.-Simon, at the siege of Yorktown.

quis d'Osmond a le Plus grand desir d'obtenir une demie heure d'entretien. Il prie ces Messieurs de vouloir Bien donner, à celui de ses gens qui Porte ce Billet, le jour où ils seront visibles et l'heure qui leur sera la Plus commode. L'empressement du Marquis d'Osmond à s'ÿ rendre ne sera qu'une Preuve Bien faible de l'envie qu'il a d'obtenir ce qu'il demande.

Addressed: A Monsieur / Monsieur franclin / à l'hotel d'hambourg / rüe jacob. / *A Paris*

Notation: D'Osmond, Paris 15 fevrier 1777

From Louis Simon[2]   ALS: American Philosophical Society

⟨Marseilles, February 14, 1777, in English: Some local merchants are sending me to the East Indies in a new ship that I am to outfit. An inquiry in England about how to equip her with an electric conductor produced the surprising answer that the British navy has not yet adopted such conductors. You are the best person to help me on that aspect of your discoveries. I should be particularly grateful for help because I was in a thunderstorm off Africa, for some twenty days without interruption, when I often saw St. Elmo's fire on the masthead and sparks on the ship's iron rods, and knew the danger I was in. The translator of this letter will also translate your reply.⟩

Jonathan Williams, Jr., to the American Commissioners   ALS: American Philosophical Society

Gentlemen   Nantes Feb. 16. 1777.

The inclosed is from Mr. Lee who set off this Morning, for Bourdeaux. The Dispatches &c. went with Mr. Morris to paimbeuf yesterday and are I hope by this time on board. I have the pleasure to inform you that an american Frigate supposed to be Capt. Weeks has sent a prize laden with Codfish into l'orient;[3] This news comes by a Gentleman who arrivd

2. He signs himself as captain of the *Pintade*, Favre, Dragon & Cie.
3. The *Polly and Nancy* had appeared off the port some time before Feb. 13. Clark, *Wickes*, p. 132.

from thence yesterday, so have no reason to doubt of its truth, but we must wait for the post tomorrow for confirmation.

I shall go to Paimbeuf tomorrow to put every thing in the most expeditious Train. It is strange that Mr. Peltier has not yet recvd. orders from Mr. Montieu relative to the purchase of the Goods to compleat the Cargo. Please to enquire into this for without such orders I apprehend it will be difficult to execute the Business. I hope you will excuse me mentioning once more that Charts are not to be had here and that 3 Weeks is the extent of Time that I allow myself to dispatch the Ship.[4] Mr. Montaudouin has recvd. a Letter from Cadiz dated 28 January which mentions that a Ship in 26 Days from Martinique brings news that the Americains have gained a great advantage over the English. I have the Honor to be with great Respect Gentlemen Your most obedient Servant J WILLIAMS

The Honorable The Deputies of the United States

Notation: Jon Williams Nantes Feby 16. 77

From Jonathan Williams, Jr.

ALS: American Philosophical Society

Dear and honored Sir   Nantes Feb. 16. 1777.

I have written the inclosed to Mr. Blunt because I thought it my duty so to do. If you don't think so, please to keep it. The one to Mr. Vaughan does not contain a word of a public nature. Please to forward it.

I have not answer'd Mr. Alexander, because I want your assistance to know how it should be answered.[5] I shall be infinitely obliged if you will favour me with a Line upon the Subject of my private concerns; tell me only what views you think are best for me to have and I am determined to know no Difficulty.

---

4. She was the *Comte de Vergennes,* soon to be rechristened *La Thérèse.*

5. This was the letter that JW had by him when he wrote BF on Jan. 25. Alexander had presumably suggested that the young man join him in some scheme of his for a tobacco contract; see JW's second request, in his letter below of Feb. 19, for BF's advice.

I have removed to another part of the Town far from Mr. Montaudoin, so send this under Covr of Mr. Shweighausser's Banker. If you will please to direct to me chez lui I shall get my letter, some time sooner. I am in haste most respectfully and affectionately Yours &c.   J WILLIAMS

Agreement between the American Commissioners and Louis-Guillaume-Servais des Hayes de La Radière[6]

AD (draft)[7]: American Philosophical Society

At Paris, this 17th Day of February, 1777. Whereas le Sr. Laradiere Major du Corps Royal du genie, in the Service of his most Christian Majesty, not having obtain'd his Leave of Absence when the Agreement between us and Messieurs le Chevalier du Portal, de Laumoy, and Gouvion, was concluded, viz. on the 13th of this Instant, could not become a Party by signing the said Agreement, but having now that Leave, is ready to enter into the same Engagements; We the undersigned do hereby agree that the same Terms and Stipulations entred into between us and the Gentlemen above mentioned, and contained in the said Agreement, shall be granted and observed, with Regard to M. Laradiere, in every Respect, he performing the same Duties therein engaged to be performed by them, which he hereby promises accordingly.

Agreemt. with M. Laradiere

Notation: Laradiere

6. La Radière (1744–79) was, like Duportail, a graduate of the military school at Mézières, and was commissioned captain of engineers in 1775. Duportail clearly recruited him after writing his letter above of Jan. 12, but when is not clear. La Radière, like Laumoy, was breveted major before his departure, and went to America as a lieutenant colonel although this agreement, surprisingly enough, says nothing about his rank. He was promoted to colonel in November, 1777, and was in charge of fortifying the Hudson Highlands; he died in service in the autumn of 1779. *JCC,* IX, 932; Lasseray, *Les Français,* I, 181–2; Elisabeth S. Kite, *Brigadier-General Louis Lebègue Duportail. . .* (Baltimore, etc., 1933), pp. 21 n, 79–90, 159–62.

7. In WTF's hand.

337

The Secret Committee to the American Commissioners

ALS: British Library; draft:[8] Harvard University Library

In the secret Committee of Congress Baltimore in Maryland

Honorable Gentlemen   Feby. 17th. 1777

We have the honor to inclose you a Resolve of Congress that is of great Importance to the public Service, which has suffered considerably the last Fall, and during this Winter, by the insufficient manner in which our Soldiers were clothed. Having found much Delay heretofore in getting Cloth made up, the Congress desire that 40,000 compleat Suits of Soldiers Cloaths may be sent. In giving directions for the making these Cloaths, it may be necessary, Gentlemen, to inform that both the Coats and Waistcoats must be short skirted, according to the dress of our Soldiery, and that they should be generally for Men of stouter make than those of France.[9] Variety of Sizes will of course be ordered.

The Eastern Ports are generally entered with so much more Safety than the Southern, that we recommend the former for these Goods to be sent to, giving Orders to the Captain to inform Congress immediately of his Arrival, either by Express or by personal Attendance. We expect this Letter will be delivered you by Capt. Johnston, Commander of the Lexington armed Vessel,[1] and as the Congress are very anxious to hear from you, it is probable Capt. Johnston will not remain long

8. Both are in the hand of Richard Henry Lee, and he signed the draft; they differ only in inconsequential details.

9. The resolution instructed the commissioners to send the 40,000 uniforms if possible, cloth for as many more, and a large quantity of blankets, stockings, flints, and lead: *JCC*, VII, 92–3. The draft lists these requirements at the foot of the page.

1. This is the first appearance of a man who will often reappear. Henry Johnson had had an earlier and disastrous voyage, when British prisoners on the privateer he commanded took her over and sailed her to England; she was anchored in the Thames, and the crew confined for a time in the hold under appalling conditions. Johnson eventually made his escape to France and so to America, where he was promptly given his new command. William J. Morgan, *Captains to the Northward: the New England Captains in the Continental Navy* (Barre, Mass., 1959), pp. 103–5.

enough in France to get either Cloth or Cloaths in any quantity, but since it is necessary for the health of the Soldiers to cover them from the Dews of Summer it will be of great Advantage to send a considerable quantity of Blankets and Tent Cloth by the Return of the Lexington, with Stockings, Flints, and Muskets with Bayonets. The Soldiers Cloaths and the Cloth should be so contrived as to reach North America by the month of September at furthest. We are with esteem, honorable Gentlemen, your most obedient and very humble Servants

RICHARD HENRY LEE
FRAS. LEWIS
WM WHIPPLE[2]

Copy.

From the Chevalier de Girard[3]

ALS: American Philosophical Society

⟨Philippeville, February 17, 1777, in French: I have heard of your arrival from Boston, and write to ask whether you can give me news of Mr. Penn, settled in the colonies and head of Pennsylvania,[4] and enable me to send a letter to him.⟩

Arthur Lee to Franklin and Silas Deane

ALS: American Philosophical Society

Bourdeau Jany. 29th

Dear Sirs   [*i.e.*, on or after February 18[5]]. 1777.

I thank you for your Letter of the 12th. I wish the news

2. For the New Hampshire delegate, who had been added to the committee the previous November, see the *DAB*.

3. A retired lieutenant colonel, who had been named a chevalier de Saint-Louis in 1760: *Etat militaire de France* . . . for 1772, p. 240; Mazas, *Ordre de Saint-Louis*, I, 519. He wrote BF twice again, both times from Paris: on June 15 asking to see him, and on Aug. 16, 1777, to recommend an unnamed officer for service in America. APS.

4. Presumably John Penn, who was still in Pennsylvania. Richard had returned to England in 1775, with considerable publicity as bearer of the Olive Branch Petition, and was still there.

5. He was in Bordeaux on the 18th: Wharton, *Diplomatic Correspondence*, II, 272. The gossip he had gathered there suggests that he had arrived some days earlier, but he could scarcely have received the commissioners' letter of the 12th, which he acknowledges here, before the 18th.

may be true. I found a Letter here from London of the 2d. which says, that Ships are actually sent for the ten thousand Germans, which with three thousand british they expect to have very early in America. That they hope for great advantages from dissentions in Pensylvania. That Burgoyne's destination is changd from Virginia to Boston. It also informs me that Cornwallis's defeat in N. Jersey is generally credited; but not a word about the retaking of Long Island.

I have desird Mr. Delap to send you an Estimate of the Exports and Imports to and from the United States within the year past; together with an Account of the heavy duties which are laid on many Articles of our commerce. As those were laid to discourage the trade when it was british, I have hopes you will easily obtain a removal of them now that reason has ceasd or indeed is rather reversd.

A ship has been lying many months at Nantes totally deserted, at the freight of the Congress of one hundred Dollars per month. I venturd to recommend the immediate sail of her, which Mr. Morris ought to have done long ago. I coud get nothing from him relative to the Cargoes detaind in Spain. It seems to me that he did not intend informing me of the agreement made with the Farmers general, which came to me thro another channel. I saw the original Agreement, in which he has engagd for all the Tobacos which shall come to the Ports of France, on account of the Congress, during the continuance of the war.

Mr. Myrcle's character is still worse here than any where else; but Mr. Morris told me, he had found him, upon enquiry, to be a very respectable man, and that a considerable House in Amsterdam had promised to advance money for him. Mr. Delap tells me, his whole time was employd here, in Houses of the lowest debauchery and drunkenness, leaving the Ship on expences and without any prospect of being dispatchd. She is in this situation now, and I am informd is a swift Sailor.[6] He

6. Merckle's ship was the *Dispatch*, Capt. Cleveland: Crout, "Diplomacy of Trade," p. 179. For the Delap firm see above, XXII, 445 n. Although it was often referred to in the plural, Samuel had been dead for some time; see Delap to Willing, Morris & Co., Mar. 30, 1776, Hist. Soc. of Pa. Lee's informant was John Hans Delap.

has undertaken to give a french Officer a lieutenant Colonel's Commission; and send him out, to the Congress.

I shall attend to your counsel, relative to the moneyd transaction; and shall be much obligd to you, at all times for your advice. I shoud submit to your consideration, whether if the demand relative to the two Ships be made and disregarded, it woud not be proper to have it publishd in the Layden Gazette, that the baseness of our Enemies may be as notorious as possible.[7] I am to go tomorrow to examine a large Fregate, which is here for sail, and which the Owners will undertake to deliver at some Port belonging to the United States. The terms and Inventory are to be remitted to you if upon examination she shoud seem likely to suit us. I have endeavord all in my power to dissuade the Owners from expecting that you will purchase her; but the zeal of those frenchmen for our interest is invincible.

I observe by the Papers, that the Agents of the Ministry are endeavoring to cover their cruelties on Long Island, by charging us with having wantonly hangd some hessian Prisoners previous to that transaction. This they are constantly repeating both in the foreign and domestic Gazettes, in order to establish it as an historical fact. I think some step shoud be taken by the Congress to publish an authentic contradiction of it, that so infamous an imputation may not go down to posterity, with whom, I hope our name will be unblemishd. It may be askd where those hessian prisoners were taken, their General not having given the least hint of any encounter before that, in which it is acknowledgd the royal Army acted so inhumanly.

The roads I have hitherto passd were exceedingly bad, and they comfort me with the information that the remainder is ten times worse. In so much that I dispair of reaching my destination till some time in march. They will not venture to travel thro the night, which delays one miserably. I shall leave this place to-morrow evening, or early the next morning. I

7. See the commissioners to Germain above, Feb. 7. The decision not to send the letter was made after Lee's departure and on Vergennes' advice: BF to Lee below, March 2. For the *Gaz. de Leyde*, and the commissioners' subsequent use of it, see Dumas' letter to them below, March 11.

have the honor to be with the greatest esteem, Dear Sirs Your most obedient Servant ARTHUR LEE

P.S. Please to remember me to Sir Roger Legrand[8] Monsr Chaumont, Mr. Carmichael and Mr. Franklin. I am much obligd to Mr. Carmichael for his Letters.

Advices from Virginia of the 20th. of Decr. mention that they had heard of the taking of Fort Washington, had raisd Six Regiments by desire of the Congress, and were perfectly unanimous. Tobacco was at 20 *s.* Sterling a hundred.[9]

Addressed: To / The Honble / Messrs. Franklin & Deane

Notation: Mr Lee / A Lee to Mrs F. and D. Bordeaux Jan 29. 77.

Robert Morris to the American Commissioners

LS: Connecticut Historical Society

Honorable Gentlemen, Philada. Febry. 18th, 1777.

By this Opportunity I forward you sundry dispatches from Congress and the Committee of Secret Correspondance still at Baltimore, and from them I have just received the inclosed resolve of Congress dated the 5th Inst. Copies of which I shall transmit you by various Conveyances, in order that you may give orders for procuring the Articles required and to have them Collected ready for Embarkation.[1] The places of their destination are not yet fixed but you will hear from the Committee or from me very soon on that subject, in the mean time the Articles may be provided and you may rest assured of our

8. The Chevalier Georges Grand.

9. This news induced the commissioners to drop their negotiations with the farmers general: BF to Lee, just cited.

1. See the committee's letter above, Feb. 17. With the present letter Morris also sent the commissioners a brief note of the same date, and presumably by the same conveyance. It enclosed a copy of their letter of credence of Sept. 30, 1776 (above, XXII, 634–5) which had been with his papers, sent into the country for safekeeping. Smith, *Letters,* VI, 316 n.

utmost exertions to make you effective remittances to answer all your Engagements.

We have at length got one of our Frigates the Randolph Capt. Biddle Cruizing on this Coast to meet any single Frigates of the Enemy and hope for good accounts from her, she sails fast is well Manned and appointed.[2] Others will soon join her and our utmost exertions will be used to put the Navy on a respectable and formidable footing fast as possible.

No event of War of any Material Consequence has happened since the last letter from the Committee. General Washington continues to Pin up the Enemy in Brunswick from whence distress obliges them to send Foraging once or twice a week, and altho they come out 2 to 3000 strong our People always attack and never fail to kill and take more or less of them. They have sent for reinforcements from Rhode Island and probably may render the Jersey War a little more serious again but our new Enlistments go on so fast we shall soon be too formidable for them in the Field unless they receive very great reinforcements from Europe, and I fancy they may not find that so practicable now as the year past. With the greatest respect and Esteem I have the honor to remain Honorable Gentlemen Your very Obedient humble Servant.

ROBT MORRIS

(Copy)

Addressed: To / The Honorable, Doctor Benjn. Franklin / Silas Deane & Arthur Lee Esqrs. / Commissioners for American affairs / Paris / by Mr. Reed.

Notation: From Rob. Morris Esqr. 18th Feby. 1777

Robert Morris to the American Commissioners

February 18, 1777 See page 342n

2. The commander was Nicholas Biddle, soon to be famous; he had been introduced to BF in London: above, XVIII, 83–4.

Thomas Morris to the American Commissioners

ALS: Connecticut Historical Society

Gentlemen   Nantes February 18th. 1777.

Since I had the pleasure to address you last, have received Mr. Deane's letter dated the 4th Instant which was delivered to me by Mr. Lee. In answer to its Contents am to acquaint you next Thursday's Post will carry you a remittance of £90,000, promised in my last. It shoud have been sent sooner, but I coud not ask payment of those the Tobacco was sold to, untill the whole was delivered, which was compleated yesterday. Captain Anderson sailed on Sunday Morning with a fair wind. Your dispatches were put in a lead box and safely conveyed onboard the Success at Paimbeuf.

I have received a letter from Captain Wickes dated at Port Louis the 14th. Instant acquainting me with his arrival there after a successful Cruize, having capturd five Brittish Vessells of which the following is a List

No. 1. The Swallow Packet bound from Falmouth to Lisbon mounted with 16 Carriage Guns and 50 Men onboard

 2. A Brigt. from Pool bound to Cadiz with a Cargo Codfish

 3. A Brigt. from Sheetland with barley bound for Cadiz

 4. A Brigt. from Dublin bound to Lisbon with wheat and flour

 5. A Ship from Bordeaux, bound to Londonderry with brandy, Claret, Rozin and Hoops

The Swallow Packet fought near 45 Minutes before she struck. Captain Wickes's first Lieutt. lost an Arm in the Action, and his Lieutt. Marines received a Musquet ball in his Wrist, which was all the damage he sustained in the engagement. Onboard the Packet many were dangerously wounded. I shall sett off in a few hours for Port Louis, and on my return shall be able to give you a more circumstantial account of this matter. In the mean time I remain respectfully Gentlemen Your most Obedient Servant   THOS. MORRIS

To The Honble. Benja. Franklin & Silas Deane Esqrs.

344

Addressed: A L'Honorable Docr. Franklin / á L'Hotel D'Hamburg rue Jacob / á Paris

Notation: Mr T. Morris Nantes Febry. 18th 1777

The Secret Committee to the American Commissioners

ALS:[3] University of Virginia Library

In Secret Committee of Congress Feby 18, 1777

Honorable Gentlemen

You will receive herewith a Copy of our Letter of Yesterday by the Lexington, with its enclosures. This goes to Boston for a Passage from thence. An armed Vessel belonging to that State will carry the dispatches and will be governed by your directions respecting her Load back, and the Time of her return.[4] Should you have failed in obtaining the Loan, or of getting the Cloth, Cloaths, &c. mentioned in the Resolve of Congress, you will please turn the Vessel over to Messrs. Thomas Morris and William Lee, or either of them to receive such Continental Cargo as they may be enabled to send in her.[5] Unless you should be of Opinion that the public Service requires that she should return immediately to North America with your dispatches, in which case you will direct what you judge best for the public good. We are with perfect esteem, honorable Gentlemen, your most obedient and most humble Servants

RICHARD HENRY LEE
FRA. LEWIS
WM WHIPPLE

Baltimore Feby. 18th. 1777

3. In the hand of Richard Henry Lee.

4. This procedure accorded with Congressional instructions: *JCC*, VII, 128–9. The duplicate went by Capt. John Adams in the *Lynch*; see Bradford to BF below, Feb. 25.

5. The committee had appointed Lee, then in England, to act as commercial agent with Morris. Smith, *Letters*, VI, 102–3; *DAB* under William Lee.

The Committee of Secret Correspondence to the American Commissioners

LS: University of Virginia Library; two copies: National Archives; draft:[6] American Philosophical Society

Baltimore in Maryland Feby 19th, 1777

Honorable Gentlemen,

The events of war have not since our last furnished any thing decisive. The enemies Army still remains encamped upon the hills near Brunswick, and still our Troops continue to beat back and destroy their Convoys insomuch that we understand their Horses dye in numbers, and we have reason to believe that the difficulty of removing their Stores, cannon, &c. will be insuperably great, until the opening of the Rareton furnishes a passage by water for their return to New York. The American Army is not numerous at present, but the new Levies are collecting fast as possible, and we hope to have a sufficient force early in the field. We see by the speech of the King of Great Britain to his Parliament that much money will be called for, no doubt, to prosecute the war with unrelenting vigor.[7] That we shall oppose with all our power will be certain, but the event must be doubtful, until France shall take a decided part in the war. When that happens our liberties will be secured, and the glory and greatness of France be placed on the most solid ground. What may be the consequence of her delay, must be a painful consideration to every friend of liberty and mankind. Thus viewing our situation, we are sure it will occasion your strongest exertions to procure an event of such momentous consequence to your Country.

It is in vain for us to have on hand a great abundance of Tobacco, Rice, Indigo, Flour and other valuable articles of merchandise if prevented from exporting them, by having the whole Naval power of Great Britain to contend against. It is not only for the interest of these States, but clearly for the

6. In the hand of Richard Henry Lee.

7. The King's speech at the opening of the session, Oct. 31, 1776, was reported in the *Pa. Gaz.*, Feb. 5, 1777.

benefit of Europe in general, that we should not be hindered from freely transporting our products that abound here, and are much wanted there. Why should the avarice and ambition of Great Britain be gratified, to the great injury of other nations? Mr. Deane recommends sending Frigates to France, and to convoy our Merchandize.[8] But it should be considered that we have an extensive coast to defend; that we are young in the business of fitting Ships of war, That founderies for Cannon were to be erected, and the difficulty of getting seamen quickly when Privateers abound as they do in the States where Sailors are, as yet, chiefly to be met with. And lastly, that our Frigates are much restrained by the heavy Ships of the enemy which are placed at the entrance of our Bays. In short, the attention of Great Britain must be drawn in part from hence, before France can benefit largely by our Commerce.

We sensibly feel the disagreable situation Mr. Deane must have been in from His receipt of the Committees letter in June, and the date of his own in October.[9] But this was occasioned by accident, not neglect, since letters were sent to him in all the intervening months, which have either fallen into the enemies hands, or been destroyed. From the time of Doctor Franklin's sailing, until we arrived at this place, the Ships of War at the Mouth of Delaware and the interruption given the Post by the enemy, added to the barrenness of events, prevented us from writing when we had no particular commands from Congress for you.

Mr. Bingham informs us from Martinique that he learned from a Spanish General there, on his way to South America, that the King of Spain was well disposed to do the United States offices of friendship, and that a loan of money might be obtained from that Court.[1] As the power sent you for borrowing is not confined to place, we mention this intelligence, that

8. In his letter of Nov. 2, 1776: *Deane Papers*, I, 339–40.

9. Deane, in every extant letter he wrote to the committee in October, protested having had no word from it: *ibid.*, pp. 228, 311, 324–5, 328, 338–9.

1. We have been unable to trace this gossip; for Bingham see above, XXII, 443 n.

you may avail yourselves of his Catholic Majesties friendly designs. Perhaps a loan may be obtained there on better terms than elsewhere.

We expect it will not be long before Congress will appoint Commissioners to the Courts formerly mentioned[2] and in the mean time, you will serve the cause of your Country in the best manner possible with the Ministers from those Courts to that of Versailles. Earnestly wishing for good news, and quickly from you, we remain with friendship and esteem, honorable gentlemen your most obedient humble Servants

> BENJA HARRISON
> RICHARD HENRY LEE
> JNO WITHERSPOON

P.S. Congress adjourn this week back to Philadelphia.

We refer you to the letter of the Secret Committee concerning the transmission of Stores by this Vessel.

Lambert Wickes to the American Commissioners[3]

ALS: American Philosophical Society

Gentlemen   LOrient Febry 19th 1777

I Wrot you Last post Informing you of the Suckces of my Last Cruize and take this Opertunity To Inform you of the Safe Arrival of All my Prizes. I Am in Great hopes youl be Able to Obtain Leave for me to heav Down and Repair my Ship at this port As that Will be Absolutely Necessary prior To my Departure from this As I Recd. a Shott in [*torn*] Bottom When the Swallo Engaged me. When I Arrivd At this port the Captns. of the Different prizes Applyed to me for Leav to Go on shore Which I Granted on thier promising me that they Would not Write to England or Else Where With out my permishon they further promised Not to Go Away or Do Any thing Disagreabl Without my Consent. Not Withstanding thier Giving me Thier joint Words on Honour that they Would

2. See the committee's letter above, Dec. 30.

3. For a fuller discussion of the difficulties described here see Clark, *Wickes*, pp. 134-7.

Comply With those Requests I find that they have at the Request of Mr. Perrit a merchant of this place Waited on the Intendant[4] To Know by What Authority they Was Detained as Prisoners in this port. I Am further Informd that they Intend Going to the Admeralty Officer at vans [Vannes] to protest a Gainst Me And Demand the Restitution of their Respecktiv Ships and Cargoes. I hope you'l take Such Steps As to prevent any Bad Consequences Arriseing from those proceadings. I Am very Sorry to See that thos Gentlemen are So Abandoned To Al Sence of Honour as I am Well Assured it Can procead from No Bad treatment that they Recd. from me as they have All Publickly Acknowledged that It Was Impossible they Could have bin better treated If they had bin taken by Thier own brothers as I have made them a present of thier Own private Adventures those belonging to the Packet Are very Considerable they Amount to Near £2700 Sterling first Cost. Mr. Perrit has bin very Acktiv in Doing me Every prejudice in his power. I Should Esteam it as a very Great favour If it is in your power to Reward him According to his Deserts.[5] I Immagine the Consequence of thier Waiting on the Intendant Will be an Order for the Enlargement of the prisoners but hope you have had Suffishent time for the Negotiateing an Exchange if it Could be Done. I Am to See the Intendant this Evening When I Shal Know his Determination and If Desired to Discharge the prisoners Shall Readyly Comply With his Request at the Same time I Shal Request that He Will order them to St. Mallo Immediately After They are Released Which I make no Doubt, but he Will Comply With. There is Several persons Now treating With me About the purchasing the Vessails and Cargoes and Am In hopes to Get Soon Clear of them on tolerable Good Terms. My Wounded

4. Naval intendants (not to be confused with the intendants created by Richelieu) were in charge of administering major ports, which Lorient was not. This "intendant," Charles-Pierre Gonet, who will appear often in later letters, was the *ordonnateur*; see his correspondence in the French naval archives, series B³, DCXL.

5. "Adventures" were goods that the individual officers had brought with them to sell on their own accounts. Perret was Schweighauser's associate in Lorient.

349

Officers are in A good Way of Doing very Well. From Gentlemen your Most Obliged Humble Servant, LAMBT WICKES

To The Honrbl Doctr Franklin Silias Dean and Arthur Lee

Mr. Montaudain and Brothers of Nantz Is Mr. Perrits Friend and a Line from you To that Gentlemen Would Get him Severally Check'd by that Gentlemen

Addressed: To / The Honbl. Docktor Benjmn. Franklin / At / Parris

Notation: Captn Weeks Orient Febry. 19th 1777

Jonathan Williams, Jr., to the American Commissioners

ALS: American Philosophical Society

Gentlemen   Nantes Feb. 19. 1777.

I went to Painbeuf on Sunday and returned hither last Evening. Mr. Peltier and myself went on board the Count de Vergennes and gave the necessary Directions. As I consider Dispatch of the utmost Consequence, I desired that as many Workmen as could be procured should be immediately employed. These are at present Scearce, but as a little more expence is no object in comparison to expedition, to insure a sufficient number it is concluded to give each one a little Gratification. I am fearfull that we shall not come within the 3 weeks I mentioned but you may depend that not a moments time shall be lost. While the Ship is preparing we shall be providing the Cargo and I intend to have the most Bulky Bales repacked but in all this I shall govern myself by my Time to which I apprehend every other Consideration should give place. I beg leave to suggest whether it would not be an additional precaution worth observing to have liberty in the Clearances to touch at St. pierre de michelon and some part of the Cargo to be aparently destined for that place, this will insure safe Conduct as far as Newfoundland and give the Captain more opportunities of getting into some part of the Massachusetts, and at the same time be a good excuse for his being so far to the Northward in case of Examination: This I humbly submit and shall not presume to add it to your directions without leave.

I have the pleasure to confirm the account of Capt. Weeks having sent in a prize laden with Codfish from Poole for Spain into L'orient, and to inform you further that he has brought in 4 more, two from England and Ireland for Cadiz, one with Barly the other with Flour, one from Bourdeaux for England with Wine and Brandy, and the Packet from Falmouth for Lisbon, this last mounts 16 Guns and engaged Capt. Weeks ¾ of an hour. Weeks I am told behavd heroically, he was the first man who boarded, and sword in hand obliged the English Capt. to strike; he had only one man kill'd, the first Lieut. lost an arm, and the Lieut. of marines has a musquet Ball in his wrist, but both are likely to do well. The Packet had many wounded but none killed, she had 50 men on board.[6] It is said that Weeks has sailed again on another cruise but of this I am not certain. Mr. Morris is going off directly for L'orient and no doubt has given you the necessary Information. I understand that the Ships cannot be disposed off in french Ports, although the Cargoes may, in this Case it would be happy if you had a sufficiency of Sailors to send them immediately to America especially the Packet which seems to be very oppertune for your purpose. I shall give you every information that comes to my knowledge, but as the Business does not come in my way I only know what passes in common with every indifferent person, so can't say what steps are intended, for every thing of this kind I must refer you to Messrs. Morris &c. &c.

I recvd. Mr. Deanes favour of the 12th and shall follow his Directions, but I apprehend it will not turn out adviseable to have anything to do with those arms.[7] I have seen some of them before and did not think them worth having, however, I

6. See Wickes to the commissioners above, Feb. 14.

7. Samples of the arms, which Montieu was offering for very little, had been sent to Paris for examination. Deane was not satisfied, and instructed jw to examine them all. Du Coudray also inspected them, and found them good. *Deane Papers*, v, 309; *Deane Correspondence*, p. 73; Du Coudray's undated memorandum to Congress, National Archives. These were the same arms, we strongly suspect, that had been offered Dubourg the year before: above, xxii, 464 n.

will have them examined very particularly, and if any of them are capable of being fitted and will stand a proof, I will report accordingly; but unless every individual Fuzil is tried and answers proof, they certainly would not be worth accepting even as a Gift. I have the Honor to be with great Respect Gentlemen your most obedient Servant   J WILLIAMS

The Honorable The Deputies of the united States

Notation: Jon Williams Nantes Feby 19. 77

From Jonathan Williams, Jr.

ALS: American Philosophical Society

Dear and honored Sir   Nantes Feb. 19. 1777.

I am very sorry to hear that you have an attack of the Gout, but I hope it will soon be over.

As to Business I must refer you to the inclosed.[8] As I suppose I am to stay here some time longer, I shall be glad to hear from you what my future Line of Life is to be, for I take it for granted that I am not to return to England again. Mr. Lee mention'd that you had views of forming some Company of french Merchts. and that I might probably have an opportunity of taking an active part in the plan; whatever it is I will do my utmost to give satisfaction. I don't know whether your hint relative to Mr. Ss Daughter was designed as serious or not, but I assure you I do not think *that* the most impracticable thing in the World; my Situation in business being settled to satisfaction, this might become an object worthy of pursuit. My former Views of this kind with Miss A I consider as totally at an end on account of the War between her Country and mine and I have long since given up every expectation of the kind. This leaves me at full liberty and I assure you that tho' I am not less sensible of Miss a's merit yet I must do justice to

8. No doubt the preceding document.

Miss S.[9] If I were settled here I imagine I could do great service to my Country but wherever you think I can be more usefull I am determined that no personal consideration shall prevent my obedience. I have written so much and so often to you that I fear I tire you with repetition, but I discover every thing that occurs to mind without m[asking?] or endeavouring to dress it with propriety, because I know you will kindly excuse whatever you find amiss and freely tell me of it. I am with great Respect Your dutifull and affectionate Kinsman

J WILLIAMS

Please to tell me what you think of Mr. Alexanders plans about the Tobacco Business.[1]

The American Commissioners to Jonathan Williams, Jr.   Copy: Connecticut Historical Society

Sir   Paris 20th Feby 1777

Yours of the 13th: is before Us. Mr. Deane wrote you on the subject of Arms &c. belonging to Mr. Montieu in Nantes[2] we wish you to send Us as early as possible an Acct. of your survey and your Estimate of the value of the Whole on the best Information You can Obtain. Also supposing the Fusils whose Barrels may answer for further Use in the Continental Army or for the Indian trade but which must be New stocked, should have their stocks Thrown away and be packed in the Closest manner, what space or how many Tonnage of Freight the Whole would Call for. The Charts and Dispatches you mention shall be procured and sent as soon as possible and should the Vessel purchased, not be sufficient to Carry the Goods supplied by Mons. Beaumarchais and the sail Cloth

---

9. BF's hint about a Schweighauser daughter was in his letter above of Feb. 5. JW's choice was the next to eldest among many sisters, and four months later she was expecting a proposal: JW to BF below, June 24. By then he was having second thoughts, and they eventually led him back to the attachment, which he here disavows, to Mariamne Alexander.

1. See the note on JW to BF above, Feb. 16.

2. Deane's letter of Feb. 11 is discussed in the annotation of JW to the American commissioners above, Feb. 19.

and Cordage &c. for two Frigates you will shorten your purchase Accordingly having an Eye to an Assortment of what
shall be sent if for more than One. We are &c.   BF
                                                    SD

We are surprised to find Ourselves among the last to be informed of so interesting a peice of Intelligence as that of the
Captures made by Capt. Wicks and wish that in future when
anything of so much Consequence happens that We may be
Notified as early as possible.

Mr. Jona Williams Nantes

Notation: Paris 20th Feby. 1777 Copy of a Lettr. to J Williams
Nantes

From Jonathan Williams, Jr.

ALS: American Philosophical Society

Dear and honored Sir   Nantes Feb. 20. 1777.
    The inclosed is in answer to Mr. Deanes Favour relative to
the Arms in Mr. Montieu's Store.[3] It has been observed to me
that Prizes instead of being brought into french ports might
be sold with secrecy and can, by landing the Goods on an
Island near the mouth of the Loire, where french Vessells might
come and take them; and perhaps in this way it might be contrived to dispose of the Ships without making a noise, but at
least they could be there easily destroyed. I mention this because I think some precaution necessary, for you may depend
that there are spies in this and other ports. One English Captain has been long suspected, and the Mayor wishes to get
some pretence to send him away, but as yet no proof can be
had. The first circumstance that will support such a measure,
will I am sure be very readily embraced. I am often applied to
for news but can give none. Lord S[tormont] is so industrious

---

3. The commissioners discussed this list in some detail in their reply
below, under Feb. 25, and enclosed a copy of it in their letter to the committee of secret correspondence of March 12 to April 4; it is now in the
National Archives.

that the London Gazette[4] when it contains anything against us, finds its way hither one or two days before any other news. The news of our Success in New Jersey has been mentioned here from several quarters but all want confirmation: I shall be glad to be informed if there is any foundation for this news. I am very dutifully and affectionately Yours &c. in haste

J WILLIAMS

Lambert Wickes to the American Commissioners

ALS: American Philosophical Society

Gentlemen,   L'Orient Feby. 21st. 1777

When I wrote you last I mentioned, being Summond to Appear before the Intendant, in regard to the Destination of the Prisoners now on board my Ship. The Intendant, then Informed me that he should come on board in Company with the Captains of the different prizes and Examine all the English, Irish and Scotch Men that was on board my Ship and all those Chose to depart was to be releas'd and would be dilivered to Captain Newman[5] and the remainder to remain on board. My Answer was that I could not Suffer any person to come on board My ship to discharge any person from her, but if he ordered me I would imeadiately Discharge all those prisoners taken in the last Cruize and take his Certificate for the Same. We have now Agreed to Wait 'till Sunday for your Answer and then Deliver the prisoners to Capt. Newman. I have also a Notification from the Admiralty Office to depart the port in 24 Hours with all my prizes. This by no Means Corresponds with your instructions to me. As we are not Allowed more than 24 hours to refit and Supply our Vessels with Necessaries, we shall send all our prizes out of the Port the first fair Wind, but shall continue here with the Reprisal, untill I receive your further Instructions which I hope will be more favourable. I have entered the Different Vessels as my Prop-

4. The government's mouthpiece.
5. Charles Newman was the only naval officer among the captives; he had commanded the packet that Wickes had taken. See Clark, *Wickes*, pp. 135 ff; *Naval Docs.*, VIII, 602, 606–7.

erty, and not as Prizes. Inclosed you have a Coppy of my declaration. Mr. Morris is here now, but has not yet Settled the Plan for Disposing of the Prizes. I am in hopes of being able to give you a full Account of the Disposal of the Whole next Week. From Gentlemen Your most obliged Humble Servant

LAMBT. WICKES

ps. Mr. Perret, Still Continued Very Active, in doing me all the prejudice he Can.

To the Honble. Dr. Benja. Franklin Silas Dean Arthur Lee Esqrs.

Addressed: To / The Honble. Dr. Benja. Franklin Esqr / at / Parris

Notation: From Capt. Weeks L'Orient 21st. Feby. 1777

From Louis Garanger

February 21, 1777 See page 432n

From J. J. Garnauld

February 21, 1777 See page 186n

From de Sparre

February 21, 1777 See page 301n

Arthur Lee to Franklin and Silas Deane

ALS: Connecticut Historical Society

Dear Sirs   Bayone Feby. 22d. 1777.

I arrivd here this day and shall pursue my journey to-morrow, and as the march is as regular as the Sun, it is agreed that the Voiturier shall place me in Madrid, in 13 days.

By Mr. Delap's account the Imports from America, I mean from the United States, amounted last year to fifty five thou-

sand pounds Sterling. He expects soon to have an exact list of
the Imports and Exports from the Custom House, and will
send it to you. He desires me to mention that the duty upon
oil being seven Livres per Quintal is so heavy as to render
that an unprofitable article of Commerce unless you can get it
removd, that unless a Certificate of its being american produce, be sent with all Bees-wax, it is subject to a duty of 25
percent and that the duty upon Fish is fifteen livres per Quintal amounting almost to a prohibition. Salmon is the only Fish
importable duty free, and that is reexported to their Islands.

Our demand upon Mr. S. has made a great noise. It was the
talk of the whole change at Nantes that we had taken up, at
once, two thousand Louis dores at Mr. Penet's and Gruel's
Banquer;[6] and I saw a Letter, of a late date, from Mr: Thoms.
Morris to a merchant at Bordeau, informing him, that we had
taken up that Sum, at his, Mr. Morris's Banker's, and that it
must be deducted out of the Sum the Merchant was to advance
us. At the same time he demands a state of Mr. Dean's account
letting the merchant, in as foolish a Letter as I ever had the
honor to read, into the Secrets of the Congress very impru-
dently. Thus those Adventurers and Sots are continually pros-
tituting the names of the Congress and of us, to exagerate
their own consequence, or cover their own little Schemes. In
every merchant's mouth of any character at Nantes and Bourdeau the names of Mr. Morris and Mr. Myrcle are absolutely
contemptible, and I assure you the censure is not a little visited, especially in the last place, upon those who appointed
them. As far as my very imperfect judgment of commerce can

6. The rumor was an exaggeration. Two thousand louis d'ors were 48,000
l. t.; what the commissioners actually had from Sollier, proceeds of the
indigo that the *Reprisal* had brought, was in instalments which came in all
to slightly over 41,000 l. t.: *Deane Papers*, v, 412. The final instalment, just
under 13,000, was received four days after Lee wrote: entry of Feb. 26,
1777, Waste Book. These payments had to finance the commission. "Though
Mr. Sollier, without business enough to pay a clerk, might be a banker in
character for Mr. Penet, lately a journeyman gunsmith at Strasbourgh,"
Deane later complained, "it was rather a mortifying circumstance to the
Commissioners of the thirteen independant United States to be dependant
on such a merchant or banker for money for their support." *Deane Papers*,
v, 413.

inform me, the credit of the Congress seems to have sufferd by their conduct, almost irreparably.[7]

I pursue my voyage quite alone, having found my nephew had little political stuff about him, so that I thought it better to leave him at Nantes under the care of Mr. Sweighausser who is a protestant.[8] I have the honor of being with the greatest esteem Dear Sirs Your most Obedient Servant

ARTHUR LEE

Addressed: To the Honble / Benjamin Franklin & / Silas Dean Esqrs

Notation: Arthur Lee Bayonne Feby 22d 1777

Jonathan Williams, Jr., to the American Commissioners

ALS: American Philosophical Society

Gentlemen   Nantes Feb. 22. 1777.

I have the honor of your Favours by Messrs. Portail &c. There is no opportunity for them to embark except via St. Domingo, unless the packet Boat should be sent. I say nothing to them of the Count de Vergennes as you do not express an Intention that they should go in her. They do not seem to like to go in a Ship under american Colours least they should be taken and their plan be thereby defeated, they therefore have thought of going by the West Indies. I beg to know whether in case they should not be able to go in this or any other way, I shall be at Liberty to take them on board the Count, they paying their passage. Four is as many as I wish to have in this Ship.

We have had bad weather for 2 Days past which has a little impeded our dispatch, but we go on as fast as we can. It is

---

7. The commissioners quoted this and the previous sentence in their letter to the committee of secret correspondence below, March 4.

8. In December Lee had sent for his two nephews, Richard Henry Lee's sons, who had been studying in England; the one he left in Nantes was Thomas, then eighteen. Cazenove Gardner Lee, *Lee Chronicles: Studies of the Early Generation of the Lees of Virginia* (Dorothy M. Parker, ed.; New York, 1957), p. 215; *Lee Family Papers,* roll 3, frames 132–3.

reported here that several Sail of english Men of War are cruising between Bellisle and Brest. This Information I thought proper to send to Capt. Weeks that he may keep a sharp look out. It is also said that a french Ship bound from the West Indies to St. Malo has been searched by an English Frigatte, and it is thought that outward bound Ships will of course meet with the same Fate. It seems to be the opinion here that these circumstances will occasion the two powers to stumble on a War whether either really intends or not. The News of our Success in Jersey, which you no doubt have heard of at Paris is thus confirmed by a Ship which arrived at Bilboa in 25 or 30 Days from Marblehead. She reports that 1800 Hessians were surprized at Trenton, on the 27. of Decr. and the whole of them with their arms &c. taken; 900 of them are said to have been killed in the action. It is also said here that the spanish Fleet has arrived at Rio de la plata. I have the Honor to be with great Respect Gentlemen Your most obedient Servant

J WILLIAMS

The Honorable The Deputies of the United States.

Notation: Mr Williams

From Nathan Rumsey   ALS: American Philosophical Society

Honorable Sir   Nantes Feby. 22d. 77.

I hope I have the pleasure of being the first who gives You the inclosed most agreable Piece of News: It is the Extract of a Letter from a Gentleman in Bayonne to his Friend in this City, which is confirmed by a Letter received at the same time with this News, from William Lee Esqr. of London, allowing for Ministerial suppression.[9] Examining the Circumstances, I think it appears to be genuine, and as such have the Honor of congratulating you upon its Existence. Messrs. Morris and Penet are at present at L'orient negociating the affair of the 5

---

9. The news, we assume, was of the Battle of Trenton. The confirmation of it in Lee's letter, Rumsey is apparently saying, was based on press reports in London that minimized the British defeat; for such reports see the *Public Advertiser*, Feb. 12, 15, 17.

Prizes, of the Capture of which you have before this without Doubt, been apprized.

One of the former Prizes of Captain Wickes is now in this Port, and Captain Pratchell, who is yet here, has made a reclamation, and demanded the Vessel. Upon his being refused the Vessel, he has obtained a summons for Mr. Penet and Self, signed by the first Judge of the Admiralty, to appear at the first Audience, and give our Reasons for detaining his Property. The sommons also includes you Sir; but doubt not but the Judge will have politeness enough to dispense with Your personal appearance.

Mr. Penet's sudden Departure for L'orient gives me an opportunity of giving you this Information. I have the Honor to be Sir Your Most obedient Humble Servant   NATHAN RUMSEY

I have forwarded the Account of the inclosed news to Mr. Lee in London with a[1] request that it may be immediately printed.

N.R.

Addressed: To / The Honorable / Doctor Benjamin Franklin / A l'Hotel D'Hambourg / Rüe Jacob / a Paris.

Endorsed: Mr Rumsey

Notation: N. Rumsey 22 Feb. 77

The American Commissioners to Lord Stormont

AL (draft):[2] Library of Congress

My Lord,   Paris, Feb. 23. 1777.

Captain Wickes of the Reprisal Frigate, belonging to the United States of America, has now in his Hands near 100 British Seamen, Prisoners. He desires to know whether an Exchange may be made with him for an equal Number of American Seamen now Prisoners in England?[3] We take the Liberty

1. Here is inserted what appears to be the letter "D."
2. It and the notation are in BF's hand. The letter was subsequently published in the *London Chron.*, Nov. 4–6, 1777.
3. Wickes' inquiry is above, Feb. 14. As he indicated to the commissioners on the 19th, he came under heavy pressure to release the prisoners, and in fact did so the day before this letter was written: Clark, *Wickes*, pp. 137–

London Mag. Feb 178.

THE R.^t HON.^{BLE}

LORD STORMONT.

David Murray, Seventh Viscount Stormont

of proposing this Matter to your Lordship; and of requesting your Opinion if there be no Impropriety in your giving it whether such an Exchange will probably be agreed to by your Court. If your People cannot be soon exchang'd here, they will be sent to America. We have the honour to be, with great Respect, My Lord, Your Lordship's most obedient, and most humble Servants

Letter to Lord Stormont

From Sarah Bache

ALS: Musée national de la coopération franco-américaine, Blérancourt, France

Honoured Sir   Goshen February 23d. 1777

We have been impatiently waiting to hear of your Arrival for some time. It was seventeen weeks Yesterday since you left us, a day I never shall forget, how happy shall we be to hear you are all safe arrived and well. You had not left us long before we were obliged to leave Town. I never shall forget nor forgive them for turning me out of House and home in the middle of Winter, and we are still about twenty four Miles from Philad. in Chester County the next plantation to where Mr. Ashbridge used to live.[4] We have two comfortable rooms, and I am as happily situated as I can be seperated from Mr. Bache, he comes to see us as often as his business will permit. Your Liberary we sent out of town well packed in boxes a week before us, and all the valuable things, Mohoginy excepted we brought with us. There was such confusion that it was a hard matter to get out at any rate, when we shall get back again I know not, tho things are altered much in our

---

40. Stormont may have expected as much. In any case he ignored the overture, as the commissioners more or less expected; see below, their letter to Wickes under Feb. 25 and BF to Lee, March 2. The problem of prisoners grew larger as time passed, and proved to be insoluble. Although a few were eventually exchanged, no reliable system for doing so was established in Europe, as it was in America. Catherine M. Prelinger, "Benjamin Franklin and the American Prisoners of War in England . . . ," 3 *W&MQ*, XXXII (1975), 261–94.

4. Jane Mecom had told BF of the move to Goshen in her letter above, Dec. 6; for George Ashbridge see XIII, 273 n.

favour since we left town. I think I shall never be afraid of staying in it again if the Enemy were only three Miles instead of thirty from it, since our Cowards as Lord Sandwich calls them are so ready to turn out against those Howes who were to conquer all before them, but have found themselves so much mistaken, their Courage never brought them to Trenton till they heard our Army were disbanded. I send you the News papers, but as they do not allways speak true, and as there may be some particulars in Mr. Baches letters to me that are not in them, I will copy those parts of his letters that contain the news. I think too you will have it more regular.

Aunt has wrote to you and sent it to Town. She is very well and desires her Love to you and Temple. We have wished much for him here when we have been a little dull, he would have seen some Characters here quite new to him. Its lucky for us that Mr. George Clymers Mr. Merediths and Mr. Buddens Families are moved so near us, they are sensible and agreable, and we are not often alone.[5] I have refused dinning at Mr. Climers to day that I might have the pleasure of writing to you and my dear Boy who I hope behaves so as to make you love him. We used to think he gave little trouble at home, but that was perhaps a Mothers partiality. I am in great hopes that the first letter from Mr. Bache will bring me news of your arrival I shall then have cause to rejoice. I am my dear Papa as much as ever your Dutifull and Afectionate Daughter

S BACHE

Addressed: Doctor Franklin / Paris

From Henry Coder
ALS: American Philosophical Society

Coder or Codere, as he sometimes spelled himself (1738–80), played a considerable part in the commissioners' early search for supplies. He was a retired army officer who came from Pézenas, in Languedoc. He had been a volunteer in the Seven Years' War and became

5. "Aunt" was of course Jane Mecom. For George Clymer and his partner and father-in-law, Reese Meredith, see above, XII, 152 n. The Buddens must have been the family of either Capt. William Budden or his brother James, old acquaintances of the Franklins: above, XIV, 279.

a lieutenant in 1775; perhaps he was soon afterward promoted (he refers to himself as a captain), but in 1776 he was pensioned off.[6] His uncle had been useful to and in the confidence of the maréchal de Saxe, and he himself had been well regarded by Louis XV; but something went wrong after the old King died.[7] Coder was now an entrepreneur. He first made contact with Franklin in January, when he warned him through Dubourg that the French weapons being shipped to America were not only defective but suicidal to use.[8] The present letter seems to have been his first direct approach to Franklin, and it was accompanied or followed shortly by three undated memoranda. One proposed to manufacture a sample of 1,300 uniforms, each batch of a hundred in different colors for a different state. The other two gave minute details of the equipment to be provided, with the cost of each item.[9]

Paris ce 23e fevrier 1777

Homme juste vertueux lisez cette lettre.
Messieurs ellie de baumon et dubourg conoissent
celui qui vous ecrit dans l'unique vue de
rendre votre voiage en frence fructueux.

Monsieur

Je vous protexte [proteste] qu'il y a en frence des hommes dans tous les etats bien disposés et tres capaples de vous scervir utilement et sans interet, mais malhureusement ce sont ceux qu'on ne vous a pas procurés, rarement ils s'offrent d'eux meme et surtout quand ils ont lieu de craindre d'etre confondus avec

6. Bodinier.
7. Coder to Dubourg, March 2, 1777, APS. The uncle was Jean-Pierre-Henry Coder, who died in 1761 as commandant of Béziers: Bodinier. Some of his relatives had to leave the country because they were Protestants, and religion may have been back of the nephew's difficulties. When the latter appealed for help to Louis XV's former valet de chambre, the baron de Champlost, he received only the cold comfort of a testimonial, dated Dec. 18, 1774; this he must have sent to BF, for it is now in the APS.
8. Coder to Dubourg, Jan. 22, 1777, Hist. Soc. of Pa. He added that Elie de Beaumont, the old acquaintance of Dubourg and BF, had furnished him the latter's address and wished to explain who Coder was. Dubourg wrote on the letter "Je ne connois ce Mr. Codere que de nom," and passed it on to BF. For the weapons see above, XXII, 464 n.
9. All three memoranda are in the APS. The contract for uniforms was eventually carried out: *Deane Papers*, III, 173, 429.

des mauvaix sujets. J'ai remits il y a un mois a Mr. ellie de
baumon, une lettre d'un manufacturié d'armes de st. etienne
que M. dubourg doit vous avoir donnée, elle a du vous convaincre et de la mauvaise fourniture qui vous a eté faite dans
ce genre et que la faute ne put pas en etre imputée aux fabri-
quans. J'ai remis aussi a M. dubourg une notte exacte de ce
que coutte au roy un soldat habillé et armé de pied en cap sauf
le fusi et la bayonete, a la marge j'indique les endroits ou on
fabrique les choses premieres propres a toutes ces sortes de
fournitures et les lieux ou on les travallie. Je le prie de vous
engagér a profitér de la reforme qui a eté faite de la regie pour
l'habillement et l'equipement des troupes[1] malgrai son utilité
demontrée pour enrollér un nombre d'ouvriers propres a l'habillement et equipement ainsi q'un ou deux commis de cette
regie reformée et d'en etablir une senblable en amerique. Par
ce moyen on n'aura besoin d'achetér yci que les objets qu'on
ne trouve pas en amerique, ce qui simplifiera la mission de
MM. les deputés du congrés qui vera arrivér avec plaisir une
compagnie d'hommes non sulement propres a travaliér l'habillement et l'equipement d'un soldat, mais en etat encore d'en
fabriquér les matieres. Je m'engage a faire cette recrue sans
qu'il y aye personne de compromits, je demande aussi dans
cette notte a vous entretenir et demontrér la facilité que j'ai de
remplir avec succés les diferents objets dont je parle et vous
confiér des choses a vous sul tres interessentes pour la prosperité des colonnies, enfin vous convaincre que je merite de
jouir de la douceur de vivre avec des hommes vertueux et
libres. Je vous engage aussi Monsieur, a prendre conoissence
d'une lettre que j'ai ecrit a M. dubourg, a ne point faire passér
des officiers avec des grades superieurs en amerique, a cause
de leurs grandes pretentions, de la difficulté qu'ils auront a
vivre en bonne intelligence avec les generaux ameriqains et
surtout dans la crainte qu'ils ne se laissent corompre, tandis
qu'on tire le parti qu'on vut d'un officier subalterne et bas
officier pour l'ordinaire plus instruit et en etat de soutenir la
fatigue. Les officiers, bas officiers et soldats que je propose

1. He was presumably referring to the centralized governmental control
over the purchase of uniforms and equipment, for which see Léon Mention,
L'Armée de l'ancien régime (Paris, n. d.), pp. 261–2.

dans ma lettre a M. dubourg d'enménér avec moi en amerique pour formér un corpts des troupes legeres seront la plus pard propres au scervice de l'artillerie et du gennie, disposés a prendre la pioche ou la charue quand il le faudra et en etat de faire des miracles en defendent la cause des insurgents (*qui est celle de tous les hommes*) dont nous meriterons la confience et l'amitié.[2] Tout ce que je propose et ay a proposé de vive voix put etre executé dans un mois. Je suis avec veneration Monsieur votre tres humble et tres obeissent scerviteur

CODER
capitaine d'infenterie
hotel d'angletere rue de seine

Monsieur le docteur de franquelin

From Coder: Three Memoranda

[on or after February 23, 1777]   See the preceding headnote

Notes on the Pennsylvania Constitution

AD (fragment): American Philosophical Society

This fragment is the only extant manuscript in Franklin's hand that deals with the second part of the Pennsylvania constitution, the frame of government. The notes might seem at first glance to be a by-product of his involvement, such as it was, with drawing up the document; and our reason for thinking that they are not requires a more detailed consideration of that process than the outline in our note on the convention.[3] The draft version of the frame of government was debated in the committee of the whole and presented to the convention on September 5, 1776. Franklin and two others were then appointed to revise the wording without changing the substance, and to have the revised draft printed for public discussion; it appeared on September 10.[4] From the 16th to the 27th the conven-

2. He elaborated this scheme in his letter to Dubourg of March 2, already mentioned; see also the annotation of his next one to BF below, under March 7.
3. Above, XXII, 512–13.
4. *The Proposed Plan or Frame of Government for the Common-Wealth or State of Pennsylvania, (Printed for Consideration.)* ([Philadelphia, 1776]). For the date of publication see William Duane, ed., *Extracts from the Diary of Christopher Marshall* . . . (Albany, N.Y., 1877), p. 92.

tion resumed debate, altered many passages, renumbered some of the articles, and added a preamble. On the 28th the frame of government and the declaration of rights were formally adopted.[5]

Franklin's notes touch on only one aspect of the constitution, the provisions for rotation in several offices. The reference to Article XIX is to the new numbering and to provisions added after September 10, when the work of Franklin's committee for stylistic revision was finished. The notes are not the sort that he would have been likely to make during the subsequent debate in the convention; they are purely factual, as if he were answering or preparing to answer questions on a specific point. The time when questions came at him was when he reached France, where the novel constitution aroused much curiosity. One of the first to evince interest was the duc de La Rochefoucauld, as witness the note from him below under Feb. 24, and it is a reasonable guess that at some time he asked about the provisions for rotation. If so this memorandum, like the Duke's note, was written before the latter's translation of the constitution appeared.

[Before Feb. 24, 1777?]

[Beginning lost] chosen an Assemblyman more than 4 Years in 7.

11. No one can sit as a Member of Congress more than 2 years successively, nor be re-elected till after 3 years of Interruption.

19 The supreme Council to be chosen 1 Member for each County annually, so as that one third be chosen yearly and the whole not changed but in three years.

Whoever has serv'd three years cannot be rechosen 'till after 4 years vacancy.

[William Alexander]: Two Memoranda

(I) AD: Historical Society of Pennsylvania; (II) AD:University of Pennsylvania Library

We have given both these documents titles supplied in the manuscripts in another hand, and date them on the assumption that they were written for the commissioners during Alexander's visit to Paris in February, which probably ended on the 24th; for he reached Dijon on the 26th.[6] While he was with the commissioners he drafted

5. Force, 5 *Amer. Arch.*, II, 34, 45–59.
6. See his letters to BF above, Dec. 22, and below, March 1.

for them the long reply to the farmers general that immediately follows those memoranda, and there is every likelihood that all three grew out of discussions held during his visit. The "Hints" are on three disparate subjects, prizes, naval gunnery, and land forces. Alexander would scarcely have gone into them unless he had learned at first hand that they were on the commissioners' minds. Neither would he in all probability have forwarded his views later from Dijon, because some of what he had to say was, coming from a British citizen, close to treason; he was well aware that spies were about.[7] The "Observations on Tobacco," although they contain almost nothing to interest spies, are not the kind of finished product that he would have sent by post; they seem to be impromptu jottings (some of them incomprehensible to us) made in the course of a meeting. These are our grounds for believing that he dashed off both memoranda while he was seeing the commissioners.

I. Hints

[Before February 24, 1777]

The advantages that will arise to the different European powers from the freedom and Independance of america, are So obvious That there can be no doubt of their Concurrence in every measure to Effectuate it, Consistent with their observance of treaties, or the timid views of Such as are affraid of War.

As the sale or Condemnation of Captures made at sea by the Belligirent Powers within the Dominions of the Newtral European Powers, is prohibited by Treaty, and this seems to be a most Important point for America as the only probable means of removing in some Degree the seat of the War[8] and the most likely to rouse the spirit of the British Nation and Compel the administration to an Equal peace, The following Considerations are submitted.

As Newtrality Implies the free admission of Cruisers and their prizes into all the Ports of the Newtral power, there can never be a want of reasons, for Unloading such prizes in a Newtral port. Any defect in the vessel will always afford a sufficient one. Nothing can prevent such defects from being repaird, as perfect newtrality requires, aids in distress (for money) in every Case where they are necessary.

7. *Ibid.*
8. *I.e.*, extending the theatre of war to Europe.

But as such repairs require time and Cargoes Suffer by detention reasons can never be wanting for shipping these Cargoes by other vessels during the detention of the prize vessels.

By the Treaty with Holland free ships make free goods,[9] and supposing this article Contested in Its full Extent, goods bear no mark of Identity but what can easily be Effaced, and It has been the practice of all Europeans at War to Cover their property in this way. Supposing difficulties to occur in unloading and loading by different vessels than the prizes, There Certainly can be none in the acquisition of Hulks for that purpose.

Queries

Were it not proper to have faithfull agents in every sea port of the principal European powers?

Woud it not be proper that one or two Cruizers have their destination in each of these ports? Will not successfull Cruizers from Each of these ports, tempt the Newtral Merchants and seamen to desire a participation in the Emoluments?

Might not prudent agents be Directed to give shares, or be entrusted with powers to assign the Entire property of Cruizers, to the subjects of newtral powers upon payment?

Woud not this augment the fund for Carrying on the War?

Woud not this by gradualy Interesting Individuals come at last to have an Influence on the Councils of the European powers?

Woud it not by irritating the Enemies of Your Country Lead Them to imprudencies, which woud Convert friends into allies?

Might not Capital be drawn from all nations for this purpose: Profit being the God of Merchants?

The Litle Effect of Distant shot at sea is so well known, both by the reason of the thing and by experience, That it may be assumed as a principle, Where there is Either wind or sea that the 5oth Shot does not take place at 3oo Yards distance.

9. For the Anglo-Dutch treaty of 1674 see Samuel F. Bemis, *The Diplomacy of the American Revolution* (revised ed.; Bloomington, Ind., 1957), p. 135.

An Engagement at sea to be decisive must then by nigh,[1] when It will be determined by the relative weight of shot thrown in from the one ship to the other.

This principle is so far understood, that it is beleivd every ship intended for action, Carries as much weight of Mette [Metal] as relative to Her strength and sailing she can bear.

But by shortening Guns of 5 or 6 feet to 3 and 4, without encreasing the thickness, will not ships carry Guns of 18 and 24 pound shot as easily as They can now do Guns of half these bores?

Will not such Guns carry point blank above the distance where guns at sea can be usefull?

N:B. The measures are assumed at random.

Have not all the Experiments made of the Effect of Guns been tried merely for Land service, and Erroneously adopted in the sea service?

Is not the object at land to give the greatest possible shock to a resisting body and at the greatest possible distance?

Is not the object at sea merely to bore a plank or Tear it, woud not the tearing one, be better than boring both sides of a ship?[2]

Woud not shortening the Guns and thus decreasing the force tend to this? And at any rate bore both sides within any distance where Shot at sea can be relied on?

Is it not Certain that the time of working and firing a Gun at Sea, is in some nigh proportion to The weight?

Was not this fact ascertaind by the famous Engagement between Captn. Falconer in a 64 Gun ship against a french 74 Gun ship on the Coast of Portugal, where by throwing in nearly 2 shot of 24 lb. in the time the french threw in one 32 pound shot he prevaild by his weight of Metal, against heavier Canon?

It is believd the history of this engagement will be found in Smolet, it is well known to all seamen.[3]

---

1. He meant to write, we guess, "be by nighing," *i.e.*, by drawing close.

2. Better because the splintering wood causes casualties?

3. The *Bellona*, 74, Capt. Robert Faulknor, captured the *Courageux* in August, 1761. See Tobias Smollett, *Continuation of the Complete History of England* (4 vols., London, 1760–61, IV, 238–43), and for a more accurate ac-

Woud not the Nation who first builds frigates of 30 Guns, 24 pounders of equal weight with the present 12 pounders prevail in all causes against ships even of 36 Guns of the present construction?

Is not some new practice necessary to give A Consciousness of Superiority, which commonly Creates a real one?

May not an Army be Compared to a parcel of Lead drops, which fired seperately will hardly pierce the skin, but when united and Melted into a Mass will produce the most Extraordinary Effects?

If additional force coud be given to this mass, without Encreasing the Bulk, The handling of it woud be equaly easy and Comodious and the Effect woud still encrease.

Is it not plain that even the best European Troops at present, are greatly Inferiour to what by accounts the ancients were, in every Essential Duty of a soldier?

Is not 5 Leagues or 15 Miles Deemd an extraordinary Good March for a body of Men, and what They can hardly exceed, for two days running, without resting a third?

Can an army now Entrench itself in the time and in the way They anciently did, where every Encampment was fortified even for a nights stay?

Is not the number of Shot fired and the small Execution in a long Batle a proof of how Imperfect modern armies are in the use of arms?

May not this Partly be accounted for, From the officers considering his Proffession, as merely an idle way of living Genteely, with too much Pay to work as a Journey Man, and with prospects too distant to Excite high ambition?

Is not the Pay of the Soldier too small to Cloth and Support Him under hard labour?

By Encreasing the Pay of the Soldier and diminishg that of the officer woud not more and better work be done?

Does not a Carpenter or Blacksmith work 12 hours a day, and keep his health and live as long as a soldier?

---

count William L. Clowes, *The Royal Navy: a History from the Earliest Times to the Present* (7 vols., Boston and London, 1897–1903), III, 306–7.

Woud not working soldiers 12 hours a day Contribute to their perfection in their art, Their Morals and even their health?

Might not lads at 16 or 17 be taught by Degrees to work as long at the business of a soldier as at any other Business?

Marching

Cannot any lad with sound limbs be accustomed to walk without great Fatigue 30 Miles or 10 leagues a day by the same progress That a nailor is taught to make 3 or 4000 nails a day?

Woud not a light dress free from ligatures Either on the arms or legs facilitate this?

Woud not an oild silk or Cloth Covering which woud reject wet facilitate this?

Woud not shoes which woud merely save the sole from being hurt, without preventing wet, facilitate this?

Might not Cleanliness be preservd by frequent washing and swimming, without Linen shirts?

Woud not a Cotton lining to such Silk or Cloth as be above described be warmer than Linen, and by attracting the moisture of the Body keep it drier and as Cleanly as Linen?

Intrenching

Coud not any lad of 17 be Soon taught to Ditch as well as a Common Ditcher?

Cannot any Good ditcher make Eight square Yards of Ditching in a day?

Coud not a body of Such, intrench themselves in two hours?

Firing

Cannot any lad be taught in a few Months to shoot a bird flying, or at least hit, a body of 4 feet dimensions at 50 yards with a bullet?

Woud not 100 Men who coud march Entrench and fire as above be equal to any 200 troops now Existing Except for the single purpose of filling space?

Is not the Success of War more determined by speedy Marches, quick and strong encampments, and superiority of Detachments than by pitchd Batles?

Is it not rare even in Batles to find a space large enough for an Army to act entirely?

Is it not on the Contrary more Common that the fate of an army is decided by the success of a part, than by the action of the whole body?

Or is it not more rare to find ground large enough for an army to act in, than an army to fill the Ground you can occupy So to act together?

Endorsed by Franklin: Hints from Mr Alexander

II. Observations on Tobacco

Observations[4]   [Before February 24, 1777]

1st. If Commissions must be paid for buying, the legal Commission in America is 5 per Centum which should be added to the Cost tho In great and Safe Business it Is sometimes done for 2½ per Centum.

2d. An Agent must also be Employed to Attend the Delivery which will be 2 per Centum. The first is only on the purchase, the last is on the selling price.

3d. The french have ever been accustomed to 4 per Centum discount for money down. After all the profit is considerable, because the fraught Insurance etc. are not advance, So that the Advance may be computed £6 for 3 months, for which the returns are the Capital, and £[*illegible*].

French ships are apt to Dammage Tobacco more than the English both on account of Their Construction, their manner of Stowing and Their manner of working at Sea. They will also Carry fewer hogsheads In proportion to their Burden.

Premiums [?] of Insurance will also probably rise.

The idea of Carrying on that trade by mutual passes appears Chimerical. The British Nation coud only agree to it on Condition that the ships returnd to Britain, in which Case she

4. They are prefaced by detailed calculations of the cost of tobacco, including insurance, shipping, etc., per hogshead of a thousand pounds. We omit these notes because they are so filled with abbreviations, in Alexander's minute hand, that we cannot transcribe them with any hope of accuracy, and because we find them largely meaningless except for their final conclusion, that the profit to be expected per hogshead is £1 17s. 4d.

woud Enjoy the monopoly of that beneficial Commerce. America can have no Object in Continuing this monopoly when she is seeking a free trade.

Whatever pecuniary Interest may be Suggested to tempt her It is to be Considerd that the British Merchant will only offer what he can afford after a large profit to Himself.

Why allow Him that profit?

If that trade[?] be to be Carried on by the Public, might it not be Converted into a Supply?

Suppose for goods delivered abroad at prime Cost, Tobacco were to be deliverd at Nantes and Bordeaux at [*illegible*] Sols putting half the fraught on the outward Cargo the fraught of the homeward might be got for 5 or at most 6 *s*. per Centum.

By Employing Foreign Ships, in case They were Seizd it woud generate questions between the Captive, and Captor, then Occasion national questions, As when the Cry of a people grows strong no Governors can resist it.

Notation: Mr. Alexanders Observations on Tobacco

William Alexander's Draft of a Memorandum from the American Commissioners to the Farmers General

Draft: American Philosophical Society; copy with one short omission: American Philosophical Society; copy with major omissions: American Philosophical Society; final memorandum: Archives du Ministère des affaires étrangères

The history of this memorandum can be reconstructed from the four versions that survive. Alexander, during his visit to Paris, first drafted it for the commissioners as their reply to the memorandum from the farmers general above, Feb. 14. He wrote it in French, unlike the preceding documents, presumably because it was intended for eventual submission to the farmers; it shows a command of the language that is fluent but far from perfect. Temple Franklin then made two copies. The first and earlier one omits Alexander's opening sentence but otherwise follows his text, with a few minor errors due to inattention; the second is drastically shortened. The version finally submitted, which bears the date of Feb. 24, follows verbatim this shortened text; but all errors in French have disappeared. What happened is clear. The commissioners quickly eliminated the blunt statement about price with which Alexander began his memorandum. They then decided to delete any discussion of specific prices, and confine themselves to the bland generalities with which Alexander concluded his statement. Finally they had this rump of a memorandum corrected and transcribed by some French amanuensis.

[Before February 24, 1777]

[L'on reponds aux propositions de la part de La Compagnie, que la prix de 4 sols la livre pour des tabacs pris dans les magazins de la Virginie et du Maryland, de meme que 6 sols par livre livrés en France ne peuvent presentement avoir lieu.[5] L'on scai actuelment que les Colons craignant la difficulté de faire passer leur produits en Europe, ont diminué de Moitie la Cultivation des Tabacs. Le prix est presentment en Europe de 15 a 20 sols la livre; aussitot que l'avis de ces prix passent en l'Americq, le prix augmentera en proportion. Les speculations qui se font par tout sur cette Article, et la Competition d'acheteurs qui en resultera, portera vraisemblablement le prix au dela de tout ce qui a eté connus jusqu'icy. Et l'on l'a vue autrefois jusqu'a 12 Sols la Livre sur le lieu, scavoir dans l'année 1759.

Sur cet fondement l'on ose doutér si les Contracteurs actuelles a 8 sols seront en etat d'acquitér leurs Engagements. Et si Ils reussissent, Ils pourront perdre Gros.

La Compagnie n'ignorent pas, que quand des vendeurs scavent qu'il faut absolument achetér, et qu'on peut donnér 8 Sols, Ils ne seront guerre disposés de vendre a meilleur marché.

Et sur le tout[6],] après avoir amplement consideré les propositions de la part de La Compagnie, L'on croit que La systeme la plus avantageuse pour Elle et pour [le] Public en Amériq est celuy dont il a été ci devant question. C'est à dire, que La Compagnie fera expediér les différentes Matiéres dont Le Congres aura besoin, suivant L'état qui Luy sera fourni par

5. This sentence, the first deletion mentioned in the headnote, embodied a conclusion that was based on news from Arthur Lee; see BF's letter to him below, March 2.

6. The bracketed passage was deleted in WTF's second draft. The remainder became the commissioners' memorandum, as explained in the headnote, except that capitalization was altered and mistakes in spelling and gender were corrected.

Leurs Plenipotentiares. Et qu'elle achetera au plus bas prix possible qu'après L'expedition ces denrees seront sur les risques du Congrès, qui seront obligé de chargér le Montant en bons tabacs de La Virginie et Mariland qu'ils acheteront au plus bas prix possible, de sorte qu'il n'y aura aucun profit pris des deux Cotés.[7] Qu'après L'expedition les tabacs seront sur les risques de la Compagnie.

La Compagnie pourra par cest moyen s'assurer d'un ample provision de matières pour la Consommation de la France sur le pied le plus médioqure que les Circonstances du tems peuvent admettre. Et se reposant sur La probité et la bonne foy de La société entiere, Elle ne Courrera aucun des risques auquel Elle sera toujours exposé en travaillant avec des particuliers.

From La Rochefoucauld   ʟs: American Philosophical Society

Thursday evening [before Feb. 24, 1777[8]]

Le Duc de la Rochefoucauld pays his respectful compliments to Doctor franklyn and beggs from him the favour of having for few moments *the Minutes of the Convention held at Philadelphia for the Pennsylvanian Legislation*. He wants of them for seeing

7. The farmers immediately turned down the suggestion that they should be responsible for delivering the supplies and bringing back the tobacco; see their reply below, Feb. 25. Lee, before leaving Paris in early February, had obtained a more specific form of this proposal in ʙꜰ's hand, which survives only as Lee quoted it: "Twenty thousand Hogsheads of Tobacco to be ready in the several public Warehouses of Virginia and Maryland, from whence the English used to take it, at the rate of 4 Sols per pound in exchange for munitions of war, Woolens, Linnens, Cloathing for the troops, tents, sails &c. These shall be purchased here by our Agents, paid for by the farmers general and transported thither in their Ships; and the exchange shall be made on this footing that for every 4 Sols contained in the invoice of such goods as the prime cost thereof, shall be delivered one pound of Tobacco, charges not to be reckoned on either side, and the expence of the transport and risque both of the Goods from France and of the Tobacco to France, to be borne by Messrs. the Farmers general." Lee's observations on the contract, April 27, 1779, *Lee Family Papers*, roll 6, frames 81–2.

8. The Duke's translation, for which he wants information, appeared under that date in *Affaires de l'Angleterre et de l'Amérique*, ɪv, cahier xvɪɪ, lx-cxxi.

and adding to his translation the subscriptions which are at the end of the Minutes, and which are not in the edition in 8°.[9]

Addressed: Monsieur / Monsieur le Docteur franklyn

The American Commissioners: Memorandum for Vergennes

D:[1] Archives du Ministère des affaires étrangères

[February 24, 1777[2]]

We have ordered no Prizes into the Ports of France, nor do we know of any that have entered, for any other purpose than to provide themselves with necessaries untill they could sail for America, or some Port in Europe, for a Market.[3] We were informed this was not inconsistent with the Treaty between France and Great Brittain, and that it would not be disagreeable to this Court; and further than this we have not thought of proceeding. The Reprisal had orders to cruise in the open Sea, and by no means near the Coast of France, and tho' we are well assured that a number of British Men of War are at this instant cruising near the Coast of France for intercepting the Commerce of America, yet if the Reprisal has taken a Station offensive to the Commerce of France, it is without our Orders or Knowledge, and we shall advise the Captain of his

9. What the Duke wished to see was *Minutes of the Proceedings of the Convention of the State of Pennsylvania* . . . (Philadelphia, 1776); what he had was *The Constitution of the Common-Wealth of Pennsylvania, as Established by the General Convention Elected for That Purpose* . . . (Philadelphia, 1776). Neither gave the names of the members who subscribed themselves; the *Minutes* had a note, which La Rochefoucauld included, that all did so.

1. In WTF's hand.

2. The "20" in the notation must be erroneous. The final sentence of this memorandum says that it was written on the same day as that to the farmers general. The latter, embedded in Alexander's longer draft above under Feb. 24, was dated the 24th.

3. This sentence plays fast and loose with the truth. The *Reprisal's* captures on the voyage from America had been sold in France, as the commissioners and Vergennes well knew, and those made on her recent cruise had been sent into French ports. BF had assured her commander, furthermore, that France and Spain would receive, protect, and supply his ship and her prizes: Wickes to the committee of secret correspondence, Jan. 24, 1777, *Naval Docs.*, VIII, 545.

Error. Though we learn his Cruise has been on the Coast of Spain and Portugal, and the Vessels he has taken, one charged with Cod fish, one with Flour, and a Packet Boat bound from Falmouth for Lisbon, demonstrate that the Cruise has not been on the Coast of France, nor detrimental to its Commerce.

We made Proposals to the Farmers General, and they returned us different ones, to which we shall this Day make our Reply and immediately afterwards lay the state of the Affair before the Count de Vergennes.

Notation: 1777. 20 février

From ———— du Breüil, fils

February 24, 1777 See page 169

The American Commissioners to Lambert Wickes

Incomplete (?) copy:[4] Connecticut Historical Society

[February 25?, 1777[5]]
Your first we did not receive till eight days after it was dated, your last of the 19th last Evening. We wish to know if the Captns. who have so little regard to their Parole sighnd a written parole or not. If they did we advise you to show it to the Intendant and desire they may be obligd to live up to it. We have applied to the British Embassader for an exchange of

4. In the hand of William Carmichael. The final sentence as it stands is an oddly disembodied conclusion; it is at the bottom of the page, lacks a period, and we suspect was continued on a sheet now missing.

5. We are almost sure that this is one of the commissioners' two letters of Feb. 25 that Wickes acknowledged in his reply below on March 5, where he responded to their advice here about written paroles, and to a recommendation of Nicholson that may well have been spelled out on the page that we conjecture is missing. The copy follows on the same page that of the commissioners to jw of the 25th. Three of their letters to Wickes have disappeared, one of Feb. 22 (but see the annotation of his reply below, Feb. 28), one of the 23d, and the second letter of the 25th. He acknowledged these respectively on the 28th and on March 3 and 5.

377

Prisoners,[6] but have receivd no answer and are apprehensive no exchange will be made. As the Sailors must on their return to England be instantly pressd if they are exchangd and return, will they not consent to enter into the Service of the united States in preference to being pressd or sent Prisoners to America, one of which must be the Consequence? We advise you in future to permit no Officer that is a Prisoner to go on Shore without a Parole written, which will oblige him to return tho' his word of honor will not. We are sorry that you should meet with difficulties in disposing of either your prizes or your Prisoners, but by treaty between France and England you may not sell [stay?] farther than is sufficient to repair and to put you and your prizes in a proper state for going elsewhere. For this you can have liberty of the Intendant. You say you have an offer made for the prizes. We do not advise you to sell at any time untill American affairs are on a more settled and regular establishment here, but on Condition of the Purchasers running all risques of any reclaimer. Respecting the Cargo's taken we are not sufficiently informd to advise you, so particular as we wish to do. But the bearer of this will afford you all the Assistance in his power, and whatever he purchases of you giving his receipt for and on account of Roderique Hortales & Co. or Mr: Beaumarchais, we will be accountable for. As to the Packet If she will answer to cruise with being refitted, we purpose that you should have her valued and the Congress to be accountable for your and Peoples shares after which that She should be fitted as soon as possible for a cruise.[7] Your first Lieutenant is wounded and the State of your Officers is not so particularly known to us. If She is equippd it will be probably at the Expence of some private

6. Above, Feb. 23.

7. The bearer of the letter was Francy, Beaumarchais' secretary, and he might have helped to deal with the problem of the ships. An order that they should leave within twenty-four hours, the commissioners knew, was on its way from Versailles; hence the suggestion that Wickes evade the order by pleading to the Intendant the need for repairs. The Captain had already done so, and had prevailed before Francy arrived. By then the *Reprisal* was being careened; the prizes, the packet among them, had vanished and were soon sold sub rosa. Clark, *Wickes*, pp. 140–50.

person, who would wish to have and must have an American to command and will be pleasd we doubt not to have an officer of your recommending. Captn. Nicholson is here at present.

Captn. Weeks

The American Commissioners to
Jonathan Williams, Jr.   Copy:[8] Connecticut Historical Society

Sir   [February 25,[9] 1777]

In answer to yours respecting the Fusils &c. we inform you that an offer being made by Mr. Montieu of the whole of his stock at Nantes at 200 and forty thousand livres made us think it worth inquiring into. Your answer and stating is particular. You say there are 15400 gun barrels for infantry 8200 ditto for Rampart Fusils &c. afterwards 7700 Rampart fusils, good, 18000 ditto to be new mounted. We understood by the first that there are 15400 barrels for infantry and 8200 for ramparts unmounted, and that the 18,000 are badly mounted. You say that all the fusils have their locks and garniture in general very capable of repair. Those to the rampart Fusils are very good. There are we find on the whole 81764 Fusils of different kinds, besides those which you say are too bad to be included and by this we understand that the 81764 have locks and garniture compleat only in want of repair. Our view in proposing to be concernd if at all in a purchase of this Store, is to have the whole at so cheap a rate That the Indian trade may be supplied out of it and a number of valuable arms &c. with a little repair supplied to the Continent. You will therefore make a second view of the whole and give us what you think of the value and as you rate the repairing low, in what time they might be compleatly repaird and fitted up. As to the charts it is difficult to procure them here, but if to be had in Paris we shall procure and send them. Your proposal of covering the voyage by Papers and orders for St. Piere and Miquelon is a

8. In the hand of William Carmichael.
9. This is undoubtedly the letter that JW acknowledged in his below of Feb. 28.

prudent Measure, but it will be necessary in the Ostensible Orders to the Captn. to direct him in case he speaks with any vessel from either of those places, or if by touching he find the Markets dull to go to St. Domingo or Martinico, and add to him to keep well on the West on account of the North and westerly winds on the Coast of America and charge him in them that if in Case of Accident He should be obligd to enter into any of the North American Ports, to be careful of offending against the Laws of Great Britain by trading or otherways, but to repair his vessel and depart as soon as possible. These ostensible orders must be in the French language. Should we fail of procuring the Charts you must try to obtain of Captn. Weeks a draught and we will supply him before his return to America. Mr. Montieu mentioned a number of sober ingenious armerers willing to go to America, that there were 10 or 18 of them with two good founders of Cannon. We wish you to inquire of Mr. Montandouine and Mr. Peltrier [Peltier] on this Subject and if you are of opinion that the State of these stores is on the whole such as to be worthy our attention, that you would make an estimate of the expence of transporting the whole. One Mr. Perrit at L'orient has been most mischeivously busy in Captn. Weeks affairs and as we are told that Mons. Montandouine has an acquaintance with him and influence over him we wish that he would advise him not to meddle in this affair.[1] We are Sir your humble S.D

B F

Mr. Williams Nantes

Notation: Dr. F. and Mr. D. to Mr. Williams

[Dumas] to the American Commissioners

ALS: American Philosophical Society; letterbook draft:[2] Algemeen Rijksarchief, The Hague

Messieurs   25e. fevr. 1777

Depuis ma Lettre du 14e. de ce mois, j'ai eu plusieurs fois la plume à la main pour vous écrire; mais n'ayant rien de pres-

1. See Wickes's letter above on Feb. 19.
2. The draft has been extensively rewritten, but in its final form differs only inconsequentially from the ALS.

sant à vous marquer, je me suis contenu, de peur d'être importun. J'espere que Mr. Franklin jouit de sa retraite en parfaite santé, et qu'il aura le loisir de m'écrire de là plus amplement, comme il me l'a promis. J'espere aussi que la santé de Mr. Deane est parfaite, et que la multitude des affaires ne l'accable pas.

J'ai écrit à Amsterdam, pour être averti lorsqu'il partira un vaisseau pour l'Amérique; en attendant j'ai souscrit pour la Gazette françoise de Leide, pour la leur envoyer. Ils me demandent aussi des papiers Anglois; mais il y en a tant, que je ne sais lequel choisir; je me rappelle seulement qu'une de mes connoissances tenoit autrefois le *London Evening post*, et devoit payer pour cela au Maître de poste à peu près 5 guinées ou 5 Livres sterling. Mr. Franklin saura cela mieux que moi; et j'attends ses ordres sur le choix.

Si Mr. Lee est encore avec vous, Messieurs, ayez la bonté de lui présenter mes respects, mes voeux pour sa conservation, et pour avoir quelquefois de ses bonnes nouvelles.

Ce n'est pas sans de fortes raisons, Messieurs, que je vous ai priés de ne mettre sur le couvert de vos Lettres que le seul nom de Mr.—*Mr. De Visme Marchand de Vin à Leide*, et de ne mettre mon nom que sur la Lettre enfermés dans le couvert. Car, depuis le passage ici de Mr. Carmichael sur-tout, je suis fort suspect à vos ennemis en ce pays. Le Juif Pinto raconte par-tout que je suis en relation intime avec les Américains, et initié dans tous leurs secrets. J'ai déjà marqué à Mr. Deane que deux, au moins, de ses Lettres avoient été ouvertes; j'avois soupçonné que cela s'étoit fait en france; mais on peut aussi l'avoir fait à La H. Après tout, les discours du Juif ne m'inquieteroient pas. Mais, ce qui est plus sérieux, c'est que l'Ambassadeur de vos ennemis s'est entretenu de moi, l'un des derniers jours de Cour, avec le Grand-Pensionaire, qu'il a prononcé plusieurs fois mon nom et que le Grand-Pensionaire lui a dit *chut*, en lui faisant remarquer qu'ils étoient écoutés par quelqu'un qui me connoissoit.[3] Ce n'est pas que je craigne que vos

3. William Carmichael, on his commercial mission to Prussia the previous autumn, had spent a month in the Netherlands: *Deane Papers*, I, 311–12, 351. For Pinto see above, XXII, 410 n. The Grand Pensionary of Holland, Pieter Van Bleiswijk, held a position that made him, next to the Stadholder, one of the most powerful figures in the United Provinces; the British Am-

ennemis m'attaquent ouvertement en ce pays; ils n'ont pas des preuves contre moi suffisantes pour cela; mais outre que vos lettres risquent d'être ouvertes et perdues pour moi, si mon nom y paroît, ils peuvent avoir la bassesse de vouloir me nuire et perdre dans la vocation qui a fait jusqu'ici ma ressource en ce pays, où la Cour est si étroitement liée avec eux, et où les plus riches rentiers sont si fort intéressés dans leurs fonds publics. Je renoncerois assurément avec joie à cette vocation précaire et désagréable, pour consacrer le reste de mes jours uniquement au service des Etats unis Américains, en ce pays-ci, en France auprès de Vous, Messieurs, par-tout ailleurs où il le faudroit. Mais vous aimerez sans doute mieux me voir dans le cas de pouvoir vous obéir au moment que vous m'appelleriez, que réduit à vous demander de m'occuper, dans le temps où je vous serois peut-être plus à charge qu'utile. Ce n'est donc point par pusillanimité, mais par discrétion pour vous, Messieurs, que j'évite de me compromettre ici; à tout autre égard je voudrois que toute la terre sût combien je me trouve honoré de la confiance et des ordres du Congrès.

Mr. Franklin m'exhorte à avoir bon courage, comme lui et Mr. Deane. J'admire leur fortitude, et ferai mon possible pour l'imiter. Vos Lettres, mes respectables amis, m'aideront beaucoup en cela. C'est un malheur pour moi d'être excessivement sensible aux désastres de mes amis; mais, d'un autre côté, si je l'étois moins, je ne les aimerois pas tant: ainsi, à tout prendre, je préfere encore cette anxiété, où j'ai du moins la douceur d'aimer, à l'ennui d'une apathie où je n'aimerois rien.

On ne parle ici que des cargaisons considérables, de tabac sur-tout, que le Congrès envoie en France. S'il pensoit à faire de-même en ce pays, je sollicite pour en avoir la factorie, avec un ami intime que j'ai à Rotterdam, qui est parfaitement au fait de la maniere dont il faut s'y prendre, tant pour la vente de ces cargaisons, que pour les retours. Les deux articles capitaux seroient le *tabac* et le *ris*, et nous devrions, autant que la chose seroit possible, les avoir seuls en ce pays, au moins

---

bassador, Sir Joseph Yorke, also exercised great influence. See Jan W. S. Nordholt, *The Dutch Republic and American Independence* (Herbert H. Rowen, trans.; Chapel Hill, N.C., and London, [1982]), pp. 15, 21.

de la part et pour le compte du Congrès. Il faudroit pour cet effet 4 Vaisseaux, bons et fins voiliers, Capitaines intelligents, allertes et sûrs, qui allassent et vinssent continuellement selon les directions dont on conviendroit. Un tel commencement pourroit avoir les suites les plus avantageuses et les plus importantes, à plus d'un égard. Une navigation, un commerce, un crédit, des ressources de tout genre &c, multipliés pour le Congrès, &c, &c. Cela mérite, Messieurs, que vous y pensiez. Ayez la bonté de m'en dire votre sentiment en réponse. Je vous aime, honore et respecte bien sincerement, Messieurs mes chers et dignes Amis Votre très humble et très devoué serviteur

ST. JEAN.[4]

Notations: St. Jean 25 fevr. 77 / 25 Feby. 1777

The Farmers General: Memorandum for the American Commissioners

AD:[5] American Philosophical Society; copy: Archives du Ministère des affaires étrangères

Du 25 fevrier 1777.

La proposition déja faite aux Fermiers généraux d'expédier des navires chargés de marchandises pour le Congrès et rapporter des Tabacs en retour, ne peut quant à présent leur convenir.

Ils s'en tiennent à celle qui leur a été faite le 12 de ce mois de la part de MM. Les plenipotentiaires du Congrès de leur livrer rendue en France une quantité de Tabac à des prix convenus au moyen de l'avance qui seroit faite au Congrès de 2,000,000 *l.t.*.

Les fermiers Généraux ont accepté cette proposition par leur mémoire du 14. Ils ont offert un prix qu'ils estiment raisonable.

C'est à cette offre que MM. Les plenipotentiaires doivent

4. Dumas had been using this alias since at least the previous autumn: *Deane Papers*, I, 371.

5. In Paulze's hand and in reply to the commissioners' memorandum of the previous day, which is embedded in Alexander's draft.

une réponse et les fermiers généraux l'attendent depuis douze Jours.

From Amelia Barry ALS: American Philosophical Society

Tunis 25th. Feb. 1777

While my Dear Paternal Friend is on this Globe and there is the shadow of a possibility of my letters reaching him duty, love and the strongest inclination impel me to trouble him with them and now he is removed from the scene of horror it is with real joy I take up the pen to tell him that no event of my past life gave me more pleasure than to hear of his safe arrival in France: but as all human happiness must be defective mine upon this occasion has received a considerable alloy by a report that you have not my Dear Sir, retired for the remainder of your life to a Country which knows and reveres your worth but are gone upon the business of the United Colonies. Tis now 3 years since you told me you would retire from publick life[6] and I was happy to read your resignations in the English Papers for I have searched and caused my acquaintance to search every gazette foreign and domestic in order to obtain from time to time some accts. of the dear Friend whose fond affection for me in the dawn of my life and kindness to me in the maturer part of it forever annexes to his very name, in my mind, sensations I have only known for my Father. Condescend then my dear Doctor to devote one quarter of an hour to your Amelia upon the reciept of this and satisfy her in the following particulars viz.

Whether you have brought my honored Mama and Mrs. Beache and her Babies with you?[7] Whether you are upon business or realy (as I hope) retired from an ungrateful world? If upon business when you think to leave Europe?

6. Either in a missing letter or when BF and Mrs. Stevenson exchanged dinners with her and her family in 1773: above, xx, 383–4.

7. "Mama" was her godmother, DF, of whose death she had not yet heard. This is Amelia's first surviving letter to BF since her marriage, but in 1774 he had forwarded to DF two earlier ones that are now lost: above, xxi, 205, 247.

Whether you have heared if my old Friend Mrs. Strettell of Philada. be living?[8] I make no inquiries further than of the health of Governor Franklin as the duties of his employment must oblige him to remain in America. And now pardon me my Dear Sir for giving you so much trouble and presuming to exact one moment of your time: but if you knew how anxious I am to be satisfied in the above particulars I am convinced you would most chearfully oblige me.

We have entertained thoughts of placing our little Amelia in a Convent in France for a few years as no advantage of Education can be procured here but thought not to send her 'till the Summer after next however if you should in the course of the approaching Summer visit the South of France I will take that time for conducting her thither in person and see you my dear Sir once more! I am sure you would be glad to see me would not you Sir? and Mr. Barry I assure you consents to my going provided I am likely to see you. Should you as I ardently wish be induced upon any occasion to go towards Marseilles let me know when you expect to be there.

As the letters I did myself the honor of writing after my arrival at Tunis may have miscarried I am to inform you Sir, that in May, 74 I was blessed with a fine little Girl who is called Philotesia Jannetta.[9] Our Consul had the honor (by my desire) to represent you my revered Friend as Sponcer. She is realy beautiful and her capacity at acquiring every thing we teach her surpasses imagination, but she is Doctor Franklin's God-daughter, and presents her dutiful compliments to you Sir.

I last March had the addition of an other Girl to my family[1] who with her brother and sisters are very well as is Mr. Barry

8. She was. Philotesia, Robert Strettell's widow, died in 1782: Charles P. Keith, *The Provincial Councillors of Pennsylvania* ... (Philadelphia, 1883), pp. 198–9 of second pagination; *PMHB*, 1 (1877), 241 n. We know nothing about the friendship except that it was close enough so that Amelia named her second daughter after the old lady; see the next note.

9. We said earlier, on the basis of church records cited in a secondary work, that the baby was Philolesia (XXI, 247 n); the error must have resulted from faulty transcription or a mistake in the records.

1. Henrietta: Lawrence H. Gipson, *Lewis Evans* ... (Philadelphia, 1939), p. 80 n.

who bids me tender you his best respects and congratulations on your happy removal from the seat of War.

Adieu my Dear Sir! Love me ever as I shall you whilst I can subscribe to that truth the name of your ever-obliged and most devoted   A. BARRY

Be pleased to direct to me under cover to Lewis Hameken Esqr. Tunis to the care of Monr Ployart Danish Consul Marseilles

From John Bradford[2]   ALS: American Philosophical Society

Sir   Boston 25th. Feby 1777

I have the Honour to transmit you this by Capt. John Adams, who goes express by order of Congress with dispatches for the Honble. Commissrs. at the Court of France, with orders to deliver them himself. The Secret Committee were desirous of making as valuable a Remittance as might be, to put the schooner in a set of Ballast, But it happens we have no Oil, pot Ash, or any other Article at market, which we usually send to the french Market. I have ship'd a hundred Tierces excellent Salmon, about three tuns Curriers Oil and a tun pot ash to the Address of Messrs. Pliarne Penet & Co. who are to advise with Wm. Lee and Thos. Morris Esqrs. if in Nants in the disposal of the small Cargo.[3]

The Board of War here have desired to have some Goods sent from France on freight, and I have given the Capt. Orders, if the Articles ship'd, be not sufficient to put her in a proper set of Ballast, to take in as much on the account of this state as will answer that purpose.[4]

The Agreeable Newes of your Arrival at the Court of France diffused a Joy throughout this Continent. May it please an

2. The Boston prize agent: above, XXII, 533 n. BF's reply is below, May 1.

3. See the note on the secret committee to the commissioners above, Feb. 18.

4. For Adams' mission see the Mass. Council to the commissioners below, Feb. 27. Bradford's letter of instructions to the Captain is in *Naval Docs.*, VII, 1293; it did not cover the orders he refers to, nor are they mentioned in the board's minutes in the Mass. Arch.

Indulgent providence to Confirm your health, that you may in the evening of Life render your Country as important Services, as you have rendered the World heretofor.[5]

You will see by the papers sir that ever since the 25th. Decr. we have been Gaining advantages of the Enemy, and its beyond doubt they are in miserable plight. General How has Staind and blasted his Character for ever, by Cruelly treating his prisoners but such is the Generosity of Americans we dont retaliate. I have the honour to be with the most profound Respects Sir Your most obedient and most Humble Servant

JN. BRADFORD

I have the pleasure to Acquaint you that family Connections here are well as is your friend Doctor Cooper. I Rejoyce that the Honble. Mr. Lee is with you, am Glad he has come out from among them.[6]

The Honble Benj Franklin Esqr.

Addressed: The Honble. Doctor Franklin / at / Paris

Notation: Bradford Boston 25 feb. 77.

From ———— Guiraut l'Aîné[7]

ALS: American Philosophical Society

⟨Bordeaux, February 25, in French: I consigned some vinegar to Dublin on the *Barbara*, Capt. Welsh. She was captured and taken into Lorient by an American ship, I have just learned, and is being held there.[8] I have the right as a Frenchman to repossess my merchandise, and ask you to have it released to the holder of my power of attorney, or to be reimbursed for its value according to the invoice that I am sending.⟩

---

5. The news of BF's arrival appeared in the *Boston Gaz.*, Feb. 10, 1777.
6. *I. e.*, left England; Lee is of course Arthur, not William.
7. A partner in an old and distinguished mercantile house in Bordeaux.
8. This assertion is baffling. We have found no record of the *Barbara* at this time; she was captured by a privateer two months later, and recaptured the following day: *Naval Docs.*, VIII, 799–800.

The American Commissioners: Memorandum for the Farmers General[9]
AD (draft):[1]American Philosophical Society

Ce 26 Fevrier 1777

Les Plenipotentiares du Congrés, apres une Deliberation maturée, ne peuvent pas accepter le Prix offert par les Fermiers Generaux, ni faire aucune autre changement dans leur derniere Propositition.

Arthur Lee to Franklin and Silas Deane

ALS: American Philosophical Society; copy: Morristown National Historical Park

Dear Sirs   Victoria,[2] Feby. 26th 1777.

I am thus far safe on my journey, which by the spur of six pistoles more I am to finish two days sooner than was at first agreed. Therefore if no accident happens, I shall reach my destination on the 6th. of next month.

In the Committee's Letter of the 23d Ocr. to me, it is said we are to negotiate with *other Nations agreable to certain plans and Instructions transmitted to Mr. D.*[3] I have none with me, nor do I remember to have seen any, but those which relate expressly to France, and that plan has been already transmitted where I am going. Nothing is more likely than that I shall be asked, what I have to propose particularly relative to this meridian. This question was put to us on our first visit to *Comprenez-vous.*[4] But the same answer will not serve here. Therefore I must entreat you to favor me with your ideas upon this particular. What alterations you think woud be proper in that plan when applyd to this country. It is best to be prepared for every favorable moment that may offer. This must plead my pardon for urging as speedy an Answer, as possible.

9. In reply to the farmers' communication of the previous day.
1. In BF's hand.
2. Vitoria, in northeastern Spain.
3. The plans and instructions were from Congress: above, XXII, 629–30.
4. "Meridian" in the old sense of region or part of the world; "*Comprenez-vous,*" we assume, was Aranda.

It woud greive me to be put to the alternative, of letting a favorable opportunity pass unembracd; or hazarding a measure, of so much moment to the public, upon my weak judgment, and very limited information.[5] With my best wishes for your health and success and begging to be remembered kindly to our friends I have the honor to be, Dear Sirs, with the greatest esteem, your most Obedient Servant   ARTHUR LEE

P.S. I write in my Chaise, from which I dare not get out for fear of the civilities of certain four-leggd Animals; which are as troublesome here, as those of the twoleggd ones are elsewhere. Dr. F. will be so good as not to forget the Covers of my Letters in future.

Addressed: To / The Honble / Benjamin Franklin & Silas Deane Esqrs

Notations: Mr Lee / Arthur Lee to BF and SD. Victoria 26. Feb 1777.

Lambert Wickes to the American Commissioners

ALS: American Philosophical Society

Gentlemen   LOrient Febry. 26th. 1777
  I hav this Day Recd. very Extraordinary Oorders from The Intendant of This port Demanding me to Leav this port in 24 Hours he Says This Order is Given in Consequence of A possitiv Order Recd, this Day from the Minester At Parris. I Asked Liberty To heav Down my Ship and Repair her on my Arrival but it has never Bin Granted.[6] On being told That I mus pos-

---

5. Lee was put to this second alternative, and drew up his own alterations; they are embodied in his plan, dated March, 1777, in the *Lee Family Papers*, roll 3, frames 149–54.
6. The "Minester" was Sartine, for whom see above, XXII, 453 n. He ordered the *Reprisal* to sail immediately unless the necessity of careening her could be demonstrated, and warned that she would be liable to capture if she cruised off the French coast; the King, he added in his own hand, intended to fulfil his treaty obligations to the letter. Archives de la marine, B[4] cxxxiv, fol. 189.

sitivly Depart in 24 Hours I Told the Intendant that it Was not in my Power to Depart in so Short A time as my Ship Was not fitt To procead to America Without heaving Down and Repairing and Beg'd he Would Send Carpenters Of to Examine the Ship and Take Thier Report Accordingly. This he Consented to and Sent them off they Return'd and told the Intendant That they thought It highly Nessesary to Carreane and Repair the Ship Before Shee Departed for America he then possitivly Refused to Grant me Liberty to Refitt Unless the Carpenter and Caulker Would Sighn A Certifycate that We Should be in Emminent Danger of Loosing the Ship If not Repaired. This Certifycate they Could not Sign, As they had not bin to Sea in the Ship and it Was not in thier power to See the Ships Bottom Without heaving her Down. He then told me I Must Depart Immediately. We are Now takeing our Water on bord and Geting Ready to procead but Shall not be Able to Sail before Friday the 28th. in the Evening and Am in hopes of I Shal have the pleasure of Receaving your orders and Instrucktions on this hed by that time but If Oblig'd to Depart Sooner or before I Recv. your orders I Shall Run into Nantz and there Enter A protest and Ask Liberty to heav Down and Repair Tho I Am Ordered by the Intendant no to go in to Any port in France. These are very Extraordinary orders and Such as I Little Exspected to Recv, in Frace. I Beg Leav to Congrattulate you on Our Late Suckces in America as I Am Informd We have Gained a Very Signal and Compleat vicktory Over our Enemies At Trentown. You'l See by my Declaration Made on my Arrival That I then mentioned my Ships being Leaky and beged Liberty To heav Down and Repair. If this favour Cannot be Granted as it is Absolutely Nessesary prior to my Departure I Should be Much Obliged If you Would forward your Dispaches as Soon and Send me of for America as Soon As possible. From Gentlemen Your most Oblig'd Humble Servant   LAMBT. WICKES

Addressed: To / The Honbl. Docktor Benjamin Franklin / At / Parris

Notation: Wickes 26 Feb. 77. L'Orient

From William Gordon[7] ALS: Historical Society of Pennsylvania

My Dear Sir   Jamaica Plain Feby 26. 1777

After having finished the enclosed I alterd my design, and concluded upon sending it under cover to you, with request that you would forward it to Great Britain by a safe conveyance:[8] if by the post via Holland, it may be best to put it under cover directed by an unknown hand, as the ministerial harpies at the London post office may have acquainted themselves with mine, or upon seeing such a quantity of writing may break it open. Wish it to get safe and soon to my friend: but have not sealed it that so you may read the contents, which must be done with allowance, it consisting much in chit chat, and not being originally intended for your inspection. There may be something new in it. I rejoy[ced in] hearing you had got safe to France. We are waiting and longing for the news of France's having de[clared wa]r against G B. Who would ever have thought thirty years back that America would have wi[shed for suc]h an event? How much in the dark are the wisest as to futurity! Dr. Cooper has married his dau[ghter to a] West India gentleman.[9] The Dr. is well; as are other friends. You will see what liberty I have ta[ken in ask]ing my correspondents to convey their letters to you, in hopes of having them forwarded by your favou[r flattering?] myself it will not be disagreeable. Wishing you the best of blessings, and praying to be remembe[red in respect]ful manner to Mr. Dean and Mr. Lee, I remain Your sincere friend and very humble servant

WILLIAM GORDON

7. The first but not the last appearance in these volumes of the man who later won fame as an historian of the American Revolution. Gordon (1728–1807) was an English nonconformist clergyman who emigrated to America in 1770 and became minister of a church in Jamaica Plain, near Roxbury, Mass. He had recently begun to collect material for his history, which was not published until 1788. *DAB; DNB.*

8. Undoubtedly material to be forwarded to Richard Price, with whom he had already been in correspondence; see his letter of Sept. 12, 1775, in the APS. Another packet for Price went with Gordon's letter to BF below, March 21.

9. Joseph Hixon; see Cooper to BF below, March 28.

391

The American Commissioners to Joseph Hynson

Copy: Yale University Library

This letter was written to a man already committed to betraying the commissioners. Their letter to Nicholson above, January 26, instructed him to buy a cutter at Boulogne or Calais and send her to Le Havre; if he failed to find a suitable one he was to try Dover or Deal. He went instead to London, met his friend Hynson there, and obtained a cutter, which was dispatched to Le Havre. While she was being loaded with the provisions, cargo, and arms that this letter mentions, the British were making arrangements with Hynson to intercept her and her dispatches at sea.[1]

Sir   Paris Feby: 27th. 1777

This by Monsr. Eyries I hope will find you at Havre with the Cutter: which you are to equip with all possible expedition for a Voyage.[2] Monsr. Eyries will supply you with the necessarys, and you will take his advice in equiping. It is proposed that she should proceed for America as soon as possible; Mr. Eyries proposes fixing eight or Ten Brass pieces of three or four pounders with other necessaries for defence against boats &c. You will be the best Judge what is suitable for her, and Mr: Eyries will be able to procure it in a manner the least liable to rumor or objections from Goverment. We shall expect from you on the Receipt of this, an account of the state of the cutter, what arming is necessary, and what goods she can carry, beside her provisions, without impeding her passage which is the first object. This we shall want to be informed of, as soon as possible immediately after which, particular Instructions with your Dispatches, shall be sent you express. You will take care that every thing be conducted with the greatest Secresy, and the choice of your Men requires your attention as several Instances of mutiny have lately happen'd. When you have consulted with Mr: Eyries and made your general arrangements, it may perhaps be as well for you to come up to Paris, leaving the Exicution in the hands of Mr:

---

1. Clark, *Wickes*, pp. 164–73; *Naval Docs.*, VIII, 568–9.
2. Hugues Eyriès (1731–84) was Beaumarchais' representative at Le Havre: Morton, *Beaumarchais correspondance*, III, 31 n.

Eyries, on the whole I think this will be the most sure mode of proceeding, as you can personally explain what may not be so proper to trust to writing, and not so easyly express'd. The sooner you can come up the better, as in case of putting in any goods by way of Ballast, the particulars ought to be fixed early. I am for Dr: Franklin and Self Sir your most obedient Very Humble Servant   SILAS DEANE

Capt Hynson

Addressed: To / Capt: Joseph Hynson / To care of Monsr Eyries

Notation: S: Dean to Capt Hynson. Paris 27h. Feby: 1777

Georges Grand to the American Commissioners

ALS: Connecticut Historical Society

Messieurs   Amsterdam le 27 Fevrier 1777

J'arrivai avant hier soir en bonne santé, avec mon Compagnon de Voyage, malgré les mauvais chemins et la difficulté des passages. Nous avons commencé à visiter les Chantiers, et nous allons tout de suite, entrer en conférences avec les meilleurs Constructeurs, pour traitter et faire metre la main à l'ouvrage; il ne manque ni de matériaux ni de bons ouvriers; M.B. parait tres content de la facon de travailler qu'il trouve bien supêrieure à celle de Françe.[3]

La nouvelle de l'arrivée de Votre Capitaine, au Port Louis, avec 5 Prises dont un Paketboat de Lisbonne, fait icy beaucoup de bruit;[4] si vous etes dans le cas d'envoyer icy par Vaisseaux Français, ou autres, les Cargaisons que Vous ne pourrés pas vendre en Françe, Vous pouvés compter que ma Maison, en tirera tout le parti possible, et Vous en rendra bon Compte.

J'ay mis ordre que Vous recevrés un Exemplaire de la Gazette de Leyden, à l'addresse de mon frere; et il importe à vos

---

3. See the notes on the agreement with Boux above, Feb. 12.
4. The news that the *Reprisal* had arrived with prizes appeared in the *Gaz. de Leyde* on March 4.

Interets que Vous m'envoyés toutes les bonnes nouvelles que Vous recevrês pour les faire insêrer dans nos Papiers Hollandais et Français, pour soutenir Votre Credit, et entretenir les bonnes dispositions des esprits dans ce Paÿs,[5] que je trouve plus favorables à Votre cause que cy devant, ce qui me fait le plus grand plaisir.

Il est fort à souhaiter que le célèbre et respectable Docteur, se détermine à venir le mois prochain, réchauffer par sa présence, et animer l'Interet que l'on prend à Vos affaires; je suis persuadé qu'il reussira à tous égards, et qu'il pourra trouver un moment favorable pour lever de l'argent chez nos Capitalistes à des conditions raisonnables.[6]

Le General Yorck vient de présenter un Mêmoire, dont je tacherai de Vous envoyer la Copie, il est si violent qu'il à aigri les Esprits et j'espère qu'on luy répondra avec la fermeté convenable; d'ailleurs on m'assure que l'on armera de nouveaux Vaisseaux de Guerre et que la résolution sera prise la semaine prochaine de faire respecter notre Pavillon sans s'embarrasser des menaçes Britanniques.[7] J'ay l'honneur d'etre avec le dévouement le plus sincêre et le plus respectueux Messieurs Votre tres humble et tres obeissant serviteur   GRAND

Je vous prie de m'informer de ce que vous aurés fait avec les fermiers Generaux, pour que j'ecrive en conséquense.

Addressed: To / The Honbles Benjamin Francklin / & Silas Deane / Paris.

Notation: Sir George Grand Amsterdam 27 Febry. 1777

---

5. Dumas gave the same advice to the commissioners in his letter below, March 11.

6. The commissioners intended to send either BF or Deane to the Netherlands; see their letter to the committee of secret correspondence above, Feb. 6.

7. On Feb. 21 Sir Joseph Yorke, the British Minister, delivered a brusque memorandum protesting the American use of St. Eustatius and the salute given there to an American warship, and threatening unspecified reprisals. The Dutch refused to be bullied, and their reply a month later was firm. Daniel A. Miller, *Sir Joseph Yorke and Anglo-Dutch Relations, 1774–1780* (The Hague and Paris, 1970), pp. 51–3.

The Massachusetts Council to the American Commissioners[8]

LS and copy:[9] American Philosophical Society; copy: Library of Congress

State of Massachusetts-Bay Council Chamber

Gentlemen   Boston, February 27th. 1777

We have lately received from the Secret Committee of Congress Seven Letters addressed to You, and they request that We would forward them by the quickest sailing Vessel to France. In Consequence of which We desired the Continental Agent here with all possible dispatch, to prepare one of the Continental Vessels for Sailing. She is now ready and is Commanded by Capt. John Adams, whom We have directed immediately upon his Arrival at Nantz to repair by Post to Paris and to deliver you the Letters himself and there receive your Answer, and be Governed by your directions touching his return, and the Port he is to come to. We wish they may arrive in Safety.[1] If the Captain should be directed to return to any of the Ports in this State, We shall expeditiously forward to Congress any dispatches you may commit to our Care. By the last Accounts from Congress We have the Pleasure to acquaint you, that they were more firmly United than ever, and that in their measures they were decisive, determinate and very Spirited. They have some time since Resolved, that Eighty Eight Battalions, should be raised for the defence of the Con-

---

8. Thomas Cushing, Sr., and David Sewall were the drafting committee: Council Records (State House, Boston) XX, 301.

9. The copy was at the head of the council's next letter below, March 31.

1. In early February Robert Morris, for the committee of secret correspondence, and the secret committee sent dispatches to the Mass. Council to be forwarded to France; Morris inquired for a vessel to carry them. On Feb. 17 the Council wrote him that John Bradford, the prize agent, was preparing a ship, and on March 11 informed the secret committee that the dispatches had gone on it ten days before. Mass. Arch., CXCVI, 241, 288; Smith, *Letters*, VI, 202–6. The ship was the schooner *Lynch*, commanded by John Adams, "as smart and as capable a man" according to Bradford, "as any in the state." *Naval Docs.*, VII, 1241. For Adams' voyage and subsequent adventures see William B. Clark, *George Washington's Navy* . . . (Baton Rouge, La., [1960]), pp. 197–200.

tinent the Men to serve for three Years or during the War. Fifteen of these Battalions are to be raised by this State, as their Quota; the Assembly are taking every measure in their Power to raise them, and hope We shall be able to Compleat them in Season. The Congress have since agreed to raise Sixteen more Battalions, and have Impowered General Washington to appoint the Officers. General Howe in Novr. and December last knowing that the Time, for which our Troops were engaged was near expiring, and that they would be most of them upon the return home, improved this opportunity suddenly to throw his Troops into the Jerseys. This manœuvre threw the People of that State into a Panic, their Militia were scatter'd and could not be rallied. This Enabled the Enemy to Traverse the whole extent of the Jerseys without much molestation, and obliged General Washington to retire to the other side of the River Deleware. But Thanks to Heaven, who has remarkably interposed in our Favour, the Scene has greatly changed, for General Washington having received a reinforcement, in the Night of the 25th. of December repassed the Deleware, attacked a large Detachment of the Enemy's Troops at Trenton, and took most of them Prisoners: and soon after when a large Body of the Enemy made an attempt to dislodge him from Trenton, He in the Night stole a March upon them passed them, and attacked and drove a large detachment of the Enemy from Princeton, who had began their March to join the Body at Trenton. He killed several hundreds and took many Prisoners and a Number of Waggons. The Enemy in the Jerseys are now Confined to Brunswick and Amboy and are said to be about Ten thousand Strong. We hear of small Skirmishes every Day in which our People have the advantage. We understand that great Dissentions and disputes have arisen between the British Troops and the Hessians: For further particulars relative to the movements, operation and State of our Army and that of the Enemy, We must refer you to the Public Prints, which We herewith Transmit. We Esteem ourselves happy, that Gentlemen of such Accomplishments and Abilities have been appointed to represent this Continent, at this Important Crisis, at the Court of France. We sincerely Wish you Success in your negotiation, and from your well known attachment to the Cause of America and from the Zeal Activity and Vigilance you have discovered in her Service, We promise ourselves that We shall soon experience the happy fruits of your exertions. The Aid and Assistance of France in this Contest in some way or other is highly necessary. We may otherwise by a further Accession of foreign Troops be overborne. It is greatly probable that unless a powerful diversion prevents, the Enemy the ensuing Summer will have in America as great a force as with all our exertions we can possibly cope with. We are under some apprehension of General Carletons Crossing the Lakes and attacking the Important post of Ticondaroga, and are forwarding Troops thither to Strengthen the Garrison. Some Warriors of the Six Nations have in the Course of this Week made us a friendly Visit and We have a good prospect of their Attachment to our Interest.[2]

The Indians likewise on the Eastern Frontiers of this State are Friendly, And We have reports, attended with some degree of Probability that the Mercenary Troops in Canada are at Variance with the British Troops there.

We have just now received a Letter from the Commanding Officer at Ticondaroga dated the 18th. instant, he writes "That Cumberland Bay in Lake Champlin was yet open, that two Frenchmen arrived there from Canada four days before who bring Intelligence of about One hundred Indians with a few Regulars being on their March for that Post, probably with a View of surprising some of our Parties: and further say that the Enemy are Posted as follows. Vizt.

150 at Montreal where General Frazer Commands
100 at La Prairie
200 at Chamillé under the now *Infamous* General Paoli[3]

2. Six chiefs of the Oneidas had come to Boston with a missionary, the Rev. Samuel Kirkland, and with credentials from Gen. Schuyler; they conferred with the Council and were sent on a tour of eastern Massachusetts and Rhode Island. Council Records, xx, 283, 287–92; Mass. Arch., cxcvi, 277.

3. How rumor brought the famous Corsican, Pasquale Paoli, to America in command of British troops we do not venture to guess. "Frazer" was Simon Fraser (d. 1777), a brigadier who had come to Canada in 1776 and was later killed in the Saratoga campaign: *DNB*.

550 at St. Johns including Sailors and Marines
300 at the Isle Aux Noix with a 12 Gun Redoubt
100 at Bojor Ville and
20 at Point au fair. The Remainder of the British Troops are billeted two or three in a House in the Vicinity of Montreal and Chamillé; and the Germans are all Cantoned in and below Quebec."[4]

By Resolves of Congress transmitted to us, we observe you are empowered and requested to procure for the Continent among other things a great Number of Fire Arms. The Public Service requires they should be sent as expeditiously as possible, and that a Considerable part of them should be appropriated to the Use of this State: in which Case it will be needful that such part should be directed to be brought into some of our Ports.

By the Return of Capt. Adams and all other Opportunities, we should be glad to be favored with such Intelligence, and Information as you shall think the Public Service makes necessary to be Communicated. In the name, and behalf of the Council of the State of Massachusetts Bay I am with great Esteem Gentlemen Your most obedient humble Servant

JAMES BOWDOIN Presidt.[5]

The Honble Benjamin Franklin Silas Deane Arthur Lee Esqrs.

Addressed: To / The Honble Benja. Franklin, Silas Deane, & Arthur Lee Esqrs. / Commissioners from the United States of America to the / Court of France / Paris.

Notation: Feby 27 1777 Lettr. from State of Massachusetts Bay

Jonathan Williams, Jr., to the American Commissioners

ALS: American Philosophical Society

Gentlemen   Nantes Feb. 27. 1777.

That you may be able to judge of the Quality of the arms when remounted I have ordered one of each to be sent by the

---

4. Quoted from Anthony Wayne to the Council, Feb. 18, 1777, Mass. Arch., CXCVI, 242–4.

5. His days in office were numbered; he attended irregularly, and later in the year he resigned because of ill health: *DAB.*

messagerie[6] which will come directed to Mr. Carmichael in the same manner as the samples of those sent by the Mercury did. The workmen are constantly at Work upon the Ship, and Shipackers are also at Work on the Bales, all is going on as fast as possible. I have the Honour to be with great Respect Your most obedient Servant J. WILLIAMS

Mr. Lesterjate went away this morning to go on board his Ship which will sail the first Wind.[7]

The Honbl The Deputies of the United States.

Addressed: A Monsieur / Monsieur Franklin L L D / a l'Hotel d'Hambourg / Rue Jacob / a / Paris.

Notation: Mr Williams Nantes Febry. 27th 1777

From [Samuel Cooper] AL: American Philosophical Society

My dear Sir, Boston N.E. Feby 27. 1777

I wrote you some Time ago, acknowledging the Receit of your kind Letter dated from Philadelphia 25th Octr. last, the Day you embarqued for Europe, and read your affectionate Leave to all our Friends.[8] We often think and talk of you, and constantly follow you with our best Wishes. I have lately heard with particular Pleasure of your safe Arrival in France, where I know you meet with many Friends, and where all Orders of People will treat you as you deserve, and I can wish you Nothing better. May Heaven preserve your Life and Health for the Sake of your Country, for which I know your Wishes are at least equal to your Abilities:

"Oh! save my Country, Heaven, will be your last."

You have doubtless heard, before this can reach you, perhaps already, from those who can best inform you, of the happy

6. Turgot had recently reformed and centralized under the government the old system of transporting packages and travelers: Larousse, *Dictionnaire universel* under Messagerie.

7. See Lestarjette to BF above, under Dec. 15.

8. An extract from BF's farewell is above, XXII, 670. Cooper's acknowledgment has disappeared; this is the first extant letter in a transatlantic correspondence that continued until his death in 1783.

Change in the Face of our Affairs since the 26th of Decr. last.
When our Army was wasted greatly, when what remain'd was
upon the Point of Dissolution, the Time of Enlistment being
expir'd, when General Lee, upon whom we plac'd large Hopes
was snatch'd from us; when Washington, whose Prudence and
Firmness can never be too much applauded was driven with
his handful of Men thro the Jersies, beyond the Delaware,
when ev'ry Thing upon which the States depended for the
Winter's Defence seem'd to fail; then a kind Providence, in
whose Blessing, in so righteous a Cause, you express'd so
firm a Dependance, signally interpos'd on our Behalf. Washington was animated to form a great and daring Design, considering his Circumstances. He attack'd the conquering and
pursuing Army; He sav'd Philadelphia; He almost instantly
clear'd the West Jersies. He reviv'd the Spirits of the States,
tho they remain'd firm, at the most pressing Season, almost
beyond Example; Since which the British Forces and their
Auxiliaries have been coop'd up at Brunswick and Amboy by
scarcely any Thing more than a Militia inferior even in Numbers. Desertions from the Enemy are now frequent. They are
straitned for Provisions and Forage. Alarms and Fatigues and
Sickness have worn their Men, and impair'd their Number.
Frequent Skirmishes, in which we have constantly had the
advantage have done the same. A large foraging Party, that
lately ventur'd but a little way from Brunswick have been drove
back with Precipitation and considerable Loss. The States are
now engag'd in forming their new Army: There are Difficulties, but not we hope unsurmountable. Washington begins to
receive in considerable Numbers the new Levies. Those from
this Quarter that are first in readiness, march to Ticconderoga.
The Lake has not yet been frozen over, and it is believ'd we
are for the present safe on that Side. Will France let such an
opportunity for her own Advantage, slip out of her Hands?
Can Britain give her an Equivalent for the Independance of
these States? Will the House of Bourbon not exert itself to
prevent any more forreign Troops from coming to America?
Can we have no Men of War to open our Ports, and Trade,
and secure our most necessary Supplies? Will not France employ it's Influence in Canada, and on the Forreigners that are

here? Many of them have already mutinied at N: York, and are confin'd in Jayls and Guardships, or disarm'd, or very narrowly watch'd by Britons. We have Reports of the same kind from Canada.

Adieu my dear Sir, for having such short Warning of this Opportunity, I write in Hast and Fear of missing it. Remember me to any Friend you see where you now are. Ev'ry Blessing attend you. Pray write me. With the greatest Esteem and Attachment, ever Yours:

Addressed: The Honle: Benjn. Franklin Esqr. LLD / In Paris

Endorsed: Dr Cooper Boston Feb. 27. 1777.

From Jonathan Williams, Jr.

ALS: American Philosophical Society

Dear and honored Sir   Nantes Feb. 27. 1777

I recvd your obliging Favour by the post to day, too late to answer it with mine to the Deputies. I am happy that you approve of my desire to settle in france, and I intend to prosecute the Scheme with Vigour. As yet I know nothing of Bordeaux so of course must give the preference to Nantes[9] I am charmed with the place and like the people, besides I think its Situation excellent for Commerce, particularly for Exportation. Mr. Montaudouin has proposed a partnership with a young man who has money, and is acquainted with those local Circumstances which a Stranger can't be supposed to know at once; but I don't like young partnerships, I have seen too many unsuccessfull ones. I will however write you farther when I am a little better informed.

My principal Reason in writing this is to give our Countryman Mr. Jones an Opportunity of paying his Respects to you, he is going to amsterdam and you may want to convey Letters or papers thither. I think him trust worthy by all I have seen, and he seems warmly attached to our Cause; he is conected in a House at St. Eustatia.

9. He must be answering a letter now lost.

Mr. Morris and Mr. Penet have returned from L'orient. I understand they do not intend to send the packet. They must inform you the Reason for I am all in the dark.

By advice from L'orient it is certain that one or two English Frigates are cruising off this Coast. I am with the greatest Respect Your dutifull and affectionate Kinsman   J WILLIAMS

Addressed: A Monsieur / Monsieur Franklin LLD / a l'Hotel d'Hambourg / Rue Jacob. / a Paris.

From [J.] Hooper

[after February 27, 1777]   See page 100n

Lambert Wickes to the American Commissioners

ALS: American Philosophical Society

Gentlemen   LOrient February 28th, 1777
I this Day Recd. yours the 22end, Which Was very Exceptable. I Wrote you Last Week Concerning the Dispossial of Our prisoners Which Was Dischargd By possitiv order from The Intendant of this port Last Satd. the 22end. I Allso mentioned In my Last of the 26th, the Difficulties of Geting Liberty to Stay in This port to heav Down and Repair my Ship Which Was Absolutely Nessesary prior to Departure for America. As the Weather Was So bad that I Could not Get it Done at Nantz I Got the Intendant to Send the Carpenters of to Make a Second Survey on the Ship the 27th, When they Stayed 4 Hours on bord and On thier Return Signed a Certifycate that they thought The Ship Would be in Emminent Danger If Sent to See Without Carreanig and Repairing.[1] On

---

1. The commissioners' "Exceptable" letter of the 22nd is now missing. In it they told Wickes, he wrote the committee of secret correspondence on the 28th, that the government had ordered the *Reprisal* to leave at once "only to Stop the Clamour of the British Ambassador," and that they hoped she would be permitted to stay: *Naval Docs.*, VIII, 624. He then arranged for the carpenters' second survey, and before it he is said to have pumped water into the hold to simulate a leak: Stevens, *Facsimiles*, II, no. 182, p. 7.

their Signing and Delivering thier Certifycate the Intendant then granted me Liberty to Enter the port to Carrean and Repair. Our prizes is All Gone So that I am in hopes All Difficulties Are Now Remooved. As there is So many Difficulties Attending our Cruizing on the Coast of Europe I hope youl Think it Best to order me Home as Soon As possible. I Shall Submit this to your judgments and Chearfully Comply With your Determinations on this Head. I have had much truble hear but Am in hopes it is Now At an End. I Cannot Giv you the particulars of Our Tranceactions Concerning the prizes but Shall Refer you to Mr. Morris for that Information but Am in hopes You Will be Well Sattisfied With our proceadings and Conduct in this Business. Pleas Let Captn. Nicholson Know I Recd. his favr. of the 22end, but have not time to Answer it by this post. I Hope you'l Obtain Liberty for me to Remain in This port Tel it Sutes you to Order me out. The Count of Marepause may be fited and Got Ready for Sea in 20 or 30 Days At furthest. From Gentlemen your most Oblig'd Humble Servant   LAMBT. WICKES

To The Honbls Docktr Franklin Silias Dean

Addressed: To / The Honbl. Doctr. Benjamin Franklin / A / Parris

Notation: Capt Weekes l'Orient Feby 28. 77

Jonathan Williams, Jr., to the American
Commissioners   ALS: American Philosophical Society

Gentlemen   Nantes Feb. 28. 1777.
    I have the honour of your Favour of the 25 by Mr. Francis.[2] As I have but a moments time I must beg leave to refer you to tomorrows post for a more particular Answer, the principal intention of this is to inform you that Mr. Morris has sold four of the prizes (all except the packet Boat) Vessells Cargoes &c. &c. for about 90,000 Livres, all risque of reclaim and every

2. Francy.

403

difficulty to be the purchasers.[3] Mr. M. tells me he has recvd. the Bills for the amount and so finished the Business.

Mr. Francis setts off this afternoon for L'orient.

As Mr. Francis communicated his Business to me I have told him of the above Sale. I have the honor to be with great Respect Your most obedient Servant.   J WILLIAMS

From Richard Bache   ALS: American Philosophical Society

Dear Sir   Phila. 28th. February 1777

I did myself this Pleasure under date of the 5th. Instant. Yesterday, via New England we had the agreeable Tidings of your safe arrival at Nantz, by some Vessel arrived at Newbury from Bourdeaux; tho' we have no Letters from you, the account comes so strait, and the news is so agreeable, that we are determined to believe it.[4] We have had a variety of reports circulated respecting you; since you left us, first you were taken and carried into Newyork, then you were taken off Bermudas, and carried to England, and a thousand such idle stories invented by Tories, to give your friends pain if possible. The Enemy still keep possession of Brunswick, they have sent for part of the Troops which went to Rhode Island, to reinforce them; part of the Hessian Troops have been mutinying, and we are confidently told that two hundred of them had laid a plan to desert, but it was discovered too soon, this however presages well. Last Sunday we had a smart Skirmish with a foraging party of about 2,000 of the Enemy, and drove them back with considerable loss, they are greatly distressed for forage for their horses, and small parties will not answer their purpose to obtain it. Since the reinforcement joined them from Rhode Island, it has been generally thought and believed that they intend pushing for this Place once more, but I think they

3. This provision accorded with the commissioners' advice to Wickes in their letter above, under Feb. 25. The packet was soon sold as well, to Bérard Frères; all were promptly renamed: Clark, *Wickes*, p. 140.

4. BF's arrival was known in Massachusetts weeks before (see the note on Bradford to BF above, Feb. 25) and was reported in the *Pa. Evening Post* of Feb. 27; the details about Bordeaux and Newburyport did not appear until March 11, in *Dunlaps's Pa. Packet*.

must wait 'till the roads get better, and by that time, I am in hopes we shall be better prepared to receive them. By the best accounts, they have lost upwards of 3,000 Men since Christmas day, without including what may have died a natural death. I cannot think that their whole force now exceeds 12,000, I mean under Howe, if so, we shall soon be a match for them by Land; and I hope that by an Alliance with the French we shall soon be a match for them by Sea.

Sally has wrote you and Benny by this opportunity. I heard from her yesterday, all well, my Love to Benny and Temple and believe me ever Honored Sir Your affectionate Son

RICH: BACHE

Dr Franklin

Addressed: The Honble. / Dr Franklin / One of the Commissioners from the / United States of America, at the / Court of France Paris

From Thomas Cushing, Sr.[5]

ALS and copy[6]: American Philosophical Society

Sir   Boston Feby: 28. 1777.

I embrace this opportunity by Capt. Adams to congratulate you upon your safe arrival in France. It gave me a sinsible Pleasure when I heard that the Congress had appointed a Gentleman of your Abilities Influence and Character one of the Commissioners of the United States of America at the Court of France. I sincerely wish you success in your Negotiations and doubt not this Country will soon realize the happy fruits and Effects of this Appointment. The aid and assistance of the Court of France will be much needed the ensuing Summer especially if Great Britain should send any considerable rein-

5. This is the first extant letter in two years from the former speaker of the Mass. House of Representatives. He had served for a time in Congress, and was now active in providing ships for the navy: *Sibley's Harvard Graduates*, XI, 389–92.

6. The copy, unsigned and differing in minor details, was attached to Cushing's letter below, March 31.

forcement to Genl. Howe. As for news I beg leave to refer you to the Letter and news papers sent you by the Council, which renders it entirely needless for me to add any thing upon this Subject. Your Freinds Dr. Winthrop, and Dr. Cooper are well, Mr. Jona. Williams and Family are all well, they send their best respects.[7]

I shall always be glad to hear of your Welfare, and as we now seldom get any News from England, any Intelligence from your part of the World will be very Acceptable, Whenever Your other Engagements will permit. My most respectful Complements to Mr. Dean and Dr. Lee. I have the Honor to be with the greatest Esteem and regard your most humble Servant   THOMAS CUSHING

Honble Benjamin Franklin Esqr.

Notation: T. Cushing Boston 28 Feb. 77

From Jacques-Alexandre Gourlade

ALS: American Philosophical Society

Monsieur   L'orient le 28 fevrier 1777
J'ai remis aujourduy a M. Lambert Wickes la lettre que vous m'avez adressé pour luy vous trouverez cy Inclus sa reponse.[8] Si en quelques choses Je pouvois vous être util disposé de celuy qui est avec respect Monsieur Votre tres humble serviteur
                                    GOURLADE

M. Bn. Francklin / a / Paris

Addressed: A Monsieur / Monsieur Francklin / A Paris

Notation: Gourlade 28 Feb. 77

From de Sparre

February 28, 1777   See page 301n

7. The Council's letter of the previous day is above. Cooper and Winthrop sent not only respects but also letters, on Feb. 27 and 28 respectively; Williams also wrote, but not until March 29.

8. The commissioners' missing letter of Feb. 22 and Wickes' reply above, Feb. 28.

From John Winthrop[1]

ALS: American Philosophical Society

Dear Sir,   Cambridge NE. Febry 28. 1777

I do most sincerely congratulate you on your safe arrival in France. Tho' nothing ever gave me greater pleasure than to hear you had undertaken a Commission in which America is so deeply interested, and which could not well have been executed without you, yet I must own I was in great pain for your safety in so long a voyage, and exposed, as you were, to peculiar danger from the enemy. The firmness of mind and ardent love of your Country, manifested on this and every other occasion, must endear you to every American, and lay this Continent under obligations that can never be forgot. May the same gracious Providence, which has hitherto protected you, succeed all your exertions in the glorious cause of liberty. We promise our selves every thing from your abilities and influence in the Court of France; and hope they will persue such measures as will effectually disconcert the plans of our enemies. Certainly, they never had so fair an opportunity of depressing and weakening their great rival. This seems to be the critical moment for them to step in; and, if they act from national views and with their usual policy, I should think they would not let it slip.

I have taken the liberty to inclose a letter to Dr. Price, upon a particular affair that he is solicitous about, and beg you will be so good as to forward it.[2]

I frequently entertain my self with the pleasing hope, that you will e'er long return to America, and have the high satisfaction of seeing your Country flourish, under your auspices, in freedom and independence; and that the circle here, whom you have honored with your friendship, will again be happy in your company.

The Council write you, by this conveyance,[3] so fully on the

1. Winthrop's correspondence with BF, like Cushing's, seems to have lapsed for some time; this is the first extant letter from him since March 28, 1775.

2. We know nothing about the particular affair, but assume that it was scientific. BF forwarded the letter, as mentioned in his reply below of May 1, 1777.

3. Above, Feb. 27.

present situation of our affairs, that I have nothing to add. With every sentiment that gratitude and respect can inspire, I am, Dear Sir Your most faithful humble servant

JOHN WINTHROP

Dr Franklin

Addressed: Hon. Benjamin Franklin Esqr / at / Paris

Notation: J. Wintrop Camb. N. E. Feb. 28. 77.

Reports from Chaumont and ——— on Uniforms

[February, 1777?]   See page 315n

From the Duc de Chaulnes[4]

AL: American Philosophical Society

Saturday evening [after February 28, 1777[5]]

The Duke's of chaulnes best compliments to Mister francklin; since every day of thise Weeck is convenient to him, after thursday to receive the Duke; he Shall take the liberty of ask-

4. BF had met the father in Paris in 1769, just before the old Duke died; see the note on BF to Ingenhousz above, Feb. 12. He may have met the son at that time, or later in London. Marie-Joseph d'Albert d'Ailly, duc de Pic-quigny as he styled himself before his father's death, had lived in England for several years; he appears from time to time in Horace Walpole's correspondence in 1764–65, usually for the scrapes into which his violent temper led him. But he had another side, as witness his election to the Royal Society in 1764, and he became a naturalist of some distinction. He apparently kept up his contacts in London, and BF must have been one of them. In the first days of the American's mission to France he and the Duke were often together, and as early as Jan. 8 Lord Stormont referred to their great intimacy: Stevens, *Facsimiles,* XIV, no. 1410, pp. 1–2.

5. This note, we are inclined to guess from its addressing BF in Passy as a member of Congress rather than its agent, belongs to the early weeks there. The dinner about which the Duke is writing may well have led to another undated communication to BF (Chaulnes was averse to dating), but we cannot be sure; it is about his dealings with Benjamin Vaughan in London, and we have elected to discuss it later in that context. See the note on BF to Vaughan below, Sept. 18, 1777.

408

ing a diner at Mister francklin according for his offer, for thursday, or fryday next, and prays him to chuse of both. The Duke is not so bold than to hope, to pass philosophicaly the after noon, but with a philosopher, and a very true one in every regard.

Addressed: A Monsieur / Monsieur francklin, membre / du congrès americain / A Pascy

The American Commissioners: Memorandum for Vergennes

AD:[6] Archives du Ministère des affaires étrangères

Memoire   Paris March 1st. 1777

In the several Memoires which Mr: Deane had the honor of presenting previous to the arrival of his Colleagues,[7] the history of the dispute between the United States of America and Great Brittain was brought down to the Time of presenting the Memoires, the situation and resources of the United States justly stated; and Conjectures as to the issue of the Campaign then depending were made, which Events have since justified; The Turn which Great Brittain then meditated, and which she would finally exert her whole force and influence to give to this War, was pointed out, Namely by an early subjugation of America to unconditional Submission by force of Arms, or an Accommodation, to be in a Situation of turning the War against France, which they would be able to enter upon with the Advantages of having their whole Force by Sea and Land ready, their Magazines Stored, and the warlike spirit of the Nation raised by civil Contest, together with additional resources from America, in a State of Peace and Amity, and ready Armed and disciplined. That Great Brittain would endeavor To give the War this direction, and avail herself of these Circumstances has with submission been pointed out, in Memoires which Mr. Deane had the honor of presenting in Addition to which Messrs.

6. In Silas Deane's hand.
7. *Deane Papers,* I, 184–95, 223–6, 252–85, 361–4, 434–42.

Franklin and Deane have only to add, that they are well assured that the present Moment labours with this Event before hinted at; and that Great Brittain is employing Art as well as force to Accomplish and compleat their favorite design. Messrs. Franklin and Deane Anxious for the Fate of their Country, and wishing to employ every means in their power to Defeat the design of their Country's Enemies, take Liberty to observe, that without supplies of military and other Stores, without Commerce established on which their resources greatly depends; and without the protection of any foreign power to their commerce, or Shipps of War, it is hardly possible for the United States to prevent for any Time this Event; nor can it be expected when considered that under all these disadvantages they have to contend with the whole Force of Great Brittain and her Allies. In Consequence of Warlike stores not being permitted to be shipp'd in French Bottoms direct for The United States, the Cannon and Stores engaged by Mr. Deane in August last are at this moment in the Ports of France; and finally obliged to send them by the West Indies, there to look for American or Neutral Ships, all hopes of their being in any Season for Service in America are lost. The Duties laid on certain Commodities coming from the Dominions of Great Brittain being continued on the same Commodities from The United States operate as a prohibition on many important Articles of the American Commerce and can be remedied only by some particular Regulation or Settlement of Rules for this Commerce. The Armed Vessels of the United States are under the Necessity of having some harbor in Europe to repair the Damages they may receive at Sea, without This it is impossible for Them to keep these Seas; and when permitted to enter the Ports of France, it is Necessary the Rules they are to Observe should be known. It is a great Disappointment to Messr. Franklin and Deane, to find that they are unable to comply with the Proposals of the Farmers General respecting Tobacco, but greatly as they are in want of Supplies they Think themselves justified in rejecting offers which must Subject their Constituents to a great and certain Loss in a Commerce which they hoped to establish on equall Terms.

Not to detain his Excellency longer than is absolutely Necessary, Messrs. Franklin and Deane propose the following Points with all submission to his Consideration.

1. Military Stores being merchandize, and subject to the same rules as other Articles of Commerce, it is asked that they may be permitted to be transported direct to the United States in French Vessels, the proprietors running the risques attending such a Voyage.

2. It is submitted whither; considering the different predicament[8] under which many Articles of the Commerce of the United States now are from what they formerly were, it is not Necessary they should be under different Regulations and consequently whither the United States may expect their proposed Treaty of Commerce and Amity with his most Christian Majesty will be accepted and approved of.

3. All prospect of Treating with the Farmers General for Tobacco being at present closed, and all hope of supply from that source defeated, Whither any other mode can be adopted for supplying France with that Article at the price it costs at its first purchase, and the unavoidable expences of transportation; that being the extent of the demand of Messrs. Franklin and Deane.[9]

4. It is requested that when Armed Vessels belonging to The United States enter the Ports of France, they may be permitted Time to repair the Damages they may have sustained, and to dispose of so much of their Effects as will enable them to do it, under such Regulations as are usual in such Cases; That the mode or Rules may be pointed out; and That they may be permitted to sell or Freight to the Subjects of other Nations their prizes, without discharging their Goods on shore, but transacting the whole on Shipboard.

5th. A Port in Europe being Necessary for the Shipps of War of the United States, and the Treaty Subsisting between France and Great Brittain not permitting one to be granted in this Kingdom; it is hoped that it will not be disagreeable That Application should be made elsewhere, and on this Subject

8. Category.

9. This paragraph may have helped persuade Vergennes to have the tobacco negotiations reopened; see the headnote on the contract below, March 24.

intreat his Excellency's advice and direction which on this and every other Concern will be attended to by them in the closest manner, as well as be received with the utmost respect and Gratitude.

Notation: 1777. 1er. Mars.

Vergennes: Memorandum for the American Commissioners

Reprinted from Benjamin F. Stevens, ed., *Facsimiles of Manuscripts in European Archives Relating to America, 1773–1783* (25 vols., London, 1889–98), xv, no. 1451.[1]

[Between March 1 and 12, 1777[2]]
Reponse aux Ministres du Congress.

1) On ne peut prendre connoissance des Operations de Commerce que des particuliers peuvent faire. On ne gêne personne à cet egard, lorsqu'on s'est renfermé dans les bornes de la Circonspection. Mais il n'est pas possible de dissimuler les expeditions qui, ayant un objet purement offensif, ne peuvent etre envisagés comme commerciales, et ce seroit se compromettre sans utilité pour la partie qu'on croiroit assister, puisque des pareils transports ne jouiroient d'aucune seureté à la faveur d'aucun pavillon, et ne pourroient etre reclamés du moins avec succés.

2) Les facilités qu'a éprouvé jusqu'a présent le Commerce de l'Amerique, ne doivent laisser aucun doute qu'on ne se prêtera à tout celle[3] d'une confiance mutuelle, lorsque le moment sera venu de se lier reciproquement par un traité de Commerce. On a déja fait connoitre les raisons qui s'y opposent dans le

1. Stevens found the memorandum, which is a copy, among the Auckland MSS at King's College, Cambridge; they were subsequently transferred to the British Library, and the Librarian has assured us that the copy has disappeared.

2. The memorandum is in answer to that from the commissioners, the preceding document, and they responded to part of it on the 12th.

3. This phrase, "à tout celle," makes no sense, and was subsequently framed in dots to indicate a copyist's error.

moment présent. En attendant, s'il est quelques Articles de Marchandise sur lesquels on demande des adoucissements, on peut les exposer, et on s'employera volontiers pour les procurer.[4]

3) On n'a rien à écrire touchant le Tabac, cet article regarde la ferme Generale.

4) Tout Batiment qui prend azile dans des ports de france y recoit, sans difficulté, les secours dont il peut avoir besoin, pour se reparer des dommages que la longueur de la navigation, et les événements de la mer peuvent lui avoir occasionné; mais ce seroit donner trop d'extension a de pareils secours, de reclamer à ce titre pour les Armateurs la faculté de faire la navette de la haute mer dans les memes ports, d'y amener leurs prizes, de les y deposer, et de les vendre meme sans rompre leurs cargaisons. Les traités qui font Loi entre les puissances, et dont la Religion des Souverains ne doit pas leur permettre de s'ecarter, s'y opposent.[5]

From William Alexander   ALS: American Philosophical Society

My Dear Sir   Dijon 1 March 1777

I got Safe here Wednesday evening,[6] after one of the Pleasantest Journeys I ever made, and made the Girls very happy with the prospect of a visit from you. If the Business of that Musty Town you reside in can admit of a few weeks interuption you will find travelling infinitely more comfortable than when the Warm weather Sets in, besides when I was a young Man making love I found litle absences and even Jealousies, Servd more to disclose the sentiments of my Mistress, than an assiduous Courtship. This is for your Grand Son.

I was thinking on the Road on your friend Dubourgs bargain, which In the way he states it is very advantageous, In so

4. This sentence was the basis for the commissioners' memorandum to Vergennes below, March 12.

5. Vergennes is referring to provisions of the Treaty of Utrecht. He expected the commissioners to be displeased with this legalism, and to use their ingenuity in suggesting ways to evade it; see his letter to Noailles, March 22, 1777, quoted in Stevens, *Facsimiles*, xv, no. 1488, pp. 1–2.

6. Feb. 26.

much that putting all Circumstances together, I am convinced it is your bargain, altho' you know nothing about it. I mean that the idea of its being a Concern of yours, which has been represented, Supported by your known friendship for him, Has led them in giving it, to think They were serving you. The Exceeding desire they Dubourg and His associate shew to have you Interested for a very trifling share, I Suspect arises more from that motive Than from any assistance you coud give in their purchases. And as for any aid from your Government, They might expect your Patronage more readily in Consequence of your friendship for Dubourg than from a trifling share in an adventure in trade. In case you therefore meditate any great Interprize for yourself I Suspect it will be necessary that you disclaim Clearly all Concern In theirs.[7]

Pray might not such a litle adventure as is proposed for you, suit Williams? He coud be of more use in the Detail Either at home or in America than your Situation permits. And I think by Combining the outward adventure with the homeward, freighting ships in place of buying, and insuring the Sale price of the outward Cargo in Europe, which Law and Custom warrants, at least in Britain, a profit might be secured against every accident, but the Breaking of the people trusted, which is working as safely as the Contingency of human Affairs will permit.

This is enough of business. But pray let me hear of you when your Grandson is not better Employd, I woud be Glad to hear what is going forward. I mean Such public matters as it is not treason to hear. And If you can give me an Address through the Channel which you know, you shall hear from me any thing that occurs worth the postage. If your Grandson will write in french it will be killing two birds with one Stone. And will you forgive me my Dear Sir for noticing, That your

7. This paragraph is Alexander at his murkiest, and the reader must guess what he meant. Our guess is as follows: BF should accept the offer from Dubourg & Debout (in which Paulze had seen no conflict of interest, as mentioned in the headnote above, Jan. 21); Congress would attribute his acceptance to friendship rather than to his minute investment, and he could dissociate himself from the scheme if the commissioners succeeded in their "great Interprize" of dealing directly with the farmers general.

papers seem to me to Lye a litle Loosely about your hand? You are to Consider yourself as Surrounded by spies, and amongst people who can make a Cable from a thread, woud not a spare half hour per day enable your Son to arrange all your papers, useless or not, So as that you coud come at them sooner, and not one be visible to a prying Eye? I understand I am put in the English papers for my visit to you, but have not yet been able to see what is said of me. If They attack not my moral Character, I Shall be easy about the rest. Before I left Paris I sent Information for Loyds of your proceedings with regard to our trade. The Girls join me in kindest Compliments to you and your Son, and be assurd that you have not a friend in the World who bears you a more tender affection than Dear Sir your most obedient humble servant   W ALEXANDER

Mr. De Morveaux book In which the Iron and Steel is treated will be publishd next week when I will send it you.[8] There is a letter perhaps more at your house for me which I beg may be returnd altering the address to Dijon.

Addressed: A Monsieur / Monsieur Franklin / a L'hotel de Hambourg / Rue Jacob / a Paris.

Notation: Alexander 1. March 1777.

From ——— Bergere

March 1, 1777   See page 170

From Jonathan Williams, Jr.

ALS: American Philosophical Society

Dear and honored Sir   Nantes March. 1. 1777.
    Inclosed are two Letters to the Deputies, one of which you will find on a particular subject, which I leave to your wisdom whether to communicate or not. I wrote it because I feared it

---

8. He was promising the first volume of a work by a famous chemist, Louis-Bernard de Guyton de Morveau, *Elémens de chymie théorique et pratique,* ... (3 vols., Dijon, 1777–8). See Alexander's next letter below, March 7.

415

might be thought neglectfull if I should hereafter be known to have omitted such information.

I am highly obliged by your kind offers of assistance and must determine in favour of nantes for many reasons. I find that with your good opinion I can be back'd by the first houses here. Mr. Montaudouin has asked me to be connected with a young man he reccommends, and Mr. Shweighausser wants me to be connected with himself.

I will write further next post. I am in haste. Your dutifull and affectionate Kinsman J WILLIAMS.

Addressed: A Monsieur / Monsieur Franklin LLD / a l'Hotel d'Hambourg / Rue Jacob / a Paris.

Notation: Mr Williams Nantes Febry 28th 1777

To Arthur Lee

ALS: American Philosophical Society

Dear Sir, Paris, March 2. 1777

We received duly yours of Feb. 14. from Nantes; and one since from Bourdeaux, dated, by Mistake, Jan. 29.[1] We are glad to hear you were got so far well on your Journey.

The Farmers General since your Departure, have been again in Treaty with us for Tobacco. We offer'd (rather rashly, I think) to deliver it in France at 8 sols. They offer'd us 5.[2] Interim we receiv'd your Intelligence of its being at 20 sh. Sterling per Cwt. in Virginia: of course we rejected their Offer; and we think of treating with them no farther, but leave them to Mr. Morris or who they please.

The Court here continue firmly of Opinion that very few Germans will go out this Year. Last Night I received a Letter from London, which mentions as confirm'd the Defeat of the Hessians at Trenton, only 300 escaping out of the Brigade, 1200 kill'd or made Prisoners; a subsequent Defeat of the 17th and 49th Regiments between Trenton and Princetown; a more

1. Both are above, the one from Bordeaux under Feb. 18.
2. The farmers actually offered six; see their memorandum above, Feb. 14.

general Action at Princetown;[3] in consequence of all which the King's Troops were evacuating Jersey as fast as they could. It is added, that the Accounts say 3 Battallions of the Hessians behav'd ill, and threw down their Arms, surrendring themselves Prisoners without Necessity, from whence it is concluded at London that they had been tampered with by "Congressional Emissaries"; and this has alarm'd the Court, and given a Distrust of Foreign Mercenaries, so that 'tis thought no more will be engag'd. All the Hessian Colours were taken, and 8 Pieces of Brass Cannon. All the Commissaries Stores assembled at Burlington for the Enterprize against Philadelphia also fell into our Hands. This News is all from London; we are yet without any direct Intelligence, therefore cannot give it as certain. I have omitted that in the two Actions, between Trenton and Princetown, and at Princetown, the English own they lost 400 killed, with 10 Officers; the Number of Wounded not mentioned. Genl. Lee is said to be taken Prisoner by the Enemy; but that News, tho' possibly true, comes so indirectly as to leave still some room to doubt. The Troops at New York were very sickly. Providence not taken nor likely to be attempted; on the contrary it is said a Part of the Fleet with some of the Troops were ordered from Rhodeisland to the Eastern Shore of Maryland, perhaps to aid the then intended Invasion of Pennsylvania.

We have heard nothing of M. Mercle since he left Paris. Consulting Mr. de V. concerning the Demand, he advis'd against making it for several Reasons, on which it is laid aside for the present. I will mention to the Congress what you propose concerning the Cruelties on Long Island.[4] I remember to have heard before I left America, that some young English Officers valued themselves on an Expedient by which they had exasperated the Hessians against the Americans while yet on Staten Island, viz. a Man happening to die suddenly in the Night, they caus'd him to be scalp'd and horridly mangled, and the

3. "Trenton" and "Princetown" and "Action at Princetown," and "Nantes" in the final paragraph, have been lightly underlined by some one, but we assume not by BF.

4. The demand was the memorial to Germain above, Feb. 7; for Lee's proposals see the letters that BF is answering.

next Day show'd him to the Hessians in one of their Uniforms, as a Hessian murder'd by the Provincials.

Sir Roger Grand and Mr. B. are gone to Holland, to forward the Business there.[5]

Capt. Wickes is return'd to L'Orient with 5 Prizes, taken on the Coast of Portugal: One a Packet from Falmouth to Lisbon, with 18 Guns and 50 Men. The others a Ship from Pool with Fish, one from Shetland with Barley, one from Ireland with Flour, and one from Bristol with Wine and Brandy. He has made near 100 Prisoners. At his Request we have proposed, to the English Ambassador here, an Exchange for as many Americans taken by the Raisonnable; but have received no Answer; indeed we did not expect any.[6] Wickes meets with Difficulties at l'Orient about his Prizes. We are solliciting here for some Favour to him, but as yet have no explicit Answer. Mr. Dean is gone again to day to Versailles. *Perhaps we might be more favour'd in Spanish Ports.* Tho' People tell us that this Court is offended with the late Conduct of Britain, (which was insolent on its supposed Success in America) and begins now to use a *Ton* that indicates a Rupture: But these are Notices not to be rely'd on.

I am now removed to Passi, but am almost every Day at Hotel d'Hambourg with Mr. Deane, who begins to talk afresh of going northward.

The enclos'd, directed to John Thomson was put into my Hands by a Person from England, who told me he believ'd it was for me. I accordingly open'd and perus'd it; and judging it by the last Paragraph to be from a Friend of yours, I answer'd it by the Return of the same Person, to Tower Hill.[7] I have since receiv'd one directed to you, which is also enclos'd.

5. Georges Grand had many Christian names, but Roger was not among them. See his letter above, Feb. 27, for his journey to Holland with Capt. Boux.

6. The proposal to Stormont is above, Feb. 23. For the captured Americans see *Naval Docs.*, VIII, 517.

7. Lee was using Thomson or Thompson as his alias: Stevens, *Facsimiles*, II, no. 154, p. 4. The "Friend of yours" who wrote him under that name, as BF realized, was Lee's brother William, who lived on Tower Hill: *The New Complete Guide to All Persons Who Have Any Trade or Concern with the City of London* ... (15th ed.; London, 1777), p. 241.

Capt. Nicholson is return'd, and the Cutter with Capt. Hynson is arriv'd at Havre. M. Hodge has not yet succeeded at Dunkirk, but expects. The taken Packet will I believe be fitted out as a Cruiser, being said to sail well.

The young Gentleman was at first a little discontented with his School, but is become better satisfied. He din'd with us last Week.[8]

Mr. Sollier has receiv'd the 90,000 Livres from Nantes for our Use. I can at present think of nothing farther to add, but that I am, with great Esteem and Regard, Dear Sir, Your most obedient and most humble Servant   B FRANKLIN

Arthur Lee Esqr.

To Claude-Carloman de Rulhière

AL: American Philosophical Society

This is Franklin's earliest surviving letter in French, and it was more consequential than it seems. The recipient, the Chevalier de Rulhière (1735–91), was a man of some distinction, a poet, historian, and diplomat, who had been the secretary of the French embassy in St. Petersburg and had written extensively on recent developments in Russia and Poland.[9] He wanted to see Franklin in order to recommend his Polish friend, Count Casimir Pulaski, but the ensuing interview must have discouraged him. The American said that he did not know who Pulaski was, declined to advance him money, but did finally agree to secure him passage on the *Reprisal* when she returned to America. He would do more than he promised, Rulhière hoped, after making inquiries about the Count and himself.[1] The hope materialized: Franklin discovered that the Pole had the support of Versailles, and recommended him to Washington with unaccustomed warmth.[2]

8. This was Lee's nephew Ludwell, sixteen at the time, whom his uncle had put in a military academy to learn engineering: *Lee Family Papers*, roll 3, frames 132–3; James C. Ballagh, ed., *The Letters of Richard Henry Lee* (2 vols., New York, 1911–14), I, 71.

9. His works were published posthumously: Larousse, *Dictionnaire universel*.

1. Stevens, *Facsimiles*, VII, no. 650.

2. Below, May 29, 1777.

A Passi, ce Dimanche matin 2 Mars pres de M. Chaumont M. Franklin presente ses Respects a M. le Chevalier Rulhiere, et sera bien aise de le recevoir ce soir à six heures, si cela est convenable a M. Rulhiere.

Addressed: A Monsr. / Monsieur le Chevalier Rulhiere / &c

Coder to Barbeu-Dubourg and Franklin

March 2, 1777 See page 441n

Lambert Wickes to the American Commissioners

ALS: American Philosophical Society

Gentlemen, L'Orient March 3d 1777
I recd. yours of the 23d Feby. by Mr. Defrancy which I am Sorry Come so late, as the Vessels are all gone. He will soon return, when I shall give you as full an Answer as I Can to all your proposals.[3] We have got up to place of Carreening and are now prepairing for that Bussiness; time is now our Own and you may order or dispose of us as you think proper. From Gentlemen Your obedient Humble Servant LAMBT. WICKES

To the Honbles: Dr. Franklin Silas Dean

Addressed: To / The Honble. Dr. Benja. Franklin / at / Paris

Notation: Capt Weekes L'Orient March 3 77

From Buisson de Basseville

March 3, 1777 See page 168

3. One of the proposals, which have been lost with the letter of Feb. 23, may have been that ships be dispatched by way of the West Indies because the direct route was at that season too dangerous; on this point the commissioners and Beaumarchais were agreed. *Deane Papers,* II, 12.

The American Commissioners to the Committee of Secret Correspondence

ALS[4] and copy: National Archives

Gentlemen   Paris 4th March 1777

We send you herewith the Draught of a Frigate, by a very ingenious Officer in this service, which appears to Us peculiarly suitable for Our purpose, and We are in hopes of being able to ship Cordage and Sail Cloth, and Anchors &c. sufficient for Five or Six such Frigates, by the Time you can have them built.[5] Though deprived of any intelligence from you since the first of last November, and without remittances leaves Us in a situation easier to be conceived than described. The want of intelligence affects the Cause of the United States in every department; what Accounts of Our Affairs arrive in Europe at all comes thro' the hands of Our Enemies, and whether defeated or Victorious we are the last who are acquainted with Events which ought first to be announced by Us. We are really unable to account for this Silence, and while We are affected with the unhappy Consequences of it must intreat the honorable Congress to devise some Method for giving Us the earliest and most certain Intelligence of what passes in America. The Ship by which this is sent is Loaded with Cloathing and Cordage and Duck. Not having a full Cargo of the former, We ordered Mr. Williams who acts for Us at Nantes to compleat with the latter, for which We have obtained a short Credit. Mr. Williams will write You by this Opportunity, he has been of great Service to Us at Nantes, and it is but justice to say that his knowledge of Business probity, Activity and Zeal for the Interests of his Country, with the good Opinion justly entertained of him by Gentlemen in Business at Nantes, render him Very serviceable in Our Affairs there, and proper to be employed in Commercial Transactions. It gives Us pain to be obliged to say, That the Conduct of Mr. Merkle is intirely the reverse. He left the Vessel he came over in at Bordeaux on

4. In Deane's hand.

5. The plan for a frigate was the outgrowth of the commissioners' agreement with Capt. Boux above, Feb. 12; see also Boux's letter to them below, April 7. They bought two tin cases to contain the designs: BF's accounts as commissioner (above p. 20), no. 10 annex, Feb. 20.

421

Expence in December last, has sent no Orders to her since, he pass'd thro' Paris in January for holland, or rather spent a Month in the City on which Journey, when, as well as at Bourdeaux his Character is marked for low Debauchery incompatible with the Gentleman or the Man of Business. Persons of such a Character giving themselves out for Agents of Congress and producing Contracts in support of their Pretensions, hurt the Commercial reputation of the United States, and can be of no service in any shape whatever. We Apprehend that Letters to Monsr. Schweighauser have not had fair play, and therefore advise You to write to him, charging the Capt. who carries Your Letters to deliver them with his Own hand if he arrive at Nantz, if at any other Port that he send them under Cover to Us. We are fitting a packet by which shall write more particularly in a few Days. Mr. Lee wrote Us last Week from Bordeaux, on his Way to Spain. We present Our most Respectful Compliments To the honorable Congress and are Gentlemen Your most Obedient and Very humble Servants

B Franklin
Silas Deane

ps. Just as We were closing this Lettr We recd. a Letter from Our Colleague Mr. Lee dated Bourdeaux 22d. Feby. 1777. He was to set out the Next Day for Madrid. The following extract of his Letter we think merits your Attention, and that we ought to transmit it.[6]

⟨Every respectable merchant in Nantes and Bordeaux holds Morris and Merkle in contempt; they have done almost irreparable harm to the credit of Congress.⟩

Notation: Franklin & Deane to the Comtee March 4. 1777

Jonathan Williams, Jr., to the American Commissioners

ALS: University of Virginia Library

Gentlemen   Nantes March 4 1777.

My two last contained the necessary Information relative to the Fuzils &c. which upon a second View I have seen no rea-

---

6. The letter, which was actually from Bayonne, is above. To avoid repetition we summarize the quoted passage.

son to alter; I am assured that there are a full number of Bay-
onetts Locks &c., rather more than less. There must be many
new Ramrods which will cost about 12 sous each at the man-
ufactury. If you make this Bargain please to be very particular
about including everything, as there are several Cases of old
Bayonets, Locks, iron Furniture &c. &c. which will sell for
something, and a few very pretty officers Fuzils which I should
be sorry to have left out; there is also a small parcell of these
arms already repaired which may be included; in short, as the
Store contains little else, the doors may be shut and the Keys
delivered at once. Mr. Peltier tells me that no armourer can
leave France without permission of Monsieur de Gribauval,
and that with that permission a good number may be procured.[7] The Man who oversees the reparation of these arms,
appears to me an excellent Fellow, and would go with proper
encouragement.[8]

I hear that St. Jean Baptiste a Frigate of 36 Guns is purchased at L'orient on your account, I suppose you are informed of this. I know no more of it than the public talk on
'Change.

I shall finish repacking those Bales that are here to day, and
then the workmen will begin to pack the sail Cloth, the Cordage is about half done and will be compleated in about 8
Days. The Ship will I hope soon be ready to take in, having
been obliged to change her masts, to recaulk her intirely, and
alter her riggin we have taken up some time, but none has
been lost.

Mr. Peltier proposes to mount 20 Guns onboard the Count
and the Captain desires to have a full Complement of men for
a Ship of that Force as he thinks we are at the Eve of a War.
Please to say if you approve of this and desire Mr. Montieu to
give similar orders.

In the order for purchase Mr. Montieu mentions 40 or 50,000
Livres, you say 60 or 80,000. What I have proposed will come

7. In 1776 Gribeauval (above, xxii, 461 n) had been named first inspector
of artillery; see Larousse, *Dictionnaire universel.*

8. He was a M. Mercier. The commissioners reached an agreement with
him summarized below, May 30; it was for work to be done at Nantes, and
left open the question of his emigrating.

to the 60,000, but I hope there will be no difficulty about the difference. It would be well however if Mr. Montieu would signify to Mr. Peltier that he may go that far. I have the honor to be with great Respect Gentlemen Your most obedient and most humble Servant   J WILLIAMS

The Honorable The Deputies of the United States.

Notation: Mr Williams Nantes March 4th 1777 [*in another hand*: to Hon: Deputies U.S.] [*illegible*]

From [Edward Bancroft]   AL: American Philosophical Society

Dear Sir   4th March 1777.

In Compliance with your favour of the 17th. ultimo. I have paid Mr. Hood twelve Guineas; Mr. Wh[arton] having represented that he could not Clear himself from hence and Convey himself to Paris with Less. I have taken his receipt for the money.[1] By Mr. Hood I shall send you the Books which were Left me sometime ago by Mr. Vaughan. I shall also send Mr. Deane a Continuation of his sett of Monthly reviews; in the Last of which you will find some further Remarks on the Dean of Gloucester's misconduct towards you. I hope that my earnest desire of refuting his Calumnies has [*not*] Lead me to mention any improper Circumstance An Apprehension of which would have induced me to have first submitted the Article to your Correction, had not Mr. Griffith's been very pressing for it.[2] I herewith inclose you two Letters from Mr. T. Walpole, in

1. Thomas Hood was a Philadelphian. He had interviewed some American prisoners in London, after giving the required assurance that he was not himself an American; when he reached Paris he made a deposition on March 29 about their treatment (University of Pa. Library); this the commissioners forwarded to Stormont with their letter below of April 2. His lie about his nationality was typical of the man. At the end of the month BF advanced him 30 louis, and the loan was apparently obtained on false pretences: Waste Book, entry of March 31. Hood went on to borrow money right and left, and generally to make a nuisance of himself; see BF to Rybot below, April 9, and subsequent volumes.

2. Bancroft was enclosing his review of Dean Tucker's latest publication, *A Series of Answers to Certain Popular Objections against Separating from the Rebellious Colonies* ... (Gloucester, 1776); see BF's marginalia above, under

one of which you will find a Draft for your Ballance. Mr. Walpole was rather Hurt by your writing on the Subject, to 176, and did not chuse to give any answer through that Channel, and on the other Hand 176 is Jealous of my intimacy with 177 and desireous that you should not Correspond with the Latter but through him. You will please therefore not to intimate that the Letters in question were forwarded by me. It is a pitiful Subject for Jealousey or Contention, but I have been most seriously applied to by 176 not to receive Letters for you from 177, a request too unreasonable to be Complied with.[3] I presume my Letters to Mr. Deane have been constantly communicated to you, and but little of News has occurred Since my Last. The Packet with Government Dispatches arived Last night, but they have given us nothing in this Evening's Gazette, a sure proof that they have nothing which they call good. I shall however collect in a Letter to Mr. D— for your and his Satisfaction such Particulars as have Come to my Knowledge and shall be happy in every Opportunity given me of approving myself Dear Sir Your most respectful, Affectionate and Devoted Humble Servant.

Addressed: Dr. F—

Notations: Dr Bancroft Mar. 4 77. / Dr Bt

From Anna Maria Clifton[4]   ALS: American Philosophical Society

Dear Sir   Philada: March 4th: 1777.

While all our *Little World* are congratulating each other on your safe arrival in France, Suffer me to assure you that none

---

Dec. 22. The review ignored the Dean's argument, except for a final paragraph, and instead took him to task for earlier attacks on BF: *Monthly Review*, LVI (1776), 145–9. Ralph Griffiths was the publisher: above, XXII, 373 n.

3. The two enclosed letters from Walpole were, we assume, those above of Feb. 2 and below of March 5, in which case the present letter was begun on the 4th and finished later. The context makes it almost certain that 176 was Samuel Wharton. 177 was unquestionably Walpole himself. A few weeks earlier Bancroft had enclosed to Deane a sketch of BF "by a son of 177" (*Deane Papers*, I, 496), and BF acknowledged young Walpole's work in writing to his father below, Dec. 11, 1777.

4. The Clifton sisters were old friends of the family, but we know little about them; incidental references are above, XVI, 262; XVII, 207. Sally Bache,

more Sincerely rejoices in it then I do. To know you are free from danger is an infinite satisfaction, to tell you so is a Pleasure I could not refuse myself. The danger with Which our Coast is surrounded would often have fil'd me with Apprehensions, but that I reflected, that if good men are the Care of Providence, you must be it's peculiar Charge.

Among the many unhappy Events of the present War, the separation of Friends is not the least. I feel this most acutely when I tell you that Mrs: Bache has removed from town, some Weeks since, and when we shall meet again the future only can determine. Notwithstanding our desire to see you, I dare not wish your return to America, but you must Permit me to say I wish I was with you in Europe, I would willingly escape from the dreadful, Terrifying consequences of War. Do me the favor to present my best Regards to the young Gentlemen. When Temple has a half-hour to throw away I should be Happy to hear from him that You are Well. In the mean time I am dear Sir with great Respect and Regard your Most obedient

ANNA MARIA CLIFTON

My Sister presents her Compliments to you, with every Salutary Wish for your Health and happiness.

Addressed: To / Doctor Franklin / Paris

Endorsed: An. Maria Clifton Philad. March. 4. 77.

From Jean-Paul Grandam

March 4, 1777 See page 170

From Jonathan Williams, Jr.

ALS: American Philosophical Society

Dear and honored Sir Nantes March 4. 1777.

I am highly pleased to find that my Inclination to settle in France meets with your approbation, and I will do my best

---

before leaving for Goshen, had sent them a number of things from the Franklin household; and they also kept an eye on the empty house. See BF to Sarah Bache, June 3, 1779, Smyth, *Writings*, VII, 347, and her letter to WTF of March 29, 1780, APS.

endeavours to preserve the good opinion you are pleased to honour me with. This place seems to me the best calculated for carrying on the american Trade, especially in time of war. I understand that all vessells that come on this coast are obliged to make Belleisle, which being just off the mouth of this River, an immediate shelter is near either in case of Chase or bad weather; while those Ships that are bound to Bordeaux or other places, have a turbulent Bay to cross, and a dangerous Coast to sail along before they can reach their port. The shallowness of the River near the Town is the only disadvantage, but where operations are to be conceal'd, the Ships being at some distance is not amiss, and with proper management and previous arrangement, this circumstance may not lessen the Dispatch. The extent of the Loire is a great Benefit, it communicates to many manufacturing Towns and by Canals joins the Seine and so goes even to Paris. It has a very rapid Stream which is the means of quick transportation, and the Goods not being jolted by land Carriage may if properly packed come in great preservation. These considerations added to my acquaintance here make me determine in favour of Nantes. Mr. Shweighausser has asked me to interest him in a House established here in my name, which I think would be of service to do as I have no capital. It will not be expected that I can suddenly run into advance because Goods are to be had here at only 4 months Credit, and I must take Care not to be an hour behind my Time on any such occasion,[5] but for selling Cargoes and laying out the amount in the most advantageous way, I think I can undertake as well as anybody, and Mr. Shweighausser will assist me in every Difficulty, besides which, (I hope you will not think me vain,) I have a very flattering reception from every part of that Family.[6]

I propose to write circular Letters to all my acquaintance in america, but a Line from you will do more good than volumes of my own, and I hope you will believe that no temptation

5. The French offered much more restricted credit than the British; this contributed to the quick revival, after the war, of Anglo-American trade.

6. A veiled reference to his hope, which did not materialize, of cementing a business connection by marrying into the family.

can make me do a dishonest or dishonorable act. I intend soon to write to Mr. A——.[7] If he is still with you please to make my best respects to him. I am most dutifully and affectionately Yours etc.   J WILLIAMS JUNR

Addressed: Doctor Franklin.

Lambert Wickes to the American Commissioners

ALS: American Philosophical Society

Gentlemen,   L'Orient 5th. March 1777
   I received two of yours of the 25th. by Mr. Defrancy who I am sorry Came so late, as our Sales were compleat before his Arrival.[8] I have strictly attended to your proposals and shall give you as full an Answer as in my power. As to Cruizing in the sound for the Baltick Ships I am afraid that will not do, as neither me nor my officers are acquainted with those Sea's, nor have we any proper Charts for those Sea's. Another objection is, the Certainty of being soon discovered, as there is such Numbers of Vessels passing and repassing constantly, the Consequence of which would be dangerous, as the passage in and out are Narrow and we should be either blocked in or taken but if you should think proper to order us on this Expedition I think it would be highly Neccessary to procure us Admittance and protection in Some of the principal Ports in those Sea's. If this Cannot be done I think it would not be Advisable to venture there. The Cruize on the Coast of Guineay I think much Safer and better, but there is Such difficultes Attending it, as cannot be got over. Our ship will not carry Water and provision enough for to Cruize, as it will be Neccessary to take 4 Months Water and provisions for that Cruize,

7. William Alexander. For our guess at what this was all about see the note on JW to BF above, Feb. 16.
8. A reference to the one letter of Feb. 25 that survives; the purport of the missing one is clear from what follows. Francy's late arrival was unfortunate because he would have bought the prizes for Beaumarchais: Morton, *Beaumarchais correspondance*, III, 66.

and we Cannot take more than 2 Months Water and provisions. If you should purchase the Marepaus, I think this Cruize would then be Advantageous[9] as the Ships Warr are all Small that is on that Coast and the Guineay Men, tho' they have all more or less Guns are not in a Condition to fight, as their Men are Generally very Sickly going off the Coast. I join with you in sentiments in regard to Cruizing on this Coast as there is very little prospect of any More Success here. I am Informed by the Officers belonging to two French Ships Warr, that arrived two days ago from a Cruize, that there is three Brittish Ships Warr Cruizing, between Cape Finnester and Ushant, one of 64 Guns one of 50 and one of 32 Guns, two of which they Saw and was told there was Another. The French Ships goes out again on a Cruize to Day. I think if a Very fast Sailing Cutter could be got and Stationed at Dunkirk they might soon make plenty Prizes by running into the Downs and Cutting Ships out from there, provided they would be received and protected in that port untill it suited you to send them off for America or Else where, And take the liberty to recommend Capt. Hinson for that service, as he is a Stout brave Man and I think well qualified for Such an Enterprize. I am very glad to hear you intend to provide for Capt. Nicholson, as I think him deserving your Confidence and make no Doubt he will Merrit your Esteem in any Station you may think proper to place him. If you purchase the Marepaus and I am appointed to Command her, I know no Obsticle in Capt. Nicholsons way, as my Officers would Chuse to Continue with me and of Course there will be room for him in the Reprisal. I think you may get the Marepaus £12,500 Sterling. She is a Very fine ship and has the Charector of a Very fast Sailor. I would recommend the purchase if Conveinient. Whatever may be your determination on those hints mentioned in your last I shall Chearfully Comply with any orders from you if in my power. The Officers do not Sign a Written parole, only give their Word of Honour, as I have wrote you fully on this head shall only Say they are all discharged. This comes by Mr. De-

9. For the proposal to buy the *Maurepas*, formerly the *St. John*, see his letter, above, Jan. 11, 14, and 18.

francy who returns emeadiately to Paris as you Trusted him I think I may safely do the same. From Gentlemen, Your Most Obliged Humble Servant.

P.S. I shall take Care not let any more Officers on Shore at all.
L.W.

Addressed: To / The Honble Dr. Benja. Franklin / at / Paris
Notation: Capt Weekes L'Orient 5 March 77

From —— Barbier de St. Georges

March 5, 1777   See page 169

From Arthur Lee   AL: American Philosophical Society

Dear Sir,   Burgos March 5th. 1777

I have been desird to stop here which is half way to Madrid, in order to negotiate with more secrecy. There appears more timidity here than with you. What I shall be able to do, I cannot yet determine, but I am told that if I proceed to Madrid it will be likely to prevent the execution of those good intentions there may be towards us.[1] I beg you will write me im-

1. An itinerary of Lee's journey, entitled "Route de Bayonne à Burgos" and undated, is in the Hist. Soc. of Pa. It shows, despite the title, that he intended to continue to Madrid by way of Valladolid, but in fact he got no farther than Burgos. When he arrived there at the end of February he received a letter from James Gardoqui, one of the sons in Joseph Gardoqui & Sons (above, XVIII, 196), who was writing from the capital to ask him, in the name of the government, to remain where he was. He promptly agreed. Wharton, *Diplomatic Correspondence*, II, 271–2. The marqués de Grimaldi, now a duke, former Spanish foreign minister and newly appointed ambassador to Rome, arrived at Burgos soon afterward with Gardoqui as his interpreter; and the three men met on March 4. Grimaldi was deaf to Lee's appeal for an open declaration of Spain's support, and insisted that the American's presence in Madrid would jeopardize secret aid; instead he should return to Bayonne. Mario Rodriguez, *La Revolución Americana de 1776 y el Mundo Hispánico: Ensayos y Documentos* (Madrid, 1976), pp. 90–3. Lee responded with two memoranda; in one he reiterated his argument for an open declaration, and in the other he insisted on remaining somewhere in Spain. Wharton, *op. cit.*, pp. 279–82. As a compromise he went back to Vitoria. Grimaldi waited to hear from the court and then joined him there in mid-March; see Lee to the commissioners below, March 16.

mediately your opinion, whether I ought to give up this point. Direct to me here.

I am assurd from the best authority, that a plan is forming for such a disposition of the forces of the two kingdoms, as will give the fullest alarm to our enemy.

If you think the enclosd is likely to be of use in augmenting that alarm, please to seal, and have it put into the post.

I suppose Mr. D. is gone. I am, dear Sir, Yours &c.

Addressed: A Monsr. / Monsr. Francois / dans le jardin

Notation: A Lee. to B.F. Burgos March 5th. 77.

From Thomas Walpole   ALS: American Philosophical Society

Dear Sir   London 5 March 1777.

It is some time since I prepared the inclosed letter in answer to that you was so kind to favour me with by Dr. Bancroft.[2] A diffidence arising from serious concern and agitation of mind on the cruel situation and melancholy prospect of affairs prevented my sending it forward which I now do as a testimony that I was both pleased and flattered by your remembrance of me, at the same time having at last closed accounts with my Associators in the Ohio purchase. I send you here inclosed yours with a circular letter and a remittance for the ballance as at foot noted, and I shall desire you will send me a receipt for the ballance of accounts betwixt us. News you will not expect from me the best friends of this Country meet often but it is only to lament its misguidance. I am with the Sincerest regard Dear Sir your most faithfull and affectionate humble Servant   THOMAS WALPOLE

The bills inclosed are Liv: 2500. 2739:16:9. ds: 29 Feby at 2 / mo. date on Lavabre Doerner & Co.[3]

Notation: Walpole 1. feby. 1777.

2. The letter enclosed was, as the notation makes clear, that above of Feb. 1.

3. The total of just under 5,240 *l.t.* represented the balance due, as mentioned in Walpole's earlier letter of Feb. 10, of £222 17s. 6d. at an exchange rate of 23.5:1; but we do not pretend to understand the date of the bills. For the Paris bankers see Lüthy, *Banque protestante,* II, 442–6.

To Richard Peters

This letter to the secretary of the American board of war was written to introduce a Frenchman who had already had vicissitudes and was to encounter many more. Louis Garanger was born about 1741 and, because of his family connections in the corps of artillery, was admitted to it as a youngster; he was on active service at the age of fifteen. His military studies brought him to the notice of members of the Académie royale des sciences, and particularly of Franklin's old opponent in electrical matters, Mathurin-Jacques Brisson.[4] Their support enabled the young man to continue his education and helped him, when he wanted to join the group that Du Coudray was taking to America, to procure leave and a brevet captaincy. He and his younger brother, breveted a lieutenant, expected to create a corps of bombardiers in the American army.

For some reason—the evidence is conflicting—the brothers did not sail with Du Coudray, but cooled their heels in Le Havre until their money ran out. In late January Louis Garanger wrote Franklin, enclosing a letter of recommendation from Brisson, and asked for help in cash. None seems to have been forthcoming, and he went to Paris to consult his sponsors. While there he left a note for Franklin, asking for acknowledgment of Du Coudray's engagement with him or at least for some authorization to go to America, and saying that he would return the next day for an answer.[5] One or more interviews presumably took place, out of which came the present letter of recommendation.

The provenance of the copy we print can be briefly explained. The brothers finally found passage for America with the marquis de Brétigney, who chartered a ship at his own expense to carry the officers and equipment needed for a corps of one hundred and thirty men. The party reached Charleston in September, 1777, but was captured at sea on the way to Philadelphia. The officers were im-

---

4. Above, XIX, 126–7 n. BF and Brisson had both attended the Academy on Jan. 15, and the Frenchman had invited him to a dinner on the 20th: Archives de l'Académie des sciences; APS.

5. Garanger to BF, Jan. 24, Feb. 21, 1777, APS. The notes explained that the brothers had arrived in Le Havre in mid-December, immediately after the *Amphitrite* sailed; they presumably did not hear of her return. Du Coudray told Congress that he had been dissatisfied with Louis Garanger's conduct in Le Havre, and did not expect him to come to America: Lasseray, *Les Français*, I, 94. Our information about the brothers comes from the notes just cited and from the summary of an undated memorial by Louis, also in the APS.

prisoned in St. Augustine,[6] and there Franklin's letter was copied and forwarded to Whitehall in a dispatch from Patrick Tonyn, Governor of East Florida. The Garangers were subsequently transferred to New York and then exchanged; the younger brother soon returned home in bad health, and the older one found only disappointments in his American service.[7]

Dear Sir,   Paris March 6th. 1777.

The Bearer Mr. Garanger, Captain of Bombardiers had as he informs me, engaged to go to America with M: De Coudray, an Officer of great Distinction in the Artillery, who is engaged in our Service, and sailed sometime since. M. Garanger not being then ready was left behind. He is well recommended to me by M. Brisson, a Gentleman of Science here, and has other Certificates of his Abilities to shew; besides that the Judgement of M: de Coudray in chusing to engage him is of itself more than a sufficient recommendation. I know nothing of the Contract between them, and must for that refer to M: de Coudray himself, who I hope is by this time safely arrived. I only beg leave to introduce him to you, to recommend him to your Civilities, and Countenance, as a Gentleman, who is zealous for our Cause, and desirous to serve it, and to request you will present him to the Board of War. I Congratulate you on the Check given to the Enemy in New Jersey, and wishing continued Success to our Arms, and to you, and Mrs. Peters Health, and Happiness. I have the honour to be, Dear Sir Your most Obedient humble Servant   (Signed) B. FRANKLIN

Copy of a Letter from Benjamin Franklin Esqr. to Mr. Richard Peters Secretary to the Rebel Board of War at Philadelphia dated at Paris March 6th. 1777.

Notations: Copy, Letter Benjamin Franklin to Richard Peters Esqr. Secretary to the Rebel Board of War / In Govr. Tonyn's (No 51) of 26 Jany. 1778.

6. The chevalier de Lalande to [d'Islé de Lamothe], March 13, 1778, Hist. Soc. of Pa. Brétigny and his subsequent adventures will appear in later vols.

7. See *JCC*, XIV, 710–11; XVIII, 863, 872–3; Fitzpatrick, *Writings of Washington*, XX, 225, 227; XXI, 210–11; XXII, 4–5; Louis Garanger's various memorials to Congress in the National Archives.

Jonathan Williams, Jr., to the American Commissioners

ALS: University of Virginia Library

Gentlemen   Nantes March 6, 1777.

The principal occasion for troubling you at present is to inform you that on account of the great Demand for Government every large anchor in this place is engaged. We shall find the other sizes easy enough, but unless you can obtain from the minister 2 Anchors of 2400 wt. and 2 of 2200 wt. our purchase I fear will be by so much incompleat.

By advice from orleans we find that 67 Bales are now loaded. 78 are on their way hither and 50 more will be dispatched in about 15 Days, this the Gentleman seems to think will be all but he can't say with certainty whether it will be so or not; these, with what we have, will make 373 Bales, and if they arrive in time to be reduced in size as I have done those that are here there will I apprehend be room enough. If this circumstance should add to our delay I hope you will not think it my Fault.

By advice from Bordeaux I am informed that a Ship is arrived at that port from Virginia with Tobacco which Brings a Virginia Gazette of the 20 Jan. containing a Letter from Gen. Washington to the Congress giving an account of the Defeat of the Hessians, the Loss is stated at 900 men.[8] The Capt. mentions that the Capture of Gen. Lee was talk'd off but nobody believed it, he adds that the americans have taken a great Quantity of Soldiers Cloathing. Mr. Lee had left Bordeaux when the post came away. I hear that the packet Boat is sold for 16,000 Livres. I expect Mr. Francis[9] here again tomorrow. I have the honour to be with great Respect Gentlemen Your most obedient Servant   J WILLIAMS JUNR

The Honorable The Deputies of the United States.

Notation: Mr Williams Nantes March 6th 1777 to Hon: Deputies U.S.

---

8. We have not traced the publication, but the letter was undoubtedly that in Fitzpatrick, *Writings of Washington*, VI, 441–4.

9. Francy.

434

From Bedaulx

March 6, 1777 See page 39

From Duportail

Copy: Archives du Ministère des affaires étrangères

A nantes le 6 mars 1777

Nous n'avons point trouvé de vaisseau ici qui allat directement a vos Colonies, et nous sommes obligés de nous embarquer sur un qui va au Cap St. Domingue d'ou tout le monde assure qu'il est très facile de passer a philadelphie. Nous sommes pourtant bien fachés de faire un tel circuit. J'apprehende que nous n'arrivions la Campagne commencée si elle s'ouvre effectivement aussitot que quelques personnes le prétendent. Comme nous nous proposons de freter a nos frais quelque petit batiment qui nous passe de St. Domingue a philadelphie, et que la tempête ou la crainte des anglois peut nous forcer de debarquer un peu plus bas que la pensilvanie, je desirerois que le Congrés prévint les Commandants de ces parties de notre arrivée, afin que nous fussions réçus sans difficulté et pussions nous faire reconnoitre autrement que par nos papiers que certaines circonstances peuvent nous obliger de jetter a la mer dans la traversée de St. Domingue.[1]

Je porte ici le nom de *Derford* Mr. de la radiere celui de *Baillard* Mr. de Launoy [Laumoy] celui de *Le thier* et Mr. de Gouvion celui d'*Olry* nous les conserverons pour plus grande sureté jusques dans votre pays, et même dans votre pays si la chose me paroit avantageuse.

Le chevalier du Portail a francklin

---

1. The party was in St. Domingue by May; Laumoy, incapacitated by sickness, was left there: see Duportail to BF below, May 15. The others landed in early June in North Carolina, and needed and received assistance in making their way overland to Philadelphia: Elizabeth S. Kite, *Brigadier-General Louis Lebègue Duportail* . . . (Baltimore, etc., 1933), p. 26.

From Nathan Rumscy

ALS: American Philosophical Society

Honorable Sir   Nantes March 6th. 77.

I am infinitely obliged to You for the agreable News contained in your favor of the 2d. Inst. and wish we may find verified with respect to it, even a Maxim of my Lord Chesterfield upon a certain Occasion, in believing only one half of what the World says.

Messrs. Penet and Morris have disposed of the Prizes in the manner you are pleased to observe, at the future Risque of the Buyers. The Packet which was the property of Cap. Wickes I understand, by some Regulations of Congress being a King's Ship, is also sold by Cap. Wickes himself and suppose upon the same Conditions as the former.

Captain Young in the Mary and Elizabeth will sail for Philadela. provided the wind answers, in 5 or 6 Days. My Compliments to Mr. Temple Franklin conclude me Honorable Sir Your most obedient Humble Servant   NATHAN RUMSEY

Dr Franklin

Addressed: A l'Honorable / Doct. Franklin / a l'Hotel D'Hambourg / Rüe Jacob / a Paris.

Notation: N Rumsey March 6. 77.

From Jonathan Williams, Jr.

ALS: American Philosophical Society

Dear and honored Sir   Nantes March 6. 1777.

Major Luttelock[2] arrived here a few days ago and I have since endeavoured to get him a passage via St. Domingo, together with the 4 Engineers, but when he found it necessary to pay his passage he told me he expected to go free and had not provided sufficient money; I can't make his passage free without paying for it myself and that I have no orders to do. He therefore waits further advice. Messrs. Portail &c. go away

2. JW never mastered the name, which was Lutterloh. See the Major's letter above, Jan. 3.

tomorrow morning. I have done all in my power to assist them and shall do the same for the Major, but I request that evry officer who is to go on the public account may have an express order, that I may not be in danger of doing wrong; and those for the Count de Vergennes I beg to be notified off. I am with great Respect Your dutifull and affectionate Kinsman

JONA WILLIAMS J

[*In the margin*:] My Love to Temple. If I have not mentioned him before it is because I have been always hurried, not because I have forgot him.

Addressed: Dr Franklin

Robert Morris to the American Commissioners

ALS: American Philosophical Society; copy: Library of Congress

Gentlemen   Philada. March 7th. 1777

I have wrote you several letters and sent you dispatches from Congress and Committee of Correspondance by Mr. Reed who will probably be longer in reaching you than this but he goes by a much safer Conveyance as I apprehend.[3] The Congress have adjourned from Baltimore to this place again but I think rather at an improper time as it appears to me that Genl. Howe is now forming another expedition against this place and I shall not think the City safe whilst the principal part of its defence depends on Militia, and altho our New Army has been recruiting a Considerable time yet we do not find them so forward as cou'd be wished, the want of cloathing &c. keeps them back a good deal, but we are spurring them on as much as possible. I do most sincerely hope you will negotiate the Loan and send out the Articles Wanted as we might then have leisure to make remittances with greater security than we can if done precipitately. We have bought considerable quantities

3. John Reed, Joseph's half-brother, was coming to France to familiarize himself with the country. An armed sloop took him and his dispatches to Martinique, whence he sailed for Bordeaux; he was in Paris by early June, when Deane recommended him to JW at Nantes. Bingham to the commissioners below, April 6; *Deane Papers*, II, 1–2, 71; Smith, *Letters*, VI, 378 n.

of produce in various parts and shall export it as fast as the times, Seasons and Enemies Ships will permit, this you may depend on, and the Produce of this Country if it coud once be exported freely will soon discharge the Debt it may be necessary to Contract.

The Committee will all be here next Week and write you fully themselves. In the mean time I remain with perfect Esteem and respect Gentlemen Your obedient humble servant

ROBT MORRIS

This goes by Monsr. Coleaux[4] who promises to deliver it and a Packet of News Papers.

The Honble Doctr Franklin, Silas Deane and Arthur Lee Esqrs.

Endorsed by Franklin: Secret Committee March 7. 77

Lambert Wickes to the American Commissioners

ALS: American Philosophical Society

Gentlemen,   L'Orient March 7. 1777

I wrote you the 3d. by post and the 5th. by Mr. De Francy. I have not received any of yours since Mr. De Francy's Arrival. I should be glad of a Line from you, informing of your intentions in regard to my further distination. We are now all ready to heave down and only Wait for good weather, the Weather has been very bad this last Week or that Job would have been done, but I am in hopes we shall be able to Compleat it in the Next Week after which time, I shall wait your Orders for the Government of future proceedings. If Capt. Nicholson can be Spared and you intend doing any thing for him here, the sooner he Comes the better. I am informed the Admiralty of Vans will Clear all our prizes out under French Coulours which is more than I expected. Please write me as soon as possible. From Gentlemen Your Obedient Humble Servant.   LAMBT. WICKES

4. For M. Couleaux, Penet's partner, see above, XXII, 469 n.

From William Alexander

ALS: American Philosophical Society

Dear Sir   Hotel de St Louis Dijon 7 March 1777

I thank you for returning me the letter that came to hand after my leaving Paris, and still more for letting me hear from you. That no news are Good News is an old proverb, very applicable to the present times. Your letter Coverd also a Blank Cover under which was an original of the Contract between Mons. Dubourg and the Farmers. I know not with what Intention it has been sent and shall therefore keep it untill You or he inform me what is to be done with it.[5]

The whole Seems to have been pretty well Considerd on the part of the sellers. Only the Alternative in favour of the Farmers in case of War between france and England to Cast the bargain,[6] seems not well advisd, the risk will not be encreased by that event and therefore the Contractors perhaps did wrong in Insisting on the right of Casting it As it gave rise to the Alternative, which throws great uncertainty on the bargain, and the farmers will only take the benefit of the Clause in case of a fall in the Market, which is the event on which the Contractors will Chiefly be anxious to maintain it. It appears to me that every ship that falls in the way of a Cruizer going to or Coming from America, under whatever Colours She Sails will be Considerd as Prize altho' Britain shoud remain at Peace with the european powers. In case of a War the Number of European privateers will be very trifling; I will venture to say within 20 from England, first because it is not the English Genius, secondly from want of hands. On the other hand the french and spanish fleet and privateers, will add Some hundred Cruizers to the defence of american trade, so that I shoud Consider the risk as rather diminishd in the voyage to and from America.

5. There must have been two originals of the projected contract, both of which have disappeared. One Dubourg left with BF, and asked to have back in his note below of March 12; the other BF enclosed in a letter to Alexander that is also now lost. The banker did not have an explanation of his copy until a month later, when he received a delayed letter from Dubourg offering him a part in the venture: Alexander to BF below, April 7.

6. The meaning, in context, must be to revise the terms.

In case Your friend from South Carolina[7] has not got the Merchandize he seeks, at Paris, He may write to Mesr. John Black & Co. Bordeaux, where I believe his business may be done. If the Comodities are to be got there, He needs no introduction. Let Him be quit Explicit to save time. He will find Mr. Black a Man of Worth, who will not trifle with Him.

I hope you have got over your money, as the Exchange is got against England 3½ per Cent by a remittance I have last post. This is a proof that the Circulation of Bank paper is mightily encreased which is the first of our many woes that will Come. We have had here a Privy Councelor of the Empress of Russia, who is positive that England will not get a Man from that Empire. The Recruiting goes on heavily in Germany and the utmost that is Expected from that quarter is 8000 Men, on the other hand they talk of stripping Ireland of ¾ of her remaining troops, and perhaps they may Supply Them by English Militia, who may be perswaded to go So far.

I sent You by a friend going to Paris the 1st vol: of Monsr. De Morveaux Elements of Chimistry which tho printed is not yet publishd and the 2d vol. is not printed. I put a Dogs ear to the part that Treats of Iron and steel, and I am apt to think he has gone further than the Russians in that article. You'l see that he makes all Iron perfect, and Consequently Inferiority of quality Implies merely a defective flux.

If you wish to know more on this subject come and See us. I beg my Compliments to Your son and all friends. I am ever with the warmest attachment Dear Sir Your most obedient humble servant   W. ALEXANDER

Addressed: A Monsieur / Monsieur Franklin / Hotel d'Hambourg Rue Jacob / a Paris

Endorsed: Mr. Alexander

Notations: Alexander W. 7 March 1777. / M. Alexander to B. Franklin

---

7. Undoubtedly William Galvan, who appears by name in Alexander's letter just cited.

[On or after March 7?, 1777[8]]

Homme juste vertueux.

Les persecutions que je ne cesse d'eprouvér, pour avoir constament fait mon devoir, le tendre et vif interet que prenent a mes malheurx, MM. turgot, malherbes, M. le marechal de soubise, MM. le marquis de castries, francès etc. doivent me faire ecouté favorablement,[9] des honnetes gens eclairés et surtout de Monsieur le docteur franklin. Vous aurez du voir par la notte que j'ai remise a M. dubourg, les grands avantages que vous retirerés da la fourniture que je propose et que je desire bien ardament que vous agreiés, persuadé que le congrés, les generaux, les soldats, en seront contents, ainsi que de voir arivér des ouvriers propres a traviliér l'habilement et l'equipement du soldat, et en etat d'en fabriquér par la suite les matieres; j'ai proposé depuis longtempts d'engagér un nombre sufisant d'ouvriers dans ce genre a passer avec moi en amerique, ainsi que cairol et ses deux fils qui attendent toujours avec impatience a roterdam, que je leur mende, si vous agréez leurs scervices.[1] Il est impossible de faire une melieure acquisition, ce que M. turgot a deja dit a M. deane[2] et je vous le

8. He was writing on a Friday, and referred to a recent letter to Dubourg. If our guess is right that that letter was the one of March 2 discussed in the note below, the earliest date for this one is the following Friday.

9. He was laying claim to an impressive list of supporters. Turgot and Lamoignon de Malesherbes were both former ministers, and Castries later became minister of marine; Charles de Rohan, prince de Soubise, was an aging courtier and a member of the *conseil d'état.* Francès had had some dealing with BF while in the French embassy in London: above, XVII, 126 n.

1. The only extant "notte" to Dubourg that enlarged on the advantages of his scheme was one of March 2, 1777, intended for BF (APS). In it Coder expatiated on the merits of his friend Etienne Cairol (or, as the latter spelled himself, Caÿrol), a cloth-maker who had been hounded into bankruptcy and then into exile in Holland, and who was ready to emigrate with his sons to America. Coder proposed to take them to St. Domingue along with his own staff of workmen and a hundred commissioned and noncommissioned officers, and from there "afronter avec joiée la ferocité avugle des anglois dans une traversée perilieuse."

2. The *Deane Papers* throw no light on what he said, for Turgot appears there only once in passing. Coder apparently bombarded the former minister with memoranda, and also left some with Du Pont de Nemours. Tur-

certifie sur mon honneur; mais comme vous seriés faché que le desir bien vif et scincere que j'ai de vous etre utile m'occasionat en heurope des nouvelles persecutions, je vous suplie d'engagér surtout M. deane (que je crois mal entoure) à ne parlér a persone de tout ce qui put avoir raport a tout ce que je propose, dans l'unique vue de rendre votre voiage en frence fructueux a vos nouveaux etats ou je suis bien decidé a allér finir mes jours. Dans cette vue et pour assurér de tout mon pouvoir, la liberté et la prosperité des etats independans de l'amerique, je doits vous representér que je scais depuis longtempts de science certaine que la majeure partie du parlement d'angletere (quoique representants d'un puple libre) c'est laissé corompre au point de favorisér le roy, secondé par les ministres, a devenir aussi despote, que les princes d'hurope. Le roy et les ministres, ivres de ce projet, enfles des succes de la dernière guere et eblouis par les richesses les ressourses et le lucxe de la mere patrie, ont trouvé aussi juste que aisé, de traitér les colons, comme un puple conquis, qui devoit s'estimér fort hureux d'etre les tres humbles scerviteurs et meme les esclaves du roy d'angletere, qui s'en seroit scervi, s'il eut reussi pour asservir le puple des trois royaumes le parlement l'etänt depuis longtempts. Il y a environ sept ants que M. ôrme, mon ami qui a epousé la soeur de milor thauren grand maitre d'artillierie dont je joints yci plusieurs lettres, ainsi que de M. matheus dont le pere a eté gouverneur de la jamaique[3] prevoioit la guere denaturée que le roy favorisé par le parlement fait aux colonies et que cette epoque seroit la ruine de l'angle-

---

got assumed that his friend would return them to the author as he was doing; "je ne suis pas à portée de lui rendre de grands services," he wrote Du Pont on May 2, "et dans le vrai, je ne le connais point assez pour en répondre." Gustave Schelle, ed, *Œuvres de Turgot* ... (5 vols., Paris, 1913–23), V, 521.

3. Orme was Robert Orme, Braddock's former aide-de-camp (above, VI, 109), who had later eloped with the sister of Viscount (later first Marquis) Townshend, master general of the ordnance. Wilmarth S. Lewis *et al.*, eds., *The Yale Edition of Horace Walpole's Correspondence* (48 vols.; New Haven and London, 1939–83), IX, 188 n; XX, 495 n. We have found no trace of "Matheus" or his father; no one of that or a similar name was governor of Jamaica.

tere. Jusqu'a ce jour M. orme a bien vû et moi je suis persuadé que le roy secondé par ses ministres, qui ont ensorsellé le parlement ne pouvant pas reussir a subjugér les colonies, se restrindra a asservir les trois royaumes, que les puissances de l'heurope ont le plus grand interet a favorisér cette revolution, et d'entretenir une guere eternelle, entre les colonies independentes et la mere patrie asservie, afin de s'enrichir et de s'-agrandir a leurs depents. La cause de la liberté comune a tous les hommes m'a inspiré ce que je vous ecris et de vous proposér des moyens qui pouront metre fin a tant des malheurx, assuré la liberté du puple anglois, qu'il devra je l'espere, aux verteux du congres et aux votres en particulié et au courage du puple ameriqain. Ces moyens sont d'apuiér la motion qu'a faite lor chatan [Lord Chatham] en ecrivant a vos amis et a ceux de la liberté en angletere d'ouvrir les yeux au puple sans perdre un moment, sur l'abominable projet qu'on a de l'servir, de prevenir le congres de vos demarches a ce sujet, qui ne manquera pas de faire tout ce qu'il feaut pour engagér la flotte et l'armée royale a ouvrir aussi les yeux, sur le dangér eminent qu'ils courent de perdre leurs libertés, en subjugent, ou ne subjugent point les colonies. Puisque le roy d'angletere ne vut point se contentér de la plasce que le hasar lui a donnée, qu'il s'en retourne dans son electorat, avec ses ministres et la majorité du parlement, qui faira des loix tout a son aise pour asservir s'il est possible davantage les pauvres anovriens. Cette revolution put s'operér sans qu'il y aye du sang rependu. L'angletere ainsi delivrée de ses opresseurs, put se reunir sans dificulté a ses amis et freres les ameriqains, aux holandois, et faire la loi a toute l'heurope qui jalouse de leurs richesses et surtout de leurs libertés, guete le moment favorable de les subjugér.

J'ai remits cette notte a M. dubourg, j'irai vous voir demain au soir samedi a passi, vous pouvés comptér homme juste, sage, et vertueux, sur codér, comme sur vous meme.

Endorsed: Codere

443

From Silas Deane

ALS: American Philosophical Society

Dear Sir   Friday Evening [March 7, 1777⁴]

I recd. This Evening the inclosed Lettrs. &c. from London. They had been opened, and when I see You, will explain by whom. I therefore broke them afresh, which impute to my impatience to know the particulars of the important Contents, on which I congratulate You most sincerely. I wish to see You early in the Morning here, as the Business I wish to confer on can be much better consulted on here, as it relates to Capt. Hynson in part; but if more Agreeable To You, will wait on You at Passy with him. I am Dear Sir Yours   S DEANE

Addressed: To / The Hone. Benja Franklin Esqr / Passy

From Lambert Wickes

ALS: American Philosophical Society

Sir,   March 7th, 1777

I should be much obliged if you would send the inclosed letter forward by the first undoubted safe Conveyance. I should not give your honour the Trouble if Could have an Oppertunity of a Safe Conveyance from this. As that is impractacable shall be much obliged for your Care of the Same. It Contains matters of Importance both to me and Mr. Johnston.⁵ From Sir, Your most Obedient humble Servant   LAMBT. WICKES

4. One of the letters that Deane was forwarding was undoubtedly Bancroft's of Feb. 28, which had been intercepted by the French: Stevens, *Facsimiles*, VI, no. 646. Accounts of the Battle of Trenton enclosed in that letter explain the congratulations to BF. Capt. Hynson, the reason for the present note, had arrived in Paris on March 6: Clarke, *Wickes*, p. 174. We assume that Deane was writing the next day.

5. The enclosure and the man to whom it was to be forwarded invite guesses. Ours, with little or no evidence behind them, are that "Johnston" was Henry Johnson, whom Wickes later consistently misspelled in that way, and that the enclosure had to do with Dr. Eliphalet Downer. Wickes did not know Johnson at this time, as far as we are aware, and certainly did not know that he was en route to France with the secret committee's dispatch above of Feb. 17. He may have known of Downer, Johnson's surgeon, who had been captured with him in their privateer, subsequently escaped to France and was in Paris by the end of March if not before (*Naval Docs.*, VIII, 723), and in mid-April joined Wickes's squadron: Wickes to BF below, April 15.

To The Hon [*torn*] Franklin

Addressed: To / The Honble. Dr. Benja. Franklin / at / Paris

Notations: Cap. Weekes L'Orient March 7. 77 / Capt Wickes

From Patience Wright   ALS: American Philosophical Society

My much Honoured Friend   Pall-mall Merch 7th [1777]

Sir, your thorow knowledg of me, and my Princples and actions makes it not nesscery for me to apoligize for writing to you.

I was very ancious for a opertunity to be of Som use in the great work of doing good to mankind. But now I see and behold gad ordreth all thing by His wise Provedence and things are all in the universial Course Set in order by him and all I Can do is only Pray for you as the means to bring about a wise and Safe Peace.

My daughter wrote to you Informing you of the Case of m. Platt now in Newgate for Rebelion Comitted in Sevannah in Georgea in year 1775[6] 4 month before the Coloney, was Declared Rebels the wondrful method taken to Convince us of our Safe Situation. I make no Doubt but your great Knowledge of human Nature and humane temper with a Desere to do all the good you Can you will so ordr that Eithr Platt be Imeadatly set at liberty or Exchangd for another prisioner or Som money be Sent to Support him in His unjust Confinement. A Letter from you to the alldmen of London or to some other of those who have Power it will Spirit up those good honest men (for Some thir are) who will Se that Justice be done if he be Brot to trial. We are now Impatient for your advise how to proced as youl See per the news papr his Case and the procedings against him. We keept in the Dark with all the movements of govrment and hope light to brake in upon us by som divine Spark Kindled in you or those providenc makes his agents.

6. See Elizabeth Wright's letter above, Feb. 13.

445

Mr. Scayr is now at Leberty to atend your Comands and if you think proper will See you.[7] My vanity promps me to think I Can entertan you if permited to write. Pray Sir Suffer me to troubel you with my Scraps of papr as I formely did in Craven Street. Small begining and Some time a Slight hint to a wise man from a honest heart may do wonders. Our Stocks is a meteriel object to our leading People and to Save ther money they Let go ther Contry &c.

Ld. Dunmore[8] Spent much time to Convince me of the week and wicked americean Rebelion this day and the Impudence of Captn. Weeks to take the Swallow Sloop war the Kings Packet and to Sell the Kings Ship at Public Sail in France is a thing he dont Like. He tells the King, "americea will very Soon be tired of doct. Franklngs Condoct" as also that thy now wish for Peace most heartly. May the great Ruler of the Earth give you health and Contune your life a Blessing to all mankind is the most heaty Prayr of sir your faithful humble servant   PATIENCE WRIGHT

I keep a Jurnal of meteriel Events and I wish to here from my Relations and friends in Philadelphia. Pray favor me with a line. My Children Joyne me in duty and good wishes.[9] All

---

7. Stephen Sayre, the American merchant and former sheriff of London (above, xx, 308), had been imprisoned in the Tower on a charge of trying to overthrow the government, and released for lack of evidence: *DAB*. On March 7 he was setting out for Paris to communicate a project to Deane, and by the 26th he was staying at the Hôtel d'Hambourg: Stevens, *Facsimiles*, XIV, no. 1446, p. 1; XV, no. 1544, p. 2.

8. The Governor of Virginia, after stubborn and unsuccessful attempts to maintain his authority there, had returned to England in 1776. *DNB*. Mrs. Wright had known him years before when he had been governor of New York: Charles C. Sellers, *Patience Wright, American Artist and Spy* ... (Middletown, Conn., [1976]), p. 108.

9. She here deleted a passage, which the APS has deciphered for us as follows: "my Son is an Exelent Portrait Painter Equal to mr West in taking likenesses. I wish you would admit him to meet [?] you and Paint you and your Friends and make him usful to you in any way you think most likely to serve his Country, my heart is full &c." See also Sellers, *loc. cit.* Young Joseph (1756–93) did come to Paris with the idea of painting BF, but not until late in 1781. *Ibid.*, p. 158.

Lettr are Said to be opend at the Post office So it is not met-eriel what I write here.

Dr. F——

Notation: Wright Pall-mall 7th. March

From Patience Wright   ALS: American Philosophical Society

My Honoured Friend,   Merch [After March 7,[1] 1777]
With the most hearty Love and confidenc in your Friend-ship, Mr. S has deservedly Recomended himself to his Contry and to your Service.

Things now are in a fare way of Coming into a Self pre-serving and Self Cure *way*. They will now with a littel of your assistance soon work their own *way*. The Spirit of honest En-glishmen seem to git the art of thinking Properly and much *now* desposd to act so, if they knew what way was best. Ther is wise and great men in England, who are Ready to Serve their Contry with your Wise Council and Some few others. In a few month, you may have Peace and happiness Restord to both of our unhappy Contrys. The gentlmen of Property from the Iland of Jemaca have com to a Resolution to Stand by america in consequence of which gov. Keath and the ad-maral Gayton are Call'd hom, and NOW is the tim to Say before the People in England that Express order went out to them at Jemaica to Seze the Vessls belonging to amerrica and take thes Property, Some Months before any actt of Parlement was made for the Same. The ordr went out in feby 4th 1775 the Actts Past the Season after[2] the metereal Cercumstanc has not allar-amd the Court what makes the Ministry Keep Platt From

1. The opening sentence speaks of Stephen Sayre, who left for Paris on or about March 7; see the note on the preceding document. But the "Barer" of this letter, referred to later, must have been some one else; what she says about him does not fit Sayre.

2. Our guess is that the sentence should end here. By "Season" she pre-sumably meant session, for she is referring to the passage of the Prohibi-tory Act in December, 1775.

Coming to a triall for fear of those profs comng out to the merchants and Peopel of *England*.

I have had the Honor to be Informd by one of the gov Council whose Intrest and health Both oblige him to own truth. You Sir are humbley Requested to urge this matter by a lette to or letters Importing what your wisdom Shall think Best. Truth Careys the Vcitory. The Peopels have been told that America Sizd the West India Property first, which was not So. But facts Properly to be Stated by you to the merchants with a demand for those Prisoners will Stope the Bosted Pride of taking up Sylas Deen and Dotr. Frankling for treason. As John the *Paintor* is to give Dignity to great Britian by his Discoveris he is to live to Confess Crimes nevr Comitted.[3]

But as the Barer may Properly be said to come to You as an asistane Sent from God to Relieve mankind and to Carey on the great work of his Providence—

Your arival at Phila was in good TIME. Your arival is in good TIME ALSO. My dream is out now this 1777 will Bring the ways of god more Clear to MAN and Prove that women are usful and may be admitted into the Bond of usful Friendship wher the good of all men are Concernd. Inclosd is a pamplet Intitld a Patrott KING which Pleas to Read as also a news Pappe with Mr. Wilks Speach, wherein Mr. Platt Case is taken up in the house Comons by him[4] and the Peopel now begin to feal thir fooly in so long Shamefuly looking upon one another. A letter

---

3. Silas Deane had employed James Aitken, better known as John the Painter, to burn British naval dockyards. Aitken did set fire to the Portsmouth yard, tried to do the same at Plymouth, and burned part of Bristol. He was arrested and convicted, and on March 10 he was hanged. William B. Clark, "John the Painter," *PMHB*, LXIII (1939), 1–23; Julian P. Boyd, "Silas Deane: Death by a Kindly Teacher of Treason?," 3 *W&MQ*, XVI (1959), 337–42. We have no other evidence that BF was thought to be involved, but a rumor that the British were attempting to extradite Deane reached Dijon before the end of the month; see Alexander to BF below, March 29.

4. The pamphlet, we assume, was the 1775 reprint of a work that BF had himself reprinted in 1749, Bolingbroke's *Letters on the Spirit of Patriotism*, which included his *Idea of a Patriot King*. For John Wilkes' discussion of the Platt case see Cobbett, *Parliamentary History*, XIX (1777–78), 29–30. Mrs. Wright may well have enclosed a clipping from the *Public Advertiser*, which printed the speech on Feb. 22.

to Sir Charls Asgall on the afairs of STOCKS, a Letter from The Emperor Germany or Some truths Properly Stated to the alldmen in London And a Letter to Ld. Temple or Gorge Germain would at this time have a blessed good efect.[5] Your own head and heart will Direct you to write to me Inclosd with proper direction which way I Cane the most honestly and most heartly Serve you by Serrving old ENGLAND. We Both Know London and wish well to mankind we have had many agreable Chatt on Publick afairs we well know what we can do and know of a truth that the great God has made us useful to our Contry.

Majr Labilear has Seven hundred men who have not bowd down to *Baäll* and I have nere five hundred in my Congregation, whose weight in the Scaile, and propely derected will turn the balanc of Power much in old *Englands* favour yet.[6]

You will find our friend the Barer of this a Stedy will Informd man whose Prudence and throw Knowledge of England and Amerrica will most Scartanly make him a object of your Cear and Confidenc you want Such a man we send him to you. We send him with a head and heart Evry way qualified to be useful in your trad, in your Countng house or at your Desk in almost any Capacity he will most faithfully Serve you and as you have Buseniss very Plenty We beg you for your own Sake as well as for us that the moment he arives you put a penn in his hand and a few gunies in his Pocket and in 3 weeks time you will See the good effects of his Politicall Skill, which from undeniable Proffts [Proofs] is good. I need not urge any thing to you who I am So well Convincd want no Spurr to great actions, only I wish to Shew you our good will and help the Glorious Cause which may god Bless and Bless you with long life and meny happy years to live and enjoy the Blessings you have so gloriously defended and assisted to Posterity. Our hearts are warm for you we are tiptoe to Come

5. The letters leave us completely bemused. So do the suggested recipients, who seem to have had nothing in common: Sir Charles Asgill, a former lord mayor of London; Earl Temple, Chatham's brother-in-law; and Lord George Germain, the American Secretary.

6. For Maj. Peter Labilliere, who was at least close to being demented, and the Biblical references here and below see Charles C. Sellers, *Patience Wright* . . . (Middletown, Conn., [1976]), pp. 114–15, 255.

to you and we Expect in July to See you COME in the Name of the Lord of host and gidion.

There is 23 more unhapy Prisoner at Portsmout and gosport and the Same perdiecterment of Mr. Platt they wish to Know what to hope from you. For gods Sake have Compasion on those Stranger whos Property is all taken from them and they in Iorns No one to Comfort them, and it is not in the powe of the People to help them without You. You must be our Delivier our Salvation depends on you and you Sir have it in your Powr to Set us all in order. You may Set us all to work in Evry mans own way to help Each other to the good of the Whole which is the Prayr of your old faithful Servnt

PATIENCE LOVELL[7]

The Bearer will inform you how these Prisoners, or any that shall be hereafter may be set at Liberty by a Letter, from some Publick Man to Public Men informing them that they may depend on Retaliation.

Endorsed: Mrs. Wright.

Jonathan Williams, Jr., to the American Commissioners

ALS: American Philosophical Society

Gentlemen   Nantes March 8. 1777.

As I don't hear farther relative to the purchase of Mr. Montieu's Fusils I conclude that you do not intend to put any on board the Count de Vergennes, so propose to put in her as much salt as will answer for Ballast. I have lately been looking over some Memoires about Mr. Montieu's process[8] and find that these Fuzils cost him at the rate of 25 sous each for those capable of repair and 10 sous each for those that are not, with a Condition that none of them should ever be sold in the Kingdom. This circumstance makes it sure that if you don't

7. She originally signed herself Patience Wright, then almost deleted the "Wright" and substituted the thin disguise of her maiden name.

8. His trial. As a result of the Bellegarde affair (above, XXII, 464) Montieu was tried before a military tribunal in 1773, imprisoned until the autumn of 1774, and fined 250,000 *l.t.* Bachaumont, *Mémoires secrets*, VIII, 198–9.

by them nobody else can (except for the negro Trade) and therefore that you will have nobody to outbid you. Mr. Shweighausser desires to know whether you approve of having Capt. Toaklys Brig sold; as she now lays at the Expence of 400 Dollars per Month, she will otherwise soon eat out her Value. The Balance remaining in his hands on the Cargo of Tobacco he tells me has been called for, and agreeable to his orders he must pay it to Mr. Pennet. I have the honor to be with greatest Respect Gentlemen Your most obedient Servant

J WILLIAMS JUNR

The Honourable The Deputies of The United States.

Addressed: A Monsieur / Monsieur Franklin LLD / a l'Hotel d'Hambourg / Rue Jacob. / a Paris.

Notation: Jona Williams Nantes March 8. 77

From Jean-Baptiste-Jacques Elie de Beaumont[9]

ALS: American Philosophical Society

Monsieur   Paris 8 mars 1777.

J'ai l'honneur de vous presenter Monsieur dufourny de villiers l'un de nos dignes Membres de la societé d'Emulation dont j'ai eu l'honneur de vous parler. Consacré aux arts par goût il ne croit pouvoïr faire un plus noble et plus patriotique usage de ses talens que de consacrer a sa patrie le buste de l'illustre franklin[1] qu'un autre hemisphere menace de nous ra-

---

9. An old acquaintance of BF; see above, XVI, 205. This is the first extant letter from him.

1. Louis-Pierre Dufourny de Villiers did execute the bust, the first of BF after his arrival in France. The artist made little mark as a sculptor but subsequently, as an architect, was prominent among the Jacobins: Charles C. Sellers, *Benjamin Franklin in Portraiture* (New Haven and London, 1962), pp. 240–6. The Société libre d'émulation, founded in 1776 in imitation of the Royal Society of Arts, was causing a considerable stir but apparently lasted for only four years: Bachaumont, *Mémoires secrets*, X, 133, 140, 146; Robert-Charles de Lasteyrie du Saillant, *Bibliographie générale des travaux historiques et archéologiques* ... (6 vols., Paris, 1888–1918), IV, xiii. Beaumont's note below, March 9, suggests to us that BF had been expected at a meeting of the society on the 8th, either as a member or a guest.

vir et qui pourtant devroit se croire citoyen du monde entier si l'estime, la reconnoissance et le respect sont des titres d'incolat et de cité. Je joins mes prieres aux siennes, Monsieur, pour vous prier de lui accorder cette faveur dont il est digne par le prix qu'il y attache et en cela je vous sollicite pour moi-même, me proposant ensuite de m'assurer d'après ce buste votre portrait pour le placer dans ma bibliotheque au rang des amis de Leur patrie et de l'humanité. J'ai l'honneur d'être avec une tendre veneration Monsieur Votre tres humble et tres obeissant serviteur   ELIE DE BEAUMONT

Addressed: A Monsieur / Monsieur franklin / A Paris

Notation: elie de Beaumont Paris 8 Mars 77

From Nathan Rumsey   ALS: American Philosophical Society

Honorable Sir   Nantes March 8th. 1777.

By the Brigantine Penet Cap. Bartlet, just arrived here in 29 Days from Boston, who sailed the 2d. Day of Feby. we have received a Confirmation of the Affair at Trenton, and the particulars of General Lee's being taken, as You will find them in the Gazette of the 6th. January herewith inclosed. The Cap. brought papers as late as the 23d. January but the inclosed of the 20th. and the 6th. include all the news of the others. As near as I can collect I think the Number of men killed, wounded and taken prisoners in the Trenton Affair including the Skirmishes of Princetown, Morristown, Hackinsack and Peek's Hill amount to about 2000.

The Captain informs us verbally that the Congress, who, by his Excellency General Washington's Letter you will perceive were Assembled at Baltimore, left Philadelphia upon General Howe's Arrival at Trenton, and that their immediate Return to Philadelphia was expected: that General Lee's being taken had greatly enraged the Populace, and that General Washington had by Flag of Truce informed the Enemy, that if they sent off General Lee for England he would hereafter give no Quarter. The French Gentleman taken with Gen. Lee is a

452

Collonel Gaiault, who sailed from hence for Phil. in a Congress Ship in August last.[2]

Not a Letter is come to Hand from Philadelphia, but in one to Mr. Penet from Boston it is said the Congress have ordered 100 Battalions to be inlisted for 3 Years: that many of those Batallions are already officered, and are filling up fast.

The Captain informs that 2 large Ships were ready to sail from Boston when he put to sea: as soon as they arrive I shall forward to You any interesting News they may bring.

I have taken the Liberty of inclosing a Letter in your Packet to Alderman Lee, the better to avoid the Nantes Post mark which I suspect condemns many of our Letters in England; it is directed, as by his Desire are all my Letters to him, to Mr. Browne. Your forwarding it will add further Obligations to those already conferred on Honorable Sir Your most obedient Humble Servant   NATHAN RUMSEY.

Addressed: To The Honorable / Doct. Benjamin Franklin / at / Paris. / per Mr. Defransey.

Notation: Nathan Rumsey March 8. 77.

From Jonathan Williams, Jr.

ALS: American Philosophical Society

Dear and honored Sir   Nantes March 8 1777.

We are informed here that a Canadian with a commission from the Congress has fitted out a privateer at Dunkirk, and after cruising sometime in the Channel has taken a very large prize and carried her into Ostend; this News seems to occasion great eagerness in some people here to fitt out privateers in the same way, if proper commissions can be obtain'd and the french Government will connive at having french Sailors on board. If you have cruising Commissions or can give them, I apprehend I could soon have several of them at Sea, and if you think the presence of an american necessary in any Enterprize of that nature which you may think proper to under-

2. For the vicissitudes of Vic Gaiault de Boisbertrand see above, XXII, 469 n.

take, you know you may command me; I am at least half of a Sailor, and would endeavour to do my duty. What I mean by this to say is that I am at your Disposal, so that no good plan may fail of Execution for want of any assistance in my power to give.

Mr. de Francy will tell you the Success of his Commission at L'orient.

The Ship Pennet is just arrived from Boston and brings papers down to the 23d Jan. some of which Mr. Ramsey sends by this Conveyance. You will see that the Capture of Gen. Lee is but too true and that our Successes in Jersey amount to 919 Prisoners at Trentown, 500 at princetown 35 at morristown 30 Tories at peeks kill and 500 at Hackinsack. I understand that this Ship is dispatched by Mr. Penets partner[3] and that she is to be followed by 2 or 3 more to his address, so we may soon expect more news.

I have this moment recd. your Favour of March 2. I thank Mr. Dean most sincerely for his Reccommendations. I shall write again per post Mr. Francy being now waiting. I am most respectfully your dutifull and affectionate Kinsman

J WILLIAMS

Addressed: D Franklin

Notation: Mr Williams

From Elie de Beaumont   ALS: American Philosophical Society

Monsieur   Paris 9 mars 1777.

Monsieur Monin de champigny officier de distinction neveu d'un homme qui a joüi de la plus haute consideration dans ce pays ci desireroit fort d'avoir l'honneur de vous entretenir et de vous presenter des vües qui peuvent vous être utiles.[4] Le vif interêt que je prends a lui me fait prendre la liberté de vous le presenter et de vous prier de l'entendre. Je comptois vous

3. Emmanuel de Pliarne: *Naval Docs.*, VII, 1000–2.

4. Louis-Antoine Monin de Champigny (born 1735) had served overseas and been retired as a lieut. col. in 1774; his uncle was Monin de Marnay, *commissaire des guerres*. Bodinier.

en parler hier, mais nous n'avons eu de vous que le chagrin de ne pas vous posseder.[5] J'ai l'honneur d'être avec une tendre veneration Monsieur Vôtre tres humble et tres obeissant serviteur ELIE DE BEAUMONT

Votre interêt pour nous vous fera apprendre avec plaisir que Madame de Beaumont (qui a l'honneur de vous faire mille complimens) et mon fils sont a present en assés bonne santé.

Notation: elie de Beaumont, Paris 9 Mars 77

From Richard Bache

ALS: American Philosophical Society

Dear Sir   Philadelphia 10th. March 1777.

We yet remain without a Line from you; tho' we have had the pleasure of hearing you were safe arrived; this is my third Letter to you, since you left us; I think I have never mentioned to you before, that Mr. Galloway, when the Enemy were at Trenton, passed over the Delaware and took protection, three of the Allens did the same, viz: John, Andrew, and Billy. They are now all in Newyork, wishing and praying, I suppose, that the Enemy may soon make a conquest of us, that they may have an opportunity of being with their Families again.[6]

Last Wednesday, Mr. Thomas Wharton Junr. was declared President of the executive Council for this State, and Mr. George

5. Doubtless at a meeting of the Société libre d'émulation, mentioned in Beaumont's note of the previous day.

6. All four had availed themselves of the pardons offered by the Howes. For Galloway's action and his subsequent career see Julian P. Boyd, *Anglo-American Union: Joseph Galloway's Plans to Preserve the British Empire, 1774–1788* (Philadelphia, 1941), pp. 53–111. The Allen brothers had supported the revolution in its early stages: John (above, XVIII, 92 n) had been on the Philadelphia committee of inspection and observation and in the N.J. provincial convention; Andrew (1740–1825) had organized a cavalry troop and served with BF on the committee of safety and in the Pa. delegation to Congress; William (c. 1751–1838; above, XXII, 428 n) had been an officer in a Pennsylvania regiment. None of the three could stomach independence. John was later attainted by the Pa. assembly but died before trial, and Andrew and William eventually retired to England. Charles P. Keith, *The Provincial Councillors of Pennsylvania* . . . (Philadelphia, 1883), pp. 145, 147–9 of second pagination.

455

Bryan Depty. President, they were proclaimed formally at the Court house.[7] The Congress have returned from Baltimore, and sit here again; they have raised the Interest on the Moneys they borrow to 6 per Cent:[8] whether this will have the desired Effect is hard to say. About a fortnight ago, we had a smart skirmish with the Enemy near Woodbridge, they were far superior in number to us, but our shot did so much more execution than theirs, that they made a very precipitate retreat, it is said, with the loss of upwards of 500 killed, wounded, and taken; we had about ten Men killed, and twice that number wounded. I left the good Folks at Goshen two days ago, very well and hearty, they join me in Love to yourself Temple and Benny. I am Dear Sir Your ever affectionate Son

RICH BACHE

Doctor Franklin

Addressed: The Honble. / Doctr. Benjn. Franklin / One of the Commissioners from the United States of America / a Paris / Via Bourdeaux.

Bordeaux 10 May 1777 Forwarded by Sir Your most obt Hble Sts.   S. & J. H. DELAP

Notation: Recd. per the [*torn*]y

From Ebenezer Smith Platt[9]

ALS: American Philosophical Society

Sir,   Newgate. March 10th. 1777.

Through the solicitations of my freinds I have made free to trouble you with thiss Packett, and to beg the favour of you to forward per first conveniant and safe opportunity the Inclos'd letters. I am inform'd you have been acquainted with a state of my Case,[1] for which reason have omited troubling you

---

7. Wharton (1735–78), easily confused with the cousin of the same name who was prominent in earlier volumes, had served on the committee and council of safety and, when elected president of the supreme executive council, became the chief executive of the state. *DAB.* For George Bryan, who had been one of BF's and Galloway's leading opponents in the old days, see above, VI, 386 n.

8. *JCC,* VII, 158.

9. See Elizabeth Wright's letter above, Feb. 13.

therewith again, and shall only give you the following Particulars (for your own satisfaction) which were not propper to be Inserted in my Case: that on the 7th. of January 1776 I left Georgea, with permission from the Provintial Congress, bound to Cape Nichola Mole,[2] but unfortunately was taken within a few hours sail of my distin'd Port, by his Majesty's Ship Maidstone, and Carried into Jamaca tho was not made a Prise off, on Account of the Vessels not being American Property. I therefore sold my Cargo, and Purchas'd a Vessell, with Intent to proceed back to America; tho was oblig'd to Clear out my Vessell for Turtling and Fishing, and as I was proceeding to Sea, was stop'd, my Vessell sold, and I detaind a Prisner in Irons, and for farther particulars I refer you to the state of my Case, which contains a true Account. Since my Confinment here I have taken every Legal step to Indeavour to be brought to tryall but could not, and fear I shall not be, as I am now detained under that Accursd, and Arbitary Law, for the suspention of the Habeous Corpus Act until January 1778,[3] until which time, if not longer I expect to remain, unless through the Blessings of God, the Americans shou'd Continue to go on with eaqual sucksess, as they have for these few months last past done, which I beleive wou'd be the meanes of Discharging me and all others, which I pray God may be the Case. From Sir Your most Obedient and Verry Humble Servant
EBENEZER SMITH PLATT

Notation: E. S. Platt from Newgate

From Elizabeth Wright   ALS: American Philosophical Society

Honourd Sir   March 10th 1777
Wee have so good an oppertunity of writing to you that it would be a Pitty to miss of it, and I cannot forbear Mentioning again to you, about Mr. Platt. He was advised by Mr. W——ks[4] to Pettition the old Baily last Session, to be brought to Tryall, and least they should Refuse it, or Plead ignorance

1. The pamphlet enclosed in Elizabeth's letter, just cited, or in her mother's of March 7.
2. Mole St.-Nicolas, on the north coast of St. Domingue, now Haiti.
3. The act that Elizabeth had mentioned, 17 Geo. III, c. 9.
4. Undoubtedly John Wilkes.

to put a Copy of it in the Papers. This He thought very Nes-scesary, that it wo'ld bc a means of his being try'd before, or Precluded the Present Act. He did, but the Attorny General imediately posted to the Court and Plead that the judges had no Right to try him there, that he had Pettition'd the wrong Court, it should have been the Court of Kings Bench (and of course be brought before my L——d M——f——d⁵). By this means he Evaded his Tryal. Since that his Lawyer has been informd thro L——d M——f——ds means, that if He would Pettition the King and take the oath of allegiance he should be set at Liberty. This all the City Patriots have advis'd him to do, alledging it would be much better than to Run the Risk of being try'd in the Kings Bench, for that if he should refuse, they would Rake Heaven and Earth to find some Proof against him, and he would be in a most terrible Situation, and they did not by any means Concieve it to be worth his while to loose his Life for that objection, or that it could be required of him by God or his Country, to So Eminently Risk it. Wee Could have wish'd to have Consulted you Sir about it but [*for*] the Distance and Uncertainty of the Way and a sort of Hury-ing fatality. The Pettition is sign'd, and the Lawyer said it was wrote in such a Manner that he did not think the Oath would not be required of him, but that Ld. M——d had given his word that he should be set at Liberty on those Conditions. How far it will be veryfied wee Cannot yet tell, but should it not sucseed, wee shall justly Reproach ourselveves for not acting with Courage and Honesty and haveing the Faith of a Daniel. Wee was the only Family he was acquainted with on his arrivall in England, therefore has placed all His Confidence in Us, and what Friends he has was cheifly Recomended thro our means, till they saw and became acquainted with Him, when He needed no other Recomendation his own innocency and integrity were sufficient. The Enclos'd is a copy of a Let-ter from him to us.⁶ I hope Sir the Bearer of this will meet

5. Mansfield.
6. A letter from Platt to Patience Wright of March 5, copied by Elizabeth and with a paragraph added by her, is now among BF's papers in the APS. The letter expanded on the advice of the "City Patriots" that he take the oath of allegiance to save his life. He still refused to do so unless the Wrights

with your approbation at least I wish it. Wee dont concieve any body more Proper or in whom wee could put more Confidence or so Capable of serving you, and know it to be his most Earnest desire to do good. I Remain Dear Sir your most Dutifull Sincere   EW

Notation: Elizabeth Wright

Dumas to the American Commissioners

ALS: American Philosophical Society; letterbook draft: Algemeen Rijksarchief, The Hague

Dear Sirs   11e. Mars 1777

Je ne saurois plus longtemps résister à la tentation de vous écrire, que j'éprouve à chaque ordinaire, et à laquelle je succomberois régulierement, si la crainte d'être importun, plus qu'utile, ne me retenoit. Enfin la joie de pouvoir vous féliciter des succès de nos amis l'emporte sur cette crainte. Trois Regiments Hessois pris à Trenton, et 3 autres, royaux, battus successivement, sont des événements avérés arrivés bien à propos, et me font augurer, non seulement que les autres, annoncés sur des fondements moins authentiques, savoir la défaite du Major Rogers, la reprise des Lignes de Kingsbridge, et le soulevement du reste des troupes Hessoises, pourroient bien se confirmer aussi. Quoiqu'il en soit, je rends graces à Dieu de ce qui est arrivé; et dans mes éjaculations mentales (car mes prieres ne sont jamais méditées, et par conséquent elles sont infiniment courtes) je lui demande à tous moments sa puissante protection pour les Etats Unis Am. Mon Epouse et ses deux fils en exhalent de pareilles; et ma fille[7] ne manque

---

approved, and begged their candid opinion. They were deeply agitated, Elizabeth added, and took further counsel with friends and in particular with Benjamin West, who reinforced what the "Patriots" had been urging. "These Arguments, Partly made converts of us (weak Women) and wee sent him Word wee thought he had best do it."

7. The draft adds "qui n'a que dix ans." This was Anna Jacoba, his older daughter: Jan W. S. Nordholt, *The Dutch Republic and American Independence* (Herbert H. Rowen, trans.; Chapel Hill, N.C., and London, [1982]), p. 48; chap. 3 is a sensitive study of Dumas.

pas, soir et matin, de demander soir et matin au bon Dieu de bons jours et de bonnes nuits pour les bons amis de Papa. Ainsi l'Amérique a pour elle, dans ces provinces, outre les voeux de tout ce qui n'y est pas directement ou indirectement intéressé en faveur de ses cruels ennemis, une petite Eglise, de 5 membres seulement, mais qui se distingue des autres, je ne dis pas par l'orthodoxie, mais par le sentiment, la simplicité et l'innocence. A mesure que nos Marchands feront avec les vôtres des affaires lucratives, et surtout lorsque nos rentiers pourront, sur des sûretés suffisantes pour capitaux et intérêts, placer chez vous l'argent dont ils regorgent, vous aurez aussi pour vous les Eglises où l'on prie avec plus de bruit et d'étalage: la superstition et l'incrédulité, l'hypocrisie même, l'avarice et la prodigalité, l'économie et le luxe, l'active coquinerie et la phlegmatique bonhommie, tout priera alors à l'envi pour l'Amérique.

L'Amb[assadeu]r A[nglais] a présenté il y a plus de 8 jours un Mémoire à nos Etats, le plus violent et le plus impératif dont on puisse s'aviser d'Etat à Etat. Le Roi son maître se plaint sur le plus haut ton, que les Am[éricains] trouvent à se pourvoir chez nos Marchands, surtout à St. Eustache, d'armes et de munitions, &c. &c.; que le Gouverneur de St. Eustache a rendu le salut à un Armateur Am[éricain] et les favorise; que par-là il a témoigné reconnoître des Rebelles pour une Puissance legitime; que les Etats doivent déposer, rappeller, punir ce Gouverneur, donner une satisfaction éclattante à l'Angleterre, prohiber efficacément les pratiques de leurs Marchands, et *NB* ne point procéder en tout ceci avec leur lenteur ordinaire, qu'autrement la bonne harmonie entre la Gr. Br. et cette Rep. sera interrompue, lui-même rappellé, &c. &c. Telle est, Messieurs, la Loi, munie, comme vous voyez, d'une Sanction formelle, que l'on vient de notifier ici, où à ce qu'on m'a assuré, les premieres têtes sont à la fois choquées de l'incartade, et intriguées comment y répondre. Comme la réponse cependant ne peut se faire sans avoir pris l'avis des provinces, on a envoyé l'affaire à chacune *ad referendum*; cela occasionnera partout des Dietes extraordinaires; et l'on est très curieux de savoir quelles résolutions elles prendront. J'ai cru cette nouvelle digne de vous être communiquée; et je ne manquerai pas, en son temps, de vous en mander les suites.[8]

Je n'ai ni écrit, ni parlé au grand Facteur depuis ce dont je vous ai rendu compte, Messieurs, faute de matiere qui puisse me donner quelque relief.

Je suis fort lié depuis quelque temps avec le Gazetier françois de Leide, qui favorise tant qu'il peut les Am[éricains], qui a déjà inséré dans ses feuilles plusieurs petits articles que je lui ai communiqués, et qui en inserera d'autres si je puis les lui fournir: il me l'a promis; et je vous conseille fort, Messieurs, de profiter de sa bonne volonté, en me fournissant de quoi lui donner (mais plus de faits que de raisonnements politiques); car sa gazette est fort répandue, tant en ce pays que par toute l'Europe, étant estimée comme l'une des plus impartiale.[9] On lui a reproché dans une lettre d'Espagne, et dans d'autres aussi, de ce qu'il n'entre pas encore assez dans les détails quant à l'Amérique.

Dieu vous donne, mes respectables Amis, santé, vigueur, et continuation de bonnes nouvelles. Je baise les mains au vénérable Docteur, et à son digne Collegue. Je sens, Messieurs, que vous m'écririez, si vous n'étiez surchargés d'affaires; mais je mentirois, si je vous laissois croire que ma philosophie me fait supporter avec résignation une longue privation de vos Lettres. Cependant quelque cheres qu'elles me soient, je ne voudrois pas, pour tout au monde, en avoir aux dépens de la moindre des affaires de nos amis; j'aimerois mieux, en ce cas, continuer de souffrir. Ceci soit dit aussi à Mr. Carmichaël, Pour lequel je joindrai un mot, si le temps me le permet, sinon, une autre fois. Ce que j'ose hardiment vous demander, Messieurs, c'est de m'aimer toujours comme je vous aime et respecte avec tous les braves Americains.

8. Perhaps he did, in a letter now lost; see BF's description of the episode to Lee below, March 21.

9. The *Gaʒ. de Leyde*, which appeared twice a week, was one of the most prestigious journals in Europe. Its editor since 1775 was Jean Luzac (1746–1807), a stalwart champion of the American cause who later corresponded with Washington and Adams. Butterfield, *Adams Correspondence*, IV, xiv–xv. The commissioners, as will be seen, accepted the invitation to contribute material.

La seule chose qui trouble la joie que j'ai de leurs succès, c'est la captivité du brave Général Lee. Son sort m'inquiete.[1]

Une autre nouvelle, que je viens de lire dans une de nos Gazettes Hollandoises, m'affligeroit beaucoup aussi, si je pouvois la croire: c'est que, selon une prétendue Lettre de New-York, du 22e. Janvier, Messieurs Allen et Galloway, tous deux Membres du Congrès, se seroient allés rendre au Ld. Howe. A moins que vous ne me la confirmiez, je ne croirai jamais une telle infamie. Vos atroces ennemis n'ont déjà que trop débité pareils mensonges. Je suis, Messieurs pour toute la vie, votre dévoué et humble serviteur   St. Jean.

[J'ai] quelques autres particularités [encore] à vous marquer. Je les dirai vendredi prochain à Mr. Carmichaël sous le couvert de Messieurs Germany Girardot et Compagnie. Ce que je lui écris est aussi pour vous; ainsi, Messieurs, s'il étoit absent, ouvrez, s'il vous plait, mes Lettres pour lui avant de le lui faire tenir.

Messieurs Franklin et Deane

Addressed: Monsieur / Monsieur Silas Deane / hotel de hambourg rue Jacob / à Paris [*in another hand:*] hotel Colbert

Notation: Dumas 11. March 77.

Thomas Morris to the American Commissioners

ALS: American Philosophical Society

Gentlemen   Nantes March 11th. 1777

I have duely received your esteemed favours of the 2d and 3d Instant the Contents of which requiring no immediate answer, the present may serve to acquaint you with the safe arrival here of the Schooner Jenifer in 35 days from Baltimore. This Vessell has brought sundry dispatches for you from Congress, and the Bearer Captain Hammond will have the pleasure of delivering them to you tomorrow Evening or on Thursday Morning. As Captain Hammond does not understand french and to obtain dispatch I have requested the fa-

1. The draft adds "plus que je ne puis vous le dire."

vour of Mr. Rumsey to accompany him to Paris.[2] The articles required by the Committee will be got in readiness immediately, so that after he has obtained your orders, he can proceed for Baltimore without delay. I remain in haste Gentlemen Your most Obedient Servant   THOS. MORRIS

To The Honble. Benja. Franklin and Silas Deane Esqrs.

Addressed: To / The Honble. Benjamin Franklin / Silas Deane & Arthur Lee Esqrs. / at / Paris. / by Captain Hammond

Notation: T. Morris 11 Mar. 77.

Jonathan Williams, Jr., to the American Commissioners

ALS: American Philosophical Society

Gentlemen   Nantes March 11. 1777.

I have began to load the Ship. The salt is at Painbeuf and we are here loading the first Lighter with some Bales and the Cordage which is near all made, the Bales that were here are all reduced, and tomorrow the workmen will begin to reduce those that are just arrived from orleans; the Letter from thence informs us that about 50 more will be ready to come away about the 15th of this month. If these should be detained and the ship ready before they arrive, I suppose we must not wait; I shall therefore hasten all I can unless you order otherwise. I beg to know whether you can obtain the large anchors, else I am afraid we shall not be able to get them. Capt. Wicks informs me that he has only a quarter Waggoner[3] that he can spare which he will send if he can find an opportunity. If you can send Charts from Paris it would be better.

A little Schooner is arrived here express from the Congress. The Capt. landed at Quiberon and now goes express with Mr. Romsey to Paris. It is said that Gen. Washington has cut off the Retreat of the English in Jersey, but the Letters they bring

2. Among the dispatches was that above, Jan. 9, from the committee of secret correspondence, where Hammond is identified. Rumsey, in a letter to his father, described his activities as the Captain's interpreter: *Naval Docs.,* VIII, 690–1.

3. A book of charts.

will give you full Information. I have the honor to be in haste, with the greatest Respect Gentlemen Your most obedient most humble Servant, J WILLIAMS JUNR

The Honble The Deputies of the United States.

Notation: Jon Williams Nantes March 11. 77

From Penet   ALS: American Philosophical Society

Monsieur   nantes le 11. mars 1777.

Mr. rumcay porteur de la presante est partie ce jour pour cerandre [se rendre] a paris avec le capt. hammond arrivant dans ce port expedie par le committé secret de philadelphie a baltimore avec des lettres pour vous Mr. Deane et Lée; nous esperons qu'il vous serat parvenus heureusement et nous attandons vos ordres et son retour pour l'expedier ausitot avec les munitions qui nous sont demandé.

Je ne vous informme d'aucunne nouvelle venant du continant en etant instruit ausi bien que moy. J'auréz l'honneure de vous dire seulement que toutes vos operations qui nous sont confié tant du Congré que des provinces sont executé avec toutes l'exactitude posible et j'ausse me flatter que lorsqu'elles vous seront connus plus particulierement elles me meritterons de plus en plus votre confiansce.

M. Th. morris depuis qu'il ai liée d'affairre avec moy tiens la conduite la plus reculliere il s'occupe du matin au soir aux affaires publicques desquelles il ai chargé et je panse qu'il vous donne un compte exacte de tous ce qui ce passe a ce sujet.

Vous auréz etté informmé sans doute de la vante des prices conduit a loriand par le Capt. Wilkes. Je me suis randue a loriand avec Mr. morris pour cette operation nous avons conduit l'affaire avec la prudansce et discrestion la plus grande. J'ay l'honneur d'etre avec un profond respect, Monsieur, votre tres humble et tres obeisant serviteur   P: PENET

Au noble Docteur Francklin

Addressed: Au noble / Docteur Francklin / A paris

Notation: Penet, Nantes 11 Mars 77

From Jonathan Williams, Jr.

ALS: American Philosophical Society

Dear and honored Sir.   Nantes March 11. 1777.

In consequence of your advice and kind offer of reccommendation, I have conversed with Mr. Shweighausser relative to a plan for establishing a House here to transact american Business. His proposition is to take the Firm of J Williams & Co. myself being the ostensible person and he the acting partner, thereby keeping it wholly seperate from his other Business.

As it cannot be expected in my Situation that I should be able to run into advances nor that Mr. S in a Time of War should suddenly transport his property into the Hands of Individuals who are strangers to him, the kind of Business we propose is to sell american Cargoes and to vest the Amount in the Manufactures of France according as shall be ordered: ready money trade was always your advice. With regard to public Business, the Congress will no doubt provide the necessary Funds if they think proper to employ us; But as some Capital is necessary for the Current Charges, Mr. S proposes to advance about 30,000 Livres (£1300 Sterling). I told him without reserve every particular relative to my Situation and he gives me a flattering mark of his Confidence in my probity and honour: if I can rub thro' the Difficultys that generaly attend the want of Capital by your friendly reccommendation and my Conduct I feel an assurance that I shall in the End make a handsome Fortune.

I inclose a Letter which I propose to have printed and circulated thro' the hands of all the principal merchants in America. I have taken the liberty to cite your name which I hope you will not disapprove but I beg you will make what alterations or additions you think necessary and return it to me with your opinion upon this whole Concern. I likewise inclose a Letter which Mr. S proposes to send in addition to mine.

I believe I inform'd you some time ago that Capt. Paddock was here, he remains still but his Vessell is ready to sail. He tells me he don't think he shall go in her.[4] I shall be obliged if

---

4. This is Seth Paddack's first appearance since the Christmas season of

you will enquire whether any more Letters are arrived for Smith.[5] I received Billys Letter by the Quaker who I have obtained a passage for. My Love to him.

I am afraid that the news I gave you from Ostend wants Confirmation.

I shall be obliged if you will write to Mr. S relative to our proposed Connection, as Things of this nature do not come so well from ones self. I flatter myself the want of a proper Establishment would be the principal, if not the only objection to a still closer Connection.

I send this by Mr. Romsey please to say all the good news that comes by him for I am surrounded every Day on Change and everybody asks for News, News! I am ever with the greatest Respect Your dutifull and affectionate Kinsman

J. Williams Junr

Addressed: Doctor Franklin

The American Commissioners to the Committee of Secret Correspondence

LS: National Archives; L:[6] British Library; copy: National Archives

Gentlemen   Paris March 12th. [–April 9] 1777.

It is now more than 4 Months since Mr. Franklin's Departure from Philadelphia, and not a Line from thence written

---

1773: above, XX, 512–13 (where we misspelled his last name, as BF consistently did). Paddack arrived in France in December, 1776, hoping to join a privateer in Nantes, but was disappointed; the vessel referred to here was presumably a substitute, and he did not sail on her. He found another privateer, out of Marseilles, and the voyage was another disappointment. Paddack to BF below, Aug. 2, 1777.

5. Presumably JW's alias. In a letter to WTF of April 9 (APS) he amplified this request: the letters were addressed to Smith at the Café royal d'Angleterre, in the Rue Jacob by the Hotel d'Hambourg.

6. The LS was extremely late in arriving, as witness the marginal note on the commissioners' next letter below, May 25. The L, headed "Triplicate" and unsigned, is apparently an original that was intercepted. It differs from the LS and copy, except as noted, only in insignificant details; from it we have silently supplied a few words now obscured in the LS.

since that time has hitherto reached either of your Commissioners in Europe. We have had no Information of what passes in America but thro' England, and the Advices are for the most part such only as the Ministry chuse to publish. Our total Ignorance of the truth or Falsehood of Facts, when Questions are asked of us concerning them, makes us appear small in the Eyes of the People here, and is prejudicial to our Negotiations.

In ours of Feby. 6 of which a Copy is enclosed, we acquainted you that we were about purchasing some Cutters to be employ'd as Packet Boats. We have succeed'd in getting one from Dover, in which we purpose to send our present Dispatches. Mr. Hodge, who went to Dunkirk and Flushing where he thought another might be easily found has not yet acquainted us with his success. We promised that when we had a Conveyance which by its Swiftness is more likely to carry safely our Letters, we would be more explicit in Accounts of our Proceedings here, which promise we shall now fulfill, as follows.

In our first Conversation with the Minister, after the Arrival of Mr. Franklin, it was evident that this Court, while it treated us privately with all Civility, was cautious of giving Umbrage to England, and was therefore desirous of avoiding an open Reception and Acknowledgement of us, or entering into any formal Negotiation with us, as Ministers from the Congress. To make us easy however we were told, that the Ports of France were open to our Ships, as Friends; that our People might freely purchase and transport as Merchandize whatever our States had Occasion for; vending at the same time our own Commodities; that in doing this we should experience all the Facilities that a Government disposed to favour us, could consistent with Treaties, afford to the Enemies of a Friend. But tho' it was at that time no Secret, that 200 Field Pieces of Brass and 30,000 fusils with other Munitions of War in great abundance had been taken out of the Kings Magazines for the purpose of Exportation to America, the Minister in our presence affected to know nothing of that Operation, and claimed no Merit to his Court on that Account. But he intimated to us that it would be well taken if we communicated with no other person about the Court concerning our Affairs but himself, who would be ready at all convenient times to confer with us.

We soon after presented several Memorials representing the State of the Colonies, the necessity of some Naval aid and the Utility to France that must result from our Success in establishing the Independance of America, with the Freedom of its Commerce. In Answer we received a positive refusal of the Ships of the Line (which we had been instructed to ask) on this Principle, that if a War with England should take place, the whole Fleet of France would be necessary at home for her Defence; that if such a War did not take place, yet while England apprehended a War, it was equally serviceable to our States that the Fleet of France should remain entire in her Ports, since that must retain an equal Force of English at home, who might otherwise go to America, and who certainly would follow thither any french Squadron.

During these Conferences, every step was taken to gratify England publickly, by attending to the Remonstrances of her Ambassador, forbidding the Departure of Ships which had Military Stores on board [*In the margin:* These were afterwards privately permitted to go, or went without Permission.] recalling officers who had leave of Absence and were going to join us, and giving strict Orders that our Prizes should not be sold in French Ports; yet that we might not be discouraged, it was intimated to us by persons about the Court, that those Measures were necessary at present, France not being yet quite ready for a War; And that we might be assured of her good Will to us and to our Cause, Means were proposed of our obtaining a large Sum of Money for present Use by an Advance from the Farmers General to be repaid in Tobacco of which they wanted 20,000 Hhds. We entered accordingly into a Treaty with that Company, which meeting with Difficulty in settling the Terms, we were informed that a grant was made us of two Millions of Livres from the Crown of which 500,000 was ready to be paid us down, and an equal Sum should be paid the beginings of April, July, and October; that such was the Kings Generosity, he exacted no Conditions or Promise of Repayment he only required that we should not speak to any one of our having received this Aid: we have accordingly observed strictly this injunction, deviating only in this Information to you, which we think Necessary for your Satisfaction, but earnestly requesting that you would not suffer it to be made publick. This is the Money which in our former Letter we mention'd as rais'd for us by Subscription.

One of the ablest Sea Officers of France, skill'd in all the Arts relating to the Marine having offered his Service to our States with the Permission of the Minister, we (enabl'd by the above Grant) engag'd him to superintend the building two Ships of War of a particular Construction, which tho' not of half the Cost, shall be superior in force and utility to Ships of 64 Guns.[7] He has built one here for the King which we are told exceeds every thing in Swift sailing. He has furnished us with Drafts which we send you, that if the Congress thinks fit, others of the same Construction may be set up in America; in which Case we have given him Expectations of being their Commodore. We have seen his large and curious Collection of Memoires containing every the minutest Particular relating to the Construction and Management of a Fleet, with a variety of proposed Improvements; and we are persuaded that he will be found a valuable Acquisition to our Country.

April 9. Since writing the above, we received Dispatches from the Congress by Capt. Hammond, others from Mr. Morris by Capt. Bell;[8] and some Copies by Capt. Adams via Boston, which on many Accounts were very satisfactory. We directly drew up and presented Memorials on the Subject of those Dispatches; We were promised immediate Consideration and speedy Answers; for which we detain'd Capt. Hammond, but we have not yet obtain'd them. We receive however continual Assurances of the Good Will of this Court and of Spain; We are given to understand that it is by their Operations the raising of German Troops for England has been obstructed; we are paid punctually the second 500,000 Livres, and having convinc'd the Ministry of the Great Importance of keeping up the Credit and fixing the Value of our Currency

7. See the commissioners' agreement with Capt. Boux above, Feb. 12.

8. Capt. Thomas Bell had received a U.S. commission for a privateering venture that Robert Morris, Deane, and others hoped to finance: *Deane Papers*, I, 477–8; Clark, *Wickes*, pp. 185–6.

which might be done by paying in Specie the Interest of what we borrow, or in Bills upon France for the Amount, we are now assured that the above mentioned Quarterly Payments shall be continued (after the 2,000,000) for the purpose of paying the Interest of the 5,000,000 Dollars you are supposed to have borrow'd, which we believe will be punctually comply'd with; and the Effect must be restoring to its original Value the Principal for which such Interest is paid and with that the rest of the Emission.[9]

We have turned our Thoughts earnestly to what is recommended to us by Congress, the borrowing £2,000,000 sterling in Europe. We first proposed to borrow it of this Court upon Interest, but were told by the Minister that it was impossible to spare such a Sum, as they were now arming at a great Expence, which kept the Treasury bare: but there was no objection to our borrowing it of private Capitalists here, provided we did not offer too high an Interest as that might raise it upon Government. We are advised to try Holland; and we have caused the Pulse to be felt there but tho' Holland at present is a little disgusted with England, and our Credit is considerably mended in Europe by our late successes, it does not yet appear to be sufficient to procure such a Loan. Spain it seems has by its punctual payments of Interest, acquired high Credit there, and we are told that by her Publickly borrowing as for herself, and privately allowing us to draw on her Banker, we might there obtain what Money we pleased. Mr. Lee was gone to Spain, before the Commission and Orders came to BF for that Station: He will give you a particular Account of his Negotiations there; We here only mention that he received the same general Assurances of the Good Will of that Court, that we have here of this; was informed that 3000 Barrels of Powder and some Cloathing were lodg'd for our Use at New Orleans; that some Merchants at Bilboa had Orders to ship for us such Necessaries as we might want; that orders would be given to allow us Admission into the Havana as a favour'd Nation; and that we should have a Credit on Holland (the

---

9. Congress, before BF's departure, had authorized borrowing the $5,000,000 through the loan offices established in each state: *JCC*, v, 845–6.

Sum not then settled) which might be expected at Paris the beginning of this Month. The Spanish Ambassador here, a grave and wise Man, to whom Mr. Lee communicated the above, tells us, that his Court piques itself on a religious Observance of its word, and that we may rely on a punctual Performance of its Promises. *On these Grounds we are of Opinion*, that tho' we should not be able to borrow the two Millions sterling recommended to us; yet if the Congress are obliged to borrow the whole 20,000,000 of Dollars they have issued we hope to find sufficient here; by way of Subsidy, to pay the Interest in full value, whereby the Credit of their Currency will be established, and on great and urgent Occasions they may venture to make an Addition to it. Which we conceive will be better than paying the Interest of 2,000,000 Sterling to Foreigners. On the whole we would advise Congress to draw on us for Sums equal to the Interest of what they have borrow'd as that Interest becomes due allowing the lenders in the Drafts 5 Livres Money of France for every Dollar of Interest.[10] And we think they may venture to promise it for future Loans, without however mentioning the Grounds we here give for making such a Promise. For these Courts have particular Strong Reasons for keeping out of the War as long as they can, beside this general One, that on both sides the Nation attacking loses the Claim which when attack'd it has for Aid from its Allies. And we have these Advantages in their keeping out of War that they are better able to afford us private Assistance, that by holding themselves in readiness to invade Britain they keep more of her Force at Home, and that they leave to our arm'd Vessels the whole Harvest of Prizes made upon her Commerce, and of Course the whole Encouragement to encrease our Force in Privateers which will breed Seamen for our Navy.

The Desire military Officers here of all Ranks have of going into the Service of the United States, is so general and so strong as to be quite amazing. We are hourly fatigu'd with

10. The recommendation to borrow £2,000,000 had been in the committee's letter of Dec. 21. The commissioners are apparently saying that, if Congress chooses to cover by domestic loans the $20 million in currency already issued, and whatever more may be needed, the French government will take care of the interest on the whole unspecified amount.

471

their Applications and Offers which we are obliged to refuse; and with hundreds of Letters which we cannot possibly answer to Satisfaction, having had no Orders to engage any but Engineers, who are accordingly gone. If the Congress think fit to encourage some of distinguished Merit to enter their Service, they will please to signify it.[1]

Capt. Wickes made a Cruise this Winter, and return'd with 5 Prizes, of the Produce of which we suppose Mr. Morris will acquaint you; for they are sold, tho' the bringing them into France has given some Trouble and uneasyness to the Court; and must not be too frequently practis'd. We have order'd him to make another Cruise before he returns to America, and have given him for a Consort the arm'd Cutter[2] Capt. Nickolson; they will sail in a few Days.

Mr. Hodge writes us that he has provided another Cutter. We intended to have employ'd one of them as a Packet, but several of yours being now here, and having lately made a Contract for sending one every Month, a Copy of which we enclose,[3] we shall make use of this new purchase as a Cruiser.

We have at length finish'd a Contract with the Farmers General for 4000 Hhds. of Tobacco, a Copy of which is enclosed. We shall receive the first Advance of two Millions of Livres next Month and we intreat you to use your best Endeavours to enable us to comply with our part of the Agreement. We found it a Measure of Government to furnish us by that means with larger Advances, as well as to obtain the Ground of some of their own taxes. And finding the Minister anxious to have such a Treaty concluded, we comply'd with the Terms, tho' we apprehend them not to be otherwise very advantageous. We have Expectations however, that in case it appears that the Tobacco cannot be afforded so cheap thro' Captures &c. Government will not suffer us to be losers.[4]

We have purchased 80000 Fusils, a Number of Pistols &c.

1. The L here adds a phrase not in the LS or copy: "and we shall take the best Advise in chusing them."
2. The L here adds "the Dolphin."
3. The contract with Chaumont below, April 1.
4. See the headnote on the contract below, March 24. The amount contracted for was 5,000 hogsheads, not 4,000; the advance was 1,000,000 *l.t.*.

of which the enclosed is an Account for 220,000 Livres. They were Kings Arms and second hand, but so many of them are unus'd, and unexceptionably good that we Esteem it a great Bargain, if only half of them should arrive.

We applied for the large brass Cannon to be borrow'd out of the Kings Stores till we could replace them, but have not yet obtain'd an Answer.

You will soon have the Arms and Accoutrements for the Horse except Saddles, if not intercepted by the Enemy.

All Europe is for us. Our Articles of Confederation being by our means translated and published here have given an Appearance of Consistence and Firmness to the American States and Government, that begins to make them considerable.

The separate Constitutions of the several States are also translating and publishing here, which afford abundance of Speculation to the Politicians of Europe. And it is a very general Opinion that if we succeed in establishing our Liberties, we shall as soon as Peace is restored receive an immense Addition of Numbers and Wealth from Europe, by the Families who will come over to participate our Privileges and bring their Estates with them. Tyranny is so generally established in the rest of the World that the Prospect of an Asylum in America for those who love Liberty gives general Joy, and our Cause is esteem'd the Cause of all Mankind. Slaves naturally become base as well as wretched. We are fighting for the Dignity and Happiness of Human Nature. Glorious is it for the Americans to be call'd by Providence to this Post of Honour. Cursed and Detested will everyone be that deserts or betrays it.

We are glad to learn the Intention of Congress to send Ministers to the Empire, Prussia and Tuscany: With submission We think Holland, Denmark, Sweden and Russia (if the Expence is no Objection) should not be neglected. It would be of great Service, if among them we could get a free Port or two for the Sale of Prizes as well as for Commerce: A Commencement of Intercourse has been made with Prussia, as you will see by the enclosed Copies of Letters between his Minister and us. We suppose as the Congress has appointed one of us to Spain, they will order another of us to some of the other Courts; as we see no utility equal to the charge, and yet some

473

Inconveniency, in a joint Commission here, where One, when freed from Commercial Cares and Action is sufficient for the Business. As soon as the Court of Spain shall be willing to receive a Minister, (which from Mr. Lee's Information seems not to be at present the Case) Mr. Franklin intends to go thither in Obedience to the Orders he has received. Mr. Lee had express'd his readiness to go to Prussia or Tuscany before the Intention of Congress to send to those Courts was known. And he waits here awhile by the Advice of his Colleagues, expecting that perhaps the next ship may bring his Future Destination.

For the procuring and sending more certain and Speedy Intelligence, We have as before mentioned entered in a Contract here, whereby we are to have a Packet boat dispatched every Month. The first will sail in about a fortnight. As we are yet without an explicit Answer from Court on several important Points, and we shall have that speedy Opportunity, we do not now enlarge in Answer to the several Letters received by Hammond, Bell, Adams and Johnson. We only now assure the Congress that we shall be attentive to execute all the Resolutions and Orders they have sent us for our Government,[5] and we have good Hopes of Success, in most of them.

For News we refer in general to the Papers, to some Letters inclosed which we have received from London. We shall only add that tho' the English begin again to threaten us with 20,000 Russians, it is the Opinion of the wisest Men here and particularly among the Foreign Ministers, that they will never be sent. The Anspachers, who were to be embarked in Holland, mutinied and refused to proceed, so that their Prince was obliged to go with his Guards and force them on:[6] A Gentleman of Rotterdam writes us, that he saw a number of them brought bound hands and feet in Boats to that Place. This does not seem as if much Service can be expected from such unwilling Soldiers. The British Fleet is not yet half mann'd. The Diffi-

5. The new instructions are discussed in the headnote above on the letter from the committee of secret correspondence, Dec. 30.

6. The incident occurred on March 8. Edward J. Lowell, *The Hessians and the Other German Auxiliaries of Great Britain in the Revolutionary War* (New York, 1884), pp. 47–50.

culty in that Respect was never before found so great; and is ascribed to several Causes; viz. a Dislike of the War; the subtraction of American Sailors; the Number our Privateers have taken out of British Ships; and the enormous transport Service. The French are free from this Difficulty, their Seamen being all Registred, and serving in their Turns. Their Fleet is nearly ready and will be much superior to the English when join'd with that of Spain, which is preparing with all Diligence. The Tone of the Court accordingly rises; and it is said that a few Days since when the British Ambassador intimated to the Minister, that if the Americans were permitted to continue drawing Supplies of Arms &ca. from this Kingdom, the Peace could not last much Longer; he was firmly answer'd, Nous ne desirons pas la Guerre, et nous ne le craignons pas. We neither desire War, nor fear it. When all are ready for it, a small Matter may suddenly bring it on; and it is the Universal Opinion that the Peace cannot continue another Year. Every Nation in Europe wishes to see Britain humbled having all in their Turns been offended by her Insolence, which in Prosperity she is apt to discover on all Occasions: A late Instance manifested it towards Holland; when being elate with the News of some Success in America, and fancying all that Business ended, Sir Joseph York delivered a Memorial to the States, expressing his Masters Indignation against them, on Account of the Commerce their Subjects carried on with the Rebels, and the Governor of Eustatia's returning the Salute of one of the American Ships: remarking that, (*if that Commerce was not stopt, and the Governor punished*) the King knew what appertain'd to the Dignity of his Crown and should take proper Measures to vindicate it. The States were much offended, but answer'd cooly, that they should enquire into the Conduct of their Governour, and in the mean time would prepare to secure themselves against the vengeance with which Britain seem'd to threaten them. Accordingly they immediately order'd 26 Men of War to be put upon the Stocks.[7]

We transmit it you some Affidavits relating to the Treatment

7. See Daniel A. Miller, *Sir Joseph Yorke and Anglo-Dutch Relations, 1774–1780* (The Hague, 1970), pp. 51–4.

of our Prisoners, with a Copy of our Letter to Lord Stormont communicating them, and his insolent Answer.[8]

We request you to present our Duty to the Congress, and assure them of our most faithful Services. With great Respect, we have the Honour, to be, Gentlemen, Your most obedient humble Servants   B FRANKLIN

                                           SILAS DEANE

Copy

To the Committee of Correspondence.

Notation: Franklin & Deane to the Comtee. March 12. 1777.

The American Commissioners: Memorandum [for Vergennes][9]

AD:[1] Archives du Ministère des affaires étrangères

             Memoire   [March 12, 1777]

While Great Brittain engross'd the Commerce of the United States, merchandize imported from thence into France was considered as British, and Consequently subject to the same duties, Customs &c, as if imported direct from the Islands of Great Brittain or Ireland. Since the separation of those States from Brittain it is presumed their Merchandize must be considered under a different predicament,[2] and it is therefore desired that untill Stable and fixed regulations respecting the Commerce of the United States can take place those Articles which come directly from the United States may be exempted from being Subject to such duties, which appear in several instances to be designed as a prohibition, particularly those on the Articles of Salt Fish, Whale Oil, Whale bone, Spermaceti, Beeswax, Peltry or Furrs, Masts for the Navy, Tar, Pitch, Turpentine, and Indigo.

Notation: 12 march 1777.

8. The commissioners' two letters, the second provoked by the Ambassador's reply, are below, April 2, 3.

9. In reply, we believe, to a sentence in Vergennes' memorandum above, under March 1.

1. In Silas Deane's hand.

2. In a different category.

Arthur Lee to Franklin and Silas Deane

ALS: American Philosophical Society

Dear Sirs: Vitoria, March 12th. 1777

In my return to this place, I receivd the joyful intelligence which I enclose; and in which I congratulat you a thousand and a thousand times. The Congress had removd to Baltimore, and General Putnam was providing for the defence of Philadelphia, before this happy change in the posture of the hostile Army. It is said that the cruelties exercised in the Jerseys, had so exasperated the People, that the Militia fought with irresistible fury. I am afraid Genal. Lee is a prisoner. Upwards of a thousand of the Prisoners in New York have died of famine and cruel treatment.

The barbarity of these Sarracen Invaders went so far as to destroy the Philosophical Apparatus at Princeton College, with the Orrery constructed by Dr. Rittenhouse.[3] The Papers say, that Genl. Howe had removed part of his baggage to Staten Island, and orderd a reinforcement from Rhode Island. There is an account in the Papers of the taking of Elizabeth Town, but that makes the number of Prisoners less than 200 among whom were 80 highlanders. The loss of the enemy in all these rencounters is stated at upwards of 2000, with Artillery, Baggage, and Stores to a considerable amount. I think we may now say the Scales are at least even, and I shall continue all my life to thank General Howe for dividing his Army, from which I always hop'd for the greatest advantages to us.

I am to wait here, an Answer to what I transmitted to Court in consequence of my conference with the Duke of Grimaldi who is to meet me here to-morrow. I have represented that my not going to Madrid will be construed a refusal on the part of Spain to receive a Deputy from the States and may therefore have a very bad effect both in Europe and America. I have askd at the same time for a credit in Holland and expect that to soften the former, they will be more liberal in the latter.[4] I

---

3. A false report; see Howard C. Rice, Jr., *The Rittenhouse Orrery: Princeton's Eighteenth-Century Planetarium* ... (Princeton, 1954), p. 44.

4. For Lee's negotiations at Vitoria see his letters above of March 5 and below of March 16.

send an Account of the late intelligence to Madrid, London and the Hague, desiring Dumas to have it inserted in the Gazettes, and translated into German to be distributed among the german troops, before they embark, with a hint that as the King of G. Britain refuses to settle a Cartel, they may remain Prisoners for life. Surely this will be a good reason for them, especially the Officers to refuse to go. I intended to have written to Mr. Dean and Sir Roger le Grand at Amsterdam to the same purpose, but I perceive by a Letter from the latter, in the post office here, going to Madrid that he is yet in Paris, which makes me suppose they have laid aside or postpond the intended journey.[5] Mr. Carmichael can assist you in contriving to distribute the Account among the german troops, from which I think some good must arise.

It seems to me that something ought to be transmitted to the States General, representing that their agreeing to let the mercenaries notoriously hird to desolate the States of America, have a passage, will be considered as a breach of that strict neutrality which the United States expect from all those nations, who woud wish to remain in Amity with them. Vatel acknowledges that granting such passage has often been warmly[?] remonstrated against; tho he maintains that it is no breach of neutrality, nor any just cause of war. I differ from him so much, that I am willing to have my name put to such a remonstrance. It is a palpable imposition upon common sense to say, that a nation who facilitates the enterprizes of my Enemy against me, preserves a neutrality: The pretence that they woud do the same for us, is incompetent; also why will it not justify the furnishing Arms, Ammunition and Provisions in the way of trade? They both stand upon the same foot, that of contributing directly to my distruction. For in what does he who opens the way to the employment of Arms &c. against me, differ from him who furnishes them?

5. The Chevalier Georges Grand (Lee consistently mistook his first name) had in fact been in Amsterdam for weeks; see his letter to the commissioners above, Feb. 27. Deane or BF had been expected to go to The Hague; see the commissioners to the committee of secret correspondence above, Feb. 6.

478

I had almost forgot to mention that the Ships which brought the news, are the Alexander, Capt. Williamson and the Charlotte Capt. Sinclair from Newberry port. They saild the 4th of Feby. and arrivd at Bilboa the 8th of March.[6]

Please to remember me to Sir Roger and all our friends. If Mr. Dean shoud go to Amsterdam, he will probably meet with a Mr. Paul Wentworth; of whom I woud advise him to be much upon his guard. I have the honor to be Dear Sirs with great esteem, Your most obedient Servant,   ARTHUR LEE

Endorsed by Franklin: Mr Lee

Notation: A Lee to Messrs F & D. Victoria March 12. 77.

From Barbeu-Dubourg   ALS: American Philosophical Society

12e. mars 1777.

J'ai l'honneur de souhaiter le bonjour à Monsieur franklin; nous avons oublié moi de lui remettre le memoire quittancé de sa Lingere, et lui de me remettre le traité original entre les fermiers generaux et moi.[7] J'ai besoin de celuicy actuellement; ainsi je le prie de me le renvoyer par le porteur.

J'ai annoncé sa visite a M. Turgot pour demain; il le recevra avec grand plaisir,[8] et je compte profiter de l'occasion, pour lui reïterer sans cesse les assurances de mon attachement sans bornes   DUBOURG

Notation: du Bourg / 12 Mars 77

6. William Sinclair sailed on Feb. 3 and John Williamson the next day, both from Marblehead; they carried cargoes of fish consigned by Elbridge Gerry to the Gardoquis. The ships returned with merchandise and naval stores, and reached Boston in mid-June. Philip C. F. Smith, ed., *The Journals of Ashley Bowen* ... (2 vols., [Portland, Me.,] 1973), II, 510–11; George A. Billias, *Elbridge Gerry* ... (New York, [1976]), pp. 74, 127.

7. The same draft contract that BF had sent to William Alexander, who had acknowledged it in his letter above, March 7.

8. This was, as far as we know, BF's first meeting with the former Minister.

From William Wilkinson[9]

AL: American Philosophical Society

Paris, March 12th 1777

Mr. Wilkinson's Compliments to Dr. Franklin and is sorry he could not find him at Hotel D Hamborg.

Twas not till this Day that Mr. W knew possitively where Dr. F was else should have sooner acquainted him that a Gentleman going to London early next Week who may be depended on will carry any Letters there carefully.

Mr. W also going himself to Nantz on Monday[1] will convey any Letters the Dr. May have to that Place.

If by the Bearer Dr. F will be so kind as fix when the Letters will be ready Mr. Wilkinson will do himself the Pleasure of waiting on him for them.

Addressed: Dr Franklin

Notation: Wilkinson

"Lettre du Comte de Chanmburg [Schaumberg]": a Satire Attributed to Franklin

Printed in [Baudouin de Guémadeuc, ed.,] *L'Espion dévalisé* (London, 1782).[2]

Franklin's contributions to the press during his first year in France, unlike his years in England, were few and far between. He helped to translate some state constitutions that were published in the *Af-*

9. A brother-in-law of Joseph Priestley and the brother of John Wilkinson, one of the leaders in developing effective iron-smelting in England. John's feuds with William drove the latter to take refuge in France, where he too had great success in iron manufacture; his foundries near Nantes became famous. *DNB* under John Wilkinson. The tone of this note suggests that he had already been in touch with BF, and he tried again to see him before leaving for Nantes; see his note below under March 18. Yet more than two years later JW gave him an enthusiastic letter of introduction to BF: April 4, 1779, APS.

1. We believe that he delayed his departure; see his note just cited.

2. The satire appeared in March, 1777, in an anonymous MS newsletter, "Bulletin de Versailles"; our effort to obtain a photocopy of the MS, now in Leningrad, has been unsuccessful, and we have only the text as published in Mathurin F. A. de Lescure, ed., *Correspondance secrète inédite sur Louis XVI*

faires de l'Angleterre et de l'Amérique; three short memoirs, one his and two perhaps his, appeared there in translation in the summer of 1777; a number of other articles in the same periodical were attributed to him, at the time or subsequently, for no apparent reason.[3] This satire was not among them; it first appeared in print five years later, and its authorship cannot be established. Another version, with minor differences, remained unpublished until 1866, and was attributed to Franklin by John Bigelow in 1874. His sole reason was the deftness of the satire. For the next eighty years, nevertheless, Franklinists accepted and at times embellished his attribution.

The fact that the essay is worthy of Franklin is no evidence that he wrote it. He certainly did not write it in this form, for the French is too finished to be his; if he was the author, what we have is a translation. We may equally well have the work of another author; several Frenchmen of the day were mordant satirists. This possibility was first raised in 1954, and subsequent research has made Bigelow's ascription look more and more flimsy. The most recent study of the subject has found no evidence whatever that Franklin was the author, and good reason to think that he was not.[4] We find this

---

... (Paris, 1866), pp. 31-3. Given the choice between that and the earliest printing, in *L'Espion dévalisé*, we have selected the latter; when it differs substantially from the former, we have so indicated in our annotation. Another and cruder satire that bears some resemblance to this one, entitled *Lettre du Landgrave de Hesse*, was published in the Netherlands in 1777; BF's copy is in the John Carter Brown Library.

3. The constitutions are discussed in his correspondence with La Rochefoucauld in this and the following volumes; his undoubted memoir is below under Sept. 8, and the two that may be his are before June 18, 1777. The *Affaires* also published in 1777 BF's "Edict by the King of Prussia" and his letters from and to Howe in 1776 (above, XX, 413-18; XXII, 483-4, 519-21). The articles attributed to him that we are convinced were not his are the following: "Extrait d'un discours prononcé par le docteur Francklin en l'honneur du Major-Général Warren ... ," II, cahier VI, pp. 26-9; "Extrait d'une gazette allemande," IV, cahier XVIII, pp. cliv-clxii; "Réflexions d'un Observateur ... ," VI, cahier XXVI, pp. viii-xxiii; "Difficultés des marches en Amérique," VI, cahier XXIX, pp. clxiii-clxx; "Caractères politiques des Américains, tracés par un des leurs," VII, cahier XXXII, pp. lix-lxiii; "Mémoire demandé," VII, cahier XXXII, pp. l-lviii; "Matroco," VII, cahier XXIII, pp. cxvi-cxxvi.

4. See Durand Echeverria, "'The Sale of the Hessians.' Was Benjamin Franklin the Author?," APS *Proc.*, XCVIII (1954), [427]-31; J. Viktor Johansson, *Sur la Correspondance littéraire secrète et son éditeur* (Göteborg and Paris, [1960]), pp. 17-29; and especially Everett C. Wilkie, Jr., "Franklin and 'The Sale of the Hessians': the Growth of a Myth," about to appear in the APS *Proc.*

conclusion, about a gem that has so long adorned the Franklin canon, both unwelcome and convincing. A negative cannot be proved, however, and we print the satire on the faint chance that it falls within our rubric.

Lettre du Comte de Chanmburg, écrite de Rome[5] au baron de Hohendorff, commandant des troupes Hessoises en Amérique.

[Before March 13, 1777[6]]

Monsieur le Baron de Hohendorff.

J'ai recu à Rome votre lettre du 27 décembre[7] de l'année derniere à mon retour de Naples. J'ai appris, avec un plaisir inexprimable, le courage que mes troupes ont montré à l'affaire de Trenton, et vous ne pouvez vous figurer la joie que j'ai ressenti en apprenant que de dix-neuf cents cinquante[8] Hessois, qui se sont trouvés au combat, il n'en est échappé que trois cents quarante-cinq. Ce sont justement seize cents cinq hommes de tués, et je ne puis assez louer la prudence que vous avez montré, en adressant une liste exacte de ces morts à mon ministre de Londres. Cette précaution étoit d'autant plus nécessaire, que les lettres adressées au ministre Anglois ne portent que quatorze cents soixante-cinq morts; il en résulteroit un différent de 462,000[9] florins à mon préjudice, puisque suivant le compte du lord de la trésorerie, il ne me revient que 483,450 florins,[1] au-lieu de 643,500, que j'ai droit de demander suivant notre convention. Vous comprenez le tort que cette erreur de calcul feroit à mes finances, et je ne doute pas que vous ne mettiez tous vos soins à prouver que leur liste est fausse et que la vôtre vraie.

5. The "Bulletin" here adds "le 18 Février." The unpronounceable "Chanmburg" is a variation of "Schaumberg," as the name appears in the other versions mentioned above.

6. It appeared in the "Bulletin de Versailles" between entires dated March 10 and 13.

7. "Octobre" in the "Bulletin."

8. "2950."

9. "483,450."

1. From "puisque" to this point is omitted. Neither version seems to make any arithmetical sense.

La cour de Londres objecte qu'il y avoit une trentaine[2] de blessés, et qu'ils ne doivent pas être payés comme morts. Mais j'espere que vous vous serez ressouvenu des instructions que je vous ai données à votre départ de Cassel, et que vous n'aurez pas cherché à rappeller à la vie, par des secours inhumains, ces malheureux dont vous ne sauriez conserver les jours qu'en les privant d'un bras ou d'une jambe; ce seroit leur faire un présent funeste, et je suis sûr qu'ils aiment mieux mourir que de vivre mutilés[3] et hors d'état de me servir. Je ne prétends pas pour cela que vous deviez les assassiner, il faut être humain, mon cher baron, mais vous pouvez insinuer sans affectation aux chirurgiens qu'un homme estropié fait honte à leur art, et qu'il n'y a rien d'aussi savant que de laisser périr tout ce qui n'est plus en état de combattre. Au reste, je vais vous envoyer de nombreuses recrues: ne les ménagez pas, songez que la gloire passe avant tout: la gloire est la vraie richesse: rien n'avilit un militaire comme l'amour de l'argent; il ne faut donc songer qu'à l'honneur et à la réputation; mais cette réputation doit être acquise parmi les dangers; une bataille gagnée sans coûter de sang au vainqueur, n'est qu'un avantage honteux, tandis que les vaincus se couvrent de gloire en périssant les armes à la main. Rappellez-vous que de trois cents Lacédémoniens qui défendoient le défilé des Thermopiles, il n'en revint pas un seul. Que je serois heureux, si j'en pouvois dire autant de mes braves Hessois! Il est vrai que leur roi Léonidas périt à leur tête, mais les moeurs actuelles ne permettent pas à un prince de l'Empire d'aller combattre en Amérique pour une cause qui ne le touche nullement; et puis à qui payeroit-on les trente guinées par homme tué, si je ne restois pas en Europe pour les toucher? Il faut d'ailleurs que je puisse vous envoyer des recrues pour remplacer le monde que vous perdez, et c'est pour cela que je vais retourner en Hesse. Il est vrai que les hommes commencent à manquer dans mes états; mais je vous ferai passer des enfans; d'ailleurs plus la marchandise est rare, plus elle se vend. On m'a assuré que les femmes et les petites filles se sont mises à labourer et à cultiver la terre, et qu'elles ne réussissent pas mal.

2. "Centaine."
3. "Inutiles."

483

Vous avez fait très-sagement de renvoyer en Europe le docteur Aumérese, qui réussissoit si bien à guérir le flux; il faut se garder soigneusement de tirer d'affaire un homme capable d'avoir le dévoiement, car il sera toujours un mauvais soldat[4]: un poltron fait plus de mal dans une affaire, que dix braves gens n'y font de bien.[5] Vous promettrez de l'avancement à tous ceux qui s'exposeront; vous les exhorterez à chercher la gloire au milieu des dangers; vous direz au major de Maundorff que je suis très-mécontent de sa conduite: c'est lui qui a sauvé les trois cents quarante-cinq hommes qui ont échappé au massacre de Trenton, et de toute la campagne il n'y a pas eu dix hommes de tué sous ses ordres. Enfin, ayez pour objet principal de tirer les choses en longueur, et d'éviter toute affaire décisive pour ou contre les Américains; car je viens de prendre des arrangemens à Naples pour avoir désormais un grand opéra italien, et je ne veux pas être dans le cas de le renvoyer.[6] Sur ce, je prie Dieu, mon cher baron qu'il vous ait en sa sainte et digne garde.

Lambert Wickes to the American Commissioners

ALS: American Philosophical Society

Gentlemen   LOrient March 13th 1777
I Take this Opertunity to Inform you Of the proceadings of the Commissary of this port[7] Which Seam very odd to me as I have Recd. no Instrucktions from you. He Sent for me to Day and told me I must Get my Ship Cleaned and put Every

---

4. "Cela fait de mauvais soldats."

5. Here three sentences appear that are omitted in our text: "Il vaut donc mieux qu'ils crevent dans leur lit que de les exposer à fuir dans un jour de combat et à ternir la gloire de mes armes. Vous savez d'ailleurs qu'on me paie comme tués ceux qui meurent de maladie et que je n'ai pas un écu des fuyards. Mon voyage d'Italie qui me coûte prodigieusement, me fait desirer que la mortalité se mette parmi eux."

6. "Cas de devoir le congédier."

7. Charles-Pierre Gonet, who first appears as an intendant in Wickes' letter above, Feb. 19.

thing on bord As fast as possible and then Departe the port Immediately. He further Informd me he Should Send persons to See That We Did not Delay any time. These are very Extraordinary orders and Such as I Should Suppose you Are Allready Acquainted With. If So Am much Surprized I Am not Informd by you in What maner or How to procead So As not to Giv Umbrage to the King or Minnisters. I Can Get the Ship Ready in 8 or 10 Days At furthest But Shall Be very Glad to heare from You As Soon As possible or At Least before I Sail. If I Should be Drove out of this port by the Commissary Without your orders I Cannot tell Where to Go to Wait your Instrucktions or Whethere to procead Directly for America or not; As I Am ordered not to Enter any french port again. I have Recd. none your favrs, Since those By Mr. Defrancy Which I Cannot Account for but hope youl Soon Write me fully and Advise in What maner to procead. From Gentlemen your most Obligd Humble Servant   LAMBT WICKES

PS Pleas answer this As Soon As possible and Exskuse it as I have Scarcely time to Write before the post Departs.

To the Honbls. Docktor Benjamin Franklin Silas Dean

Addressed: To / The Honbl. Docktor Benjain Franklin / Paris

Notation: Capt. Wickes 13 March 77.

From ——— Baud   ALS: American Philosophical Society

⟨Paris, March 13, 1777, in French: A person now in the provinces, about whom the duc de La Rochefoucauld can tell you,[8] has asked me to make you some proposals that I think will please you. Kindly tell me when I can discuss them with you at Passy.⟩

8. Possibly the chevalier de Cambray, an engineer. La Rochefoucauld rarely supported a volunteer for service in America, but made an exception of Cambray; see BF to Washington below, Sept. 10, 1777.

Alexander Small on Franklin's Views of Ventilation: Extract of a Memorandum

MS and copy:[9] Library of Congress

Dr. Small has not appeared in this series since 1772. By then he had known Franklin for more than a decade,[10] and they presumably continued to see each other in London. At some point, before or after the American left for Philadelphia, his friend went to Minorca as an army surgeon.[1] We conjecture that he composed this portion of his memorandum during the winter of 1776–77, and that it was what he promised to forward to Franklin in his letter of March 15, immediately below; he had a draft before him, he said there, and these pages are likely to be it because they do not mention, as later pages do, anything after 1776. Small worked over his paper for years, and on two occasions Franklin was involved; but the finished product was not published until William Temple Franklin included it in his grandfather's works in 1819.[2] We do not know when Small noted the observations by Franklin that he quotes or paraphrases here, and we cannot attempt to distinguish between the ideas of the two.

Of Ventilation

[Before March 15, 1777?]

I do not know that we have, in any author, particular and separate directions concerning the ventilating of hospitals, crouded rooms, or dwelling-houses; or the making of proper drains for carrying off stagnant or putrid water. The want of such general information, on these subjects, has induced me to endeavour to recollect all I can of the many instructive conversations I have had upon these matters with that judicious and most accurate observer of Nature, Dr. Benjamin Franklin. I do this, in hopes that either the Doctor himself, or some other person well qualified for the task, may follow the ex-

9. The first part of the MS, in an unknown hand, is followed by extensive revisions and additions in Small's hand, relating to the pages of the draft that we do not print. The copy was made by WTF, probably much later when, as mentioned below, he published the memorandum.

10. See above, IX, 110 n; XIX, 105 n.

1. He remarks, in a part of the MS omitted here, that he arrived on the island as surgeon for the royal artillery: WFT, *Memoirs* (2nd ed.; London, 1818–19), VI, 184.

2. *Ibid.*, pp. 173–94. The occasions of BF's involvement, in the 1780's, will appear in our subsequent vols.

ample set in so masterly a manner, by Sir John Pringle, Bart. when speaking on the Preservation of the Health of Seamen.[3]

It has long been observed, that if a number of persons are shut up in a small room, of which the internal air has little or no communication with the external, the respiration of those who are so confined renders, by degrees, the air of that room effete, and unfit for the support of life.

Dr. Franklin was, if I mistake not, the first who observed, that respiration communicated to the air a quality resembling the *mephitic*;[4] such as that of the *Grotto del Cane* near Naples. The air impressed with this quality rises only to a certain height, beyond which it gradually loses it. The amendment begins in the upper part, and descends gradually, until the whole becomes capable of sustaining life. The Doctor confirmed this, by the following experiment. He breathed gently through a Tube into a deep glass mug, so as to impregnate all the air in the mug with this quality. He then put a lighted *bougie* into the mug; and upon touching the air therein, the flame was instantly extinguished. By frequently repeating this operation, the *bougie* gradually preserved its light longer in the mug, so as, in a short time, to retain it to the bottom of it; the air having totally lost the bad quality it had contracted from the breath blown into it.

At the same time that the lower part of the air is thus affected, an acrid noxious quality may be communicated to its upper part, in the room; occasioned by the volatile putrescent effluvia of the persons inclosed therein. "It is surprising, says Sir John Pringle, (in his Observations on the Diseases of the Army, 4th Edit.[5] p. 109) in how few days the Air will be corrupted in close and crouded wards; and what makes it hard to remedy the evil is the difficulty of convincing, either the nurses or the sick themselves, of the necessity of opening the windows and doors, at any time, for a supply of fresh air."

---

3. John Pringle, *A Discourse upon Some Late Improvements of the Means for Preserving the Health of Mariners* (London, 1776). The speech was delivered on Nov. 30. Small must have received it, and written this part of his MS, at the end of 1776 or soon thereafter.

4. *I.e.*, carbon dioxide.

5. London, 1764.

It may be inferred from the above account of *mephitic* air, that such air can be but little altered by a Ventilator in the cieling of a room; and Dr. Franklin justly concluded, that, in crouded rooms, and especially in bed-rooms, in dwelling-houses, a current of air should be kept up in the lower part of the houses [*interlined*: rooms], to carry off what is thus affected. He approved of the use of chimneys for this purpose, especially when the current is quickened by a fire. Even when there is not any fire in the chimney, a current of air is constantly kept up in it, by its ascending or descending in the flue, as the weight of the internal or external air preponderates. This creates a kind of tide in the flue, conducing much to the healthiness of the air in rooms: and hence we may see the injudiciousness of having chimney-boards which fit closely and thereby prevent a salutary circulation in the air. Hence also, in warm weather, we may account for liquors, or other things, kept in a chimney, being cooled; and more so, if means are used to create an evaporation around them.

Every person has an atmosphere of his own, heated by the warmth of his body, which can be dissipated only by a motion in the circumambiant air. Thus, in warm weather, wind cools the body, by carrying off the personal atmosphere; and by promoting, at the same time, a more free evaporation of the effluvia arising from the body. This creates a greater degree of coolness on the skin. The personal atmosphere can be but little affected by a ventilator in the cieling of a room, unless the admission of external air is so directed, as to act principally on the air surrounding those in the room. Dr. Franklin, when consulted on Ventilating the House of Commons, represented, that the personal atmosphere surrounding the Members might be carried off by making outlets in the perpendicular part of the seats, through which the air might be drawn off by Ventilators, so placed as to accomplish this without admitting any by the same channels. It will appear from what has been said, that windows placed high in the walls of churches, or in rooms intended for large assemblies, can contribute but little towards correcting the *mephitic* quality of the lower part of the air, or towards carrying off the personal atmospheres.

The experiments made for ventilating crouded rooms, by

that most beneficent of men, the reverend Dr. Stephen Hales,[6] bring evident proof how much the upper part of the air, in such places, is vitiated by the volatile putrescent effluvia arising from the persons present in such rooms. He at the same time shewed an easy and effectual way to carry off such vitiated air. His Ventilators were, however, attended with the inconveniency of occasioning smokey chimneys, by drawing off so much air, that there was not a suffiency left, to keep a current strong enough to carry the smoke up the chimney, unless a door or window was left open. The circulating Ventilators in windows were intended for refreshing the air in rooms, without affecting the current of air up the chimney: but they did not affect the *mephitic* air, nor the higher air, near the ceiling of lofty rooms, which is most vitiated with putrescent particles, and they were besides, often out of repair.

Instead of either of these, Dr. Franklin proposed, that openings should be made close to the ceilings of rooms, communicating with a flue, which should ascend in the wall, close to the flues of the chimneys; and, when it can be done conveniently, close to the flue of the kitchen-chimney; because the fire burning pretty constantly there, would keep the sides of the flue warmer than those of the other chimneys; whereby a quicker current of air would be kept up in the ventilating flue. Such a flue might be carried from the vaults or under-ground offices. This would render them dryer, without altering their temperature much, as to heat or cold. These ventilating flues would cause a constant discharge of the volatile putrescent effluvia, without interfering with the current of air up the chimneys; while the current towards the chimney would carry off the *mephitic* air below. These ventilating flues would be peculiarly beneficial in bed-rooms of which the ceilings are low.

Dr. Franklin mentioned an instance of a number of Germans, who, on their arrival in Pensilvania, were obliged to live in a large barn; there being at that time no other place of residence, fit for them. Several small windows were made on both sides of the barn, under the eaves. These windows were

6. For the famous physiologist and writer on ventilation see above, IV, 315 n, and the *DNB*.

kept constantly open, even during a severe frost in the winter; and this, without any detriment to the health of the Germans. Prejudice, said he, has raised so great a dread against cold air, in England, that such openings would make every person shudder at the thought of being exposed to so great a degree of cold: and therefore I did not dare to recommend a practice, the good effects of which I had known. The Dormitory for the youths of Westminster School, is a similar instance: for the glass put in their high lofty windows is soon broken, but seldom repaired: yet without prejudice to the health of the youths.

There is a channel, by which much of the vitiated air escapes, and is but little attended to. Whoever looks at the cielings of rooms in old houses, will soon discover the traces of the rafters, by a difference in colour, in parts of the cieling: for wherever there is not a solid resistance to the passage of the air, much of it gets off, through the ceiling, and deposits in it part of its contents, which discolours the intervals between the joists. In the British Museum, there is a remarkable instance of the inconveniency of the want of this outlet. The ceiling of one of the rooms, in that house, is covered with a picture, or painted cloth. This room continues warm, with little fire; but the air soon affects the respiration of Valetudinarians; as was often remarked by that accurate observer, Dr. Gn. Knight, late principal Librarian.[7]

An attentive observer will soon be convinced, that there is a current of warm air which ascends in the room from the chimney while a fire burns. Dr. Franklin shewed that this was the case, by the following experiment. He suspended, by a thread, a piece of pasteboard, cut in spiral form. The thread was fastened to the chimney-piece, so that the pasteboard, drawn out into a spiral form, came near to the edge of the chimney. The constant current of warm air, heated by the fire, gave a continued circular motion to the pasteboard. This warm air ascending to the ceiling, there spread, and kept a constant motion in the upper part of the air. The warm air thus ascending, coming into contact with the cool walls, and being thereby

7. Gowin Knight, F.R.S., a friend of Fothergill and an authority on magnetism: *ibid.*

To ———⁸　　　　　　　　　ALS (draft): Library of Congress

Sir,　　　　　　　　　　　Passy, March 15. 1777

We are much oblig'd to M. De la Haye and his Friends for their Offer of Supplying the Americans with Merchandize, and we desire them to accept our Thanks; But it does not suit us to enter into any Engagements of the kind; We as Commissioners from the Congress have no Orders for purchasing other Goods than what are necessary for the Arming and Clothing of the Troops and fitting out the Ships of the United States: and that Commission will not be continued when private Merchants shall supply Quantities of Goods sufficient, as the Congress do not desire to interfere with Merchants in Commerce. The Trade and Ports of the States are open to the Merchants of France; and M. De la Haye and his Friends may send thither and sell what Goods they think proper, and purchase for Returns the Produce of the Country, in which they will receive all the Protection the Force of the States can give them, and probably may make considerable Profit. But it is not to be expected of us to engage them Payment in Money at Paris, nor to find Sureties there for such Payment. If those who are to have a Profit in furnishing the Goods will not for the sake of such Profit give us Credit, how can we being Strangers here desire others to be our Guarantees, and hazard themselves for nothing? In short We chuse to purchase as our Funds arrive and to avoid Debts. I am, very respectfully Sir, Your most obedient humble Servant　　　　　　　　　　　B F

8. The letter gives no clue to the recipient, who seems to have written BF in the name of a consortium of merchants. Charles-Marin de La Haye, the apparent leader of the group, was one of the farmers general and, like most of them, a man of great wealth: Yves Durand, *Les Fermiers Généraux au XVIIIe siècle* (Paris, 1971), pp. 451–2, 474–5.

From Paulze

AL: American Philosophical Society

Paris le 15. mar de 1777.

M. Paulze fait mille complimens à M. francklin. Il lui envoye le projet du Traité entamé par M. Grand.[9] Si M. francklin et son collegue approuvent les dispositions il voudra bien en instruire M. Paulze le plutot possible afin que cette affaire puisse etre entièrement terminée dans le courant de la semaine prochaine. Les conditions sont les memes que celles qui ont toujours eté d'usage en angleterre et en Ecosse.

The American Commissioners and the Farmers General: Proposed Tobacco Contract

D: American Philosophical Society

Du 15 Mars 1777

MM. Les plenipotentiaires du Congrès ont propose de livrer aux fermiers généraux dans le courant de cette année 4000 B. de Tabacs rendus dans les ports de france au prix de 8 s. la livre de Tabac net poids de Marc.

Ils ont demandé qu'il leur fut avancé par les fermiers generaux La Somme de Deux millions de Livres, dont moitié seroit remise dans trois mois et l'autre moitié trois mois après et dont le remboursement seroit fait en Tabac avant la fin de l'année au prix de 8 s. la livre comme il est expliqué.

Des considérations particuliéres ont suspendu l'exécution de cet arrangement qui peut être conclu dans ce moment.

Si MM. Les plenipotentiaires sont toujours dans les memes dispositions, ainsy qu'on vient de l'annoncer aux fermiers généraux, ils sont pries de reponde le plutot possible et pour prevenir toutes difficultés sur les clauses du Traité, on en joint icy les conditions.[1]

---

9. The proposed contract immediately follows, because it was the enclosure with this note. British intelligence reported that Georges Grand had been acting as intermediary in the negotiations: Stevens, *Facsimiles*, III, no. 277, pp. 9–10; VII, no. 705, p. 5.

1. These were slightly modified in the final contract below, March 24.

[Art. 1°]

MM. Les plenipotentiaires. . . .[2] Tant en notre nom que comme fondés des pouvoirs du Congrès des Provinces unies de l'amérique septentrionale, auquel où besoin seroit ils nous promettront faire agréer et ratifier la convention, vendront et s'engageront de livrer dans le courant de la présente année 1777 a MM. Les fermiers Generaux de france la quantité de quatre mille Boucauds de Tabacs des crus de York et James Rivers rendus dans Les ports de france.

Art. 2°

Le prix des Tabacs ainsy livrés demeure fixé a 8 s. la livre poids de Marc Tabac net ou de 40 *l.t.* du cent pezant livré dans les magazins des fermiers généraux.

Art. 3

Tous les Tabacs avariés pourris ou gattés, seront couppés et rejettés du poids de payement suivant l'estimation qui en sera faite amiablement par experts, ou il sera convenu d'une refraction particuliere pour en tenir lieu.

Art. 4

Il serà encore deduit a titre d'allouance et bon poids 4 pourcent et 8 L. par boucaud pour echantillons et 2 pour-cent d'escompte pour prompt payement sur le prix des factures.

Art. 5

Pour acquitter le prix des 4000 B. de Tabacs MM. Les fermiers generaux s'obligeront de remettre à la disposition de MM. Les plenipotentiaires deux millions de Livres tournois payables moitié dans trois mois à compter du jour de la convention, l'autre moitié trois mois après, a compter du jour du premier payement.

Art. 6

Dans le cas où le congrès pourroit expedier en france une quantité de Tabacs plus considerables, tout ce qui excedera 4000 B. ou quatre millions pezant de Tabac Net, sera aux même

2. The suspension points are in the original.

494

prix et conditions remis aux fermiers generaux qui en payeront la valeur en argent ou en Lettres sur leur Receveur general a Trois usances suivant l'usage.

Notation: Contract with Farmers General

Baron Schulenburg to the American Commissioners[3]

Reprinted from Benjamin F. Stevens, ed., *Facsimiles of Manuscripts in European Archives Relating to America, 1773–1783* (25 vols., London, 1889–98), VII, no. 656.[4]

Messieurs   Berlin Le 15e. Mars 1777

J'ai recu la lettre que vous m'avez faite l'Honneur de m'addresser le 14 passè et Je n'ai pas manquè d'informer Le Roi de L'empressment que temoignent les Colonies Angloises de L'Amerique septentrionale, a ètablir avec nous un commerce Libre et reciproque.

Sa Majestè m'a paru recevoir avec plaisir les Assurances des dispositions favorables où les Colonies sont a cet egard et Je ne doute point que, toujours attentive a ètendre ce Commerce et a augmenter le bonheur de ses peuples elle ne seroit bien aisè, qu'une pareille Liaison peut avoir Lieu. Cependant Messrs. comme vous ètes entierement au fait des affaires Vous sentirès mieux que moi toutes les entraves qui generoient ce Commerce dans les Circonstances prèsentes. Le Roi par la situation de ses Etats n'ayant point de Flotte en mer pour faire respecter son Pavillon, nos Vaisseaux qui voudroient essayer de parvenir jusques a Vous s'exposeroient a une perte certaine, et quand meme on voudroit se servir d'un pavillon ètranger il pericliteroit tousjours par les Flottes d'Observations Britaniques.

Je ne Connois point de Port en Amerique ou nos vaisseaux pourroient dècharger, et St. Eustache meme n'offre point d'asile assurè, puisque dans ces environs il ne [n'y] a pas moins de 90 vaisseaux Anglois qui ne Laisseroient jamais passer nos Marchandises, ni celles qu'on voudroit prendre en retour.

---

3. In reply to their letter above of Feb. 14.
4. The MS was in the same collection as Vergennes' memorandum to the commissioners above, under March 1, and like it has disappeared.

Il seroit donc a mon avis, bien plus naturel que les Colonies qui ont le plus grand intèret de trouver un debouchè a leurs produits superflûs et a les Changer contre les Manufactures qui leur manquent, connoissant d'ailleur par experience tous les dangers et les moiens de les prevenir, après avoir reussi a faire entrer leurs vaissaux dans les ports de France essaiassent de se frayer un chemin jusqu'a nous; de nous porter les produits dont nous avons besoin et prendre en exchange celles des nos manufactures qui pourront leur convenir, ou bien de trouver quelque autre port de L'Europe ou ce Commerce d'èchange puisse se faire Librement.

Ce me paroit a present la seule voie de mettre en train une Liaison de Commerce entre *les deux Nations*: mais si vous pouvès Messieurs me fournir d'autres eclaircissements et des moiens de surmonter les difficultes mentionnèes, Je les recevrai avec plaisir, et J'en ferai L'usage le plus convenable au vue des vos Commettants et a celles du Roi mon Maitre. J'ai L'Honneur d'etre avec un consideration tres distinguèe Messieurs Votre tres humble Serviteur   LE BARON DE SCHULENBURG.

A Messieurs Messrs. Franklin & Deane a Paris

Copy

Lambert Wickes to the American Commissioners

ALS: American Philosophical Society

Gentlemen.   L'Orient March 15th 1777.

I wrote you last post informing you of my disagreeable Situation, Also Mentioned the proceedings of Mr. Gonnett the Commissary of this Port. He Still continues to threaten driving me out imeadiately. If the threats and abuses of this Buissey person cannot be stop'd I should be much oblig'd for your Instructions and am in hopes you'll either dispatch me imeadiately for America or procure me Admittance in some other Port where I shall be better received and kinder treated than I have been here. You may rest Satisfied that no proceedings of mine has meritted Mr. Gonnetts treatment as I have always behaved with all the Complisance in my power to that Gentleman which I am afraid will be out of my power to continue longer as it Vexes me very much to be treated in this Manner and I would not Submit to it elsewhere. Please let me know what News there is from America. From Gentlemen, Your Most obedient humble Servant   LAMBT. WICKES

To the Honbles. Dr. Benja. Franklin & Silas Dean.

Addressed: To / The Honble. Dr. Benja: Franklin / at / Paris

Notation: Wickes 15 March 77.

From Alexander Small   ALS: American Philosophical Society

Dear Friend   St Philips Minorca March 15th 1777

The most upright Intentions cannot command Success. The Shallow Ken of Man cannot penetrate into futurity; and cannot therefore ascertain what is, or is not most beneficial to Societies. What we have here to do, is to act the most consistently with our Judgment of Circumstances. I know you have done this.

Britain is most certainly hurting herself by an enormous Increase of her Debt; and is perhaps a just Scourge in your Country, for the excessive Luxury and Dissipation you were running into. This Scourge will restore you to your Senses; and will Send every Man to live Soberly and dilligently under his Vine.[5] Had not this scourge been inflicted, your growing Luxury and Effeminacy would have rendered you an easy Prey to some future enterprising Genius. Your Children will not soon forget what has now happened, which may the longer preserve a Love of Liberty among them. On the whole I do not know whether I should condole with you, or congratulate. Friendship, at any rate demands my trying whether this can come to your hands. I have delayed writing for some time, in hopes I might have your Direction. As this has not happened, I have directed my Letter so as to carry it among your Philosophical friends. I dare say the Ami des Hommes,[6] and his

5. "Judah and Israel dwelt safely, every man under his vine and under his fig tree." I Kings, 4:25.
6. The elder Mirabeau: above, xv, 182 n. BF and Dubourg had called upon him in late December: Mirabeau to Dubourg, Dec. 30, 1776, APS.

497

friends live in friendship with you. An Account of your and Family's Health, will give great pleasure to Dear Sir Your Affectionate and faithful friend ALEXR SMALL

P:S: When I settled in this Island, I soon found the want of duely Ventilating our Hospitals. This set me on recollecting what I had learned from you and having drawn it up in the best Manner I could, I sent a Copy of it to our Friend Sr. J: Pringle.[7] I have not heard from him since. If this reaches your hands, I will send you a Copy of it, that you may yourself put the finishing hand to it, if greater Concerns give you Leisure. What can be a greater Concern than to give Relief to the Sick? You remember Cicero's expression; Homines nulla in re propius ad Deos accedunt, quam Salutem Hominibus dando. Vale! et Sit Sana Mens in Sano Corpore![8]

This will be now probably delivered to you by a worthy friend of Mine, and Fellow Labourer here, Mr. MacNeille.[9]

Addressed: A Monsieur / Monsieur Benjamin Franklin / L:L:D: et de l' A: R: S: Etranger / a Paris

Notation: Small Alexander March 15. 1777.

Arthur Lee to Franklin and Silas Deane

ALS: American Philosophical Society

Dear Sirs: Vitoria March 16th. 1777

I have receivd an answer from the Court, thro the Duke de Grimaldi, to this effect. That the reasons for wishing me not to come to Madrid are insuperable. That the States may depend on the sincere desire of Spain to see their Liberties establishd and to assist them as far as his own situation will permit. For this purpose I had only to direct the House of

7. See Small's memorandum above, before March 15.

8. *Homines enim ad deos nulla re propius accedunt quam salutem hominibus dando:* "in no way do men draw nearer to the gods than in giving health to their fellow men." *Pro Ligario,* XII, 38. The second sentence, "Farewell, and may you be of sound mind in a sound body," is an adaptation of Juvenal, *Satires,* X, 356.

9. This second postscript is written under the address.

Gardoqui to supply us by every opportunity with whatever Spain offers [us] for our use. That 3000 Barrels of powder and some cloathing were deposited at N. Orleans for us,[1] that we shoud be receivd at the Havannah as the most favord Nation, and that the Count d'Aranda woud have directions to supply me with credit upon Holland.

I asked to what amount. He replyd that was not settled, nor coud be, till they heard of my acquiescence, which he was to announce immediately, and then I might rely upon the directions being at Paris by the 1st. of next month. He desird I might not even go to Bilboa, as that woud occasion the Port, which was now unobservd, to be watchd, and render the supplies more precarious.[2]

I am now settling a Cargo with Mr. Gardoqui, which is to be dispatchd as soon as possible. This will keep me here till the 21st. and I shall be at Bordeau the 26th. where I may hear from you if necessary, and if you write I beg to know where I may find you in Paris where I expect to be on the 2d. or 3d.

Mr. Gardoqui informs me that he has orders to load the three vessels at Bilboa entirely with Salt. I shall however recommend to all the Captains the receiving such Supplies for the general Congress, as he shall send. One of the Captains reports, that Genl. Washington had offerd to exchange three hessian Officers for Genl. Lee which Howe refusd, and had so disgusted the hessian troops that they threatnd to lay down their arms.

I desird the Duke's opinion relative to our right to demand the Vessels betrayd to England, and to remonstrate against the States general granting a passage. He said he thought we shoud

1. These supplies had begun arriving early in the year, and the Americans subsequently put them to use. See Samuel F. Bemis, *The Diplomacy of the American Revolution* (revised ed.; Bloomington, Ind., 1957), p. 90; George M. Waller, *The American Revolution in the West* (Chicago, [1976]), p. 35.

2. Grimaldi, after talking with Lee at Burgos, wrote for further instructions from his successor as foreign minister, the conde de Floridablanca. These were dispatched on the 10th, and were behind Grimaldi's assurances in the interview described here. See Lee's letter above of March 5; Wharton, *Diplomatic Correspondence*, II, 282–3, 290–6; Mario Rodriguez, *La Revolución Americana de 1776 y el Mundo Hispánico: Ensayos y Documentos* (Madrid, 1976), pp. 94–7, 100–2.

succeed in neither, because, as he conceivd the practice of Nations woud justify both England and Holland, but more especially as our independency was not yet acknowlegd.

I was particular with the Duke, that the credit shoud be to all or any of us, so that if any accident shoud happen to me upon the road, the business might not be delayd. I have the honor to be, with the greatest consideration, dear Sirs, your most obedient Servant ARTHUR LEE

N.B. I have not receivd a single Letter either from Paris or Madrid, since I left Bordeau. Will you be considering whether I can be of service at Florence or at Berlin, that I may not be idle?

Addressed: The / Honble / B. Franklin & S. Dean Esqrs.

Notations: A Lee March 16. 77. to BF & SD. Victoria / Mr. Lee / Letters from A. Lee to BF. & SD.

From Louis-Pierre Penot Lombart (or Lombard), Chevalier de Laneuville[3]   ALS: American Philosophical Society

Moster   A Paris ce 16. mars 1777.

The desire of the glorÿ, and of be serviceable to a nation whom defend her libertÿ, is the onlÿ mover wich embolder us and decide mÿ brother and me to go to boston for offer our service to a people whom we have in admiration.

We will not emploÿ bÿ ÿou the waÿ of the protection and recommendation. A man aproved of her nation is not made for to be persuaded through some like means.

---

3. Created a chevalier de Saint-Louis the year before. He and his brother, René-Hippolyte Penot Lombart de Noirmont, did leave for America, and landed in South Carolina from a sinking ship the following September without papers or, Laneuville said later, a word of English. (He wrote the present letter, but could have copied a translation.) The two became inspector and deputy inspector general of Gates' northern army, and in 1778 Laneuville was commissioned brigadier general. He resigned and returned to France in 1779 with Lafayette; his brother remained and rose to be a lieutenant colonel. Lasseray, *Les Français*, II, 349–58; *JCC*, XI, 466, 498–500; XII, 1010; Fitzpatrick, *Writings of Washington*, XII, 223–4; Laneuville's memorandum for Bancroft, *c.* Oct., 1779, APS.

27 year of service, the degree of major which I have obtained through the good testimonÿ which have been give of me to minister of the war, Chevalier de St. Louis, nephew of moster Merlet maréchal de camp,[4] an Enthusiasme natural for a good cause, some zeal, some good will, some young age some good health are the onlÿ title which I will to improve bÿ you.

We nor demand nor silver, nor advance for go to boston; if I have not the degree of colonel I take the field as volunteer.

It is in these sentiment as I have the honour to be, in there joining these of the muster perfected esteem Moster Votre tres humble et tres obeissant Serviteur   LANEUVILLE

Notation: Leneuville

The American Commissioners: Memorandum for the Farmers General   AD (draft):[5] American Philosophical Society

March 17, 1777

Messrs. Franklin and Deane, having considered the Proposition of the F G dated the 15th Inst. and willing to serve and oblige them, will agree to the Articles proposed with this Addition, viz.

Article 7.

If the Tobacco in America can be purchased at such a Rate, as that with the Addition of all Charges and Losses in purchasing and transporting it to France and delivering it there, it shall appear to have cost less than 8 *s.* the pound, Messrs. F. and D (who do not desire to Gain by this Contract) agree that there shall be an equal Abatement of the Price, so as that the F.G. shall pay no more than the exact Cost. And on the other Hand

4. He and others wrote Washington to recommend Laneuville. Congress, in acknowledging Merlet's letter, referred to him as the quartermaster general of the French army, which was probably an error arising from an earlier position that he had held. *JCC,* XI, 499; *Etat Militaire de France* . . . for 1775, p. 122.

5. In BF's hand. The escape clause proposed here was abandoned in the final contract below, March 24.

if it shall be found to have cost more, the F.G. (who do not desire that Mcssrs. F. and D. should be Losers by their Contract,) agree to make an Addition of Price sufficient to equal the Difference.

In confiding in the Justice and Honour of the Company, that if on making up the Accounts it shall appear that the Tobacco with all the necessary Charges and the Losses, did bona fide amount to more than the 8 *s.* per lb. a reasonable Compensation will be made.

It is to be wish'd that the first Payment could be prompt, and the 2d at the Expiration of 3 Months.

From ———— Gastebois

March 17, 1777   See pages 170–1

The American Commissioners to Vergennes

ALS:[6] Archives du Ministère des affaires étrangères; copy:[7] Archivo Historico Nacional

On March 14 the commissioners received their first dispatches from America. Among them was the letter above of December 30 from the committee of secret correspondence, enclosing the Congressional authorization to offer Versailles territorial inducements to enter the war. Deane promptly informed Vergennes that the commission had received new instructions, and requested an audience. No answer came for three days, during which Deane and Franklin must have composed this letter between them. Deane alone signed it and took it to Versailles on the 18th; Franklin was suffering from gout. On the 19th, having failed to see Vergennes, Deane forwarded the letter.[8] The bait that it offered was declined, on the ground that the time for discussing such matters was not yet ripe.[9]

6. In Silas Deane's hand. We have silently supplied a few missing words from the ALS as reproduced in Stevens, *Facsimiles*, VII, no. 659.

7. Which omits the complimentary close, "We have the honor," etc., to the beginning of the postscript.

8. *Deane Papers*, II, 23, 25. With the letter Deane enclosed two proposals for raising a £2,000,000 loan without involving the government: *ibid.*, pp. 28–9.

9. Doniol, *Histoire*, II, 325.

Sir   Versailles, 18th. March 1777.

We have lately received an Express from The Congress of the United States of North America containing some new instructions to Us the purport of which it is proper your Excellency should be acquainted with. The Congress tho' firmly determined to maintain as long as possible their independance, whether assisted or not by any other power, yet for the sake of humanity wishing universal Peace would not for the Advantage of America only desire to kindle a War in Europe, the Extent and duration of which cannot be Foreseen. They therefore, on this Account, as well as for Reasons of Respect to the King whose Character they venerate do not presume to propose that France should enter into a War merely on their Account. But if France to obtain satisfaction from Brittain for the injuries received in the last War, commenced by that Nation, or for any other just causes, should think it right to improve the present Occasion, in declaring War against Great Brittain, we are directed to induce if it may be the more early Declaration to offer the following Advantages, in Addition to those of Commerce already proposed.

1st: That the Object of the War be to obtain for France satisfaction for the Injuries aforesaid, and for the United States the Establishment of their Independance with a reduction of the British Power for the Security both of France and America, to which Ends it is proposed, that the Conquest of Canada, Novascotia, Newfoundland, St. Johns, the Floridas, Bermuda, Bahama and all the West India Islands now in Possession of Brittain be attempted by the joint Force of France and the United States and in case of Success, half the Fishery of Newfoundland together with all the Sugar Islands shall thereafter Appertain to France,[1] the rest to the United States; and the Trade between the Kings Dominions and the United States shall thenceforth be carried on by the ships of said Dominions, and of the United States only.

2d. That in case it is agreed that the Conquest of the british Sugar Islands be Attempted, the United States shall on timely

1. Congress had instructed the commissioners to offer the British West Indies only if the fisheries alone proved insufficient: *JCC*, VI, 1056.

notice, furnish provisions for the Expedition To the Amount of Two Million of Dollars, with six Frigates mann'd of not less than 24 Guns each, with such other Assistance as may be in their power, and becoming good Allies.

3d. That as a close connection is understood to subsist between France and Spain, and that their Interests are the same it is also proposed by the Congress, that in case Spain shall enter with France into the said War, the United States will if thereto required, declare War against Portugal (which has already insulted their Commerce) and will continue the said War for the total Conquest of that Kingdom, to be added to the Dominions of Spain.

4. That a Peace shall not be made but by mutual consent. But if it be determined by his most Christian Majesty to remain in Peace with Great Brittain, the Congress do then pray that his Majesty would use his influence with Europe for preventing the further Transportation of foreign Troops into America to serve against the United States, and to obtain a recall of those already there. And having unbounded Confidence in the Kings Goodness and Wisdom they pray his Advice in their present Circumstances, whether to apply to any of the other Powers of Europe for Auxiliary Aids, or to make Offers of Peace to Brittain on Condition of their Independancy being Acknowledged. In neither of these points would the Congress take a Step without consulting his Majestys Ministers, and We hope for a favorable Answer. We have the honor to remain with the most profound Respect Your Excellencys most Obedient and most Humble Servants

> SILAS DEANE in behalf of himself and B. Franklin
> Commissioners Plenipoten[tiary]
> for the United States N America

To his Excellency the Count de Vergennes

P.S. The Congress and the People of the United States continue unanimous in their Opposition to the claims of Brittain, and are fully determined to assert their own independancy to the last; there is no doubt but Brittain would on certain Commercial Terms, acknowledge their independance, if the United States can have no aid from France directly, and if no encouragement can be giv'n to receive support in a short space of Time; as the United States wish for nothing, so much as Peace and Liberty; They wish, and ask for advice, under those Circumstances, whether they should, through the Freindly interposition of His Most Christian Majesty, or otherways, make Offers of Peace, to Great Brittain on that Condition, of their independance, or pursue the War, and risque the Event.[2]

Notation: 18. mars 1777. envoyé avec la lettre ci après No 77 la traduction suit 71.

Debrissac de Saxey[3] to the American Commissioners

ALS: American Philosophical Society

Gentleman,   St. Quentin 18th. Martz 1777.

I congratulate myself very much of the happiness of your acquaintance on my last Stay in Paris of your token of friendship of your trust and the preference you are willing to give us of the orders for you or friends when they wille call for concerning the linen of this fabrick. You ought to receive in this month your commissions from America. I take the liberty of remembring you your promise on that account and the inssurance we give you, to have for your Interest the best regard; we hope then you will not forget it on the first occasion.

I intend to pass the next easter days to Abbeville and to intertain Mr. Vanrobais and neveux[4] of your good disposition for them; no doubt they will be very sensibles on it.

I perceivd with great satisfaction as well by the publicks papers, than the particulars letters your success and prosperity in America, accept of my compliment on it, remaining with a

2. Congress had authorized the commissioners to threaten a "reunion" with Great Britain, but had said nothing about its being conditioned on an acknowledgment of independence: above, XXII, 628.

3. A leading textile manufacturer in St.-Quentin; he was a close relative of Anthony Benezet, as the latter subsequently explained in asking BF to forward a letter to him: Benezet to BF, July 12, 1781, Hist. Soc. of Pa. The present overture led nowhere.

4. Another textile firm: *Almanach des marchands,* p. 3.

great esteem, Gentleman, Your most Obediant and humble Servant.   DEBRISSAC DE SAXEY

Addressed: A Messieurs / Messieurs francthlin Et Deane / a l hotel d'hambourg rue de / Luniversite faubourg St Germain / a Paris

Notation: De Saxy 18. March 77

Jonathan Williams, Jr., to the American Commissioners   ALS: American Philosophical Society

Gentlemen   Nantes March 18. 1777.
     In answer to my Express, Capt. Wickes informed me that he should set off the next morning for Paris: his Letter is dated the 16th.[5]
     The inclosed was this day received from Mr. Lee under Cover to Mr. Shweighausser; please to deliver it.
     Capt. Young still remains windbound. A Ship is arrived in the River from america, but as the Capt. is not yet come up we do not know from what part, it is supposed to be a Ship that sailed with the Brig that last arrived from Boston. Not having the Honor of any of your Favours since my last I have only to add that I am with the greatest Respect Gentlemen Your obedient Servant   JONA WILLIAMS

The Hon. The Deputies of the United States.

Addressed: A Monsieur / Monsieur Deane / a l'Hotel d'Hambourg / Rue Jacob / a / Paris

Notation: Mr. Wms. Nantes March 18th. 1777

From William Wilkinson   AL: American Philosophical Society

                    Tuesday Morn. 8 oClock [March 18,[6] 1777]
M. Wilkinsons Compliments to D Franklin. He calld twice on Sunday at Hotel D Hambourg and as he leaves Paris Tomor-

5. The commissioners had received Wickes's letter of March 5, with his advice about a cutter based on Dunkirk, and had summoned him to Paris to consult; see Clark, *Wickes*, pp. 179–80.

6. He was planning, when he sent his note above of the 12th, to leave for Nantes on Monday the 17th. This second note is clearly about the same trip, which we assume he postponed for two days.

row for Nantes requests the Letters for that Place may be given the Bearer.

Addressed: Dr Franklin

In another hand: Hotel d'Autriche dans la Rue Traversière St. Honore

Thomas Morris to the American Commissioners

ALS: American Philosophical Society

Gentlemen   Nantes March 19th. 1777

I had the pleasure to address you last on the 11th. Instant by Captain Hammond, who I understand arrived safe at Paris on Thursday Evening last, and make no doubt duely delivered the sundry dispatches he brought with him from America for you. Any intelligence they contain, and that you may think proper to communicate, shall be greatly Obliged to you for. Yesterday the Ship Versailles Captain Chapman arrived here in 40 days from Boston and by him I received the inclosed letter, which is recommended in a particular manner to our care by the President of the War Office,[7] as containing Papers of the greatest importance, and request the favour of you to cause it to be safely delivered as directed. Captain Chapman brings a paper with him dated the 27th. Jany. wherein it mentions Genl. Howe having sent a Flag of Truce to Genl. Washington requesting a Cessation of Arms 'till the 1st. of the ensuing month. Captain Bartlett in the Brigantine Penet will sail for Boston in about 10 days from this date for your government in writing by him and I beg leave to assure you that I am with much respect Gentlemen Your most Obedient Servant

THOS. MORRIS

The Honourable Benja. Franklyn, Silas Deane & Arthur Lee Esqrs. at Paris

Addressed: The Honourable / Benja. Franklin, Silas Deane & / Arthur Lee Esqrs. at / Paris

Notation: T. Morris Mar 19 77

7. The Mass. board of war. Its letter to Chapman is printed in *Naval Docs.*, VII, 1035.

To Arthur Lee

ls: Harvard University Library; draft:[8] Library of Congress

Dear Sir,   Passy, March 21. 1777.

We have received your favours from Victoria and from Burgos.[9]

The Congress sitting at Baltimore, dispatch'd a Packet to us the 9th. of January, containing Accounts of the Success at Trentown, and subsequent events to that Date, as far as had come to knowledge. The Vessel was obliged to run up a little River in Virginia to avoid some Men of War, and was detained there 17 Days, or we should have had these advices sooner. We learn however thro' England, where they have News from N. York to the 4th of Feby. that in Lord Cornwallis's Retreat to Brunswick two Regiments of his Rear Guard were cut to pieces; that General Washington having got round him to Newark and Eliz. Town, he had retired to Amboy, in his Way to N. York; that Gen. Howe had called in the Garrisons of Fort Lee and Fort Constitution, which were now possess'd by our People: that on the New-York side, Forts Washington and Independance were retaken by our Troops; and that the British Forces at Rhode island were recall'd for the defense of New York.

The Committee in their Letters mention the intention of Congress to send Ministers to the Courts of Vienna, Tuscany, Holland[1] and Prussia. They also send us a fresh Commission containing your name instead of Mr. Jefferson's; with this additional Clause; "and also to enter into and agree upon a Treaty with his most Christian Majesty or such Person or Persons as shall be by him authorized for that purpose for assistance in carrying on the present War between Gr. Br. and these united States." The same Clause is in a particular Commission they have sent me to treat with the Court of Spain, similar to our common Commission for the Court of France; and I am ac-

---

8. From which we have silently supplied a few words now missing in the ls.

9. Above, Feb. 26 and March 5 respectively.

1. A slip of the pen; he meant Spain.

cordingly directed to go to Spain; But as I know that choice was made merely on the supposition of my being a little known there to the great Personage for whom you have my Letter,[2] (a circumstance of little importance) and I am really unable thro' Age, to bear the Fatigue and Incommodities of such a Journey, I must excuse myself to Congress; and join with Mr. Dean in requesting you to proceed in the business, on the former footing, till you can receive a particular Commission from Congress, which will no doubt be sent as soon as the Circumstances are known.

We know of no Plans or Instructions transmitted to Mr. Dean, but those you have with you. By this Packet indeed we have some fresh Instructions, which relate to your Mission, viz. that in case France and Spain will enter into the War the United States will assist the former in the Conquest of the British Sugar Islands, and the latter in the Conquest of Portugal, promising the assistance of 6 Frigates manned, of not less than 24 Guns each, and Provisions equal to 2,000,000 Dollars;[3] America desiring only for her Share what Britain holds on the Continent; But you shall by the first safe opportunity have the Instructions at length. I believe we must send a Courier.

We are ordered to borrow if we can £2,000,000 Sterling, on Interest. Judge then what a piece of Service you will do, if you can obtain a considerable Subsidy, or even a Loan without Interest.

We are also ordered to build 6 Ships of War. It is a pleasure to find the things ordered which we were doing without orders.

We are also to acquaint the several Courts with the determination of America to maintain at all Events her Independance. You will see by the Date of the Resolution relating to Portugal, as well as by the above that the Congress were Stout in the midst of their Difficulties.

It will be well to sound the Court of Spain on the Subject of permitting our arm'd Ships to bring Prizes into their Ports,

2. Don Gabriel Antonio de Bourbon: above, XXII, 62, 298.
3. The assistance applied only to the West Indies: *JCC,* VI, 1056–7.

condensed, becomes heavier, and so falls along the sides of the walls. Also the glass in windows, being exposed to the temperature of the external air, in cold weather, becomes colder than any other part of the room; the warm air coming into contact with the glass is more condensed than the air in any other part of the room, and therefore more sensibly descends; as may be seen, by approaching a lighted *bougie* to a window. The flame is then carried downward by the air, or, if the flame is extinguished, the smoke will more clearly shew this truth, by descending along the window, till it meets with air of an equal temperature. This will be the case, however tight the window; and the more so, the brighter and stronger the fire is, and the colder the external air: the circulation of the air being thereby quickened. This accounts for the familiar caution of avoiding to sit in or near a window. This circulation of the air is yet more evidently proved by the following instance. When there is a bright strong fire, in a close room, open the door, and present immediately a lighted candle to the upper part of the door: the flame will bend outward; though warm air in the higher part rushes out. Lower the candle gradually, and the strength of the current outward will lessen by degrees, as the candle is lowered, till it comes to a space in which the flame shall rise upright: continue to lower the candle, gradually, and then the current of cold air, inward, will gradually increase, and more strongly bend the flame of the candle inward. This will be the case even in frosty and windy weather. May it not be inferred from this circumstance, of so strong a current of air outwards, in the upper part of the door, that an opening over, or in, the upper part of the door, in the ward of an hospital, might be of advantage; especially if there is no ventilating flue in the ceiling? By such means, a circulation of the air in the upper part of the ward could be constantly kept up; and thereby a vent would be given to the volatile putrescent particles. This vent might remain open at all times, without any prejudice to the patients.

with the Request. While we are asking aids it is necessary to gratify the desires, and in some Sort comply with the Humours of those we apply to. Our Business now is to carry our point. But I have never yet changed the Opinion I gave in Congress, that a Virgin State should preserve the Virgin Character, and not go about suitering for Alliances, but wait with decent Dignity for the applications of others. I was over-ruld; perhaps for the best. With the greatest Esteem, I am ever Dear Sir Your most obedient humble Servant   B Franklin

Honorable Arthur Lee Esqr.

Notation: March 21st 1777

From Barbeu-Dubourg   ALS: American Philosophical Society

21e. mars 1777.

Je vous supplie, Monsieur, de vouloir accorder une audience favorable a Mr. Le Baron de fray de qui j'eus l'honneur de vous parler dernierement et qui ne forme que des demandes tres impetrables en faisant des offres tres avantageuses de services importans par l'experience et les talens dont il a fait preuve en divers pays.[5] J'ai l'honneur d'etre avec autant de reconnoissance que d'attachement Monsieur et cher Ami, tout a Vous

Dubourg

Addressed: A Monsieur / Monsieur Franklin / maison de Mr. de Chaumont / A Passy

Notation: dubourg 21 Mars 77

5. Joseph-Pierre-Charles, Baron de Frey (1740–96), was a Swiss soldier of fortune, a veteran of the Austrian and then the Polish service. Saint-Germain recommended him to BF, who is said to have given him a letter to Washington. De Frey joined the American army as a volunteer in September, 1777, and eventually was in the Yorktown campaign. Lasseray, *Les Français,* I, 222–4.

From François Baudin[6]   ALS: American Philosophical Society

⟨St. Martin, Isle de Ré, March 21, 1777, in French: This island is well situated for importing from America, and exporting more cheaply than from Nantes or Bordeaux. Captain William Moore of the *Dauphin*[7] left here on the 19th carrying salt furnished by my friends the Delaps, and with notes on the island's advantages for your commerce. He prefers our brandy to that of Bordeaux; it is as strong as cognac and is free of export duty. French manufactures may also be exported cheaply from here. MM. Sellonf & Cie.,[8] who forward this letter, will vouch for me, and I am known in Nantes, Bordeaux, and La Rochelle; I ask only the usual two percent commission.⟩

From William Gordon   ALS: American Philosophical Society

My Dear Sir   J[amaica] P[lain] March 21. 1777

I trouble you afresh with a packet designed for our friend Dr. Price. Be pleased to peruse the letter and papers ere you forward them to him. I wished to put both parties out of conceit with Mr. Hutchinson, which I think will be effected by what is in Edes's papers, and will be confirmed in two or three subsequent ones.[9] Such a man ought to have no supporters

6. A merchant who was so pushing in his effort to drum up trade for himself that he annoyed fellow merchants on Ré, the island off La Rochelle. In the summer of 1777 two of them wrote a letter, which eventually found its way to the commissioners, to say that Baudin was making contact with American ship captains, when they put in at St. Martin, on the pretense of having orders from Congress that they should apply to him. Fairholme and Luther to J. R. Hamilton, July 15, 1777, APS. In 1780 Baudin's son requested BF's help to settle in Pennsylvania; eight years later the father asked to be U.S. consul on Ré, and cited his services to American shipping and sailors. Sept. 12, Oct. 18, 1780, APS; to Congress, July 8, 1788, National Archives.

7. The *Dolphin*: Smith, *Letters*, III, 377.

8. A Parisian banking firm: Lüthy, *Banque protestante*, II, 437–8.

9. "Both parties" were presumably America and Britain. In June, 1775, Gordon began to edit and publish in Benjamin Edes' paper, the *Boston Gaz.*, extracts from letters of Hutchinson that had recently come to light; these were soon reprinted in London. Gordon's account of the episode is in *The*

but two upright posts with one across it. Hope you will find time, and honour me so far as, to write me a few lines, agreeable to what is mentioned in Dr. Price's; communicating some important information proper for the history of these times. May you enjoy your health and live to be more serviceable to America than ever! Present my respectful compliments to Mr. Dean and Mr. Lee, the latter I am not known to except it may be by name. Expect that Dr. Cooper writes by the present opportunity.[1] I remain with sincere respect your very humble servant and friend WILLIAM GORDON

The Continental lottery will succeed according to appearances. No tickets are yet come to Boston, which I suppose is owing to their rapid sale in and about Philadelphia.[2] Ten thousand would probably go off in the Massachusetts very soon.

Addressed: The Honle Dr Benjamin Franklin

Notation: W. Gordon March 21. 77.

From the Baron de Würmser[3]

AL: American Philosophical Society

A Paris ce 22 mars 1777

Mr. Le Baron De Wurmser Lieutenant général des armées du roy prie Monsieur Le Docteur Frankelin de vouloir bien lui

---

History of the Rise, Progress, and Establishment, of the Independence of the United States ... (4 vols., London, 1788), II, 28–31; see also Bernard Bailyn, *The Ordeal of Thomas Hutchinson* (Cambridge, Mass., 1974), pp. 334–7.

1. He did; the letter is below, March 30.

2. Congress had established the lottery to raise money and control the inflation of paper currency. The tickets reached Boston by the end of the month; the agent for selling them was Jonathan Williams, Sr.: *Boston Gaz.*, March 31, April 7, 1777. See also Lucius Wilmerding, Jr., "The United States Lottery," *N.-Y. Hist. Soc. Quarterly*, XLVII (1963), 5–39.

3. Christian-Louis, baron de Würmser, was a man of some distinction, lieutenant general since 1762 and now commanding the régiment d'Alsace. He had been one of the first recipients of a military order of merit created in 1759 for foreign officers who, as Protestants, were ineligible for the order of Saint-Louis. *Etat militaire de France* ... for 1777, pp. 75, 228; Léon Lecestre, *Liste alphabétique des officiers généraux jusqu'en 1762* (Paris, 1903), p. 108; Mazas, *Ordre de Saint-Louis*, I, 498–500.

donner demain dimanche 23 mars une audience de cinq minutes. Il se rendra ches lui a Passy entre 10 et 11 heures du
matin.[4]

Il auroit eu L'honneur de lui demander son jour s'il n'etoit
pas obligé de passer la Semaine prochaine a Versailles.

From the Baron de Würmser

March 23, 1777   See the previous note

The American Commissioners and the Farmers General: Contract for Tobacco

Copy: Library of Congress; copy: National Archives[5]

In the light of the previous negotiations, this is a remarkable document for the commissioners to have signed. It passed over in silence
two main points on which they had been seeking concessions: insurance and transportation; by agreeing to deliver the tobacco in
France they tacitly assumed the risks of the sea and responsibility
for shipment in American bottoms. Last but not least, they agreed
to a fixed price, although they had known for a month that commitment to that price might be ruinous.[6] As late as March 17 they had
insisted on an escape clause,[7] yet a week later they signed the contract with no such clause.

If the Americans carried out the terms, Arthur Lee said later, they
would lose two million livres; if they did not carry them out, and
"there was not the remotest possibility that they would," the breach
of faith would jeopardize any future loans from the farmers general.
All the commissioners achieved was to get their hands on the first
instalment, a million livres. "If it was rash at first, it was infinitely
more so after information they had received" of rising prices in

4. He was delayed by pressing business, and wrote to BF the next day to
postpone the interview to seven that evening. APS.

5. Other copies, in French, are in the APS and the Harvard University
Library.

6. See above, the first note on their memorandum of Feb. 24 and BF to
Lee, March 2.

7. See their draft memorandum of March 17.

Virginia.[8] The point was well taken, assuming that the contract was what it seemed. But was it?

The advance was made on conditions that both parties must have known were unlikely to be fulfilled; hence fulfilment could not have been the prime consideration. The commissioners suggested as much a few weeks later, though in guarded fashion, when they sent news of the contract to the committee of secret correspondence: they hoped, presumably for the record, that the terms would be carried out even though disadvantageous; but the central point was that Vergennes was using the contract as a further means to finance the American cause. He had assured them, they implied, that if the tobacco could not be delivered at the stipulated price "Government will not suffer us to be losers."[9] The Minister presumably gave a similar assurance to the farmers general, for he seems to have been behind the whole affair.[1] It was not a business deal to procure tobacco, but a political move, like the formation of Hortalez & Cie.; the purpose was to conceal a government subsidy of a million livres.

That purpose was secret, and the commissioners only hinted at it in writing to the committee. On the surface they negotiated a bona fide contract, thereby opening themselves to Lee's later criticism. Whether or not he learned their real reasons for what they had agreed to in his absence, the apparent rashness of the agreement was a weapon against them; and by the time he made his observations in 1779 he was looking for any weapon. His attack was apparently justified but essentially irrelevant, for it was directed against what had happened on the stage. What mattered was behind the scenes.

[March 24, 1777]
Contract betwixt the Farmer's General of France and Messrs. Franklin and Deane.

Article 1st. The undersigned, as well in our names, as in virtue of the powers vested in us by the Congress of the United Colonies of North America, do promise and obligate ourselves to deliver in the course of the present Year 1777 to the

8. Lee's observations on the contract, April 27, 1779, *Lee Family Papers*, roll 6, frames 80–6.

9. Above, p. 472.

1. A further indication of Vergennes' role is his use of Georges Grand, his confidant, in the revived negotiations that led to the contract. See Paulze to BF above, March 15.

Farmers General of France, at the ports of that Kingdom, five thousand Hogsheads; equal to five Million pounds of Tobacco, of the Growth of York and James River.

Article 2d. The price of the Tobacco so delivered shall be eight livres[2] for every pound Mark of Nett Tobacco, or forty livres for every hundred pounds, weighed and delivered into the Stores of the Farmers General.

Article 3d. All the Tobacco, which is damaged, rotten or spoiled, shall be cut off and deducted from the payment according to an amicable estimation made by proper judges; or in lieu of this mode it shall be subject to a general Refraction.

Article 4th. There shall be also allowed, and deducted for full weight four per Cent; two per Cent on the Amount of the Invoice for prompt payment, and eight livres on every Hogshead for samples.

Article 5th. In payment of the above five thousand hogsheads of Tobacco, the Farmers General shall, on account of Congress either pay into the hands of a Banker to be named by Messrs. Franklin and Deane, One Million of Livres; or accept Bills drawn by those Gentlemen, through their receiver General at Paris during the course of the ensueing month, to the above amount; and another Million of Livres shall be paid on the arrival of the first Vessels, laden with Tobacco, and delivered on Account of this Contract: which two Million of Livres, shall be the full and complete of the five thousand hogsheads, or Fifty Million pounds marc of Tobacco, to be deliver'd on Account of Congress, at the price of eight Sols per pound, as above stipulated.

Article 6th. Should Congress send to France, a further quantity of Tobacco, whatever exceeds the amount of the two millions advanced by the Farmers General, shall be delivered to them by Messrs. Franklin and Deane, at the same price, and conditions, and the Cost thereof shall be paid by the Farmers General, either in money or in bills, at three usances drawn on their receiver General.

Article 7th. And the undersigned Farmer General in Virtue of the powers given to me by my Company do obligate my-

2. An obvious error; "sols" appears in the French copy in the APS.

self in their name to the full and entire completion of these presents.

Done by duplicate at Paris on the 24th. March 1777.

(Signed) B. Franklin
S. Deane
Pauleye [Paulze]

From the Comte de Clermont-Tonnerre[3]

ALS: National Archives

De paris ce 24 [29?][4] mars 1777

Mr. dorset, Monsieur, qui vous remettra cette Lettre est un officier qui s'est fait une reputation dans le service.[5] Il est homme de condition sans fortune et plein de Zele pour son metier. N'etant point dans la position de faire un chemin aussi prompt qu'il le desireroit dans les circonstances actuelle du service de france, il voudrait que ses services pussent vous etre agreables. Le suffrage des chefs sous les ordres desquels il a servi depuis dix huit ans est un titre avec lequel il peut les offrir partout. Mon pere le Marechal duc de Tonnerre et toutte ma famille y prennent le plus grand interest. En un mot il desire vous entretenir et quoique je n'aye pas l'avantage d'etre connu de vous il a desire ce petit mot de Lettre pour vous faire connaitre qu'il ne se presente pas a vous sans etre connu, et sans avoir autant de droit qu'aucun autre a ce que vous croirés pouvoir faire pour lui. Je suis avec le plus parfait devouement Monsieur Votre tres humble et tres obeissant serviteur

Le Cte. de Clermont Tonnerre

3. Charles-Henri-Jules (1720–94), a lieutenant general and the eldest son of the aged Gaspard, duc de Clermont-Tonnerre (1688–1781), senior marshal of France; for both see the *Dictionnaire de biographie française*, and for the duc *Etat militaire*, 1777, p. 54.

4. The digit can be read as either "4" or "9"; the former seems to us more probable. In any case the note was obviously written before BF to Washington of the 29th.

5. François-Joseph Dorset or d'Orset (born 1743) was clearly a protégé of the house of Tonnerre, and BF was averse to antagonizing the influential. For that reason, we assume, he gave Dorset the noncommittal letter to Washington just cited.

From Germany, Girardot & Cie.[6]

L: American Philosophical Society

⟨March 24, 1777, in French: They have sent a letter for Franklin received from Strasbourg, and will forward the reply when notified.⟩

To Michael Hillegas[7]

ALS (draft): Library of Congress

Dear Sir, Paris, March 25. 1777.

The Bearer M. de Bert de Majan, has been bred in the Military Line, and is esteemed here to be skilful in his Profession. As such he is recommended to me by the Count de Rochechouart, Lieutenant General in the King's Armies. He is desirous of entring into our Service in America, the Grenadier Regiment of Colmar, in which he was a 2d. Lieutenant, being disbanded. I do all I can to dissuade foreign Officers from going over, knowing the Difficulty of placing them there; but the Desire in some is too strong to be overcome by Reason. You can have no Conception of the Numbers that are continually applying, to be sent thither, and whom I am oblig'd to refuse, as they generally want Advance-money, and a Promise of Commissions, which I am not empower'd to give. This Gentleman goes at his own Expence; and as he speaks German, I thought it more likely that he might on that Account find Employment.[8] I have therefore consented to give him a Letter of Introduction, acquainting him at the same time that I could promise him nothing. You are acquainted with that Language, and I therefore beg leave to introduce him to you, and to recommend him to those Civilities which his Zeal for

6. Deane's bankers, who had become BF's; see above, p. ooo n and Girardot de Marigny to BF, Feb. 6.

7. For BF's old acquaintance see above, XVI, 8 n. Hillegas was now an important figure as continental treasurer.

8. Claudius de Bert de Majan joined Washington's army, served throughout the war, and was a founding member of the Cincinnati. Lasseray, *Les Français*, I, 129–30. On Oct. 1, 1777, the abbé Bert de Majan wrote BF from Molsheim, near Strasbourg, to ask for news of his brother and enclose a letter to be forwarded to him. APS.

our Cause, and his Character as a Gentleman of Family and personal Merit, besides his being a Stranger, undoubtedly entitle him to. You will also be so good as to present him to the Board of War. With great and sincere Esteem, I have the Honour to be Sir, Your most obedient and most humble Servant

B F.

Michael Hillegas Esqr Treasurer to the United States of America

To [Penet]   ALS (draft): Library of Congress

Dear Sir,   Passy, near Paris, Mar. 25. 1777.

The Bearer, M. de Bert, is desirous of going to America. He goes at his own Expence, but will want Advice about his Passage. As he is your Countryman, I cannot do better for him, than to introduce him to you and to recommend him to your Civilities, as a Gentleman of Character and Merit.[9]

I receiv'd your Favour by Mr. Rumsey,[1] and am glad to hear of your Welfare, and that your Operations for the Congress go on well. There is no doubt, but that finding themselves faithfully serv'd, their Confidence in you must increase proportionably. I am, Sir, Your most humble Servant

B FRANKLIN

Recommendations

The Committee of Secret Correspondence to the American Commissioners

LS: American Philosophical Society; copy: Library of Congress

Sir: Philadelphia March. 25. 1777

We are commanded by Congress to transmit Copies of their Resolve of the 13 instant to all the Gentlemen abroad that hold correspondance with any of their Committees. The Necessity of Such a resolution and due attention to it, is fully

---

9. De Bert de Majan and Penet were both Alsatians.
1. Penet's letter above, March 11.

evinced by the heavy expence america has been put to by many Gentlemen received into their Service, who have found it impossible to render themselves usefull for want of the Language and we think this the most likely means to save others the charge and trouble of a long voyage, as well as the mortification, of being disapointed in their expectations. You will therefore serve all such and oblige us by discouraging their coming to America for Military employment.[2] We are sir Your Obedient Servants. By order of the Committee of Secret Correspondance   ROBT MORRIS

Addressed: To / The Honorable Doctr Benjn Franklin / Silas Deane & Arthur Lee Esqrs / Paris

Notation: Secret Committe March 25 1777

Jonathan Williams, Jr., to the American Commissioners

ALS: American Philosophical Society

Gentlemen   Nantes March 25. 1777.

I am still without any of your Favours which I confess gives me great uneasiness as I am apprehensive that my Letters have miscarried. The last I received from Mr. Deane which was 23 days in coming encreases this Suspicion: if you have not received one by every post this must be the Case as I have written by every one.

I have the pleasure to inform you that the anchors are arrived from Spain and those we wanted are procured. I have also received the Charts Capt. Wickes mentioned to have sent; but those Mr. Deane sent are not to be found.

I long since thought that the officers of Mr. DuCoudrays party were either gone or had given up all thoughts of going, but there are now 7 of them with 2 Servants who apply for passage, and say they have received advice that they were to pass on board the Count de Vergennes. The answer given them is that no person is to go in that Ship without particular

2. For the problem that these foreign applicants created in America see Freeman, *Washington*, IV, 419–20; Smith, *Letters*, VI, 486 n. Congress resolved to discourage all except those with the highest recommendations and a mastery of English: *JCC*, VII, 174.

orders. I therefore beg to be informed whether you will consent to this or not and if you do, whether their passages are to be gratis or not.

Please to send a Copy of the orders properly signed. I have a Copy but it will not be of any effect without your signature, please to have the word *Jack* (for the Signal,) translated *petit pavilion* and not *flamme* which signifies *pendant*:[3] I took this liberty with those given to the Capt. of the Mercury.

I send this Letter under cover to Mr. Montieu to be sure that you have it. I request to have a particular Direction for my future Letters. I have the honour to be with great Respect Gentlemen Your most obedient and most humble Servant

JONA WILLIAMS JUNR

The Honorable The Deputies of the United States.

Notation: From Mr. Williams March 25. 77.

From La Rochefoucauld   AL: American Philosophical Society

Ce Mardi matin [March 25, 1777[4]]

Le Duc de la Rochefoucauld fait bien des complimens à Monsieur le Docteur franklin; il le prie du lui donner des nouvelles de sa goutte; il a l'honneur de lui envoier la Nouvelle Constitution de Delaware, et si Monsieur franklyn le trouve bon, il ira la rechercher Jeudi matin à Passy, si Monsieur le Docteur y est encore, ou à Paris.[5]

From Jonathan Williams, Jr.

ALS: American Philosophical Society

Dear and honored Sir   Nantes March 25. 1777.

I am extreemly uneasy at not hearing from you particularly in answer to mine relative to Mr. Shweighaussers proposals

3. A pendant or pennant was flown only on a ship commissioned by the government.

4. The Duke's note below of the 26th, a Wednesday, was clearly the immediate sequel to this one.

5. La Rochefoucauld's translation of the Delaware constitution was subsequently published, under the date of May 8, 1777, in the *Affaires de l'Angleterre et de l'Amérique*, v, cahier XXI, iii–xxx.

which seems to surprise him, and I am fearfull it will make some impressions unfavourable to the notice and Friendship you have hitherto honoured me with. I who know how many things you have to attend to and being conscious of not having intentionaly deserved your displeasure cannot allow myself to interpret it in this way. I am also beset with politicians who are forever asking for news and it is with the utmost difficulty that I can make them believe that I have none, as they think I keep it secret: I was yesterday spoken to in this manner by the mayor of the City.

I shall be much obliged to my good Friend Temple if he will write to me when you are too busy to do it.

I have received a Letter from Major Lutlock[6] in which he says that an order had arived from the English Embassador, but that he was luckily on board the Ship, else he would have been obliged to return to his Regiment. I hope the Ship is by this time gone. I am with the greatest Respect Your dutifull and affectionate Kinsman J WILLIAMS JUNR

Addressed: Doctor Franklin

From Jean-Jacques Caffiéri[7]

ALS: American Philosophical Society

De Paris ce 26 mars 1777

M. Caffieri a l'honneur de soiter [souhaiter] le bonjoure a Monsieur franklin et Le pris de lui faire dire quel jour il voudra bien lui donné, pour La derniere séance.

Addressed: A Monsieur / Monsieur franklin / A Passy

From La Rochefoucauld

ALS: American Philosophical Society

Paris. 26. Mars. 1777.

Mr. Dean vient de me dire, Monsieur, que vous alliez demain à Versailles; ainsi je n'irai point vous chercher à Passy, comme

6. Lutterloh.

7. For the famous sculptor see the *Biographie universelle*. He was making the monument to Gen. Montgomery that Congress had commissioned, and was also completing a bust of BF: Charles C. Sellers, *Benjamin Franklin in Portraiture* (New Haven and London, 1962), pp. 116–18.

je l'avois compté; mais, comme je pars demain pour aller passer quinze jours à Rouen où est mon Régiment, je vous serois bien obligé, si vous avez bien voulu jetter les yeux sur la traduction de la Constitution de Delaware, de vouloir bien me la renvoier avec vos corrections, parce que je m'occuperois pendant mon séjour à Rouen à la faire copier pour la publier à mon retour.[8]

Voici une Gazette Américaine que M. Dean m'a donnée parce qu'elle contient la constitution du Maryland; mais il n'y en a que le commencement, et, comme vous devez, à ce qu'il m'a dit, avoir la suite, vous me feriez plaisir de me l'envoier, parce que, pendant mon séjour à Rouen, je traduirai cette piece, et la constitution de la Virginie. A mon retour, je vous rendrai tous vos livres; mais en attendant je vous prie de me renvoier avec ma traduction les deux *Remembrancer* qui y étoient joints, et dont j'aurai encore besoin.[9]

Si vous ne pouviez pas me renvoier tout cela ce soir, je vous prie de me mander à quelle heure je pourrois les envoier chercher demain matin.

Permettez moi de vous demander si vous avez nouvelle que les differentes colonies aient accepté *l'Acte de Confédération* que nous avons vu ici, et si l'acceptation est pure et simple, ou avec des changemens.[1] Recevez, je vous supplie, l'hommage des sentimens d'estime et d'attachement avec lesquels j'ai l'honneur d'être, Monsieur, votre très humble et très obeissant serviteur, LE DUC DE LA ROCHEFOUCAULD

Ma mere me charge de vous faire ses complimens.

Notation: de la Rochefoucaut Paris 26 Mars 77

8. The Duke had suggested coming to Passy in his note of the previous day about the constitution of Delaware. The visit to Rouen was in his capacity as colonel of the regiment de la Sarre, a command he had held for a decade: Joseph Ruwet, ed., *Lettres de Turgot à la duchesse d'Enville . . .* (Louvain and Leiden, 1976), p. 184.

9. The Virginia declaration of rights and form of government appeared in London in Almon's *The Remembrancer . . .* , III (1776), 221–3; IV (1777), 65–9.

1. The Articles of Confederation had not yet been submitted to the states: above, XXII, 572.

Jonathan Williams, Jr., to the American Commissioners

ALS: American Philosophical Society; letterbook copy: Yale University Library

Gentlemen   Nantes March 27. 1777.

When the Count de Vergennes was bought it was thought that she would be much too large for her Cargo, and you in consequence ordered purchases sufficient to fill her. In determining what would be sufficient, we had only for our guide the goods that were left here, and those advised from orleans, and we made our arrangements accordingly; we were soon after advised of upwards of 100 Bales more than we expected 70 of which are arrived, and 50 were to be dispatched the 15th Inst. These we found we could make room for by reducing their size and taking away the useless straw. By advice from orleans yesterday we find that instead of 50 there are 80 Bales now on their way, and that 80 more are soon to follow. Now it will be impossible to put these on board, and we cannot alter what we have done; the Cordage is made to order and the greater part is already on board, the sail Cloth is all in Bales ready to be shipped, and the greater part of the anchors are gone to the Ship: there is therefore no otherway to do than to put as much as we can on board this Ship, and to buy another for the rem[ainder] which (if you make the Bargain) may convey the Fuzils &c. &c.

I am particular in this detail that you may see how our operations have been conducted, and I hope you will not blame me though I own it would have been better [as] matters have turned out if we had not thus increased the Cargo. But not forseeing this, I flatter myself you will allow that we could not have done otherwise. I have the honor to be with great Respect Gentlemen Your most obedient Servant

J WILLIAMS JUNR

The Honorable The Deputies of the United States.

From Jonathan Williams, Jr.

ALS: American Philosophical Society; letterbook copy: Yale University Library

Dear and honored Sir   Nantes March 27. 1777.

I received a Letter from Mr. Dubourg desiring me to be concerned in his plan. I have given such an answer as any one who knows not what the particulars of the plan are would naturaly give. I refer him to you, and if any rational Scheme can be made out I will under take as far as you advise, but must first request your opinion relative to Mr. Shweighausser proposals which perhaps may not interfere with the other plan. I am with the greatest Respect Your dutifull and affectionate Kinsman   J WILLIAMS JUNR.

Addressed: Doctor Franklin. / a l'Hotel de Hambourg[2] / Rue Jacob / a / Paris

[The American Commissioners]: Memorandum [for Vergennes]

AD:[3] Archives du Ministère des affaires étrangères; copy: Harvard University Library

March 28. 1777.

On the 19th of November, the Congress resolved, That

100 brass Cannon	3 pounders	
50	6 pounders	
50	12 pounders	
13	18 pounders	
13	24 pounders	

In all 226 Pieces, be provided as Field Artillery; and this Order is sent to us.

It is probable that when this Resolution was taken, the Congress had not heard of the Number of Field Pieces then about to be sent from France, which being all 4 pounders will

---

2. If JW had not yet heard of the move to Passy, small wonder that he felt out of touch.

3. In BF's hand.

probably supply the Demand for the 100 three pounders, and 50 six pounders: but the others, viz.

50 .... 12 pounders
13 .... 18 pounders
13 .... 24 pounders

In all 76 Pieces, will be wanted. And we desire to know whether they may be borrowed from the King's Magazines, on Condition of being replac'd as fast as the Founders can make them? For otherwise we cannot have them in time for this Campaign.

On the 29th of November the Congress ordered the Secret Committee to provide as soon as may be Arms and Equipage for 3000 Horse.

The Committee have written to us to make this Provision in France, and transport the same to America.

We have provided the Pistols. We request to know whether the other Arms, viz. Carbines, and Swords, with Belts, and every thing but Saddles can be borrowed from the King's Magazines, on the same Condition as above-mentioned for the Cannon?

And whether two or three Ships of War can be borrowed to convoy the Merchant Ships that shall carry them?

On the 23d of December, the Congress resolved, that their Commissioners in France be instructed and authorized to borrow on the Faith of the United States a Sum not exceeding Two Millions Sterling, for a Term not less than Ten Years, upon Interest.[4]

Advice is requested upon this Head.

Robert Morris to the American Commissioners

ALS and copy: University of Virginia Library; copies: American Philosophical Society (two), Library of Congress

Honorable Gentlemen   Philada. March 28. 1777.

I wrote you a few lines the 7th Inst. by Monsr. Coleaux and

4. The three Congressional resolutions, Nov. 19, Nov. 29, and Dec. 23, may be found in the *JCC*, VI, 963, 992, 1036–7.

sent you the News papers to that time; by this Conveyance I send another packet of them under Cover to Mr. Delap at Bordeaux. There are only two Members of the Committee of Correspondance here at present, the rest being absent on leave.[5]

Genl. Howe's army in the Jerseys still remains inactive, and greatly distressed for want of Forage and Fresh provisions which they cannot obtain in any tollerable plenty as our Army are posted all round them, have removed most of the Hay, Corn and Provisions that was near Brunswick and never suffer a Foraging party of the Enemy to stir out but they attack them and altho' they come out strong enough to drive our People from their Posts very frequently, yet it has always happened the reverse, for they are constantly driven back into Brunswick with considerable loss of Men Horses, Waggons &c. Their Situation is disagreable and for that and other reasons I cannot think they will be Content with it much longer, especially as desertion is become frequent amongst their best British Troops, the Grenadiers, more or less of them, come over to us every Week. You being at so great a distance may probably think we ought to have destroyed Mr. Howe's Army by this time, and we undoubtedly shou'd had we an Army to do it. But when it is considered that Genl. Washington has drove them from their Cantonements on Delaware to Brunswick and confined them there the whole winter, during which he has killed and taken between 3 and 4000 of their Men, 4 to 500 Horses, a Number of Waggons and considerable quantities of Stores, Cloathing &c., kept them pent up in a place where they are Ill supplyed with provisions and other Necessarys which has produced desertion, discontent and sickness, it will astonish all mankind to learn that he had not during that whole time one half their Numbers in the Field, and the greatest part of the Troops he had, consisted of raw Militia that never saw a Gun fired in anger untill opposed to this very formidable army. It is now evident to all America that if in the beginning of this Contest we had enlisted our army for a

5. Morris' colleague was John Witherspoon. The only other member of the committee who had not resigned from it or ceased to attend Congress was Richard Henry Lee, who returned from leave in early April. Burnett, *Letters*, II, lvii, lxxi.

Number of Years or during the War, Genl. Howe cou'd not have wintered here unless as a Prisoner, but alas our Army were disbanded by the nature of their enlistments when they cou'd have been most usefull and the militia are too much their own masters to expect from them a steady adherence to the extream Fatigues of a long and hard Winters Campaign. They turn out for a month or six weeks shew great Bravery whilst they stay, but curiosity once being gratifyed and some feat performed to make a good story at home, they become impatient to return to their Familys and neither perswasion nor principle can detain them. For this reason Gen. Washingtons army since Novr. last has consisted every month of fresh raw hands, a constant shifting Scene of comers and goers, you might suppose him 10 to 15 or 20 thousand strong by the Commisarys and Quarter Masters returns but never 5000 by the Adjutant Generals for he never had so many at any one time with him. These constant movements of Militia and the large Bountys and high wages given them has hurt the recruiting service exceedingly for those that would have enlisted, by turning out as militia for a short time have got more money than their pay and Bounty as soldiers wou'd amount to and they are more their own Masters. In short the Systems adopted by Congress respecting the Army were formed without experience and have not been equal to what was expected from them. They are now and for sometime have been Correcting their errors, so that I hope to see a formidable army under wise and wholesome regulations in a very short time as the General is now drawing all the new recruits together and as his hands are strengthened with sufficient powers I have no doubt he will do business with them this summer if the Numbers raised are sufficient to Face the Enemy and this I am inclined to believe will be the case. The Garrison at Ticonderago will be strong enough to dispute the passage there with Mr. Carleton and if you do but effect an European War to employ the British Navy, this Country will become Free and independant in a shorter time than cou'd have been expected. I fancy Genl. and Ld. Howe have it in View to attack this City. They may possibly get possession and if they do it will probably bring on their ruin, for they will there raise a Nest of Hornets that they dont expect and are taught to believe very differently. I am most truely Gentlemen Your Obedient humble servant. ROBT MORRIS

From Samuel Cooper   ALS: Henry E. Huntington Library

My dear Sir,   Boston N.E., 28th. March 1777.
If this Line ever reaches you, it will be deliverd by Mr. Joseph Hixon, a Gentleman born in Montserrat, and whose Estate lies in that Island. Bound from thence on Business to London, by the Way of Corke, He was taken by an American Ship of War and brought to this Port in October last. I need not mention the Opinion I have entertain'd of his Probity and Worth, when I acquaint you that I have given my Daughter and only Child to him in Marriage. He does not mean to go to France, but should he be cast there in these tempestuous Times, your Advice and Countenance where he may need them will particularly oblige me.[6] Wishing you Health and good Things, I am with the greatest Regard Your obedient humble Servant   S.C.

The Honle: Benjn. Franklin Esqr.

From ——— de Jousserant

March 28, 1777   See page 169

6. Hixon (d. 1801), a prosperous merchant and slaveholder, returned to Montserrat soon after marrying in January Abigail Cooper, Samuel's surviving child (Judith Cooper Johonnot had died). He was a sot, according to Abigail Adams, and was soon discovered to have a dark-skinned "wife" and five children at home. Butterfield, *Adams Correspondence*, II, 202.

From François-Léonard-Pierre-Auguste Tissot[7]

ALS: American Philosophical Society

⟨Geneva, March 28, 1777, in French: I send you my thanks for seeing me. If your grandsons ("vos fils"), before returning home, wish to visit the districts to which I have come to wait for better times, I will show them how much I appreciate a person with your greatness of soul.⟩

To George Washington

ALS: National Archives; AL (draft): Library of Congress

Sir   Paris, March 29. 1777.

The Bearer, Monsr. Dorcet, is extreamly desirous of entring into the American Service, and goes over at his own Expence, contrary to my Advice (as I apprehend you have already more foreign Officers than you can possibly employ) and without the smallest Expectation given him by me of his obtaining a Place in our Army. This at least shows a Zeal for our Cause that merits some Regard. He is recommended to me by the Count de Clermont-Tonnerre, Lieut. General, and Son of the

---

7. He signed himself Tissot Grenus, the name by which he was normally known. He was a Swiss (1732–1810), who had served in the Dutch army and retired to Geneva in 1775; three years later he published there his *Cahiers militaires portatifs, contenant une nouvelle idée sur le génie et plusieurs autres pièces intéressantes* . . . , which was subsequently reprinted in England. *Dictionnaire historique et biographique de la Suisse* . . . (7 vols., Neuchâtel, 1921–33), under Tissot. Two other notes from Geneva followed this one, of June 26 and July 28, 1777 (APS). In the first the Colonel mentioned two small works that he was about to give to the printer, and a proposal that he was making to BF about them. That proposal, now attached to the second note though it probably came with the first, he had hoped to give to the commissioners before he left Paris, as he told "mon bon amy le Chevalier G: actuellement a A:," meaning Georges Grand now in Amsterdam. It advertised his forthcoming *Cahiers* as a textbook that every officer should have, and offered to come to Paris at the commissioners' expense so that they could examine and, if they wished, purchase the MS; 7,000 copies, he estimated, would be needed for the American army. The second note asked for BF's answer as soon as possible.

premier Marechal de France; whose Letter I enclose.[8] I therefore take the Liberty of introducing him to your Excellency; and that is all I presume to do, knowing myself to be no Judge of military Merit, if I were otherwise acquainted with the Gentleman. With the greatest Esteem and Respect, I have the Honour to be, Your Excellency's most obedient and most humble Servant   B FRANKLIN

His Excy. Gen. Washington

Notation: Genl. Washington, Paris March 29, 1777 respecting Monsr. Dorset. (omitted)

From William Alexander   ALS: American Philosophical Society

Dear Sir   Dijon, 29 March 1777

I leave no letter from you unanswerd, but wait your orders about what is to be done with the tobacco Contract which Lyes still here. There is a story current here that the British Ministry have applied to have a Mr. Dean deliverd up on a pretext that He was Concernd in Burning Portsmouth,[1] which Calls to a mind a story that happend a good many years since. A Person I think his name was Rice had forged a Power of attorney by which he transferd Some stock belonging to a Lady at the Bank of England. He Escaped to French Flanders and the British Minister applied to have Him deliverd up as Guilty of a public Crime. The Duke de Choiseuil Then French Minister, askd the Ambassador whether If Such a Crime had been Committed in France, England woud deliver the Culprit. He was answerd fairly by the Ambassador, that He coud not by the Laws of England, upon which he was told that for this time the Request Shoud be Complied with, but that in future it never shoud, as England was only to Expect in such Cases, what she woud do to other powers.[2] This anecdote may be

8. It is above under March 24. When Dorset reached America, he found that BF's advice had been all too sound: there was no opening, and he returned disappointed to France. Lasseray, *Les Français*, I, 184–5.

1. For this affair see the note on Mrs. Wright to BF above, under March 7.

2. John Rice was returned to England, tried, and executed. *Gent. Mag.*, XXXII (1762), 599; XXXIII (1763), 42, 207–10; *London Chron.*, May 3–5, 1763.

depended on and may perhaps serve the French Court for an answer, in case They do not Chuse to Comply with the request, nor to give a bolder one. The Girls[3] and my best wishes attend you and your Grand son. I am with the most sincere attachment Dear Sir Your most obedient humble Servant

WILL ALEXANDER

Had it been practicable to get a French subject from England D'eon certainly woud have been applied for.

There was a scots Man of the Name I think of Gordon tried and Convicted in France for some Public crime of this nature and the evidence came home to Mr. Walpole then Chargés d'affaires.[4]

Addressed: A Monsieur / Monsieur Franklin / a L'hotel d'Hambourg / Rue Jacob / a Paris

Notation: Willyander 29. March 1777.

From Jonathan Williams, Sr.[5]

ALS: American Philosophical Society

Honored Sir   Boston March 29th. 1777
    Doubtless you will be pleas'd to hear that notwithstanding the Calamities of human life in general and the State of War this Country is in by Which we among a number of Innosent

---

3. Presumably the two daughters referred to in his letter to BF above, Dec. 22.

4. For the Chevalier d'Eon, who was perpetually in hot water with the French court, see Lauraguais (?) to BF above, under Dec. 21. Gordon, we are inclined to think, was the Alexander Gordon, banker in Boulogne, who was involved in the early 1720's in the conspiracy to bring back the Pretender, but as far as we know never came to trial. He is referred to obliquely in appendices D and E of *A Report from the Committee Appointed by Order of the House of Commons to Examine Christopher Layer, and Others* ... (London, 1722); see also John M. Bulloch, *Bibliography of the Gordons* ... (Aberdeen, 1924), p. 6. Walpole was Horatio or Horace (1678–1757), Sir Robert's brother, who was sent on a diplomatic mission to Paris in 1723 and soon became the British envoy: *DNB*.

5. This is the first extant letter from BF's nephew since March 1, 1776, when he was in exile from Boston during the British occupation.

ones have Suffer'd great Loss and Damage yet we are all well in good Spirits and Choose rather still to Suffer than Submit to lawless Power.

My Son John being in the prime of Life and out [of] Busness was Desirous to go to France to se his brother. I thinking it would keepe him out of harmes way and possible his Brother might help him to some Imploy I Consented to his going though it seemes hard as I have but two Left out of seven to part With both but as he was a Merchant from his birth he might Git acquaint'd with the Language and methods of Trade in France and in future Open Some Scene of Busness either with his Brother or me or both.[6] Your kind Notice and advice to the Lad will ad to the many Obligations allready Conferd on Your Dutyfull Nephew and Most Humble Servant

JONA WILLIAMS

NB your Connections at Phila. Where [were] all well a few Days ago. I Should as I ever did Esteem it a honour to be favour'd with a Line from you, it Gives us all Pleasure.

Addressed: The Honble / the Honble: Benjamin Franklin Esqr / Paris

Notation: J. Williams le pere Boston March 29 77

From Jonathan Williams, Jr.

ALS: American Philosophical Society; letterbook copy: Yale University Library

Dear and honored Sir.   Nantes March 29 1777.

I have not anything worth troubling the Deputies with by this post; the intention of this is only to inform you that Capt. Paddock has applied to me to know if he could get a passage in a French Ship to america and to be her pilot on the Coast. I have said nothing of the Count de Vergennes, but if the Dep-

6. For John Williams the younger (1756–94) see above, I, lvii n, lviii, and for his death date the [Boston] *Independent Chron.*, April 21, 1794. The births of the other nine children are noted above, XXII, 69 n. Josiah died in 1772, and four of his brothers no doubt predeceased him.

uties think proper it may be of Service to engage him as her pilot.

I hear to day that you have had the Gout very bad which I suppose is the Reason that I have not heard from you. I hope it is now over and that I shall soon of [have] the pleasure of a Line. I am with the greatest Respect Your dutifull and affectionate Kinsman   J WILLIAMS JUNR

Addressed: A Monsieur / Monsieur Franklin LLD / a l'Hotel d'Hambourg / Rue Jacob. / a Paris. / ou chez Monsieur / de Chaumont a / Passy.

Notation: From Mr: Williams Nantes March 27 1777 and Do. March 29

From [Samuel Cooper]   AL: American Philosophical Society

My dear Sir,   Boston N.E. March 30th. 1777.

I have wrote you within a few Weeks a Number of Letters,[7] and long to receive one from you. I know you will give me that Pleasure as soon as an Opportunity and your many and weighty Employments will allow. I had some Expectation of receiving one by a Ship from France, arriv'd a few days ago at Portsmouth, with a French Gentleman, Who appears to be a General in the American Army, and an Officer of Artillery.[8] This Vessel brought twelve thousand Muskets, a thousand Barrels of Powder, Woollens &c., a most seasonable Supply, as we began to find it difficult to supply the Levies for the new Army with good Arms, without leaving the Militia more bare than we could wish. The Continent would be glad an hundred Thousand Muskets were imported: As great Numbers have been ruin'd, lost, or taken by the Enemy. Last Evening we had the agreable News that two more Ships from France with military Stores were arriv'd at Falmouth: of what kind or Quan-

---

7. The two that survive are above, Feb. 27 and March 28.

8. The ship was the *Mercure*, and had arrived on March 17; the general was Preudhomme de Borre and the artillery officer Mauduit du Plessis: *Naval Docs.*, VIII, 140–1.

tity we are not yet inform'd: and a Letter receiv'd this Day here from Philadelphia mentions a Vessel from the same Quarter, and same Kind of Lading, as taken near some southern Port, after landing her Papers and Passengers, by a British Man of War.[1] We have also this Day an Account that the Enemy have proceeded from N. York up N. River, and burnt some Stores left at Peek's Kill under a small Guard. The Armies on both Sides have remain'd quiet in their Winter Quarters for more than two Months except Skirmishing amongst forrageing Parties &c. which have in almost ev'ry Instance turn'd out to our Advantage. The last that happen'd, was not far from Amboy, and more important than common. It was something similar [to] the Lexington Fight, the Enemy retiring before our Militia, with some new rais'd Forces, for many Miles, and with the Loss of five hundred kill'd, wounded, and taken.

By a Letter lately received from Genl. Washington He thinks it probable that the British Forces, under Howe will proceed as soon as the Season will allow for Philadelphia, and endeavor the Reduction of that City; and that a considerable Part of the Army in Canada, will come down St. Lawrence River, to join him. But by the Remaining of the British Forces under Lord Piercy, at N. Port, where they have winter'd, and there being as yet no Appearance among them of any Design to quit that Place, should any Body of Troops come by St. Lawrence, perhaps they may make a Junction at N. Port, or near it; and the Design may be to act upon the Defensive in Canada, and to have an Army in N. England at the Time that Howe is acting to the Southward.[2] A little Time, however, will open their Design. I hinted to you in a former Letter, that our Levies met with some Obstructions, and went on more slowly than we could wish, from Reasons that you will easily apprehend; I hope however we shall soon surmount all Difficulties. We are told here that the Quotas of several southern States

1. For the ship captured in the south see *ibid.*, p. 147.

2. Washington's letter of March 13, not in Fitzpatrick, was to Bowdoin as president of the Mass. Council: Mass. Arch, CXCVI, 290–1. Lord Percy (above, XXI, 333 n) had succeeded to the command at Newport, which the British had occupied the previous December.

are already compleated; and tho our Army is not fully rais'd, it is, and will be daily increasing: and is now at last a permanent one: so that we expect Washington will soon be able to take the Field with such a Force as immediately to impede, and before long effectually to stop the Progress of the Enemy. The Price of ev'ry Thing in the States, as might naturally be expected in our Circumstances is greatly advanc'd. Congress seems not inattentive to the Support of it's Currency. The Loan Office in this Town receives large Sums at 6 per Cent and the Lottery Tickets have a surprizingly rapid Sale. I have good Information that the southern States, instead of being depress'd, are only more firm and decisive by the late Irruption into the Jerseys. The indiscriminate Devastation and Plunder of the British and Hessian Troops there, and the unexampled Cruelties perpetrated by both, have induced many, who were dispos'd to favor them, or were at best lukewarm, to enter now into the most resolute and zealous Opposition.

France cannot expect long to avoid a War with Britain but upon Concessions that must finally ruin her. She never had a fairer Opportunity for taking a decisive Part. Should the British Forces prevail here, the opportunity is gone. When our Army is compleated, a French Fleet of the Line, as there are but few large British Ships here at present, might strike a Blow at N. York, and upon our Coasts that might go near to determine the Dispute at once. Her Influence at the same Time, might perhaps be employ'd with no small Efficacy upon the Canadians, the Indians, and even the forreign Troops in British Pay. Her secret and her open Operations united, might produce great Things. This is the Language of many here: With what Propriety you can best judge. I send this, by Mr. Cushing, a young Gentleman much esteem'd here; a Son of our Friend, the Honorable Mr. Cushing, late Member of Congress, who goes to France on Business.[3] I am my dear Sir, with the greatest Esteem and Attachment Your's

Endorsed: Dr. Cooper, March 30, 1777

3. See the senior Cushing's letter below, March 31.

From Silas Deane

ALS: American Philosophical Society

Sir   Sunday, March 30th. 1777

Inclos'd is a Letter from Mr. Williams which Appears to have shared the Fate of my last To have been opened. I have wrote him a long Letter this Morning, on the Magazine. Rumsay sets out Tomorrow, and Hood, and others on Tuesday. The Letter and Dipositions for Lord Stormont, and the Memorial for the Portugal ambassador I take leave to remind you of. I sent you Lettrs from Mr. Boux which I wish may be answered by Tomorrows post.[4] I have many Letters to answer, or I would come out. I have wrote to Alderman Lee by last Nights Courier.[5] I am your most Obedient Very Humble Servant

S DEANE

Addressed: To / The Honble Dr Franklin

The Massachusetts Council to the American Commissioners

LS: American Philosophical Society; copy: Library of Congress

Gentlemen   Council Chamber Boston March 31th. 1777

Above you have a Copy of our last,[6] since which we have received from the Secrett Committee of Congress Three Letters addressed to you, and they request that we would forward them by any Vessel going to France, but under the Care of a discreet Person to be employed by us at Continental Expence to go Passenger. We have employed Mr. Thomas Cushing junr. for this purpose, and have committed these dis-

---

4. The commissioners' letter to Stormont, which enclosed depositions, and to the Portuguese Ambassador are below, respectively April 2 and 26. Capt. Boux's letters have disappeared; they were presumably about the shipbuilding agreement mentioned in his below of April 7.

5. The letter, which notified Lee of his appointment as joint commercial agent with Thomas Morris, has disappeared; for Lee's description of it see Worthington C. Ford, ed., *Letters of William Lee* . . . (3 vols., Brooklyn, N.Y., 1891), II, 586–7.

6. Of Feb. 27, above.

patches to his Care, and have directed him immediately upon his Arrival at Nantz to repair by Post to Paris, and to deliver you the Letters himself, and there receive your Answer, and be Governed by your directions, touching his return, and the Port he is to come to. If you should committ any dispatches to him, We doubt not they will be taken due Care of, and if you should direct him to return with them to any Port within this State, we shall forward them with all possible Expedition to Congress. Such Intelligences or Information as you can Communicate consistant with the public Safety, we should be glad at all times to be favour'd with: We have at present nothing new to Communicate. We have sent you some of the latest Newspapers by Mr. Cushing. In the Name and behalf of the Council I am with great respect Gentlemen your Most Obedient Humble Servant JAMES BOWDOIN Presidt.

Honble. Benjn. Franklin, Silas Deane and Arthur Lee Esqrs.

Addressed: The Honle. Benjn. Franklin, Silas Deane & Arthur Lee Esqrs. / Commissioners from the united States of America to / the Court of France / at / Paris

Notation: Commit of the State of Massachusetts March 31. 1777

From Reinier Arrenberg[7]   ALS: American Philosophical Society

Monsieur   Rotterdam 31 Mars 1777
   C'est en qualité de Second Secretaire de la Societé Physique Experimentale Batave a Rotterdam, que j'ai cherchai, il ÿ a longtemps l'occasion pour vous ecrire, car j'avois la commission de vous envoyer les deux volumes des Actes de la Societé, mais je ne l'ai pu faire jusqu'ici, parce que je ne scavois

7. A Rotterdam book-dealer and printer (1736–1812) and the editor and publisher of the *Rotterdamsche Courant*; he also printed the proceedings mentioned below of the Batavian Society of Experimental Science, of which BF had been a member since 1771 (above, XVIII, 100 n).

pas votre adresse.[8] Mais il y a encor un autre raison, pour moi en particulier, qui m'oblige de prendre la liberté de vous ecrire, c'est Monsieur pour vous solliciter de m'indiquer une voye par laquelle je pourrois recevoir des nouvelles de l'Amerique: car etant Gazettier de cette ville, il faut que je me contente seulement avec des Nouvelles que je recois par Angleterre ou avec les Gazettes Angloises qui sont si partiales qu'on y peut presque pas compter, et parceque les Americains ont en Hollande beaucoup des Amis, qui sont fort portes pour leur affaire, je voudrois donc bien satisfaire a la desir de ceux qui veulent avoir des Nouvelles veritables de la part des Americains: Si vous voulez en consequent m'honorer avec votre Correspondance ou me montrer quelqu'un en France, qui etoit en etat de me fournir des Nouvelles Americaines et les Actes du Congres, qu'il voudra publié, vous m'obligerez infinement, pouvant etre assuré de la plus soigneuse Silence.[9] Je payerai aisement tous les fraix qu'y viendront et recompenserai lui, qui vous voudrez emplöyer de m'ecrire. Il ne seroit même pas mauvais pour les Americains, a ce que je pense, que les Hollandois etoient mieux instruits de les affaires en Amerique, afin qu'il ne croiront pas les fausses Nouvelles qu'on distribue en leur desavantage. En esperant d'etre honorér avec quelque reponse, j'ai l'honneur d'etre avec une profonde estime Monsieur Votre tres humble et tres obeissant serviteur

REINIER ARRENBERG

P.S. Mon adresse est seulement Reinier Arrenberg à Rotterdam

Addressed: à Monsieur / Monsieur Benjamin Franklin / a / Paris

Notation: Reinier arrenberg Rotterdam 31 mars 1777.

---

8. The volumes, the first two of the *Verhandelingen van het Bataafsch Genootschap der Proefondervindelijke Wijsbergeerte te Rotterdam* (Rotterdam, 1774–75), were finally sent to BF with the letter from Lambertus Bicker below, May 23, 1777. The present letter went by an intermediary; see Suard to BF below, April 9.

9. BF responded, for on May 24 Arrenberg acknowledged receipt of his letter and enclosed papers. The printer became one of the major disseminators of pro-American material in the Netherlands.

From Thomas Cushing, Sr.

LS:[1] American Philosophical Society

Sir, Boston March 31 1777

The above is a Coppy of mine of the 28 ultimo by Cap. Adams. This will be delivered you by my son, whom the Council of this State have Employed at the Continental expence to proceed to France and to deliver You a number of Letters which they have lately received, from the Secret Committee of Congress. I think myself happy that he will be under your Eye and direction while at Paris. I beg leave to recommend him to your Care and Patronage, not the least doubting but you will from time to time give him your best advice as to his Conduct and behaviour while with you, and that you will afford him your kind assistance in improving this tour to his best advantage. He is to be under your Directions with respect to his return, but if you should not have occasion to send him back soon and there is any Bussiness during his tarry in which you can employ him for the publick service, he will chearfully obey your Orders.[2] Any kindness you may shew him or any Favors you may grant him shall be remarked with Gratitude by, Your most humble servant THOMAS CUSHING

PS. I beg leave also to recommend to your Freindly Notice, Mr. Henry Newman, a nephew of mine who goes to France in the same vessell with my son upon Bussiness of his own.[3]

Hon. Benj Franklin Esq at Paris.

---

1. The body of the letter is in the same unidentified hand that copied Cushing's letter above of Feb. 28; the postscript is in Cushing's.

2. Little seems to be known about young Cushing except that he had married in 1772 and had recently been commissioned in a Boston regiment. James S. Cushing, *A Genealogy of the Cushing Family* (Montreal, 1905), p. 188; *Massachusetts Soldiers and Sailors of the Revolutionary War* . . . (17 vols., Boston, 1896–1908), IV, 304. His trip to France was probably connected with his father's shipbuilding interests. He was in Paris by late spring; BF wrote to his father on May 27 that he expected the young man to go to Nantes with JW to acquaint himself with the merchant community there. Six months later Cushing was again in Paris and again setting out for Nantes: *Deane Papers*, II, 256. He sailed for home in February, 1778, and reached Portsmouth, N.H., on May 1: Butterfield, *Adams Correspondence*, III, 19–20.

3. Henry Newman was born in 1756; his mother was the sister of Mrs. Cushing. *Report of the Record Commissioners of the City of Boston* (39 vols.,

The American Commissioners and Chaumont: Draft
of a Contract for Packets   AD:[4] American Philosophical Society

[March,[5] 1777]

Les amis du Congrès proposent a ses deputés en france d'expedier touttes les semaines un paquebot de 60 tonneaux au moins pour Boston pour porter leurs depesches et la personne a qui ils les confieront.

Les deputés seront libres de charger dans chasque Paquebot vingt tonneaux de Marchandises qui seront estimés 80000 *l.t.* et pour lesquels ils payront 10% de fret comptant.

Si le Congrès s'en rapporte a la personne qui sera indiquée pour l'achapt de ces Marchandises le choix les Bons d'aunages et le credit feront un benefice de plus de 10% de différence que si elles etoient acheptées de la seconde main.

Les amis du Congrès s'obligeront a ne charger que dix tonneaux de Marchandises en plus des vivres dans chasque Paquebot pour leur compte afin de conserver tout l'avantage de la Marche.

Il en sera de mesme pour le Retour de Boston en france et le Congrès poura charger vingt tonneaux de Marchandise en payant un fret de 10% et il poura faire suivre ses depesches par la personne a qui elle jugera apropos de les confier.

Le premier paquebot partira dans quinze jours. Les autres suiveront de semaine en semaine a l'exception de la seconde Expedition qui ne partira qu'au commencement de may.

Endorsed by Franklin: Mr Chaumont's Proposal for Paquets

Boston, 1876–1909), XXIV, 289; above, XVIII, 265 n. Newman remained in Nantes when his cousin went to Paris, and returned home with him. BF to Cushing, just cited; *Deane Papers*, III, 446–7.

4. In Chaumont's hand.

5. The draft was probably composed in the latter half of March. The commissioners had previously intended to use the cutters that they were purchasing as packets; see the second paragraph of their letter to the committee of secret correspondence above, March 12. Their decision to convert the cutters into warships opened the way to Chaumont's negotiations, which culminated in the more modest contract printed below, April 1.

From Louis-Guillaume Le Veillard, Enclosing [Madame Brillon] to Him: Two Notes

(I) ALS and (II) AL: American Philosophical Society

These notes are the earliest surviving record of Franklin's relations with neighbors in Passy who came to be close friends. Both lived near his new quarters in the Hôtel de Valentinois and were well acquainted with his host, Le Ray de Chaumont. Le Veillard (1733–94), often referred to as "le grand voisin," had married a wealthy wife and administered her dowry, the famous and fashionable mineral waters of Passy and their elegantly landscaped grounds, which sloped down to the Seine. Anne-Louise Boivin d'Hardancourt, who had become on her marriage in 1763 Madame Brillon de Jouy (1744–1824), was a celebrated performer on the clavichord, as appears between the lines of her note, and on other instruments.[6] Franklin had already been to call on her and her husband, but she was still shy with him. She must have been writing, therefore, soon after he moved to Passy, and we are assigning the two notes to his first month there.

I.

Monsieur   Passy ce Lundy [March? 1777]

Je viens de recevoir une lettre de madame Brillon a laquelle je ne puis repondre qu'avéc vostre secours. J'ay l'honeur de vous l'envoyer; je n'appuyerai point une requête que celle qui la presente rend aussi séduisante qu'il est possible; si seulement vous pouviez luy donner le samedy vous me feriez grand plaisir parceque j'aurais aussi l'avantage de passer une partie de cette journée avéc vous. Je suis avéc respect Monsieur Vostre tres humble et tres obeissant serviteur   LE VEILLARD

Madame Brillon compte certainement que monsieur vostre fils voudra bien vous accompagner.

Notation: le Veillard

II.

Ce lundi matin [March ? 1777]

Vous me rendriés un vrai service mon voisin, si vous pouviés me faire avoir les airs ecossois que mr. franklin a bien voulu

---

6. Antoine Guillois, "Inauguration de la plaque Franklin," Soc. hist. d'Auteuil et de Passy, *Bulletin*, no. XV (March, 1896), 100; Lopez, *Mon Cher Papa, passim.*

Madame Brillon's House and Gardens at Passy

promettre de me donnér; j'essayerois de les jouér, et d'en com-
posér dans le mesme genre! Je désire que mon talent pour la
musique plaise a mr. franklin, ce n'est point affaire de vanité;
je n'en ai jamais mis a jouér mieux du clavecin que quélques
autres, c'est uniquement l'envie de delassér un moment un
grand homme de ses occupations, et de me procurér le plaisir
de le voir: si mr. brillon n'étoit point incommodé, il auroit été
lui rendre sa visite, et l'invitér si cela pouvoit lui convenir, a
venir disnér avéc vous a la maison le jour qu'il sera curieux de
me dire si je jouë bien ou mal, les airs écossois! Il faut que
vous nous rendiés le sérvice de lui faire cétte proposition, il
seroit important pour moi de sçavoir son jour, pour avoir pagin[7]
qui surement lui fera plaisir a entendre! Adieu mon aimable
voisin: s'il étoit possible que ce fut vérs la fin de cétte semaine,
cela arrangeroit pagin.

Je compte bien aussi vous priér de me menér faire visitte un
jour a mr. franklin; je veux y allér avéc vous, parceque si je
suis timide comme le jour qu'il m'a fait l'honneur de venir
chés moi, vous qui sçavés ce que je pense, vous le lui dirés, et
je n'y perdrai pas!

Addressed: A Monsieur / Monsieur Le veillard / A Passy

Contract between Chaumont and the American Commissioners

ADS: New York Public Library; DS and AD (draft):[8] American Philosophical Society

Paris ce 1er. avril 1777.
Conventions de Messieurs Frankelin et Dean et Lee[9] deputés

7. "Père Pagin," a violinist who was part of the Brillon circle: *ibid.*, p. 30.
8. The ADS is in Chaumont's hand. The AD is in BF's; it has numerous
differences in wording, is unsigned and undated, and lacks the final paragraph. An English version in Deane's hand in the APS, dated March, 1777,
is not a translation but a listing of the terms, and mentions that three agree-
ments—presumably duplicates—were signed on the same day. Undated
copies of this English version are in the APS and the National Archives.
9. "& Lee," added by BF, reappears as his interlineation wherever the
commissioners are named later in the document; he has made the same
change in the DS. Lee probably returned from Spain and signed the ADS and

du Congrès des etats unis d'amerique avec le Sr. Leray de Chaumont.

Le Dit Sieur de Chaumont equipera tous les mois a compter du mois de may prochain pendant un an, un pacquebot ou vaisseau propre a porter les Depesches des Dits Srs. Deputes de france en amerique et de l'amerique en france, lequel pacquebot pourra porter plus de trente tonneaux d'effets sans que cela puisse Nuire a sa Marche la plus avantageuse.

Le Dit Sieur de Chaumont fera la depence de chasque voyage pour l'equipement vivres avances et gages de l'equipage et touttes autres depences quelconques.

Les Dits Sieurs Frankelin Dean et Lee decideront du port de destination en amerique pour la plus grande seureté de livraison des depesches et des Marchandises qu'ils envoyront.

Les Dits Sieurs auront le droit de charger chasque pacquebot en allant et en revenant de vingt tonneaux d'effets consignés a qui ils jugeront apropos et aussi d'y faire passer sans fraix un homme qui sera chargé du soin des depesches et des effets.

Les Dits Sieurs payront au Dit Sieur de Chaumont pour chasque voyage qui commencera en france et finira en y revenant d'amerique huit mil livres; lesquels payments seront faits trois mois après chasque depart de france et soit que le Pacquebot arrive ou non, la ditte somme sera acquise au dit Sr. de Chaumont sans retour.

Les Dits Pacquebots ne pourront estre retardés etant prest a recevoir les effets par les Dits Sieurs deputés ou leurs proposés [préposés] soit en france ou en amerique et la ditte somme de huit mils livres sera Neammoins payé a mon dit Sr. de Chaumont quand mesme les Dits Pacquebots partiroient a vuide.

Les Dits Pacquebots avec tous leurs Equipages seront aux risques de mon dit Sr. de Chaumont, et les effets chargés en chasque Pacquebot par les Dits Sieurs Frankelin Dean et Lee seront a leurs risques.

DS on April 3; on that day the commissioners sent their letter to Stormont without his signature, but it is on a receipt by them the same day (Yale University Library).

Le Dit Sr. de Chaumont sera libre de charger sur chasque Pacquebot ce qu'il voudera pour son propre compte sauf toujours la meilleur Marche des Dits Pacquebots.

Si Mon dit Sr. de Chaumont etoit empesché par ses superieurs d'expedier les Dits pacquebots, il en sera dechargé par les Dits Srs. Dean Lee, et Frankelin sur les preuves qu'il leur en produira et si le Congrès revoquoit les pouvoirs des [Dits] Sieurs Frankelin Dean et Lee la resiliation auroit egalement lieu.

B FRANKLIN
SILAS DEANE
ARTHUR LEE
LERAY DE CHAUMONT

Jonathan Williams, Jr., to the American Commissioners

ALS: University of Virginia Library; letterbook copy: Yale University Library

Gentlemen   Nantes April 1, 1777.

I received your favour of the 27 ultimo advising of the purchase of the arms &c. in Mr. Montieu's magazine, which as soon as possible shall be all counted and the real quantity of each kind with the Tools &c. &c. exactly asscertained. In looking over your Letters I observe you have made a mistake of the pen in adding the Number of Fusils in my list where you say you find 81,764 of different kinds; if you will please to recur to that list you will find that all the Fusils and musquets, (exclusive of those that are too bad,) amount to only 75,644, the remainder are pistols and side arms. I hope however this mistake will not affect your Bargain, and that, whatever number you supposed them to be of, there will be a proportionable allowance for all that fall short, for as you made the Bargain agreeable to the List there can be no doubt but the number should be made good. Least I should have made this error myself I send you another Copy of my list;[1] there

1. The copy has disappeared, but the original list was enclosed in his letter above of Feb. 20 and is extant; it gave the figure that he says was erroneous, 81,764.

and there dispose of them. If it cannot be done openly, in what manner we can be accommodated with the use of their Ports, or under what Restrictions. This Government has of late been a little nice on that Head; and the orders sent to L'orient have occasioned Capt. Wickes some Trouble.

We have good advice from our Friend of Amsterdam that in the height of British Pride on their Summer success, and just before they heard of any Check, the Ambassador Sir Joseph York had been ordered to present a haughty Memorial to the States, importing that notwithstanding their promises to restrain their Subjects from supplying the Rebels, it was notorious that those Supplies were openly furnished by Hollanders at St. Eustatia; and that the Governor of that Island had returned from his Fort the Salute of a Rebel Ship of War, *with an equal number of Guns.* That the King justly and highly resented these Proceedings, and demanded that the States should by more severe Prohibitions restrain that Commerce; that they should declare their disaprobation of that insolent behaviour of their Governor, and punish him by an immediate Recall. Otherwise his Majesty, who knew what appertained to the Dignity of his Crown, would take proper Measures to vindicate it. And he required an immediate answer.[4] The States coolly returned the Memorial with only this Observation, that when the Respect due to Sovereigns was not preserved in a Memorial, an answer to it ought not to be expected. But the City of Amsterdam took fire at the Insolence of it, and have instructed their Deputies in the States to demand Satisfaction, by the British Courts' disavowal of the Memorial and a Reprimand of the Ambassador. The States immediately ordered a number of Men of War to be put in Commission. Perhaps since the bad News is come, England may be civil enough to make up this little Difference.

Mr. D. is still here. You desire our advice about your stopping at Burgos. We agree in opinion that you should comply

4. See Dumas to the commissioners above, March 11. The news in the rest of the paragraph was perhaps also sent by Dumas, but if so in a later letter that is now lost.

may be more than it contains, and there may be less. Mr. Peltier thinks the Gun Barrells will turn out more but it is the Inventory only that must determine it. I shall inclose it as soon as it is taken, in the mean time I have desired that the workmen may continue their reparations till I have your orders relative to the whole. I have been over the Store to day with Mr. P. to examine what things there are that do not belong to this concern. There are 297 new Fusils (the same as those sent in the Mercury) which have been sold and paid for some months since, but remain here at the desire of the purchaser, and a few trifling articles that have no relation to arms which Mr. Peltier thinks cannot be understood as being in the bargain. It does not appear to me your intention that they should be included, so I do not contradict him; but there are about 100 doz. of Knives, 240 common iron hilted Swords, and about 400 slight Fuzils, all new, made at Mr. Montieus manufacture and sent hither for the negro Trade, which Mr. Peltier likewise thinks should not be included; but these I claim, particularly the Fuzils and swords as I think they come within the letter at least of the order: it remains with you and Mr. Montieu to determine to whom these belong. In the other points we are agreed, and except as above the Store and all its contents are on your account; the Time it is taken for will expire at the end of this year, if you mean to keep it longer for this or any other purpose, it should be known now as this is the Season when all Leases &c. are renewed. I shall observe your directions about the Cutter when she arrives.

I have not the honour of anything from you by this post, but Mr. Peltier has received advice that the destination of the Ship is changed, and that instead of going to Boston she is to go to St. Domingo and there to be unloaded.[2] Mr. Montieu

2. The ship was the *Comte de Vergennes*, rechristened the *Thérèse*; she did not finally sail until April 26. Beaumarchais had referred to her by her new name in mid-February and in early March had consulted the Minister, who presumably said that he did not wish to be associated with her. The change in destination was due to the value of her cargo, which consisted in part of the commissioners' purchases and in greater part of Beaumarchais' (a division that raised acute controversy when she returned to France with a new cargo); both parties agreed that she should not arrive on the American

likewise mentions that the 7 officers and 2 Servants are to have their Passages in her. To all this I can say nothing as I have not your orders, and it is by them only that I shall be governed.

While I have the honour of your commands I will do my utmost to give you satisfaction, and I flatter myself you will allow that wherever the operations I have directed have turned out wrong there has been no intentional Fault, for had I known that the ship would be sent to the West Indies I should not have put the salt on board; but should have ballasted her with Bricks, which in that Country are valuable while the other is of little worth. In the States you know it is exactly the reverse and I supposed the Ship would go directly thither. I have the honour to be with the greatest Respect Gentlemen Your most obedient and most humble Servant   JONA WILLIAMS JUNR

An american Ship is arrived at Quiberon[3] but it is not yet known what news she brings.

Notation: From Mr. Williams Nantes April 1st. 1777. to Hon: Deputies U. S. Fusils in the Magaz.

From Penet
ALS: American Philosophical Society

Monsieur   Nantes le 1er. Avril 1777

Celle ci est pour avoir l'honneur de vous prevenir qu'il vient de nous arriver deux Navires, l'un de la Caroline que nous avons expedié en Octobre dernier et l'autre de Philadelphia expedié par Messrs. Nixon & Co.[4] Les lettres nous ne sont pas encore parvenue. S'il y en a pour vous nous aurons l'honneur de vous les adresser ausitôt; nous venons d'expedier le Navire le Penet chargé pour la Province de Massachusets Bay, rien autre à vous mander pour le present.

---

coast at the height of the enemy's cruising season. Morton, *Beaumarchais correspondance*, III, 59, 61; Stevens, *Facsimiles*, XIV, no. 1445; XV, no. 1526.

3. Doubtless the *Lynch*, Capt. Adams; see the Mass. council to the commissioners above, Feb. 27, and JW to the commissioners below, April 2.

4. For John Nixon (1733–1808), a Philadelphia merchant who had served with BF on the Pa. committee of safety, see the *DAB*.

Monsr. Williams est toujours à Nantes il se porte bien. Nous continuons toujours en consequence de votre Lettre signé de vous Messrs. Dean et Lee à lui compter tout l'argend qu'il nous demande, jusqu'à present nous lui avons fournis quatre vingt louis, nous desirons savoir si vous jugés apropos de continuer; lorsque vous voudrez m'honorer de vos nouvelles vous pouvez m'ecrire en anglais, je sai le lire. J'ausse toujours vous demander une part dans votre amitié en laquelle j'ai toute ma confiance et que je conservrai respectieusement par la zèle et interest que j'aurai toute ma vie à servir avec fidelité votre nation à laquelle je suis entierement devouë. J'ai l'honneur d'etre avec respect Monsieur Votre trés humble et trés obeissant serviteur   P. PENET & Co.

Addressed: A / L'Honnorable / Doctr. Franklin / A Paris

Notation: Penet, Nantes I Avril 77

Seth Clark: Receipt

April 1, 1777   See page 584n

The American Commissioners to Lord Stormont

ALS: the Johns Hopkins University Library; AL (draft):[5] Library of Congress; copy: Public Record Office.

My Lord,   Paris, April 2. 1777

We did ourselves the Honour of writing some time since to your Lordship on the Subject of Exchanging Prisoners.[6] You did not condescend to give us any Answer, and therefore we expect none to this.[7] We however take the Liberty of sending you Copies of certain Depositions, which we shall transmit to Congress:[8] whereby it will be known to your Court, that the

5. The ALS and AL are in BF's hand; to the latter he has added "return'd with Insult."

6. Above, Feb. 23.

7. They had an answer of sorts; see their letter to Stormont below, April 3.

8. Two of these depositions, made on March 30, are printed in *Naval Docs.* VIII, 723–4. For the third, by Thomas Hood, see the note on Bancroft to BF above, March 4.

United States are not unacquainted with the barbarous Treatment their People receive, when they have the Misfortune of being your Prisoners here in Europe: And that if your Conduct towards us is not altered, it is not unlikely that severe Reprisals may be thought justifiable, from the Necessity of putting some Check to such abominable Practices.

For the sake of Humanity it is to be wish'd that Men would endeavour to alleviate as much as possible the unavoidable Miseries attending a State of War. It has been said, that among the civilized Nations of Europe, the ancient Horrors of that State are much diminished. But the Compelling Men by Chains, Stripes, and Famine, to fight against their Friends and Relations, is a new Mode of Barbarity, which your Nation alone has the Honour of inventing. And the sending American Prisoners of War to Africa, and Asia, remote from all Probability of Exchange, and where they can scarce hope ever to hear from their Families, even if the Unwholesomeness of the Climate does not put a speedy End to their Lives, is a Manner of treating Captives that you can justify by no Precedent or Custom, except that of the black Savages of Guinea. We are, Your Lordship's most obedient humble Servants B FRANKLIN
                  SILAS DEANE

Rt. honble. Lord Viscount Stormont

Notation: Dr. Franklin and Mr. Deane Letter to Lord Stormont April 2d. 1777.

"Model of a Letter of Recommendation of a Person You Are Unacquainted with."

AL: (draft): Library of Congress; copy: Morristown National Historical Park

Sir   Paris April 2, 1777
The Bearer of this who is going to America, presses me to give him a Letter of Recommendation, tho' I know nothing of him, not even his Name. This may seem extraordinary, but I assure you it is not uncommon here. Sometimes indeed one unknown Person brings me another equally unknown, to rec-

ommend him; and sometimes they recommend one another! As to this Gentleman, I must refer you to himself for his Character and Merits, with which he is certainly better acquainted than I can possibly be; I recommend him however to those Civilities which every Stranger, of whom one knows no Harm, has a Right to, and I request you will do him all the good Offices and show him all the Favour that on further Acquaintance you shall find him to deserve. I have the honour to be, &c.

Notation by William Temple Franklin: Model of a Letter of Recommendation of a Person you are unacquainted with.

To [Anne-Robert-Jacques Turgot, Baron de l'Aulne⁹]

AL (draft): Library of Congress

Sir,   Passy, April 2. 1777

M. Cenis¹ being at Bourdeaux, will easily find Ships there bound to some Part of North America, as I am told that scarce a Week passes, in which a Vessel does not sail thither from that Port. He should get the Assistance of some Merchant in agreeing for his Passage, and in purchasing the Provisions for his Voyage: And he ought to take a Sum of Money with him to subsist on, in case he does not soon find Employment, it being by no means certain that he will. On the contrary, I know there are many now there who cannot be employ'd, and

9. This note must be in response to Turgot's recommendation of Crénis, now lost, that BF forwarded to Washington with the letter that follows.

1. Martial-Jean-Antoine Crozat de Crénis (1739–85), a former captain of French dragoons who had served in the Legion of Corsica, had been trying for many months to join the Americans. As early as June, 1776, Turgot had tried to get him a colonelcy, and in July Dubourg had asked Vergennes to expedite his passport. By November, 1777, Crénis was with Washington's army; he was described, though not by name, as a relative of Turgot with great pretensions, intent on using the connection for all it was worth. He was eventually breveted lieutenant colonel, and apparently returned to France in 1779; Congress paid him $1,000. Stevens, *Facsimiles*, VIII, no. 757, pp. 3–4; IX, no. 887, p. 3; Gustave Schelle, *Œuvres de Turgot . . .* (5 vols.; Paris, 1915–23), V, 492, 496; Lasseray, *Les Français*, I, 175–9; *JCC*, X, 138; XII, 1143–4.

who subsist only by the charitable Courtesy of the Inhabitants. It is therefore with great Regret that I give Letters of the kind; as I see that too much Dependance is plac'd upon my Recommendation; and I am afraid of encouraging People to make so long, so expensive and hazardous a Voyage, which may end in Poverty and Distress. Those who have always liv'd in this Country, where Interest and Solicitation do almost every thing in procuring Places, very naturally conclude, that it is the same every where: But it is not so in a new Republick. Some Popularity is necessary in procuring Employment, and generally a Stranger must be a little known before he can be appointed. With great and sincere Respect I have the honour to be, Sir, your most obedient and most humble Servant

To George Washington   LS and AL (draft): Library of Congress

Sir,   Paris, April 2. 1777.

As I see that the Congress has resolved upon raising 3000 Horse for the ensuing Campaign I hope M. de Cenis[2] the bearer of this Letter, may be of great Use in forming some of the Troops, as he is acquainted with that Service, having been a Captain of Dragoons. He goes over at his own Expence, without the least Encouragement or Promise from me, which indeed I have no Authority to give. This shews a Zeal for our Cause, which has considerable Merit. I cannot speak of the Gentleman from my own knowledge but I send you inclosed the Recommendation I have received of him from Monsr. Turgot, late Comptroller of the Finances, and one of the most respectable Characters of this Nation: I refuse every day Numbers of Applications for Letters in favour of Officers who would go to America, as I know you must have more upon your Hands already than you can well employ; but M. Turgot's Judgement of Men has great Weight with all that have the honour of knowing him, and I am confident that an Officer of his recommending will be a valuable Acquisition to our

2. Crénis. Congress had decided the previous November to raise the cavalry: *JCC*, VI, 992.

Army.[3] With the most sincere Wishes for your Prosperity and Happiness, I have the Honour to be Your Excellency's most obedient and most humble Servant   B FRANKLIN

His Excelly. Genl. Washington

Notation: from Doctor Franklin

Jonathan Williams, Jr., to the American Commissioners

ALS: American Philosophical Society; letterbook copy: Yale University Library

Gentlemen   Nantes April 2. 1777.

I had the pleasure of writing to you yesterday since which Capt. Adams is arrived express for [from] Boston and now setts off with his packets for Paris.

If I did not think myself absolutely obliged to stay here untill I have orders to return I should be tempted to set off with him, as a few hours Conversation might be of Service as to matters of Business, and far less troublesome to you than writing.

I have began to take the Inventory,[4] which I apprehend will require some days to compleat. I have the honor to be with great Respect Gentlemen Your most obedient and most humble Servant   J WILLIAMS JUNR

Please to turn over

PS I open this Letter to acknowledge the Receipt of yours of the 25 which I will answer particulary by tomorrows post. I have at present only time to say, That the Tin Case with the Charts and Letters never came to hand.[5] What I mean by proper

---

3. Washington, in his reply, professed respect for Turgot but urged BF not to give countenance to any volunteers: below, Aug. 17, 1777. BF usually discouraged such offers, as mentioned in the introduction, and we assume made this exception because of Turgot. But he made another at about the same time, for a German who seems to have had no prominent sponsor; see the note on Burdett to BF below, April 5.

4. Of Montieu's arms.

5. The letter from the commissioners is missing. The tin case was probably one of the two they had bought to contain Boux's shipbuilding plans.

order is orders signed by you, which I suppose necessary to give validity, if not I have a Copy here, but as the Destination is changed I suppose the orders will be Entirely altered. I will observe all your directions and am with great Respect tho' much in haste Yours as before   J WILLIAMS JUNR

The Honble The Deputies of the United States.

Addressed: The Honble Silas Deane Esqr / Hotel de Hambourg / Rue Jacob / Paris.

Notation: Mr. Williams April 2. 77.

From Jan Ingenhousz   ALS: American Philosophical Society

Dear Sir   Vienna April 2th. 1777

I recieved a note from the post office of Paris, that a lettre directed to me has been put in the bureau without the postage being payed, and is therefore not forwarded. I have immediately given ordres to my banker to pay the postage. As I have reason to suspect, that this lettre is yours, the more so, as the last lettre I recieved from you, has had the same fate, I think it my duty to acquaint you with it.[6] I set out for Ratisbon the 12th of this month and will remain there with the Prince of *Taxis* during may and a part of juin. From thence I have a good mind to set forwards for Holland, England and France if I can manage it with my Royal Mistriss. My only desires to go to France are for to have once more the satisfaction to see you, and to be an eyewitness of you being in good health and happy.

Tho I am absent, lettres directed to me at Vienna will allways come to right.

The Emperour did set out yesterday morning for Paris, and will not return before july,[7] which I take for a convincing proof of a peacefull disposition among the European Powers. I hope, this Happiness will soon befall your natif country, and I languish to hear Soon, that your advice and counsel, not enough attended to before, will at last bring upon both nations a last-

6. See BF's reply below, April 26.
7. For the visit see Saul K. Padover, *The Revolutionary Emperor: Joseph II* . . . (London, [1934]), pp. 117–29.

ing peace and happiness. I am with the Greatest respect Dear Sir Your most obedient humble servant   J. INGEN HOUSZ

Addressed: à / Monsieur / Monsieur Benj. Franklin / Membre de l'Academie Royale / des Sciences de Paris &c. &c. / à Paris

Notation: Dr Ingenhause Vienna 2d April 77.

From —— la Barberie

April 2, 1777 See page 171

The American Commissioners to Lord Stormont

Printed in *The London Chronicle*, November 4–6, 1777.

My Lord,   Paris, April 3. [1777]
    In answer to a letter which concerns some of the most material interests of humanity, and of the two nations, Great Britain, and the United States of America, now at war, we received the enclosed indecent paper, as coming from your Lordship,[8] which we return, for your Lordship's more mature consideration.

B. FRANKLIN, S. DEANE.

The American Commissioners: Receipt for Money from the French Treasury

April 3, 1777 See page 199n

8. The paper was the reply, written on the outside of the commissioners' letter above of April 2: "The Kings Ambassador receives no Letters from Rebels but when they come to implore His Majesty's Mercy." Stormont read and copied that letter for Lord Weymouth; he then resealed it so that it appeared to be unopened, and returned it with his comment by the bearer, William Carmichael. Stevens, *Facsimiles*, xv, no. 1507. The commissioners sent the letter and comment to Congress, which ordered publication; both appeared in Philadelphia in early August and in London two months later. *JCC*, VIII, 599, 601; *Pa. Gaz.*, Aug. 6; *London Chron.*, Oct. 9–11, 1777. The commissioners did not send Congress this riposte, apparently, and we have not located it in MS; it has, however, the hallmarks of authenticity.

From Silas Deane

ALS: American Philosophical Society

Sir   Thursday Morning [April 3?, 1777]

I think it will be Necessary To have a Copy of the Contract with Mr. Chaumont sent to Mr. Williams and also to the Secret Committee.[9] As you have [*torn*] Original I wish they may be made out to go by the Express. I am Sir Your most Obedient and very humble Servant   S DEANE

Addressed: To / The Honl / Benja Franklin Esqr / [*illegible*] Passy

From Peter P. Burdett[1]

ALS: American Philosophical Society

Dear Sir   Rastadt in Germany 5 April 1777

Upon the News of your arrival in France I did myself the honor of writing to you at the particular request of their Highnesses the Prince and Princess of Baaden, as well as from the pleasure I felt upon your return to Europe.

This letter in all probability never reached your hands, or if it did, the multiplicity and importance of your present engagements, it is natural to suppose leaves you no time for less important correspondence.

The American cause findes in me a very weak friend indeed, but yet, a strong well wisher in their favor; whether my partiality arises from other motives than that I have the pleasure to be acquainted personaly with some of the Principal and most active men in their cause or, from the cause it self, is of no consequence. It has however given me frequent occation to speak before the Margrave warmly in their favor, and contrary to my intentions has at the same time inspired a certain officier in the service of his serene Highness with a strong desire of Embarking on the American side of the Present war.

9. The copy of the contract with Chaumont of April 1, for which Deane is asking, was finally sent to JW with the commissioners' letter below of May 1, which was a Thursday. He could conceivably have made this request of BF early that morning, but a much more likely time is some Thursday in April. We assign it to the earliest one according to our practice.

1. The cartographer and engraver, who had migrated to Germany in the service of the Markgraf of Baden: above, XX, 370–1; XXI, 386–8.

He is a Gentleman of the Rank of first Lieutenant speaks French and is a German, is well acquainted with the Use of the Theodilite and other Instruments of Engineering.

Under an opinion that I can serve the Cause of America without injuring the service of my Gracious Prince and Patron, I presume to recommend this Gentleman to your Friendly Notice. Should such service be wanted in America and my friend actualy embark for that Continant I shall reinforce his expedition and Recommendations with Letters to Mr. John Adams and several other of my old friends in America firmly perswaded that his prudence valour and Merit will not disgrace those who have promoted his Honor and Interest.[2] I am Dear Sir with the utmost affection your Sencere and Most Humble Servant P P BURDETT

PS I believe it needless to say that I should be unwilling to have all the subject of this letter known to my Prince.

I must not trust the direct-post carriage. The Bearer Monsieur Kornmann[3] who brings you this will also receive and forward to me the Honor of your answer, addressed to Rastadt per Strasbourg.

Addressed: To / Doctor Francklin / Paris

Notation: Burdett P.P. 5 April 1777.

2. We can only guess who the man was. Our grounds for guessing are that BF made an exception at about this time to his rule against recommending volunteers, and that the exception was a German. In late April he paid 240 *l. t.* to Henrich (*sic*) Klein to enable him to enter the service of the United States. In the late summer Klein delivered to John Hancock a letter of recommendation from BF, and soon afterward appealed for money; he had used up what he had in getting from Hamburg through Europe to Boston. The following June Congress allowed him $500, for which he was to be accountable. Waste Book, entry of April 29; Klein to John Hancock, Aug. 5, 1777, National Archives; *JCC*, XI, 662. This scrappy evidence indicates that Klein was one of the few Germans who entered the American army.

3. Doubtless a member of the famous Strasbourg banking family, which had a branch in Paris: Lüthy, *Banque protestante*, II, 325.

From Aimé (or Amé)-Ambroise-Joseph Feutry[4]

AL: American Philosophical Society

Ce 5 avril 1777.

Feutry aura L'honneur de se trouver demain dimanche chez Monsieur de Francklin &c. à Passi; il a celui D'envoyer encore un mémoire en attendant plusieurs autres qu'il va copier incessament. Il assure ici Mr. de Francklin de ses sentimens d'estime, de Respect, et de l'envie extrême qu'il a de Jouir un moment du bonheur de voir un homme aussi vertueux que Célebre.

From ——— Montée

April 5, 1777   See page 171

To ——— Lith

ALS (draft):[5] Library of Congress

Sir,   Passy near Paris, April 6. 1777

I have just been honoured with a Letter from you, dated the 26th past, in which you express your self as astonished, and appear to be angry that you have no Answer to a Letter you

4. Feutry (1720–89), born at Lille, abandoned a legal career to become a writer. He began publishing in the early 1750's, largely verse, and made a name for himself. He was also interested in ballistics and invented a number of military machines, which cost him much of the income from his literary works. Larousse, *Dictionnaire universel*; *Dictionnaire de biographie*; Henri Pajol, *Feutry, sa vie et ses ouvrages* (Lille, 1854). As a friend of the Chaumont family, he composed *poèmes de circonstance* such as a verse to Mme. Foucault, Chaumont's daughter (dated May 2, 1777 and among BF's papers in the APS); he was thus part of the Passy circle when BF joined it. Feutry's admiration for him (the last sentence of this note is not mere rhetoric) shone through his published works and helped to burnish the American's halo. For the next four years Feutry sent him letters, memoranda, and verse. BF reciprocated with his own works, and doubtless saw him frequently; but no letter of his to Feutry is extant.

5. The MS is headed by a later note of WTF, which he published with it in his *Memoirs*, I, 320–22: "The following Letter ... was addressed by Dr. Franklin to an impertinent and unknown applicant; and contains some wholesome Advice in a tart and pithy style."

wrote me of the 11th of December, which you are sure was delivered to me.

In Exculpation of my self, I assure you that I never receiv'd any Letter from you of that date. And indeed being then but 4 Days landed at Nantes, I think you could scarce have heard so soon of my being in Europe.

But I receiv'd one from you of the 8th of January, which I own I did not answer. It may displease you if I give you the Reason; but as it may be of use to you in your future Correspondences, I will hazard that for a Gentleman to whom I feel myself oblig'd, as an American, on Account of his Good Will to our Cause.

Whoever writes to a Stranger should observe 3 Points; 1. That what he proposes be practicable. 2. His Propositions should be made in explicit Terms so as to be easily understood. 3. What he desires should be in itself reasonable. Hereby he will give a favourable Impression of his Understanding, and create a Desire of further Acquaintance. Now it happen'd that you were negligent in *all* these Points: for first you desired to have Means procur'd for you of taking a Voyage to America "*avec Sureté*"; which is not possible, as the Dangers of the Sea subsist always, and at present there is the additional Danger of being taken by the English. Then you desire that this may be "*sans trop grandes Dépenses*," which is not intelligible enough to be answer'd, because not knowing your Ability of bearing Expences, one cannot judge what may be *trop grandes*. Lastly you desire Letters of Address to the Congress and to General Washington; which it is not reasonable to ask of *one* who knows no more of you than that your Name is Lith, and that you live at Bayreuth.

In your last, you also express yourself in vague Terms when you desire to be inform'd whether you may expect "*d'etre recu d'une maniere convenable*" in our Troops? As it is impossible to know what your Ideas are of the *maniere convenable*, how can one answer this? And then you demand whether I will support you by my Authority in giving you Letters of Recommendation? I doubt not your being a Man of Merit; and knowing it yourself, you may forget that it is not known to every body; but reflect a Moment, Sir, and you will be convinc'd, that if I were to practice giving Letters of Recommendation to Persons of whose Character I knew no more than I do of yours, my Recommendations would soon be of no Authority at all.

I thank you however for your kind Desire of being Serviceable to my Countrymen: And I wish in return that I could be of Service to you in the Scheme you have form'd of going to America. But Numbers of experienc'd Officers here have offer'd to go over and join our Army, and I could give them no Encouragement, because I have no Orders for that purpose, and I know it extremely difficult to place them when they come there. I cannot but think therefore, that it is best for you not to make so long, so expensive, and so hazardous a Voyage, but to take the Advice of your Friends, and *stay in Franconia*. I have the honour to be Sir, &c.   B. FRANKLIN

Answers[6] to an impt. Letter.

William Bingham to the American Commissioners

ALS: Connecticut Historical Society

Gentlemen   St Pierre Martinique April 6th 1777
Herewith you will please to find Triplicate and Copy of my two last Letters to Mr. Deane;[7] but as they are addressed to

6. At the foot of the letter BF drafted another version, which he then deleted. It is prefaced by "rather this, shorter," and reads as follows:
Sir,   Passy, near Paris, April 6. 77
Your Letter of Dec. 11. never came to my hand, but I have receiv'd two Letters from you, one of Jan. 8. desiring to know whether you can be convey'd to America *avec Sureté, sans trop grandes Depenses*, and one of March 26. wherein you enquire whether you may expect to be receiv'd in our Troops *d'une maniere convenable*. In answer I can only say, that to the common Dangers of the Sea is now added the Danger of being taken by the English; that the Expence of your Journey to the Sea Side and Passage over will be about 100 Ducats; and that a Number of experienc'd Officers have already gone thither more than can possibly find Employment. I cannot therefore advise you to prosecute your Scheme: but thanking you for your good Will to our Cause, I wish you a better Situation than you could have probably met with in America. I have the honour to be
7. Presumably those of March 21 and 29; he also wrote on the 9th: *Deane Correspondence*, pp. 79–84.

559

him in an official Capacity, I have thought proper to place them under your Notice, and shall in future do myself the honor of directing my Letters in the like manner, as I am informed by my last Dispatches from Congress, that you are jointly appointed Commissioners for the United States of America, at the Court of Versailles.

The Armed Sloop Independance arrived here yesterday in which came Passenger Mr. Reed. My Orders from Congress are to facilitate his Passage to you, with the greatest Expedition; Accordingly he embarks this Day in a Vessel bound to Bordeaux. This Gentleman will deliver you the present, and also some Dispatches from Congress, which I was desired to forward to you.

The Situation of Affairs in America you will be sufficiently instructed in, by these Enclosures, so that I think it needless to dwell upon the Subject. I herewith have the honor to inclose you an Extract of a Letter from the Honorable Committee of Secret Correspondence as well as Copy of one from the Honorable Robt. Morris Esqr.[8] The Dispatches which are referred to in the Beginning of the last Letter from Capt. Biddle, I have not as yet received, but wait for them with the utmost Impatience, as I imagine they must be of a very serious and important Nature, by reason of their chusing so respectable a Conveyance.[9]

It gives me Pain to acquaint you of the unfortunate Capture of the Ship Seine Capt. Morin. She was taken the Evening of her Departure and carried into Dominica, and this Morning, I heard of the melancholy News. I am extremely happy that I have taken out of her so considerable and valuable a Part of her Cargo.[1] What will be the Result of this affair, I cannot as yet determine.

I shall take every Step that Prudence can point out to recover her. If Capt. Morin has been sufficiently cautious in de-

8. The committee's letter, we assume, was that of Feb. 1 and Morris' that of the 26th; they are printed respectively in Wharton, *Diplomatic Correspondence*, II, 256 and *Naval Docs.*, VII, 1296–7.

9. The frigate *Randolph*, Capt. Nicholas Biddle: *ibid.*, pp. 1210–11.

1. The *Seine* was one of Beaumarchais' ships; see Stevens, *Facsimiles*, III, no. 241; *Deane Correspondence*, pp. 81–2; *Naval Docs.*, VIII, 280.

stroying the Letters and Orders which had a Reference to his Voyage to Boston, and has carefully preserved those that respect his Destination for Miquelon, I hope upon a spirited Application from the General, She will be given up. I have just sent off an Express to his Excellency, giving him a circumstantial Account of this Affair. I shall do myself the honor of writing you more fully upon the subject in a few Days.

I have been under the Necessity of advancing a considerable Sum of Money to Mr. Davis, who came Passenger in this Vessel. He had an unlucky Run of Play and enter'd into other Expences unknown to me. The following Extract of a Letter wrote by Mr. Carmichael and addressed to the Committee of any District, where the Ship might arrive, was the principal Cause of my making him so great an Advance; "The Gentleman who comes out Passenger Mr. Davis, is recommended to Congress by the Commissioners here, which Sanction will no doubt obtain for him all Civility and Assistance on your Part."

After which I could not think of refusing his Demand and consequently subject him to a Detention, after the Vessel he had came Passenger in, had sailed. He informs me that he has, or will have, a considerable Sum of Money in Mr. Deanes Hands, which he means to apply to the Purpose of liquidating this Account.

His Receipt for the Money I have herewith the honor to inclose you, as well as that of Capt. Morin for the Amount of what I advanced him for his Vessels Use.

Mr. Davis is now a Prisoner at Dominica, and I imagine his situation will again demand[?] a helping hand.

By the last Letters that I have received from the honorable the secret Committee of Congress, they mention that I may expect very large Quantities of Arms, Ammunition, Soldiers Cloathing &c. will be Sent out to my Address, in Order to be forwarded to the Continent, and that they shall constantly keep sending out Armed Vessels to receive them. I seriously recommend to you this Mode of Conveyance, as the most proper to facilitate a Supply of these necessary Articles, and to insure their safe Arrival. Very few French Masters of Vessels are acquainted with the Coast of America, and admitting they were, large Ships cannot take the Advantage of running into small

Inlets and Harbors as lesser Vessels may. Besides all the Continental Vessels sail with skillfull Pilots, which greatly lessens the Risk.

I have the pleasure to inform you, that the Congress has returned to Philadelphia. I have the honor to be with great Respect Gentlemen Your obedient humble servant

WM BINGHAM

Notation: Mr. Bingham March 6th. 1777

To the Conde d'Aranda

ALS: Archivo Historico Nacional; ALS (draft): Library of Congress

Sir,   Passy, April 7. 1777.

I left in your Excellency's Hands, to be communicated, if you please, to your Court, a Duplicate of the Commission from the Congress, appointing me to go to Spain as their Minister Plenipotentiary. But as I understand that the Receiving such a Minister is not at present thought convenient, and I am sure the Congress would have nothing done that might incommode in the least a Court they so much respect, I shall therefore postpone that Journey, till Circumstances may make it more suitable.[2] And in the mean time, I beg leave to lay before his Catholic Majesty, through the Hands of your Excellency, the Propositions contain'd in a Resolution of Congress, dated Dec. 30. 1776, viz.

"That if his Catholic Majesty will join with the United States in a War against Great Britain, they will assist in reducing to the Possession of Spain the Town and Harbour of Pensacola, provided the Inhabitants of the United States shall have the free Navigation of the Missisipi, and the Use of the Harbour of Pensacola; and they will (provided it shall be true that the King of Portugal has insultingly expelled the Vessels of these

2. The commission arrived on March 14, and BF originally hoped that Lee might substitute for him; the hope vanished when Lee's letters made clear that no emissary would be welcome. See above, the commissioners to Vergennes, March 18; BF to Lee, March 21; Lee to Franklin and Deane, March 16. BF apparently meant what he said about postponing rather than canceling his journey; see the note on Sarsfield to BF below, May 26.

States from his Ports, or has confiscated any such Vessels) declare War against the said King, if that Measure shall be agreable to and supported by the Courts of Spain and France."

It is understood that the strictest Union subsists between those two Courts; and in case they should think fit to attempt the Conquest of the English Sugar Islands, the Congress have farther propos'd to furnish Provisions to the amount of Two Millions of Dollars, and to join their Fleet with 6 Fregates of not less than 24 Guns each, manned and fitted for Service; and to render any other Assistance which may be in their Power, as becomes good Allies, without desiring for themselves the Possession of any of the said Islands.[3]

These Propositions are subject to Discussion, and to receive such Modifications as may be found proper. With great Respect, I have the Honour to be Your Excellency's most obedient and most humble Servant   B Franklin

His Excelly the Comte d'Aranda

Boux to the American Commissioners

ALS: American Philosophical Society

Le 7. avril 1777.

Je vous est rendu conte Messieurs Du premier marché aresté pour la construction D'un Vaisseau,[4] et c'et avec un plus grand plaisir que je vous ennonce la parole donnee pour un segond, qui ne coutera que 200 milles florins, c'est a Dire plus de 35 milles franc de france de moins que le 1er.[5]

---

3. Congress had made Spain only the quoted offer, and had envisaged joint action with France alone: *JCC*, VI, 1056–7. Vergennes kept in close touch with Aranda, and had the proposals made to France translated for him; see Doniol, *Histoire*, II, 322–3, 325.

4. In one of the letters, now lost, to which Deane referred in his to BF above, March 30.

5. Roughly £18,000 or 425,000 *l.t.*; the first ship was therefore costing more than 460,000 *l.t.* Georges Grand had claimed, as Arthur Lee remembered later, that each frigate could be built in Amsterdam for £6,000 or 142,000 *l.t.*; at about this time he or Boux asked for an advance of 300,000 *l.t.*, which the commissioners made a few weeks later. Lee, *Life of Arthur Lee*, I, 337–8; *Deane Papers*, III, 166, confirmed by an entry of April 19 in Grand's accounts with BF and Deane (above, p. 22).

J'espere que cette semaine les deux contrats seront passé pour l'execution de ces deux Bastiments; ce segond marché Double mon travail, que je vouderois pour Beaucoup estre finy car jean est [j'en ai] pardesus les ôreilles, de plus d'une semaine je n'aurois encore finy; alors j'irois a Lahaie y voir notre Embassadeur, pour le disposé a lever les petites Diffigultes au cas qu'il en surviennent, sen [sans] cependant le metre Dans mon secret. Cela finy je croy n'avoir rien de mieux a faire que de Vous rejouaindre ma presence n'etant plus utille ysi, elle Vous causeroit des Dépenses sans fruit et nuiroit d'aillieur au secret necessaire De la reusite que nous désiron.

Par des Informations que j'ay prise vous ne pouvé rien entreprendre Dans le nord, mais si le Besouin est aussy pressent que je le croy vous pourriée vous procurer quelques Bastiments a Livourne, a Genne, ou dans les autres républiques de la mediterranee, quelques constructions y seroient infiniment faciles. Des negosients de marseilles pourroient vous donner sur cela les Instructions nécessaires. Il seroit Desirable que vous puissiée vous procurer la connoissence de Mr. Guis negotient a marseille,[6] personne ne feroit mieux que luy ce que Vous pourriée désirer. La construction de deux Vaisseaux en france est la chosses la plus aizee. Le port de Lorient vous ôffre De plus grandes facillites que tout autres. En ce qu'il y à un negotient qui fait ce genre de commerce, on ne sera point etonné de la grandeur de ces Bastiments puisqu'il en vient de faire d'eux a deux batries. Mr. De Chaumon par ces connoissences a Lorian, peut faire reusir cette affaire. Il faut seulement qu'il paroissent etre fait pour son conte ou celuy de tout autre personne sans que le ministaire soit prévenu que c'es pour vous car dans ce cas tout seroit manqué. Si les chosses prenoient cette tournure nous pourrion avoir 4 Vaisseau en etat de partir de Lorian Du 1. au 15 Jenvier prochain. Je jure que cette marechaussee feroit une rude police, sur toutes vos côtes, ne perdé pas un moment à entamer cette affaire; c'es une des plus importantes que vous puissiée faire; si a cela ce jouint

6. For Guieu & Cie., one of the major houses in the city, see Charles Carrière, *Négociants marseillais au XVIIIe siècle* . . . (2 vols., Marseilles, [1973]), II, 922.

l'execution en amerique Des plans que je vous est adressé, je ne doute pas que l'annee prochaine vous ne soyee maitre de toutes vos mers. C'es de la que depent l'independance de l'amerique. Vous connoissé la seincerité des sentiments tres disteingue avec lesques je suis Messieurs Votre Tres humble et tres obeisant serviteur BOUX

Notation: Boux, 7 avril 77

From William Alexander ALS: American Philosophical Society

My Dear Sir   Dijon 7 April 1777

Your letter of the 4th came to hand this morning and I immediatly Called at the post office, where I found Monr. Dubourgs letter which woud have remaind there untill Doomsday as I am neither known, as Marchand, nor Americquain. The post goes only Tuesday So I expect to save a day by sending you this by my Friend Monr. de Montarché formerly intendant de St. Domingue a very worthy and Ingenious Man, who will be probably Employd in the Finances which he has studied and understands I believe well relative to his own Country.

Inclosed is my answer to Mr. Dubourg with His Contract. When I wrote you on that affair I had really no desire or Expectation of going into business again in that shape. But If I do, the object must be such as will Justify me in it, and I do not think less than 15 without risk woud do. They will probably think it too high, both now and after the Execution, however Successfull I may prove. I myself however allowed much more in proportion, to a Young Man who had neither the Years Experience, nor any other merit but that of Executing orders, during the Last War, on a similar scheme in the W: Indies. His name is stewart now secretary to the Government of Bengal. I notice that You have also made an Agreement with the F:G: but If it is for your Constituents do not you think it may Embarrass them to act in a Copartnary which must be the Case if you join with the others? I presume They woud send home the produce of taxes, and study objects very Important for Them, but not purely Comercial.[7]

On the other hand it is Clear that a purchase managed by one and the same Channel, will be made Cheaper than where there is a Competition. Your measures are likely however to be so much Better taken than Theirs, that the Advantages woud probably be on your side, or to speak more properly the Disadvantages woud be on theirs. And therefore considering the thing merely in a Mercantile light, They shoud be obliged to buy the Copartnary.

It is impossible in a letter to give You any of the Numerous details that are necessary to be Attended to In such an Adventure. The General outline that I have Conceivd is this. That one very stout ship shoud be fitted out for a reason to be afterwards mentiond, and this ship may be Employed on Some such objects as Galvin's,[8] which will give a large Command of funds abroad indeed the Greatest part of what will be necessary for the Interprize. The Insurance will be done Cheap by such a vessel and on that account a heavy fraught may be put on the outward Cargo to defray the Charges of outfit. But the great object of such an Equipment is to have 250 good seamen in America to Navigate home prize ships to be bought there. During Last war I did in that way things that look like romance. I would propose with this preliminary to send out only 1000 tuns of shipping from France loaded with salt to Clear

7. We assume that this passage refers to BF's taking part in Dubourg & Debout's tobacco scheme while contracting with the farmers general. Alexander had discussed that possibility, in almost incomprehensible terms, in his letter above of March 1; and his meaning here is at least as obscure because none of his pronouns has a clear-cut antecedent. If "They" in the final sentence are Dubourg & Debout, or the farmers, then "home" is France, "the produce of taxes" is either tobacco paid as taxes in America or French domestic taxes on tobacco, and the "objects" studied are perhaps the complications with Britain if the crop is shipped in French bottoms. But by this time the farmers, at least, had made crystal clear that such shipments were out of the question, and Alexander might be expected to have known as much from BF's missing letter.

8. William Galvan, with a privateer's commission from the Governor of South Carolina, had sailed to France to obtain military stores for the defense of Charleston. *Naval Docs.*, VIII, 467; Stevens, *Facsimiles*, II, no. 151.

out for French ports[9] so as to run no risk but on the American Coast, to send 1000 tuns from Holland with sail Duck and Cordage to supply the prizes which will be Entirely destitute. If you are not unfortunate I think the vessels may be bought in America and sold in France so as to pay litle or no fraught for the Tobacco home. The purchase of the Tobacco or the knowledge of the Plan of it shoud be Intrusted with only one person, who shoud after visiting the Country employ people on the spot two or three on every River to buy limited quantities Suitable to the ships that are ready, and these orders to be Extended from time to time as ships are got. The tobacco to be only paid on delivery. Each of the ships from France and Holland Shoud also Carry out 10 or 12 Supernumerary hands to be Employd homeward in the same way, both to secure matters in Case of Ships being lost or taken and to save the Risk of navigation outward in many ships. In this way I think in the Course of 6 Months 13000 hogds. may be shipd to Insure the delivery of 10000 hogds. or it may be pushd faster or Slower agreeable to Circumstances. A number of objections may be started to this proposal. But I think they can all be obviated. Even the difficulty of Conveying Inteligence to get Insurances made in time, which is none of the easiest. I propose to fraught few ships in france because They are not Carriers and a great number woud raise fraughts besides I hold it not bad policy to Interess as many nations as possible in your Comercial Affairs. Perhaps one or two Danish and Swedish vessels might not be amiss and They might be got Cheaper than in France. What are fraughted in this Country will come very dear. In Britain we Count a ship of 200 tuns 400 hogds. Here she will not Carry perhaps 300 hogds. even with the necessary precaution of attending to Her Dimmensions at fraughting. But dear as They will be, it will be Cheaper than buying and outfitting in France, besides that buying, woud employ Capital, which shoud be kept for more Important purposes. I am affraid your Friends will not keep Their secret as you will do. Now were it known It woud start Tobacco 50 per Cent. The reason why I woud not purchase more than half a

9. In the West Indies.

years supply is That I woud take the benefit of two Crops for the whole order, and next Crop is only made in October. Ships will besides come home safer in winter than Summer.

We have got a third story which I Suspect has some foundation That a new treaty is going forward between France and Britain. It is said both are to Disarm by Sea in a Certain Ratio and that France is to fish on the Banks at large, In which case there will be peace for at least another year. Talking of fleets I know not If you ever attended to the way of fleets drawing up and engaging at Sea. One great Absurdity has been handed down by our Ancestors which is the Commanders engaging in the Center of Their squadrons by which They can neither see nor know what passes at any distance. I have mentiond this to some of our best sea Men who were struck with it. But no Admiral Dare propose to rectify it, because it might reflect upon His spirit. But If the Admirals were to hoist their Flags in the rear onboard of frigates which are placed to repeat signals, They coud see and Direct every thing cooly, and I am perswaded in that Case we never woud have complaints of the Misbehaviour of Captains and Admirals which happens at present in almost every action. If Ever I live to be Ld. High Admiral this practice Shall be Introduced. I know not If I mentiond to you, that the American plan of Debauching the sea Men to Carry in Ships, Is at Great length Explaind in Loyds book. I have seen your Correspondence with Ld. How in the English papers and like it much.

I have been looking into the Ancient Wars and find the loss of troops by Sickness and desertion was much the same as in modern times and much more bloody on the part of the vanquish'd. But you must come to the period where the War lasted Campaigns.

Pray are we to see you here or not? This and for 3 weeks to come will be the best time both for travelling and for Privacy, as we have a vaccation of the Parl[iamen]t.

Your Campaign in America is I Suppose now opend. I take it for Granted General How will still Aim at offensive operations, but If nothing decisive Happens, I hope and believe the next that is 1778 will be the Last land Campaign from England. For unless the troops can live upon the Country no nation can Stand the Expence of Carrying provisions for an

Army 1000 leagues. I beg my best respects to your Son and am Joind by the Girls in the kindest wishes for you and Him. I am ever with the warmest Attachment Dear Sir Your most obedient humble servant W ALEXANDER

One Circumstance has weight with me in insisting upon Terms were I to undertake an affair of this kind. I believe Mr. Dubourg a very worthy Man the other Concernd I have barely Seen. But as They are all Ignorant There cannot be the same satisfaction in doing business with or for Them, as If They were Conversant In it. Ignorance produces indecision and Suspicion, two very disagreeable Companions in such a Journey. I am very Glad to learn that Williams is Likely to obtain a reasonable setlement at Nantes. He understands every thing relative to shipping well and I am Satisfied the Concern or any Concern coud not be in worthier hands.

I am Glad that you are pleasd with De Morveaux book, you will like the Man still better when you know Him. I will send you the second volumne whenever it is printed.

I most heartily thank you for your news. I have got within these two days most agreeable News from Granada, which give me a fair prospect of being once more a great That is an Independent Man.[1] This Campaign promises to be an Important and I hope will prove a decisive one, after which there will be only a Privateering war, which will be Continued because our Rulers will not have humility enough to make Peace. Mr. Montarché I find just now will be latter than the post. So I send it in that way. The Girls join me in their best wishes for your health and prosperity and I am ever with the warmest attachment Dear Sir Your most faithfull humble Servant W ALEXANDER

As I write by post I send Mr DuBourgs letter Seperate.

Addressed: A Monsieur / Monsr Franklin / a l'hotel d'Hambourg / Rue Jacob / a Paris[2]

Notations: W. Alexander Dijon. / W. Alexander 7. April 77.

1. He is referring to some development in the legal action against him in the island courts, for which see Price, *France and the Chesapeake,* II, 699.

2. Alexander went on using this old address throughout the spring; see below, June 19. Did he possibly think that his correspondence would be safer with Deane, who still lived at the Hambourg, than if sent to Passy?

From Feutry ALS: American Philosophical Society

Monsieur Paris ce 7 avril 1777.

Voici ce que vous avez eu la bonté de paroître desirer; je copie quelques mémoires relatifs aux machines de guerre. J'aurai L'honneur de vous Les donner Jeudi à 11 heures, à L'hôtel de hambourg.[3] Je cherche aussi à rassembler une partie de mes foibles productions, que je n'ai pas sous La main, et j'ose à L'avance, Monsieur, vous demander La permission de vous en faire hommage. J'ai fait part à M. Le Marquis de Puységur, Lieutenant général, avec Lequel Je vis tous les Jours, du bonheur que j'ai eu de faire connoissance avec un grand homme. Il m'en fit son compliment sincere. Il a eu L'honneur de vous voir chez M. Le comte d'hérouville qui m'honore également de ses Bontés.[4] Ils pourroient tous deux, au besoin, vous rendre compte de mes moeurs belgiques,[5] et de mes petits talens. Je suis avec autant d'admiration que de respect et une envie extrême de mériter votre estime Monsieur Votre très humble et très obeissant serviteur FEUTRY

From Feutry ALS: American Philosophical Society

Monsieur Paris ce 8 avril 1777.

En attendant L'honneur de vous revoir Jeudi matin à L'hôtel de hambourg, à 11 heures, et de vous remettre quelques mémoires &c. J'ose vous adresser une douzaine de mes fables

3. Two of these memoranda, now among BF's papers in the APS, were presumably the enclosures. One was a plan for a four-wheeled war chariot, and the other for a gigantic floating battery; Feutry subsequently published both in his *Supplément aux nouveaux opuscules* (Dijon, 1779), pp. 45–54.

4. Hérouville de Claye has already appeared in Le Roy to BF above, Nov. 28. For Jacques-François-Maxime de Chastenet, marquis de Puységur (1716–82), like Hérouville a general and author, see Larousse, *Dictionnaire universel*. The marquis, as suggested here, was Feutry's patron and also seems to have been his mainstay; after Puységur's death in 1782 Feutry retired from Paris, went into a long depression, and in 1789 hanged himself. See *ibid.* and Feutry to [BF?], March 9, 1782, APS.

5. Feutry used the adjective, at a time when there was no Belgium, to denote the virtues of the ancient Belgae in contrast to Parisian decadence; see the next letter.

nouvelles qui paroîtront bientôt avec une vingtaine d'autres dans Le 2e volume de mes opuscules pöétiques et philologiques.[6]

Je regarde Le jour où j'ai eu Le bonheur de vous connoître, Monsieur, comme Le jour Le plus heureux de ma vie. Vous avez fait une impression profonde et durable sur une ame Belgique, encore sensible, et que paris n'a point corrompue. Adieu. Je suis avec un respect sans bornes Monsieur votre très humble et très obéissant serviteur   FEUTRY

From the Chevalier de Mazancourt

[c. April 8, 1777]   See page 169

From the Comtesse de Mazancourt

April 8, 1777   See page 169

From Charles [?] Rybot[7]   ALS: American Philosophical Society

Sir   Hotel de Luynes. Paris 8th April 1777

I did not imagine you would have hesitated to pay me the trifling sum I disbursed for Mr. Wood,[8] as had I not assisted him he must (as himself declared) have staid at Calais till you had, which besides the expence, might have been detrimental to your concerns by the delay; tis true I have no immediate call upon you, but as a man of known integrity; I am persuaded you would not have me be a sufferer, by an act, from

6. The MS of the twelve fables is now among BF's papers in the APS. They were part of a collection of thirty-two with which Feutry opened his *Nouveaux opuscules* . . . (Dijon, 1779), a continuation of his *Opuscules poétiques et philologiques* . . . (Paris and The Hague, 1771).

7. A Londoner, to judge by BF's reply the next day. The uncommon name suggests that he was some relative of Francis Rybot, a Spitalfields weaver and merchant listed in *Kent's Directory* . . . for 1776.

8. BF's answer of April 9 makes clear that this was Thomas Hood, who first appeared in Bancroft to BF above, March 4.

which you reaped the benefit. I should have declined troubling you further on this Head, but I forgot to desire the Letter Mr. Carmichael left with you, which, do me the favor to deliver the bearer, if you do not chuse to pay him the money. If you do, he has my receipt and you will thereby oblige Sir Your most obedient Servant,   Cs RYBOT

Addressed: A Monsieur / Monsr. Le Dr. Franklin / a Son Hotel / a Passy.

Notation: Rybot.

From Jonathan Williams, Jr.

ALS: American Philosophical Society; letterbook copy: Yale University Library

Dear and honored Sir   Nantes April 8. 1777.

I thank you for your kind favour of the 30th Ultimo and am happy to find that you are recovered from the Gout.

I will observe your alterations in the circular Letters which please to return as expecting them again we did not keep Copies. Whatever Business you please to throw in the way of Williams & Co. shall be carefully executed. With regard to the alderman[9] perhaps that might be made agreeable on all sides by his joining us in the Business of your contract, especialy as I hear Mr. Morris is engaged, or about to be engaged with Mr. Gruel and Mr. Penet. The inclosed is from Mr. Hood he desires me to request you to answer it soon. Monsr. de Chantay brought a Letter from you dated 22 Jan. reccommending him to me for a passage, he says he has been sick ever since which is the reason he did not come sooner.[1] I have offered to assist him in getting a passage in an american Ship or in a french one via St. Domingo, the first is too hazardous, the other too

9. William Lee.

1. The disappearance of BF's letter leaves us with no clue to Chantay's identity except the inference that, because he was recommended, he must have been well connected.

far round. I can do no other so I imagine he will return to paris. Potter and his Companion have never appeared.[2]

I have ordered the Public advertizer and the London Evening post for ½ a year certain and so on 'till forbid, they shall be regularly conveyed to Congress. The first paper you know is in favour of Government the latter is strong on the other side, I therefore chose them as the truth may lay between. It is said that an american privateer of 20 Guns is arrived at Bordeaux with a prize, but I don't know that it is more than report. I am with the greatest Respect most dutifully and affectionately Yours   J WILLIAMS JUNR

Addressed: Doctor Franklin.

To Charles [?] Rybot[3]   ALS (draft): Library of Congress

Sir,   Passy, April 9. 1777.

I believe it is very unusual for one Man to pay another's Debts without being desired so to do by the Debtor, or knowing that he acknowledges the Sum demanded to be due. Mr. Hood is as much a Stranger to me as he is to you. You have lent him 3 Guineas: I have lent him 30, supposing him an honest Man: By the Account you give me of his Treatment of you, and which I do not doubt, he appears to be otherwise; and from the Falshoods he told you and wrote to you there is reason to question the Truth of what he has said of his Estate and Ability to pay. These are certainly no Inducements to me to advance more on his Account. The Letters he brought for me were of small Consequence and the Packets contain'd only Newspapers: The Benefit therefore which you suppose I receiv'd by your helping him on to Paris, is vastly less than the Damage I shall suffer by his coming thither, if I am not repaid. And I imagine that if a Man intrusted with carrying Letters to you, should obtain a Credit by shewing them, you would hardly think yourself oblig'd to pay his Debts. In the Memorandum you left with me, you have not given your Address in London.

2. See the headnote above, Feb. 14.
3. In answer to Rybot's letter of the day before.

Send me that, if you please. I shall take the same Care and Pains to recover your Money as my own, and when recover'd shall faithfully remit it to you. This seems to me all that you can fairly desire of Sir, Your most obedient humble Servant

B F

Mr. Rybot

Notation: Answers to Rybot & DelaHaye[4]

From —— Butor

April 9, 1777 See page 169

From Feutry

AL: American Philosophical Society

[April 9, 1777[5]]

Feutry supplie Monsieur de Francklin &c. de vouloir accepter cette foible marque de son estime et de son respect. Ce Robinson et ces opuscules pourront peut être amuser ses petits Enfans.[6] A demain à onze heures Jeudi matin hôtel de hambourg.

Feutry attend ses autres ouvrages, moins frivoles, mais peutetre plus tristes, pour des français S'entend.

From Jean-François Georgel

ALS: American Philosophical Society

Hotel de Soubise ce 9 avril 1777.

L'abbé Georgel demeurant ches S.A. Mgr. le prince Louis de Rohan et cy devant chargé des affaires de france a la cour de Vienne a L'honneur d'adresser a Monsieur francklin le jeune homme porteur de ce billet. Il est breton, de parens d'extrac-

---

4. Presumably Charles-Marin de la Haye, the farmer general. No letters between him and BF are extant, but see BF to unknown above, March 15.

5. This and Feutry's two previous letters mention meeting BF at eleven Thursday morning, clearly Thursday, April 10.

6. *Robinson Crusoé, nouvelle imitation de l'anglois* (2 vols.; Paris and Amsterdam, 1766).

tion Noble et ancienne. Destiné a être officer dans le regiment de dragons de la Rochefoucault ou il etoit Cadet gentil-homme, il vient de subir la réforme. La forme actuelle du Militaire francois ne lui montrant qu'une perspective très eloignée et brulant du desir de se signaler, il s'offre a passer en amerique si Monsieur francklin veut bien lui assurer un grade et un traitement. Il a du talent et a eu une tres bonne education: il etoit cy devant page de S.A. Mgr. le prince Louis de Rohan pendant L'ambassade de ce prince a Vienne, et s'est distingué dans tous les exercices qui préparent au penible Metier des Militaires.

Monsieur francklin voudra t-il bien se rapeller que l'abbè Georgel a eu L'honneur de le voir et de lui remettre une lettre de Mr. Le Docteur Ichquenauss?[7] L'abbe Georgel offre a Monsieur francklin L'hommage de sa respectueuse consideration.

Addressed: A Monsieur / Monsieur Francklin / hotel dupon Mahon [?] / Rue Jacob

Notation: Georgel, Paris 9 Avril 77

From Jean-Baptiste-Antoine Suard[8]

ALS: American Philosophical Society

⟨Paris, April 9, 1777, in French: Sends a letter from M. Arrenberg of Rotterdam, entrusted to his care and addressed to Franklin; please acknowledge its receipt.⟩

From Barbeu-Dubourg

ALS: American Philosophical Society

Dear Sir [*c.* April 10,[9] 1777.]

Je partois pour Passy, lorsque ma femme s'est trouvée si mal qu'elle a eté obligée de se mettre au lit. A peine a t'elle deux

7. The letter above of Jan. 4, as Ingenhousz explained in his of Jan. 29.

8. For the writer, academician, and censor of the theatre (1733–1817) see Larousse, *Dictionnaire universel.* The letter he was forwarding is above, March 31.

9. Two clues to the date are in the first paragraph. One is his wife's illness: on May 27 he wrote Coder that it had been going on for forty-

jours par semaine d'une santé passable; c'est ce qui m'a empeché d'avoir l'honneur de vous voir depuis si longtems. J'attens impatiemment des reponses de Dijon et de Nantes.

Voicy une lettre que je reçois dans le moment, qui etoit
tellement cachetée que je n'ai pu en defaire la 1e. envelope
sans dechirer la seconde. J'ignore l'adresse de M. Thomson
pour la lui faire tenir.[1] Je vous prie de vous en charger, ou d'en
charger mon domestique a son retour. J'ai l'honneur de vous
souhaiter le bonjour, une parfaite santé et de bonnes nouvelles; et de vous reïterer les assurances de mon inviolable
devouement   DUBOURG

Notation: du bourg

Jonathan Williams, Jr., to the American Commissioners

ALS: University of Virginia Library; letterbook copy: Yale University
Library

Gentlemen   Nantes April 12 1777.

When I wrote last the Cutter was arrived tho' I did not
know it. As soon as I received your orders I lodged the necessary ones at painbeuf for the Capt. when he should arrive.
He had then come up to town and of course did not receive
these orders 'till he returned to his Vessell.[2] This little accident
has been attended with no other disadvantage than the loss of
2 or 3 days time.

I have got her in an unfrequented part of the River, where

seven days (APS), and he numbered them, it may be reasonably assumed,
from when she took to her bed. The other, which suggests a *terminus ad
quem*, is his awaiting an answer from Dijon, in other words Alexander's
response to the tobacco scheme of Dubourg & Debout: that response was
in Alexander's letter to BF of April 7, and Dubourg could scarcely have
learned of it by the 10th. JW also responded from Nantes, but we do not
know when; see his letter to BF below, May 7.

1. The letter was to Arthur Lee under his alias, for which see the note
on BF to Lee above, March 1.

2. The Captain was Samuel Nicholson. See the headnote on Wickes to
the commissioners below, April 15.

the necessary alterations to receive 8 3-pounders 4 2-pounders for bow and stern Chases and 10 Swivels will be made as soon as possible, in the mean time the most cautious steps are taking to secure the Crew. When this Vessell is ready for the Sea, she will still be French property and apparently bound to Gorée,[3] when american Colours are hoisted the real design can be no longer conceal'd; for fear of difficulty with the Commissaires in altering the property again, it may be necessary to have a hint from Authority that the officer may venture to shut his Eyes: of this you are the best Judges. Capt. Nicholson desires me to ask for a Commission for a Lieut. There are on board the Cutter two young Fellows named Fay and Antoine Rozet, who were given to understand by Mr. Ariez at Havre that they were to pass to america in this Vessell passage free.[4] They call themselves officers, and say they have received 50 Crowns (petits ecus) advance. I know nothing more of them, but least they should injure us by chattering I told them that I would write to you and act as you may order with regard to their passages in some other Vessell, telling them that this must depend on their discretion. I hope this will keep them quiet for 8 days at least, but I have promised nothing. If you know anything of them and think them worth the expence, I dare say they would be glad of a steerage passage in some american Vessell, in the mean time I will try to persuade some Captain to take them for the Service they will be able to do on board. Mr. Hood has applied to me for money. I told him that I apprehended your orders for advances had reference only to his passage, and the necessary expences, that as soon as I could obtain a passage for him upon an estimate of this I should pay

3. An island off Senegal, adjacent to the present Dakar, that was a center for the slave trade.

4. JW's debonair attitude toward the spelling of French names makes for obscurity. The young men had been sent by Hugues Eyriès, Beaumarchais' agent. They were in all likelihood the chevalier de Failly, captain in the régiment d'Anjou, and a lieutenant in the same regiment by the name of Onrazat: *Etat militaire* for 1777, p. 204. Failly had applied to join Kalb's party, initially scheduled to leave from Le Havre; he seems instead to have made his own way, and he was commissioned in the American army in August, 1777. Friedrich Kapp, *The Life of John Kalb* (New York, 1870), pp. 80, 300; Lasseray, *Les Français*, I, 211–12; *JCC*, VIII, 607, 638.

them and take his note as you order, but that I should not think myself justify'd in advancing any indefinite Sum. I received Mr. Deans favour by Monsr. Olsenne[5] and shall give him all the information relative to american Commerce that I can. I have the honour to be with great Respect Gentlemen Your most obedient and most humble Servant   J WILLIAMS

The Honorable The Deputies of the United States

Notation: Mr. Williams to Hon: Deputies U.S (12 April 1777.)

Jonathan Williams, Jr., to the American Commissioners
Letterbook copy: Yale University Library

Gentlemen   Nantes April 12. 1777.

Since writing by this days post I have received the inclosed plans and Memorandum from Messr. Jean henry Wilfelsheim & Compy.[6] who wish to be employed to build in some port in the Baltic Sea ships of war on account of the Congress if they or you for them will give orders. They say that they can do this in a very advantageous manner that being the Country for Wood Iron Hemp and naval Stores. If you think such an undertaking worth prosecuting and will either keep the Plans for your own Government or will send them to the Congress they are at your Service (but if you at once decide not to have any thing to do in the Business it is desired that they may be returned). If you desire particular proposals I will examine into the whole Intention but without your permission I did not think proper to make farther Enquiry as it may only give False expectations. In the mean time I think it my duty to communicate thus Far and have the honour to be Gentlemen &c.

It is reported to day that a privateer called the Dr. Franklin has carried 3 prizes into Bayonne.

5. Ozenne, of Charet & Ozenne, a Nantes firm that will reappear in later vols.

6. Wilfelsheim was a German who had become a banker in Paris: Lüthy, *Banque protestante,* II, 531, 695 n. He had, to judge by JW's letter below of April 28, a junior partner in Nantes.

From Jonathan Williams, Jr.

ALS: American Philosophical Society; letterbook copy:[7] Yale University Library

Dear and honored Sir   Nantes April 12. 1777.

I am obliged to you for mentioning the welfare of my Friends which gives me great satisfaction.

The many Instances you give me of your friendship demand my warmest gratitude and lay me under indispensable obligations to endeavour to merit your Favour by my conduct, which is the only return I can make.

The circumstances you mention for my private Government shall be attended to with Caution and whatever Business falls into my hands I will endeavour to execute *well*. The Goods you will have occasion to ship I suppose will be such as the public service requires, I therefore at this time can't forbear observing that as it requires a great deal of time to convey the Goods from the different parts of the Kingdom to the place of shipping, the orders should be given so early as to give time for this transportation that a Ship may not be waiting on expence. These orders should also be divided according to the seasons in which they will probably arrive else the Goods will come indiscriminately and there will be winter ones in summer and summer ones in winter. I take the liberty of making this observation because I have an Instance of this before me the Cargo now shipped on board the Count de Vergennes consisting of both linnens and woolens for Winter.

The young Gentleman who delivers this is from Mr. Schweighaussers' Counting House, I send it by him because the packet is large for the post, and because he is desirous of having it to say that he has seen Dr. Franklin. In return for a great deal of good nature and civility I could not refuse what will give you no trouble, and what he will think a very great Favour. The Gentleman who gave me the inclosed plan is connected with the House mentioned, and I think him a very worthy good man.[8] The House I understand is a very good one,

---

7. Lacking the first two paragraphs and the final one.
8. See the preceding document.

but if you think any thing about the plan I will endeavour to get the best Information. I am with the greatest Respect and Esteem dear and honored Sir Yours most dutifully and affectionately   J WILLIAMS JUNR

Addressed: Doctor Franklin.

From ———— de Gailhard

April 13, 1777   See page 171

From Antoine Court de Gébelin[9]

ALS: American Philosophical Society

Monsieur   Paris 14e. avril 77

Je prens la liberté de Vous recommander un jeune Suisse, M. Guez, de Lausanne fils d'une ancienne connoissance de M. Hutton, et d'un de mes Amis, reçu Chirurgien à Montpellier, qui vient de quitter sa Patrie pour aller offrir ses services dans les Colonies Angloises qui vous doivent tant. Je verrai avec la plus vive reconnoissance, tout ce que l'illustre Docteur Francklin voudra bien faire en faveur de ce jeune homme dont le Pere etoit deja très distingué dans la Pharmacie et qu'il a eu le malheur de perdre depuis quelques années.[10] J'aurois eu l'honneur de vous le presenter moi même si je n'etois retenu dans ce moment par les soins qu'exige l'impression et la composition du 5e. vol. du Monde Primitif; c'est mon Beaufrere qui me remplace à cet egard et qui saisit avec empressement cette occasion de Vous rendre ses devoirs.

Il vous parlera aussi, Monsieur, d'un de nos Amis communs M. Pierre *Dutilh* de Bordeaux, Negociant habile et de la plus

9. This old friend of James Hutton, the Moravian leader (above, XIX, 342 n), soon became closely associated with BF through the Masonic Lodge of the Nine Sisters. We print his letter out of the usual order because it helped to elicit the one from BF that follows.

10. Charles-Antoine Guez or Gueux (born 1754) was the son of Louis-Guillaume, a Lausanne apothecary who died in 1772. Young Guez was apparently still at home in mid-March, 1777. Eugène Olivier, *Médecine et santé dans le pays de Vaud au XVIIIe siècle* (Lausanne, 1939), pp. 955–6. He left for America with BF's recommendation (the following letter) and got as far as Nantes, where JW turned him into a German named Gueznt: to BF below, Aug. 28, 1777.

grande probité qui seroit très flatté d'etre honoré des commissions de vos Negocians, surtout pour les vins, Eaux de vie, epiceries &c. et dont on seroit certainement satisfait; je vous aurois aussi beaucoup d'obligation si vous vouliez bien nous faire donner à cet egard les renseignemens necessaires ou faire recommander notre Ami.[1]

Je profite de cette occasion Monsieur pour vous faire presenter le 4me. Vol. du Monde Primitif ouvrage pour lequel vous m'avez fait l'honneur de souscrire.[2] J'en devrois faire passer un aussi à M. Rush, qui est egalement souscripteur.

Si les Colonies etoient dans un Etat plus tranquille, j'oserois esperer que Vous auriez la complaisance d'interesser vos amis à cette Souscription. Personne ne le merite plus par l'estime et la veneration avec lesquelles il a eté dans tous les tems Monsieur Votre très humble et très obeissant serviteur

COURT DE GEBELIN

Notations: Court de Geblin 14 avril 1777. / A. Guez de lausanne en Suisse

To Richard Bache

ALS: American Philosophical Society

Dear Son, Passy, near Paris, April 14. 1777

The Bearer Mr. Guez, being well recommended to me as a skilful Surgeon, and otherwise of good Character for his Morals and Prudence,[3] I recommend him to your Civilities and Advice, which as a Stranger he may have occasion for: And as he has not sufficient to pay his Passage here, and will not be able to provide such a Sum immediately there, I desire you to advance it for him out of my Money left in your Hands, and take his Bond for repayment in a Year. I request likewise that

1. Among BF's papers in the APS is an undated request from one Brethon, "ancien medecin Du roy a st. Domingue," for letters to four substantial firms in New England that BF had mentioned to him; Pierre Dutilh is equipping a ship to send there. Brethon, we assume, was Gébelin's brother-in-law, and wrote just after the interview mentioned here.

2. BF had subscribed to the *Monde primitif*, presumably in 1772 in response to Hutton's letter above, XIX 342–6, and had recently spent 36 *l.t.* for vols. III–V: Waste Book, entry of March 14, 1777.

3. One recommendation was the letter preceding this one; BF's phrasing suggests that Guez had others as well.

you will endeavour to introduce him to some Employment either in the Army or Navy; or if those are full, into some Town or Place where one of his Profession may be wanted. Ben and Temple continue well, with Your affectionate Father

B FRANKLIN

R. Bache, Esqr

Addressed: To / Richard Bache, Esqr / Philadelphia

From the Comtesse Conway

ALS: American Philosophical Society

Sir   A ville d'avray ce 14 avril 1777

I Commence to read, and write a litle the english but I Know not Speak yet that language; wherefore, I bold not, to go See you, nevertheles I pray you of Signify to me the a day, and a hour where I Can render my homage to you; I am the wiffe of thomas Conway departed by l'amphitrite, for to aid his Brother americains, end to Share the glory with them. I wait the honour of your answr with impatience. I am Sir With the best great veneration your humble Servante.   D B[4] CONWAY

Addressed: A Monsieur / Monsieur franklin / maison de mde [madame] de valantinoix / at passi

Notation: Countess Conway

From Paul Veron[5]

ALS: American Philosophical Society

Monsieur,   Paris ce 14. Avril 1777.

Mr. Monge de Beaune vient de m'envoyer par sa lettre du 11 du courant la lettre que j'ay l'honneur de vous acheminer par la presente, en me recommandant de vous la remettre en main propre, s'il m'est possible.[6] Comme j'ignore votre ad-

4. Du Bouchet. She was the sister of Denis-Jean-Florimond du Bouchet, who had accompanied Conway to America and served with distinction there: Lasseray, *Les Français*, I, 264–6.

5. Or Véron, a Parisian banker mentioned in Lüthy, *Banque protestante*, II, 343, 396 n.

6. Gaspard Monge (1746–1818), the famous mathematician and inventor of descriptive geometry, was the successor at Mézières of the abbé Nollet,

resse, Monsieur, j'ay envoyé aux informations, d'un côté, l'on m'a dit que vous etiés souvent à la campagne, d'autres m'ont dit qu'ils ne sçavoient point votre demeure. Mais m'ayant été assuré que Ms. Grand et Cie. avoient l'honneur d'etre connus de vous, et qu'ils pouroient vous voir soit en ville ou à Passy, sous peu, j'ay crû Monsieur ne devoir pas hesiter de leurs remettre le presente contenant la ditte lettre qui m'a été adressée pour vous, avec priere de voulloir bien vous l'a faire parvenir aussitost qu'il leurs sera possible.

Mon dit Sr. Monge m'avoit indiqué de m'informer de votre demeure chez Mr. Kornemann, ce qui ne m'a point reussy n'ayant point trouvé ces Messieurs.[7]

Le dit Sr. Monge me marque qu'il est prié de la part des personnes qui luy ont envoyé cette lettre de leur en procurer reponse, si cela est possible; si vous souhaités Monsieur me la faire tenir, je l'achemineray aussitost que je l'auray recuë pourquoy vous avés cyaprés ma demeure. J'ay l'honneur d'etre Monsieur Votre trés humble obeissant serviteur   PAUL VERON

Paul Veron negt. Ruë St. Martin visavis celle aux ours à côté du caffé maillard

Addressed: A Monsieur / Monsieur Franklin / *à Paris.*

Notation: Paul vron Paris 14 avril 1777.

From ——— Brethon

[after April 14, 1777]   See page 581n

Lambert Wickes to the American Commissioners

ALS: American Philosophical Society

This letter speaks of preparations for a major American naval move, Wickes's cruise in the Irish Sea. The commissioners had summoned him to Paris in mid-March, and out of their consultations had come

---

BF's old opponent in electrical matters: Larousse, *Dictionnaire universel.* The letter Monge was forwarding by Veron has apparently disappeared.

7. Kornmann should not have been difficult for a fellow banker to find; he undoubtedly belonged to the Paris branch of the famous Strasbourg firm: Lüthy, *Banque protestante,* II, 325.

the plan for the cruise. The tiny squadron was to consist of the *Reprisal* and a cutter, renamed the *Dolphin*, which had been intended for a packet and was now converted into a warship under Nicholson's command. The idea of buying a frigate was dropped; but the brig *Lexington* had arrived with blank naval commissions from Congress, and Wickes's suggestion here that she be added to his squadron was promptly accepted.[8]

Gentlemen   Nantes April 15th, 1777

We Arrivd hear Late Last Wendnesday Night; and the Cutter Got up to pileren[9] thursday and friday We Went on bord her in order to Give the Nessesary orders for fitting her. After Doing this We Went Down to Pain Beaf in order to procure All the American Seamen in our power. We Was tolerable Suckcesfull. We have Now Nine Americans Engaged Includeing Captn. Clarke and the Docktor.[1] The Captn. and the Crue that Came from Haverdegrass in the Cutter is Inclined to Giv us Sum trouble but I Am in hopes We Shal be Able to take Such Measures as Will prevent them from Doing any Dammage.[2] The Cutter is a fine Stout vessail And much Better than I Exspected She Would be for the purposes intended. We Shal mount her With: 10 Carage Guns And 12 Swivels and About 30 men. She is Now in the Carpenters Hands and I Am in hopes We Shall be Able to Get her fitt for Sea in 6 or 7 Days. I Shall Remain hear With Captn. Nicholson Until he Gets things in A fair Way and then Make the Best of my Way

8. See Clark, *Wickes*, pp. 187–93. The author argues that the commissioners' underlying purpose in ordering the cruise was to provoke war between Britain and France. But such evidence as he adduces is in later statements by Wickes and Carmichael; we have found none at the time to support his contention.

9. Le Pellerin, down river from Nantes. "We" were Wickes and Nicholson.

1. Seth Clark was a merchant captain who had been captured by the British and escaped, and had come to France with Nicholson; on April 1 the commissioners had advanced him 18 guineas (his receipt is in the Library of Congress). The doctor was Eliphalet Downer, formerly surgeon on Henry Johnson's privateer, who had also escaped from England. Nicholson selected Clark for first officer and Downer for surgeon. *Ibid.*, pp. 169, 183, 191; *Naval Docs.*, VI, 517, 531; VIII, 723–4.

2. The French crew had signed on for a voyage to America in a packet, and had no stomach for serving on a warship. *Deane Correspondence*, pp. 91–2.

for L'Orient. I think our Little Squadren Would Receive a very Nessesary Addition of Streng if joind By Captn. Johnston of the Lexington if he is Not Distened for Any Particular Service or Cruize Would be Glad if he Would join me. I think you Would Do very Well to procure the Kings Pass for All persons Who Comes from parris to this With your Dispaches or Any other Urgent Business Where Dispach is Required. I think this hint Nessesary on Account of A Number of Delays that We met With from the postmasters and post Boys Comeing Down, and I Beleav We Should hardly Got here yet if We had not forced them to procead by Beating and hard Threats. From Gentlemen your Most Obligd Humble Servant

LAMBT. WICKES

Addressed: To / The Honbl. Doctr. Benjamin Franklin / Paris.
Notation: Capt. Wickes April 15. 77. Nantes.

From Nathan Rumsey

ALS: American Philosophical Society

Honorable Sir   Nantes 15th. April 77.
   The dispatches by Mr. Cunningham[3] arrived safe late on Sunday Night. The Packet falls down the River to day, and if the wind continues fair, will sail tomorow.

3. The first appearance of a ship captain who later made major trouble for the commissioners. Gustavus Conyngham (1747–1819), an Irish-born Philadelphian, had been marooned in Europe when the British blockaded his ship and its cargo of war supplies in the Texel. He got to Dunkirk and there met William Hodge, who was purchasing cutters for the commissioners and apparently recommended him for command of one of them. Conyngham was commissioned, returned to Dunkirk soon after carrying these dispatches to Nantes, took over a lugger renamed the *Surprize*, and on May 1 left for his first cruise. Helen Augur, *The Secret War of Independence* (New York, etc., [1955]), pp. 82–4, 176; Robert W. Neeser, ed., *Letters and Papers Relating to the Cruises of Gustavus Conyngham, . . . 1777–1779* (New York, 1915), pp. xxix-xxx. The choice of Dunkirk as a base was imprudent to a degree. The town, so long a bone of contention between France and Britain, had been demilitarized under the Treaty of Utrecht; its status had been confirmed in the peace treaties of 1748 and 1763, and a resident British commissioner ensured compliance. Fred L. Israel, ed., *Major Peace Treaties of Modern History* . . . (4 vols., New York, 1967), I, 207, 282, 313. The cruise was being prepared under that official's eyes, and had serious diplomatic repercussions.

I have my faults, and perhaps they are conspicuous but Nemo nascitur sine Vitiis.[4] I doubt not but Ennemies have made a Handle of them to rob me of your favor and good Opinion for the Loss of which I am sincerely sory. My Views at leaving my Native Land were to serve it; they shall be the same on my return; and I hope my general Behaviour will be such as to merit again Your approbation. As far as my Assistance may be necessary to forward the Dispatches to Congress, it shall be heartily given.

I wish you all possible success in your laudable Commission and have the Honor to be Sir Your most obedient Humble Servant   NATHAN RUMSEY.

Doct. Franklin

Addressed: A l'Honorable / Doct. Benjamin Franklin / A l'Hotel D'Hambourg / Rue Jacob / a / Paris.

Notations: N. Rumesy 15. April 77. / Rue Royal Place de Louis 15.

From the Comte de Sarsfield

April 15, 1777   See page 231n

From Jonathan Williams, Jr.

ALS: American Philosophical Society; letterbook copy: Yale University Library

Dear and honored Sir   Nantes April 15. 1777.

I am fearfull you will think me too troublesome in so often diverting your attention from other important concerns, but I can't help requesting your opinion on the inclosed articles before I consent to them, as when I am once engaged I must continue, and it is too important on my side to agree without the necessary previous Consideration. Please to return the Circular Letters.

4. "No one is born without faults." Horace, *Satires,* I, 3:6.

Your Favour of 20 March is but just come to hand. I am with the greatest Respect most dutifully and affectionately Yours

J WILLIAMS

Addressed: Doctor Franklin

From Feutry   AL: American Philosophical Society

[After April 15, 1777[5]]

Feutry est venu pour avoir L'honneur de voir Monsieur de Franklin et de se rappeller à son souvenir. Il joint ici une nouvelle Traduction de Richard que M. Quétant, son ami, Lui a confiée pour la faire voir à Monsieur de Franklin; il Le supplie de vouloir bien la lui renvoyer dans quelque Jour.[6]

Feutry fait remettre ses canons en Etat de paroître et de tirer; il aura L'honneur d'en instruire Mr. de franklin aussitôt qu'ils seront prêts.[7] Il ose ici L'assurer de son profound respect et de son sincere attachement.

Maison de M. de Cormainville, Maréchal de Camps, Barriere ste. anne, à La nouvelle france.

5. A covering letter of this date from Quétant to Feutry was enclosed with the MS and is now in the APS; the translator expressed the "plaisir que j'ai à satisfaire votre empressement," and we are confident that the same sense of haste led Feutry to forward the documents to BF within a day or two.

6. For Antoine-François Quétant, the playwright, see Larousse, *Dictionnaire universel*. He was sending his translation of "Father Abraham's Speech," which was published before the year was out; see Feutry to BF below, Nov. 14, 1777.

7. As early as 1754 Feutry had made a model of a small light cannon, which could be disassembled to be carried in parts, and had tried intermittently since then to have his invention tested. No one except the marquis de Puységur seems to have given him any encouragement. See his *Supplément aux nouveaux opuscules*, pp. 22–6, 30–6, and the article on him in the *Dictionnaire de biographie française*. During the summer of 1777 he had two shells and two pierced bullets made for the model; BF apparently promised to subsidize the work, for seven years later the ammunition-maker asked him for reimbursement: Chevalier to BF, May 16, 1784, APS.

From Antoine-Joseph Raup de Baptestin de Moulières[8]

ALS: American Philosophical Society

Monsieur   Le 16 avril 1777.

Dès que les Etats-unis de l'Amerique commenceront a jouir de la tranquilité qui, selon toute apparence, va bientôt succeder a la plus injuste et la plus revoltante de toutes les Guerres, Leur premier soin sera sans doute, de se livrer plus vivement que jamais au goût que vous leur avés donné pour les sciences et les arts, sans lesquels un Etat ne saurait etre florissant; c'est vous, Monsieur, qui les avés portés dans cette nouvelle republique dont le bonheur comme la Gloire seront egalement votre ouvrage, Et tout ce qui peut tendre à leur accroissement est fait pour vous interesser.

C'est a ce titre, Monsieur, que je vous prierais de m'accorder un moment pour conferer avec vous sur un objet qui y est relatif. Je suis avec autant de respect que d'admiration, Monsieur votre tres humble et tres obeissant serviteur   Baptestin

From ——— Desegray[9]

AL: American Philosophical Society

Ce 16 Avril [1777?[1]].

M. Desegray, Neg[ocian]t de St. Malo, logè à *Paris à l'hôtel de Nock, rüe de Richelieu, No. 154*, est venu pour presenter ses Respects à Son Excellence, et pour luy remettre la lettre cy jointe.

8. Baptestin (1747–1827) was a writer, at the beginning of a career as essayist and historian that stretched over the next half-century; see J.-M. Quérard, *La France littéraire* . . . (10 vols., Paris, 1827–39), VI, 337. His works are there listed under Moulières, and in the catalogue of the Bibliothèque Nationale under Raup.

9. The senior member of the St. Malo house of Desegray, Beaugeard fils & Cie., which later corresponded extensively with the commissioners as their unofficial agent in St. Malo. A letter from the firm of April 8, 1778 (APS), indicates that it had connections with Schweighauser.

1. A later year is unlikely. In the first sentence Desegray seems to be introducing himself, and BF would have known who he was as soon as the commissioners began to use the firm in July, 1777.

Il la prie de vouloir bien, s'il veut faire reponse à cette lettre, l'envoyer chez luy à l'hôtel susdit, ou de luy faire sçavoir si et quand il pourra venir la prendre à Passy.

Notation: DeSegray.

From ——— Franquelin

ALS: American Philosophical Society

Monsieur   A paris ce 16 avril 1777.

La crainte de troubler vos grandes occupations m'a empêché jusqu'à ce jour de me présenter devant vous: mais pressé par ma famille, j'ose donc vous prier de me permettre d'avoir l'honneur de vous voir pour verifier si effectivement nous sommes descendus de la méme souche, comme plusieurs de mes parents me l'ont asseuré; peut-etre n'esce que le desir qu'ils ont, ainsi que moy, d'appartenir à un grand homme. J'ay l'honneur, en attendant votre moment, d'etre avec un tres profond respect Monsieur Votre tres humble et tres obeissant serviteur   FRANQUELIN
avocat au parlement de paris[2] rüe de Bercy fauxbourg St. Antoine

Notation: Franquelin. 16. Avril 1777.

From Louis Gioanetti Pellion

April 16, 1777 See page 169

From the Chevalier de Basserode

April 17, 1777 See pages 169–70

2. A position that he had held since 1768: *Almanach Royal* for 1777, p. 331. In an undated memorandum, doubtless enclosed with this letter, he traced his line back to a merchant who settled in Picardy about 1710, and suggested that BF write the local curé for birth and death records. APS.

From Feutry

AL: American Philosophical Society

Monsieur   Ce jeudi matin de bonne heure, 17 avril 1777.

J'ai eu, hier, L'honneur de vous adresser quelques mémoires; j'ai celui de vous envoyer une Bagatelle qui vous prouvera du moins que je desire Le bien. J'attends toujour vos ordres et suis très Laconiquement, très Belgiquement, et très respectueusement Monsieur votre très humble et très obeis-\ sant   )

P.S. Quand j'aurai sous La main mes autres ouvrages, qui forment sept à huit volumes, j'aurai L'honneur de vous en faire hommage.

Notation: Feutry

The American Commissioners to the Comte de Mercy-Argenteau[3]

ALS:[4] Haus-, Hoff-, und Staatsarchiv, Vienna; draft:[5] Library of Congress

Sir   Paris, April 19. 1777

By direction of the Congress of the United States of America, we have the Honour of informing your Excellency, that they purpose to send a Minister to your respected Court, with all convenient Expedition, properly impower'd to treat upon Affairs of Importance.

In the mean time we beg the Favour of your Excellency to inform your Court, that we are instructed and authorized by the said Congress to sollicit its Friendship, to request that it

3. Florimond-Claude-Charles, comte de Mercy-Argenteau (1727–94), had the dual role spelled out in the address on the letter, of representing both the Emperor Joseph II and his mother, Maria Theresa. The two courts were distinct, and Congress had authorized a minister to the first (along with the Prussian and Tuscan) but not the second. The commissioners are lumping them together, and in the second paragraph mention specifically "the Subjects of Austria," *i.e.*, of Maria Theresa.

4. In BF's hand.

5. Partly in an unidentified hand and partly in BF's, and endorsed by him "Draft of Letter to Ambassadors 1777."

would afford no Aid to their Enemies, but use its good Offices to prevent the Lending of Troops by other Powers to be transported to America for their Destruction; and to offer the free Commerce of the said States to the Subjects of Austria; which Request and Offer we now hereby make, and we beg your Excellency would transmit the same to the Ministers of your Court, for their favourable Consideration. With great Respect we have the Honour to be Your Excellency's most obedient and most humble Servants   B FRANKLIN
                                                    SILAS DEANE
                                                    ARTHUR LEE

Commissioners Plenipotentiary from the United States of North America

His Excelly. M. le Comte de Mercy-Argenteau, Imperial Ambassador.

Addressed: A son Excellence / M. le Comte de Mercy-Argenteau / Ambassadeur de l'Empereur, & de sa / Majesté Imperiale, Royale & Apostolique / l'Imperatrice Reine de Hongrie & de Bohéme / &c. / à Paris

The American Commissioners to Baron Schulenburg

Copy: National Archives; two copies: Harvard University Library

Sir,   Paris 19 April 1777.
We received the letter which you did us the honour to write to us of the 15th Ultimo and should earlier have replied particularly thereto, but from the daily expectation we had of recieving orders from Congress of the United States on this important subject. We have their commands to inform his Prussian Majesty's Ambassador here,[6] that they propose to send a Minister to your respected Court with all convenient expedition properly impowered to treat upon affairs of importance, and that we are in the mean time instructed and authorised by the Congress to solicit the Friendship of your Court, to request that it would afford no aid to their enemies, but use its good

6. Baron von der Goltz.

offices to prevent the landing of troops by other powers to be transported to America for their destruction, and to offer the free Commerce of the United States to the Subjects of Prussia. We have taken the earliest opportunity of obeying these commands. But considering the great importance of establishing a free commerce between the two Countries as soon as possible, and confident that every objection may be obviated, and the wished for intercourse opened and established on the most certain and beneficial grounds to promote the Interest of both Countries, We propose that one of us shall wait on your Excellency as soon as conveniently may be done, to explain personally the Situation of America, the nature, extent, and importance of its commerce, and the methods by which it may be carried on with Prussia to mutual advantage. In the proposed interview we are confident the Difficulties mentioned by your Excellency may be surmounted, and a very considerable part of American Commerce be turned to Prussia by measures neither dangerous nor expensive. We have the honor to be &c.　　　　　　　　　　　　Signd B. FRANKLIN
　　　　　　　　　　　　　　　　　　　　S. DEANE
　　　　　　　　　　　　　　　　　　　　ARTHUR LEE

To his Excellency Baron Schulenburg at Berlin

Notation: Letter from the Commissioners in France to Baron Schulenburgh apr 19th. 1777. inclosed in a Lees Letter apr 8 1778[7]

7. Presumably the letter to the committee for foreign affairs printed in Wharton, *Diplomatic Correspondence*, II, 542–3.

From François[8] de Brahm

ALS: American Philosophical Society

Monsieur   Coblence Le 20 d'avril 1777

Mon fils qui est oficier de S. el. E.[9] de Treves, mais qui est pressentement au service de la Republique d'amerique, en qualité de capitaine d'artilerie à demandé à l'electeur son Maitre la permission, (qui'il n'avoit que pour deux ans,) d'oser rester jusqu'a que la geure soit finie, et il vient aussy de la recevoir. Elle est cy jointe, avec une lettre de moy, et de mes autres enfans. Je vous suplie dont [donc] de lui faire parvenir ces ecrits, aussy-tot qu'il sera possible. Vous m'obligerés infiniment, etant avec parfait Estime Monsieur votre très obeissant serviteur   DE BRAHM

                                    capitaine de S. el. E. de Treves.

Notation: De Brahm Coblence le 20 d'avril 1777.

The American Commissioners to Henry Johnson

ALS:[1] Public Record Office

Sir   Paris April 21st: 1777

You are directed to call on Capt. Wicks on your return, and inform him that We have pursuant to his proposal,[2] ordered the Lexington, under your Command to proceed with him on the Cruise on which he is bound; you will agree with Capt. Wicks, on the place of your Rendevouz, your Signals &c. which you are to take in writing, and carefully attend to. You will also follow such directions, as he shall give you in writing,

---

8. Given as Franz by Horst Dippel, *Germany and the American Revolution, 1770–1800* . . . (Chapel Hill, N.C., [1977]), p. 118 n.

9. The abbreviations cannot be deciphered with assurance, but we take them to mean "Son excellence l'Electeur." Ferdinand-Joseph-Sébastien de Brahm, about whom the father is writing, was a captain of engineers in the service of South Carolina until he became a continental major in 1778; he held that rank through the war: *JCC,* x, 150; xxi, 843. See also Lasseray, *Les Français,* i, 134–5.

1. In Deane's hand.

2. In his letter above of April 15.

and by no means suffer yourself to be separated from him, if you can avoid it; should you miss seeing him on your Return, the Letter delivered you for him must be given to Mr. Williams, of Nantes, and if he is not actually sailed, and there is a probability of your joining him in season, you are to write to him from Nantes, informing him in what Time you may be able to join him, and asking his directions express. But should you neither meet with him at Nantes, nor receive Letters from him you will get ready for Sea, as quick as is possible, and Sail from Bourdeaux to the Entrance of the Channel, where you will cruise for a few Days, more of less as the Winds &c. shall with the advice you may receive direct you; thence you will continue your Course up the Irish Sea, keeping a good look out, lest you get deceived by a Vessel of Superior Force under the Mask of a Merchantman. You will Cruise here, in case you do not meet with Capt. Wicks, for Three or four Weeks after which return to Nantes or Morlaix or Rochelle and send us an Account of your proceedings. Should you meet with Capt. Wicks you are to consult with him and attend carefully to the Instructions he shall give you. In Case of making a Prize leave not more than Two or three at the most of the Prisoners on board her, and guard carefully the rest, send her if taken at the Mouth of the Channel to Bayonne, or Bilboa, if the Winds are favorable, and you receive no News, particular, of danger in crossing the Bay, otherways to *L'Orient*, or *Morlaix*. At Bilboa, address to *Messrs. Gadoroqui & fils*. Order your prize Masters to keep what prisoners they may have committed them in the strictest manner consistent with humanity, and neither permit them to go on Shore on their Arrival untill after the Sale of the Prize, or to hold conversation with your People on board. Should you by any Accident, fail of meeting with Capt. Wicks at Nantes, or of receiving his Directions, or joining him you will calculate your cruise at the furthest, not to extend beyond Four or Five Weeks. You will order your Prize Masters instantly on their Arrival to inform us of their Situation and Proceedings. At Nantz, they must address Themselves to Mr. Williams, and At Bordeaux to Messrs. Delaps. It will not be prudent to send prizes far up the Channel. On your return from the Cruise you will give us direct and immediate

intelligence of your Situation and proceedings, as well as by every other Opportunity in your Way. But as We have established an Express between this and Nantes it will not be Necessary unless on some extraordinary emergency for you to leave your Vessel to come up to Paris. We have wrote Mr. Delap to Furnish you with the Necessaries you may want at Bordeaux for use of the Vessel and must Urge you to make all the dispatch in your power, and the most Vigilant Attention to avoid future deceptions, and to obtain reparation for those you have already suffered. You are to converse with Messrs. Delaps, and every other Person at Bordeaux, as if you were bound directly to America, and if Letters are offered you, take them, but excuse yourself as To Freight. Your People must not know, but that you are bound for America, but by no means admit passengers. We are wishing you a successful Cruise sir your most Obedient and Very humble servants   B Franklin
Silas Deane
Arthur Lee

Capt. Johnson

Addressed: To / Capt. Henry Johnson / Commander of the /Briga. Lexington

Endorsed: No 2 My Orders from the Commissioners at Paris April 21st: 1777

From Jabez Maud Fisher[3]   AL: American Philosophical Society

Monday April 21. Rue Jacob. Hotel de la grande Bretagne
Mr. Fisher presents his respectful Compliments to Dr. Franklin, and informs him that he shall set out for London on Thursday next, when if Dr. Franklin should have any Com-

---

3. A Quaker merchant in London. He had been born in Philadelphia and had three brothers there, who soon after this were arrested as Loyalists. Jabez may have shared their sympathies; in any case he lived in England, except for a brief sojourn in New York, from 1775 until his death in 1779. *PMHB*, IV, 408; XLI, 277. He had arrived in Paris on April 10th, and Silas Deane immediately became suspicious of the "subtle, shrewd Fellow": *Deane Papers*, II, 44–5. BF doubtless knew of those suspicions when he returned his cautious reply, the following document.

mands to his particular Friends Dr. Forthergill and Mr. Barclay or any other of his Friends, Mr. Fisher will with great Pleasure take them under his Care and deliver them with Fidelity. If Dr. Franklin should not incline to write and has any verbal Message to deliver to those Gentlemen, Mr. Fisher would do himself the honour to wait on him for that Purpose.

Mr. Stevenson and Mr. Lownds present their respectful Compliments.[4]

Addressed: Dr: Franklin / Passy.

Notation: Mr Fishers Note

To Jabez Maud Fisher[5] AL: Historical Society of Pennsylvania

Passy April 21. 77.
Dr. Franklin presents his Respects to Mr. Fisher, with Thanks for his obliging Offer of taking Letters under his Care to the Dr.'s Friends in London: but apprehending that a Correspondence with him at present may be attended with some inconvenient Circumstances to his Friends there, he has generally avoided writing to any of them since his Arrival in France, except in Answer to Letters received. He is however much oblig'd to Mr. Fisher, and wishes him a good Journey. He only requests Mr. Fisher would present his affectionate Respects to Dr. F. and Mr. B.

Compliments to Messrs. Stevenson and Lownds.

Addressed: Mr Fisher / Paris

---

4. "Lownds" was doubtless Charles Lowndes, former secretary to the treasury (above, XIII, 87 n), whose family had once occupied Fothergill's house: R. Hingston Fox, *Dr. John Fothergill and His Friends* ... (London, 1919), p. 24. Stevenson we cannot identify.
5. See the preceding document.

From ——— de Bragelonne[6]

ALS: American Philosophical Society

⟨Bordeaux, April 21, 1777, in French: M. Delap has promised to forward you my letter and the attached memorandum.[7] I am a man of standing, an old soldier allied with the most respectable houses in the kingdom and descended from generals. An impoverishing lawsuit has compelled me to put to use my observations made during many campaigns. The memorandum will show you the importance of my ideas, and your country needs to profit from those wise in the military art.

After more than thirty-five years of work I have perfected a new gun carriage. I have other suggestions as well, even more advantageous for your cause, but let us begin with this one. I will explain it to M. Delap, who, though young, strikes me as knowing the ways of the world. Please give him any directions needed for reducing the delays that usually ruin such cooperative ventures.⟩

From Feutry

ALS: American Philosophical Society

Monsieur,   Paris ce 21 avril 1777. au Soir

Donner un petit pois pour une grosse fève, comme dit un ancien proverbe Belge (et je suis de cette bonne Nation) voilà mon histoire avec vous. J'ai eu L'honneur de vous adresser une partie de mes foibles ouvrages, et vous me gratifiez de vos oeuvres scientifiques! J'ose encore, Monsieur, vous envoyer

6. He signs the letter "De Bragelonne de filley de la Barre &c." We suspect that he was identifying himself as the son-in-law of Pierre Filley de la Barre (died 1779), for whom see the *Dictionnaire de biographie*.

7. The latter, endorsed by BF "Projet d'un nouvel Affut," is also in the APS. On May 24 Bragelonne wrote again from Bordeaux (APS), this time in high dudgeon. I am sure, he said, that you received my letter and memorandum, and had assumed that they would be appreciated. If you had troubled to answer, I should have raised other points of great importance to your countrymen. Now, not having had the courtesy of a reply, I too shall keep silent, and find other use for my talents, reflections, and proposals. BF endorsed this letter "Projector."

La bagatelle ci Jointe, dont L'avertissement seul et l'introduction, doivent, ou peuvent se lire. J'attends, de flandres, mon *choix d'histoires morales*, en 4 parties, et mes *mémoires de La cour d'Auguste* (*Octavien César*) pour Les mettre à vos pieds.[8] Daignez, Monsieur, me donner Le jour, Le moment précis, où je pourrai avoir Le bonheur de vous voir, de vous admirer, de vous entendre et de m'instruire. Si je L'osois, je dirois, ici, *Barbarus hìc ego sum, quia non intelligor illis.*[9] Je suis avec autant d'estime, d'attachement, que de respect et de vénération Monsieur votre très humble et très obéissant Serviteur   FEUTRY.

Maison de Mr. de Cormainville Maréchal de Camps, ès armées du Roy. Barriere ste. anne, à la nouvelle france.

From La Rochefoucauld   AL: American Philosophical Society

Lundi matin [April 21, 1777[1]].

Le Duc de la Rochefoucauld fait bien des complimens à Monsieur le Docteur franklyn, et le prie de vouloir bien, s'il a achevé de lire la Traduction de *la Constitution de Virginie*, la lui renvoier, parce qu'il voudroit avoir le tems d'y faire quelques corrections, pour lui demander, s'il est nécessaire, quelques derniers éclaircissemens Vendredi; il espere et Madame sa mere aussi que Monsieur le Docteur [*se rappelle?*] l'engagement qu'il a pris de venir diner avec eux ce jour là, et d'amener Monsieur son petit fils.

Si Monsieur franklyn a la suite de la Constitution de Maryland, le Duc de la Rochefoucauld lui sera obligé de vouloir

---

8. *Choix d'histoires tirées de Bandel . . . Belleforest . . . Boistuau . . . et quelques autres auteurs . . .* (4 parts in 2 vols., London and Paris, 1753); *Mémoires de la cour d'Auguste, tirés de l'anglois du Dr. Thomas Blackwell* had been through three editions between 1754 and 1768.

9. "Here I am the barbarian, because I am understood by no one": Ovid, *Tristia*, V: 10:37. He presumably means to imply that only BF understands him.

1. BF almost certainly returned La Rochefoucauld's translation, as requested here, with his note below of April 25; we therefore assume that the request was made the previous Monday.

bien la lui renvoyer, et lui renvoier aussi les deux *Remembrancers* qui contiennent celle de Virginie.[2]

Notation: de la Rochefoucaut

From Benjamin Sowden[3]   ALS: American Philosophical Society

Sir   Rotterdam April 21 1777

As a proper apology for this intrusion, permit me to inform You, that tho' not honoured with your personal acquaintance, I have an high respect for your Character, founded on your well earned Fame, and the perusal of your useful and ingenious works. I am also under some obligation, for your readiness, about ten Years since, and in Answer to a Letter with which I troubled You, in furnishing me with such Authorities, concerning the non existence of a Town in the County of Glôster in North America, where a vision was said to have happened to one Chamberlain A Minister; as enabled me effectualy to crush a *Fabula anilis*, that had made many silly good people in this Country half frantick with Enthusiasm. Forgive, Sir, this strain of *Egotism*, which in the present Case cannot well be avoided, while I proceed to inform You, that for these last 28 Years, I have been Minister of the English Presbyterian Church on the Dutch establishment, in this City; that I am intimate with Dr. de Monchy, medical Professor of this Town, and with Your old Friend Dr. Kippis,[4] nor am I totaly unacquainted with that excellent Man Dr. Price, to whom I have lately forwarded some Letters that reached me by way of France, and whom I have desired, in Case he apprehends any thing from Ministerial vengeance, to come and reside here.

These Circumstances however, Sir, would not have induced me to trouble You, had I not been prompted by the Reverend

2. See the Duke's note above, March 26.

3. He became a channel for disseminating pro-American material (see his letter below, June 7, 1777), and the correspondence opened here continued until Sowden's death in June, 1778.

4. We have found no trace of the silly fable. For François de Monchy, the Rotterdam physician, and Andrew Kippis, the London clergyman, see above, respectively XIII, 484 n, and XV, 85 n.

Mr. Gordon of Jamaica plain near Boston, with whom I was formerly intimate in England, and who has corresponded with me during the 9 Years that he has resided in America. In a Letter that reached me the week before last (inclosed in one to a Mr. Tabor[5] of this place) by way of Paris, he complains that for a year past, he has not received one Answer to the many Letters he has sent me, and desires me to send my future Letters for him to You. This, Sir, is a Liberty I dare not presume to take unless I previously obtain your permission. If I am so happy, my Letters for him shall be sent open to You, that you may see what I write, and be sure of Your Man. As they will contain nothing but a recital of publick affairs here; and in England, relative to America, there will perhaps, be several things in them that you would be glad to see, and to the perusal of which you are heartily welcome. The favour of forwarding my Letters to Mr. Gordon will be peculiarly acceptable at this time by reason of the departure of my good Friend Mr. Rumsey. With him I had an acquaintance here, and a correspondence ever since his residence at Nantes, which by the sudden and melancholy Death of his Father, demanding his return home, is now broken off, so that I cannot, as formerly, send my Letters by that Channel. In Case You permit me to forward my Letters for him, or Mr. Gordon, to You, I shall probably trouble You once every 5 or 6 weeks, and, if the connection of the post office here with that of Paris will permit, shall frank my Letters.

This being an introductory Letter it is proper to close it with my name, and equaly proper, beset as You are with Lord Stormont's Spies, to send it inclosed by a Merchant of this City to his Correspondant in Paris, to be by him delivered at your lodgings, and, if possible, into your own hands. But if You permit me to write again to You, and will furnish me with any particular address, for the sake of greater safety, I shall not in future put any name or place of abode, an omission that, after this hint, will amply answer the purposes of both.

In return, Sir, for the trouble I am now giving you, I can

5. After Sowden's death this friend of his, Samuel Tabor, wrote BF about the correspondence: Aug. 16, 1779, APS.

only say, that if You think I can serve You in transmitting any Letters You want to have forwarded to any of Your old Friends, by a very secret and safe mode of conveyance, or in forwarding any Letters from them to You, by the same mode, I am much at Your service, and that, if I know myself, You may depend upon the most confidential honour and secrecy. Please to direct to me thus: *A Monsieur Monsieur Sowden à Rotterdam.* Should any Letter come inclosed to You from America with no other address than *A Monsieur Monsieur,* upon it, please to supply my name and place of abode, and dispatch it by post.

We have an excellent Paper published twice a week in this Country. It is printed at Leyden, and is known here by the name of the French Leyden Gazette, tho' it is entitled *Nouvelles extraordinaires de divers Endroits.* If it reaches Paris, I would by all means recommend it to Your perusal. It contains a faithful and judicious compend of English news, and abounds with pertinent remarks. I once more entreat You would excuse this trouble, and also to do me the justice to believe that, with a most sincere esteem, and profound respect, I am, Sir, Your very humble Servant   BENJN SOWDEN

PS. Excuse my sealing this with a wafer. I was desired to do it for the greater conveniency of inclosing.

Addressed: A Monsieur / Monsieur Le Docteur Franklin / à / Paris / [*In another hand:*] Legrand fils negociant rue St. Denis presque visavis celle de la heaumerie a Paris.

Notation: Ben. Sowden Ap. 21. 77

To [Pierre-Joseph Perreau⁶]   AL (draft): Library of Congress

Reverend Sir,   Passy, April 22. 1777

Mr. Mercley whom your Reverence mentions as having made Promises to Monsieur your Brother, was employ'd as a Mer-

6. Also spelled Perrau; his Christian names are supplied from Joseph-Marie Quérard, *La France littéraire* (10 vols., Paris, 1827–39), VII, 63. He was Bishop of Tricomie or Tricomia in Palestine, one of nine French bishoprics *in partibus infidelium,* from 1775 until at least 1789: *La France ecclésiastique . . .* for 1778, p. 19; *Almanach royal . . .* for 1790, p. 69.

chant to purchase some military Stores for the Congress, but I know of no Authority he had to engage Officers of the Marine, or to make any Promises to such in our Behalf.[7] I have not myself, (as I have already had the Honour of telling your Reverence) the least Authority from the Congress, to make Promises to Officers to encourage their going to America; and since my Arrival in France I have constantly dissuaded all who have applied to me, from undertaking the Voyage, as I knew how difficult it would be for them to find Employment, a few Engineers and Officers of the Artillery excepted, who are gone. Nevertheless, if your Brother continues resolv'd to go thither, at his own Expence, and the Risque of finding or not finding Employment which I cannot advise him to do, I will give him Letters of Introduction to Gentlemen there, recommending him to their Civilities; but I must at the same time caution him against having any Reliance on those Letters as a means of procuring him a Command in our Armies, since I am by no means sure they will have any such Effect. I will, if you please, give him a Letter to Gen. Washington; but then I should have the State of his Services to enclose; and if accompanied with Recommendations from some General Officers of Note, it will be so much the better. My Door is never shut to your Reverence when I am at home, as I am almost every Evening. With great Respect I have the Honour to be Your Reverence's most obedient and most humble Servant.   B F

Bishop of Tricomie

Notation: Letter to Bishop of Tricomie

From Jonathan Williams, Jr.

ALS: American Philosophical Society

Dear and honored Sir   Nantes April 22. 1777.

You reccommended Mr. Hood to my Civilities and assistance in getting a passage to america. The assistance he wants is Cash, which you say nothing about. Mr. Dean gave me

7. John Philip Merckle, the unreliable Dutchman, had reportedly promised one French officer a lieutenant colonelcy: Lee to BF above, under Feb. 18.

orders to pay his passage &c. but he since writes angrily about him. I am however trying to get him a passage in the first Vessell to america, he wants to wait for a Phila. Ship but I do not think myself justifiable to advance for him while on Shore, therefore must tell him he has nothing to expect from me after the Vessell I procure a passage for him in has sailed, if he does not go in her. He depends much on hearing from you and requests me to press an answer which is the principal Reason for troubling you at present. I am with the greatest Respect Your dutifull and affectionate Kinsman   J WILLIAMS J

Addressed: Doctor Franklin.

From Joseph Cauffman[8]   ALS: American Philosophical Society

Sir.   Vienna 23 of April 1777.

Difference of station, the most honourable place, you hold in one of the most glorious causes, which man e'er beheld from the very creation of the world, and the numberless occupations, which the love of Mankind and our dear Country has conferred upon you, restrained a long time the ardent desire I had of writing to you. However at length I thought it an essential part of my duty to pay my respects to a man, for whom, tho' I had never the honour to know him, I have always nourished the highest esteem and veneration, not only as one famous in litterature and of the most unblemished character, but much more as one, to whom Posterity is so much indebted for his glorious endeavours to maintain the liberty of almost one quarter of the World. Surely then, Sir, you'll not take amiss my boldness, especially if you consider that presumption itself, if well grounded, is laudable. I was born in Philadelphia, and sent abroad in the most tender years to imbibe knowledge, particularly in the medical way. I have studied a considerable time in this University, where I have had the satisfaction to see my labours crowned with honour. My

8. A young Philadelphian who was an acquaintance of Ingenhousz and had recently graduated from the medical school; see Ingenhousz to BF above, Nov. 15.

only wish and desire is to prove one day or other serviceable to my Country, for which, tho' my youth and my not having accomplished my studies till now have rendered me hitherto incapable, I should be happy in spending the rest of my days, my repose and blood.[9] Let our foolish modern moralists ridicule love for one's Country as much as they please, I shall always think it the first duty of Man to serve his Country, as much as ever lies in his power, it being the dictate of reason, Nature and own proper instinct. Though I have not had the honour to serve America in person, still I have the satisfaction to think, that I am in some measure concerned. The present war has put me into somewhat critical circumstances, as my Father has been therby hind'red in sending my remittances; however I glory in this small misfortune, as I am at least in some respects touched by the present calamities. How happy should I be if I could partake of everything in person! It is cheifly for this reason that I make bold to trouble you with the present. I have applied myself with an indefatigable zeal to my studies, in order to prove one day or other a worthy citizen of America, to which the success I have had in 'em convinces me I can be serviceable at least in the branch I profess, witness the inclosed attestations, which I thought myself bound by duty to send you, that you may be convinced of my sincerity and nothing less than boasting. One of 'em is from the renowned Dr. De Haen, the other from the learned Dr. Stoll his successor;[1] I have particularly studied Anatomy and

9. Perhaps he did. He is said to have returned to America, been commissioned surgeon of the new continental frigate *Randolph*, Capt. Nicholas Biddle, and been killed in March, 1778, when she engaged a ship of the line and blew up: Theodore F. Rodenbough, *Autumn Leaves from Family Trees* . . . (New York, 1892), pp. 17, [25]–30. Unfortunately for this story, the *Randolph*'s surgeon had another name: William B. Clark, *Captain Dauntless: the Story of Nicholas Biddle* . . . ([Baton Rouge, La.,] 1949), pp. 199, 201. But Cauffman, though his background and training should have destined him for prominence, seems to have disappeared from sight at that time. Possibly he shipped on the *Randolph* in some other capacity; her records are incomplete.

1. Anton De Haen (1704–76) came to Vienna from The Hague in 1754 as professor of medicine and was, like Ingenhousz later, physician to Maria Theresa. He was succeeded in the chair of medicine by Maximilian Stoll

Surgery thinking that the Army will stand in most need of these two branches. If therefore you find my presence of the least service in the present contest, I am ready to return to my native shore by such means, as you shall be pleased to prescribe to me, being much more contented with a less lucrative but still more glorious station, than with the most brilliant office, which I have reason to expect in this University, for our Country is always to be prefered to any other whatever in the world, especially when it is engaged in an affair that concerns it's aras et focos.[2] But should you think it more adviceable for me to remain some time longer in Europe in order to enable myself in some other branch &c. &c., I submit to your advice and judgment, only beseeching you to point out some way, by which I may be supplied from my Father with necessary remittances towards the prosecution of what you may advise me. If you should desire to be informed on any matter whatever in or concerning the Austrian Dominions &c., which can be of any service to our Country, you can but command. No pains shall be thought too great, no stone left unturned, to procure you proper information; and tho' you may be, as is natural, somewhat diffident in trusting any thing to an unknown person, still you'll certainly always find in me a faithful and an honest man. Put me to the trial, and let the event speak. This is but a hint of what could with reason be enlarged. I have given no description of my Family, as I suppose it known to you: all we have to boast of is honesty, and this, I think, is sufficient in the depraved age we live in.[3] Nor do I immagine that my being educated in the catholic religion will prove any obstacle to serving my Country, and doing the duty of an honest and worthy citizen. I cannot persuade myself, that such

(1742–88), a former Jesuit who did not receive his medical degree from Vienna until 1772. *Nouvelle biographie universelle*, XXIII, 56–8; XLIV, 520–2. Haen's attestation, in French, was written in May, 1776, and Stoll's, in Latin, in March [?], 1777; both are in the Hist. Soc. of Pa.

2. Freely, hearths and homes.

3. Honesty was backed by considerable means. Joseph T. Cauffman (1720–1807) emigrated from Strasbourg to Philadelphia in 1749 and became both prosperous and influential, although he was a Roman Catholic and during the Revolution held strong Loyalist views. Rodenbough, *op. cit.*, pp. [13]–15.

great and thinking men, under whose direction America so gloriously proceeds, will any ways oppose my ardent desires for so trivial a reason. Certainly the many able pieces which they have bestowed on the public to the admiration of all Europe, convince me of the contrary. But to make an end to tatling, I finish by beseeching you to second the wishes of one, who would be happy in contributing something to american liberty, and showing on all occasions the high esteem he has for a man, whom the Almighty has bestowed on our Country as it's Saviour and protector. Sir I remain with due respect your ever Devoted Servant,   JOS. CAUFFMAN

P.S. I make bold to beg the favour of a line or two at leisure in answer to the inclosed. My directions are A Mosr. Jos: Cauffman. M.D. et Membre de la faculte de Vienne chez Monsr. de Stoll Professeur en Medicine a Vienne en Autriche.

NB. Many able officers, even of rank, who have served in both of the last wars in Germany have expressed a desire of taking part in the present contest, provided they had previous intelligence of the conditions, upon which such a step could be undertaken. Several have beged me to write to you on this topic, which I have done by way of hint in compliance to their repeated requests.

I beg you would forward the inclosed attestations either to America, or send me them back to Vienna: if you send any to America be pleased to direct 'em to my Father.

Notation: Caufinan 23 April 1777.

To La Rochefoucauld and the Duchesse d'Enville

AL: Bibliothèque municipale, Mantes

Passy, April 25. 77.

Mr. Franklin rejoices to hear that Monsr. le Duc de Rochefoucauld, and Madame la Duchesse d'Enville, in whose Welfare he is much interested, are both on the Recovery.

Art. 4. M. F. thinks the Error is in the Number of Districts, which ought to have been 24.

Art. 9. Is also misprinted. It should have been that two Members are to be removed at the End of every Year.

Art. 13. The Word *Fees* does not signify a constant Salary, but a particular Sum allow'd by Law to be receiv'd by an Officer, for every Act done by him in the Execution of his Office, which Sum is usually proportion'd to the Trouble of each Act.

Art. 19. The Intention of the Exception is to reserve to Virginia the free Navigation of those Rivers, which are the Boundary between that State and Maryland; but not to exclude Maryland from the Navigation of the same Rivers.[4]

In the Money of the Massachusetts Bay, *Old Tenor* signifies the State of Depreciation their Money was in, when a Shilling Sterling was equal to ten Shillings of their Paper. This State of Depreciation continuing a long time, the Prices of everything were conformable to it, and the People being accustomed to reckon in that Money, continued to do so after the Paper was all call'd in and destroy'd. *Lawful Money* only now passes there, which is reckon'd by adding one third to Sterling Money: Thus the third of a Guinea is seven Shillings sterling, which being added to Twenty-one Shillings, makes 28*s.* the Value of a Guinea in lawful Money, according to the Act of Parliament of Queen Anne. *Old Tenor* is now only *Money of Account*, no real Money of the kind now actually existing.[5]

Mr. F. will be glad to hear when the Health of his Friends is perfectly re-established.

4. La Rochefoucauld numbered the paragraphs of the Virginia constitution as printed in the *Remembrancer*, IV, (1777), 65–9; BF was suggesting changes before the Duke's translation was published. Article 4 concerned members of the state senate; Article 9 provided for removal by the legislature of members of the privy council; Article 13 had to do with constables' fees, and Article 19 with navigation of the Potomac and Pocomoke Rivers. The Duke embodied BF's corrections: *Affaires de l'Angleterre et de l'Amérique*, v, cahier XXII, lv–lxxx.

5. For a discussion of the eighteenth-century monetary history of Massachusetts see Andrew M. Davis, *Currency and Banking in the Province of the Massachusetts-Bay*, Amer. Economic Assn. *Pubs.*, 3d ser., I (1900), no. 4.

Henry Johnson to the American Commissioners

ALS: Connecticut Historical Society

Hon'ble Gentlemen   Nantes April 25th 1777

I arrived here Thursday Morning 4 O'Clock where I found Capt: Weeks was gone for L'Orient.[6] Have sent Express as I was much fatigued, Shall wait here for Capt. Weeks's orders, which when I receive shall instantly set off for Bourdeaux and make every possible dispatch agreeable to your Instructions.[7]

Capt: Hammond has not as yet gone he now lays at the mouth of the Loire. You'll perhaps be surprized at that, he was time after time forewarded off the small draft water there was on the bar a little below this Town, except Spring Tides, however being obstinate his Vessel grounded on said bar, and he lost them fine Easterly winds.

Capt: Adams is below, has taken the precaution, has been ready some time to take in Goods and complained to me Yesterday of the backwardness of the Agents here, he is determined he says to follow his Instructions from Congress and when your dispatches arrive he'll Stake [take?] in Stone ballast and proceed imediately, as he is determin'd not to have any thing said after his departure, of his not having acted with that necessary precaution that is required in this Case. I from Capt. Adams inform'd Mr: Morris of this and that his Vessel was ready to take the Goods, and had actually been several times to let them know it, and they put him off. Mr. Morris answer was he thought Capt: Adams had no right to expect any Goods, as he bro't no Cargo,[8] and if they put any Goods on board it would be on advance. However Since which Capt: Adams, has told me that they are to send the Goods to day. He Capt: Adams complains much.

Now Gentlemen, If you think I am too busy, in speculating into any matters where you are not personally yourselves (as I shall as I long as I have that pleasure of serving the Honbles

---

6. Thursday was the 24th. Wickes had left Nantes some hours before; see the following letter.

7. Above, April 21.

8. He had in fact brought a small one; see Bradford to BF above, Feb. 25.

the Congress I shall ever do) till I have your orders to the Contrary as I think it the duty of every officer in the Service, and knowing the imediate want of the many Articles (Capt: Adams can take) on the Continent I thought it a great pity that Vessel should go without the Goods. And respecting the Conduct of the other Captains You'll be pleased if you think I am too officious in these matters to acquaint me of it. Shall be every opportunity troubling you with my Scrawls, if anything turns up. And with wishing you all Gentlemen, every possible blessing you can ask for, With due Respect Your Very Humble Servant: HENRY JOHNSON

Notation: Capt. Henry Johnsen Nantes April 25. 1777. To the Commissioners? [*In another hand:*] Capt Johnson

Lambert Wickes to the American Commissioners

ALS: American Philosophical Society

Gentlemen,   L:Orient 25th April 1777
I left Nantz a Wednesday Evning to Come here and by a letter from you and one from Capt. Johnston I find he Arrived at Nantz soon after my departure. I returned an Answer to Captain Johnston and desired him to Come imeadiately and Join me, but have Since received a Possitive order from the Commissary of this Port to depart the Port in 24 hours.[9] In Consequence of those orders Write by this Evnings Post desireing Capt. Johnston to Join me at St. Auzear,[1] as Soon as Possible. As Capt. Nicholson is not yet ready I think it will be best place to Meet and depart from. You may depend on my Utmost attentions to your orders and Make no doubt We shall be able to give Satisfaction if we are not taken. There is three Brittish Ships War Cruizing in the Bay, which has been seen last Monday Evning. A Prize Sloop Arrived here yesterday, taken by Capt. Thompson of the Brig Rising States from Boston, this was the third Prize taken by her, Since her departure

9. The commissary was acting on orders from the naval ministry: *Naval Docs.*, VIII, 765.
1. St. Nazaire?

from America. This Prize is from Lisbon bound to London, loaded with Fruit and Wine.[2] I shall leave this Port to Morrow or Next day if the Wind and Weather Permits and go imeadiately for St. Auzear, where I will inform you of my further Proceedings. From Gentlemen Your most humble Servant

LAMBT. WICKES

To the Honbles. Benja. Franklin Silas Dean Arthur Lee Esqrs.

Addressed: To / The Honble. Dr Benja. Franklin / at / Paris

Notation: Cap. Wikes L'Orient Ap. 25. 77.

From the Vicomte de Sarsfield

April 25, [1777 or 1783]   See page 231n

From Rodolphe Valltravers

AL: American Philosophical Society

Our predecessors' introduction of Valltravers, at the time when he and Franklin were acquainted in London, called him "a shadowy, though well-meaning, figure."[3] Although he is still somewhat shadowy, we now know more about him. He was born in Berne in 1723 and died in 1814 or 1815. He came to England in 1750, was naturalized in 1757, and the next year married Jane Fisher, the daughter of an M.P. and presumably the "Mrs. V." of this note. In 1762 he returned to Switzerland; five years later he was back in London, connected with the legations of Bavaria and the Palatinate. After 1777 he seems to have lived most of the time on the continent, exploiting his wide connections with Europe's leading intellectuals, from Linnaeus to Rousseau.[4]

He and Franklin were out of touch, as far as we know, from 1768 to Valltravers' appearance in Paris in the spring of 1777. The present note inaugurated a series of letters from him that continued for years.

2. The *Rising States*, Capt. James Thompson, had captured the sloop on the 12th and three days later had herself been captured: *ibid.*, pp. 763, 768–9, 791 n.

3. Above, XIV, 24 n.

4. Gavin R. de Beer, "Rodolph Valltravers, F.R.S.," Royal Soc. *Notes and Records*, IV (1946), 216–26.

The Swiss was full of schemes for aiding the American cause, and they soon exhausted Franklin's patience. "I have long since been tired of the Acquaintance and Correspondence of Mr. V.," he wrote in 1783. "Having but a small Remnant left of Life, I cannot afford to attend to his endless Discourse and numerous long Letters, and visionary Projects. He wants to be employ'd in our Affairs, but he manages his own so badly that one can have but little Confidence in his Prudence."[5]

Passy, apl. 25th. 1777.

Valltravers has called on Messr. Franklin, to pay his Respects, and to inform Them of what is come to his Knowledge, and of what Steps he has taken, since their last Interview. He goes to Versailles, where Business may, most probably, detain him till Monday next. He takes his quarters at Versailles, *chés Delcro, au Juste*, where the Doctor's Commands will be received with due Attention. His Return to Paris, if joined by his Ladies, will lead them over Marly and St. Cloud, St. Germain, Bois de Boulogne, &c. V.'s Stay at Paris is likely to continue some Time; But his Ladies leave it next Week, on Account of Mrs. V.'s State of Health.

Notation: Valtravers.

The American Commissioners to [the Conde de Sousa Coutinho[6]]

LS and draft:[7] Library of Congress

Sir   Paris, April 26. 1777.

The Congress of the United States of America have seen a paper purporting to be an Edict of his Portuguese Majesty, dated at the Palace of Ajuda, the 4th. of July, 1776. in which

5. BF to Ingenhousz, May 16, 1783, Smyth, *Writings*, IX, 42.
6. The Portuguese Ambassador to Versailles, who remained there for years; Jefferson referred to him in 1785 as a "torpid uninformed machine": Boyd, *Jefferson Papers*, IX, 61. The commissioners were carrying out their instructions (above, Dec. 21) and were apparently not satisfied with the Ambassador's reception of their letter, for they redrafted it a few months later and sent it directly to the Portuguese court: below, July 16, 1777.
7. From the draft, in BF's hand, we have silently corrected a few slips of the pen in the LS.

the said States are treated with Contumely, their Ships however distress'd, forbidden to enter any Port in his Dominions; and his Subjects every where forbidden to afford them the least Shelter or Relief.[8] But as this Instrument has not been communicated to the Congress with any Circumstance of Authenticity, and appears only in the Gazettes which frequently containing fictitious Pieces are not to be rely'd on; as a long Friendship and Commerce has subsisted between the Portuguese and the Inhabitants of North America, whereby Portugal has been supplied with the most necessary Commodities in Exchange for her Superfluities, and not the least Injury has ever been committed or even offered by America to that Kingdom; the United States can scarce bring themselves to believe that the said Edict is genuine, and that Portugal which but little more than a Century since, was with respect to its former Government in a Situation similar to theirs,[9] should be the first to reproach them with it as a Crime that rendered them unworthy the common Rights of Humanity; and should be the only Power in Europe that has rejected their Commerce and assumed to judge of their Cause, and condemn them without Authority, Hearing or Enquiry: We therefore being Ministers of the Congress of the said United States have been charged by them to represent to his most faithful Majesty their sincere desire to live in Peace with all Mankind, and particularly with his Nation; that if he has been by their Enemies surprised into the issuing such an Edict, he would be pleased in his Wisdom to reconsider and revoke it; and that he would henceforth permit the continuance of the said Friendly and Commercial Intercourse between his People and theirs which has ever been so advantageous to both: This Representation we now take the Liberty of making to your Court through the Medium of your Excellency; and whatever might have been its Reception if it had been made before the late Change,[1] we do not now

8. See above, XXII, 645.

9. The revolution against Spain in 1640 began a long war of liberation, in which Portugal was dependent on foreign assistance.

1. The death of King José the previous February, which ended the long ministry of the marques de Pombal, brought to the throne Maria I together with her husband, Pedro III, as king consort.

allow ourselves to doubt of its having in due time a favourable Answer, being persuaded from the equitable Character of the present Government, that the Measure in question cannot be approved of, and such unworthy Treatment continued towards an inoffensive and Friendly People. With great Respect, we have the Honour to be Your Excellency's most obedient and most humble Servants, B FRANKLIN
SILAS DEANE
ARTHUR LEE

Commissioners Plenipotentiary for the United States of North America

His Excellency the Ambassador from Portugal

Notation by Franklin: Portugal [*In another hand:*] Letter from Commrs to the Ambassador from Portugal, at the Court of France. [*In a third hand:*] Ap. 26. 77.

To Jan Ingenhousz   ALS: Henry Huntington Library

My dear Friend,   Passy, near Paris, April 26. 1777
I find by your Favour of the 2d Inst. that my Letter to you had been stopt in the Post Office. I am sorry I omitted Payment of the Postage; it was thro' Ignorance.[2] As you mention having order'd your Banker to forward it, I hope you have it before this time. I shall take care of this.

It is probable that I shall remain here still some Months, so that if you resolve to call at Paris in your Way to England, I shall once more enjoy the very great Pleasure of seeing you in this World.

As to the Peace you so much desire between America and England, there is at present no Appearance of its soon taking Place. The several States having separately, during Years past, and the Congress for the whole, sent Petitions, Remonstrances, and humble Addresses without Number: to the King and Parliament, which were all treated with Contempt, and answered only by additional Injuries, no farther Proposition

2. Perhaps mixed with absentmindedness, because BF had been so long accustomed to the franking privilege?

is to be expected from them, especially since they have settled their new Government, after being compelled to relinquish and renounce their Connection with Great Britain. And I imagine Britain is yet too proud to make any reasonable Propositions on her Part, and has not yet suffer'd enough by the War; which I therefore [*think?*] is likely to continue a long time, as we on our part are every Year in a better Condition to support it.

Here is nothing new in the philosophical Way, or I should have a Pleasure in communicating it to you. The Emperor is arriv'd, and very industrious in seeing every thing worth a Sovereign's Notice: The French appear to be much pleased with him.

I hear sometimes of our Friend Sir John, by means of M. Le Roy: but my Regard for him prevents my writing to him directly, as his having any Correspondence with me would if known be certainly made use of against him by his Enemies, and hurt him with the King;[3] &c. I am ever, my dear Friend, Yours most affectionately   B FRANKLIN

William Bingham to the American Commissioners

ALS: Connecticut Historical Society

Gentlemen   St Pierre Martinique April 26th 1777

Herewith is Copy of my last Respects; Since which have received very little News from America. A Letter from Mr. Morris of March 1st mentions, "that on Sunday last, there was a smart Skirmish between a considerable Body of the Enemy, and a Party of our Troops near Brunswic; Our Loss was inconsiderable, but not so with them; they lost a great many Men, both killed and wounded;" it adds, "these frequent Skirmishes make Soldiers of our People and the Enemy is daily render'd weaker by them."

The Ship Seine I believe will be condemn'd, notwithstand-

3. Since 1774 Sir John Pringle had been the King's physician.

ing the General's Application,[4] and the Nature of her Clearances; The Answer the General obtained from the Governor of Dominica was, "that this Affair did not come under his Cognizance, nor within his Jurisdiction, but rested altogether with the Judge of the Court of Admiralty, over whose Decisions he had no Influence or Controul;" this being the Case, and this Court being so unequitably established, that the Judge shares in the Profits of the Condemnation, I think there is no Prospect of a Recovery; Matters have now taken such a Turn, that the smallest Pretext is sufficient for the English to seize and condemn the Property of the French Merchants, who cannot even transport the Produce of America from one Island to another, without a Dread of the Consequences. Indeed several Vessels have been lately carried into Dominica for no other Reason whatsoever; After their Trial is finished, I will duly inform you of the Result.

I have heard that a Ship called the Colbert, loaded on Account of the Congress at Havre de Grace, with Arms, Ammunition &c.; touched at Guadeloupe, Stayed there but a few Hours, and then took her Departure for America. I wish She had called in here, as the General has promised me, that upon all such Occasions, he will give Orders for a Frigate to convoy these Vessels clear of the Islands.[5] Indeed it was not without consulting with him and the Intendant, that I changed the Ship Seine's Clearances; I was confident they would stand her in no Stead, when She arrived upon the Coast of America, which to all Appearance would have been the Scene of greatest Danger.

I was induced to give the Pilot who entered on board this Ship, an Order on the Council of Safety in any Port he might enter, from this Consideration, that several Persons who had engaged in the Same Way, after being paid their Stipulated Sum, had entered on board the Privateers, and were never

4. The General was Robert d'Argout, commanding on Martinique: above, XXII, 444 n. His application had, as Bingham expected, no effect; the *Seine* was condemned and then commissioned as a British warship: *Naval Docs.*, VIII, 950.

5. D'Argout's blanket promise drew a severe reprimand from Sartine: *ibid.*, VI, 583–4.

heard of afterwards; and as this Man was absolutely necessary for the purpose of facilitating the Voyage, I thought the best way of retaining him would be to secure to him the Payment of his Money in America, after he had performed his Contract.

My positive Orders and his own personal safety both pointed out to him the Necessity of destroying this Paper, at the Appearance of the least Danger. The Infatuation which led him to keep it, I cannot account for.

Every Circumstance operates against this Vessel; more especially one that no less surprizes than afflicts me, which is, that Mr. Davis who behaved with Such a manly Fortitude upon his being first made Prisoner, has, either from the Persuasions of Interest, or Motives of Fear, relinquished his Pretensions to our Service, and has become our open and avowed Enemy. He has basely betrayed the Trust that was reposed in him and has laid open the History of this Affair, as far as had come to his Knowledge.

Such perfidious and treacherous Conduct cannot even be approved of by our Enemies. Altho they may love the Treason, they will detest the Traitor, and the Name of Such a Man, if not too insignificant to blot the Page of History, will be handed down to Posterity with distinguished Infamy and with the Curses and Execrations of all honest Men; tis Said that he has taken the Oath of Allegiance and Fidelity to his Britannick Majesty.

I have herewith the honor to inclose you Copy of the Opinion of Council, which Capt. Morin consulted in regard to this Affair; likewise the General's Letter to the Commandant at St. Pierre Miguelon, wrote upon the Occasion of altering the Ships Clearances.

Capt. Morin has conducted himself So ill in the Management of this Voyage, that if I thought his Owners could derive any Advantage from the Capture of his Vessel, I Should be led to believe that he acted from a Sinister Motive. Instead of steering the Course which would naturally have carried him out of the Way of Danger, he chose that which would lead him into the midst of it for when he was taken, he was entering the Channel betwixt this Island and Dominica; A Light which he kept burning in his Caboose the whole Evening and by which he was discovered and pursued, adds Strength to my Conjectures and almost confirms my Suspicions. I have the honor to be with great Regard Gentlemen Your obedient humble Servant   WM BINGHAM

Messrs. Franklin Dean and Lee Commissioners from the United States of America, at the Court of Versailles

Notation: Mr. Bingham 26th April 1777

From Jean Annet Chabreu Duparquet

April 26, 1777   See page 170

From Feutry   AL: American Philosophical Society

Ce samedi 26 avril 1777.
Feutry supplie Monsieur Franklin de vouloir bien accepter L'ouvrage ci Joint. Il aura certainement L'honneur de se rendre, demain dimanche, à sa gracieuse invitation. Il assure ici Mr. Franklin de son Respect, de sa vénération et du desir sincère de mériter son estime et son amitié. &c.

Lambert Wickes to the American Commissioners

ALS: American Philosophical Society

Gentlemen,   L'Orient April 27th. 1777
I wrote you last post acknowledging the receipt of your letters by Capt. Johnston and informing you of my Intentions to proceed to Nantz and there wait the Arival of Capt. Johnston. I am very Sorry to inform you of the Mutiny that has happend amongst my People since my Arrival, they have all refused to go to Sea untill they received their prize Money; With much threats and a promise that the prize Money should be paid before they left Nantz, have prevailed on them to go to Nantz, but do not expect to get them from there till they are paid. As the time they ship'd for was One Year, which is now expired, I hope you'll be punktual in giving orders to Mr.

Morris for paying them as soon as We Arrive in order [to] prevent delays, I think this will be Necessary in order to prevent any dispute between Me and Mr. Morris. The People has promised to Continue in the Ship and behave well provided they receive thier Money and if not, I shall be under the disagreable Nessesity of Proceeding directly for America, with a few the People I Can get to go with me, which will not exceed 30 or 40 Men. I have this day received my certain Orders from Mr. Gonet, Commissary of this port ordering me out this day and not to offer to Cruize or make any Prizes on the French Coast on any pretence whatever. These orders was handed to me to Sign which I refused to do and told the Commissary I would comply with those orders, as far as was Consistant with my orders from the Honble. Continental Congress of the United States of America. I told him that I never had Cruized on the Coast of France or Made Prizes on Said Coast, nor would I do it. I should be glad to receive your Advice on those different Subjects as soon as Possible.

I Also take this Oppertunity to recomend Mr. Gourlade to your honours Particular Notice and think him Worthy of your Utmost Confidence and hope for the future you'll render him every Service in your Power, as he has been very Active in rendering me every Service in his power. I have made him my Confident in regard to Prizes and the Signals to be made by them agreable to a requ'st in a paragraf of your last letter to me. If they should fall in here I make no doubt but he will do every thing in his Power to give you Satisfaction and hope you will favor him with your Instructions in regard to the Sale of the Prizes that may Come in here. Mr. Gonets orders was in writing, that he wanted me to Sign but I told him I could not Sign them or receive orders from him or Mr. Sartine or any other Person except the Honble. Congress or their Commissioners. I imagine you'll hear this from the Minester at Paris, which makes me more particular in my Answer. From Gentlemen Your most Obedient Humble Servant

LAMBT. WICKES

P.S. If you should have any other business to Transact I think Mr. Gourlade the most proper Person you Can Imploy at this

Port. I have had Ocasion to take Mony of Mr. Gourlade, to pay the Ships disbursments and he would have Advanced the Money to pay the People but I did not like to give a Bill for So large a Sum without your Orders.   L:W:

Addressed: To / The Honble. Dr. Benja. Franklin / at / Paris

Notation: Wickes 27. April 77.

From Jean-Jacques Bachelier[6]

ALS: American Philosophical Society

Monsieur   Ce 27. avril 1777.
    Dans la crainte d'avoir mal datté La lettre que j'ay eu l'honneur de vous ecrire et a Mr. de chaumont Je vous adresse celle cy pour vous assurer que c'est lundy 28 avril que Mr. Parens[7] nous attant a sevres ou nous devons diner chez luy. Je vous prie d'en faire part a Mr. Le Ray de chaumont. Je suis avec Respect Monsieur Votre tres humble et tres obeissant serviteur
                                            BACHELIER

Addressed A Monsieur / Monsieur frankelin / chez Mr. Le Ray De / chaumont / *a Passy*

Notation: Bachelier, Paris 27 Avril 1777

From ——— Eÿraut

April 27, 1777   See page 170

6. A painter (1724–1805), and the director of the *ateliers de décoration* at Sèvres: Larousse, *Dictionnaire universel.*

7. Parent, intendant of the Sèvres porcelain manufactory: *Almanach royal* for 1777, p. 471.

Feutry: Verse for Franklin's Portrait[8]

DS: American Philosophical Society

Passy, ce 27 avril, 1777.
Vers à mettre sous le Portrait de Monsieur de Franklin etc.

Honneur du Nouveau Monde et de L'humanité,
ce sage aimable et vrai Les guide et les éclaire;
comme un autre Mentor, il cache à L'oeil vulgaire,
sous les traits d'un Mortel, une Divinité.

Par son très sincere et très humble admirateur   FEUTRY

Notation: Verses

The American Commissioners to [the Committee of Secret Correspondence[9]]   Copy: Harvard University Library

Gentlemen   Paris, April 28 1777
We wrote to you pretty fully on the State of Affairs here, in ours of the 12th of March and 19th of this Month, since which there has been little Alteration. There is yet no Certainty of a

---

8. Augustin de Saint-Aubin, engraver for the King's library, was making the print, based on a sketch by Charles-Nicolas Cochin. These verses were designed for that engraving, but it went on sale the following June without them; they were later attached to another, by Juste Chevillet from the Duplessis portrait painted in 1778. Charles C. Sellers, *Benjamin Franklin in Portraiture* (New Haven and London, 1962), pp. 227–8, 247–9. BF sent the Chevillet print to Mrs. Jay, with the comment that "the Verses at the Bottom are truly extravagant. But you must know that the Desire of pleasing by a perpetual use of Compliments in this polite Nation, has so us'd up all the common Expressions of Approbation, that they are become flat and insipid, and to use them almost implies Censure." To John Jay, June 13, 1780, Columbia University Library.

9. The letter says that it is to the secret committee, but the phrase was often used for the committee of secret correspondence. We believe that this is a case in point. One reason is the subject matter, which deals with more than commercial affairs. Another is the reference to the commissioners' letter of March 12 and April 19, which fits (on the assumption that "19" is a copyist's error) the long letter to the committee of secret correspondence above, March 12 to April 9; no letter to the secret committee during that period is extant.

620

William Carmichael

sudden Declaration of War, but the Preparations go on vigorously both here and in Spain, the Armies of france drawing towards the Sea Coasts, and those of Spain to the Frontiers of Portugal; and their fleets fitting in the Ports: But the Court still gives Assurances of Peace to the British Ambassador, The Nation in general all the while calling out for War.

We have receiv'd the Resolution of Congress of Feb. 5. for sending over a great Quantity of Cloathing upon the Credit of the States, in Case We cannot borrow Money of the Government to pay for them. We wrote before that the Loan proposed was at present impracticable; and we have not yet receiv'd the Credit We expected from Spain; the Arms We have bought, Ships building and the Brass Cannon ordered will demand great Sums; But as We shall receive a Payment from the farmers general next Month, and hope you will be very diligent in sending Remittances, We shall go as far upon our Credit as it can carry us, in sending the Cloathing required. Flints sufficient, we apprehend are already gone.

We have according to Orders notified the several Courts of the Intention of Congress to send Ministers to them: and delivered a Remonstrance to the Portugueze Ambassador concerning the Proceeding of that Court. As the Minister for Prussia may not soon arrive, and that Court has shewn a Disposition to treat, by entring into a Correspondence with us, We have thought it might be well that one of us should visit it immediately to improve its present good Dispositions and obtain, if possible, the Privilege of their Ports to trade and fit Ships in, and to sell our Prizes. Mr. Lee has readily undertaken this Journey, and will soon set out for Berlin, with Mr. Carmichael, who has already been there and pav'd the Way, and whom we recommend to Congress as a faithful serviceable Man, that ought to be encouraged.[1]

Hon. the Secret Committee.

(Copy)

Notation: Dr Franklin believes there was some additions made to this Letter before it was sent, but is not certain.   W.T.F.

---

1. William Carmichael had been serviceable in more than his recent mission to Berlin. In March he had a series of interviews in the Place Vendôme,

Jonathan Williams, Jr., to the American Commissioners

ALS: American Philosophical Society; letterbook copy: Yale University Library

Gentlemen   Nantes April 28. 1777.

The Thérese sailed as I wrote last and was at St. Nazare the 26th, the Wind continuing fair she has no doubt continued her route. You may date the Departure of Capt. Hammond at nearly the same time as the Therése overtook him at St. Nazare. I have a Letter from Mr. Rumsey which says he expected to sail the next day.

We have received accounts that the rising States Capt. Thompson a privateer from Boston has brought into L'orient an english Ship from Lisbon with 84 pipes of wine and a Quantity of Fruit: this may be depended on [*In the margin*: This I find a mistake.²] The privateer went out again to sea,

---

first with Thomas Jeans, Lord Stormont's chaplain, and then with the Ambassador's secretary, Horace Saint Paul, in which he received overtures for an Anglo-American accommodation; he attended these meetings with the commissioners' full knowledge and, before the end of the series, on instructions from Vergennes. He rebuffed the overtures. They were accompanied, he said later, by the offer of a handsome income, to be paid him anywhere in the world and whether or not the negotiations succeeded, as a reward for his good offices. —— to Carmichael, [*c.* March 24, 1777], University of Pennsylvania Library; Stevens, *Facsimiles*, VII, nos. 672, 675; Wharton, *Diplomatic Correspondence*, II, 308–9. Did he in fact keep his political virtue as spotless as this implies? The evidence, all from the British side, raises some doubts. He had promised his bosom friend Joseph Hynson, the latter reported to his British employers, to let him steal any papers that might be useful to him. Whether or not this promise led to the interviews in the Place Vendôme, Jeans' account of the first one suggests overtures that had nothing to do with an Anglo-American rapprochement. Stevens, III, nos. 246, 248, pp. 3–4; VII, no. 670, pp. 17–25. The British clearly had hopes of Carmichael.

2. JW, when he found his mistake, deleted the sentence that follows: "Mr. Morris and M. Penet are I hear gone to L'Orient I suppose to take the disposal of the prizes on themselves."

'tis said to bring in two other Vessell she had taken; this seems to be conjecture only.

I wrote some time since that the lease of the Magazine and outhouses should be renewed now if at all, as it will expire in a few months. Another person has applied for it. I therefore beg to know by return of post whither you will continue it or not. I understand the shortest term is 5 years, it now stands at 1800 Livres, this is high, but in my opinion you will not find another in Nantes that will answer your purpose so well on every Account.

I mentioned the other day the number of Bales now here, since which we have advice of 40 more being shipped from orleans and it does not appear that this is all.

I leave this Letter to go by the post tomorrow, as I am going to Painbeuf immediately to dispatch Nicholson and I do not intend to return 'till I have seen the last of him.

After he is gone and his accounts settled I shall have little to do, therefore with your permission I will come for a few days to paris to give a full account of all my proceedings and to make what other commercial arrangements you may think proper to honour me with.

The arms I ship by Adams will go on board to day. He is ready for his dispatches. I have the honour to be with the greatest Respect Gentlemen Your most obedient Servant

J WILLIAMS

The Hon The Deputies of the united States.

Notation: Nantes, J. Williams 28 Ap. 77.

From Jonathan Williams, Jr.

ALS: American Philosophical Society; letterbook copy: Yale University Library

Dear and honored Sir   Nantes April 28. 1777.

I have spoken to the Gentleman who gave me the plan. Mr. Anthus the second in the House has thoughts of going into that Country soon, in the mean time they will make the necessary enquiries relative to Seamen. I understand the place they propose to build in is not in the Government of Sweden but of prussia.[3]

I have returned the articles to Mr. S. to make the additional one relative to the dissolution in case of its not answering. As to Capital he observed it would be as much as would be wanted in the manner we propose to do Business there being only the ordinary charges requisite to be paid, and as to advances that should never be wanted, the Goods being arrived.[4] I have the highest Confidence in Mr. Alexanders Sagacity and wish you to send the articles to him: I want to converse with you and him which is better than writing.

I am obliged to break of being just setting of to Painbeuf. I am ever most dutifully and affectionately Yours

J WILLIAMS JUNR

I sent your Letter to Mr. Rumsey

Addressed: Doctor Franklin.

[The Marine Committee of Congress] to the American Commissioners
Copy: National Archives

Gentlemen   April 29th 1777.

Should you see this Letter it will be forwarded to you by Thomas Thompson Esqr. Commander of the Raleigh, Frigate in the Service of the United States of America. This Ship was built in New Hampshire where is no Foundreys for Casting Cannon and the distance from the places where they are Cast

3. The plan was for shipbuilding, and "that Country" was presumably Prussia. The commissioners had had Sweden in mind; one of them should go there, Deane had recently proposed to Gérard, to oversee the construction of three ships of fifty to sixty guns. Jean Anthus was second in the House of Wilfelsheim, and was subsequently associated with Wilfelsheim's brother in Nantes. See JW's second letter to the commissioners above, April 12; *Deane Papers*, II, 44–6; Lüthy, *Banque protestante*, II, 695 n.

4. This business arrangement with Schweighauser, even more sketchily adumbrated in earlier letters from JW, never progressed beyond the planning stage, doubtless because the young man was appointed three days later the commissioners' agent in Nantes; see their letter to him below, May 1.

to Portsmouth where the frigate now lies is so great that we think it better to put on board such Guns as can be got for her in the neighbourhood and send her to france to be compleated, than to Hall them by Land such an amazing distance, or than to trust them by Water to her, or her along the Coast to them, now that the enemies Ships are so numerous and powerful at the Mouths of our Bays and Harbours.[5] We have ordered her to Brest as the most suitable Port for supplies. Captain Thompson will transmit you an Indent of all the Guns, Stores and Materials he wants and we hope you may procure and order for his being Supplied out of the Kings arsenals or Stores. Orders are given to the Commercial Agents to pay your drafts for the amount of such supplies, but if you cannot obtain them in the way proposed you will write to the said Agents William Lee and Thomas Morris Esqrs. to purchase every thing necessary on the best terms and in the most expeditious manner they can.

We have told Captain Thompson if you have any particular service, Cruize or enterprize, to point out for the benefit of these States, that he should obey your Orders; otherways to return to America well manned and fitted cruizing on our enemies ships the whole voyage. You will therefore write to him giving such Instructions as you may think best calculated to promote the honor, Interest and welfare of these States. With great esteem and regard we remain Honorable Gentlemen Your obedient Servants

The Honorable Benjamin Franklin Silas Deane & Arthur Lee Esqrs.

5. Thomas Thompson, an immigrant Englishman, had supervised the construction of the *Raleigh* before being named to her command. William James Morgan, *Captains to the Northward: the New England Captains in the Continental Navy* (Barre, Mass., 1959), p. 68. For the troubles in arming the frigate see William M. Fowler, Jr., *Rebels under Sail . . .* (New York, [1976]), pp. 239–44.

From the Marquise de Sainneville[6]

ALS: American Philosophical Society

Au chateau de vincennes ce 30 avrille 1777

N'esce pas trop presumer, Monsieur, que d'imaginer qu'a ma recommendation vous voulussiés bien vous interesser, pour un officier, qui ne demande qu'a mériter aux yeux de votre nation?[7] L'etat de ses services qu'il vous remêttera Luy même, avec cette Lettre, vous prouvera sa capacité, et si vous avés La bonté de l'écouter, il ne vous Laissera pas de doutte sur sa bonne volonté. Les personnes qui s'interessent a Luy et qu'il vous nommera, vous certifirons de son honnesteté, et d'une délicatesse, qu'il porte a l'héroïsme, enfin Monsieur, il a le plus grand désir de se rendre utile, et tout ce qu'il faut pour se rendre interessant. Je ne doutte pas que cet officier, pour lequel je vous demande votre protection, ne vous soit une nouvelle preuve que je ne m'interesse que pour de bons sujets. Mr. L'abbé raynal à bien voulu vous rendre ce témoignage de Mr. le chevalier dannemours mon parent pour lequel vous avés eü la bonté de me donner des lettres de recommendation pour philadelphie, j'ignore si il est arrivé dans cette ville. Si par les personnes a qui vous L'avés adressés, vous en avés des nouvelles, vous me ferés grand plaisir, Monsieur, de m'en faire part. J'ay l'honneur d'estre avec bien de La reconnoissance et de La vénération, Monsieur, votre tres humble et tres obeissante servante

JARENTE DE SAINNEVILLE

Acknowledgments of Poetic Offerings to Franklin: Five Models
Drafts: American Philosophical Society

These drafts are impossible to date, except perhaps in a general way. Four of them were composed after Franklin's move to Passy at the end of February, and are in the hand of Le Veillard, his friend and neighbor there. The fifth is in the hand of the abbé Martin Lefèbvre

---

6. See the note on d'Anmours to BF above, Jan. 17. BF's reply to this letter is below, June 6.

7. Lauron; see his letter to BF below, June 3.

de la Roche, a house guest of another neighbor, Mme. Helvétius;[8] it does not mention Passy, but is so close to the others in substance that it would appear to have been written at about the same time. If there were any particular period when Franklin was inundated with verses, these replies might be assigned to it; but the effusions that survive are too scattered to offer a clue. The only remaining clue is that he apparently did not draft the notes himself and then have them corrected, as he did with later exercises,[9] but prevailed on friends to write them for him; this lack of confidence in his French suggests an early date, and we are therefore assigning the models to the first months in Passy.

I.

Monsieur   Passy ce [*blank*]
Je me rejouis pour ma patrie de ce qu'elle a éxcité assez d'interest parmi les guerriers de l'europe pour engager un grand nombre a sa deffense; je vous remercie en particulier, Monsieur, de vos intentions pour elle et je reçois avéc reconnoissance les vers que vous voulez bien m'addresser, mais malheureusement je n'ai pas assez d'usage du françois pour en connoître tout le prix; je souhaite que vous soyez bientost delivré des contradictions que vous éprouvez et je suis Monsieur Vostre tres humble et tres obeissant Serviteur   B.F.

II.

Passy ce [*blank*]
J'ay l'honeur de vous remercier, Monsieur, des vers que vous m'avez addressés, je n'ai point assez de connoissance de vostre langue pour en sentir tout le prix et vous donner mon avis sur leur impréssion, mais je ne puis qu'estre reconnoissant des sentiments que vous temoignez pour ma patrie et pour moy. Je suis tres parfaitement Monsieur Vostre tres humble et tres obeissant Serviteur   B.F.

Notation: Models of Notes written for Dr. F.

8. For the abbé see Lopez, *Mon Cher Papa*, p. 248.
9. *Ibid.*, pp. 71, 73–4.

III.

Passy ce [*blank*]

J'ay l'honeur de vous remercier, Monsieur, des vers que vous m'avez addressés, je n'ay point assez de connoissance de vostre Langue pour en sentir toutes les beautés, mais je ne puis qu'estre reconnoissant des sentiments que vous temoignez pour ma patrie et pour moy. Je suis tres parfaitement Monsieur Vostre tres humble et tres obeissant Serviteur   B.F.

IV.

Passy ce [*blank*]

Je n'ay pas, Monsieur, assez de connoissance de vostre langue pour sentir tout le merite de la poësie française, j'ay cependant l'honeur de vous remercier des vers que vous m'avez ad-dressés et des sentiments qu'ils expriment pour ma patrie et pour moy. Je suis tres parfaitement Monsieur Vostre tres humble et tres obeissant Serviteur   B.F.

V.

Je vous suis obligé, Monsieur, du beau poëme que vous m'avez envoyé. En le lisant, j'ai eu regret de ne pas assez bien con-noitre vôtre langue, pour mieux sentir et aprétier vôtre ou-vrage. Je vous remercie en particulier de m'y avoir nommé, en parlant de plusieurs gens celebres de vôtre Nation. J'ai l'hon-neur d'être avec estime M.   B. FRANKLIN[1]

1. Penciled in another hand.

Index

"Father Abraham's Speech" (BF), Quétant translates, 587 n
Faulknor, Robert, Capt., R.N., captures French ship (1761), 369
Favre, Dragon & Cie., 335 n
Fawcett (Faucit), Col. William, recruits German mercenaries (1776), 203.
Ferdinand, Duke of Brunswick, mentioned, 111
Fergusson, Elizabeth Graeme: H. Fergusson requests information about, 58; Hamilton inquires about, 93; J. Ritchie befriends, 162 n
Fergusson, Henry Hugh: requests interview, information, 58; sends news, 88–9; Hamilton inquires about, 93; letters from, 58, 88–9
Feutry, Aimé (Amé)-Ambroise-Joseph: sends works to BF, lvi, 557, 570–1, 574, 590, 597–8, 617; biog. note, 557 n; inventions of, 557 n, 570, 587; and Puységur, Hérouville, 570, 587 n; death of, 570 n; on virtues of Belgians, corruption of Paris, 570–1, 590, 597; forwards Quétant translation, 587; receives BF's scientific works, 597; verses by, for BF portrait, 620; mentioned, 40 n; letters from, 557, 570–1, 574, 587, 590, 597–8, 617
Fielding, Henry, mentioned, 326 n
Fielding, John, refuses to meddle in Platt case, 326
Filley de la Barre, Pierre, mentioned, 597 n
Firearms. See Arms; Fusils.
Fisher, Jabez Maud: offers to carry letters to London, BF declines, 595–6; brothers of, arrested as Loyalists, 595 n; letter from, 595; letter to, 596
Fisher, Jane, marries Valltravers, 610
Fisheries, off Newfoundland, division of: proposed, between France and U.S., 97, 503; rumored, between France and Britain, 568
Flagg, Jane, grandniece of BF, greetings to, marriage of, 34
Florida, East and West, proposed Franco-American conquest of, 503
Floridablanca, Jose Moñino y Redondo, conde de: replaces, sends instructions to Grimaldi, 173–4 n, 192 n, 499 n; Ternant praises, 192
Folger, John, ship captain, expected to leave

for Nantucket, 258
Fort Constitution, N.J., reported retaken, 508
Forth, Nathaniel Parker, BF warned against, as British agent, 49, 50 n
Fort Independence, N.Y., reported retaken, 508
Fort Lee, N.J.: captured by British, 52; reported retaken, 508
Fort Washington, N.Y.: in campaign of 1776, 52, 89, 99, 342; reported retaken, 508
Fothergill, John: Fisher offers to carry BF letter to, BF declines, 595–6; mentioned, 36 n, 490 n
Foucault, Mme. (daughter of Le Ray de Chaumont), Feutry verse for, 557 n
Fox, Charles James: meets BF, lvi, 92 n, 227; Strahan's opinion of, 227
France: BF's arrival in, xlix–l, lv–lvi, 23–4, 26, 28, 79, 115, 386, 399, 404: supposed, real reasons for, xlix, 79, 115, 162–3, 216, 310–11, 384: effect of, in England, 62; immediate military aid from, urged on ground of self-interest, 55, 96–8, 108, 261–2, 265–6, 346, 409–10; offered territorial inducements to enter war, 97–8, 502–4; government versus public opinion in, 105; supposed influence of, on Canadians, Indians, British mercenaries, 536; rumored treaty between Britain and, 568; BF on use of compliments in, 620 n. See also Army, French; Commissioners, American, to France; Duties; Farmers general; Joseph II; Louis XV, XVI; Navy, French; Ports, French; Trade; Vergennes.
Francès, Jacques Batailhe de, Coder claims support of, 441
"François," BF's alias, 151 n, 235, 306
Francy, Jean-Baptiste-Lazare Théveneau de, Beaumarchais' secretary: suspected, 49; expected, arrives in Nantes, 207, 229, 253, 378 n, 404, 428–9, 438; Montaudoüin criticizes, 247; carries letters, 300, 378 n, 403, 420, 428–30, 438, 454, 485; at Lorient, Nantes, 404, 434, 453; mentioned, 434
Franklin, Benjamin: has meager command of French, l, 38, 419, 627–8; besieged by favor-seekers, liii–liv, 168, 244; cool toward Beaumarchais, lv; on former Anglo-

641